Designing
INSTRUCTIONAL
SYSTEMS

Designing
INSTRUCTIONAL
SYSTEMS

Decision making in **COURSE** planning
and **CURRICULUM** design

A J Romiszowski

**KOGAN
PAGE**

To John Hamer, who started me on this road;
Tom Gilbert and Bob Horn, who pointed the way;

and Anne Howe, Barbara Atherton, Lina Pastor
and Nick Rushby, who helped me get there.

Reprinted 1988, 1990, 1992, 1993, 1995, 1999

First published in Great Britain in 1981 and reprinted 1981 and 1982 by
Kogan Page Ltd, 120 Pentonville Road, London N1 9JN

First paperback edition published in 1984 and reprinted 1986 and 1987 by
Kogan Page Ltd

British Library Cataloguing in Publication Data
   Romiszowski, Alexander Joseph
   Designing instructional systems.
   I. Curriculum planning
   I. Title
   375   LB1576
   ISBN 0-85038-787-6

Published in the United States of America by
Nichols Publishing Company, Post Office Box 96, New York, NY 10024

Library of Congress Cataloguing in Publication Data
Romiszowski, A J
   Designing instructional systems
   1. Instructional systems – design
   I. Title
   LB1028.35.R65   371.3'07'8   80-13524
   ISBN 0-89397-181-2

Printed in England by
Clays Ltd, St Ives plc

Contents

Preface

This book deals with large-scale or macro-level instructional design, which is referred to by other authors variously as curriculum development, course design, training system design or instructional systems design.

The emphasis throughout the book is on the application of a *systems approach*, which implies both a way of thinking about the problem and a methodology for seeking and developing solutions. Thus the approach of the book is problem-oriented.

The successful problem-solver requires more than a technique or procedure. He requires experience of similar problems, some general principles that he can apply to the class of problems and a great deal of creativity to develop an optimal method of solving *each problem*. This book brings together the theories and practical experience that have been built up by instructional technologists over the last two decades, the techniques that are currently most used for the analysis of problems in education and for their solution, and a range of new ideas specially developed by the author to encourage the creative element (so often missing from educational materials).

This book is intended for anyone involved in instructional design. It is designed on a 'grid' structure to facilitate the reader's choice of chapters. Those who wish to gain a general overview may concentrate on the chapters at the *theory base* and *analysis* levels (see the grid below). Those more practically concerned with course design will find much of use in the *synthesis* and *evaluation* levels. Those who wish simply to discover 'what's new' in this book and its treatment of instructional design will find what they are seeking principally in the *analysis* and *evaluation* levels.

Those who wish to study the book in its entirety have two options: either they may read the chapters in sequence, or they may first read the *theory base* chapters and then proceed to the more practical chapters.

These are the planned options. The reader will no doubt work out his or her own reading plan to suit specific requirements and interests.

In the opening chapters a five-stage general procedure for problem-solving (by means of the systems approach) is outlined. In most large projects, involving a team effort, responsibility for the various stages may be subdivided in a variety of ways. To deal in depth with all the stages in one volume would make the book unwieldy, both in size and in the proportion of the content that would be of relevance to any one member of the team. As it is common in such teams to distinguish between the functions of curriculum developers (or course designers), producers of materials and resources, the actual teachers or instructors who use the system and the managers who make the system work in practice, it was decided to concentrate in this book on the area of interest of one of these four groups: the curriculum or course designer. All four areas of activity are covered in outline to establish the general context, but we enter into detail on those functions normally referred to as course design.

A companion volume is planned which will deal in detail with the functions of the other three essential human elements in an instructional design team.

The intended application

This book promotes an open minded approach to instructional design. No hard and fast procedure is suggested. Rather, a range of techniques is presented, to act as a 'tool box' capable of being used to tackle a wide variety of instructional design tasks, both in the context of formal education and in vocational and industrial training. The emphasis is on the skills needed to choose appropriate tools for the problem being tackled.

The term 'skills' is used in this context to emphasize that knowing the techniques is not enough; one must develop competence in their use and this is best done through practical experience. No book can, by itself, provide the experience necessary to develop practical competence. It can, however, act as a guide and a handbook.

The use of conceptual schemata

To assist the decision making process, a number of concept maps or schemata are developed and are presented in the appropriate chapters. The background to these schemata is presented in the theory base chapters. We have chosen to use conceptual schemata as 'job aids' because the instructional design process is a complex, heuristic process, more akin to solving new maths problems or playing chess than to simple algorithmic procedures such as cancelling fractions or playing noughts and crosses. One must consider many factors in combination when making an heuristic decision. The schemata developed in this book attempt to visually present the principal factors and the ways in which they interact.

There are many ways of storing and cross-referencing knowledge. It is said that no person's conceptual schemata are identical to any other person's. We all make our own mental maps to interrelate what we have learned. The reader should therefore treat the schemata presented here not as the last word on the subject, but rather as the beginning. The reader should critically appraise the schemata presented and should adapt them, if he sees the need, to better suit his own way of thinking. To stretch an earlier analogy, if the specific techniques listed in the directory sections of some chapters are the tools in the instructional designer's tool box, the schemata are aids to organizing and planning the job and selecting the most appropriate tools. There is seldom one best way to do this, that suits all craftsmen equally. But there are certain general principles that the craftsman should bear in mind when designing his own best way.

The schemata presented are, after all, merely a way of structuring the factors that I consider of importance for instructional decision making. The reader may feel that I have missed an important factor, or given undue weight to another. In such cases, I would be most happy to receive readers' comments and suggestions. Conceptual schemata are living structures which can, and indeed should, adapt to new insights or information. There is no doubt that my own schemata, presented here, are still open to modification. Any feedback is thus most welcome.

The overall grid structure on which the chapters are organized, which is presented below, serves to locate specific chapters and to define their function in overall general terms. Some readers may, however, welcome a more detailed overview to the content and the structure of specific chapters or sections. The three content maps which follow the grid may serve this function. They illustrate the interrelations between the principal topics covered in each of the main sections of the book. Use of these, together with the index at the back of the book, may serve as a quick means of locating topics of special interest.

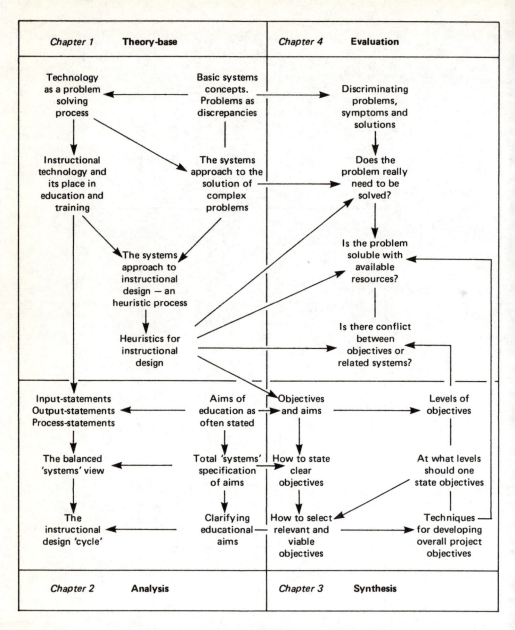

A summarized content map of Part 1: define the problem

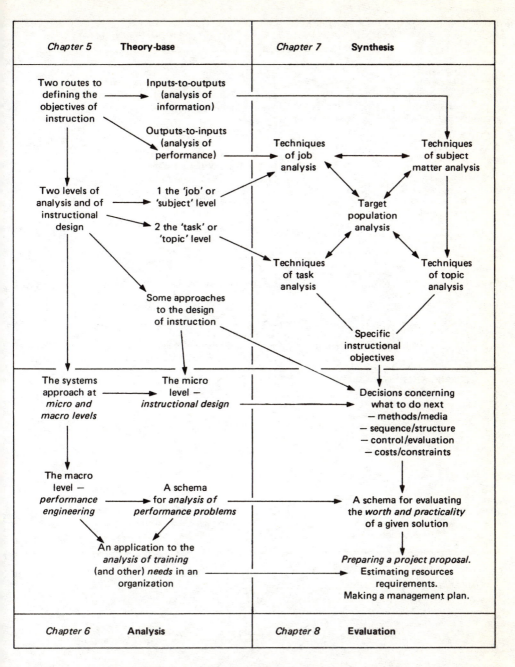

A summarized content map of Part 2: analyse the problem

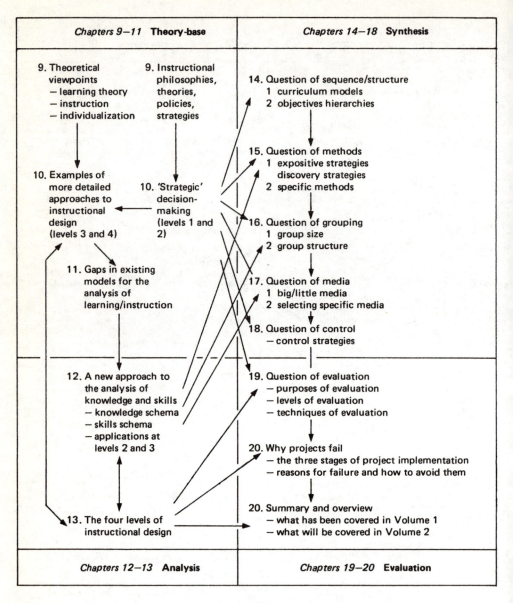

Chapters 9–11 **Theory-base**	Chapters 14–18 **Synthesis**

9. Theoretical viewpoints
   — learning theory
   — instruction
   — individualization

9. Instructional philosophies, theories, policies, strategies

14. Question of sequence/structure
   1 curriculum models
   2 objectives hierarchies

10. Examples of more detailed approaches to instructional design (levels 3 and 4)

10. 'Strategic' decision-making (levels 1 and 2)

15. Question of methods
   1 expositive strategies
     discovery strategies
   2 specific methods

16. Question of grouping
   1 group size
   2 group structure

11. Gaps in existing models for the analysis of learning/instruction

17. Question of media
   1 big/little media
   2 selecting specific media

18. Question of control
   — control strategies

12. A new approach to the analysis of knowledge and skills
   — knowledge schema
   — skills schema
   — applications at levels 2 and 3

19. Question of evaluation
   — purposes of evaluation
   — levels of evaluation
   — techniques of evaluation

20. Why projects fail
   — the three stages of project implementation
   — reasons for failure and how to avoid them

13. The four levels of instructional design

20. Summary and overview
   — what has been covered in Volume 1
   — what will be covered in Volume 2

Chapters 12–13 **Analysis**	Chapters 19–20 **Evaluation**

A summarized content map of Part 3: designing a solution

PART 1
Define the Problem

Overview

Chapter 1. Examines the similarities and differences between 'education' and 'training', defines the term 'instruction' as used in this book and introduces 'systems thinking' as a unifying set of concepts and techniques for instructional design.

Educational technology is treated as a multi-faceted concept and the more restricted concept of 'instructional technology' is identified as the principal area of interest of this book. Nevertheless, related technologies (eg for the control and maintenance of performance, for organization development, etc) will be considered in order to give a total view of the design of instructional systems.

Any technology is seen as the creative application of knowledge (science) to a practical purpose (or problem). The systems approach is put forward as the most adequate general methodology for such creative problem-solving. The systems approach is seen as very much a *heuristic* process, rather than an algorithmic sequence of steps.

Thus the purpose of the book emerges as the presentation of heuristics for the application of the systems approach to the design of instruction. Each of the five main stages of the systems approach is seen to involve all of the three types of thinking generally associated with problem-solving and productive or creative activity: analysis, synthesis and evaluation.

The charts at the end of this chapter summarize some of the heuristics that will be examined and applied in more detail in later chapters. These charts also serve to illustrate the overall structure of the book.

Chapter 2. Analyses how problems differ in terms of the system characteristics that are used to define the problem (inputs, processes or outputs).

A brief analysis of theoretical viewpoints on learning and on instruction (both in the education and training contexts) attempts to explain the past tendency towards undue stress of one system characteristic at the expense of the others. A more balanced, total-system viewpoint is proposed.

The design of instruction is seen as a cycle of activities which should consider inputs, processes and outputs in relation to each other.

Chapter 3. Delineates general aims and precise objectives. Instructional objectives are seen as micro-level objectives which should generally contribute to the achievement of other macro-level objectives of the wider systems (society, organization or the individual). A method for the statement of objectives and for the examination of their relevance, measurability and viability is presented.

Some difficulties and objections to the use of performance objectives are examined. However, it is shown that they are necessary as controls at every stage of the systems approach. The tables (or maps) at the end of the chapter present some ways of overcoming the difficulties in using performance objectives.

Chapter 4. By means of several analogies and case studies, this chapter attempts to encourage the reader critically to evaluate problems and their proposed solutions. It shows that problems are not always quite what they seem to be when first presented. The need to analyse the problem and to pre-evaluate any proposed solutions by reference to the context of the wider system is stressed. The case studies present some techniques for such pre-evaluation, such as the preparation of systems diagrams, consideration of hypothetical 'before' and 'after' steady states in the system, etc. One encounters the need sometimes to restate the problem before attempting to solve it.

1. Instruction, Instructional Systems and the Systems Approach

1.1 Education and training: a question of goals

'Training' is akin to following a tightly fenced path, in order to reach a predetermined goal at the end of it. 'Education' is to wander freely in the fields to left and right of this path — preferably with a map.

This quote is the only thing that has stuck in my mind, from an otherwise forgotten lecture I attended some time in the early 1960s. I cannot even remember the theme or the speaker's name. Perhaps they were rendered insignificant by the philosophical depths of this opening statement. It says in two sentences what many writers have tried to say in whole books.

At about the same time, Professor B F Skinner, the father of programmed instruction, was somewhat less generous when delivering a lecture at University College, London. While discussing the use of precise objectives as the key to efficient instruction, he concluded by saying that

those of us who know where they are going, and can define the path that leads there, are in the business of training, whereas those who neither know their destination nor the means of getting there are in education.

Who sets the aims? This somewhat extremist view would not be shared by most educators. They would claim that they do have some idea about their ends and the means of reaching them, but that their ends are general and there are many means of reaching them. Certainly, it is true that some educators have argued strongly against predetermined aims. They consider that it is the learner who should establish his own aims, with only minimal guidance from the teacher. Once the learner has established his aims, he should merely be given the resources required to discover the means of achieving them. This 'free discovery' movement has its supporters, but is by no means the mainstream of educational thinking.

Who chooses the means? At the other extreme, the various multi-media, personalized or resource-based schemes which have recently gained popularity offer the learner a variety of pre-prepared paths towards predetermined goals. The learner may choose his route, but he always ends up at the same place. In between these extremes are a number of other models in which both goal-setting and path-choosing are joint teacher/learner activities.

The education-training continuum Where exactly to draw the line between training and education in this continuum is not clear. But perhaps it is also not important. Perhaps it is more important to realize that most teaching/learning situations contain something of each.

Even if we are primarily concerned with herding the learners as fast as possible along that tightly fenced path, we seldom achieve our goal without some straying along the way. The fences may be hedgerows, interesting and nutritious in themselves. And in practice the fences are not learner-proof. Many gates and gaps appear along the way, allowing all to glimpse the wonders that lie in the fields and some to stray in and perhaps be left to wend their own way.

If on the other hand we are concerned primarily with the open fields, we have to consider the question of the map. Should we provide one? If we do, we should first make sure that our learners can read the map. Maps have conventions and learning to read these conventions and so to interpret the map constitutes training, at least in so far that it involves predetermined goals. Thus whether we adopt the multi-media or 'orienteering' approach (by specifying the learner's goals and giving him the freedom to choose what he considers the most efficient route) or the free-discovery 'tourist' approach (in which both goals and routes are at the learner's discretion) there is nevertheless an obligation on the part of the teacher first to make certain that a satisfactory standard of 'map-reading' has been achieved.

If we are not concerned with the tourists or the boy-scouts, but with the 'real' explorers who must find their way through previously uncharted territories (researchers and scientists for example) we cannot and indeed do not wish to provide a map. But this does not eliminate the training element. The pioneer must have appropriate terrain-reading skills, adequate survival skills and map-drawing skills, in order that he may return successfully from his voyage and then inform others how to follow in his footsteps. Much of these skills he would gain most effectively through pre-planned, goal-oriented teaching, ie through training.

1.2 Instruction: what this book is about

As most training involves some unplanned learning (educational effects) and most education involves some planned, goal-oriented teaching (ie training) the value of these two terms as discriminators is somewhat dubious. Indeed perhaps the simple view that 'education is what goes on in schools and training is what goes on in industry' is as useful a definition as any. The use of the term 'instruction' may help to both distinguish and unite the two processes.

A working definition

By 'instruction' we shall mean a *goal-directed* teaching process which is more or less *pre-planned*. Whether the goal has been established by the learner or by some external agent such as a teacher or a syllabus is immaterial. What is important is that a predetermined goal has been identified.

		Specific objectives exist?	
		Yes	No
Pre-planned study resources exist?	Yes	Instruction	Visits to theatre/museum, study tours, library, etc
	No	Projects apprenticeships, research, etc	Incidental learning

Figure 1.1 *A definition of instruction*

Whether the routes to the goal are then unique or various, whether they are prescribed by the instructor or chosen by the learner is immaterial. What is important is that pre-planning has taken place to establish and test out viable routes, or failing this, that pre-planning has taken place to enable the learner to test out the viability of any route he proposes to take, to check his progress along the way, and to 'map' it so that he (or others) may retrace his steps.

Instructional systems design

It is thus the presence of precise goals or objectives (however arrived at) and the presence of careful pre-planning and testing out that shall be taken as the main characteristics of our use of the term 'instructional system'. Instructional systems design is therefore a three-phase process of establishing precise and useful objectives, planning viable routes and testing them out. We shall be concerned with analysis, synthesis and evaluation.

However, we shall make it our business to attend to the needs of the signpost-following 'traveller-in-a-hurry' who seeks the shortest path to his objective, the 'orienteer' who wishes to examine and compare all possible routes, and the 'tourist' who is not yet sure at which of the many attractive objectives open to him he will decide to aim. Thus we shall not be concerned with only one recipe for instruction. We shall examine when and how the instructional system should establish the objectives, and when and how the learner should do this for himself. We shall examine ways of signposting clear pathways to these objectives and of helping learners to keep moving efficiently along the path. We shall also examine ways of producing clear maps which show the learner various objectives and various ways of reaching them. We shall consider how to teach the learners to use the maps efficiently, and touch on the way one should develop the 'pioneering' skills the learner needs when signposts and maps prove inadequate.

This book will be concerned with task-centred learning, with subject-centred learning and with life-skill-centred learning (insofar as the source of objectives is concerned) with programmed and with student-directed learning (insofar as the choice of route is concerned), with individualized self-instruction, media or resource-based learning and teacher-led group instruction (as far as the choice of transport is concerned) and with mastery-learning and experiential learning (as far as the control of progress is concerned).

1.3 Systems thinking

To avoid the potential confusion of so many approaches and techniques (and so much jargon) one unifying set of concepts has been adopted: the concepts of systems thinking and systems analysis. Most of the models for instruction described in this book can be explained, as least up to a point, by the use of systems terminology. All the approaches to design can be shown to be variants of the systems approach to problem solving, an approach with applications in many other fields besides education and training. The remainder of this introductory chapter will illustrate how systems concepts can act as a unifying terminology in instructional design.

The concept of system　　The term 'system' describes a rather abstract concept. Traditional definitions, such as 'a set of components or elements, interacting together towards a common goal' do not get us very far towards understanding the concept.

To a large extent, a system exists because someone has defined it as such. This is, of course, a generalization. Some systems define themselves. A bicycle is a system with very clearly defined components — wheels, pedals, chain, handlebars, etc. Most people would agree as to the purpose or goal of a bicycle (to provide a means of propelled transport) and on the essential components of a given type of bicycle. However, one might consider the bicycle as but one component of a wider system (of a man-machine system, for example, whose objective is to maximize the efficiency of transformation of the man's energy into the bicycle's motion) or an even wider system (the bicycle is one component in a city's transport system, which involves cars, trucks, trains, buses, roads, etc). Alternatively, the three-speed gear in the hub of the back wheel can be considered a system on its own, and quite a complex system at that.

Thus, for our practical purposes, a system exists because we have chosen to consider it as that. We have drawn the boundary that limits the extent of the system, thus defining the components, or sub-systems that compose our 'system of interest'.

Once defined in this way, we can identify the principal connections between this system and its environment, the inputs from the environment to the system and the outputs from the system to its environment (see Figures 1.2 and 1.3).

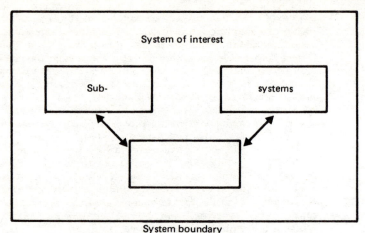

Figure 1.2 *Some basic systems terminology*

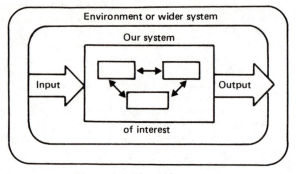

Figure 1.3 *The wider system*

The purpose or objective of a system   This is a step towards identifying the purpose or objective of a system. Apparently, purposeless systems do exist, both natural (what is the purpose of a particular rock formation?) and man-made (for example, certain bureaucratic data collection systems). In the first case, perhaps we are simply unable to identify the higher purpose of some natural systems, or perhaps none indeed exists. In the second case, however, it is highly doubtful that a man-made system without a discernible purpose was worth making. The purpose may no longer be clear because circumstances have changed (the environment no longer requires the outputs of our system) or because the purpose was very personal (a work of art). But whoever designed and made the system must have had some purpose or objective in mind. The sole exception to this rule might be the class of 'accidentally' made systems: new ecological systems brought about by pollution or rape of natural resources, new social systems arising in reaction to rampant civilization. These were not so much designed to supply the environment's observed needs, but arose in response to changes in the environment.

The 'black box' concept   In either case, however, we can identify the reason for the existence of the system (or the need for a new system) by examining its relationship to its environment, the inputs and the outputs. Hence the concept of the 'black box'.

In the words of the system engineer's anthem:

'A system is a little black box, Of which we don't unlock the locks,
But find out what it's all about, By what goes in and what comes out.'

The first step in systems analysis is to define the system of interest, its boundaries and the chief inputs and outputs across these boundaries. Quantifying these inputs and outputs defines the purpose and to some extent the efficiency of the system. This cartoon illustrates a system, a black box.

Deduce the purpose of the black box by comparing the input and output

Figure 1.4 *Input/output analysis using the black box concept*

Its purpose is fairly obvious, a transformation in weight. Its efficiency seems quite reasonable too. How it achieves this transformation is not clear: by exercise, by chemicals, by starvation? But for many purposes it may be unimportant to understand the processes. As long as the relationship input 'x' → □ → output 2/3 'x' or some other criterion of efficiency is maintained (and there are no complaints or undesirable side effects) then all is well. Your doctor will continue to recommend the treatment. But you, as a potential part in the raw material being processed might think differently, you might like to know what privations you are about to undergo. You may wish to prise the lid of the black box and examine what is inside (see Figure 1.5).

Things may be more complex than expected. There may be various sub-systems, each with its own objectives contributing to the overall objective. There may be alternatives for you to choose between, or feedback paths to recycle you as required. You, as a free agent in this example, are free to accept or reject the treatment. A successfully designed system involving humans should, apart from achieving its objectives, also be acceptable to the majority potential clients. Certainly a point to consider in designing educational or training systems.

However, as a general rule we should avoid opening up the 'black box' unless this proves to be really necessary. We shall see in a moment how to tell when this is necessary.

Control by feedback

Once we have defined the outputs and know the capability of our system, we usually have some means of controlling the output from outside the black box. The doctor in the example above may control the number of days of treatment he prescribes. A listener may control the waveband, tone and volume of a radio without the need for any knowledge about how a radio functions. A ministry of education may (to a point) control the output of a school system by manipulating output criteria, input resources and capacity without detailed knowledge of the instructional processes going on in the schools. A teacher may (also to a point) control the learning of a student by observing the outputs (new capabilities or behaviours) and manipulating the inputs (type of information, type of task, frequency and repetition, duration of practice, etc) without any detailed knowledge of the internal learning processes that are

Figure 1.5 *Detailed systems analysis:*
opening the black box

going on inside the student. In all these cases, one is applying control by
feedback (see Figure 1.6).

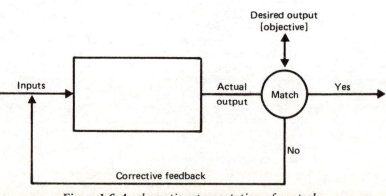

Figure 1.6 *A schematic representation of control*
by feedback

It is only when this mode of control fails that we have a system malfunction, which might possibly justify the time and effort of detailed system analysis. When normal controls fail, the Ministry of Education begins to be interested in the nuts and bolts of curriculum design, teacher training, teaching methods and other aspects of the process. Only when the teacher has exhausted his own resourcefulness in adapting instruction, guiding, explaining, demonstrating, motivating, etc, should he begin to look for system malfunctions in the students, and for this he may well need the expert help of the school psychologist.

1.4 Defining problems in systems terms

Problems, like systems, exist in the eye of the beholder, when he expresses dissatisfaction with things as they are. One man's problem may be another's panacea. The raising of compulsory schooling from age 15 to 16 may have helped to solve problems of youth unemployment (a source of dissatisfaction to society in general) but created problems for already resource-starved schools (a source of dissatisfaction to many teachers). The poor performance of students in, say, mathematics, may be a source of dissatisfaction to the teacher, but not necessarily to the students, who have a different set of priorities. The non-observance of safety regulations is seen as a problem by the company's safety officer (and he may propose solutions such as training or tighter supervision or fines) but the staff, being paid on a piecework basis, do not share his dissatisfaction (indeed they may view his proposed solutions as problems and seek other counter-solutions).

An observed discrepancy
'Real' problems are those that generate enough dissatisfaction to justify that something should be done to reduce them. Someone is sufficiently dissatisfied with 'what is' in order to pay the cost of achieving 'what should be'. This cost may be simply the inconvenience caused by a simple change, or it may be a complex of real costs: time, money, and other resources required to develop and implement a solution. The amount one is prepared to pay is a measure of the 'worth' of a successful solution. One may sometimes be able to objectively calculate this worth, from the value of changing the 'what is' into 'what should be'. In industry and commerce, productivity increase, reduction in waste or overtime or turnover can all be quantified to establish the worth of a successful solution (perhaps training is the solution). In general education, it is somewhat more difficult to establish the worth of an innovation, but this is no excuse for not trying. One way of setting about it is to use our black box concept (see Figure 1.7).

Cost and worth

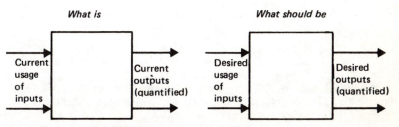

Figure 1.7 *Procedure for defining problems*

First, identify the system which best defines the problem in input/output terms. Second, define the problem as a *discrepancy* between the *current* state of the system and the *desired* state. Do this in *input/output* terms only. If you find difficulty in doing this you are probably looking at the wrong system.

Third, attempt to quantify the worth of the change which you would accept as measure of a successful solution. For example:

What is:　　　　　poor productivity (100 units/man day)
　　　　　　　　　high scrap wastage (20 per cent of raw material)
　　　　　　　　　high labour turnover (50 per cent per annum)
What should be:　other companies achieve up to 150 units/man day
　　　　　　　　　no obvious reason for more than 5 per cent waste
　　　　　　　　　reasonable labour turnover (20 per cent per annum)
Worth of:　　　　extra productivity £100,000 per annum
　　　　　　　　　reduced scrap £20,000 per annum
　　　　　　　　　reduced turnover (more difficult to estimate) £30,000 per
　　　　　　　　　annum

Total worth of a successful solution £150,000 per annum.

Do not confuse aims and means

Notice that we have not mentioned any specific solution, nor should we at this stage. Indeed that is a thing we should avoid lest we fall into the trap of mixing up problems and solutions, confusing aims and means. This is easily done. Just consider some current 'hot' issues:

☐ Raise the school leaving age
☐ Extend the availability of abortion
☐ Modern mathematics
☐ Falling educational standards in schools.

Only the last one of these is stated in 'problem' terms. All the others are solutions to some implied but unstated problems. The abortion 'problem' (the term is deliberately misused here) may be discussed on religious grounds, on demographic grounds, from a feminist viewpoint and so on. Each of these starting points is really a different problem. The Church's dissatisfaction with what is is quite different (in kind as well as quantity) from population planners' or feminists. There are three distinct viewpoints giving rise to three different problems and what to do about abortion enters into the discussion only as a part of a possible solution.

Solutions seeking problems

At least, that is the way it should be. However, all too often, people make premature decisions about the form of the solution before they have really got to grips with the problem. Worse still are those who see themselves as having a mission or who are selling an idea, for they have a vested interest in clouding the problem and concentrating on the solution. The education and training field has been plagued with more than its fair share of solutions looking for problems.

☐ Educational television
☐ Programmed instruction
☐ The discovery approach
☐ Individualization of instruction.

These are just some current movements which, though adequate solutions to certain specific problems, have tended to be sold as general, across the board approaches to improving education.

The systems approach to problem solving

One should note here that there is a time and a place for solutions seeking problems. Much research concerns itself with searching for new practical applications of a given phenomenon or product. The results of such research generate new possible solutions to as yet unstated problems. But effective problem-solving is concerned with the selection of the best solution from among alternatives. The criteria for such a selection to be made must spring from the specific problem. Hence the emphasis on first defining the problem. Thinking in systems terms helps us to *define the problem* as clearly and as completely as possible. It also helps us to *analyse* the problem in order to *identify* possible alternative solutions. It helps us to *select* among the alternatives and to *develop* the most viable solution 'mix'. Finally it helps us to *implement* the solution and to *evaluate* its effectiveness and its real worth and to *rethink* if necessary.

This approach to problem-solving has been termed the 'systems approach'. It has been used successfully in vastly different areas such as electronic engineering, product design, economics, military projects, ecology, education and training. The one thing in common between these areas is that they are concerned with complex systems. Hence the systems approach is essentially a way of thought, a tendency to think about problems in systems terms. But it is also a methodology: scientific method applied to complex systems. It follows the general stages of

- ☐ problem definition (in systems terms)
- ☐ analysis (to generate alternatives)
- ☐ selection and synthesis of an optimal solution
- ☐ controlled implementation
- ☐ evaluation and possible revision.

1.5 Educational technology

Technology The creative application of science to industrial (or any practical) purposes.

Science Any body of tested knowledge, which may be expressed in the form of a set of general principles.

Why the controversy about educational technology

Educational technology is a term which has been used (and abused) in so many contexts that it can mean all or nothing: 'all' in the sense that any planned innovative activity in education has at times been termed educational technology; 'nothing' in the sense of nothing new.

The term has generated an extraordinary amount of controversy, accompanied by a rich philosophical (and emotional) literature. Yet looking at the dictionary definitions quoted above, one is hard pressed to understand why. Why should the concept of 'the creative application of science' to *educational* purposes generate so much heated discussion? Well, of course, it does not. It is the misunderstanding of the concept that creates disagreement. This misunderstanding arises from two sources:

1. The different concepts that different people hold of technology.
2. The different concepts that they hold of education.

Controversy about education

The variety in this latter concept has already been touched on in this chapter. The very fact that aims of education is a topic which has generated its own rich literature from Plato to Whitehead and is a subject considered worthy of deep academic study in most teaching/education programmes suggests that any technology of education should be as rich and varied as the aims. In short, what science we apply and how we apply it will depend on our own particular educational purposes. This implies a complex, multi-faceted technology. Inevitably, as in most other areas of human activity, conflicts of purpose lead to differences in opinion as to methods. This acts as a source of intellectual friction, giving rise to some of the controversy surrounding educational technology. But it does not explain the intensity of the argument.

Controversy about technology

The various concepts of 'technology' add to the confusion. For some reason, this term has acquired emotional implications which often seem to impede rational thought. The definition quoted above is a *process* definition: it is something that is done. Furthermore, it is something that people do by applying what they know, and they do it creatively.

Technology as a product or as a process

Yet for some, technology is a *product* rather than a process. It is something which exists. You can see it, touch it, measure it. We note this in the recently coined 'high technology, intermediate technology, low technology' continuum, which classifies solutions to problems according to whether they are highly mechanized and automated at one extreme or little mechanized and labour-intensive at the other. Much is talked now of 'appropriate technology' particularly in connection with development projects in the Third World. What this means is the choice of appropriate technological solutions (whether high, low or intermediate) for the problems encountered, taking into consideration all relevant and related factors. Thus a highly automated solution may not be the most appropriate for a country with a largely unemployed population, a mechanically sophisticated solution for a country whose politics creates difficulties for the importation of necessary spare parts or indeed a highly labour-intensive solution for a country whose religious or social structure is unfavourable to such occupations. Such choices imply an intelligent analysis of the real situation (problem) and a creative search for an appropriate solution. This is very much a *process*.

So appropriate technology is a process concept. High or intermediate technology is a product concept. It is very easy to point out a host of poorly designed, poorly thought out technological products: machines which do not do what they should, or do not do it well, industries which create more problems than they solve. It is perhaps an understandable human error to pass from the criticism of some poor *products* to a general criticism and rejection of the *process*. Such a rejection of technology has occurred in the minds of some people. Technology is seen as a monster which threatens all the values of society, a dehumanizing influence which must be resisted.

The origins of educational technology

1. The product concept

Technology has entered education in both the product and the process sense. We see this in the two definitions of educational technology (1) and (2) suggested by Lumsdaine in 1964. Educational technology (1) is the hardware or product type. It is the use of equipment (as opposed to humans) in the teaching process. At the low-technology end of the spectrum the products are chalkboards, wallcharts, simple models and real objects. At the intermediate level we have such items as the overhead projector, slide and film projectors, simple teaching machines and any other presentation hardware essentially still under the control of the teacher. At the high technology end we have packaged distance education through radio or television, complex teaching or simulation devices, computer assisted instruction and dial-access information systems. The progress from low to high is marked by increased complexity and sophistication of the hardware and increased need to pre-programme and pre-prepare the message content (software) by specialists, thus leading to a progressive change in the role of the human element in the system (teacher) from planning/ executing to selecting/managing.

2. The process concept

Educational technology (2) is the software or process type. It is concerned with the development of learning experiences, through the application of the sciences of learning. This definition is in general terms very much within our own definition of technology as a process. How it was depicted by Lumsdaine in 1964 was however somewhat limited by the very 'state of the technology' at that time. The science that had most concerned itself with learning was of course psychology and this had tended (and still tends) to concentrate on the study of individuals learning relatively simple content under controlled conditions. The strong influence of reinforcement principles was being felt in the learning sciences field and 'programmed instruction' was the technological product currently in vogue. Thus unfortunately, though perhaps unavoidably, the process concept of educational technology became intertwined with the product concept of step-by-step programmed learning materials.

Despite the efforts of writers such as Susan Markle (1969) to establish that 'programming is a process', the general view of 'programmed instruction' held by non-specialists (ie by teachers rather than programmers) is very much a *product* view. Perhaps there has been more success in Britain than in most other countries in establishing the *process* view of programming, as evidenced by the title of the Association for Programmed Learning and Educational Technology where the two concepts are used almost as synonyms. In the United States on the other hand, several attempts have been made to coin new phrases that would sort out the confusion.

Growth: new names and techniques

The earliest (and perhaps the one to which Lumsdaine's second concept owes its origin) is Gilbert's (1961) 'Mathetics' system. Launched in a specially published *Journal of Mathetics* this was heralded as 'the technology of education'. It is a system of task analysis, behaviour classification and learning exercise design, based on tested principles of learning and behaviour, and a considerable amount of commonsense: in short the 'creative application of science . . . .' Where it fell short was in its view of education. Even Gilbert himself later (1969) retracted his claim that this was a total technology of education. However he says that whereas in 1961 we were not ready to launch such a total technology, now (in 1969) we know enough to enable us to do so. We will investigate Gilbert's technique in detail in later chapters. For now, it suffices to comment that a technology is never *total* just as science or knowledge is never complete. It would be more useful to talk of the *power* of a technology: what complexity and variety of problems is it capable of solving. We can note the attempt to increase the power of a technology in the work of Robert Gagné and his collaborators at Florida State University over the years. Gagné's original classic *The Conditions for Learning* (1968) outlines a technology for the development of teaching/learning experiences (events) based very much on the same scientific principles as Gilbert's, but with an extension into the area of cognitive (conceptual) learning which Mathetics appears at first sight not to consider. By the 1970s Gagné's thinking has expanded to embrace other principles of learning, developed by psychologists such as Piaget and Bruner, resulting in a more powerful technology, capable of being applied to a wider range of educational purposes (Gagné and Briggs 1974). The rather mechanistic term of 'instructional engineering' has been coined at Florida State for this technology, in yet one more recent attempt to flee from the confusions of the term educational technology.

But confusion continues . . .

As an example of this confusion, and the serious consequences it can have, one may quote from the strong attack on the educational technology approach made by Hamblin (1974). In his otherwise excellent book on the evaluation and control of training Hamblin devotes a whole chapter (the last one) to a criticism of educational technology and the educational technologist. He examines the two concepts already discussed above, and also the third meaning, or 'educational technology (3)' suggested by Davies (1971). This is based on a wider organizational view (a systems view) of the problem under attack, which Hamblin rejects as being 'difficult to pin down' and 'capable of criticism due to the inadequacies of the systems theory of organization'. Whereas one must agree that the sciences of education are in many ways incomplete and inadequate (and therefore any application of these sciences must also be limited in its power) these are insufficient grounds for the rejection of a concept as an ideal for which to strive.

Educational technology seen as 'mass production'

Be that as it may, Hamblin appears to reject this wider concept and identifies educational technology (2), the one derived from programmed instruction, as the true definition of what educational technologists do. He then says 'educational technologists seek to advance the technology of education.' What such a phrase means is not at first clear (surely, from the process definition of technology, an educational technologist would seek to advance the efficiency of certain educational purposes). From what follows, his meaning becomes clear. He quotes Joan Woodward's work (1965, 1970) on the relationship between technology and organization, that

> . . . production systems which are technologically the most advanced are also the least adaptable and work to the longest time scale of decision making. These are the process industries (chemical plants, oil refineries and so on) in which vast resources are invested in the creation of a closely programmed and tightly controlled process which will continue to perform the same task over a very long period.

In contrasting such mass production systems with unit production systems 'in which every production task is different from the previous one', Hamblin sees the educational technologist as seeking to move education in the direction of mass production while the 'discovery learning' and 'interactive skills' camp is trying to move it in the direction of unit production.

Thus Hamblin's assumptions appear to be:

The implied criticism of educational technology . . .

1. 'Technology' is a measurable product or characteristic of a system, identified by the degree of mechanization/automation/pre-programming present.
2. All 'technologists' have a vested interest in applying high technology solutions rather than low technology ones.
3. In the specific case of education, therefore, all educational technologists seek to make educational systems more mechanized/automated/ pre-programmed/dehumanized.

. . . and the defence

An alternative view of the situation might be as follows:

1. Technology is a process of creatively applying certain known and tested principles (science) to a given practical purpose (or problem). (Thus technology is scientific method in a practical situation.)
2. All technologists should have an interest in developing the most appropriate solution to the given practical purpose or problem. (Thus technology must search all possible avenues and will borrow principles from a variety of bodies of science, depending on the nature of the practical situation.)
3. In the specific case of education, therefore, educational technologists should develop and apply methods which are appropriate to the educational purpose or problem under study. (Thus, the limits to what an educational technologist might do are established by what he knows, and the purposes are established by his, or his boss's, view of education.)

How developed and powerful is educational technology?

Do we really have a usable technology of education or of training at the present moment? How powerful is it?

The sciences of human behaviour, psychology and sociology, are as yet quite young. Few well-tested and generalizable principles exist, as compared to such sciences as physics, chemistry, or even biology. It is interesting to compare the situation in biology about 100 years ago with the present state of development of the science. A century ago, Linneaus was busy classifying living organisms, constructing a (by no means perfect) taxonomy. Today we can explain nearly all of the phenomena of life by a few basic principles (DNA, RNA, etc) and some say we are on the verge of creating life.

In psychology today, we are just at the stage of developing (by no means perfect) taxonomies of learning. Who knows where we shall be in 100 years, but it is not surprising that some authors consider it premature to claim the existence of an all-embracing technology of education.

1.6 An analysis of the growth and development of educational technology

Behavioural technology

There are some areas of learning psychology where coherent sets of principles are emerging. The first area to be practically exploited was operant conditioning, very successfully in the control and modification of behaviour under clinical conditions (treatment of neuroses, stuttering, etc) and perhaps rather less successfully at the beginning for teaching new behaviours in education (Skinner's linear programmes).

This latter application grew and flourished for a decade or so and then appeared to stop. Some would even claim that 'programmed instruction is dead'. But this is not so. Linear programmed texts may be on the wane but principles of programming continue to develop and to be applied to the production of a variety of other products including:

☐ Individualized/personalized instruction
☐ Competency-based education
☐ Learning modules, etc.

These principles, or in other words, the process of programmed instruction, involve the detailed analysis of behaviour (both the behaviour to be learned and the previously existing behaviour of the learner). Thus it gained the name of 'behavioural technology'. Some prefer the term 'behavioural engineering'. The approach popularized particularly by the work of Gilbert (1961) on Mathetics and the later work of Mechner (1965) is extremely detailed and systematic.

A micro technology
One could refer to it as a micro technology because it carries the analysis of behaviour to a micro level. Indeed, as we shall see in later chapters, the power of this technology lies in its ability to discover the most obscure cause of learning difficulty both in the topic to be learned and in the individual learner.

However not all learning presents obscure learning difficulties. Some learning is only moderately difficult, and some is very simple. Moreover, not all learning tasks (particularly the higher order ones such as problem-solving) are easy to analyse in terms of basic behavioural patterns.

Instructional technology
Therefore, alternative approaches to instructional design have arisen, some simpler and faster, some better able to deal with higher order learning. The theoretical base has also strengthened. Recent work by psychologists as varied as Bruner (1966) and Gagné (1974), by cyberneticians such as Landa (1976) and Pask (1976), and by practical practitioners such as Gilbert (1969), Horn (1969) and several prominent commercial companies (eg Praxis Corporation in the USA and Learning Systems in the UK) has enriched the technology of instruction both in terms of basic principles and specific practical techniques.

Increase in scope and power
Whereas it may be premature to claim the existence of a well-developed technology of education, a technology of instruction exists here and now. It is both powerful and versatile, capable of being used creatively for the solving of instructional problems. Though perhaps not as micro as the behavioural analysis approach, the technology still operates at a detailed level and with problems that are amenable to instructional solutions.

Performance technology
However, this proved not to be enough. Particularly in industrial training (where instruction is furnished as a solution to a real problem in the hope of a quick return in the form of improved job performance) it was often noticed that instruction was not the only possible, nor always the best solution to a job performance problem. Other possibilities such as motivation, better selection procedures, job reorganization and better supervision are sometimes more appropriate. How to select the most appropriate solution? The technology expanded.

Extension at the 'front end'
A technique variously called 'front-end analysis' (Harless 1968) or 'performance problem analysis' (Mager and Pipe, 1970) was developed to do just that: to analyse performance problems at the front end of the instructional design process in order to avoid the possibility of developing training where no training is needed. The full potential of this technique is yet to be realized. It can serve, in an expanded form, as the basis of a methodology for training needs assessment (developed by the author and presented in later chapters). This methodology has the advantages that it considers alternatives to training as well as training, attempts to construct a multi-disciplinary complete solution to the performance problems in an organization and in so doing breaks down the barriers to horizontal communication and cooperation which so often exist in organizations, between training department, organization and methods, work study, etc.

The author believes there would be much potential in attempting to extend the technique to education as well. All too often people are taught things that they could find out otherwise, do without, or work out for themselves. Too often one sees the school made responsible for attaining objectives which could be much better attained through other sub-systems of our society.

What about the 'rear end'   One aspect, which the author considers to be still rather weak in education and training is the implementation and management of instructional systems, particularly on a large scale and in the long term. There are innumerable cases of projects that started life with great promise but later failed to fulfil this promise. As in general only the human elements in an instructional system are variable (the materials stay the same), the reasons for such decline in efficiency must lie with the humans, teachers, possibly students and definitely managers. We shall deal with this aspect later. However there is much to learn yet concerning the maintenance of performance and the multiplication and large-scale dissemination of training.

Towards a technology of human resources development   Progress is being made in this aspect, because learning is not the only aspect of human behaviour that has been receiving the attention of scientists in recent years. We have now at least embryonic technologies of human development (both personal development and development in group interactions), of manpower planning and forecasting, and of organizational development. All these technologies can interact and contribute to strengthening each other. Malcolm Warren (1978) writing in the 1978-79 *International Yearbook of Educational and Instructional Technology* is most optimistic on this point. He says:

> The technologies needed to manage effectively an organization's other resources — physical, technical and financial — have been known and refined over many years. The technologies relating to the management of personnel are of more recent development and are not nearly as well tuned. Until recently, there has been no centralizing theory or sets of theories which provide an integrating 'glue' for focusing on human resources management.
>
> What is occurring to make human resources management a possibility is the merging of two themes. The first theme is the development of a theory base relating to individual behaviour, particularly the way in which adults learn and respond to their environment. The second theme is the development of theories relating to the way in which organizations of individuals behave, both within the organization's own system and in their response to their environment. The significance of this merger of theories about individual behaviour and organizational behaviour does not stem from the desire for an academically acceptable general theory of human resources, but rather from the growing evidence that combining knowledge about individuals and about organizations into a single set of activities leads to measurably improved performance by the organization.
>
> Where in the past specific programmes or actions have failed to fulfil their promise of improved performance, an integration of the various elements that go into human resources management has demonstrated long-term results reflected in the profit and loss statement of the firm.

Any such integrated technology of human resources management must include a comprehensive technology of training, capable of dealing with the types of training that Hamblin claims to be exactly opposed to current educational technology practice, the learner-controlled, learner-developed type or training situation. But educational technologists are there already. Warren (1978) also comments on this:

> There has been another shift in focus, particularly in private sector learning situations. This shift towards the individual learner controlling his or her own learning processes is changing not only the technologies of instruction but also the very role of the technologist. This new role of 'facilitator' is still poorly defined and the techniques and skills required to carry out the role effectively are not fully understood. The objective, however, is clear: to provide learners with the tools and resources they need to meet learning objectives and performance outcomes which they themselves have developed or have shared in developing.
>
> Learner control places entirely new demands upon the training function. Since its role is to facilitate learning and skill-building, it must be able to produce instruments and processes which will enable the learner to assess accurately needs, set objectives, self-evaluate learning, identify resources, access those resources and

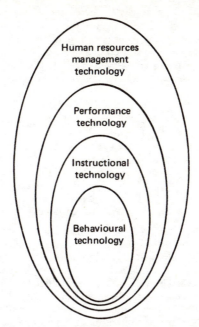

Figure 1.8 *The technology of human resources management contains performance technology which contains instructional technology, etc, as components*

demonstrate successful accomplishment of learning objectives. At the same time, the training function continues to be accountable for the development of instructional units, with the added requirement that those units be devised in such a manner as to be available to the learners in sequences and timing that they control.

It is in the application of learner-controlled instruction to management development that the impact of the human resources management model is most clearly felt. First of all, management development is seen as the means to accomplish two ends. The first is the improvement of performance of the individual in his or her present position. The second is to provide the learning or behaviour necessary to qualify that individual for selection for a promotional position.

The requirement that a management development function be able to respond to individual development needs has created in some organizations a new kind of institution. Rather than providing a classroom curriculum, the new institution acts as a resource centre in which learning units of various kinds from magazine articles to computer assisted response sets are available at the discretion of learners. The centre becomes a place where an individual manager has access to many of the resources he or she needs to complete his or her development plan. The challenge facing the management development function in this case is providing the indexing and instrumentation needed to make use of the resource centre easy for the participant.

Where might trainers learn something about the running of learning resources centres? From educational technologists working in elementary and secondary schools, and in a few universities. This may be one area of development where education is actually ahead of industry. Resource-based learning is a 'here and now' in British education, and has been for over a decade.

1.7 The systems approach

Origins of
the systems
approach

The systems approach was born in the field of systems engineering and was
first applied rigorously to the design of electronic, mechanical, military and
space systems. Here it got involved with man-machine systems and from there
it was a short step to organizational and management systems. It began to be
used in training and then in education from the late 1950s and early 1960s.
What was new was the systematic methodology; the general approach is as old
as scientific method itself and has been practised by a few enlightened souls for
generations.

The use of
flow charts
to describe
the systems
approach

The proponents of the systems approach present their methodologies,
generally in flow chart form. Two examples are shown below (see Figures 1.9
and 1.10). Both attempt to illustrate the stages that should be followed to
identify the training or educational needs (define the problem), analyse thes
needs in order to transform them into objectives (analyse the problem), design
the instructional methods and materials (develop a solution), implement
experimentally and finally evaluate the course.

The
limitations of
flow charts

However, such flow chart presentations are an ineffective, indeed a
somewhat misleading, way of explaining the systems approach:

1. They give the impression of a more or less linear, step-by-step process,
   where one step is completed before the next one is commenced. This is
   not in fact the case. Problem-solving involves a lot of jumping forward,
   based on sudden insights, and feeding back to complete or alter earlier
   steps. The flow charts should have arrows (perhaps dotted to indicate the
   occasional use of these paths) from every block to every other block,
   both forwards and backwards. But this would make the diagrams so
   cluttered as to be unreadable.
2. They give the impression that most of the analysis happens at the
   beginning, the synthesis or design stages about the middle and evaluation
   mainly at the end of the process. In reality, systems thinking (the
   application of the systems approach) involves the exercise of these **three**
   types of intellectual activity at all stages throughout the process.
3. Finally, such flow charts have tended to give the impression that the
   procedure is mechanistic, that there are precise rules for the carrying out
   of each stage, as in the case of a flow chart of a computer procedure.
   Some rules do exist but these do not cover all eventualities. Some step-
   by-step procedures exist but these are more to guide one's thinking
   rather than to take over the thinking process. The systems approach to
   problem-solving is not *algorithmic*; it is *heuristic*. (These terms are used
   here in the sense in which they are used in mathematics.)

Algorithmic
procedures

An algorithmic problem-solving procedure is one which, if followed
correctly in the appropriate circumstances, is bound to lead to the correct
solution or outcome. The example below (Figure 1.11) shows (in flow chart
form) the algorithm for calculating capital gains tax liability. If followed
correctly it is bound to give a correct solution. (Incidentally, such binary
[or yes/no] flow charts have of recent years been referred to as algorithms and
have found many applications in training both as design tools and as means of
communication.) We shall be using such flow charts extensively. However, we
should note that they are but *one* way of *representing* algorithms. The
algorithm is the procedure being represented and this may often be done just
as effectively in simple prose (as in cook book recipes) by check-lists (as in
aircraft maintenance) or by other forms of charts and decision tables (we shall
meet some of these later in this book).

Heuristic
procedures

A heuristic problem-solving procedure is one which is based on general
strategies rather than precise rules. Using these strategies improves the chances
of coming up with a solution, but does not guarantee a correct solution. Many
mathematicians would not **grace** algorithmic procedures with the name

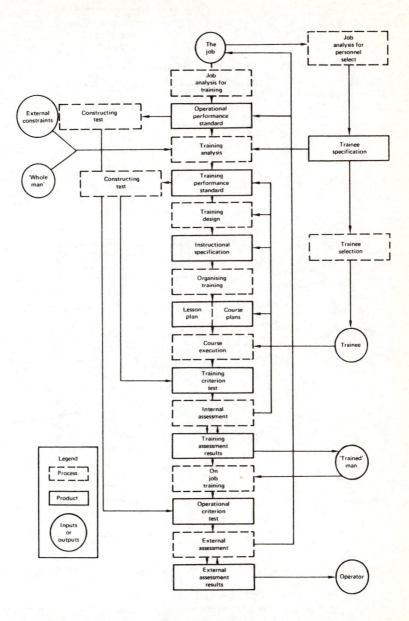

Figure 1.9 *A flow chart illustrating the systems approach to course design (as used for training in the Royal Navy)*

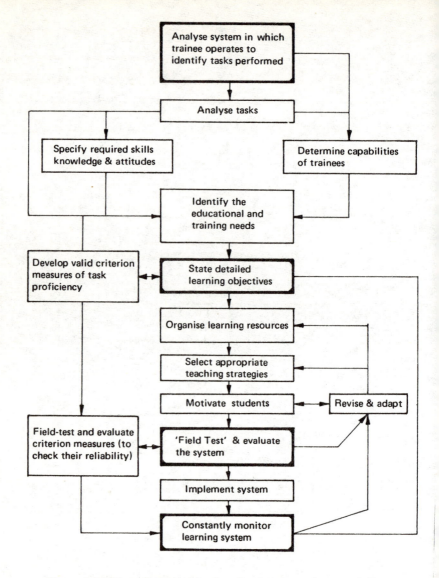

Figure 1.10 *Flow chart used to describe a system of course design*

'problem-solving' but would reserve this term for such problems where there is
no algorithm (ie where heuristic approaches have to be used). This is the case
of solving a new problem, rather than repeating a well practised procedure.
While the study of heuristics goes back to at least Descartes and was very
popular among nineteenth-century mathematicians, it was not very well
documented or taught (problem formulation and problem-solving are still the
weakest parts of mathematics instruction from primary through to university
levels). This is partly due to neglect — an excellent book by Polya entitled
How to Solve It, which sets out some powerful heuristic strategies for
mathematical problem-solving, has been on the market for 30 years (Polya
1948).

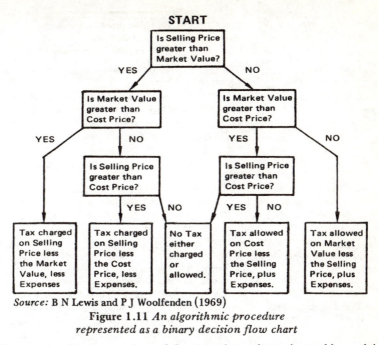

Source: B N Lewis and P J Woolfenden (1969)

Figure 1.11 *An algorithmic procedure represented as a binary decision flow chart*

We reproduce here a summary of the stages in mathematics problem-solving and the heuristic strategies (or key questions) that Polya suggests for each stage, for two reasons:

1. The problem-solving stages outlined by Polya are remarkably similar to those we have outlined for the systems approach. Polya does not use this term. It was not in widespread use in 1948. However, he does use 'scientific method'. We would certainly classify Polya's method as an application of the systems approach to mathematical problem-solving.
2. The questions, or heuristics, listed by Polya would certainly defy any attempt at being flow charted. For any given problem you would use the questions as an organic system of inquiry, in any order and as often as required, and not all questions for all problems. Although some structure exists it is rather loose and certainly not linear. This emphasizes the limitations of the flow chart as a means of describing the systems approach, and illustrates the way that I have attempted to structure this book. In the rest of this chapter I shall outline some heuristics which can help in the solution of problems in the education or training areas.

As a sort of footnote, it is worth making six observations:

1. Polya's book remained in its first hardback edition from 1945 until 1957. Since then, it has gone into paperback (1971) and several editions, sales being stimulated largely by the adoption of the book as a set book by the Open University. An example of a good idea before its time, lying dormant, or of the general inertia and unwillingness of educational systems as a whole to improve themselves?
2. One does not need to stick to mathematics to illustrate algorithmic and heuristic processes. Lewis and Horabin (1969) produced an algorithm which guarantees that the user will not lose a game of noughts and crosses (see Figure 1.13). If both players follow the algorithm, they draw every time which rather takes away the point of the game. This is a game of skill in which the number of options open to a player at any one time

HOW TO SOLVE IT

UNDERSTANDING THE PROBLEM

First.
You have to *understand* the problem.

What is the unknown? What are the data? What is the condition? Is it possible to satisfy the condition?
Is the condition sufficient to determine the unknown?
Or is it insufficient? Or redundant? Or contradictory?
Draw a figure. Introduce suitable notation.
Separate the various parts of the condition.
Can you write them down?

DEVISING A PLAN

Second.
Find the connection between the data and the unknown.
You may be obliged to consider auxiliary problems if an immediate connection cannot be found.
You should obtain eventually a *plan* of the solution.

Have you seen it before? Or have you seen the same problem in a slightly different form?
Do you know a related problem? Do you know a theorem that could be useful?
Look at the unknown! And try to think of a familiar problem having the same or a similar unknown.
Here is a problem related to yours and solved before. Could you use it? Could you use its result? Could you use its method? Should you introduce some auxiliary element in order to make its use possible?
Could you restate the problem? Could you restate it still differently? Go back to definitions.

If you cannot solve the proposed problem try to solve first some related problem. Could you imagine a more accessible related problem? A more general problem? A more special problem? An analogous problem? Could you solve a part of the problem? Keep only a part of the condition, drop the other part: how far is the unknown then determined, how can it vary? Could you derive something useful from the data? Could you think of other data appropriate to determine the unknown? Could you change the unknown or the data, or both if necessary, so that the new unknown and the new data are nearer to each other? Did you use all the data? Did you use the whole condition? Have you taken into account all essential notions involved in the problem?

CARRYING OUT THE PLAN

Third.
Carry out your plan.

Carrying out your plan of the solution, *check each step*. Can you see clearly that the step is correct? Can you prove that it is correct?

LOOKING BACK

Fourth.
Examine the solution obtained.

Can you *check the result?* Can you check the argument? Can you derive the result differently? Can you see it at a glance? Can you use the result, or the method, for some other problem?

Source: Polya (1945, 1957)

Figure 1.12 *Polya's approach to mathematical problem-solving: an example of the systems approach in practice?*

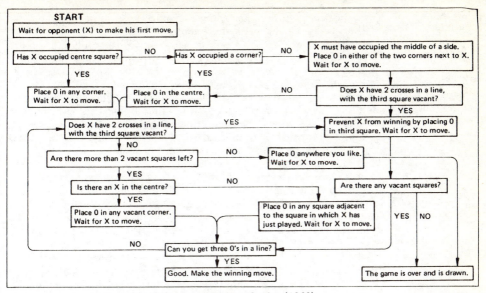

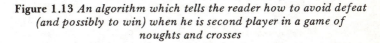

Source: B N Lewis and P J Woolfenden (1969)

Figure 1.13 *An algorithm which tells the reader how to avoid defeat (and possibly to win) when he is second player in a game of noughts and crosses*

is very limited indeed. A player wins by being the less careless of the two, or by not understanding the finer points (knowing the algorithm).

However, those familiar with more complex games, such as chess, bridge, or even draughts or monopoly, will realize that the variety of options open to a player during a game is so large (there are always so many moves to consider) that it would be totally impractical to follow an all-embracing flow chart. Indeed it may be impossible to construct such a chart in the first place. General principles or hunches based on past experience have to be used. The player with the better grasp of the principles and with more experience at playing thoughtfully (including the careful analysis of games and evaluation of moves) generally wins.

Even chess-playing computers operate on heuristic rather than algorithmic principles. They make their moves according to certain general strategies, weighing up alternatives in the light of limited available data. They are as good as (a) the general strategies programmed into them and (b) their ability to 'learn' the opponent's strategies and use this information to adapt their own. They can construct and modify a model of their opponent using this model as a factor in their decisions.

3. Many problems can be solved by either algorithmic or heuristic approaches. The motor mechanic or TV repairman may be taught an algorithm, a step-by-step procedure for fault finding. This logical procedure should guarantee that he locates a fault in a reasonable time, as compared to random checks. But as his experience grows, he develops heuristic approaches. He forms conceptual models of certain types of car or TV set made up of sets of principles such as 'in this car this type of symptom generally means this fault'. These heuristics do not guarantee a solution. But once a sufficient number of such heuristic principles have been learned, the repairman jumps to conclusions and more often than not is correct, thus reducing the average fault finding time. Although algorithmic procedures are easier to learn and apply initially, heuristic procedures are more efficient in the long run.

4. Thus, the efficient use of heuristic procedures depends on:
   ☐ Knowing the heuristics or principles
   ☐ Using them to form a model of what the probable solution will be like, and
   ☐ Modifying the model as necessary in the light of experience as the problem-solving process continues.

   Even the major stages or steps (define the problem, analyse it, develop solutions, etc) merge into each other. In order to select the right questions to ask when defining and analysing the problem, it helps to have already formed a tentative model of possible solutions. Thus Step 3 starts before Steps 1 and 2 are completed, and so on.

5. As already stated the systems approach is primarily an heuristic procedure. Step-by-step procedures exist for certain activities (eg for task analysis) but these are only at the level of collecting or organizing information. What to do with the information is not governed by an immutable algorithm. Creative solutions pop up as sudden flashes of insight (and one then back tracks to check them out for viability) rather than as a result of plodding carefully and completely through each step in sequence. Apart from an overall methodology, one needs some basic models, experience in adapting them to specific situations, and the ability to jump backwards and forwards in the design process, without losing sight of the total 'wood' whilst studying some aspect of a particular 'tree'.

   This is where systems concepts and systems thinking play their role. The systems approach is one part of methodology to five parts of systems thinking.

6. However, as always, it is much easier to explain and present a methodology than a way of thought. Moreover, a methodology is easier to present step-by-step rather than all at once. The following sections of the book deal with each step in detail. Some 'tools' which can assist in the planning, the documenting and the communication of one's thinking are introduced in each section. Case studies are used to illustrate these tools in action and also, when possible, to illustrate the heuristic and creative aspects of the process.

1.8 Heuristics for instructional design

In order to give an overview of the following sections, the remainder of this chapter lists some of the key questions or heuristics which the instructional systems designer should use in order to maximize the chances of a successful solution to the original problem, not a part solution, inadequate by itself, nor a solution to another different problem, or an inefficient or unduly expensive solution.

The questions are illustrated by examples taken from both training and education at both macro (large scale instructional systems) and micro (single instructional problem) levels.

Map 1.1 *Heuristics for instructional design: define the problem*

Key questions/actions	Comments and examples	
	Education	Training
Step 1: Define the problem		
Analysis		
Is it really the problem (or a symptom of a more fundamental one)?	Is 'poor maths teaching' the problem or just one symptom of 'inadequate resources for maths teaching'? Is 'lack of creative thinking ability' just one symptom of inadequate curricula?	Is falling sales a performance problem or a general market trend? Is low productivity a human performance problem or is the organization at fault?
Who sees it as a problem? Why is he dissatisfied? Are these sufficient grounds to proceed?	Some teachers see any innovation as a problem. Distrust of change.	A manager sees certain behaviour as a problem just because it is different.
What extent of dissatisfaction? What will he pay for a solution? (What is a solution worth?)	Educational systems are notorious for identifying problems they are unwilling to tackle. The education 'industry' has the lowest index of investment in research and development.	Often the worth of a solution to a human performance problem is directly calculable in terms of increased productivity reduced wastage, time, etc.
How does this compare to the worth of other problems that one might be attacking instead?	It has been said that if one tenth of the funds which used to be spent on school milk had been spent on appropriate research and development the poor literacy and numeracy performance of British school children would have been a thing of the past.	Generally there are more problems than resources. Defining priorities for training is an integral part of training needs analysis in any organization.
Synthesis		
State what is and what should be in precise and measurable terms. Avoid statements which imply specific solutions. State the 'real life' or 'job' objectives. (What should a solution achieve?)	'Is': low numbers of maths graduates 'Should be': double the number of maths graduates. Avoid at this stage: 'improve the training of maths teachers' 'extend the hours devoted to maths'. A 20 per cent increase in graduates each year for the next four years.	'Is': poor productivity, high waste of material 'Should be': 50 per cent up on productivity 30 per cent down on waste. Avoid at this stage: Introduce bonus payment schemes. Tighten up on supervision, etc. Productivity to rise by 50 per cent within six months. Waste cut by 30 per cent within four months.
Evaluation		
Consider the probability of success in developing a solution. (Are there other systems with conflicting objectives? Are there any environmental constraints which make it improbable/impossible to achieve objectives?)	More than a 20 per cent increase per year is not possible because time is needed to extend facilities. Maintaining a 20 per cent annual increase is improbable because of other openings for appropriately qualified entrants.	Other similar firms have much higher productivity and lower waste. No specific reasons seen why we cannot emulate them. Other priorities make it impossible to start working on this problem for three months.
Estimate the probable cost of a solution. (Is the cost more or less than the worth? By what margin?)	The cost of a 20 per cent annual increase in maths graduates is high. What will be the drop-out and wastage rates?	The worth in this case is £2.5 million in a year. It is unlikely that a solution would cost more than a few per cent of this to develop.
Estimate the relative worth of solving this problem as opposed to using the same resources on some other problem (priorities).	Would it make more sense to concentrate our resources on adult retraining and functional maths courses?	Is this an exceptional problem? Are there others like it?

Map 1.2 *Heuristics for instructional design: analyse the problem*

Key questions/actions	Comments and examples	
	Education	Training
Step 2: Analyse problem and select solution		
Analysis		
What is the underlying nature of the problem? Information or performance deficiency?	Often, in education, problems appear as an information deficiency: □ 'insufficient is known about . . .' □ 'I wish to know about . . .'	Generally in 'training' we meet performance deficiency problems (eg 'He is not performing up to required standard').
Is instruction an appropriate solution (or part of a solution)? What other solutions are appropriate? What combination or mix of solutions is appropriate?	Analysing the information will indicate what parts of it really need objectives-oriented teaching (ie instruction) and which parts simply need dissemination.	Analysing the performance problem identifies to what extent instruction can be expected to solve it and what contributions job design, motivation, supervision, information, feedback, etc may make.
For instructional solutions: Where do the objectives come from? Who defines them? What are the instructional objectives? What are the learners' entry levels?	Analysing information in order to establish instructional objectives can start from the content itself or from the general skills that the information is to foster.	Performance objectives are derived directly from the job or task. Various levels of analysis can be used depending on the degree of task complexity.
Synthesis		
Design, in general terms, all solutions which appear possibly appropriate. Identify the resources required for developing, producing and implementing each solution.	For information problems apart from instructional solutions might include reference, descriptive, publicity or impact, feedback, or experiential solutions.	For performance problems apart from instructional solutions might include job redesign, information feedback, organizational development, etc solutions.
If an instructional solution is selected: state in detail the specific instructional objectives at the task or unit level. State the prerequisites for each task or unit. Develop test items for post-test and prerequisite test.	A unit is a coherent block of information relatively self-contained eg 'Roman Britain' in a history course. Generally a student would learn several units, and each unit would have several specific objectives.	A task is a coherent set of activities or operations, generally carried out together towards a common objective. Generally in order to master the task the student must also master some specific information.
Evaluation		
Consider the advantages and disadvantages of alternative solutions in terms of: □ probable effectiveness □ probable cost □ probable development difficulties □ probable implementation difficulties □ possible control difficulties □ possible evaluation difficulties □ other factors considered important (eg political, ethical) □ possible side effects (new problems) If possible, try out or simulate the solutions before making a final decision.	Effectiveness may be measured directly on the objectives of the unit, or on the potential for transfer of skill to a different situation. This is particularly valued in education. Development and implementation difficulties arise in schools due to unpreparedness of staff to change or to accept innovations. Preparing the ground is very important. Control, political and ethical factors often render a solution unacceptable in a school environment although it may be acceptable elsewhere. The converse is also sometimes true.	Keeping theory content to only the 'necessary and sufficient' for executing the task is an important factor in the cost/effectiveness of training. Development and implementation of objectives-based instructional systems is facilitated if the organization already operates on a management by objectives basis. Labour relations, trade unions and industrial law must be considered very carefully.

Map 1.3 *Heuristics for instructional design: develop a solution*

Key questions/actions	Comments
Step 3: Develop the solution	**The education/training division hardly applies as from now on we are in the business of instruction**
Analysis	
In order to teach each unit or task what are the 'enabling' or sub-objectives that must first be mastered and the type of learning that they represent?	May be done by behavioural analysis (Gilbert). Sometimes easier to do as a hierarchy (Gagné). In addition to Gilbert's behavioural types, Gagné uses some learning categories more concerned with higher verbal learning and thinking. Best done by behavioural analysis (Gilbert) for practical and perceptual tasks. Identifies the chains (procedures), discriminations and generalizations (concepts) involved in learning the task.
Do the potential learners exhibit any preferences for learning styles, past habits and interests related to the objectives of instruction, sources of interest in the topic to be taught? How much new material can be safely presented in one exercise?	The objectives of this stage of the learner analysis are the same for any course of instruction: ☐ Learning preferences and styles may influence choice of plans, strategies, tactics and media of instruction. ☐ Past habits and interests, similar material learned before may indicate sources of 'competition' ('need to unlearn or to discriminate similar content) or of 'facilitation' (common material, useful known examples, analogies) between the objectives to be achieved and past learning.
Analyse the sub-objectives in order to identify the exercises, their sequence, and the strategies and tactics to be used in each.	☐ Sources of interest will help to include motivational material and also to sequence the course so that it shows 'relevance'.
Synthesis	
Select an overall basic course *plan* (or plans). List the enabling or sub-objectives, grouping them into *learning exercises*. Select suitable *strategies* and *tactics* for each exercise. Sequence the exercises for both efficient learning and instructional convenience. Decide the communication *media* and student *grouping* for each exercise/set of exercises. Develop the exercises and the necessary material.	There are many different *plans*, some veering towards the 'mastery learning' philosophy (eg Keller Plan) others towards 'experiential learning' (eg simulation games). An exercise is the basic unit of instructional development. Once its content (its objectives) have been defined and a suitable *strategy* selected, the exercise is developed according to the rules of that strategy. Only two strategies will be considered here. The inductive (exemplified by the behavioural analysis model of exercise design) and the deductive (exemplified by the various guided discovery models). *Tactics* depend on the content and objectives of specific exercises — there are too many to list here. Several factors control sequence — logic, motivational interest, relative difficulty, type of learning, grouping of similar strategies, etc. *Media* and *group size* selection is controlled by the strategies/tactics previously selected. Also interacts with the sequencing question, to avoid unnecessary frequent changes of methods/media. It is now a question of development according to plan.
Evaluation	
Test out all decisions and all exercise materials produced *as soon as possible*. Do not wait until the course is complete. Prepare a developmental testing timechart as the main control instrument for Step 3. Revise as you go along and try to generalize what you discover in order to apply it to later exercises.	Developmental testing can be done with small groups or even individuals. If samples of the real population are not available, better to use approximate substitutes and make allowances than to delay evaluation. Constant formative evaluation is the key to the productivity, motivation and in-service development of the instructional designer.

Map 1.4 *Heuristics for instructional design: implement experimentally*

Key questions/actions	Comments/examples
Step 4: Implement and test the solution	
Analysis	
What is the structure of the wider system into which the one under design is being implanted? Is is likely to be hostile? Will it possibly reject the new system?	In Step 1 we considered whether the overall objectives (the problem to be solved) were compatible with other objectives of related systems. Now we are considering whether the *means* adopted to achieve these objectives are compatible with the wider system. Of course this should be done, at least in part, well before the completion of Step 3, to avoid unnecessary changes, an illustration of how the five steps overlap in practice.
Who will be involved in operating or interacting with the new system? Are they fully informed? Have they been involved actively? What is their attitude?	The human elements in the new system and in its environment are the most unpredictable. Every possible effort should be made, in good time, to enlist full support and develop full capacity of all the human resources concerned. This again should be started way back at Step 1.
Who will be managing the system? Has he the necessary management tools? How will he monitor the day to day operation of the system? How will he rapidly distinguish problems of faulty design from faulty operation?	There is a lot to be said for using the course developers as the course managers during initial trial runs. They are closest to the course materials, and should be closely involved in trial applications, as it is they who can best identify problems in the design and develop remedies.
Synthesis	
Design the run-in implementation of the instructional system. Inform/motivate/involve/train all concerned.	If instructors who did not participate in course development are used, then particular care must be taken over 'selling' them the system, training them in their roles and monitoring their performance.
Design the management system. Ensure that it is capable of monitoring results on a regular basis and is acceptable to the wider system. Motivate and train the personnel concerned.	The management system must be able to process evaluation data efficiently at this stage, to avoid delays that might clog up the system. A system of management drastically different from the norm in the wider system may cause unexpected problems from unexpected sources.
Evaluation	
Monitor results on a regular, management-by-objectives basis. Analyse operational difficulties and their causes. Evaluate the probable effects of any such difficulties on final results. Take immediate remedial action whenever this is possible.	Regular meetings of all concerned, checking and auto-evaluating progress, and setting short-term management goals. Whenever possible, systematic 'formative' evaluation should be carried out right from the commencement of implementation. If cumulative weaknesses are threatening to bring training to a halt, it is necessary to plan remedial actions at once.

Map 1.5 *Heuristics for instructional design: evaluate and revise*

Key questions/actions	Comments/examples	
Step 5: Evaluate and revise	Education	Training
Analysis		
What are the most appropriate measures and instruments for immediate formative evaluation? Can we make the measures reliably and use the results? What are the most appropriate measures and instruments for long-term formative and summative evaluation? At what level do we need to evaluate? Can we make the measures reliably and use the results?	Formative evaluation is performed to improve or form the product. We want results capable of being fed back immediately and usefully into the design process. The measures looked for would be learning objectives achieved and learner reactions, and occasionally expert comments.	
	Summative evaluation is performed to sum up or report on a product. This may be necessary for some management decisions (eg whether to discontinue a project) without any formative intent. But in general, any long-term evaluation should be so planned as to give useful formative data. The data collected in the long run should enable one to perform job-performance evaluation, organizational effects evaluation, ultimate benefit evaluation and cost/benefit evaluation.	
Synthesis		
Prepare the necessary evaluation instruments.	Many of these would (or could) be prepared at early stages of the design process, in Steps 2 and 3.	
Plan the necessary processing mechanisms and feedback channels rapidly to use evaluation data.	This need to plan for feedback is often overlooked, with the result that data piles up, creating work without any useful result (as feedback eventually comes too late, if at all).	
	The preparation of long-term evaluation instruments in the 'pure' education field is very difficult as there is no long-term performance or effect on which the instructional system is based. Course graduates may go into various occupations. We have only very indirect measures of probable long-term effects.	The preparation of long-term performance evaluation instruments, cost-benefit measures, etc is relatively easy in 'hard' industrial training, where performance equals productivity, etc.
Evaluation		
Validate the evaluation instruments to establish levels of validity and reliability.	This is an important, yet often omitted action. It is particularly important in the case of instruments measuring indirect data such as measures of attitude, measures of general educational benefit, etc.	This is not so important in 'hard' training situations, as the instrument often directly measures the performance specified in the objective.
Process and evaluate the data collected. Make formative decisions and feed these back into the design process.	In the 'steady state' when a system is installed and operating well, this stage becomes the process-control stage. As long as nothing unusual happens, evaluation simply continues at a level sufficient to control outputs via input manipulation.	

1.9 Levels of instructional design

The level of detail to which one may have to go in order to develop a satisfactory instructional solution to a given problem may vary. Occasionally one only needs to develop clear *instructional objectives*. Usually, these are then used as the basis for a detailed *instructional plan*, or curriculum, which specifies sequence, content, methods, media, etc. Sometimes one needs to develop detailed *lesson plans* for each lesson, specifying the precise tactics to be adopted at each stage of the lesson. Sometimes one needs to prepare special *instructional materials* in a variety of media.

We plan to examine all four of these levels of instructional design, but to do this thoroughly in one volume is not practical. The more detailed and practical aspects of instructional design will, therefore, be covered in Volume II, while here we examine the initial decision making processes. The table below shows how the two volumes will cover the whole instructional design process, and how their structure relates to Polya's problem-solving methodology.

Polya's main steps in problem-solving	Main stages in the systems approach (Stage 3 is expanded into four levels)	Main sections of 'Designing Instructional Systems'
Understand the problem	1. Define the problem (decide whether it is worth solving)	*Volume 1.* Part 1
	2. Analyse the problem (determine the role of instruction)	Part 2
Devise a plan	3a. Select solution(s) (determine objectives of instruction)	
	3b. The solution (develop a plan or curriculum)	Part 3
Carry out the plan	3c. Steps (prepare detailed lesson plans)	*Volume 2.* Part 1
	3d. Develop resources (prepare instructional materials and media)	Part 2
	4. Implement the system (bring together all parts of the solution)	Part 3
Look back	5. Evaluate the results (monitor, control and improve the system)	

Figure 1.14 *Structure and content of* Designing Instructional Systems *and* Producing Instructional Systems

2. Approaches to Problems in Education and Training

2.1 Macro and micro problems

The macro level

In Chapter 1 we defined 'training' rather glibly as a goal-oriented process (following a fenced path to a predetermined goal) and education as a process which may not necessarily have a specific predetermined end goal ('wandering in the fields to left and right of the path'). However this is not strictly true. If

Education as a sub-system of society

we study the pronouncements of educators on the aims of education, we encounter a variety of goals, albeit stated in general terms. These goals are generally, though not always, stated in relation to the learner, the individual undergoing the educational or training process.

Examples of aims of education not stated in direct relation to the learner include references to the role of education as a leveller of society, as a source of opportunity for a better life, as a means towards the effective use of a nation's human resources, as a tool for maintaining society's traditions, customs, beliefs and social structures, or alternatively as a tool for revolution to change society's beliefs and structure. Such aims are stated at the macro level, treating society as the system of interest, and specifying the inputs to society that the education sub-system should be producing.

If these inputs are not forthcoming, we perceive a problem. The characteristics of this problem may be *quantitative* (eg insufficient number of qualified engineers, insufficient number of married women working due to lack of kindergarten facilities, etc) or *qualitative* (eg inadequate levels of literacy, numeracy, etc among school leavers, inadequate levels of participation in society's political, social or cultural aspects by sections of the population; inadequate knowledge and understanding of one's civil rights and obligations by the society's citizens, etc).

Training as a sub-system of industrial organizations

A similar level of aims of training can be encountered in an industrial or commercial organization, or indeed in a sector of industry (as for example the sectors of industry catered for by the industrial training boards in Great Britain). The aims of training, at this level, may be specified in terms of opportunities for the workforce in general to progress within the industry, for the industry to keep its position and maintain its standards in relation to the competition, or for the industry to change and evolve in line with new market needs and new production technologies. Once again, these aims may have quantitative characteristics (this is the area for human resources or manpower planning) and qualitative characteristics (this is the area of job performance definition and evaluation). When the reality does not match the aims, we perceive a problem.

The complexity of the systems and their problems

Let us not make the error of considering the industrial organization that much simpler than society, by thinking only in terms of training for the job. An industrial organization also has its own culture, with norms, standards of behaviour, organizational structure, etc. Just as the social system attempts to use the education sub-system to maintain the *status quo*, or to change it in a controlled manner in specific directions, so the organization system attempts to use the training sub-system to maintain or change its structure (this is the area for organization development).

So once again, taking the systems view, the similarities between education and training are seen to be of perhaps more significance than the differences. One might, in passing, point out one particular similarity. Both society and industrial organizations often tend to expect more than is reasonable from the education/training sub-systems.

The complexity of the probable solutions

The problems (discrepancies) at the society or organization level are usually multi-faceted, resulting from a combination of causes. The solutions should therefore be multi-faceted, combining various actions. Rarely is education or training a complete solution to a problem in society or industry. But people often talk and act as if this were so. One potential advantage in taking the total systems view of the problem is that in so doing one avoids the dangers of ignoring other (non-educational/training) solutions to our problems or of specifying unrealistic, unattainable aims for our educational or training systems. We shall examine this more closely in later chapters. But first let us consider education/training problems at a more detailed level.

Aims stated in non-learner terms can be conceptualized as desired goals of the educational or training system, as a whole. They state the type and quantity of *output expected* (eg 4000 qualified engineers per annum, decrease of illiteracy from 25 per cent to 10 per cent of the population within 15 years, etc); or the type and quantity of *input expected* (eg an increase of 200 per cent in the annual intake of children to kindergartens, a cut of 20 per cent in the annual supply of trained teachers for elementary schools, etc); or the type of *structure and processes* which should exist (eg the system should be organized on comprehensive lines with no streaming or division according to abilities; students should proceed at their own pace as indicated by their success in mastering the objectives rather than on the basis of their success relative to other students in their age group; the traditional norm-referenced process; etc).

Aims of education

As we proceed to a more detailed level of analysis, we find that the aims of education are expressed more in terms of the learner. We still find examples of aims stated in input, output or process terms, but in all cases they are related more directly to the child, the student, the trainee. As examples we may turn to recent reports and acts of education. Here we encounter:

> *Input statements* such as: 'The purpose of education is to provide the nurture and environment which will enable the child to grow eventually to full stature . . .' (*Norwood Report* 1943: *Curriculum Examinations in Secondary Schools*).
> *Process statements:* 'all boys and girls . . . need to develop capacities for thought, judgement, enjoyment, curiosity . . .' (*Newson Report* 1963: *Half our future*).
> *Output statements:* 'certain skills of communication in speech and writing, in reading with understanding and in calculation involving number and measurement' (*Newson Report* 1963).

In other words, at this level, the aims of education are stated (albeit still in very general terms) as:

☐ What to provide for or do to the learner
☐ What the learner should develop in the way of internal capacities
☐ What the learner should be able to do as a result of learning.

A discrepancy between the actual situation and that defined by the aims is perceived as a problem.

How do we measure the processes?

But here we strike a difficulty. We can perceive the inputs to the learner, and the outputs from the learner, but we cannot directly perceive the processes going on inside the learner. We can only *infer* what these processes might be from our observations of the inputs and outputs. What can our learner do to convince us that he is thinking or judging, enjoying or being curious? What information does he use, and in what order, or how structured, in order to make optimal learning progress? What are the input/output relationships that we can observe, document, measure and use as guides for future educational

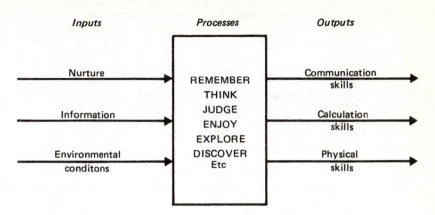

Figure 2.1 *A model for classifying educational aims*

actions? In terms of measuring learning, we are in a sense forced to adopt an input/ouput analysis approach. We can only measure the effects of learning by observing the learner's capabilities for behaviour, or performance, under specific conditions. And we can measure the efficiency of the learning process by observing the inputs used to achieve effective learning. These inputs include the content of education (the information supplied, its structure, etc) and the organization of the environment (the way that the information is made available, the way the supplementary guidance or feedback is given to the learner, etc). In effect, the learner is a black box and any problems perceived are seen as:

☐ Instructional output or performance problems: discrepancies between the actual behaviour capabilities and the desired behavioural capabilities *after learning*.
☐ Instructional input or information problems: discrepancies between the actual and desired information content and/or its structure.

2.2 Some basic viewpoints on the aims and problems of education

Internal learning processes do exist — One should mention here that the impossibility of directly observing the internal learning processes does not mean the denial of their existence, any more than the impossibility of directly observing the detailed structure of matter denies the existence of atoms, protons, neutrons, electrons and so on. We infer the existence of these particles from their observable effect and every so often we are led to postulate the existence of yet other particles to explain yet newer phenomena, which we were hitherto unable to measure. So in learning, we infer the existence of internal capabilities (intelligence, short- and long-term memory, etc) and processes (thinking, problem-solving, etc) from their observable effects. As our capability to measure the effects of learning improves, new phenomena lead us to postulate yet other capabilities or processes.

Many learning theories: a result of the 'youth' of psychology — However improbable, it is theoretically possible that progress in measurement of physical phenomena may one day lead physicists to revise their theories of atomic structure. After all this has happened several times already. There was a period when the 'solid ball' model was the one subscribed to by most physicists. A similar situation of controversy exists among learning theorists and models of the learning process. The 'youth' of psychology as a science is mirrored in the variety of models of learning and the difficulty of measuring the effects of learning with sufficient precision to determine which model is correct. Indeed, probably no existing model is correct, but is only a facet of a more complete, as yet not fully understood, model. If in the much more advanced and precise science of physics new discoveries are still being made which result in modifications to our models of the structure of matter, it would be foolish indeed to expect a different, better defined situation in the very young and as yet imprecise science of learning.

The tendency toward schools of thought

However human nature must have its way. Just as physicists have staked their reputations on the validity of one particular model of the atom, just as so many famous biologists staked their reputation on the authenticity of the Piltdown skull (because it supported their model of the evolution of man) so, throughout this century, educational psychologists have staked their reputations on the authenticity and universality of particular models of the learning process.

The input/ output model

As a reaction to this trend, some behavioural psychologists, notably Professor B F Skinner, adopted the input/output approach, ignoring the internal processes completely. Skinner preaches that one can control and predict learning entirely by the observation of behaviour and the relationships that exist between specific inputs (stimuli), specific output (responses) and the consequences (reinforcers) which follow. We note an analogy between Skinner's 'stimulus/response/reinforcement' cycle, and the system engineer's 'input/output/feedback control' cycle. However, Skinner has been unjustly accused of denying the existence of internal learning processes and capabilities. He never denied their existence; he simply found it unnecessary to consider or to define them in order to analyse, predict and control learning.

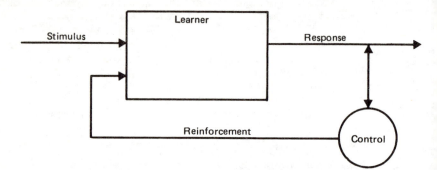

Figure 2.2 *Skinner's input/output model of behaviour control*

This is not all that surprising. The electronics engineer can measure the performance of a given circuit, can predict its performance in new situations, and can construct more complex circuits by combining simpler ones, without the need to tear apart the circuits into their individual components.

The people who need this information are the designer of the components (who must select materials according to their basic electrical properties and put them together so that the intended electron flow patterns may take place), the development engineer (who seeks better ways of achieving results, by modifying the structure of existing circuitry), and the maintenance engineer (who must troubleshoot, identify, interpret the faults and repair the faulty components).

An analogy between Skinner's model and engineering practice

By analogy, the learning engineer who limits his activities to measuring the learning effects of particular teaching activities, or to predicting, on the basis of past measures, the effects of teaching/learning activities, or who constructs more complex teaching/learning systems by connecting together previously tested component activities, has little need of learning theories which deal with the internal processes of *learning*. What he needs are theories of *instruction* dealing exclusively with factors outside the learner.

Only if he intends to improve existing learning processes (that is to redesign the learner), or to repair defective learning processes (to apply some form of thereapy or treatment to transform the poor learner into a good learner) would he need to understand the functioning of internal learning processes. We have hardly got to that stage of sophistication, but there are indications that we are heading in that direction.

Recent work in cybernetics, simulating human learning processes by machines, is giving new insights into the probable organization of human learning. Recent emphasis on 'learning to learn' attempts to apply what little we know about the internal learning processes to enabling the learner to improve his own learning efficiency. Some, little publicized, work is going on into direct actions to improve learning capability by surgical or chemical means. This indeed raises the question of just how far should we go in this direction. What are the moral and ethical implications?

Alternatives to the Skinner model

The opposition in viewpoints between the *gestalt* psychologists and the behaviourists as regards the form of the learning process have led to partisan adherence to specific instructional models such as the conditioning model, the discovery-learning model, the expository learning model, and many others. We shall return to consider the pros and cons of some of these models in later chapters. For the time being, all these are classified as one approach to the problems of instruction: the process-oriented approach which considers the choice of teaching strategies above other considerations.

The process-oriented approach

The work of such educators as Jerome Bruner (1966) is an example of an approach which seems to consider the processes adopted for instruction as the most important and first consideration of the instructional designer. This is not so in reality, as Bruner's views regarding the processes which should be adopted in teaching are based on his views of what is important as the *outputs of learning*. For Bruner, the important results of a child's education are not specific items of knowledge, or specific job-related skills, but generalizable skills which may be applied to life in a variety of ways.

The learner should be instructed in such a way that he can continue to learn, without instruction, in the future. Such skills as identifying relevant information for a given problem, interpreting it, classifying it in a useful way, and discovering interrelations between new and previously learned information emerge as important outputs of the instructional process. Observation of how learners tend to learn these skills most efficiently led Bruner to specify the instructional processes which should be adopted. Bruner stressed (perhaps overstressed) the process aspects of his approach, in reaction to the tendency, prevalent at the time and brought about by the behavioural objectives movement, to stress the output aspects.

The output-oriented approach

The behavioural objectives movement of the 1950s and 1960s is linked with the programmed instruction movement, although its origins are independent. Bloom's taxonomy of educational objectives in the cognitive domain was published in 1956 and was the reflection of widely accepted ideas by test designers in the United States at that time. The work of designing the taxonomy was stimulated by the needs of a common language and

The behavioural objectives movement

methodology in the design of multiple choice objective tests, already accepted on a large scale before programmed learning was introduced. However, the advent of programmed learning and its emphasis on the analysis of behaviour gave new stimulus to the objectives movement, whose creed was that before you do anything about the content or process of instruction you should be sure of the final learning outputs that you wish to achieve. As Mager (1961) put it 'if you don't know where you're going, you're likely to end up some place else'.

Much effort was given during the 1960s to the definition of specific objectives in measurable (and that meant behavioural) terms. The task proved more difficult and time-consuming than might have been imagined. Most progress was made in defining the lower level, simpler objectives, while the higher level, more complex ones (yet exactly those most prized by educational theorists) were left largely undefined. The link between the objectives movement and the programmed instruction movement did not help the image, as the published programmes were also largely concerned with simple rote memorization or 'reproductive' learning (with relatively few good examples of programmed problem-solving). As the movement grew, so did the number and variety of objections. We shall examine some of these more closely in Chapter 3.

Some of the objections to the 'objectives first' or output approach to instructional design strengthened the ranks of the process approach school, tending to lose sight of the fact that their principal theorists (eg Bruner) had not been overlooking outputs but merely concentrating on those outputs they considered important yet neglected. They also tended to lose sight of the original motives for the objectives movement, which was a dissatisfaction with the previous exaggerated emphasis on content or inputs.

The inputs-oriented approach

The inputs approach, although not referred to by this name, has been the main approach to educational course design since the birth of organized institutionalized education. When education was reserved for a small élite of rich individuals whose livelihood did not depend directly on the skills that they gained from the process, it was perhaps reasonable to ignore the outputs and the process. The outputs were defined by the values of society — the concept of the 'educated man' — and this concept was largely defined by the educators themselves. The processes were those best known to the educators, usually those by which they had themselves learned.

The subject discipline tradition

As educational provision spread, and 'an education' became even more a key to status in society, the selective nature of the game tended to play down even more the importance of processes and outputs. The object of the game was to do well in comparison to others, and to be selected for the next rung on the promotional or social ladder. So as long as the instructional process was the same for all and the measures of success the same for all, it was a fair game. The game continues to this day. National examinations still sometimes reflect the personal tastes of the examiner. (How often do we still hear complaints that the examination was totally unexpected because there had been a change in the examiner.)

The denial of output standards

Examination results are still scaled to the norm expected. If an abnormal number of students do well, the examination was too easy and the scores are scaled down accordingly, and if an unusual number do badly, results are scaled up. Where is the incentive to improve the teaching process? It exists on a local scale perhaps, to improve one school's exam record as compared to another's. But an across the board improvement in teaching would wreak havoc with the system (or would simply be absorbed by rescaling the results). When a more effective method of programmed, computer-managed instruction was used to

The inconvenience of improved processes

teach the structures option in an engineering course at Aston University, the results of the students in the structures examination were so outstanding (as compared to their results in other subjects and as compared to the results of other universities on the same examination) that the students were accused by the examining board of having stolen the examination paper. When the reality was explained, the examination board reacted by suggesting a special, more difficult, examination paper for the group (Croxton and Martin, 1970).

2.3 Industrial training

Early origins

While all this was going on in formal education, vocational education or training was developing along somewhat different lines. The trade guilds, were the guardians of standards in professions as diverse as silversmiths, shoemakers and law. The trade apprenticeship was the process almost universally adopted: instruction by the 'master' or 'sitting next to Nellie' are alternative names for this process, mirroring different points of view as to its effectiveness. Outputs were never lost from view. After all, a craftsman is always judged by the products of his work (though this may be more difficult to define in the case of a solicitor than of a shoemaker). However, unfortunately, another output factor crept in to confuse the issue: the quantity of skilled craftsmen in a given profession that the market could absorb. In order to protect existing members, the guilds had to control the output of new craftsmen, and this they did by two means: the insistence on long periods of apprenticeship and the maintenance of artificially high, even irrelevant standards. Thus, in vocational training also, the need for more relevant, better defined output criteria, or for better, more efficient instructional processes was not seen as of great importance. Once again there was a tendency by the master to control the inputs by reference to what he knew best or what he liked doing best.

With the coming of the industrial revolution, however, the need for large-scale, efficient training became more marked, and this tendency was accelerated during the two world wars when the military forces of all the nations involved suddenly needed efficient instructional processes to meet clear and specific instructional objectives.

It was in this period and in this context that many of the procedures for systematic instructional design were born, particularly the techniques for defining and refining instructional objectives (eg job analysis, task analysis, skills analysis, etc).

The present situation After World War II, the lead taken by the armed forces was followed up first by industry and then by education. The input-oriented approach to course design was challenged by the objectives movement and its output-oriented approach. This was accepted in industry with little reaction on the whole, but in education the excesses of the objectives movement led to the process-oriented approach. Once again human nature had its way and the rival factions defended the superiority of the discovery approach or the expository approach irrespective of the aims or content of the course.

2.4 Trend towards the systems view

Only in the last decade or so has a more balanced or systems view come to the fore. In education, one of the most influential of recent writers has been Robert Gagné. He has taken ideas from the behaviourist camp, the *gestalt* camp, the humanist camp and, more recently, from the cybernetics camp and combined these ideas into one theoretical approach to the design of instruction.

In training, there has been a realization that not all of an organization's human resources goals can be achieved by job-related instructions, nor even by training (which includes such non-instructional means as study visits or planned job experience) but that other non-training, development activities are needed to adapt the individual to his working group and to the culture of the organization. The planning of such developmental activities often starts by defining the process to be used and only later considers the best inputs (information content) and outputs (indication of success). Such experiential approaches to personnel development in industry are akin to the traditional exposure approaches used in such subjects as literature, musical appreciation or drama, which typically follow the design pattern of 'how can we involve and interest the learners' (the process), 'what content shall we select' (the inputs) and 'how can we get some idea of the success of the exercise' (the desired outputs).

The design cycle So what is important is not whether you start by defining course objectives (outputs) or course content (inputs) or the methods to be used (processes), but that you define all three in relation to each other. This can conveniently be done as a cycle of activities, illustrated in Figure 2.3. The arrows indicate a preferred, though not obligatory route to follow. Where you start depends on how the problem first presents itself.

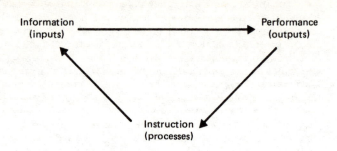

Figure 2.3 *The design cycle*

Performance problems It may present itself as a discrepancy between actual and desired *performance* on a particular task or group of tasks. Thus just by defining the problem, one defines the objectives in performance terms. By analysis of these objectives and comparison with experience of similar problems one designs or selects appropriate instructional methods, and these in turn indicate the information, concepts and examples that should be included in the course.

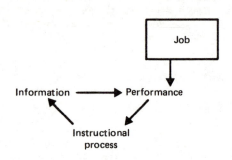

Figure 2.4 *Starting the cycle by defining the outputs*

Information problems Alternatively the problem may present itself as a discrepancy between how much is known and how much should be known about a particular subject or topic. We can label this an *information* problem. Analysis of the information discrepancy should reveal indicators of how we can judge whether a particular individual exhibits the information gap or not. These indicators are invariably in observable 'behaviour' or 'performance' terms, otherwise we would not be able to measure them, and their use to us is exactly as a means of measuring success. Whether we name these indicators our objectives or, alternatively, reserve this word for some general internal capability (eg the student should be able to solve everyday problems in a creative manner) and consider the measurable performances as mere samples of this capability, is not very important. What is important is to reach agreement on how the internal capability will be externally measured. Having defined the measures, one proceeds to define the methods or processes as before. We may indeed then be led back to consider the information content in more detail, selecting now the specific examples or topics which are best suited to the objectives and methods defined.

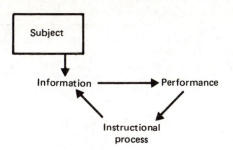

Figure 2.5 *Starting the cycle by defining the inputs*

Learning process problems

       Occasionally the cycle may start off with the 'process'. The problem presents itself in terms of a discrepancy between the instructional methods currently employed and those which should be employed. There is need for some caution here. Is the discrepancy observed due to an obvious mismatch between the methods employed and the objectives of the course? Or is it observed due to a preconceived notion of which methods are 'good' and which are 'bad'?

       The former case implies the presence of defined objectives. So there may be no need to complete the cycle. One may merely redesign the methods in the light of the objectives and this may also suggest detailed modification in the content.

       The latter case however implies a preformed opinion as regards the solution, irrespective of the problem, the type of mentality which suggests the panacea approach: programmed instruction for every training need, the discovery approach as an overall and universal strategy, etc. This approach does not necessarily follow our cycle, nor any other systematic model of instructional design. But it is quite legitimate to have only a general statement of educational aims (unquantified outputs) and to use this to make decisions about the general form of the methods in order to select and organize the information content, and only then to return to the objectives and to develop quantified performance indicators in the light of the methods and content selected.

       In spite of what Mager says, it may be legitimate to select a means of transport before deciding exactly where you want to go. This is when the experience of the journey is in itself the main aim of the exercise. But someone

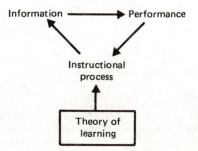

Figure 2.6 *Starting the cycle by defining the*
learning and instructional processes

still needs to decide on a destination and route before starting the journey. Otherwise the journey does not get under way. So once again, we follow through the three steps of the design cycle (see Figure 2.6).

We conclude this chapter with some tables, summarizing and illustrating the three starting points for our analysis of educational aims in order to define precise educational objectives.

Map 2.1 *Analysing the aims of education (input, process and output statements)*

Educational aims as given	On first viewing an educational aim, it may appear to be stated predominantly in terms of *output/input* or *process*, or a combination). The black box under consideration is the individual in society − the learner. One should attempt to complete and clarify the problem statement. One way to do this is to analyse the given statement of the problem into these three categories. Below are some examples taken from various reports of English government committees.
Examples:	
1. Stated in input terms	'The purpose of education is to provide the nurture and the environment which will enable the child to grow aright and to grow eventually to full stature, to bring to full flowering the varying potentialities, physical, spiritual and intellectual of which he is capable as a member of society.' (*Norwood Report: Curriculum and Examinations in Secondary Schools*, 1943).
	This statement says the purpose is to provide *inputs*, in order to promote certain internal *processes*. Nothing about outputs.
2. Stated in process terms	'All boys and girls need to develop, as well as skills, capacities for thought, judgement, enjoyment, curiosity . . .' (*Newson Report: Half our Future*, 1963).
	'It is important that they should have some understanding of the physical world and of the human society in which they are growing up' (*Newson Report: Half our Future*, 1963).
	These statements refer to internal processes or capabilities. They say nothing about how we will measure these capabilities (the outputs) nor what we need to do to develop them (the inputs).
3. Stated in output terms	'. . . certain skills of communication in speech and writing, in reading with understanding and in calculations involving number and measurement' (*Newson Report*, 1963).
	'They will need as always to be able to live with their fellows, appreciating and respecting their differences, understanding and sympathizing with their feelings. They will need the power of discrimination and when necessary to be able to withstand man's pressures' (*Plowden Report: Children and their Primary Schools*, 1967).
	These statements, while still very general, do (because they are stated in output terms) give some idea of the way in which the authors envisage evaluating the success of education. One can imagine categories of measurable performance (communicating, calculating, interacting, analysing feelings) to be used as criteria of success. Nothing is said about the general capabilities (thinking processes) required, nor about the way of teaching them (the inputs).
Comments	1. Whereas the examples quoted are of a very general nature, not necessarily intended to be used directly for the generation of instructional objectives, it is obvious that the statements which say something about the outputs expected, are of more help to the instructional designer.
	2. One notes a tendency, in the reports quoted, to move from input/process-oriented statements (in earlier reports) to process/output-oriented statements in later reports. This would appear to be a symptom of the general trend towards greater objectivity and results consciousness in education.
	3. However, the instructional designer (or indeed any teacher or course planner) generally needs to define more precisely each general aim, before he can derive specific course objectives. Which types of education skills? What level of written communication skill? What type/strength of pressure should the learner be able to withstand? We need to define and agree the *outputs* fairly precisely, even at this early stage.

Map 2.2 *Clarifying educational aims (use of the systems analysis chart)*

Introduction	A useful tool for clarifying educations aims is to complete a chart, listing the input, process and output components of the aim, as given, and then completing the components, particularly the output components, until the statement is precise enough to enable long-term evaluation criteria and instruments to be developed from it. The statement should then also be complete enough to enable one to develop precise course objectives.		
The chart	The chart shown below is our standard systems analysis chart. The system under consideration is always the *learner*. Processes are therefore internal learner capabilities. These may be observed as outputs (ie behaviours or performances). The educational system should supply the necessary conditions or inputs. In the examples which follow the italicized statements are taken from official reports.		
Examples	**Input**	**Process**	**Output**
1. *Norwood Report* (1943)	Provide nurture Provide necessary environment Definition of necessary — physical environment — social/spiritual environment — intellectual environment	To develop Physical, spiritual, intellectual potentialities/capacities.	Reasonable standards (for the individual) of increased strength, coordination, standard, visual perception, musical perception. Reasonable standards (for the society) of 'moral behaviour', self discipline, religious beliefs, treatment of others. Reasonable standards (for the individual and for society) of intellectual behaviour, calculating, communicating, reading, problem solving.
2. *Newsom Report* (1963)	Definition of the main subject areas from which to draw the content; the examples on which to practise thought, judgement, etc. The concepts/principles of the physical/human sciences to be included.	Capacities for thought, judgement, enjoyment, curiosity. Some understanding of the physical world, and of human society.	Skills of communication in speech and writing, in reading with understanding, and in calculations involving number and measurement. Standards for assessing judgement, enjoyment, curiosity. Definition of the aspects of the physical world and of society which should be understood and the level of understanding.
Comments	1.	The above examples are not presented as complete analyses, but only as examples of how to complete a given statement. No judgement is passed on the statements as given. Therefore, no comments are made on the *processes* specified in the original statements. Of course, in practice, one could apply value judgements to the statements, modifying them substantially. In this case, one would be *developing* educational aims of one's own, as opposed to *clarifying* somebody else's.
	2.	In a given practical curriculum design project, one would generally start with somebody else's general aims (eg from official reports, from the project sponsors, etc) and would need to clarify and complete them. It pays to do this early on in the project and to agree the clarified aims with the project sponsors, to avoid the possibility of serious divergences between the objectives you develop and the real needs.
	3.	There is a definite interrelationship between input and output. Specific outputs (final performances) define the needs for specific inputs (conditions — physical, organizational, etc) to enable learning to take place. This is the time to identify such relationships, so as to avoid the specification of objectives which require non-existent/unobtainable conditions for their achievement. Most current educational systems exhibit a marked lack of compatibility between desired aims and existing conditions. Avoid this in your project by carefully analysing the input/output interrelationships.
	4.	In general, it is more logical, and easier, to first define/clarify the desired outputs, and the necessary input conditions (eg define the life-skills, then the subject matter of the course). This is however often reversed in education, when one starts with a defined input (eg algebra, latin, sociology) and then proceeds to define the outputs one will measure (specific calculating/problem-solving, ability to translate/write, ability to explain certain phenomena).

3. The How and Why of Performance Objectives

3.1 Aims and objectives in education and training

Whatever you feel about the strength of objections to objectives let's be clear about one thing: the denial of behavioural objectives does not mean that none is being achieved. The teacher who refuses to identify his objectives is nevertheless acting as an agent of change on the behaviour of his students (Derek Rowntree, 1974).

We have already referred to objectives on several occasions. Sometimes we have used other terms: aims, goals, purposes. It is time to tighten up our usage. It has become customary (at least among educational technologists) to use the term 'educational objective' in a precise way, whereas the other near synonyms are used less precisely.

Aim: a general statement

Thus, an educational aim, goal or purpose can be a fairly general statement of intent, not necessarily stated in a systematic way. An educational objective (or instructional objective) on the other hand, is a *precise* statement of intent, stated in a *systematic* way.

An aim may be stated in *input* terms (eg to teach history; to spread the gospel), or *process* terms (eg to solve maths problems). An objective is always stated in *output* (or product) terms. It is also stated more precisely. For example, the aim 'to solve maths problems' would transform into an objective (or rather a set of objectives) thus:

Objective: an output statement

1. Given maths problems of the following types (specify).
2. The students should solve them.
3. To the following standards of speed and accuracy (specify).

Instructional objectives describe the outputs of the instructional process

Such statement of post-instructions or terminal behaviour became commonly used in the 1960s. The particular systematic format illustrated here was popularized by Robert Mager's booklet *Preparing Instructional Objectives* (Mager, 1962).

The essential ingredients in a behavioural objective, according to Mager are:

1. A statement of what the student should be able to do at the end of the learning session (the terminal behaviour).
2. The conditions under which he should be able to exhibit the terminal behaviour.
3. The standard to which he should be able to perform (the criteria).

Mager-type statements of objectives

For example: the student (1) should be able to find the square root of any number (2) using tables of square roots or logarithm tables and (3) getting the answer correct to three significant figures nine times out of 10.

Transforming aims into objectives

Transforming the other aims mentioned above is more difficult, as apart from making the statement more precise, we have to transform the input or process statements into an output statement, and there are many ways in which this could be done. However, it can be transformed into an output statement once we form some idea of 'where we are going', in this case, once we are clear *why* we wish to teach history. If, for example, we accept that history should be taught so that it is relevant to today's life and times and should be useful to the learner in his everyday life, then one possible form of output statement would be:

1. Given a current political, social or economic event and prior teaching or relevant historical events.
2. The student should identify the similarities and differences between the current events and relevant past events, construct a hypothesis to explain or predict the results of the current event and justify his hypothesis by reference to historical evidence.
3. He should be able to do this to the satisfaction of the teacher, which would be assessed by the following criteria: at least 60 per cent in agreement with the teacher's own viewpoint or with reality. In the other 40 per cent of cases the student can explain to the teacher's satisfaction the source of the divergence of opinion.

In becoming precise, the statement has become somewhat unwieldy, but this is unavoidable in some cases. Other examples of aims transformed into objectives are included in Map 3.1.

3.2 Extending the statement of objectives: the test instrument

Mager's instructional objectives are stated in terms of student *behaviour* or *performance* because this is the only type of *output* from the student which can be observed in order to infer whether learning has taken place. If the student could not exhibit the behaviour before instruction took place and now he can, the instructional process had some effect.

But was it as effective as we had hoped? We can only judge this if we have a *standard* or *criterion* which we can use to compare the actual behaviour with the desired behaviour (the objective).

Finally, if the actual terminal behaviour does not match the objective, can we be sure that it is due to the student not having learned? There are at least two other alternative possibilities:

1. He *chooses* not to exhibit the behaviour (although he could if he wanted to). This is a problem of motivation/cooperation/attitude which we will come back to later, but for the moment ignore.
2. He knows how to but he does not have the necessary tools/data/time. He has not been supplied with the necessary *external* (environmental) *condition* for satisfactory performance.

The three components used by Mager

Hence, the need for Mager's three components (see Figure 3.1) of a precise instructional objective:

Behaviour: to specify what we are going to observe and measure.
Standard: to enable us to assess the effectiveness of the learning.
External conditions: to ensure that any 'under-performance' is not due to causes other than 'under-learning'.

A fourth component: the test instrument

It is by now quite clear that one use of precise objectives is to provide the basis for measuring the results of instruction (the other main use is to make sure that the methods and content of instruction are relevant). So some writers (eg Miller 1962, Armstrong *et al* 1970) have suggested that it would be useful and yet more precise to include a fourth type of component in the statement of objectives: a description of the way in which the behaviour will be measured. Some behaviours can be observed directly (eg kicking a football) but others only when special conditions or instruments are arranged (eg testing an attitude may require a questionnaire, or a confrontation to be prepared).

To some extent, the 'conditions' item may already imply what means of measurement is to be used, but this is not always so. In any case, it is quite useful to give some systematic thought to the means of measurement to be used, as sometimes in practice certain procedures are impractical, too costly, unreliable, etc. For example, in the case of the history objective mentioned

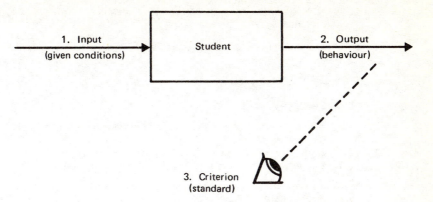

Figure 3.1 *Components of an instructional objective*

above, it is not yet clear whether our evaluation is to be a one-off examination, which presents certain events to the student and asks him to explain them through his knowledge of history (the student knows that the examination is coming and prepares himself accordingly), or whether (as the original aims seems to imply) history is to be a useful tool throughout life and therefore we should evaluate the course by a long-term observation of how the student reacts to or explains current events out of school. This latter test instrument may be theoretically more valid, but is probably quite impracticable. A similar problem occurs in practical skills — do we test on simulated exercises or follow up job performance — and even more in the case of attitudes: will the sales girl who 'knows' that the 'customer is always right' continue to act accordingly even in extreme real-life circumstances.

So let us adopt a four-point format (see Figure 3.2) for instructional objectives:

☐ Necessary external conditions
☐ Desired performance (or behaviour)
☐ Standard (or criterion)
☐ Instrument (or method) of evaluation.

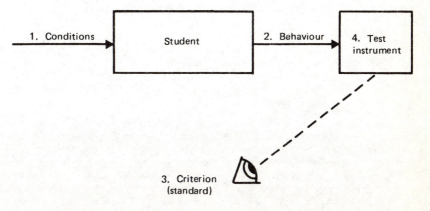

Figure 3.2 *A four-point format for instructional objectives*

It is quite useful to lay out the statement of objectives in a four-column format, as shown overleaf:

Given the following external conditions	The student will	To the following standard	As measured by the following method

Doing this:

- ☐ Saves a lot of writing. You avoid rewriting the linking words and phrases of the statements
- ☐ Helps to ensure that all four components have been defined
- ☐ Enables several checks to be made as will be explained below.

3.3 Levels of objectives

The history objective mentioned above has the appearance of an end-of-course objective. Indeed, its very statement implies that other sub-objectives must also be taught to enable this objective to be achieved. The necessary conditions state 'prior learning of relevant historical facts'. There will obviously be many of these in the course. Some may be grouped in a given unit or lesson, say on the French revolution. These unit or lesson objectives will include remembering what happened, explaining what happened, suggesting what might have happened if circumstances had been somewhat different, and so on. So each lesson has its own set of sub-objectives as well as its terminal objective.

Similarly, at the other end of the scale, the course objectives contribute to (are sub-objectives of) the school's (institution's) objectives. These in turn are (or at least should be) sub-objectives of the educational system's objectives. So just as we have systems within systems, we have objectives within objectives. We could specify objectives at a variety of levels, starting from the objectives of society and going on down to specific objectives for each teaching act that will be performed. A similar hierarchy of levels of objectives exists in the industrial training field, matching the hierarchy of systems: market, industry, specific organization, job, training (course), unit, lesson, etc (see Figure 3.3).

3.4 When and how to state precise objectives

Two questions arise:

1. How to specify objectives at these various levels? Are the methods the same as those already presented?
2. Whether to specify objectives at these various levels. Do we really need to be so careful about specifying our objectives? When is it useful and when superfluous?

Taking the questions in reverse order, one only needs to specify objectives if one is serious about achieving them. One can not evaluate the attainment of a general, loosely stated aim without first transforming the aim into a precise measurable statement (ie objective). Some authors argue that one can avoid specifying objectives altogether by developing test items or exercises directly from general aims. This is true in a sense, but the test items are another way of stating the objectives, or rather of giving an example of the objectives. Our format for stating objectives (the four-point format) is almost a test item. All one needs is to insert specific examples of simultaneous equations, current events and so on. One might add that a test item by itself (eg explain the causes and effect of the French revolution) is not sufficient to evaluate the relevant course unit. We also need a marking scheme (standards or criteria) and the

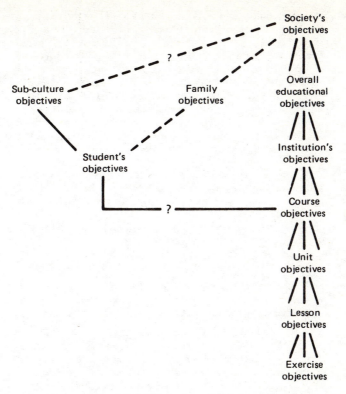

Figure 3.3 *Hierarchy of training objectives*

certainty that prior learning necessary as a prerequisite for this task had been learned (conditions). So by the time we have added to our test item in this manner, we have a statement as complete as our four-point format for objectives.

So, as a general rule, state objectives:

Use clear objectives to aid clear communication

1. When you wish to establish agreement between the people involved in the project (team members, trainers and clients, teachers and students). It is much easier to agree or disagree with a statement as precise as a behavioural objective. It is easy to overlook a source of disagreement if only general aims are stated.

State objectives at the levels at which you plan to evaluate

2. When you are responsible for ensuring the achievement of the objectives. A course examiner may require to state only the terminal course objectives, because this is the level at which he will evaluate. The achievement of these objectives depends on lower level lesson objectives or topic objectives. The course designer will need to specify these (and in so doing he needs to refer to the level above the course objectives). Each lesson or topic has its own set of lower level objectives. If the course designer is descending to the level of detailed instructional exercise design, he will also specify the lesson's sub-objectives, because each instructional exercise will need to be tested and evaluated. If, on the other hand, the course designer stops at the point of overall lesson planning, and leaves the detailed lesson planning to individual teachers (as is the case in most curriculum projects) then perhaps he may also leave the task of stating the sub-objectives to the teacher. But someone will need to state them if serious evaluation and revision of the lesson is foreseen.

In general, therefore, one would state objectives at the levels at which one is working. However, in order to check the viability of one's objectives, one should compare them with higher level objectives. If these have not been stated precisely, it may be useful to clarify them before proceeding to lower levels.

Taking the other question of how to state objectives at higher levels, the answer is simple. Use the same four-point system. After all, a system objective or purpose (we defined earlier) is always discernible from an analysis of the inputs and the outputs. In the case of instructional objectives, the conditions are the necessary inputs and the terminal behaviour is the desired output from the learner. Thus, Mager-type objectives are but a special case of system objectives — instructional system objectives. We can approach any other system in the same way.

We can ask the same questions of any system or project: what are we really interested in? Not, for example, 'advise the government on the setting up of an apprenticeship scheme' but 'the government will set up an apprenticeship scheme'.

So, first ensure that *final* project objectives describe things which will be happening as a result of the project. Second, ensure that these statements are in clear, precise and measurable terms, so that they can be used later for the control and evaluation of the project. Or, to put it in the systems terminology:

1. Objectives are the desired outputs of systems.
2. Comparison of desired output and actual output can be used to evaluate and control the process in the system.

Let us consider the stating of objectives in measurable terms a little more closely. In the case of objectives concerned with human beings, invariably the output is behaviour. So we can state quite categorically that objectives of human systems should be stated in terms of performance or behaviour. In the case of organizations we could argue that perhaps the structure of the system is what interests us. Our objective might be that we change the structure of the way that employer/worker negotiations take place, or we change the management structure of our company.

Project
objectives
are usually
stated in
terms of
expected
system
performance

But is this really our main objective? Or do we restructure in order to change the outputs (the *performance*) of our system? We are making the suggestion here that in nearly all cases the main objective of any project can be stated, and indeed ought to be stated, in performance terms. There are rare exceptions to this principle. But let us ignore the exceptions and establish four rules:

1. State the main objectives of the project in performance terms. Thus, 'school building complete' is not a main objective, although it may be a sub-objective. However, 'school turning out 200 craftsmen per year' could be our main objective.
2. State clear criteria of the performance that is required. In the last example, turning out 200 craftsmen per year is a sort of criterion, but it is not yet sufficiently clear because we do not know what type of craftsmen, and what skills and what standard of excellence these craftsmen should attain.
3. State exactly how the achievement of the objective will be measured. What are the instruments or sources of data which will be used? Are they available, reliable and not too costly? Are we going to measure our output of 200 craftsmen by a head count of the number of certificates issued at the end of the year (easy and cheap but not too reliable), or are we going to measure how many of them actually seek and obtain employment in the industry for which they have been trained (a more reliable indicator but much more difficult to measure)?
4. State the assumed necessary external (environmental) conditions. What inputs must the system receive in order to be able to produce the desired

outputs? For example, producing 200 craftsmen per year requires the recruitment of 200 plus (to allow for wastage) trainees with satisfactory prerequisites and this depends on the recruitment drive of the organization, competition from other schools and from other industries and professions seeking similar trainees, etc.

3.5 Selecting project objectives

Relevance viability and measurability

The idea of desired output leads us to consider a further point: someone must *select* the objectives. A decision has to be made that one objective is more worthwhile pursuing than some other possible objective. In this context, it helps to consider a given possible objective in terms of whether it is:

☐ *Relevant.* Will achievement of this objective contribute to the broader (perhaps more woolly) aims which the wider system has? Would other objectives be more relevant? Would they achieve the broader system's objectives more directly?

☐ *Viable.* Do we have the means to achieve the objective? Is there *conflict* between this objective and other objectives of the system?

Viability

Suppose you are planning a rural education project in a country with large tracts of underdeveloped farming areas. Due to rapid industrialization in the last few years, a great urban drift has resulted in slum areas around the cities. It would seem quite possible that a village-based development model and a 'back to the plough' policy for agriculture with low mechanization would be the ideal solution to some of the problems that you have observed. Now it would seem that such objectives could be very relevant to the problem as observed. Certainly such objectives could be measurable (how many people have gone back from the town to the country as a result of the project?). However, would such objectives be viable? Would they not involve a total change in government policy? Even if the government would be prepared to implement this policy, would the people concerned really be interested in going back to the land?

Relevance

Now let us consider a project (in the same country as the urban drift example quoted above) in which a mass adult literacy campaign seems to be a reasonable objective for which to aim. Is it viable? The government wants it, we have the resources and we have data that many illiterate adults would welcome the chance of learning to read. Is it measurable? Yes: how many people have in fact learned to read? Is it relevant? It *seems* to be relevant. However, let us consider some points in more detail.

First, what are the wider objectives? Some of these may be educational equality based and our literacy campaign is very much in line with those. However, consider the problem of urban drift in the last example. One result of increased literacy will be to encourage more people to leave the land and to go to the cities and look for jobs. And yet one of the wider system's objectives is exactly opposite to this.

Second, we might ask whether the best way to eliminate illiteracy will be to spend our resources on adult literacy campaigns. Perhaps spending our money on improving the educational system, to cut down evasion and drop out, will reduce the illiteracy rate faster for less money than the project we are actually planning. So the relevance of this objective is not at all clear and certainly needs very detailed analysis.

Measurability

Finally, let us consider measurability. Our aim now is to improve industrial relations. Now this is not very clear as an objective as yet, but we shall try our best. Is it relevant? The answer certainly seems to be yes. Of course it depends on the prevailing conditions of industrial relations. Is it viable? Well, assume that employers and government and workers are interested in improving industrial relations and that you already have the resources with which to do this. Is it measurable? It is not very clear at the moment. We need to define our objective with much more precision in order to find out exactly how we are going to measure it. One measure might be the number of man-days lost in strikes during the next year. Now this may be a reasonable measure for the whole country. It is a global measure. But it is not much good for a particular firm who hopes that even if there are no strikes, the present level of industrial relations would nevertheless improve. Perhaps we have to use some subjective criteria. How does management feel about the state of industrial relations in the firm? Now the problem here is, can we standardize criteria sufficiently to be able to rely on them?

3.6 Checking objectives for compatibility

The objectives at various levels in a system, or at various stages in a project must be compatible. Sub-system objectives contribute to the achievement of wider system objectives. The objectives of one project activity are prerequisites of the execution of certain subsequent activities. Various techniques exist for ensuring this compatibility. In project management, the use of project network flow charts and of 'management by objectives' techniques is recommended. Another technique, useful at the project definition stage, is the objective matrix.

We may extend our four-point format for the specification of objectives at any level in our system. The result is a matrix similar to that shown in Figure 3.4.

How to read the matrix The objectives matrix shown here is of course a sample, showing only one lesson objective (among many) of one course (among many) of the training department of one organization. But it does serve to illustrate the value of specifying objectives at various levels, in relation to each other.

First, the objectives at lower levels should contribute to the achievement of objectives at higher levels. They should do so in the most direct and economic way possible. We have here a method of deciding between alternative objectives for our system, which of them contribute better to the achievement of the objectives of the system (of which our system is but a component). Second, there should be no conflict between the objectives at various levels. They should not have incompatible outputs and should not be in competition for the same scarce resources (in our example is the training department's need for instructors in conflict with the service department's need for the same scarce human resource — skilled maintenance engineers?). The criteria should not be out of phase (one should not overtrain nor undertrain). The methods of measurement should not be incompatible (course evaluation should simulate real job conditions whenever possible).

How to construct the matrix A study of the cells in our matrix should reveal any glaring sources of conflict or incompatibility between objectives (see Figure 3.5).

3.7 Objections to objectives

The objectives movement has generated many reactions and objections: 'writing clear objectives is difficult, if not impossible, in some educational subjects'. One should not predetermine everything in education, and anyway it is the student, not the school who should determine his own educational objectives, it is argued. By specifying objectives one emphasizes the trivial aspects of education and overlooks the really important, long-term goals. Backing up these philosophical and technical objectives are practical ones, such as 'the preparing of objectives is very time consuming, and the benefits do not justify the effort', or 'what are the benefits', or 'do precise objectives help the teacher to teach.'

Several writers (eg Popham 1968; Rowntree 1974) have analysed these objectives, it is argued. By specifying objectives one emphasizes the trivial because they are simply not true, or because even if there is some truth behind them, the positive advantages of working with objectives outweigh the negative

System level	Necessary input conditions from environment	Desired outputs	Standards (criteria)	Measuring (evaluation) instruments
Electronic industry	Continued 5 per cent pa economic growth (GNP)	Increased sales of electronic equipment	Ten per cent pa increase production and sales (total value)	Study of nationally published statistics
Organization X	Necessary bank approval for loans Necessary recruitment of manpower	Increase in colour TV Production sales and after sales service	Twenty per cent pa for next three years	Production department statistics
Training department of Organization X	Necessary manpower resources New recruitment and selection policy etc	TV maintenance engineers	Forty per annum next year rising to 60 per annum in two years time Capable of repairing 20 typical faults per working day	Training department statistics On-the-job performance evaluation
Course	The necessary prerequisites in trainees Laboratory and workshop facilities	Trainees can — locate — identify — repair faults in a a colour TV	Average 10 minutes per fault Location 100 per cent; identification 100 per cent; repair 80 per cent correct	Using a special TV set programmed to simulate faults manufacturer's models A, B and C
Lesson	A fault of type X in a colour TV model A	Identify the type of fault	Correctly in under one minute	Practical laboratory test on faults simulator, model A
Individual lesson exercise	A live circuit and a multi-test meter	Measure the voltage and resistance between any two points	To 5 per cent accuracy 10 seconds per measure taken	Practical test using real test meter and a variety of standard circuits

Figure 3.4 *An objectives matrix for a hypothetical training design project (an extract)*

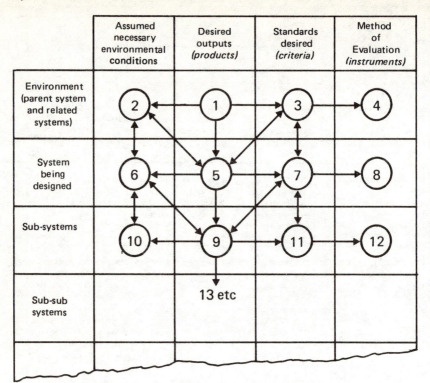

	Assumed necessary environmental conditions	Desired outputs *(products)*	Standards desired *(criteria)*	Method of Evaluation *(instruments)*
Environment (parent system and related systems)	2	1	3	4
System being designed	6	5	7	8
Sub-systems	10	9	11	12
Sub-sub systems		13 etc		

The numbers 1, 2 . . . etc and the arrows indicate the sequence of completion of the matrix. Double-headed arrows means check for compatibility and replan if necessary

Figure 3.5 *Sequence in completing the matrix*

aspects. Let us look critically at some of these objections.

Objection 1: stating performance objectives is difficult and sometimes impossible

It is difficult to state clear and precise objectives in some areas of education (not so in industrial training). This is partly because of the traditional heritage of subject disciplines and the resultant divergence of teacher's opinions about *why* they teach a subject. The difficulty is not to state a precise objective, but to agree that this is the most worthwhile objective to pursue. This agreement is easy in the training situation because one can refer to the needs of the *job* for which the trainee is being prepared. We can observe job performers and measure the knowledge and skills they use in performing the job. It is relatively easy in the case of an organized scientific subject, or mathematics, as most teachers of such subjects agree more or less on why they teach the subject.

Think of a 'notional' job . . .

They can imagine, with relative ease, the typical real-life situation in which mathematics is used. They can form a conceptual model of the 'notional' job that the school leaver will perform. In lower school, when planning mathematics for all, we can form a useful model of our job by investigating the calculations that a typical citizen must perform in order to survive in our modern society. In upper schooling, mathematics is for specialists. The notional 'jobs' are further study of mathematics as a specialist, or use of mathematics as a tool in engineering, economics, sociology, etc.

. . . or think why and how a subject is taught

But some might reject the idea of starting by defining a notional job performance. They might argue that history is not taught to be useful but because it is interesting in itself. There is a certain amount of difficulty in following this position by a decision to put history as an obligatory part of any school curriculum. However, if history is an option for students to choose then this position is quite tenable. However, few students would choose the option if it were dry and boring. So what makes history interesting? What content is worth including? How should it be presented and taught? Can we call it teaching if we have absolutely no objectives? And how will we measure our success at making it interesting? So it is really difficult to get away from the need for objectives. But in this case both the types of objectives stressed and the routes to specifying objectives may be different. One may stress the affective (attitudinal) objectives more than the cognitive. One may get at the objectives from the content of the subject itself, rather than from an analysis of an imaginary master performer. But in all cases it is *possible* to state precise objectives.

Objection 2: One should not pre-determine everything in education

But is it *desirable* to state precise objectives in all cases? Are there not many educational side-effects which are difficult to pre-specify but are nevertheless beneficial? Yes, no doubt there are. But who says that teachers should not follow up such unplanned opportunities when they occur? Does the specification of what is *obviously* intended prevent one from adding to it along the way? However, if the primary objectives are not specified in clear and measurable terms, there is quite a danger of making so many interesting unplanned sojourns on the way, that we never actually reach our destination. And furthermore we may never even know we have failed to reach it. Or, more likely, we (the teachers) will know, because we have unstated objectives, but our employers and our clients (the students and their parents) will not know. How can they? There was no clear specification, no 'contract' of what was to be achieved. How convenient for the teacher! Is this one motive behind many of the objections to objectives?

Objection 3: the student should be free to choose his own learning objectives

In education this may be partially true (not entirely and certainly not to any great extent in training). However, the student usually arrives with not very clearly formed objectives. He knows neither the options open to him, nor what is involved in following them up.

The democratic view of student-directed learning carries with it a moral obligation to help (not to force) the student. And one way of helping a student decide among his options is to present them to him clearly. What better way of doing this than by furnishing clearly specified objectives for each option.

One should also point out that by making some decisions, the student abdicates the right to make others. A student may choose freely to study sociology. Within the course he may have a free choice of course options. If, however, he chooses the statistics option, it is quite unrealistic to think of him then choosing which specific objectives he should achieve within the option. As the statistics option is a sub-system of the course, related to other options, it must produce certain specific outputs which are governed by the overall subject structure of sociology and the specific structure of this course in sociology. The student cannot choose intelligently exactly which statistics techniques he should master. If he had this capability, he would not be a student of the type who requires instruction. He would be an advanced researcher working entirely on his own. By denying the need for pre-specified objectives on democratic grounds one is denying the need for teachers.

Objection 4: performance objectives emphasize the trivial levels of education

It is true that many published sets of behavioural objectives do appear to concentrate on low level rote learning and simple application skills. Is this because the stating of behavioural objectives forces one to look down to this level and this level only? Or is it that much teaching has always been down at this level? Look at typical school examinations: can we really blame the objectives movement for uncovering what was previously hidden?

But can we construct higher order objectives? Certainly we can. Tools to assist in this have been around for some time, such as Bloom's taxonomy (Bloom *et al*, 1956). The objectives movement has made educators climb upwards, to the achievement of more worthwhile, higher order objectives. This climb is not easy, but we are beginning to make it, which is better than the previous situation when we talked higher order (eg problem-solving) objectives but 'taught' to lower order (eg story telling objectives). (See Maps 3.7 and 3.8 for an outline of the categories of Bloom's taxonomy.)

The use of such techniques as the specification of a master performer model, or the completion of an objective matrix to identify the interrelation between course objectives and the wider system's objectives helps us to look upwards.

Objection 5: the benefits do not justify the time and effort involved in preparing detailed performance objectives

It is true that the specifications of detailed objectives can be time-consuming. The author worked for a time with a team of teachers in California specifying objectives for Project PLAN, a computer-managed system of instruction developed by the American Institute for Research, in conjunction with Westinghouse Corporation. The team of twenty or so teachers (led by Bob Mager) worked throughout the summer of 1967 to establish the objectives for the elementary mathematics and English language curriculum. After further field trials and use in dozens of schools (when the objectives suffered various revisions) Westinghouse eventually published two books of objectives for mathematics and English respectively. Was the effort worthwhile? Project PLAN is now used by hundreds of schools throughout the USA and elsewhere. (The author even encountered its use in Saudi Arabia in 1970.) Many teachers are reaping the benefits of the time and effort put in by the original team. In such a situation, this objection does not stand up.

It is more difficult to defend the time involved when the project is restricted to one course or one school. Will the use of the objectives justify the effort of producing them? Observe what has happened through the use of objectives-based training in industry, commerce or the forces. There are dozens, perhaps hundreds, of case studies which document the savings in training time, in resources devoted to training, in reduction of post-training errors, in reduction of manpower turnover, etc, which have resulted when existing training courses have been revised through a systematic analysis of their objectives. Training by objectives is a proven cost-effective approach in industry.

The problem in education is to prove a similar return on investment. The value of achieving certain educational objectives (of the trivial, easily measurable type) is obviously not very high. But in most objectives (especially in the case of the long-term objectives of the institution or the educational system) it is extremely difficult to even approach an estimate of the contribution that improved teaching might have had towards their achievement. But perhaps, by looking at the proven value in industry, we might at least believe in a similar value to be gained in the less strictly measurable areas of education.

In any case, a large-scale adoption of objectives-based curricula in education and the derivation of these objectives through systems analysis techniques (eg the objectives matrix) will make the results of educational effort and change more measurable in the future.

Objection 6: once produced, the objectives are often not used in the actual teaching process

It would be particularly difficult to justify the effort if the product is not used. But why should objectives not be used in actual teaching? One reason is that teachers, who have neither the time nor the inclination to develop their own objectives, are reluctant to use those prepared for them by others. Such teachers justify their rejection by many technical reasons, all open to easy refutation. The real reasons are always attitudinal, arising from the fear of being measured, from the fear of extra work, or from the jealous guarding of the principle of academic freedom (which was never meant to imply freedom to be incompetent). It is interesting to note here the acceptance by just about all British (and many overseas) universities of the Open University texts and other teaching materials. These are in the main objectives-based and have proved to be (in many subject areas) the best available texts on the market. Thus hundreds of university teachers have, indirectly, accepted the use of instructional objectives and have subjugated their academic freedom to academic excellence. The Open University has managed to influence university teaching more than generations of governments, academic boards and staff development schemes. Here, objectives are being used in practice, even if rejected at a philosophical level.

3.8 The systems approach is based on objectives

One can counter philosophical arguments by philosophical arguments. If one subscribes to a problem-solving approach (and that implies, in complex problems, a systems approach), one must use objectives at each and every stage of the problem-solving process. Objectives are the cornerstone, the keystone, one might even say the philosopher's stone of problem-solving. If we follow the stages of the systems approach we use objectives at each and every stage.

Stage 1: define the problem

A problem is a discrepancy between the actual situation (what is) and the desired situation (what should be). In defining what should be, we define the *objective* of our problem-solving project. This is the overall objective of the project. It should already however be:

☐ *Relevant* to the solution of the problem without creating new problems in related systems or the wider system.
☐ *Viable* in the sense that the necessary resources and 'climate' exist for achieving the objective.
☐ *Measurable* so that we know when to stop.

The important output here is a set of *agreed* objectives (between all concerned in the project).

Stage 2: analyse the problem

In considering how to reach the overall objective, inevitably one specifies intermediate or enabling objectives, the stepping stones by which one will proceed and judge one's progress. These should also be relevant (sequentially), viable and measurable. Each of them may be achieved by alternative paths perhaps, but we cannot consider the alternative solutions until each key step is defined in terms of its desired outcomes.

Stage 3: develop the chosen solution

In the context of instructional design, objectives are used in at least two important ways. First, the interdependence between the intermediate or enabling objectives helps to establish the best sequence for instruction. Second, the types of objectives to be achieved help to define the instructional methods to be used.

Stage 4: implement the solution

The intermediate objectives, and their sequence form the basis of an implementation plan, a plan for management by objectives which will enable one to monitor the progress of the project on an ongoing regular basis.

Stage 5: evaluate and revise

The basis upon which evaluation is carried out and revision decisions made is governed by reference to the original overall objective and the intermediate objectives later developed from it.

3.9 Summary and preview

This chapter has dealt largely with the basic concept of instructional objectives; how they are stated, how they relate to objectives at different levels in the system or project, and the difficulties encountered in, and objections posed to, the use of precisely stated objectives. The aim has been to illustrate that the benefits outweigh the difficulties. If a systems approach is to be employed, one cannot avoid the use of objectives as a principal tool throughout the process.

Approaches to the selection of objectives

The mastery performance approach

The practical aspects of how to derive objectives have so far only been touched upon. As we are dealing in this section of the book with stage 1 of the systems approach, we have restricted ourselves to the definition of the problem, that is the establishment of the overall objective. In the industrial training context this is usually easy. We look at the job that the trainee will do. We have seen that in education this can be done also, by the definition of a notional job and its master performance.

Other approaches exist in education. One of these is by transforming the general aims of a particular course into more precise objectives. We have seen some examples of this approach in this chapter (eg the history aim). Further examples and techniques are included in Maps 3.3, 3.4 and 3.5

The subject matter analysis approach   Another way of establishing educational objectives is to start from the content (often already defined by the course syllabus which one inherits) and derive 'what is worth teaching and testing' from this. One might derive what is worth teaching from what is actually tested by analysing existing examinations. This is often done and equally often bemoaned.

'Teaching for the exam' is seen as a necessary but definite evil by many teachers. But it is only an evil in as much as the objectives which the examination tests are 'evil' or rather the extent to which they are not in agreement with the objectives held dear by the teacher. So if the teacher can bemoan the examination he should be able to do better. But examination setting has not proved to be all that simple a task. All too easily one falls into

The use of a taxonomy   the trap of testing what is easy to test and measure rather than what is really worthwhile in the subject. A certain amount of training and discipline is needed to keep from falling into this error, and a methodology helps. So does a common language to describe the desired outcomes of education (see Maps 3.5 and 3.6).

Tools to aid the definition of objectives   Hence, we have attempted to establish a language and a means of classifying different types of objectives, so that, starting from the subject as a whole, we can:

1. Decide what is worth teaching and testing in general terms, and communicate it to others who may be involved with us in the project.
2. Having gained their approval to the general statement, return to the subject and select topics or examples which can be used either to teach or to test the general objectives.

To help one do this, several tools have been developed, the best known and most used (and abused) being Bloom's taxonomy of educational objectives (Bloom *et al* 1956) for intellectual (or cognitive) objectives. These works attempt to establish a hierarchy, or sequential classification, of types of objectives, which should enable the objectives developer (and test designer) first to achieve agreement on the level of objective to be achieved, and then to 'search' the subject for suitable teaching and testing content.

A summary of Bloom's taxonomy is included in Maps 3.7 and 3.8. Its detailed use will be discussed further in Part 3, as will the derivation of intermediate objectives by any of the routes indicated above.

Map 3.1 *Transforming aims into objectives*

Examples	Aim	Objective
From mathematics	The aim is that students should learn to attack any geometry problem in a systematic yet creative manner, applying the principles of problem-solving	*Given conditions* 1. A well defined geometry problem of a type unfamiliar to the student 2. Prior mastery of the necessary theorems *Product (performance)* 1. Develop alternative strategies for solutions of the problem 2. Select the most 'elegant' solution, applying the relevant theorems *Standard* Quantity — minimum two possible solutions/problem, problems/hour Quality — 80 per cent correct solutions, 60 per cent judged of above average elegance (by a skilled mathematician)
From history	History should be taught so that it is relevant to today's life and times. Students should find history useful	*Given conditions* 1. A current political social or economic event 2. Prior teaching or relevant historical events *Product (performance)* 1. Identify the similarities and differences between the current event and relevant past events 2. Construct a hypothesis to explain/predict the results of the current event 3. Justify his hypothesis by reference to historical evidence *Standard* At least 60 per cent in agreement with teacher's viewpoint or with reality. In the other (40 per cent) cases he can explain, to the teacher's satisfaction, the source of divergence of opinion
From industry	The skilled craftsman should use his equipment, tools and materials with efficiency and economy	*Given conditions* 1. A technical drawing or specification of a component 2. A variety of possible tools and adequate raw materials *Product (performance)* 1. Produce a work-plan to economize time and materials 2. Execute it, produce the component *Standards* 1. Not more than 15 per cent below the set target standards for — time — scrap material 2. Meeting fully all the tolerances and quality standards set out in the technical specification

Map 3.2 *The level of aims or objectives*

Introduction	The distinction between aims and objectives is not based on the *level at which* they are defined, but on the *precision with which* they are defined. Both aims and objectives may exist at various levels. Lower-level aims/objectives are always derived from the higher levels. The hierarchies in education and training are surprisingly similar.
Levels of educational aims or objectives	Societies' aims and constraints determine Educational system's aims (objectives) determine Institutional (school) aims (objectives) determine Curriculum (course) aims/objectives determine Course unit (subject) aims/objectives determine Lesson (topic) objectives (aims) determine Specific learning (exercise) objectives (aims)
Levels of training aims or objectives	Organizational environment's (market) aims and constraints determine Organizational (industry's) aims/objectives determine Job (occupation) performance aims/objectives determine Training (course) objectives (aims) determine Course unit (module) objectives (aims) determine Lesson (session) objectives (aims) determine Specific learning (exercise) objectives (aims)

Map 3.3 *Procedure for transforming general aims and poorly stated objectives into performance terms*

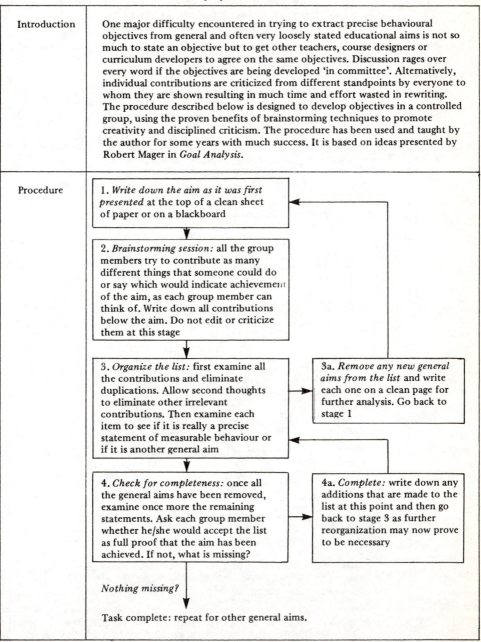

Introduction	One major difficulty encountered in trying to extract precise behavioural objectives from general and often very loosely stated educational aims is not so much to state an objective but to get other teachers, course designers or curriculum developers to agree on the same objectives. Discussion rages over every word if the objectives are being developed 'in committee'. Alternatively, individual contributions are criticized from different standpoints by everyone to whom they are shown resulting in much time and effort wasted in rewriting. The procedure described below is designed to develop objectives in a controlled group, using the proven benefits of brainstorming techniques to promote creativity and disciplined criticism. The procedure has been used and taught by the author for some years with much success. It is based on ideas presented by Robert Mager in *Goal Analysis*.

Procedure

1. *Write down the aim as it was first presented* at the top of a clean sheet of paper or on a blackboard

2. *Brainstorming session:* all the group members try to contribute as many different things that someone could do or say which would indicate achievement of the aim, as each group member can think of. Write down all contributions below the aim. Do not edit or criticize them at this stage

3. *Organize the list:* first examine all the contributions and eliminate duplications. Allow second thoughts to eliminate other irrelevant contributions. Then examine each item to see if it is really a precise statement of measurable behaviour or if it is another general aim

3a. *Remove any new general aims from the list* and write each one on a clean page for further analysis. Go back to stage 1

4. *Check for completeness:* once all the general aims have been removed, examine once more the remaining statements. Ask each group member whether he/she would accept the list as full proof that the aim has been achieved. If not, what is missing?

4a. *Complete:* write down any additions that are made to the list at this point and then go back to stage 3 as further reorganization may now prove to be necessary

Nothing missing?

Task complete: repeat for other general aims.

Map 3.4 *From aims to objectives to content*

1. The output → input route (the concept of the master performer)	
Introduction	The output → input route from aims to objectives starts by defining and agreeing the desired final performances to be achieved by learners (at this stage still in fairly general terms). Then the necessary inputs to the teaching/learning situation are identified. These inputs are of various types: — physical environment (equipment, etc) — social environment (grouping, locale, etc) — instructional environment (teachers, other media) — informational content (the subjects/topics) — time required for learning. All these are theoretically controllable by the course designer, and will be controlled/selected by reference to the predetermined desired outputs. This approval gives rise to the concept of the 'master performer'.
The master performer (definition)	The master performer is a model. He is the model with which we shall compare the real people who leave our educational/training system. He is not the best existing performer, but the 'typical' performer which we hope to create. Like the 'average man', such a typical performer may not be any one identifiable real person, but a general statement of the performances and standards expected of the successful course graduate.

Examples	1. The mastery performance approach is almost traditional in industrial or vocational training. We wish to train gas welders. Therefore we observe a competent welder (not the best but the adequate performer) to identify the tasks he performs and how he performs them. Further analysis reveals the basic knowledge and skills he requires in order to perform, and hence by comparison with the existing levels of relevant knowledge/skills in our trainees, we derive both the detailed objectives (outputs) and the content, methods, equipment needs (inputs) of training.
	
	2. In formal education this approach is less common, but quite feasible. Its practical use was well illustrated by Tom Gilbert (1966) when discussing 'why teach a subject matter' by reference to history. Gilbert proposed four alternative models of the master performer.
	
	  (a) *The storyteller:* he who can use what he learned of history and of the methods of historians in order to transmit it to others (eg many teachers)
	  (b) *The archivist:* he who can use what he learned of history and of the methods of historians in order to continue the study of history (to research, discover, document history)
	  (c) *The history maker:* he who can use what he learned of history in order to create history (eg the revolutionary)
	  (d) *The problem-solver:* he who can use what he learned of history in order to better understand and predict the problems/social phenomena of today.

Comments	1. Gilbert's titles for his master performers have the ring of job titles. They beg the questions: Do such jobs exist in our society? Should society encourage the existence of such jobs? Gilbert himself rejects the models (a), (b) and (c) as adequate reasons for teaching history to *all* children on the grounds that:
	
	  (a) The storyteller job is not practised by many (should perhaps be part of teacher-training, etc) in a society based on mass media.
	  (b) The archivist job is also a specialism for the few who make history their profession.
	  (c) The history maker is generally a troublemaker.
	
	He therefore recommends model (d) the problem-solver as the most adequate to justify history as a standard part of the curriculum. He then argues that (and shows how) one can develop detailed performance objectives from this model.
	
	2. Whether one agrees or not with Gilbert's analysis is not of importance. One could select an alternative model, or a combination of several, or define yet other different master performers. But, in so doing, one is still following the same approach (ie output → input). Having defined/selected your own definition of master performance in general terms, as above, the process of rendering this statement more precise will produce specific performance objectives. These objectives will identify the historical content worth including in the course.
	
	3. There is a definite analogy here between the master performer → specific objectives → historical content stages and the job → tasks → knowledge/skill stages of training design which we shall explore later.

Map 3.5 *From aims to content to objectives*

2. The input → output route (taxonomies of objectives)	
Introduction	The input → output route from aims to objectives would seem to be the traditional way that education (as opposed to training) has been planned. It is embodied in the subject or discipline-based approach, which has dominated educational planning until very recently. Having paid lip service to broad educational aims or ideals, these are not used as the starting point for planning but are (if at all) used only much later in the design process. The subject takes over as the starting point for design. Decisions are made on such inputs as: ☐ subjects to be included in the curriculum ☐ relative importance and therefore the time devoted to each ☐ relative importance of the various topics ☐ resources needed for the topics (teachers, time, equipment) ☐ content or syllabus (the topics to be taught or 'covered'). Only at a later stage are the outputs considered (tests and examinations). It is at this stage that it sometimes becomes apparent that the content selected does not lend itself well to developing the sort of output performances that our broad educational aims imply. Discrepancies appear between the aims subscribed to and the actual objectives examined for. To overcome such deficiencies of the old, traditional planning process, various attempts have been made to develop tools for the matching of content based objectives to more general educational aims. Perhaps the most used of these are the taxonomies of educational objectives, developed by Bloom, Krathwohl and others (Bloom *et al*, 1956; Krathwohl *et al*, 1969). However, many other taxonomies/tools exist.
The purpose of an objectives taxonomy	*Subject* Set of teachable topics, methods, skills, etc / *Aims* The broad educational goals we wish to achieve Selection → *Course* *Content* ← → *Objectives* (These should be compatible) ← Definition Given a subject area (from which it is possible to select the precise content of a course) and given broad, general objectives or aims, we need (a) a common language among teachers to *define* broad aims in terms of specific testable performances (b) a methodology for the *selection* of specific content from any subject area, which is compatible with the teaching and testing of these performances.
The components of a taxonomy	Any such taxonomy therefore should: (a) Define the common language, the concepts to be used in the statement of aims and objectives (such concepts as knowledge, skill, attitude, understanding, comprehension, capability, thinking, etc) (b) Define a methodology by which 'useful' content may be identified and selected. This is often defined in the form of an *objectives hierarchy* which identifies lower level objectives which are implied by a given higher level objective. Thus, subject content contributing to these lower level, or enabling objectives is useful and should be included in the course. Also the instructional sequence is implied by the hierarchy.
Example of the use of an objectives taxonomy (much simplified)	*Aim* speak foreign languages fluently. *Common language* (restricted to the example only). *Complex procedures*: sets of activities, involving decisions or control of quality. *Discriminations*: identifying differences between similar stimuli. *Methodology* *Rule* (for teaching complex procedures which involve discrimination as part of the decision-making process) — teach the component discriminations before teaching the complete procedure. *Application to our example:* students should be taught to discriminate correct and incorrect pronunciation in others (eg from tape recordings) before being given practice in speaking a foreign language.

Map 3.6 *Existing approaches to the classifying of educational objectives:*
an overview

Introduction	Several ways have been suggested for the classifying of educational aims and objectives. ☐ By immediacy: long-term/immediate ☐ By performance-type: eg cognitive/affective/psychomotor ☐ By source: eg life-skill/methodological/content.
Immediacy	Objectives are classified into: Long term: knowledge and skills useful throughout life Medium term: what is to be gained specifically from schooling Course: what the course will teach/test Unit: what the unit will teach/test Lesson: what the lesson will teach/test Specific behaviours: the steps of a given lesson or exercise. This is useful for the purposes of curriculum design/sequencing such a classification is used, for example, as a basis of the procedures suggested by Briggs, Gagné and others (1970) in their *Handbook of Procedures for the Design of Instruction*.
Performance type	Such a classification is usually combined with a set of rules (a taxonomy) for matching the teaching methods and testing instruments to the objective type. A simple classification, commonly used, is into Cognitive objectives — to do with thinking Affective objectives — to do with feeling Psychomotor objectives — to do with doing. Another is the even more common terminology of knowledge/attitudes/skills. This appears to be the same as the former, but its usage varies. For example calculating skills are *cognitive* objectives. More detailed classifications, according to type have been developed by: Bloom *et al* (1956): taxonomy of cognitive objectives Krathwohl *et al* (1964): taxonomy of affective objectives Simpson *et al* (1967): taxonomy of psychomotor objectives. Other approaches have sprung from the (stimulus/response) behaviour school. These include Gilbert (1961): chains, discriminations and generalizations, and Gagné (1965): hierarchy of learning categories. These will be explained in more detail later.
Source	Educational aims spring in general from the felt needs of individuals as members of society, and from the aims of that society (unlike training objectives which spring directly from the needs of specific organizations and specific jobs in those organizations). Thus a particular aim might be derived from a need of society or from a need of the individual. These needs may be phrased in terms of input (content or information) or alternatively in terms of process (thinking capabilities) or in terms of products (specific skills, performances). One classification (see Rowntree 1974) which mirrors these divisions, uses the terms: *Life-skill* objectives: skills practised in everyday life when interacting with other people, specific situations, etc. These would include cognitive, psychomotor and affective life-skills. *Methodological* objectives: ways of thinking about and acting on information, the specialized modes of inquiry and ways of knowing which are embodied in various subject disciplines. *Content* objectives: 'the student's ability to recognize and expound the concepts, generalizations and principles that make up the substance and structure of his subject area.' The principal use of this classification is to ensure that all three sources of *possible* objectives are considered when selecting worthwhile objectives for a course.

Map 3.7 *Objectives in the cognitive domain*

Summary of the taxonomy: Handbook I (Bloom *et al* 1956)

Introduction: This table is presented here as an example of a taxonomy of objectives. It is the best known of the existing taxonomies. (The use of the taxonomy is discussed in Parts 2 and 3.)

Descriptions of the major categories in the cognitive domain	Illustrative general instructional objectives
Knowledge. Knowledge is defined as the remembering of previously learned material. This may involve the recall of a wide range of material from specific facts to complete theories, but all that is required is the bringing to mind of the appropriate information. Knowledge represents the lowest level of learning outcomes in the cognitive domain.	Knows common terms Knows specific facts Knows methods and procedures Knows basic concepts Knows principles.
Comprehension. Comprehension is defined as the ability to grasp the meaning of material. This may be shown by translating material from one form to another (words to numbers), by interpreting material (explaining or summarizing), and by estimating future trends (predicting consequences or effects). These learning outcomes go one step beyond the simple remembering of material, and represent the lowest level of understanding.	Understands facts and principles Interprets verbal material Interprets charts and graphs Translates verbal material to mathematical formulas Estimates future consequences implied in data.
Application. Application refers to the ability to use learned material in new and concrete situations. This may include the application of such things as rules, methods, concepts, principles, laws, and theories. Learning outcomes in this area requires higher level of understanding than those under comprehension.	Applies concepts and principles to new situations Applies laws and theories to practical situations Demonstrates correct usage of a method or procedure.
Analysis. Analysis refers to the ability to break down material into its component parts so that its organizational structure may be understood. This may include the identification of the parts, analysis of the relationships between parts, and recognition of the organizational principles involved. Learning outcomes here represent a higher intellectual level than comprehension and application because they require an understanding of both the content and the structural form of the material.	Recognizes unstated assumptions Recognizes logical fallacies in reasoning Distinguishes between facts and inferences Evaluates the relevance of data.
Synthesis. Synthesis refers to the ability to put parts together to form a new whole. This may involve the production of a unique communication (theme or speech), a plan of operations (research proposal), or a set of abstract relations (scheme for classifying information). Learning outcomes in this area stress creative behaviours, with major emphasis on the formulation of new patterns or structures.	Writes a creative short story Proposes a plan for an experiment Integrates learning from different areas into a plan for solving a problem.
Evaluation. Evaluation is concerned with the ability to judge the value of material (statement, novel, poem, research report) for a given purpose. The judgements are to be based on definite criteria. These may be internal criteria (organization) or external criteria (relevance to the purpose) and the student may determine the criteria or be given them. Learning outcomes in this area are higher in the cognitive hierarchy because they contain elements of all of the other categories, plus conscious value judgements based on clearly defined criteria.	Judges the logical consistency of written material Judges the adequacy with which conclusions are supported by data Judges the value of a work by use of internal criteria Judges the value of a work by use of external standards of excellence.

Map 3.8 *Objectives in the affective domain*

Summary of the taxonomy: Handbook II (Krathwohl *et al* 1964)

Introduction: The second handbook of 'Bloom's taxonomy' deals with attitudes and values. Both these handbooks will be discussed further in Parts 2 and 3.

Descriptions of the major categories in the affective domain	Illustrative general instructional objectives
Receiving. Receiving refers to the student's willingness to attend to particular phenomena or stimuli (classroom activities, textbook, music, etc). From a teaching standpoint, it is concerned with getting, holding, and directing the student's attention. Learning outcomes in this area range from the simple awareness that a thing exists to selective attention on the part of the learner. Receiving represents the lowest level of learning outcomes in the affective domain.	Listens attentively Shows awareness of the importance of learning Shows sensitivity to human needs and social problems Attends closely to the classroom activities.
Responding. Responding refers to active participation on the part of the student. At this level he not only attends to a particular phenomenon but also reacts to it in some way. Learning outcomes in this area may emphasize acquiescence in responding (reads assigned material), willingness to respond (voluntarily reads beyond assignment), or satisfaction in responding (reads for pleasure or enjoyment). The higher levels of this category include those instructional objectives that are commonly classified under 'interests', that is, those that stress the seeking out and enjoyment of particular activities.	Completes assigned homework Obeys school rules Participates in class discussion Completes laboratory work Volunteers for special tasks Shows interest in subject.
Valuing. Valuing is concerned with the worth or value a student attaches to a particular object, phenomenon or behaviour. This ranges in degree from the more simple acceptance of a value (desires to improve group skills) to the more complex level of commitment (assumes responsibility for the effective functioning of the group). Valuing is based on the internalization of a set of specified values, but clues to these values are expressed in the student's overt behaviour. Learning outcomes in this area are concerned with behaviour that is consistent and stable enough to make the value clearly identifiable. Instructional objectives that are commonly classified under 'attitudes' and 'appreciation' would fall into this category.	Demonstrates belief in the democratic process Appreciates good literature (art or music) Shows concern for the welfare of others Demonstrates problem-solving attitude Demonstrates commitment to social improvement.
Organization. Organization is concerned with bringing together different values, resolving conflicts between them, and beginning the building of an internally consistent value system. Thus the emphasis is on comparing, relating and synthesizing values. Learning outcomes may be concerned with the conceptualization of a value (recognizes the responsibility of each individual for improving human relations) or with the organization of a value system (develops a vocational plan that satisfies his need for both economic security and social service). Instructional objectives relating to the development of a philosophy of life would fall into this category.	Recognizes the role of systematic planning in solving problems Accepts responsibility for his own behaviour Understands and accepts his own strengths and limitations Formulates a life plan in harmony with his abilities, interests and beliefs.
Characterization by a value or value complex. At this level of the affective domain, the individual has a value system that has controlled his behaviour for a sufficiently long time for him to have developed a characteristic 'life style'. Thus the behaviour is pervasive, consistent and predictable. Learning outcomes at this level cover a broad range of activities, but the major emphasis is on the fact that the behaviour is typical or characteristic of the student. Instructional objectives that are concerned with the student's general patterns of adjustment (personal, social, emotional) would be appropriate here.	Displays safety consciousness Demonstrates self-reliance in working independently Practices cooperation in group activities Demonstrates industry, punctuality and self-discipline Maintains good health habits.

4. The System in Its Environment

4.1 The problem and its context

What is the problem as it is first presented? A medical analogy

We have already defined our use of the word 'problem' as a discrepancy between what is and what should be sufficient to cause dissatisfaction. The person who is dissatisfied and observes the discrepancy is said to have the problem. But can he always define it?

A man goes to see his doctor because he is dissatisfied with his state of health. 'I have this problem, doctor — I suffer regularly from headaches. Can you give me a really effective analgesic?' The patient has specified the problem as he sees it and is even suggesting the solution. The doctor, however, will examine the patient more thoroughly. He will ask when exactly the headaches occur (during reading, in stressful situations, etc) and will look for possible causes of

Symptoms and causes

the headaches. The doctor is treating the headaches as *symptoms* and is looking for *causes*. He may find, for example, that poor eyesight is the cause of the headaches and will set out to treat this. The doctor sees the problem as a discrepancy between the patient's actual eyesight condition and the desirable condition. By suggesting the use of glasses, he treats the problem rather than the symptom. He may dig yet deeper and wider to discover that the poor eyesight is a symptom of a yet more fundamental problem, such as the patient's working habits and life-style. He may recommend appropriate solutions, to avoid further deterioration of the eyes (and perhaps other related symptoms too). He may suggest a change of job, for example. At yet another level, he may identify the problem of this patient as an example of a class (or occupational disease) and recommend changes in the structure or procedures of a whole industry.

The wider system

Our doctor, in the above example, is engaging in problem definition, through systems analysis. He is considering the wider context in which the problem, as first presented, is embedded. He is discovering that problems, as first encountered, are often only symptoms of more general problems. He believes that he should attempt to treat the problem and not just the symptoms. Of course, he will recommend an analgesic (in the short term), at the same time prescribing glasses (medium term) and a change in habit together with eye-improving exercises (long-term solution). He may never be able to do much

The sphere of influence

about the occupational disease aspects of the problem, as they will be outside of his sphere of influence. He may merely advise his own patients concerning the dangers they are facing, or publish articles in an attempt to alert employers.

Discriminating problems and solutions

The good doctor is also careful to avoid being misled by the patient who arrives already 'knowing' what is the matter. The doctor must steer his way through to identifying the fundamental problem and to prescribe appropriate treatment, without upsetting or alienating the patient.

The client-consultant relationship

This delicate patient-doctor relationship is not unlike the client-consultant relationship that exists in management consultancy (see Figure 4.1). The same balance of diagnostic/analytic skills and bedside manner is required. The same types of question are asked.

☐ Is the 'problem' really a problem?
☐ Is it a symptom of a deeper problem?
☐ Is the deeper problem soluble by me?

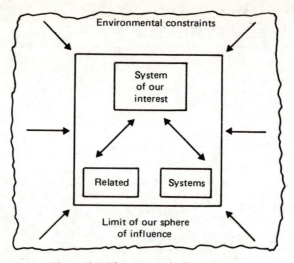

Figure 4.1 *The system in its context*

☐ Is it worth trying? Who will pay?

In order to answer these questions, it is necessary to take the broader view of the problem in its context. We attempt to analyse the wider system, to identify the causes of the problem under study and to assess whether these causes can be eliminated, or at least partly controlled, by us. This enables us to define the limits of the sphere of influence within which we must work to solve the problem. We have defined certain environmental constraints which we must take into consideration.

Let us illustrate the process in action, by a few case studies.

4.2 Case studies in problem definition

Case study 1: the 'long hair' problem The training department of a motor car firm in which the author once worked was asked (told) by one of the directors to 'do something about the long hair of the apprentices'. This was in the early 1960s when long hair was just 'coming in', so the apprentice age group tended to stand out as being the only group in the factory with a predominance of 'hairy freaks'.

The problem, as presented, appeared to be:

What is: long haired apprentices.
What should be: short haired apprentices.

Even the most cursory analysis of the content of the problem, as in Figure 4.2, illustrates why the obvious 'solution' of ordering the apprentices to cut their hair was impossible. The apprentice needed long hair to be accepted in the *younger generation system*, which, as far as he was concerned, was a more important system than the *factory*. Furthermore the apprentice, within the factory, was a part of the *workforce* sub-system, whose relationship with the *management* sub-system was such as not to allow the issuing of orders such as cut your hair without solid justifications. These are both environmental constraints, outside our sphere of influence. Perhaps the problem will turn out to be insoluble, or perhaps it is not worth solving (depending on whether you take the director's viewpoint, or that of a disinterested outside observer)..

However, perhaps there are more fundamental problems behind the long hair problem. An analysis of the apprentices in the organization revealed only one possible justification: danger of accidents when working with high-speed machinery. Obviously, instructor efficiency, learning efficiency, productivity,

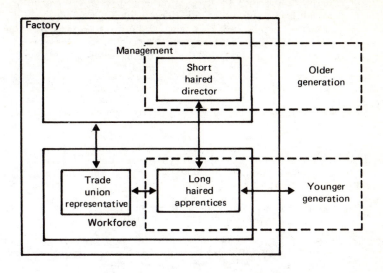

Figure 4.2 *The factory and the wider system*

dexterity or strength are not affected by the length of the apprentice's hair. Other personal appearance factors do not count for much as the apprentice does not interact directly with the clients of the motor car firm. So the problem was restated as:

What is: danger of work accidents due to long hair.
What should be: no danger of such accidents.

When presented with the analysis and the restated problem, the director in question concurred (and this proved to be his downfall). The problem as now stated opened itself to a variety of solutions: (various ways of keeping hair out of machines) and some of these solutions are capable of being implemented without entering in conflict with the wider objectives of the worforce sub-system. The solution adopted was to decree that apprentices, before working on any high-speed machinery must either:

(a) get their hair cut short, or
(b) wear a hair net.

The workforce response was 'OK but you must provide the hair nets.'
A special cap was designed, rather like a foreign legionnaire's peaked cap with a flap at the back which pulled up to gather in the long hair. Far from 'shaming the boys into getting a haircut' the cap became a status symbol even with shorter-haired apprentices. The problem, as restated, was solved. The original pseudo-problem no doubt continued to be a source of dissatisfaction to the director, but the 'bedside manner' of the training department staff left him no option but to live with his problem.

Case study 2: the teaching effectiveness problem
Each year, reams of paper are devoted to the 'problems' of teaching and learning, thousands of hours of lectures are given to trainee teachers on 'teaching method', several books are published. Yet the problems remain and appear undiminished. Are we attacking the problems correctly? Are the problems soluble? Do they indeed exist? Do the 'owners' of the educational system (ie society at large) really see the problem as some of us (teaching professionals) see it. To us, poor system performance, as exemplified by poor

examination pass results, is a source of dissatisfaction, but what about the super-system (society)? Certainly, whatever it 'says', society does not behave as if the performance of the educational system were a source of dissatisfaction. It does not spend a very large proportion of the resources devoted to education in attempts to improve the system. The size of the educational industry is quite staggering. Austwick (1972) described it as follows:

> I would ask you to imagine a major national industry, with an annual expenditure of about 2500 million pounds, a workforce of about 400,000 and a further 100,000 trainees. The manufacturing time for each product varies between 10 and 20 years and a further 10 or more years are required for evaluation afterwards. The number of items going through the system at any one time is of the order of eight million. The industry itself is very old but has been expanding rapidly during the past 100 years and seems likely to go on doing so. If you ask for a specification of any of the products of the industry you will be told that this is not available, being still under discussion! The industry has no central board of directors, but during the past 25 years has had 15 successive general managers — an average of about 20 months each!
>
> The 'industry' which satisfies these conditions is of course the educational system of England and Wales.

The level of investment in educational research and development

Depending on their technological complexity most manufacturing industries spend between 2 per cent and 15 per cent of their total turnover on research and development. The medical industry (drugs, pharmaceuticals) is one of the biggest spenders in this field. In many respects the medical and educational industries are very similar, and with the food industries, they have the greatest influence on the well-being of man. They are also very similar in their direct action upon man as an individual: diagnosis of individual needs, presentation of individual treatments, construction and control of appropriate environments, etc. Yet while medicine invests heavily in research and development, education hardly does at all. Till quite recently, Britain spent upwards of £50 million a year on school milk. This measure, necessary immediately after the war, outlasted its usefulness by years, contributing to the health problems of obesity, now more serious than malnutrition among British schoolchildren. This expense represented about 2 per cent of the annual educational budget. Yet the total expenditure on research in education is several times less than this, only a fraction of one per cent. When the then National Council for Educational Technology obtained a research budget of £2 million over several years for computer-based learning, it made headline news.

Why the super-system does not really want to improve the efficiency of education

Yet there is ample evidence to suggest that a reasonable level of investment in research and development would reap benefits in education, as it has in other industries. Why then do we not see an effort made? It would seem that education does not wish to improve, that the problems of educational efficiency to which lip service is paid by successive ministers of education are merely pseudo-problems. As an example of the reasons behind this, let us investigate one case: high drop-out rates from a course caused by difficulties in learning, attending regularly and so on. Typical examples of British courses with high drop-out rates are the Ordinary and Higher National Certificate courses. These are for people who are in full-time employment in industry, so are run in the evenings or on a sandwich basis. No doubt this aspect contributes to the average annual drop-out rate of between 25 per cent and 30 per cent of students. But overloaded curricula, poor learning conditions, poor equipment, scarce learning aids and poor teaching also play their part. These courses are designed to run over five years, three years up to ONC or a further two years to obtain the HNC. As a result of the drop-out rates and examination failures, only about 8 per cent of those who start the course obtain a Higher National Certificate within the five years. This number swells a little later on, owing to second attempts. The process seems terribly wasteful. Why is nothing done to improve the situation? Let us suppose that we could halve the annual drop-out rate from 30 per cent to 15 per cent, what then? Twice as many students would be studying for HNC in the fourth and fifth year, requiring twice as many classrooms, laboratories and workshops, teachers etc. Nearly three times as many would graduate. Can industry use that many graduates?

Thus there are constraints both within the system (available resources) and in the super-system (in this case industry) which militate against anything being done to improve the situation.

Year	Drop-out rate	
	30%	15%
1.	100	100
less drop-outs	−30	−15
2.	70	85
less drop-outs	−21	−13
3.	49	72
less drop-outs	−15	−11
4.	34	61
less drop-outs	−10	−9
5.	24	52
less drop-outs	−7	−8
Number sitting HNC examination	17	44
Number passing at first sitting (at 50 per cent norm-referenced passing grade)	8	22
Maximum number in HNC course: 4th and 5th years combined	58	113

Figure 4.3 *Number of trainees in ONC/HNC courses; over a hypothetical 5-year period at annual drop-out rates of 30 per cent and 15 per cent (per 100 trainees entering)*

Case study 3: the adult literacy problem

Many countries are very concerned about the levels of illiteracy of their adult population. Either because schooling opportunities did not exist, or because existing facilities were inefficient, a proportion of the population (in some countries quite considerable) reaches adulthood without acquiring the basic skills of reading and writing. This is bemoaned from two standpoints:

Arguments for a high level of literacy

1. That the lack of these skills makes the person almost unemployable in a developing and industrializing nation. The concept of functional literacy stems from this: each citizen should at least reach that level of literacy which will enable him to hold down a job and fulfil his obligations to society (eg write a cheque, pay his taxes, etc). We might label this the human resources standpoint, which views the population as an important resource which society should use efficiently in order to reach its objectives.
2. That the lack of literacy skills closes many doors of self-improvement for the person. In a society as large and complex as most modern nations, the village-level techniques of education and training through personal example and word-of-mouth are ineffective. Not only is there not enough time to learn all that is required for modern living in this way, but there are also many things which can only be effectively learned through reading and writing. We might call this the humanist standpoint, which views the individual as the important system, and is concerned with improving his capabilities of interaction with his environment.

Whichever of the two standpoints one favours, there seem to be strong reasons for doing something about the adult literacy problem.

One country which has put a lot of effort into solving the problem is Brazil. For some years now, an organization called MOBRAL (Brazilian Movement for Literacy) has been running schemes of adult literacy training throughout the country. The stated aims of MOBRAL are to eliminate adult illiteracy by the turn of the century. The techniques MOBRAL uses involve the use of many volunteer teachers, the media, other local and national resources, and are reported to be very successful. Indeed the MOBRAL model has been copied and adapted by several other Latin American and African nations. MOBRAL has become a Brazilian export.

Can it achieve its objective, however? A little bit of systems analysis casts strong doubts on the possibility of MOBRAL *on its own* ever eliminating illiteracy. What do we mean by eliminating in this context anyway? Surely we do not mean that there will be not one illiterate person in the country. Rather, we must have an idea of the percentage of the population which we will tolerate as illiterates. For example, the problem could be stated as:

What is: X per cent of adults over 15 years are illiterate.
What should be: no more than Y per cent of the group should be illiterate.

One really also needs to define illiterate in quantifiable and measurable terms, but we will come back to this point later.

Let us build up a hypothetical systems diagram, based on simplified figures (but figures not far from the Brazilian reality). We shall imagine a 'steady state' before the implementation of adult literacy schemes, which was giving a level of 50 per cent adult literacy. This was arrived at as shown in Figure 4.4. For every 100 children reaching school age, 90 enter some form of schooling. The other 10 do not (mainly because of no local facilities) and very few of these (a negligible proportion) manage to become literate through their own efforts by the time they reach the school leaving age of 15. Of the 90 who enter schooling, only 50 are literate by the age of 15. This is largely due to heavy drop-out and the process of repeating a grade if standards are not reached (half the nation's schoolchildren are in the first grade). This figure represents a 50/90 or 55.5 per cent efficiency level for the school system.

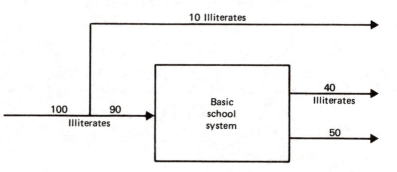

Figure 4.4 *Steady-state before implementation of adult literacy programme*

Let us now state our problem as:

What is: 50 per cent of adults (15+) are illiterate.
What should be: 10 per cent or less of adults (15+) illiterate.

In order to solve the problem, we construct an adult literacy programme. We implant this system in our hypothetical society and link it to existing systems as shown in Figure 4.5. This shows a new hypothetical steady state when the problem is 'solved' as we have 90 literates being outputted for every 100 new children entering the system. Notice that we have assumed no change in the efficiency of the school system. What does this imply for the efficiency of the adult literacy programme?

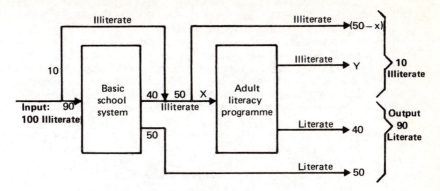

Figure 4.5 *Steady-state (hypothetical) after the adult literacy programme has been implemented and has reached its objective of maintaining a 10 per cent or less output of illiterates (ie 10 per cent of all children born will remain illiterate)*

Given 50 illiterates aged 15 or over, it must produce 40 literates. This may be achieved in several ways.

1. The programme manages to 'catch' all 50 (ie x = 50). Then in order to output 40 literates, the programme must work at 80 per cent efficiency.
2. It may catch only 40 (any less and it could not reach its target output). This implies an 80 per cent success rate in attracting adults into the programme. But it also implies an impossible 100 per cent efficiency for the programme.
3. Any intermediate stage between 1 and 2. For example, if the adult programme was as successful as the school system in capturing the illiterates (90 per cent), then it would have to operate at a 40/45 or 89 per cent efficiency).

None of these three situations are in the realms of probability. It is unlikely that the percentage coverage of any adult education system could even equal that of the normal school system, given that the former is voluntary and the latter is compulsory, and that *all* those who nevertheless managed to evade the compulsory system are in the clientele.

It is also unlikely that an adult programme could be over one and a half times more efficient than the school system (80 per cent to 90 per cent as compared to 55 per cent) given that adults as a rule have more learning difficulties, and the 'natural' good learners have in the main succeeded in the schools, and the ones we are now dealing with are the poorer learners who have already experienced failure (unless of course there were to be a breakthrough in instructional methods).

Finally, one should note that the throughput capacity of the adult programme in our example is about half that of the school system. This will represent quite a high investment.

Look at other sub-systems and alternative courses of action

The systems analyst/project planner may well ask at this stage such questions as: 'Should we not do something, about the efficiency and coverage of the school system, at the same time as (or even before) we implement an adult literacy programme?' 'If there are techniques which can give 80 per cent or more efficiency in the teaching of reading and writing, would it not be more economical to spend our resources on implementing these at the school level?' He may even be led further into systems analysis, to consider whether he ought to be designing adult literacy programmes at all? He might, for instance, get more interested in the efficiency of the school system. Do we have a steady state? Is the school system keeping up with population growth? Is it in fact deteriorating? What can we do to close the gap here, thus automatically reducing the adult literacy problem?

He may even start questioning the validity of the problem. Is it really the problem he should be devoting his attention to? He may note that illiteracy is predominant in the rural areas and in the poorer quarters of the country. He may note that the justifications for 'total adult literacy' do not apply there: life is still lived at the village level. He may note that the population is largely (over 70 per cent) urban and that this has been a recent phenomenon caused by urban drift from the rural and poorer areas. It seems therefore that to some extent the adult illiteracy problem solves itself in the cities. Is it that once in an urban environment, the pressures of job-hunting and simply living create motivational conditions facilitating the rapid learning of essential survival skills

Look at the super-system

(like reading and writing)? Or do rural dwellers, who have learned to read and write now find themselves equipped to seek their fortunes in the industrialized cities?

Yet the cities have high levels of unemployment. Literacy is not enough. It only supplies the tools for further learning. So the migrant is still largely unemployable. The shanty towns grow up around the city. Some of the shanty dwellers soon cannot even afford to travel to the city to seek work, nor back to their original homes. They are trapped. Malnutrition and disease spread.

Compare objectives for compatibility and examine the long-term value to society

At this point our systems analyst gets involved in comparing the objectives of other systems. He examines the interaction between the educational system and the industry, social welfare, demographic and other systems. He may well lose interest in the adult literacy problem, as being of low priority in relation to other problems he has identified. Or he may look at the problem in a new light. Is the success of adult literacy programmes in the rural areas actively encouraging urban drift? Do they do more harm to society than good? How could we counteract any possible harm? Should we, for example, only offer literacy training as part of a vocational training programme? Should we be concentrating more on programmes that would keep rural dwellers on the land?

Examine the long-term value to the individual

He may take the humanist viewpoint and come up with other questions. How many of the adults who go through the programme later have any opportunities to use their new skills? How many are once again effectively illiterate after a year or two? Are any parallel projects in action to make good books, of the appropriate level of difficulty, available at little or no cost? Should we not be thinking of travelling libraries, for example? Of promoting the production of books and literature relevant to the rural dweller's interests? Of creating a 'need to read' in rural as well as urban areas.

Examine the economic benefits and real costs

Finally, he must also take the economist's viewpoint, and determine what the society can afford to do. Among the alternatives, what are the priorities? What are the super-system (society and state) objectives which govern these priorities? Are these objectives realistic in the light of world trends? Should we, for example, be as strongly wedded to the industrial development model of progress as we are?

Establish the limits of one's sphere of influence

How far our analyst goes into his investigation of the wider system will depend on the limits of his sphere of influence. He may of course theorize, as we have done. He may write articles to influence others indirectly. But insofar as his own actions are concerned, there is a very definite limit to what he can or cannot do.

If he is an instructional designer, he will stop at reformulating the project objectives in input-output terms. For example, he may set a realistic standard of efficiency for the adult literacy programmes of say 70 per cent. He can only inform superior sytems how this will influence the attainment of overall objectives related to literacy levels.

If he is responsible for the whole adult literacy programme, he may prescribe the covering, the throughput, and therefore the cost necessary to achieve a given objective.

If he is the minister of education, he may determine the allocation of resources to this project, as opposed to others, the integration of this project with others, and the overall objectives of the educational systems of the nation. He may question the national objectives, but only if he were to be elected president next time round (or turn revolutionary) would the national objectives enter into his sphere of influence.

However, in order to act wisely within your own sphere of influence, you need to analyse and understand the objectives and the functioning of related systems outside your influence. In the long run, no one will thank you for establishing unrealistic objectives.

Case study 4: the course design problem

Lest the last case study seemed to be way outside of your own spheres of influence, let us examine a case closer to home. The problem is one of designing a new course. The example is at university level, but similar examples can be found at all levels of education.

Some years ago, when working at one of the polytechnics formed in England in the late 1960s, I was responsible for running a unit, which, among other tasks, offered an educational technology service to all other courses, both ongoing and in the process of development. This service was not concerned with providing slides or transparencies (a separate audiovisual aids unit looked after all this) but with the provision of advice and help in the selection or development of course objectives, teaching methods, evaluation methods and so forth. Therefore, particularly when new courses were being planned, the unit was often consulted (and sometimes it poked its nose in even though unasked).

On one occasion, I was participating as a member of a course design team planning a part-time master's degree course in business studies. The team had already met a few times when I joined it and a scheme was already at an advanced stage of planning. Basically, the course was to have a pyramidal curriculum, with broadly-based general studies in the first year, tapering upwards to greater and greater specialization in second and third years.

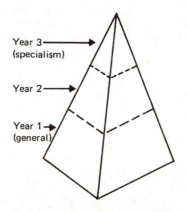

Year 3 (specialism)
Year 2
Year 1 (general)

Figure 4.6 *The pyramidal curriculum model*

The team had just reached the stages of defining the specialization or rather specializations, as it was soon decided that the college could offer three choices of specialization. Thus the concept of the three-peaked pyramid was launched on an unsuspecting world. I missed a couple of meetings, during which the team suffered some other changes in personnel (and changes of heart) which led to a revision of basic ideas about the course: participants were to start by studying a special area of their choice and, as their knowledge and interest grew, they would naturally become involved with related subjects until in the last year of the course they would be ready to take in the whole area of

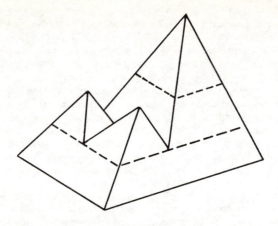

Figure 4.7 *The three-peaked pyramid*

business studies as an integrated subject.

Thus I was suddenly confronted by an animated group of academics discussing in all seriousness the finer points of the 'inverted three-peaked pyramid' curriculum. By now the working strategy of the group was obvious: 'what teachers have we available, how much time can they devote, what can they teach to fill the time', tempered with a few philosophical viewpoints which changed with the absence or presence of the stronger personalities among the team members.

From an educational technologist's viewpoint this was all wrong, so naturally I went into the attack with some unpleasant questions like:

> Who is the course being designed for? Where do they come from? What are their present jobs? What are the promotional channels they would hope to follow? What topics do they need to learn to facilitate these ambitions? How much time would *they* need to learn? Do they really need a three-year part-time master's course, or only a one-year diploma? Perhaps our plans are too academic? Would it be a good idea to do a market survey of local industry to establish the true needs of our potential clients?

My suggestions were not received as a good idea at all. The reactions were almost hostile.

> We, as specialists in the academic study of business, know best. We already know enough about local industry's needs. Anyway it is not relevant what local industry thinks it needs; we know what they *ought* to think. And, furthermore, the very fact of having an MSc is the important key to promotion, irrespective of what was studied and learned.

Anyway, I persevered and over the weeks the minutes of past meetings and announcements of future meetings developed a strange tendency of not reaching my pigeonhole. As far as the rest of the crew were concerned, the educational technology approach was 'not wanted on voyage', they could plan and steer their course quite happily in their own way.

I was quite intrigued by the extent of the resistance encountered, especially as business study and management people should have been very much in tune with an objectives-oriented approach to design. So why the resistance in this particular case? A bit of systems analysis soon revealed the causes.

In my enthusiastic naivety, I had been working from a rather simplistic view of the polytechnic as a sub-system of the local community (as far as part-time courses are concerned, this is very much so, as one only services people who can travel in easily after work). Certainly insofar as inputs are concerned, these

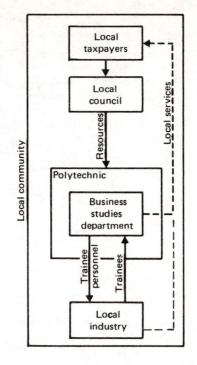

Figure 4.8 *'Naive' model of the polytechnic in its local community*

are in the main local community taxes.

As far as outputs are concerned, those of the business studies department are largely absorbed by the local industry sub-system. Therefore, it seemed to me paramount to consider the client's needs in designing the new course. However, there was another viewpoint, much more important (as it happened) to the head of business studies. The polytechnic is also a sub-system of the tertiary education system, and here things were happening which strongly affected the polytechnic sub-system.

The new polytechnics are controlled, in terms of courses offered, degrees, standards, etc by the Council for National Academic Awards (CNAA). This council had only recently authorized the submission of proposals for higher degrees.

Representation on the CNAA was from the whole tertiary education system, but dominated by the older, more traditional (more academic) universities. Approval of plans therefore depended heavily on their academic worth. Furthermore, approval was important for the growth and survival of the polytechnic. Through its general policy for tertiary education in the polytechnics, the CNAA was effectively rationing the number of licences for courses in any particular area (all part of so-called manpower planning). A competitive situation was created between the polytechnics.

Therefore, to succeed in obtaining approval, the academic worth route was the one to follow. Relevance to actual needs of local industry was to be given lip service of course, but would not be allowed to cloud the real issues.

Also, one should not overlook the situation within the polytechnic itself. Because of the recent amalgamation of several institutions into one new polytechnic, several departments, among them business studies, found themselves severely overstaffed. Hence another source of pressure for new courses (in the long run). But, in the short term, the actual planning process and the administrative tasks involved were welcome buffer functions that

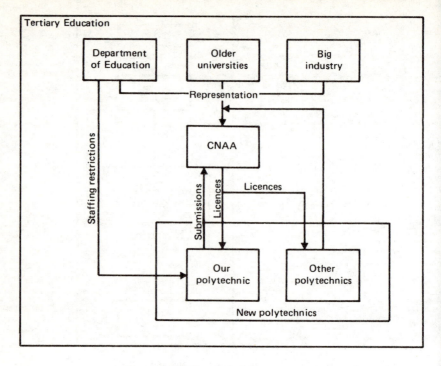

Figure 4.9 *Influence of the super-system*

soaked up surplus human resources, rather than returning them to the general
resources pool where they may be consumed irretrievably by other
departments, or worse still, lost entirely to the system. The polytechnic
management was also interested in maintaining, or indeed increasing existing
resources. The various pressures therefore amounted to 'new course approvals
at all costs' as an aim, and 'maximize the man-hours used in course
development, while not delaying the final approval date' as a methodology.

This is, of course, a gross oversimplification of the reality. A full analysis
of the interactions between the system and sub-system involved would reveal
yet other sources of pressure for particular courses of action. And the situation
was not quite as one-sided as I have suggested. Some weight was being given to
the needs and interests of local industry and of the potential student
population. These factors, though theoretically of high priority, were in reality
given low priority due to other very real and very important factors concerned
with the very survival of the institution.

However, perhaps some rigorously applied systems analysis, somewhat more
thorough than quoted in the example above may have helped to maintain a
better equilibrium between the various factors involved. Could we not have
systematically planned a *trade-off* between the needs of the local community
and the needs to satisfy the CNAA. Even if no diminution in man-hours were
obtained (or desired) could not the work of the course design teams have been
more useful, both in terms of the quality of the final product (the course
submission) and in terms of what the individual course design team members
got out of the experience by way of insights and techniques for future similar
activities (see Figure 4.10).

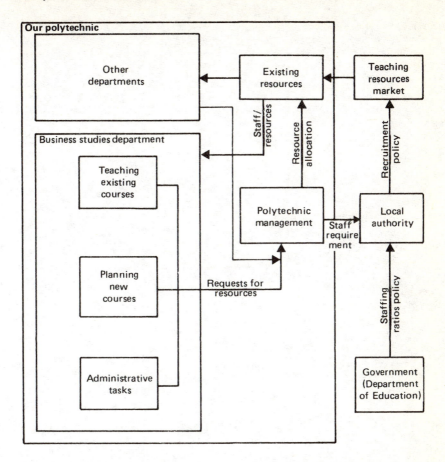

Figure 4.10 *Influence of related systems*

PART 2
Analyse the Problem

Overview

Chapter 5. Defines two 'roads' of instructional design: via the analysis of the performances required (the outputs), and via the analysis of the information content proposed (the inputs). Two levels, or depths, of initial analysis are identified in each of these roads and are termed 'level 1' and 'level 2' analysis. The object of each level of analysis is considered and some common approaches are examined.

Chapter 6. Presents a schema and some practical techniques for the analysis of performance problems (front-end analysis) in an organization. Extends the schema to form a conceptual model for the application of the systems approach to the assessment of training (and other) needs in large organizations.

Chapter 7. Presents (in information mapping form) a number of practical techniques for the analysis of jobs and tasks (performance) and the analysis of subject matter and specific topics (information). The role of target population analysis at both levels is illustrated.

Chapter 8. Presents a conceptual schema for the analysis and evaluation of alternative solutions to a given problem. The evaluation is performed by considering the 'worth' of a solution when compared to the 'cost' of the problem and the cost of developing the solution. A further consideration is the viability, or practicality, of a given solution. It is suggested that a formal evaluation of worth and practicality should be performed early in the instructional design project and that the client should be involved in this activity in order to obtain his support for the proposed form of solution, to secure the necessary resources for developing the solution and to establish a realistic time-plan and project management plan.

5. From Project Objectives to Instructional Objectives

5.1 The roads to instructional design

In the previous section, we made a distinction between two categories of problems which may face the instructional designer:

Knowledge and information

1. Those that present themselves in performance terms: a discrepancy between what the learner can do and what he should be able to do (output problem).
2. Those that present themselves in information terms: a discrepancy between the actual and desirable levels of knowledge or information about a subject (input/problem).

The word knowledge should not be used as a synonym for information or content (although it is used commonly in this way, eg the existing *knowledge* about quasars), because it is confused with the use of knowledge with reference to a particular person. Existing knowledge about quasars is external to me. What I know about quasars is inside me.

So, taking *me* as the system of interest, let us standardize our usage as:

Information: information which exists.
Knowledge: information stored in me.

The previous section restricted itself to stating the problem — defining actual and desired system states in terms of input and output. The only analysis that was done was input/output analysis and systems analysis applied to the wider system, in which our system of interest is embedded. So, if I am the system of interest, we came to a conclusion that I need either to:

(a) receive certain information which I have not got, or
(b) improve my performance of certain tasks.

Two roads to instructional design

The problem may combine both aspects. Indeed, very often in order to improve performance, I must gain certain information. On the other hand, in order to gain certain information, I may not need to change my performance, but in order to show that I have gained the information, to show that the information has been stored, to show that I now possess knowledge, I will be called upon to perform certain observable acts. Thus, there are always both input and output aspects to a problem. The division used here is for convenience, as the techniques of analysis are somewhat different depending on whether we decide to tackle first the input aspects, or the output aspects. However, we shall see that just as all roads used to lead to Rome, all the techniques of analysis tend towards the same goal, the definition of the specific learning problems of individual learners.

Levels of analysis for instructional design

However, one does not always need to go all the way along the road. There are several levels of analysis that one may perform. Sometimes, quite a superficial analysis is sufficient to show what to teach and identify; the 'what' is so simple that there is really no need to proceed to a 'how to teach' level of analysis. On other occasions, a slightly deeper analysis is sufficient to identify that ready made solutions (training modules, texts, etc) exist, which are compatible with the particular needs of the problem. Further analysis is required to produce solutions (modules, texts, etc) which are perfectly suited to the problem. But even here one can analyse to various depths. For example, the detail of analysis needed to prepare a lesson plan for a skilled teacher is less than that needed to produce all the exercises that the lesson should contain. And, finally, the level of analysis needed to take into consideration the individual learning differences between students is deeper still.

Avoid too much analysis We do not always have the resources (time, skills) nor the need to go all the way. We can often output from analysis into the development of instruction at quite an early stage. And if the nature of the problem is such that we can do this with success, we save a lot of time and effort in solving the problem. We should remember the heuristics for problem-solving that Polya suggests (see Chapter 3). We should always be looking for familiar aspects of the problem. Perhaps we have solved a similar problem before, or perhaps we know where to borrow a solution. We should constantly be seeking ways of avoiding an unnecessarily deep analysis. In the chapters that follow, stress will be placed on this aspect by dividing the analysis and the instructional development procedures presented into levels of detail and suggesting ways in which one can successfully output at an early stage.

5.2 Level 1 analysis

Let us outline a little more clearly the two roads to instruction that I have mentioned. One begins with a subject (information to be communicated). The other begins with a job (tasks to be performed). A subject is made up of a quantity of items of information, grouped in interrelated chunks or topics. A job is made up of a quantity of actions to be taken, also grouped in interrelated chunks or tasks. Not all the topics in a subject may be worth teaching. Some may be irrelevant to our aim in communicating the subject, others may already be known and do not need to be communicated anew. Similarly, not all the tasks that make up a particular job may need to be taught. Again some may already be known: performance is adequate. Others may not merit teaching because, although unknown at present, they are so simple and obvious that doing the job will be all that is required to learn them. Others are practised so rarely that there is no point in learning them (one will forget anyway before the opportunity to practice occurs), and other methods of ensuring job performance (job aids) must be looked for.

So, whether we start from the subject or from the job, the first level of analysis has the objectives: to identify the component units that most interest us (from an instructional design point of view). We are in fact performing a systems analysis, our system of interest being either the subject or the job. We are using these terms in the wider sense. A subject need not be a recognized school subject such as history or anthropology. It can be any coherent body of information such as 'What there is to know about the community we live in'. A job need not be a recognized job for which people are employed, such as motor mechanic or dentist, it may be an imaginary or notional job, such as 'a solver of real-life problems'. The main and critical difference is simply that subjects specify information and jobs specify performance.

Figure 5.1 attempts to summarize the aims of level 1 analysis and the essential similarity in the structure of subject analysis and job analysis.

The diagram identifies our principal area of interest as *designers of instruction*. In the wider problem-solving context, we would be interested in the other pathways that branch off from the main road, and may get involved in designing job aids or reference manuals, systems of job supervision and performance maintenance, simple information dissemination media or systems of information storage and retrieval. However, let us concentrate for the time being on the main purpose of this book, which is the design of instruction.

The techniques of level 1 analysis We identify in level 1 analysis either: (a) the tasks worth teaching and not yet mastered by typical trainees, or (b) the topics worth teaching and not yet

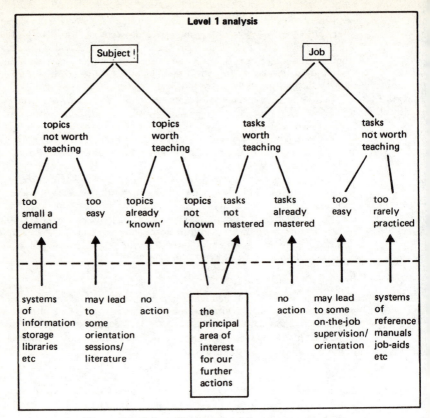

Figure 5.1 *Job analysis and subject matter analysis:*
a similar basic structure

known by typical students (or quite likely a combination of both in many projects). To do this we will need to apply several types of analyses.

A word concerning terminology. The literature of educational technology is full of names for analysis techniques, but there appears to be little standardization or coherence in the use of these terms. Take the case of the term 'task analysis' for example. To some authors this means taking a task and identifying the component steps or operations that compose it. To others it signifies the previous stage, identifying those tasks in a job. Yet others (eg Davies 1971) use the term in a general sense to include all manner of analyses, including analysis of jobs, subject matter, topics, etc.

We will reject this general use, as it will be useful to us to make several names which identify what is being analysed and at what level of detail the analysis is being performed, and we will standardize our terminology by always referring to the thing being analysed (the *system of interest*) in the name. Thus the analysis of 'x' will be termed 'x' analysis.

At this level therefore, we will need to carry out:

Analysis of
— job
— subject
— learner

(a) *job* analysis to identify the tasks worth teaching, and/or

(b) *subject/content* analysis to identify the topics worth teaching, and always

(c) *clientele* analysis (or *target population* analysis) to identify the gap which exists between actual and desired levels of knowledge or performance. Thus, we will define the 'knowledge deficiency' or the 'performance deficiency' in our clientele. These deficiencies will enable us to sort the task/topics worth teaching into those to be taught and those already learned.

Various specific techniques have been developed to perform these analyses. Job analysis may be performed by observing the job, by interviewing people connected with the job, by having a go oneself and so on. Different approaches collect different types of data and present it in different ways. (Some specific techniques are discussed in Chapter 7.) Subject content analysis may be performed by constructing topic lists, topic names, topic networks and so on. Generally these are constructed by experts in the subject (with help perhaps from an instructional designer), unlike the case of job analysis which generally is performed by a specialist in analysis (with help from experts in the job). These differences are partly the result of historical accident (the different ways in which educational and industrial organizations are structured) and partly due to intrinsic differences in the two processes of analysis (it is rather difficult for a layman to 'observe' a subject in the way that he can observe a job).

The clientele or target population analysis is the one most often overlooked at this stage. Yet it is obviously important to verify whether the topics or tasks we are identifying really need to be taught. In some cases, one may be able to perform this shallow level of target population analysis without ever meeting the target population. One takes the word of the experts regarding what is difficult to learn, what students typically bring to the course in the way of previous learning, what previous experience do job recruits typically have (this can indeed be specified and controlled by recruitment and selection procedures). If such indirect techniques prove unsatisfactory, or we cannot be confident of discovering the knowledge/performance deficiencies, we may need to interview and indeed test samples of the target population. One important product of this first level analysis is to specify realistic entry standards (or prerequisites) for the instructional system we are planning to develop.

5.3 Level 2 analysis

The passage from level 1 to level 2 analysis is easy to identify. It is when we shift our attention to a new system of interest. On the information side this will be the topic. On the performance side, the task. But note that it will not be *all* the topics or *all* the tasks identified at level 1. This is an important point which cannot be overstressed. Much time is wasted in projects analysing in depth all the topics/tasks and later on finding that little use is made of the analysis data because the difficulty of the problem did not warrant the depth of analysis. Thus at each level there should be a sorting out into priorities of the elements being identified.

In the model we are building up therefore, we perform level 2 analysis only on the tasks/topics identified at level 1 as:

(a) Worth teaching, and
(b) Not known/mastered.

We now wish to know the structure of these topics/tasks in order to decide:

☐ What to teach (instructional objectives)
☐ To what standard (criteria for evaluation)
☐ In what sequence.

Task analysis A task is a coherent set of activities (steps, operations or behaviour elements) which leads to a measurable end result. The steps of a task are therefore interrelated. There is a sequence of performance, albeit this sequence may have branches to deal with alternative cases or examples. For example, the task of connecting an outside caller to the correct internal extension (from the 'job' of a telephonist/receptionist) is a sequence of steps, with some branches, depending on whether the caller asks for a specific extension number, or for a person by name, or simply poses a question or problem not knowing to whom he really wishes to speak. Similarly, the task of solving quadratic equations (from a hypothetical or notional job of 'passer of secondary school mathematics examinations') is a sequence of steps, with alternative branches at some points, dependent on whether the equation has factors or whether the formula has to be used.

These examples also illustrate a further characteristic of a task. There is a specific triggering event or triggering stimulus which starts off the execution of the task, and a specific product or terminal event which indicates that the task is complete.

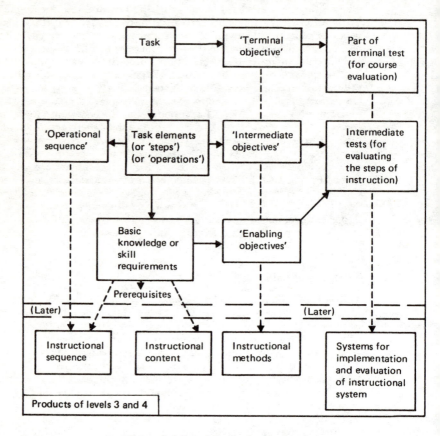

Figure 5.2 *Level 2: Analysis of tasks*

Thus, analysing the task, we encounter a set of steps to be performed and an operational sequence (which may or may not be the best instructional sequence, as we shall see later). Also, as the task has a specific triggering event and a specific terminal event, it is almost child's play to transform a task (once identified) into an objective. The form of the objective will be:

Given	Performance	Standard	Instrument
The triggering event	Perform the task	To achieve the standards indicated by terminal event	Observation of real-life/simulated performance of the task

Naturally this is a job-performance objective, or an end-of-training objective. The actual learning of the task will entail the achievement of lower level, intermediate objectives, as yet to be defined. These intermediate objectives are derived with the same ease from the task steps, or elements, and will be used to prepare test items to be used during the instructional process, to evaluate progress from one step to the next.

However, there is often a hidden element of knowledge or basic skill (eg perceptual acuity) necessary to perform certain task elements. These are also looked for at this stage, identified, listed and then transformed into *enabling objectives*. An enabling objective is one that does not appear in the task analysis as a step or operation, but which should be mastered by the trainee *to enable him to learn* certain elements of the task.

Notice that we are here crossing the border from task to topic analysis, in the case of the identification of necessary knowledge and the transformation of this knowledge into behavioural objectives.

Products of task analysis Thus, as Figure 5.2 indicates, the outputs of task analysis establish:

☐ The objectives (what to test)
☐ The tests themselves (usually produced at this stage)
☐ An operational sequence
☐ The prerequisites for the course.

These outputs may help, in later stages, to establish:

☐ The implementation/evaluation system
☐ Instructional methods
☐ An instructional sequence
☐ The content of the course.

Topic analysis A topic is made up of a coherent set of elements (or teaching points or rules) which are interrelated into a sequence or a 'structure' (a complex set of interrelationships which are not perhaps sequentially structured). For example, the topic of Ohm's law was analysed (Thomas *et al* 1963) into a teaching sequence of 29 teaching points or rules by a matrix method of investigating their interdependence. However, at first glance the topic is made up of a complex interrelationship between four basic concepts — electrical charge, electrical current, potential difference and resistance. In this case, there is no operational sequence in the sense of an order of performance of the elements. However an intellectual study of the topic, by experts, will reveal a logical sequence of interdependencies (one concept cannot be explained adequately without the use of another, so this one must be explained first.

Definition of topic Unfortunately it is more difficult to standardize a definition of a 'topic'. In the example quoted above, Ivor Davies (1971), when representing the rule-set as an example of topic analysis, used the following terminology (in an awkward attempt to use the same terms for both practical tasks and conceptual subject matter):

Topic (eg theory of conservation of energy) made up of
Duties (eg Ohm's law) made up of
Tasks (eg concept of electrical charge) made up of
Rules (eg an electrical charge is produced by friction).

However this terminology cuts across some of the terminology we have already established (topics and tasks are at about the same level of breakdown, one describing information, the other performance) and further terminology we shall establish (rules are made up of concepts, not concepts of rules).

Accepting the fact that 'theory of conservation of energy' is not normally recognized as a complete subject (though it could be, logically), but is a part of the recognized subject physics, we need a term for this level. But just as duty is used in job analysis for an intermediate stage between job and task (a group of tasks which do not form a complete job, but could do so logically) we shall use an intermediate term such as unit to identify a major part of a subject, which nevertheless is still composed of several topics. Thus, in the case above, we have:

> *Subject* (eg physics) made up of
> *Units* (eg theory of conservation of energy) made up of
> *Topics* (eg Ohm's law) made up of
> *Elements of information* (eg concepts or groups of concepts [schemata], facts or groups of facts) made up of
> *Definitions and examples* (these will be very specific to each element).

We can now define our use of topic as a coherent set of informational elements (factual and conceptual, terms which we shall define precisely later on) which lead to a measurable change in the state of knowledge of the individual. Here we meet a difference between task and topic. We can observe the execution of a task and measure the end product. As we saw, it is child's play to write a terminal objective for a task. But we cannot directly observe changes in the state of knowledge of an individual. What we need are external indicators of internal change. Previously the student did not understand Ohm's law. Now he does. How do we know? How can we tell? Obviously by setting him a *test* to perform, a task which will demonstrate in an observable and measurable way a *performance* which we are prepared to accept as *evidence* that the student has reached the new state of knowledge that we desire.

We may also wish the student not only to have knowledge (to be able to recall or explain) but also to use the new knowledge in a variety of ways (to develop skills in the use of his knowledge). This will require different types of performances, as evidence of different intellectual (or cognitive) skills.

The problem of transforming the information (topic or element) into performance or behaviour has not always proved easy (as already discussed in Chapter 3 on objectives). The difficulty has not been so much the writing of a performance description or objective, as the achievement of agreement among teachers on a particular set of behaviours being *indicative* of the presence of a determined level of intellectual knowledge or skill. Part of this difficulty results from a real divergence of opinion as to the aims of education, but part has been caused by communication problems, because of sloppy concepts and misunderstood terminology.

Use of a taxonomy

There have been several attempts to remedy this situation, by the development of techniques and tools that would standardize procedures and terminology. The earliest and still perhaps most used tool is the taxonomy. A taxonomy is a classification system which standardizes nomenclature, classifies examples unambiguously and establishes a hierarchy of interrelationship between groups of ideas, species, things, etc. The first of these in the educational objectives field was Bloom's taxonomy of the cognitive domain (Bloom *et al* 1956). It was followed by several others (Krathwohl, Bloom *et al* for the affective domain 1964; Harrow 1972 for the psychomotor domain) and various adaptations (eg Drummeller 1971).

Summaries of the two major taxonomies, together with examples of objectives are presented in Maps 3.7 and 3.8 in Chapter 3.

The aims of Bloom's taxonomies

The ideas behind the use of these taxonomies are described by Bloom (1956) as follows:

> The major purpose in constructing a taxonomy of educational objectives is to facilitate communication. In our original consideration of the project we conceived of it as a method of improving the exchange of ideas and materials among test workers, as well as other persons concerned with educational research and curriculum development. For instance, the use of the taxonomy as an aid in developing a precise definition and classification of such vaguely defined terms as 'thinking' and 'problem-solving' would enable a group of schools to discern the similarities and differences among the goals of their different instructional programs.

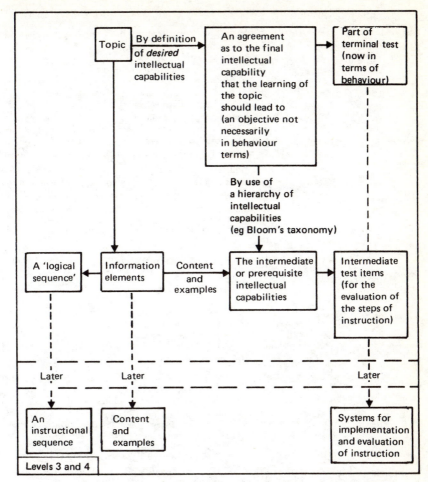

Figure 5.3 *Level 2 analysis of topics by use of Bloom's taxonomy and similar tools*

Set at this level, the task of producing a taxonomy, that is, a classification of educational outcomes, is quite analogous to the development of a plan for classifying books in a library. Or, put more abstractly, it is like establishing symbols for designating classes of objects where the members of a class have something in common.

Of course, such a classification procedure cannot be a private fantasy since it is of value only if used by the workers who wish to communicate with each other. Thus, the classifications 'fiction' and 'non-fiction' are of value only if librarians use them. Acceptance of such classifications by potential users is likely to be facilitated if the class names are terms which are reasonably familiar to them and if these terms are given precise and usable definitions.

In summary then, the major task in setting up any kind of taxonomy is that of selecting appropriate symbols, giving them precise and usable definitions, and securing the consensus of the group which is to use them. Similarly, developing a classification of educational objectives requires the selection of an appropriate list of symbols to represent all the major types of educational outcomes. Next, there is the task of defining these symbols with sufficient precision to permit and facilitate communication about these phenomena among teachers, administrators, curriculum workers, testers, educational research workers, and others who are likely to use the taxonomy. Finally, there is the task of trying the classification and securing the consensus of the educational workers who wish to use the taxonomy.

The value of Bloom's taxonomies

Have these tools served their purpose? There are opposed opinions. Drummeller (1971) considers that the answer is a qualified yes. In justifying his own modifications he evaluates the original taxonomy of the cognitive domain as follows:

Criterion 1: Can the classification be clearly differentiated? Research indicates that examination questions and statements of objectives can be classified within the confines of the taxonomy, by independent raters, with a high degree of agreement. Such research is reported in the handbook, and in more recent studies by Stoker and Kropp (1964), and Louise Tyler (1966). Factor analysis studies by Milholland (1966), however, indicate that the taxonomy categories are not functionally independent.

Criterion 2: Is the taxonomy comprehensive enough to provide educators and researchers with all the categories they need to develop curricula and construct adequate examinations? All of the studies reported under Criterion 1 indicate that the taxonomy is comprehensive, to the extent that practically all of the questions which appear on examinations from the elementary through the professional school can be fairly readily classified into the system.

Criterion 3: Are the categories compatible with the existing language of the educational discipline? If a taxonomy gives narrow, specific meaning to common general terms within the discipline, it frequently creates a barrier to communications, making an élite out of the initiated.

Criterion 4: Is there a real order among the phenomena represented by the terms? With reference to the Bloom taxonomy, the answer to this is a qualified yes. Research by Ayers (1966) provides statistical evidence for the hierarchical structure of the taxonomy. In other words, learnings on the lower levels of the taxonomy tend to be prerequisites of the mastering of objectives on the higher levels.

Criterion 5: Does the structure of the taxonomy make a significant contribution to the education discipline which is above and' beyond the categories defined? It seems readily apparent that the Bloom's taxonomy has clearly fulfilled a genuine and long-felt need for a systematic approach to the classifying of educational objectives, and the testing for such objectives. It could be, however, that Bloom's entire *Handbook*, rather than the taxonomy itself, is the key to its success.

Other writers have been more critical. Peters (1969) referred to the taxonomy as 'a dog's dinner — full of muddled concepts'. Williams (1977) criticizes it as follows:

The taxonomy is complex, necessitating a substantial amount of time for initial mastery, and decreasing the likelihood of retention and, therefore, of regular use. Second, even experienced users of the taxonomy have difficulties in agreeing on the classification of objectives or test items into the categories of the taxonomy. Finally, the taxonomic categories generally are defined in terms of the intellectual processes required of learners rather than in terms of the observable characteristics of tasks presented to learners in the form of objectives or test questions. A typology with categories defined in terms of concrete characteristics of tasks structured by teachers not only should lead to better inter-rater agreement in classifying objectives or test items, but also should provide instructors with more guidance in producing tasks or objectives which fit each category.

The task analysis approach to topic analysis

William's suggestion that a classification based on behaviours (outputs) rather than intellectual processes, underlines the other mainstream of development of tools for the analysis of subject matter. Instead of analysing the topic into information or knowledge elements, transform it directly into a task and analyse the task into its subsidiary or intermediate behaviours. We can see this alternative in Figure 5.4.

The mathetics approach of Gilbert

This approach was not invented by Williams. It is the basis of the behavioural analysis approach which grew up in the 1950s and 1960s. One early methodology, *Mathetics* (Gilbert 1962), maintained that all observable behaviour can be represented as combinations of three basic behaviour patterns

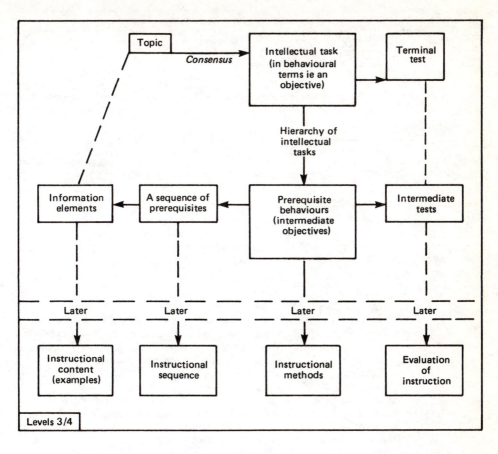

Figure 5.4 *The task analysis approach to topic analysis*

— chains, discriminations and generalizations. He developed precise rules for teaching each of these types of behaviour (and typical combinations). He also used the concept of the master performer, the person (either real or imaginary) who performs at the level of competence desired after training. Instead of specifying lists of discrete objectives, Gilbert suggests the preparation of a behavioural 'prescription', a map of all the separate behaviours that make up mastery of the task being analysed. This prescription establishes both the task elements and their operational sequence. As each task element (or operant) is described in stimulus/response terms (ie in input/output terms), the prescription serves as a substitute for a statement of objectives (or at least the conditions and performance parts). The other components appear later in the teaching prescription (see Figure 5.5).

We shall be discussing the mathetics approach in more detail later. Suffice it to say for the moment that it was not very widely accepted in educational circles, at least partly because (being based on Skinnerian ideas) it totally disregards internal learning processes. It was more accepted in training applications and still is the basis of the methodologies of some of the most successful training consultancy organizations. However Gilbert (1969) demonstrated how the master performance principle can be applied to the

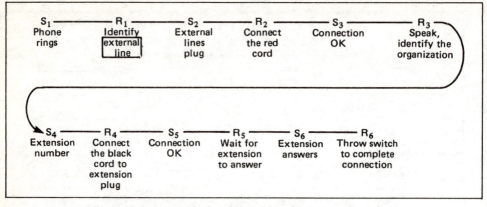

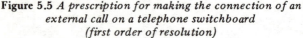

Figure 5.5 *A prescription for making the connection of an
external call on a telephone switchboard
(first order of resolution)*

derivation of useful and relevant objectives in such subjects as history (see the
discussion in Chapter 3 and Map 7.19).

This approach attempts in level 1 analysis to transform the subject into a
hypothetical or notional job and henceforth to treat the analysis process more
as one of job/task analysis than of topic analysis (though one must return to
the subject matter for the content and examples to put in the teaching
exercises).

**Gagné's
approach
(learning
categories)**

Gilbert's approach and Bloom's approach are at opposite extremes of a
continuum of techniques for subject/topic analysis. A hybrid approach was
popularized by Gagné (see Figure 5.6). He expanded Gilbert's list of three
types of behaviour to eight, extending to simpler behaviours of signal learning
(classical Pavlovian conditioning) and simple stimulus/response learning (or
discrete associations) and upwards to more complex 'thinking' types of
behaviours (learning of rules or principles and problem-solving). In his book
The Conditions of Learning (1965) Gagné develops definitions of each
category of learning in observable performance terms (one difference from
Bloom's taxonomy). He also develops detailed suggestions for the *internal*
(student 'readiness') and *external* (instructional) conditions that must be met,
category by category, for effective learning to take place. Thus Gagné's
approach goes much further than Bloom's in that (like Gilbert's) it deals with
the design of the *instructional process* as well as the evaluation instruments
(Bloom's taxonomy only really deals with the latter).

Like Gilbert's approach, Gagné's methodology springs from the subject/
topic to deal in terms of performances at the earliest possible moment.
However, rather than analysing the behaviours into their minutest elements (in
the stimulus/response prescription), Gagné classifies some aspects of behaviour
as examples of one particular category, then proceeds to look for component
behaviours at lower levels in his hierarchy, which would be prerequisites of the
mastery of the originally identified behaviour, building up in this process an
objectives hierarchy. Derek Rowntree (1974) gives a neat example quoted
here:

> Suppose we have as our objective that the student should be able to state the time
> as so many hours o'clock in terms of hours and minutes (eg 8 o'clock or 4.37)
> reading from a conventional 12 hour clock. (Needless to say there is no intrinsic
> value in this objective; if all clock faces were replaced tomorrow by digital
> indicators it would then be of antiquarian interest only.) Once we start analysing

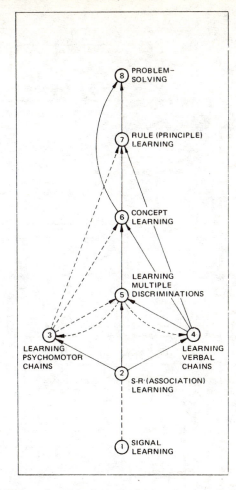

Figure 5.6 *How the eight learning categories described by Gagné relate to each other (higher categories require prior mastery of relevant lower ones)*

back through the behaviours that lead up to this performance (see Figure 5.7) we find that two streams of enabling objectives immediately begin to form and that these in turn have several tributaries. Thus, we can trace back, discovering the succession of objectives the student needs to have achieved prior to being able to decide on the hour . . . Eventually we get down to quite lowly abilities (eg say the number represented by the numerals one to 12 or recognize that clocks show the time) which may or may not already be in his repertoire.

Analysis *à la* Gagné can be enormously productive, whether applied to the wider objectives of a course or to the objectives of a smaller unit of learning. First, it clarifies our thinking on prerequisites (or entry behaviour) — the abilities with which the student should (or does) come to the learning situation. Gagné suggests that we take our hierarchy and draw a line across at the point below which are the abilities students are assumed to possess before embarking on the learning and above which are the abilities they will learn).

Rowntree's last comments illustrate another advantage of this approach over the use of Bloom's taxonomy — the built-in target population analysis. Just as at level 1, here at level 2 one should keep the student firmly in the picture. It is necessary to continue the target population analysis to a greater level of detail, so that we may identify task elements or information elements that

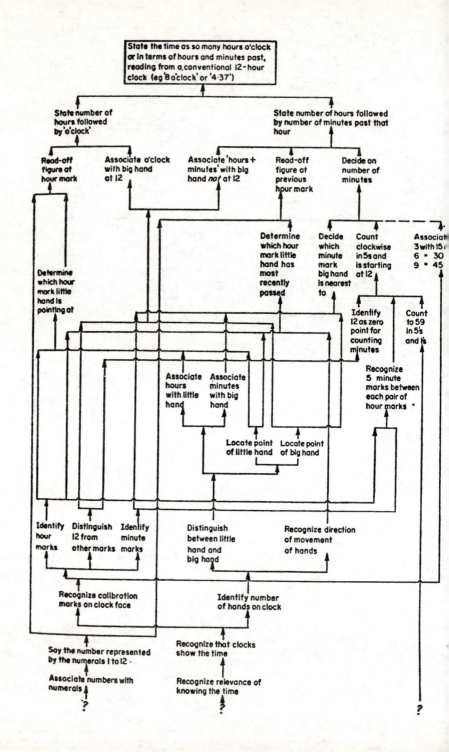

Figure 5.7 *A Gagné-type topic analysis*
(from Rowntree 1974)

do *not* need to be taught (because they are known already or extremely simple), and thus avoid wasting time in analysing them further.

We have now seen how Gagné's approach allowed the establishment of what to teach (and what to assure as prerequisite), and in what sequence. The aspect of standard of performance is overlooked though this must of course be defined, if only through intuition, in order to generate actual test items.

The aspect of how to teach, which Gagné's methodology examines as well, we shall leave as a topic for level 3 analysis.

5.4 Summary

Level 1 analysis

So, let us summarize where we are. At level 1 we broke a job into its constituent tasks, or a subject into its constituent topics. These were sorted into those worth teaching and those which for a variety of reasons are not worth teaching formally by the process of planned instruction. If we were to stop at this point of the analysis our *product* would be not unlike a traditional course syllabus (a list of teachable topics) or a training specification (overall training objectives).

We could at this point also convert our topic list into terminal objectives using plain commonsense (which is what most examiners have been doing over the ages) or with the help of a job aid (eg Bloom's taxonomy). Stopping at this point, we could delegate the rest of the instructional design process to the instructors themselves who may do it well or badly depending on their experience and talents. Typically, they would slavishly apply certain global instructional strategies which they favour (eg the demonstration method, the discovery approach, etc) throughout the whole course. (See Chapter 15 for a discussion of these strategies.)

Level 2 analysis

Level 2 analysis follows on from level 1. It is an alternative to the intuitive instructor-executed instructional design. However, it takes time and should therefore be justified in specific cases (which is not difficult to do).

1. Starting with the teachable tasks or topics these are broken down into their elements (task analysis or topic analysis).
2. Alongside the breakdown process, there occurs a build up or sequencing process, because the steps of a task, or the elements of a topic, are interrelated in some *operational or logical sequence.*
3. Still alongside these breakdown/build up processes, there occurs a further stage of the *target population analysis*, started in level 1. We examine the task/topic elements and once again classify them into those requiring formal instruction (teaching and testing individually) and those which only need 'telling' and practice together with other elements (these are the easy-to-learn and well-known elements). These elements nevertheless form part of the instructional prerequisites.
4. In the case of task analysis, the tasks worth teaching are transformed into terminal objectives and the elements worth teaching into intermediate objectives, which will be tested at key points in the course (this is usually quite easily done). A further look at the elements to be taught, reveals hidden *enabling objectives*, which may be informational (knowledge) or performance (basic skills).
5. In the case of topic analysis, the topics worth teaching are transformed into terminal objectives, and the topic elements into intermediate objectives. Techniques commonly used to help one do this (it is not as easy as in the case of task analysis) are based on Bloom's taxonomy, on a definition of a hypothetical master performer (thus turning a topic analysis into task analysis) or (an intermediate method) by the use of a hierarchy of learning categories (eg Gagné 1965, Merril 1973, Williams 1977).
6. All the lower level objectives thus derived are compared yet once more

with the model of the target population to identify which enabling objectives are to be thought and which may be safely required as prerequisities.

6. Is Instruction the Solution?

6.1 Approaches to the analysis of human performance problems

Level 1 analysis generates objectives at the job performance or subject mastery level. Level 2 analysis transforms these real-life objectives into instructional objectives, sorting out those that are worth teaching from those that are not. The criteria for this sorting out which we considered in the last chapter were:

- ☐ Are the objectives already known/mastered?
- ☐ Are they so easy to achieve that formal instruction is not called for (we simply need to inform the student what is expected of him and he will perform, since he already has all the component knowledge and skill requirements).

In order to establish the teaching worth of an objective, one questions or observes trainees and trained, collecting data for each task or task element, under headings such as:

- ☐ Frequency of performance
- ☐ Criticality of an error
- ☐ Difficulty in avoiding errors.

The logic is that frequently performed, critical and difficult tasks are obviously worth teaching (high priority in our 'worth league') whereas at the other extreme, rarely performed, non-critical and easy tasks are of low priority. Intermediate cases lead to intermediate decisions concerning whether or not to instruct and also give some clues on how to organize any proposed instruction.

However, training consultants in the industrial and commercial training field began to realize that such an approach sometimes led to training that was obviously not necessary (the instructor discovered that the trainees knew more about the task than he did) and, at other times, theoretically very effective training failed to eradicate the poor job performance that had instigated its design. So there was obviously more to analysing problems of poor performance than simply looking at the apparent difficulty of a task.

Praxeonomy More sophisticated approaches to the analysis are required. Several training consultancy companies in the United States have developed techniques. Tom Gilbert, as ever in the forefront (and as ever fond of coining new and complex jargon), developed the technique of 'praxeonomy' and set up the Praxeonomy Institute to exploit it (Gilbert 1967).

In this approach, Gilbert presents four rules:

1. D=M—I (deficiency = mastery — initial repertory). We have already met this in level 1 analysis, as the difference in performance between the master performer and the target population.
2. Discriminate accomplishment and acquirement. A small difference in acquirement (what a person has learned) can make an enormous difference to accomplishment (what we can perform). To identify training needs one needs to measure acquirement, not accomplishment. This is not necessarily directly observable from performance on the job (which is accomplishment).

3. Discriminate knowledge deficiencies and execution deficiencies. An execution deficiency is when someone *knows* how to do something right, yet he does it wrong. He may do this for several reasons. Gilbert suggests inadequate feedback on his performance, interference between tasks, tasks which are punishing to perform right, and lack of motivation. To separate the two sources of deficiency, Gilbert suggests we ask 'could he do it if his life depended on it?'

4. Establish economic priorities (P = VN/c) or priority (of eliminating a deficiency) = value to be gained x number of people/cost of instruction.

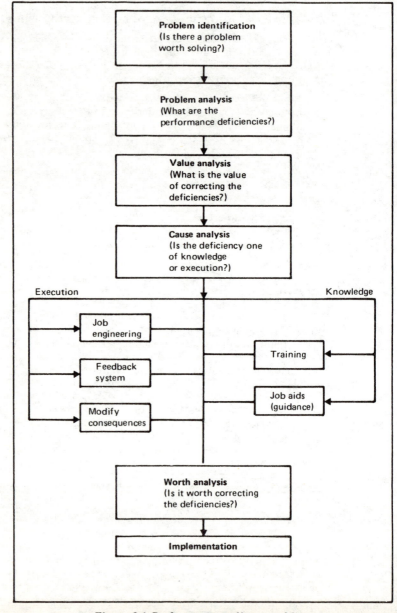

Figure 6.1 *Performance audit as used by Praxis Corporation*

Approaches to front-end analysis

In this chapter we shall concentrate on Rule 3 which really governs whether instruction is *at all* indicated as a solution to a given performance problem, or whether we should be planning other types of solutions, and what are these other types.

Similar techniques have been used by other practitioners. Harless (1968) calls his approach front-end analysis, a much more descriptive term than Gilbert's for a very similar technique. Harless argues that it pays to analyse the need to train before launching into the production of expensive training systems ('an ounce of analysis is worth a pound of programming').

In 1970, Robert Mager put pen to paper and popularized Gilbert's knowledge/execution analysis technique (as he had earlier done for behavioural objectives) under the title of *Analysing Performance Problems* (Mager and Pipe, 1970). He tried to present it in the form of an algorithmic flow chart or binary decision tree. However, this is not a very successful presentation as one can see (Figure 6.2) because the analysis process being depicted is not totally algorithmic in nature. There are bits and pieces of decisions hanging loose from the main trunk of the logical tree, like fallen leaves. This is not a criticism of the analysis process or the book, which is an excellent, clearly written and

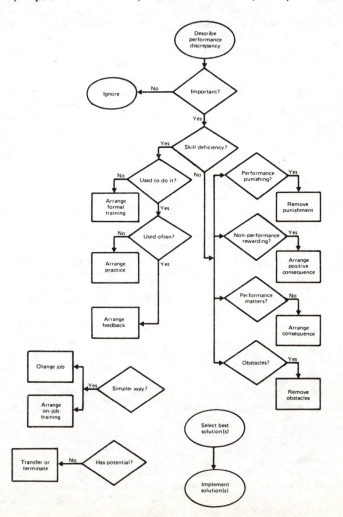

Figure 6.2 *The Mager and Pipe model (1970)*

(as always) entertaining presentatation full of convincing case studies and practical examples. However, the use of the algorithmic presentation may be misleading, by suggesting either that the 10 outcomes (eg remove punishment) are the only possible ones, or (more seriously) that because they are up different branches of the tree they are mutually exclusive. They are not. The answer to 'skill deficiency?' may be 'yes' so we are led to consider whether 'he' could have forgotten. The answer to 'used to do it' is 'no'. So we opt for training. But in reality, apart from this (correctly diagnosed) cause of poor performance, there may be others. There are obstacles to performance (poor tools), punishing aspects (correct performance entails much physical discomfort) and it does not seem to matter whether the job is done correctly or not (poor supervision), etc. So the individual is trained, transfers to the job and continues to perform poorly. Back to the drawing board (or rather the tree).

6.2 The systems approach applied to performance problem analysis

In teaching the front-end or performance analysis technique to training personnel, we have found it useful to get away from the linear or branched tree presentation to a more integrated, organic one, which would encourage rather than inhibit the combination of two or more part-solutions into a 'best solution'. After all, the systems approach suggests the search for alternatives and the subsequent selection/combination of these into an optimal solution 'mix'.

Alternative levels for system analysis
It may help to conceptualize the jump that is being made, in systems terms. The traditional job/task analysis approach assumes that instruction will probably be necessary. It remains only to define the objectives and content of this instruction. Perhaps as a result of the influence of the teaching profession in formal education, the training profession in industry tended to see its role as the increase in the amount of training offered. Whether this was due to an empire-building mentality or to a genuine belief that any (reasonably well designed) training *must* be beneficial to the individual and the organization, is not a relevant question to pursue here. Suffice it to say that much unnecessary training was (and still is) perpetrated on the human resources of many organizations.

The jump referred to is from one system level to another in the analysis of the problem. The traditional approach seems to begin with the training problem dumped on the desk of the training manager. He may well apply a systems approach to the problem, neglecting to notice that training problems cannot exist until the training exists and proves problematical (in the context above he is really presented the task of designing a training *solution* to an as yet unanalysed problem).

Micro level
So our manager analyses the job, related subject matter and the typical trainees expected to take part in the training (for training there will be!). He (1) defines the problem by deriving certain training objectives, (2) analyses these objectives to arrive at alternative training solutions, makes a cost-effectiveness study to select a particular solution or solution mix (but all the components in the mix are types of training), then (3) he designs and produces this solution, (4) implements the training, (5) evaluates it and finds that all the trainees reach a given standard on all the objectives. The only cloud which appears to dim this bright picture is the poor level of subsequent job performance of the trainees. The solution is to jump to the wider system and analyse the real roots of the performance problem. One might jump higher still and analyse the organizational environment, to establish that the supposed performance problem is not really something quite different.

Macro level
The steps of the systems approach will now follow the same pattern, but at a higher level. We can see the difference comparing the two flow charts (Figures 6.3 and 6.4).

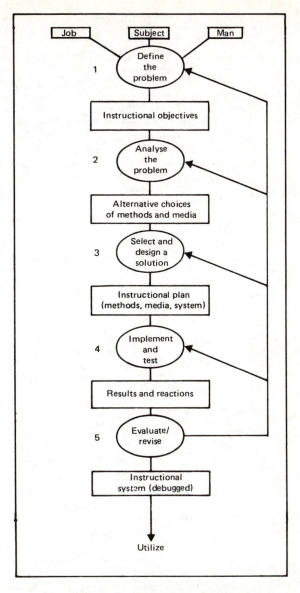

Figure 6.3 *Systems approach at the micro level –*
applied to instructional design

Step 1 will involve redefining the problem in quantifiable terms, establishing clear and measurable job performance objectives and identifying the environmental conditions which are required to make these objectives relevant and viable.

Step 2 will now be the analysis of the performance problem to identify all possible solutions and solution components, to evaluate the alternatives and to select the optimal mix of solutions (instruction, plus other types of training/development activity, plus other actions such as organizational change, job design, modified selection procedures, etc).

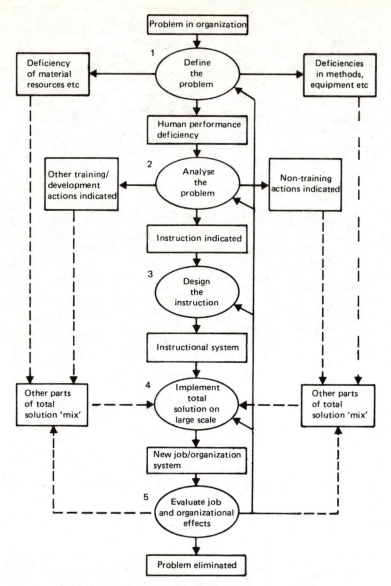

Figure 6.4 *Systems approach at the macro level –*
applied to the solution of any problem in the organization

Step 3 All the components of the mix will now need to be developed in
coordination (and they may be the responsibilities of different departments
in the organization). Let us concentrate on the instruction component
however. If there is an instruction component to develop, its contribution
to the total solution (ie the job performance objectives) is by now defined.
We are therefore at the same point (in principle) as we started from in the
first flow chart. We would now:

☐ Develop instructional objectives
☐ Generate alternatives for instructional methods/media
☐ Develop the chosen solution

☐ Implement experimentally
☐ Evaluate.

So all of the micro level application of the systems approach is compressed into step 3 of the macro level application.

Step 4 In parallel to this activity, the other components are undergoing a similar process of systems development. Large-scale implementation brings together the various (already validated) components of the solution, and implements them jointly in the real organizational setting.

Step 5 Evaluation now occurs at the organizational and long-term effects level, to check that all aspects of the original diagnosis and the developed solutions are correct.

Let us now concentrate on step 2 of the macro level problem-solving approach. Since we wish to encourage rather than to inhibit the creative search for multi-faceted, multi-disciplinary solutions, we shall use a structural presentation of the analysis process, rather than a linear, semi-algorithmic approach.

6.3 Analysis of performance problems

The roots of the performance problem may be in the performer or in his environment. We should examine both, keeping in mind that the roots may be embedded in both of these sectors.

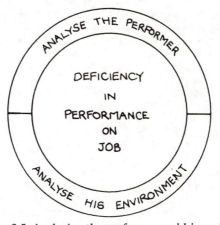

Figure 6.5 *Analysing the performer and his environment*

Analysing the performer sector we wish to investigate if he ever/never could perform satisfactorily. If he never could perform, then it looks like a training solution will be necessary. But wait! Maybe he has not got the prerequisites necessary to enter the training programme? If this is so, perhaps we can teach these too (but this may involve going back so far as to render the option uneconomical). The alternatives are transfer to simpler jobs or job redesign to eliminate the particular difficulty, which may be as simple as the division of tasks between supervisor and supervised (see Figure 6.6).

Could he ever perform the job well?

If on the other hand, the trainee has the prerequisites, we may consider instruction or other training alternatives. These other training alternatives may be as simple as the arrangement of opportunities for practice on the job (appropriate when the tasks are very easy to learn and there is no great danger or economic loss involved if the trainee makes a mistake). A slightly more sophisticated approach is to ensure that this on-the-job practice is performed under the supervision of an experienced person (who is not in any way trained

Does he have the prerequisites?

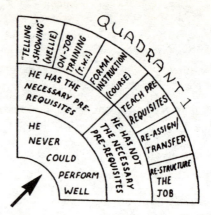

Figure 6.6 *Quadrant 1 of job performance schema*

as an instructor). This method is much maligned but often quite an adequate and economical training method. More sophisticated is the approach illustrated by the TWI training method. Only when the learning difficulty of the tasks justifies it should one invest in complete off-the-job programmes of carefully designed instruction.

What is the frequency of his performance?

On the other half of the upper sector (see Figure 6.7) we have a series of alternatives, depending on the frequency of performance and other subsidiary factors specific to each case. If certain tasks in the job are performed only on infrequent occasions then there is a chance of forgetting or part-forgetting how to perform. One solution is to arrange for more frequent practice by regular recycling or retraining sessions. This approach is indicated particularly when rapid reactions to infrequently occurring situations are required. There is no time to stop and refresh one's memory at the instant when the performance is called for. Examples are firefighting skills, warfare skills, self-defence skills, etc. However in many cases there is no such need for split-second reaction. The performer can take a reasonable amount of time to react to the situation. In such cases the expense of regular recycling can often be avoided through the provision of reference material on the job. Such job aids may be relatively complex and complete, as for example the workshop manual used by a motor mechanic when servicing or repairing an unfamiliar model of motor car, or can be quite a short, condensed list of key points in the form of a flow chart, checklist, diagram or wall chart. Examples include the lubrication charts for specific models of car often encountered on garage walls, wiring diagrams and parts lists, the checklist of operations that an aircraft mechanic must always complete when performing any servicing operation (to make absolutely certain that no step is omitted) and the aids to diagnosis, often in algorithmic flow chart form now so popular with computer and systems personnel and even used by doctors for medical diagnosis.

If, on the other hand, personnel used to perform well but now performance has deteriorated and the poorly performed tasks are performed quite frequently, then it is not forgetting that is causing the deterioration. Two very different causes may be at work. The job may be intrinsically boring, leading to a deterioration in interest and motivation, or the job may be in itself quite interesting and the performer may be quite motivated, but a sort of performance drift is occurring because the performer is insufficiently aware of the results that he is achieving. In the first case, appropriate solutions would

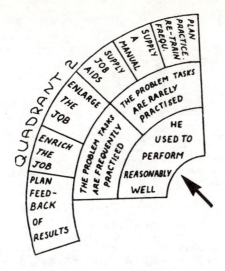

Figure 6.7 *Quadrant 2 of job performance schema*

try to make the job more interesting. Two well-known approaches, which both have their own literature are job enlargement and job enrichment: (Paul and Robertson 1970; King Taylor 1973; Thornley and Valentine 1968). Yet other approaches to making jobs more satisfying include job rotation and working in groups (see Figure 6.8).

What feedback does he receive?

In the second case, when the performer is not bored by his job but simply does not have information regarding the results of his performance, the solution is to provide such information by the installation of effective systems of information feedback. In a case known to me, the performance of the cost estimates department of a large steel fabrications company had drifted to danger point because the cost accountants working there were never informed of the final real costs of the projects that they had estimated. Over the years the cost accountants had developed 'quicker and better' methods of estimation which much increased the speed of their work and of which they were most proud. They were far from unmotivated and certainly not uninformed (as became painfully obvious when they were sent on a refresher course and taught the instructor a thing or two). The solution finally adopted was to feed back actual costs to the person that had made the estimate and to ask him for an analysis of the causes of any discrepancies. This simple change in procedure enabled the accountants to constantly monitor their own performance, to identify and improve those short cuts that really worked and to avoid those which did not.

The performer analysis schema

Thus we now have a complete upper sector of our schema (see Figure 6.9). This sector considers the performer and what he brings to the job in the way of necessary skills, knowledge and aptitudes. Our discussion has illustrated the value of asking certain key questions about the tasks in the job, questions that we have already met in our earlier discussion of level 1 and 2 analysis. These questions are:

1. *Frequency of performance:* to help decide between planned practice, retraining, manuals, job aids, job enlargement/enrichment and improved feedback solutions (note that other considerations enter here in the choice between specific solutions, but the frequency question helps initially to decide between two main categories of solutions).
2. *Criticality*, or the importance of good performance, which helps here in

---

Job rotation

One method of increasing variety in work is for people to rotate between jobs. This is usually done at regular intervals ranging from a few hours to several weeks, and is sometimes arranged on a less formal basis.

Job enlargement

This involves amalgamating several tasks into a single job, eg, instead of staying at one station and completing one-third of the tasks on every car, doing all the related tasks on every third car.

The intention of rotation and enlargement is to break monotony and relieve pace by lengthening cycle times. There can be some widening of interest. But it should be noted that if tasks have no intrinsic interest, are unrelated to one another, and are very short-cycle, combining them in either of these two ways may simply distract and annoy.

Job enrichment

A job may be enriched by an individual undertaking greater responsibility, eg, by organizing and checking his own work, or by being involved in decisions about planning and organizing the work of his unit. The content of the work is changed by extending the opportunities for decision and judgement. Job enrichment programmes attempt to build in, over time, scope for development of an individual's skills to provide a sense of personal achievement.

Group work

This approach entails dividing all the tasks into logical groups which reflect the informal group structure among the people doing them. Without an increase in autonomy, group working may not of itself significantly improve job satisfaction. What it usually provides, however, is an opportunity for the question of job satisfaction to be re-examined.

Autonomous working groups

This entails giving groups of employees wide discretion for planning and organizing work among themselves. The traditional role of supervisor changes to one of giving advice and support to the group. The group has clear goals, such as producing a specified number of units per week or completing a certain volume of work, while the means by which they are achieved are left very much to the group. An advantage of autonomous group working is that individual workers have some degree of choice as to whether they perform a large number of tasks or only a limited number.

Source: Adapted from HMSO 1975

Figure 6.8 *Some ways of making work more satisfying as defined by the Tripartite Steering Group on job satisfaction*

deciding the feasibility of less formal training solutions or of less controlled anti-forgetting measures (such as simple job aids rather than systematic and regular retraining). Note that a further useful question to ask in this specific context is concerned with the speed of reaction that is required.

3. *Learning difficulty*, which should throw light on the question of necessary prerequisites and whether, for the type of human resources that are coming forward to do a certain job, it is feasible to teach the prerequisites or whether this would prove to be less economical than other solutions connected with improved selection criteria or with job redesign.

Similarly, in the lower sector (see Figure 6.10), we encounter a series of solutions to unforeseen consequences (contingency management solutions) and a series of solutions to poorly planned work methods and organization.

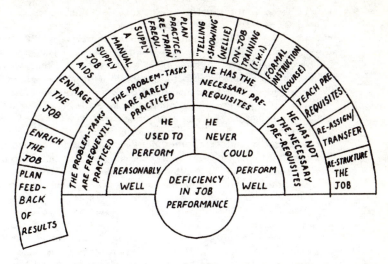

Figure 6.9 *Upper sector of job performance schema*

What are the consequences of performance?

Taking first the consequences of performance, we note an overlap with the previously discussed sector: there may be no consequences to his performance as far as the performer is concerned. If he never knows the final results of his work, how can he try to improve his performance? If no one else in the organization seems to be taking an interest in his performance, why should he strive to improve it? So there are two aspects to 'no consequences', one concerned with establishing standards and furnishing results so that the performer has the tools necessary for self-evaluation and self-improvement, and the other concerned with showing that 'somebody cares' about the standard of his performance. This second implies a system of reward for good performance (not only financial rewards but also rewards of a social nature — recognition, approval and encouragement of the desired performance).

1. No consequences

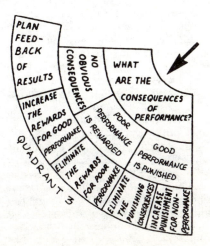

Figure 6.10 *Quadrant 3 of job performance schema*

2. Poor
performance
rewarded

Analysis of the consequences of desired performance often reveals severe weaknesses in the reward structure, particularly the unplanned (social and work environment-generated) rewards. Undesirable performance is often rewarded unwittingly, as in piece-work payment schemes which are designed to encourage fast work and high productivity, but as a by-product encourage sloppy or downright dangerous work practices which save time. In one motor car bodywork factory, despite the most careful attention paid to all aspects of safety, despite all machines being equipped with the best possible safety guards, many serious accidents occurred every year. It was found that the cause of this was the piece-work payment system. Rather than lose one piece of car bodywork because of a badly positioned metal panel in the press, men were vaulting the safety guards as the press was in operation in a last-minute attempt at readjustment, and were sometimes just that second too late in getting out again; rather than lose production they risked losing a piece of their arm.

Poor performance, or the failure to perform, are often reinforced socially, as in the case when it has become a tradition in a particular work environment to work without the use of safety clothing or equipment. Anyone using the safety equipment is ridiculed by his workmates while the non-use is rewarded socially by the acceptance of the worker by his mates as a 'real man'. I once worked on a project preparing a training course for post office workers in the UK. This course included training in the use of equipment for testing whether there were any toxic or explosive gases trapped in underground installations before the man went down the manhole. The equipment was quite complex and we decided to perform an analysis on the job. However, this soon revealed the important information that hardly anyone uses the equipment although all the telephone maintenance vans were equipped with it. The men preferred to 'use their nose' as a test device: this was much quicker (one type of reward for non-use of the equipment) and was the traditional way employed by the senior and more experienced members of the team (creating another source of social reward for the new worker). In terms of ensuring the desired performance, the training aspect was quite dwarfed by the contingency management aspect of overcoming the negative consequences.

3. Good
performance
punished

Finally, many instances can be quoted of the desired performance being unwittingly punished. The performer knows quite well what is expected of him, but the actual performance is physically uncomfortable or socially threatening. The performer attempts to avoid the punishing or threatening aspects of the job and this results in poor job performance. An example quoted by Gilbert (1967) concerns maintenance personnel of a company specializing in the installation of air conditioning systems in office blocks. These systems often got blocked (always in the summer of course) which required the maintenance personnel to apply heat with a blowlamp to the blocked pipe (always in some cramped, unventilated, already hot cupboard or underfloor duct) until the salts causing the blockage had all entered back into the solution. This required time and the pipe invariably became partially unblocked long before all the salts had dissolved. The man tended to stop applying heat as soon as the circulation restarted, rather than continuing for another half hour or so in extremely uncomfortable conditions in order to make absolutely sure that the blockage was completely eliminated, with the result that in a week or so the pipe would block again requiring a further visit from the maintenance team. As in this case there was no way of eliminating the punishing consequences of desired performance (how do you stop an underfloor duct from being hot and cramped?) the adopted solution was to create a threat of equal punishment for non-performance, not by inventing disciplinary threats but by an organizational change which made each maintenance man responsible for a certain group of installations. Thus poor performance on the first visit bore the penalty of an early future visit to do the same uncomfortable task again and to face the same irate customer again.

My own experience includes a somewhat more subtle case, involving the performance of bank managers. The objective was to get the managers to lend money more creatively in support of new, untried, potentially high risk industrial projects. Pamphlets, pep talks and training seminars had already been tried with very little result. Analysis of the consequences soon showed that there were no obvious consequences for the manager resulting from good performance, but the occasional bad debt (which would increase if the high risk lending policy were followed) invariably led to unpleasant repercussions. Thus a two-pronged solution was adopted, involving the orientation of top management as regards their reaction to bad debts (apply critical analysis and constructive suggestions rather than disciplinary measures) and the installation of a feedback and reward system to reinforce the desired behaviour (publishing and circulating reinvestment data to all branches, publishing articles on successful reinvestment case studies, making reinvestment count as one factor in a manager of the year competition, etc).

How is the job organized?

Passing now to the sector of analysis dealing with the internal organization of the job, we enter the fields traditionally occupied by work study, methods study, organization and methods and, more recently, organizational development. All these disciplines have their own literature and a host of techniques too numerous to describe fully in this book. Suffice it to say that problems which at first present themselves as potentially requiring a training solution, often on more careful analysis are found to have job organization aspects as well. The problem may lie in the physical and practical aspects of the job (bad equipment, poor layout, poor lighting, uncomfortable conditions, etc) or in the methods used (inefficient methods, unnecessarily tiring methods, inefficient sequence of operations, poor division of tasks, etc).

Note that some of these causes may have the results of making the job unnecessarily dissatisfying (see Figure 6.9) or may create unpleasant or punishing consequences resultant from desired job performance (see Figure 6.10).

Alternatively, one may identify problems in the managerial organization of the job (see Figure 6.11). The problem may be poor supervision, no clear job targets, no measurement of job performance against targets, etc. Or it may lie in the basic management organizational structure relating the performer to his superiors. To quote the gospels: 'No man can serve two masters'. Whereas this

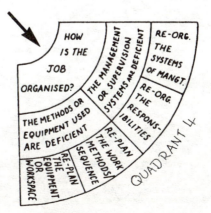

Figure 6.11 *Quadrant 4 of job performance schema*

is somewhat of a generalization (most matrix-based management systems include line responsibility and project responsibility) it is essential that in cases of mixed responsibility, the different aspects of a job for which different managers are responsible are clearly delineated and the job is organized so that the performer does not encounter a conflict of responsibilities. (Give to Caesar what is Caesar's and to God what is God's?) Mager (1970) quotes a neat example of this: the case of a medical technician who must perform certain tasks which involve continual painstaking attention over a period of time (preparing samples for microscopy) whilst he is also called to attend to a variety of other urgent tasks in the casualty ward at unpredictable intervals. Such 'task interference' inevitably results in poor job performance.

Note again that some of the causes mentioned will result in the creation of demotivating job conditions, jobs which appear to be of no consequence or where the avoidance of job performance is more rewarding/less threatening than the execution of the desired job performance.

The complete performance analysis schema

We have now completed constructing an analysis schema for performance problems. We call it a schema because that is what it is intended to be, an interrelation of the many aspects that might contribute to any given performance problem.

The schema (Figure 6.12) is not necessarily complete. As any conceptual schema it is subject to constant adaptation as new phenomena or new information is encountered. However, we believe it will be easier for the reader to adapt a schema as presented here than to adapt a semi-algorithmic presentation (eg Mager's) which carries with it the connotation (as do all

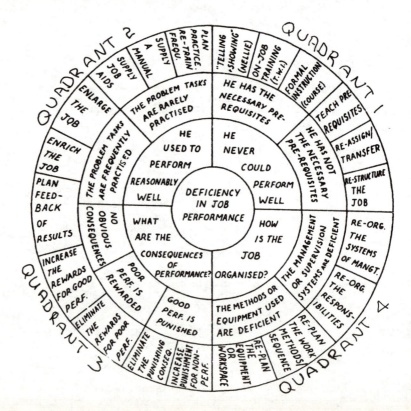

Figure 6.12 *An analysis schema for performance problems*

algorithms) that every problem has a unique and predictable solution.

Systemic thinking

The schema emphasizes the flexibility and the overlap that exists in the process of selecting a solution. No sequential steps of analysis are implied. Rather, the reader is encouraged to think *systemically* of all the factors in relation to all the others. Theoretically, almost any combination of almost any of the 20 types of solution listed in the outer rim of our circle could be selected as a specific 'total' solution to a specific complex, multi-faceted performance problem. In practice, some of these solutions are mutually exclusive so the sum total of viable alternative choices is considerably less than the theoretical total number of possible combinations (640,000) but would still remain in the thousands.

A plea for a multi-disciplinary approach

Finally the schema emphasizes the importance of a multi-disciplinary approach and the prerequisite of effective horizontal communication and cooperation in the organization, so as not to artificially restrict the choices of solution open to us. Figure 6.13 emphasizes this point. We remove the outer ring of solutions and replace it by an indication of the six types of support services which might exist in a typical large organization and which might be concerned with developing certain types of solutions to performance problems. Any combination of these six types of intervention might be quite a viable total solution to a given problem. This gives us a total variety of 63 different combinations of departments (or 63 different possible structures for the plan which is to solve the problem). Any lack of horizontal cooperation will severely limit this variety. It is not uncommon to meet instances in reality where this variety is limited to one, for example the problem is first brought to the notice of the training department so you can be quite sure that a training solution will be produced (a purely training solution).

If there is one thing that renders systemic thinking impossible, it is the compartmentalization of one's problem-solving schemata into watertight compartments.

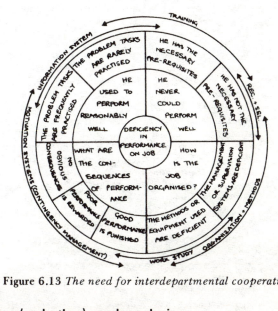

Figure 6.13 *The need for interdepartmental cooperation*

6.4 Training (and other) needs analysis

I was recently involved in the planning and implementation of a system of training needs analysis for a large group of companies employing some 80,000 persons. It was a good opportunity to attempt to install a system of performance problem analysis, based on the methodology described above.

The organization did not have any working system of regular job performance evaluation, and the various companies of the group were extremely varied in their approaches to training (if indeed they had one), the data which they kept regarding personnel problems, operational problems and so on.

As it was already planned to train several training officers, who would, among their other duties, perform training needs analyses in their companies, we incorporated the performance analysis methodology as a part of the training needs analysis methodology (which should perhaps now be called a training and other needs methodology).

In adapting the method to the needs of a large organization, one had to take another look at the system, but this time the wider system. We found ourselves analysing not only obvious skill and knowledge deficiencies but just about every other possibly imaginable type of problem that a large organization can have. Slowly a practical methodology emerged, which seems to be working reasonably well and is having quite unexpected success in breaking down the barriers to horizontal communication between departments, from which the organization used to suffer severely. The methodology will not be presented here in full but rather the theoretical thinking behind it will be explained, as it is an extension of the approach adopted to performance problem analysis.

Typical approaches to training needs analysis

As training is generally held to impart knowledge and/or skills, the implied problem that the training needs exercise sets out to solve could be stated in the form of a discrepancy between the existing (what is) levels of knowledge or skill of certain groups of the workforce, and the desired (what should be) levels. We may note a hint of a suggested solution in this statement. Training is the solution, for which problems are being sought. This in itself may not be bad, as long as it does not encourage the needs assessor to force training solutions on problems that do not warrant them.

Unfortunately, quite often the techniques applied for training needs assessment actively promote the solutions-seeking-a-problem syndrome. Among such techniques we can mention:

1. The *course menu* approach adopted by many companies. The training department draws up a catalogue of training schemes and courses (both internally organized and externally available) which it circulates to all departments down to supervisor level, inviting management and supervision to identify useful programmes and propose participants from their staff. This suffers from several weaknesses. Staff who are not training experts are expected to match their inexpert judgement of the training needs of their staff to the ill-defined objectives or content of the training programmes listed. It also encourages the use of training 'because it is there', irrespective of whether there are any benefits to be gained. This was quite an economically useful exercise in the early days of the Industrial Training Boards in the UK. Any training (even unjustifiable and ineffective) could be claimed for in the training grant (currently in Brazil the exercise is even more profitable, as companies may discount double the cost of any training from their income tax bill). However, these are artificial and transitory situations, which vanish as one develops the means to check the quality and usefulness of the training, as well as the quantity. The longer-term value of the course menu approach is very doubtful.

2. The *training needs prescription* approach. Management and supervision are requested to complete a questionnaire or form, specifying their projected manpower needs for a period (say one year or six months) ahead, and the training/development needs of existing staff. The exact format and content of such forms varies, but typically they may request a specification (in both quantity and type) of the training needs of the department or section. Often, the probable recruitment sources of new

staff are indicated, sometimes also the selection criteria which should be applied are given. The type of training may be stated in subjects or topics or else in the form of objectives.

The weaknesses of this approach are similar to the menu. Staff are requested to make judgements of training objectives or content, without necessarily having the skills required to do so. Also, the returns from each department tend to be parochial. Each sub-system states its needs without too much concern for how these relate to other sub-systems. It often proves difficult for training departments to analyse the returned forms and integrate them into a coherent company training policy and programme.

3. The *job performance evaluation* approach. This is based on a regular evaluation and report of the performance of each company employee by his superior. In theory these reports should serve as the basis for, among other things, the design of individual training or development programmes for each employee. In practice, the amount of data generated in a company of any size is such that it becomes difficult to handle unless some sophisticated methods of data processing are used, and these generally mean that the data has to be categorized in such a way that much of the individualized nature of the approach is lost. If the procedure is restricted to the appraisal of key personnel, as opposed to all personnel, (the rest being treated as occupational or job groups) the data becomes more manageable. This approach is certainly a better way of assessing the training needs than the previous two, as generally the analysis of the job performance evaluation, with a view to specifying training, is performed by specialist training staff. However, it shares one weakness with the other two, namely that it amasses a mass of data from all departments of the organization, which then has to be sorted through without any basis upon which to assign priorities. As the amount of data is often very large, the training staff may spend a lot of time on relatively low-priority problems before unearthing a high-priority one. This approach should be used as part of a broader and more flexible systems approach.

The systems analysis approach

The systems analysis approach recommended here attempts to create a basis for establishing priorities among the problems to be tackled, thus enabling the training department to get on with the solution of high-priority problems, while still collecting data and analysing lesser-priority problems. The stages of the approach are as follows:

Stage 1: Identify problems and priorities

1. Build a functional model of the organization. Identify the chief functions performed by the organization and draw a functional flow diagram to illustrate how they interact with each other. This diagram may be devised from the organization chart, but it would not be exactly the same, as several functions are occasionally grouped in one department of a company. The object of identifying all the functions is to then identify sources of information.
2. Identify the most reliable sources of information for each of the functions identified. This would include the people responsible for the execution of the function, departmental reports, documents, financial statements, etc.
3. Interview and study these sources, from the following standpoints:
    (a) What are the problems (present and future) that you see in the internal operation of the function?
    (b) What are the problems (present and future) that other functions with which you interact may cause for you?
In systems terms, this amounts to asking: what is wrong with the processes operating within the sub-system? What is wrong with inputs from other sub-systems? These are the two factors which may influence

the outputs from the sub-systems.

4. Identify the human resources aspects of these problems? Attempt to specify these in terms of both the quantity and the performance requirements:

      eg What is — current quantity of human resources
                  — current quality of performance
      What should be — quantity
                    — quality of performance.

5. As the analysis progresses, function by function, it is useful to complete a control chart, like the one shown in Figure 6.14.

6. Establish a priority among the problems. This would be on the basis of:

      Worth — what will the organization gain by solving the problem
      Urgency — is the problem present/future, growing/static, etc.

		Existing problem	Predicted problem
Problem inside department	Deficiency cost to company number of people urgency		
Problem when interacting	Deficiency cost to company number of people urgency		

Figure 6.14 *A control chart*

Thus we see that a human resources problem may be quite complex. It may be composed of four key factors:

☐ The type or quality of persons required for the job
☐ The quantity of persons available for recruitment and training
☐ Existing problems of job performance or of recruitment/selection
☐ Future needs to be created by changes in or growth of the organization.

All four of these interact and are present to a greater or lesser extent in any human resources problem area. We may visualize this as in the circular diagram (Figure 6.15). The object of the circular presentation is to emphasize the organic integration which exists between the factors. We shall be using this form of circular presentation frequently. As an example of the integrated, complex nature of most human resources problems, consider the possible effects of a new product being launched; new operative level staff to be recruited and trained in new techniques; existing supervisory/management staff to be prepared for the changes; internal transfer/retraining to be arranged for staff becoming redundant due to the product change; new attitudes to be formed; labour turnover rates to be predicted; etc.

In order to identify all the possible factors of the problem, the training needs analyst must understand it in depth. He may at this stage need to refer to (or to perform if one is not in existence):

☐ An analysis of the existing job or jobs. The results of such an analysis are usually presented as a job description, which lists all the tasks and duties involved, together with necessary explanatory details and also the characteristics required of the person performing the job.

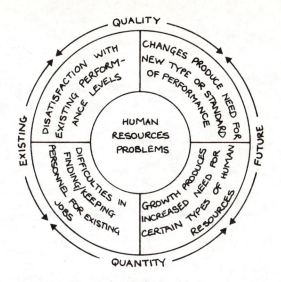

Figure 6.15 *A schema for analysis of human resources problems*

☐ A synthesis (or modelling) of the future job.

When stage 1 analysis has indicated that because of technological, organizational or policy changes a new job will be created requiring a new, hitherto unused, type of trained person, a prerequisite to analysing the type and availability of recruit is to form a clear idea (model) of the tasks he will perform. This we shall call a job synthesis (as opposed to a job analysis) as it involves the putting together of the tasks that a new process requires (ie one or more proposed job descriptions).

This job description, whether of an existing job, or a model of the future job, can be used to estimate to what extent training should be considered with other approaches. Using the job description, one thinks through the supply/demand aspects, the performance deficiency aspects and the staff development aspect of the problem. Doing this may suggest potential sources of difficulty, which may be avoided by redesigning aspects of the job even before it passes from the theoretical model stage. To think through an analysis of this sort effectively in general requires a fairly experienced analyst, who can identify analogies between the job being studied and similar situations he has encountered. This is what we shall call stage 2 of our system for training needs analysis. Having identified the most important aspects of the problem in stage 1, we now proceed to a more detailed analysis of the relevant aspects. There are three routes and we may need to follow one, two or all of them. Whichever of the three routes are followed, one is led to consider if training is really a part of the optimum solution, and, if so, what are the desired outputs of the training?

Stage 2: Analyse the problems

While stage 1 is continuing, one can proceed to the more detailed analysis of an already identified high-priority problem area.

As the flow chart (Figure 6.16) indicates, stage 1 may have defined the problem in terms of:

☐ Poor performance of existing human resources
☐ Inadequate numbers (now or in the future)
☐ New types of human resources need
☐ Or any combination of these.

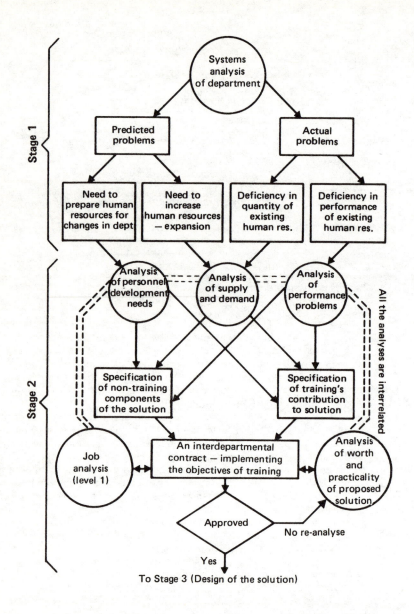

Figure 6.16 *Systemic analysis of training (and other) needs*

Taking each of the three contributory factors in turn, we see the need to perform some further analysis before deciding whether training is required, let alone the type of training.

Performance problems

1. *Analysis of performance problems (discrepancies).* Poor on-the-job performance at any level in the organization may have many causes, other than a lack of knowledge and skill. Therefore there may be many other solutions appropriate, other than training. Some components of non-training solutions are:
   ☐ Selection of a different category of person
   ☐ Improved supervision
   ☐ Redesign of the job
   ☐ Modified working conditions
   ☐ Modified job-reward systems
   ☐ Improved on-the-job information exchange.

   We have already discussed performance problem analysis in detail earlier on in this chapter (see Figures 6.12 and 6.13).

Supply and demand

2. *Analysis of supply and demand.* When in stage 1 the problem is identified as primarily one of quantity, it is necessary to analyse *why* there are difficulties in obtaining sufficient numbers (or why we may anticipate difficulties). Taking the job as the system of interest, one needs to analyse the current or proposed human resource inputs in terms of the criteria one should apply in selection and the availability of such personnel on the labour market. This must consider both job requirements and external constraints, such as other similar organizations looking for the same type of human resource (and possibly offering more attractive conditions). So we need an analysis of the job in terms of the conditions it offers, both within the job and within the organization as a whole. Is the job as interesting to do as it might be? Are general working conditions as good as they might be? How about industrial relations and social services? How about the rewards, both financial and status? How does the job compare with similar ones on the market? How does it match up to the general social status aspirations of the type of person required to do it? As Figure 6.17 suggests, all these factors interact with each other. Only by considering them as a total system can one identify to what extent training would form a part of the solution. Training plays its part in cutting the time needed to reach 'experienced worker standard', in cutting frustrations and errors on the job, in reducing the minimum selection criteria, and so on. But training is seldom the total solution (and what training to use is yet to be determined).

Personnel development needs

3. *Analysis of personnel development needs.* Changes or growth in the organization bring about a whole variety of needs for changes in the knowledge, skills and attitudes of existing staff, as well as possible needs for an expansion of existing staff. Whereas the aspect of new staff should first be tackled by a supply/demand analysis, the aspect of existing staff requires a consideration of the training and/or education that existing staff will need. We say education, as this aspect of the problem often requires some changes of attitudes, or simply information about the proposed changes, as well as specific job-related training or on-the-job experience. It is here that one may identify the need for orientation or appreciation courses/seminars which are not strictly speaking 'training'. They are 'browsing in the fields' as opposed to 'following the path'. We shall refer to this mixture of training and education for the future as development. One may require to develop a man to prepare him for:
   ☐ promotion within his department
   ☐ changes in the organization of his job or his department
   ☐ changes in technology or in methods/techniques — changes due to growth of a department.

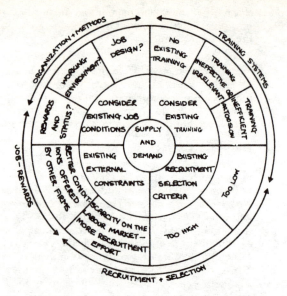

Figure 6.17 *Schema for analysis of supply and demand*

Figure 6.18 attempts to illustrate the complex, integrated nature of these factors. For example, a change in the technology/products could imply promotion for some, retraining for others, increased responsibility for yet others, and changes in organizational structure for all.

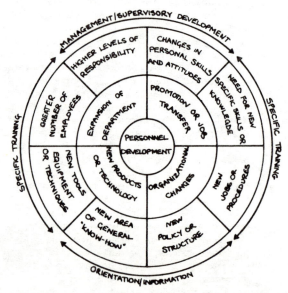

Figure 6.18 *Schema for analysis of personnel development needs*

Define overall project objectives

The extent and depth to which one would need to perform the three types of analysis described here will depend on the characteristics of the problem under study. These analyses are but steps to the specification of useful training objectives. The final step of stage 2 attempts to define these objectives. Naturally, all of stage 2 should be performed by interaction with the persons concerned, the management and supervision staff of the department concerned, the job performers (if they exist) and so on. But not all information will exist in the department (for example, supply/demand information may have to be sought outside the organization).

However, the last step in stage 2, the determination of what training, *must* be performed in conjunction with the department. It should be seen as a sort of contract:

— A successful solution to the problem involves other factors as well as training, therefore
— All these factors should be tackled in a coherent, integrated way, so that
— The final solution will be a combination of several actions, among them training, so
— The objectives of the training to be developed are conditional upon other actions also being performed successfully, and . . .
— These actions are the responsibilities of other departments/services/ individuals in the organization, so
— We should establish, jointly, objectives for the various components of the solution and work as a team to develop it, so
— We shall distribute responsibility for achieving the objectives as follows, and
— We shall have regular review meetings to monitor and evaluate progress.

In other words, the end of stage 2 lays the groundwork for a management by objectives approach to developing and implementing the solution, which by now has been sketched out.

Thus, the overall training objectives will be set jointly by training designers and the 'clients' in job performance terms, more or less as follows:

Given the following conditions for viability (to be achieved by other non-training actions):	The training department will provide a flow of persons capable of performing the following tasks:	To the following standards of: ☐ productivity ☐ quality ☐ speed, etc Flow criteria ☐ So many per year/ month/week, etc

If this is done, subsequent job performance evaluation of training is simply a question of comparing actual performance to the predetermined standards and checking against the conditions for viability to identify the probable sources of poor performance. The statement also gives the training designer clear indication of overall training objectives, both in quality and quantity.

Stage 3: the development of the training

The third stage involves the preparation of concrete proposals for the training to be developed, and once these are approved by management or client the development of the training system.

This is now the specialist task of the training department, and is dealt with fully in other chapters (in this book and in Volume II). The process is presented here in summary in Figure 6.19. Note that before launching into expensive training development an overall training proposal should be submitted for approval to those who will be paying the bill.

The end of stage 3 is marked by the existence of a fully validated training system, ready to be implemented on a regular and large-scale basis. By now any other actions of a non-training nature (that were specified in the contract which closed stage 2) should also have been taken. Only then are we really ready to pass on to stage 4: full-scale implementation.

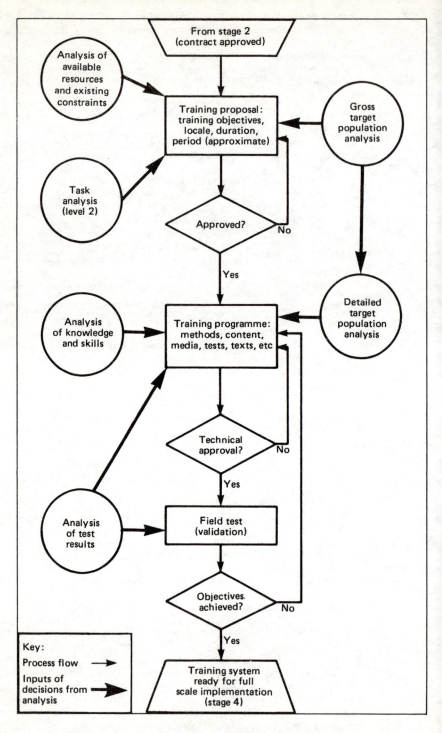

Figure 6.19 *Developing concrete proposals for training*

Note finally that the stages in this model are following the five-stage model of the systems approach outlined earlier. Stage 5 will be the full-scale evaluation of whether the originally diagnosed needs have been satisfied. This will be done through a job performance evaluation system.

7. Techniques and Procedures for Analysis at Levels 1 and 2

Chapter 5 presented an analysis of what we have called level 1 and 2 analysis. This chapter presents a synthesis of some of the techniques and procedures which may be used in practice to perform these analyses.

Information mapping: the chief features
As this chapter is intended to be used for easy reference, the 'information mapping' method of organization and presentation has been adopted. Each page is a self-contained table, or 'map', designed to present a single element of information (eg a concept or a procedure) comprehensibly and in a standard format. This format is based on 'blocks' of information, separated from each other, each block having a specific function in the communication, which is clearly stated in a marginal heading. Thus the reader may quickly identify those parts of the total communication that are of relevance to his needs and may concentrate on these. Whenever appropriate, the maps are cross-referenced to enable the reader to move backwards and forwards through the chapter.

Other features of information mapping
Some of the features of information mapping, as suggested by the inventor of the method (Robert Horn 1969, 1974), are absent from this chapter. These include the use of review tests and feedback questions. However, we shall use the technique more rigorously in later chapters. We shall also examine the technique in more detail in Volume II. We begin with a diagrammatic statement of the contents and structure of the chapter.

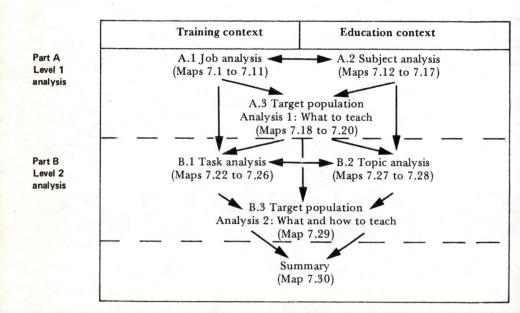

Part A Level 1 analysis

Part B Level 2 analysis

Map 7.1 *Job analysis as a tool for defining objectives: an overview*

Introduction	Much confusion reigns over the use of terminology such as job analysis, task analysis, occupational analysis, skills analysis, etc. Some authors use them almost as synonyms. We shall try to be more careful and shall always refer to the *thing being analysed*.
	Example: Analysing a *job* into duties, tasks, etc — *Job analysis* Analysing one of the *tasks* into its component steps — *Task analysis*
	Thus job analysis stops once we have established the structure of the job. Once we concentrate our attention on a specific task in the job, we commence task analysis.
	This section therefore stops when we have identified the tasks (*all* tasks or only the *problem* tasks) in a given job.
Use of job analysis in instructional design	As a part of the instructional system design process, job analysis is a tool which helps to define instructional objectives, in cases when the post-instructional or real-life objective is the performance of a specific job. The word 'job' should be taken in a wide sense here to include real jobs and notional jobs. The criterion to apply is that there are specific activities (tasks) to be performed, leading to specific measurable results (outputs, outcomes).

Examples of jobs (real and notional)	Real jobs — Postman
	                     — Teacher of French
	                     — Barman
	
	Notional jobs — Solver of quadratic equations
	                     — User of one's civil rights
	                     — Follower of the highway code
	
	This second group is, if you like, the performance content of education.

Structure of Part A	We shall explain job analysis, as practised for real jobs; consider the analysis of subject matter in education; extend its use to the group of 'notional' jobs, and consider how to select what to teach.
Content of Part A	A.1 *Job analysis* 7.1 Overview 7.2 Structure of jobs 7.3 Concept of task 7.4 Concept of occupational groups 7.5 Concept of job analysis/synthesis 7.6 The job description 7.7 The job specification or task list 7.8 How to perform a job analysis: (1) Basic steps 7.9 How to perform a job analysis: (2) Questions to ask 7.10 Techniques of data collection: (1) From managers/supervisors/specialists 7.11 Techniques of data collection: (2) From the job and the performers A.2 *Subject analysis* 7.12 Overview 7.13 Analysing the structure of a subject: (1) Hierarchical structures 7.14 Analysing the structure of a subject: (2) Topic maps or networks 7.15 Analysing the structure of a subject: (3) Conceptual models 7.16 Analysing the structure of a subject: (4) Venn diagram techniques 7.17 Analysing the structure of a subject: (5) Syllabus networks A.3 *What to teach* 7.18 Selecting the topics worth teaching 7.19 Using the 'master performer' concept 7.20 Target population analysis at 'level 1'

Map 7.2 *The structure of a job*

Introduction	The terminology used in describing jobs or occupations is extremely varied and no standardization seems to exist. However, there is general agreement on the overall hierarchical structure into which most jobs can be analysed. As the structure is more important than the exact names used for the components, we present the following terminology without apologies.
Structure of a job	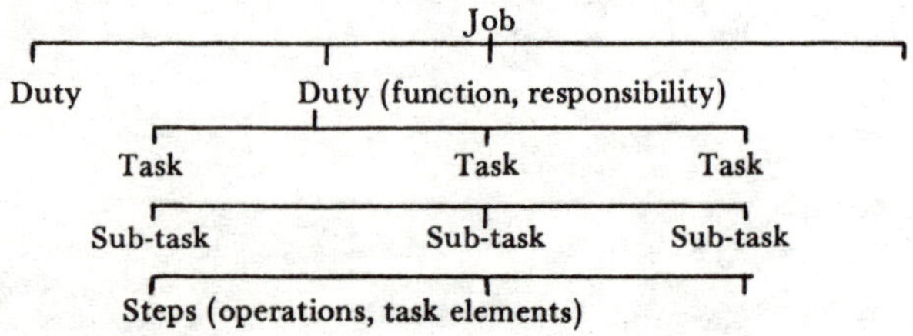 Job Duty Duty (function, responsibility) Task Task Task Sub-task Sub-task Sub-task Steps (operations, task elements)
Example 1	Job: Service station mechanic. Duties: Diagnose and repair engine faults, check and maintain wheels and tyres, check and maintain steering, etc. Tasks: Repair punctures, balance wheels, adjust brakes, etc. Sub-tasks: Remove wheel, remove tyre and tube, locate puncture, etc. Steps: Check wheels, loosen nuts, locate jack, jack up car, remove nuts, etc.
Simpler job structure	In some simple jobs, the job/duty distinction may be unnecessary. For example, many garages employ a man who specializes in maintaining wheels and tyres. A tyre sales depot would employ only such men.
Example 2	In this case, the structure becomes Job: Check and maintain wheels and tyres Tasks: eg Repair punctures Sub-tasks: eg Remove wheel Steps: eg Loosen nuts
Example 3	In very highly specialist jobs, the structure may be yet further condensed. In a large tyre firm, there is a specialist puncture repairman. Job: Repair punctures Tasks: eg Remove wheel Steps: eg Loosen nuts
Comments	1 The job varies at the duty level and at the step/operation level in this hierarchy, but all authors seem to use the term *task* in more or less the same sense. 2 The 'jobs' in the three examples above all really do exist. They all belong to the same cluster of jobs, which might include others such as forecourt attendant, tyre sales technician, highway patrolman, etc (the same occupational group) and they also share some tasks in common. (See definitions of *task* and *occupation*.)

Map 7.3 *Tasks*

Introduction	We see that tasks are the basic building blocks of both jobs and occupations. It would be just as well therefore that we can recognize a task.
Definition	A task is a small unit of behaviour (or performance) which: (a) has a specific identifiable triggering (or stimulus) event which starts it off; (b) is composed of a series of actions (steps, operations) which are related in some way (sequence, time, purpose); (c) has a specific identifiable final result (or terminating event) which indicates that the task is complete.

Examples	Performance	Task?	Why?
	1. Service station mechanic	No	Does not specify a performance
	2. Check and maintain wheels and tyres	No	Various triggering events for various different unrelated actions, eg — flat tyre — wheel wobble — uneven tyre wear, etc
	3. Repair puncture	Yes	(a) Flat tyre on car (b) Sequentially related actions to be taken (c) Repaired when stays inflated
	4. Remove wheel from car	Yes	(a) Damaged wheel on car (b) Sequential steps (c) Damaged wheel on bench
	5. Remove tube from wheel	Yes	(a) Damaged wheel on bench (b) Sequentially related steps (c) Wheel, tyre and tube separated
	6. Chock wheels	No	No meaningful sequence of separate actions worth considering. (There are triggering and terminating events, but they are rather trivial: (a) no chocks (b) chocks

Comment	Note that our definition is still flexible. It does not distinguish between tasks and sub-tasks. The specialist 'job' of 'puncture repairman' is also a 'task' when rephrased 'repair puncture'.

Map 7.4 *Occupation (occupational group)*

Introduction	We saw that various similar jobs may exist, because of differences in the distribution of duties and tasks among individual workers.
Definition	An 'occupation' or 'occupational group' is a group of related jobs (a job cluster) which: (a) contain some common or similar tasks (b) require the same or similar knowledge and skill from the performers.

Examples	Occupation	Job cluster
	Motor vehicle maintenance and repair	☐ Service station mechanic, engine tuner, puncture repairman, lubrication bay attendant, motor vehicle electrician, body repairman, etc
	Catering	☐ Cook, barman, pastrycook, wine waiter
	Teaching	☐ Mathematics teacher, English teacher, junior school teacher, infant school teacher
	Supervision	☐ Paint shop supervisor, production supervisor, typing pool supervisor, chief salesman

Use	The concept of an occupational group is useful in the design of vocational education and training. A job exists in the context of a particular organization. A job with the same name in a different organization might in fact be quite a different job (a different set of duties and tasks). An occupation is independent of a particular organization. It defines what is common among the various related jobs. Vocational training/education seeks to identify the common base (knowledge, skills) required to practice any of the jobs in an occupational group, and then to provide appropriate instruction.
Comment	In order to define the content of required training for a given job one would analyse the job and then define the learning objectives. To define the content of required training for an occupation (vocation) one would need to analyse a representative sample of the jobs in the job cluster that define the occupation, and then look for the common core of learning that is required. This is the main difference between job analysis and occupational analysis.

Map 7.5 *Job analysis and job synthesis*

Purpose	To determine what is involved in the execution of a given job:
	    Job analysis — investigation of an existing job
	    Job synthesis — planning of a future job.

Definition	Job analysis (or job synthesis) is the *process* of examining an (existing) job or planning a (future) job. This process goes on in the *head* of the analyst. It is not a specific document, nor a fixed and rigid procedure, although it may lead to a final document, which may be standardized in format (generally called the job description or job specification).
Process	Involves the interviewing/observing of all concerned with the job — those who do the job (or will do it), those who manage/supervise it, those who plan/design it. 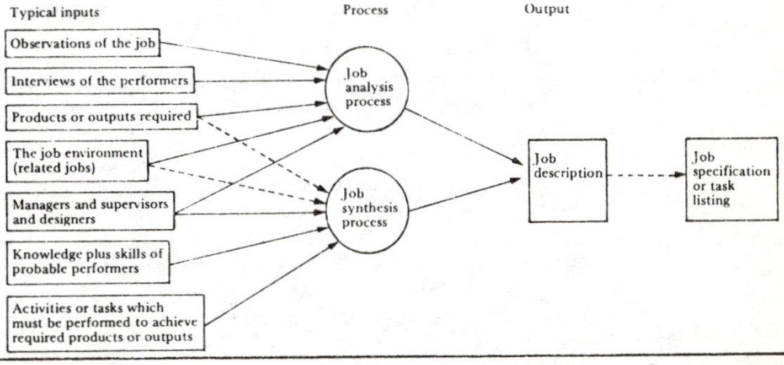
Products	The products of job analysis/synthesis may be presented at two levels of detail: (a) Job description level: Specifying the purpose or function of the job, the physical conditions and the principal duties and responsibilities. (Such a statement is usually adequate for the formulation of recruitment advertisements etc.) (b) Job specification, or task detailing level: In addition to the above information, a full listing of all the tasks to be performed, together with observations concerning the type of tasks, their difficulty/frequency, etc and necessary performer characteristics. (Information necessary for selection and training decisions.)
Inputs	The inputs shown in the diagram above are only the most obvious and common ones. Particularly in the case of the design or synthesis of a new job, a variety of other inputs and experience and imagination are required. The designer may have to decide whether to give all the tasks to each worker (the job-enrichment approach) or whether to divide them among several workers (the production-line approach). He will design one, two or several jobs. In order to make such decisions efficiently, he will need to study other similar projects in the past, the motivation level of workers, local customs and culture, salary and bonus systems, etc.
Comments	1. When analysing existing jobs, one often comes up with ideas for job redesign/improvement (job synthesis). Special departments often exist with the express aims of job improvement. The trainer will often need to cooperate with other specialists in order to plan the 'best' solution to a human performance problem. How to identify such 'multi-disciplinary solutions' is dealt with later. 2. The trainer may often receive previously prepared job descriptions. He will usually however need to perform his own task detailing and in so doing will check the reality of how the job is done with the ideal of how it is described in the job description. Any observed discrepancies should be resolved and approved by the trainer's clients or sponsor before continuing to further stages of instructional design. Otherwise, the training provided may diverge from that desired by the client and the trainer will have no cover for his decisions.

Map 7.6 *Job description*

Definition	A document explaining in a concise and clear way the chief characteristics of a given job (existing or planned):
	(a) To supply information to prospective job candidates.
	(b) To establish position of job in the organization, and have salary levels, benefits, lines of responsibility, etc.
	(c) To act as a basis for the preparation of recruitment literature.
	(d) To act as a basis for the design of selection criteria.
	(e) To act as the basis for the design of staff training or development.

Example	
	1. This example shows a commonly used way of presenting a job description. Note that the duties and responsibilities are stated in quite general terms. All the tasks involved in, say, running the office, are not specified.
	This job description would serve quite well for purposes (a) to (c) above, but has insufficient information for purposes (d) and (e).
	2. This example is couched in general terms, concentrating on the duties that are performed and the skills and capabilities that are necessary in order to perform them. It says nothing about job conditions nor about lines of responsibility within the organization.
	This job description would not be very helpful for purposes (a) and (b), but serves well for purposes (c) to (d).
	(From Mager, R F and Beach, K M *Developing Vocational Instruction*)

Example box 1:

Job description

Title:	Shorthand typist.
Departments:	All
Function:	To establish and maintain effective communications between her principal and other people concerned with the latter's work.
Hours of work:	8.30 am to 4.45 pm Mondays–Thursdays. 8.30 am to 4.15 pm Fridays, ie 37½ hours plus overtime as required.
Responsible to:	Principal.
Responsible for:	Office junior.
Authority over:	Office junior.

Duties/responsibilities:
1. Comply with company rules, regulations and working practices at all times.
2. Present a good image of the company to people outside.
3. Handle business correspondence.
4. Deal with visits/meetings.
5. Attend to principal.
6. Run the office.
7. Deal with messages and queries.

Source: Boydell, I H (1973) A Guide to Job Analysis BACIE

Example box 2:

Radio and television service technician

A radio and television service technician may be required to install, maintain and service amplitude and frequency modulated receivers, transistorized radios, monochrome and colour television systems, high fidelity amplifiers and tape recorders. He is able to read circuit diagrams and codes of values and to select component substitutes.

The radio and television service technician's work requires meeting the public both in the repair shop and on service calls. In order to service home receivers or equipment, he may be required to drive a car or truck. He must be able to tolerate heights, as antenna installations on rooftops are often an everyday occurrence. A service technician who establishes his own business may need to know how to maintain business records and inventory.

Comments	
	1. It is of course quite easy to devise a format for job descriptions which combines the features of both examples shown above. Such a format might include:
	☐ Job title and other identifying information
	☐ Function or purpose of the job
	☐ Where and when practical
	☐ Responsibilities and duties
	☐ A full list of the tasks which compose each duty
	☐ A list of physical, mental and personal attributes which the job demands.
	Such full job descriptions are defended on the grounds that they serve for many purposes and so, once prepared, may be filed and referred to as and when required. Many standard forms exist, some quite complex, for the preparation of such 'complete' job descriptions.
	2. However, although it is undoubtedly useful to refer to such a document if it exists, it always needs some checking (for changes) and rewording (to enable one to understand the document and complete the data needed for the current purpose). Contrary to expectations, a general job description is seldom complete when used for a specific purpose. Nearly always, further information is required and much listed information is irrelevant.
	3. *Analysis is a tool for making decisions, not for filling in forms. Keep it simple and avoid the collection of too much data 'just in case it may prove useful'.*
	Only collect the data relevant to your problem.
	Keep the job description short.

Map 7.7 *Job specification or task list*

Introduction	Following on the comments made regarding the specificity/generality of a job description (keep it general but short), one usually needs to collect further information, more specific to the problem or project being studied, in order to complete the job analysis. This should however be done with a specific purpose in mind. For example, to answer such questions as: ☐ What training shall we give? ☐ How much training? ☐ Should we give any training at all? One would seek data of quite a different type than if the main purpose of the study were to answer: ☐ What is this job worth (how much to pay)? ☐ How can the working methods be improved? ☐ Why is there an excessively high rate of turnover? In what follows, we assume that the main purpose of the analysis is to aid in the making up of *training-related decisions*.
Definition	A job specification (for training-related purposes) consists of a list of the tasks that make up the job (or in complex jobs with several duties — the tasks for each duty), together with other information that the analyst considers will help him in later decision making.
Example 1.	This commonly used layout lists the tasks for each duty and alongside, the knowledge and skills required to execute the tasks. The example distinguishes practical skills and social skills. Other similar formats do not make this distinction, or else include yet more columns for 'general knowledge' and 'attitudes'. An interesting question (to consider later) is how one identifies the knowledge/skill/attitude requirements. By intuition or by some formal procedure? Another is: how do you know whether you need to teach the knowledge/skill/attitude? *Extract from job specification (Catering officer)* — table with columns: Duties/responsibilities and tasks, Knowledge, Skills, Social skills. *Source: Boydell, T H op cit*
Example 2.	This example also lists the tasks, but alongside considers quite different data: how often is the task performed, how important/disastrous are errors in performance, and how difficult is it to learn? This data is used to decide whether a task: — does not warrant any further analysis; — appears to require training; — appears to require other measures to be taken. Thus, in theory, the tasks can be shortlisted and ordered in some form of priority *before* a detailed consideration of the knowledge/skill/attitude requirements is made. (a) It tends to avoid the deeper analysis of tasks that do not merit it. (b) It tends to avoid the development of training for tasks that do not require it. *Electronics technician* table follows. *Source: Mager, R F and Beach, K M (1967)*

Extract from job specification (Catering officer)

Duties/responsibilities and tasks	Knowledge	Skills	Social skills
1. Administer day to day running of unit as directed by the General Manager			
1.1 Ensure high standards of hygiene and cleanliness are instituted and maintained	Statutory and company hygiene requirements. Inspecting standards	Inspection	Motivating, advising and/or correcting staff
1.2 Ensure that quality, preparation, presentation and service are maintained within company standards	Company standards. Methods involved	Inspection	Motivating, advising and/or correcting staff
1.3 Ensure supervisors and chefs are aware of responsibilities and duties	Job descriptions of chefs and supervisors	Work organization. Systematic planning	Liaising and communicating with chefs and supervisors
1.4 Ensure that letters of complaint and all other letters receive an internal acknowledgement and then are immediately referred to General Manager	Company standards. Company procedure. Own job description	Investigation of complaints. Dealing with faults. Written communication	Diplomatic skills
etc	etc	etc	etc

Electronics technician

No	Task	Frequency of performance	Importance	Learning difficulty
1.	Troubleshoots and repairs malfunctioning equipment	Everyday occurrence	1	Difficult
2.	Reads electronic schematics	1 to 10 times a day	2	Moderate
3.	Performs chassis layouts	Once a week	2	Easy
4.	Uses small hand tools	Continuously	1	Easy
5.	Checks electronic components	Frequently	1	Moderate to very difficult
6.	Replaces components	Once in a while	2	Easy to moderate
7.	Solders various components	Frequently	2	Moderate
8.	Recognizes the applicability of electronic test equipment	Once in a while	2	Difficult
9.	Interprets test instruments	Frequently	1	Difficult
10.	Performs calibration of test equipment	Once a month	3	Difficult
11.	Interprets and records test data	Once in a while	3	Easy to moderate
12.	Specifies and orders electronic components	Frequently	3	Easy

Map 7.8 *How to perform a job analysis: basic steps*

1.	Check and agree your terms of reference with your boss/client.
	
	What: Which job/jobs are to be analysed?
	Why: For what purposes are the descriptions to be used?
	How: What are the limits of your freedom of action to:
	  ☐ suggest changes in job methods?
	  ☐ redistribute tasks among performers, etc?
	Who: Who may be consulted for information/approval/advice/assistance?
	When: How much time (and other resources) is it reasonable to spend on the analysis?

2.	Check and study existing documentation related to the job. This will include manuals, standards, trade literature, etc. In particular, verify: ☐ Does a job description already exist? ☐ If so when was it prepared and why? ☐ Have many changes occurred since then? ☐ Do any job standards exist? ☐ Are they achieved? ☐ Do any written procedures exist for any parts of the job? ☐ Is it likely that they are followed? ☐ Have any other departments investigated the job (work study, organization and management, etc)? ☐ If so, where is the documentation of these studies?
3.	Enlist the support of all concerned, who have been identified in step 1. This should include people at the following levels: Senior management — who approve the time and resources used in the analysis (both the analyst's and the analysed). Middle management — who will be one of the sources of information. Supervisors — an even more important information source. The performers — often the prime information source, and easily upset if not fully informed of the purposes and proposed benefits of the analytical exercise. If hostile this source becomes untrustworthy/useless. Trade unions — also easily upset if not kept in the picture and very concerned with issues such as upgrading/downgrading of jobs/pay scales, etc. Specialists — in the design of this job, its equipment, and of jobs in general (work study, ergonomics, in order to validate check and advise on the results of the analysis.
4.	On the basis of steps (1), (2) and (3), now begin to complete the picture by first holding discussions with managers, supervisors and specialists. These discussions may be informal, unstructured, or (better) may be structured in several ways (eg DACUM process; critical incident method).
5.	You should by now have a draft job description and job specification, which mirrors how the job *should* be done (as seen by specialists, management, supervision). Now verify the accuracy of your draft descriptions by observation of the job. Study the job performers and the products of the job. Compare with your draft procedures and standards. If no discrepancies are encountered, you have finished this stage. Type the documents.
6.	However, generally some discrepancies are noted. Investigate these by discussions with the job performers, to find out why they do things the way they do. If they do not (or will not) tell you, try the job yourself. Make a fool of yourself — it helps to get people talking.
7.	Return with any important discrepancies to management and specialists. Attempt to resolve the differences. Repeat the cycle several times if necessary and produce final and agreed job descriptions/job specifications, etc.

Map 7.9 *How to perform a job analysis: questions to ask*

About the job as a whole	☐ What is the job? Its purpose? Its products? ☐ What are the required standards of job performance? ☐ How does actual job performance match up? ☐ Is the job stable/changeable with time? ☐ How does the job fit into the organization? What are the avenues of responsibility/authority? ☐ What are the working conditions, hours, etc? ☐ Are any special or unusual physical/intellectual/personal characteristics obviously required in order to perform the job? ☐ What are the duties/functions/responsibilities that are to be performed? (In the case of less complex jobs, involving only a few duties, what are the tasks performed?) Answers to these and related questions will enable you to draft a job description.
About each duty	☐ What is the *importance* of this duty to the job? If performed badly, how serious are the consequences? ☐ What is the *frequency* of this duty? Is it high frequency (daily), medium (weekly) or low (monthly)? ☐ What is the *difficulty* of this duty? How frequently do errors actually occur? Does it take excessive time to complete? Do the performers complain? Answers to these three questions will enable you to establish a *priority for attention* among the job's duties. A duty which scores *high* on all three counts obviously deserves urgent and careful analysis. A duty which scores *low* on importance *and* difficulty may not need any further analysis. No action may be required. For those duties that are deemed to require further analysis, ask: What are the tasks that are to be performed? In some cases there are alternative or occasional tasks, rarely practised (eg emergency procedures). Make sure you do not miss them.
About each task	Repeat the three questions: ☐ How *important* is the successful performance of the task to the success of the duty/job? ☐ How *frequently* is the task performed? ☐ How *difficult* is this task to perform? Answers to these three questions will enable you to establish a priority among the tasks. Tasks scoring low on all counts (particularly on importance and difficulty) may not need any further action at all (eg new trainees will learn them rapidly on the job, without any formal training). Tasks scoring generally high ratings, will require training or other action to be taken and this will usually require further analysis of the task (task analysis).
Comment	The procedure described here is designed to eliminate unnecessary analysis. At every stage of breakdown, attempt to establish priorities so that you spend your valuable analytical time/skills on those duties/tasks that are causing problems. Avoid analysis for the sake of analysis.

Map 7.10 *How to perform a job analysis: techniques of data collection*
1. From managers, supervisors, specialists

Unstructured direct interviews	Useful as a first step — to get started if little documentation exists. Not very reliable unless several informants are interviewed and their replies compared. More reliable for the products/standards of a job (the things that management directly measure) than for the detailed steps of execution (where management often have only a faint idea of what actually goes on in the job — often their ideas are wrong or out of date). If possible it is better to structure the interview in some way.
Structured group workshops (eg DACUM)	Rather than using individual interviews better to get several managers/specialists to work together to define the job. ☐ In a group they tend to open up more. More information is generated. ☐ The information is cross-checked and complemented by other group members. ☐ The group members can be organized to do the documentation for you. One way of doing this is to use a card system. First get the group to generate the job's duties and write each one on a separate card. Then, for each duty, write the tasks on separate cards and order them beneath the duty card. Thus a dynamic model of the job's structure is created and modified until agreement is reached. The cards may be laid out on a table or pinned to a wall. One version of this procedure has been given the acronym DACUM (Designing a Curriculum). It is a useful technique for the analysis of jobs, tasks and knowledge structures. We will discuss it in more detail later.
Critical incident interviews	This interviewing technique concentrates on the exceptions rather than the norm. It is particularly useful for establishing the importance and the difficulty of a task or duty. Analysis of a critical error pattern will give measures of both the consequences of poor performance and the frequency with which they occur. In order to be reliable, the technique must investigate a reasonably large number of incidents. This renders it an unsuitable technique for infrequently performed tasks. However, in the right situation, critical incident analysis can be quite accurate and very quick.
Input/output analysis	Managers and supervision are geared to supplying the necessary resources for a job and measuring the job's products. This is how productivity, profitability, efficiency, cost-effectiveness etc are established. A useful and quick technique to get started is to get management opinion about the current input/output situation of the job. Are the products up to standard? Is the use of resources within normal limits? If not, what can we infer about the job processes? Now let us check our hypotheses on the job.

Map 7.11 *How to perform a job analysis: techniques of data collection*
2. From the job and performers

Direct observation	The most commonly used method for practical jobs. Usually the first method to be adopted. But a bit of prior document analysis and work with supervision can simplify this stage and cut the time invested drastically. Rigorous observation of complex and high-speed tasks can be very time consuming. Keep it to a minimum. Aids to observation (eg filming) are sometimes used, but the cost is rarely justifiable.
Performer interviews	It is usually necessary to question the performer being observed as to why he performs a task in a particular way. This is seldom obvious from direct observation. Often the performer does not readily explain why — either because he is hostile or apprehensive, feeling perhaps that his position is threatened if he divulges all, or because he is not consciously aware himself of certain cues which control how he performs a task. In the former case, first put the interviewee at ease. Dispel his worries about the implications of the study. Show him what a fool you are by (deliberately) exaggerating your lack of understanding of the job, introducing deliberate mistakes in your analysis, etc. This tactic usually opens the floodgates of information.
Having a go yourself	If the performer *cannot* tell you clearly how he performs his job, then have a go yourself and cast the performer in the role of instructor. Perhaps he cannot explain verbally, but he can demonstrate in practice. Once again you can try the tactic of the 'deliberate mistake' to create opportunities for interventions by the performer and to boost his self-confidence and technical superiority.
Simulation or comparison techniques	When a job does not yet exist (ie we are involved in a job synthesis) we usually limit ourselves to working with the managers/specialists who 'want' the job. However, it is sometimes possible to simulate the job (in order for example to estimate the difficulty of tasks). Alternatively, if a similar job already exists (one with many identical/similar tasks), it may be possible to analyse this job and to estimate the differences with some degree of reliability.
Questionnaire techniques, job diaries, etc	Questionnaire data is of limited value in job analysis. It is usually rather too general. The large number of job performers who can be reached by a questionnaire in a short time appears to be an advantage. But this is not so. The large amount of data generated is often biased to an unmeasurable extent, takes an inordinate amount of time to process and is not necessary for the sort of decisions made as a result of job analysis. Somewhat better written techniques are the structured periodic ones, such as keeping a diary of management activities or activity sampling.

Map 7.12 *Subject analysis: an overview*

Introduction	The methods used for the preparation of a syllabus are various. We shall illustrate in the next few tables some of the more objective techniques, which can be used as part of a systems approach to instructional design in courses of an educational nature. In such courses (as opposed to hard training courses), it is not always common (nor indeed necessary) to start the instructional design process by stating objectives.
Two routes of instructional design	In Chapter 2 we identified the instructional design process as a cycle of activities. The two most valid starting points for this cycle are either: (a) a set of required skilled activities (a job) (b) a body of information to còmmunicate (a subject) 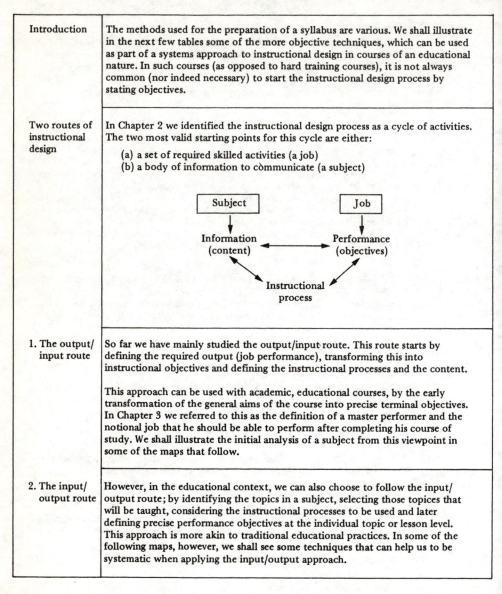
1. The output/input route	So far we have mainly studied the output/input route. This route starts by defining the required output (job performance), transforming this into instructional objectives and defining the instructional processes and the content. This approach can be used with academic, educational courses, by the early transformation of the general aims of the course into precise terminal objectives. In Chapter 3 we referred to this as the definition of a master performer and the notional job that he should be able to perform after completing his course of study. We shall illustrate the initial analysis of a subject from this viewpoint in some of the maps that follow.
2. The input/output route	However, in the educational context, we can also choose to follow the input/output route; by identifying the topics in a subject, selecting those topices that will be taught, considering the instructional processes to be used and later defining precise performance objectives at the individual topic or lesson level. This approach is more akin to traditional educational practices. In some of the following maps, however, we shall see some techniques that can help us to be systematic when applying the input/output approach.

Map 7.13 *Analysing the structure of a subject to define the 'topics worth teaching' 1. Hierarchical structures*

Introduction	An expert in a particular subject will form an opinion on 'what is worth teaching' largely on the basis of the *structure* of the information that composes the subject. Certain key concepts or topics that interrelate with many others, or which explain many phenomena, or which are a rich source of examples, would be considered as more worth teaching than rarely used peripheral information.
Mapping out the structure of the subject	In order to identify the key concepts or topics in a subject, one may attempt to map out the structure of the subject, using some form of pictorial representation. A visual representation of the structure is an aid both to the analysis of complex subject matter and to the communication of what is worth teaching and learning (to other teachers and also to students).
How to map out a hierarchical structure	One may use a family tree approach to represent the topics which compose the subject. One may descend to lower levels, identifying sub-topics, just as we saw in the case of job analysis. Jobs generally have a hierarchical structure, the job being the sum of a particular set of tasks and each task being the sum of a set of sub-tasks and so on. Subject matter structure can also be presented in this way. This is particularly useful when the subject contains a system of classification which is to be communicated.
Example	In the example below, several key concepts (eg active, direct, etc) are used to analyse the subject (individualized instruction) into a hierarchy of topics (instructional methods). This hierarchical structure may then be used to order the presentation of the subject in an organized manner.

Individualized instruction

Individual — Class

Active — Responsive — Permissive

Active		Responsive		Permissive	
Direct	**Indirect**	**Direct**	**Indirect**	**Direct**	**Indirect**
Tutorial	Dalton plan	Montessori School	Responsive environment	Students' school (know place)	Selected programme (electives Meadowbrook School)
'Private lesson'	Winnetka plan	Leicestershire plan	Simulation	Personal programme (with counsellor)	Independent programme (with adviser)
Apprenticeship	IPI	Cooperatively designed programme	Games	The Everdale Place	'Quest phase' Melbourne School
Remediation	Programmed — linear — branching — adaptive			Non-directive teaching	
Protege	SRA				
Prescriptive teaching	Reading lab				
	Correspondence course				
	Independent study (part of a course)				

An elementary classification of individualized instructional programmes (adapted from Gibbons [1971])

Map 7.14 *Analysing the structure of a subject*
2. Topic maps or networks

Introduction	Most subjects that are worth teaching have a more complex structure than do jobs. Not only do the topics add up to form the subject, but they also relate to each other in complex ways. Often the justification for teaching a particular body of information lies in the value to be gained from the investigation of these complex relationships. In such cases the analyst should attempt to visualize the complexity of the structure.
Example 1.	This analysis by Clarke (1970) of a part of primary school mathematics clearly illustrates the importance of certain key topics (eg sets), and gives many insights into possible teaching sequences and revision points. 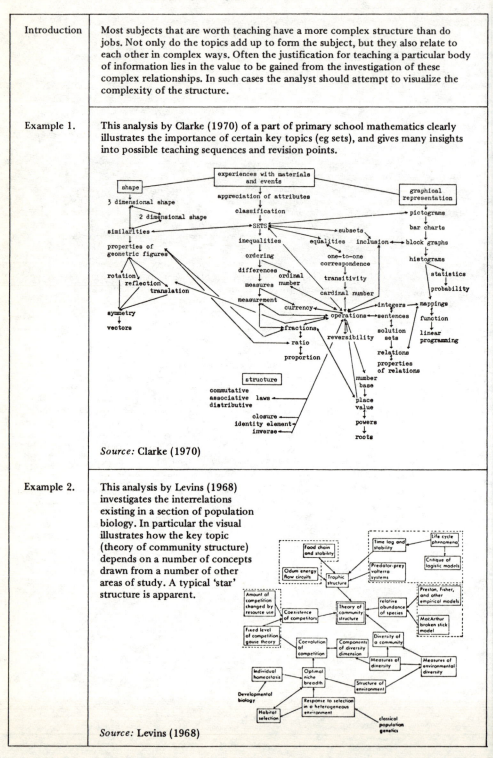 *Source:* Clarke (1970)
Example 2.	This analysis by Levins (1968) investigates the interrelations existing in a section of population biology. In particular the visual illustrates how the key topic (theory of community structure) depends on a number of concepts drawn from a number of other areas of study. A typical 'star' structure is apparent. *Source:* Levins (1968)

Map 7.15 *Analysing the structure of a subject*
3. Conceptual models

Introduction	This approach is similar to the previously illustrated networks of key topics, but it is a little more rigorous. As Neil (1970) puts it, the 'stringing together of a series of topic headings by means of arrows is no more than a structured index or contents list'. Such a network often does not communicate much about the *types* of relationships that exist (except perhaps to experts or to the one person who drew up the network). Neil suggests the need for two refinements: (a) the need for a classification of the types of possible relationships, together with a language (notation) for representing them, and (b) the need for rules, for the clear visual presentation and organization of the resulting models (he calls this 'graphic topological design').
Example	The following example (Neil 1970) illustrates the attempt at clear layout and the use of a notation for different types of relationships. A well-designed conceptual model should be read in the same way by anyone who 'knows the rules and the notation'.

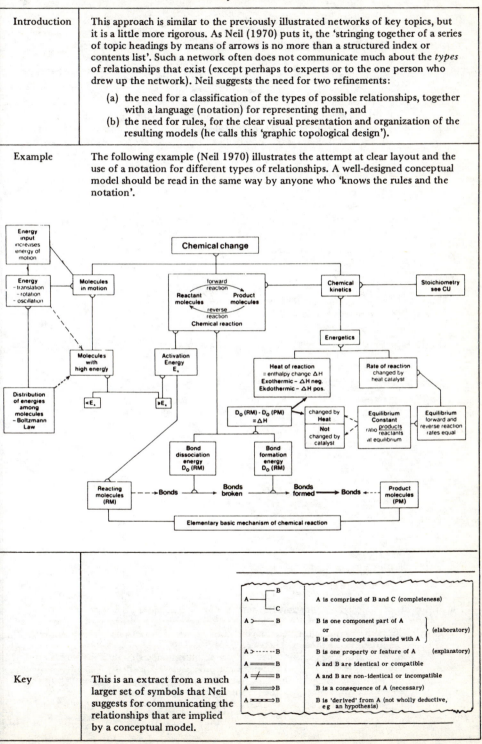

Key	This is an extract from a much larger set of symbols that Neil suggests for communicating the relationships that are implied by a conceptual model.

Map 7.16 *Analysing the structure of a subject*
4. Venn diagram techniques

Introduction	The Venn diagram, used in mathematics to illustrate the composition and interrelation of sets, can be a powerful tool for the analysis of subject matter. We have already used this technique in a rather crude way when defining our terms (instruction, instructional technology, etc) in the first chapter of this book. In more rigorous, closely defined bodies of information, the Venn diagram technique can be developed to a highly sophisticated level, both for the analysis and for the communication of the structure of a subject (or a topic).
Example	This approach was used by Godycki (1968) at the Pedagogical Institute of Warsaw, Poland, for the analysis of physics and chemistry concepts and their presentation as an organic whole, by means of a so-called 'structural notation' based on the Venn diagram. The example shown here is taken from Godycki and Romiszowski (1970) and shows the development of a structure which relates all the concepts involved in the law of conservation of energy.

We shall use the following notation: E=work, F=force, l=distance, m=mass, t=time, v=velocity reached during the time (t) (we shall take the initial velocity to be zero), $\bar{v}$=average velocity during the time (t), a=acceleration.

Traditional notation   *Structural notation*

1. Force equals mass times acceleration.

   F = ma

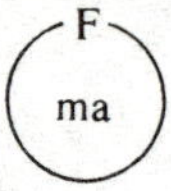

2. Work done equals force times distance.

   E = Fl
   E = mla

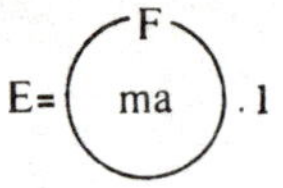

3. Distance moved equals the average velocity times the time in motion

   l = $\bar{v}$t
   E = ma$\bar{v}$t

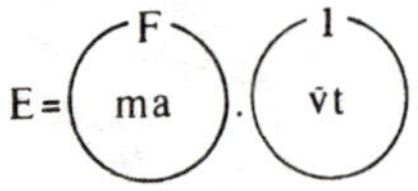

4. Acceleration equals velocity change per unit time. Average velocity equals the final velocity less the initial velocity divided by 2. When the initial velocity is zero, we have:

   a = (v−o)/t = v/t
   $\bar{v}$ = (v−o)/2 = v/2

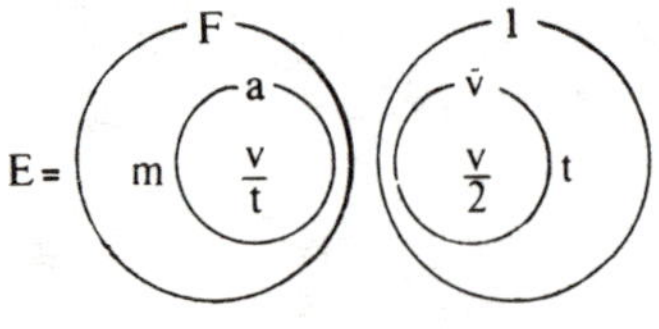

5. Thus E = m.$\frac{v}{t}$.$\frac{v}{t}$.t

   Cancelling: E = ½mv^2

Comments	1.	The structural notation illustrates the fairly symmetrical structure of the relationships between the concepts involved (nearly all the areas of science investigated by this method have, curiously enough, yielded symmetrical, easily memorized structural diagrams).
	2.	In addition to the five equations used to build up the structural diagram (E=Fl; F=ma; l=$\bar{v}$t; a=$\bar{v}$t; v=$\bar{v}$/2) one can directly 'read-off' from the diagram a further ten relationships which would normally have to be individually derived by the process of substitution in equations (the ten equations are: F=mv/t; l=vt/2; E=F$\bar{v}$t; E=Fvt/2; E=ma$\bar{v}$t; E=mavt/2; E=mal; E=mvl/t; E=mv$\bar{v}$; E=mv^2/2).

Map 7.17 *Analysing the structure of a subject*
5. Syllabus networks (PERT charts)

Introduction	This is a special form of representing the structure of a subject which uses the techniques of network analysis (or PERT). It differs from the examples so far presented in that it represents the sequence of the topics in the course.
Method of construction	Once the 'topics to be taught' have been identified (perhaps by one of the methods outlined previously or perhaps more by intuition) the analyst considers the interrelationships between them and asks: (a) what is the earliest time at which I could teach this topic, and (b) what is the latest time by which the topic must be learnt. The answers to these questions place the topic in the network in relation (both sequential and parallel) to the other topics (and even related subjects, if the network is big).
Uses	The process of preparing the network: ☐ Reveals the logical sequence and interrelation of the topics in the subject ☐ Reveals the various routes and sequences that are available for learning the subject ☐ Reveals topics which are loosely connected and perhaps redundant ☐ Reveals missing topics, necessary to forge links and improve the sequence. The final network may be used as an analysis tool, a teacher's guide, a student's guide or a course control document. Much has been done to develop the use of this technique in education by Wyant (1971, 1972, 1973, 1974) and by Vaughan (1972).
Example	This network was produced by Wyant to plan and control an individualized course in educational technology. *Source:* Wyant (1972)
Comment 1.	Network analysis (PERT) is a powerful technique of project planning and control, resources scheduling, etc. In the context of syllabus planning, only some aspects of the technique are fully used. It can be used more fully for the overall planning and implementation of educational or training projects. Its use for this purpose will be illustrated in Volume II, where the reader will also find a short self-instructional course on the technique.
2.	For the purpose of syllabus analysis and curriculum planning, the group dynamics technique DACUM gives results very similar to the PERT method.

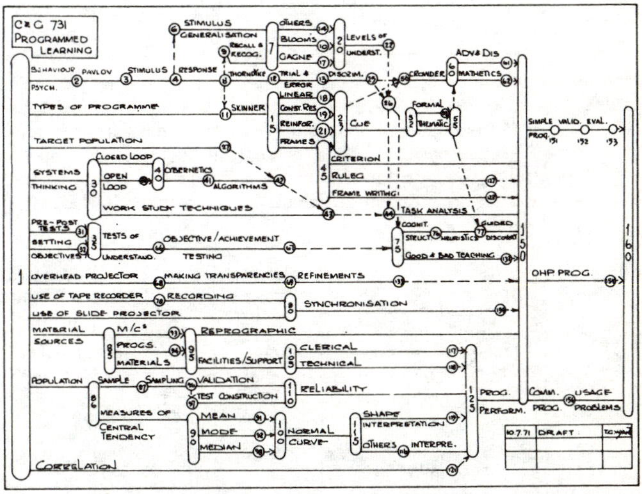

Map 7.18 *Selecting the 'topics worth teaching'*

Introduction	The techniques for analysing subject matter that have been presented in the last few maps, answer the question 'what is' the subject. To this extent they are analogous to the job description in job analysis. We followed this stage by performing a job specification (or task listing) and it was at this stage that the tasks worth teaching were identified (see Map 7.7). Similar methods may be used to identify topics worth teaching.
The content-based approach	This approach uses the content of a topic as a means of assessing its value to a curriculum. In effect, one performs a rapid topic analysis, listing the useful knowledge, skills and attitudes that a student might be expected to gain through study of the topic. The final decision in this approach depends very much on the subject matter expert who is doing the analysis and *what he sees to be useful* in his subject. If he has no well formed concept of what the *students* might find useful, the resultant curriculum may lack relevance.
Example	Subject: history

Topics	Knowledge	Skills	Attitudes
The slave trade	Origins of ethnic mix in Americas	Reading world map	Towards racial differences
	Colonialism	Analysing causes of racial problems	Towards individual freedom
	Man's inhumanity to man		
Piracy	Relations between the imperial nations	Discriminating legal and illegal aggression	Towards international terrorism
etc			

The 'reasons for learning' approach	This approach attempts to establish clear and agreed reasons for the teaching of the *subject* (taking into consideration why the student should wish to learn it) and then using these reasons to analyse the worth of each topic in the syllabus. This approach is akin to the analysis of frequency, importance and difficulty of a task. However, the factors influencing the worth of a topic in an educational course are much more varied. Those included in the example below are not exhaustive.
Example	

Topic	Relevance to today	Use in everyday life	Transfer value	Promotes learning skills	Promotes problem-solving
French revolution	Soviet, Latin American, etc revolutions French politics today	Low	Moderate	No	Yes

Map 7.19 *Using the master performer to define the topics worth teaching in a course*

Introduction

The concept that you form of mastery performance can be used as the principal guide for subject analysis and for the selection of worthwhile topics for the curriculum. This approach has been pioneered by Tom Gilbert (1969). His example of the various master performers that one might imagine for a hypothetical history course was discussed in Map 3.5.

Mastery performance in the educational context

As most educational courses do not prepare students for a specific job, one must imagine a notional job that the graduate of our course might perform. Note that whereas in the training context the master performer exists and can be easily observed and analysed, in the educational context he is often an ideal not usually encountered. Furthermore, often the mastery performance which interests us is an internal thinking process and is not directly observable. We need to look for it by asking our performer suitable questions or by setting him appropriate tasks.

Identifying the tasks of mastery performance

This is analogous to the preparation of a job analysis, with one important difference. As our notional job does not exist in reality, there is no finite limit to the tasks our master might perform. We are in fact looking for *typical tasks* which could be used to evaluate our students. We are, indeed, plunging straight into the preparation of performance objectives. It is useful to have some form of tool to organize and document our reflective search for mastery performance. One such tool, developed specifically for the problem-solver type of performance, is a matrix like the one shown below. We have used history as the example, but the idea may be adapted to many other subjects. To complete the matrix, one searches the subject (history) for specific topics that illustrate a cause/effect (or other) relationship with specific current events. Noting these topics in the appropriate cells, we construct a syllabus that is related to our concept of mastery performance.

Example

Events in history	Current events	Wars	Revolutions	Coups	etc	Economic booms	Depressions	etc	Social health	Population	Customs	Migrations	etc	Religions	Revivals	Intolerance	etc	etc
Military	Wars																	
	Revolutions																	
	Coups																	
	etc																	
Economic	Booms																	
	Depressions																	
	etc																	
Social	Health																	
	Population																	
	Customs																	
	Migrations																	
	etc																	
Religious	Revivals																	
	Persecution																	
	etc																	
Legal etc	etc																	

Map 7.20 *Target population analysis at level 1*

Introduction	Throughout the process of instructional design, one should keep in mind the final consumer of the course — the student or trainee. It is never too early in the process to begin to analyse his characteristics, needs, habits, levels of knowledge or skill, etc. Rather than a definite stage on its own, this analysis continues throughout. It is a good idea to remember, right at the outset that our 'client' (who is commissioning the course and paying the bill for instructional design) is not necessarily one and the same as the 'consumer' and he may well have different viewpoints and motivations. This has been whimsically termed the 'dog-food syndrome'. While satisfying the client, do not forget the consumer.
Definition	The term 'target population' will be used to denote the 'consumer' of the course we are designing — the students or trainees that we expect (we are aiming) to cater for.
Purpose	The chief purposes of an analysis of the target population are: (a) to determine the 'entry level' to the course (what can we assume concerning the initial levels of relevant knowledge or skills) (b) to determine the structure of the course (what existing attitudes, habits, study skills or relevant experiences do we expect and how will these influence instructional design). At level 1, the information sought is fairly general (which of the tasks/topics identified as worth teaching *actually need to be taught*). In addition, in the educational context, one needs to check that the topics *we* think are worth teaching, are considered to be *worth learning* by the *target population*.
Methods	In general, one would investigate, therefore: — what the target population *have done* in the past (experience); — what the target population *can do now* (that is relevant); — what the target population *tend to do* (attitudes and habits). The table below suggests some of the investigations that might be carried out at level 1.

Information required	Suggested methods of collection	
	Educational context	**Training context**
What they have done		
(a) Previous learning	Analysis of curricula and results of any past courses	Restrict analysis to prior job-related learning
(b) Previous relevant performance	Interview teachers familiar with the target population	Teachers and/or supervisors who know the TP
What they can do now		
(a) Knowledge/skill related to the planned course	Interviews of a sample of the TP (best leave formal diagnostic tests to a later stage)	Observation of on-the-job performance of a sample of the TP plus interviews perhaps
(b) General skills, learning skills, etc		
What they tend to do		
(a) Interest in course and in study generally	Try to discover the TP's objectives. Perform a consumer survey	Study the job's market, turnover rates, motivation, rewards, etc
(b) Existing learning styles and habits	Informal interviews with teachers who know the TP and with samples of the TP	

Map 7.21 *Level 2 analysis: an overview*

Introduction	We have studied techniques for the analysis of jobs and the analysis of subject matter. We ended up with a list (or diagram) of the topics or the tasks that compose the subject or job. We also made a gross selection of those topics/tasks that appeared 'worth learning/teaching', eliminating from the list those that are obviously already mastered, those that are very easy or those that are not at all important and those that are practised/used very rarely. The remaining tasks/topics are important, often used and present some learning problems to typical students and so are worthy of further analysis.
Do not over-analyse	It cannot be overstressed that detailed analysis is an expensive activity (in terms of time and the required quality of analyst). Thus, the preliminary sort-out at level 1 does not necessarily mean that no mention at all will be made of the known/easy/rare tasks or topics in the course we are designing. They may certainly be included in order to paint a complete picture. But they will not form an important part of the main course activities and, being easy or rarely used, do not therefore warrant the expense of further analysis.
The 20/80 principle	Some training companies (notably Iconotrain of South Africa) apply a rule that as, in practice, about 80 per cent of the time on most jobs involves the 20 per cent most frequently used tasks, one should attempt to limit initial training to that important 20 per cent, leaving the remainder to be gained through supervised on-the-job experience. Whereas such a rigid principle would not be applicable in the educational context, it is as well to remember even there that a course overloaded with rarely used content will inevitably appear irrelevant to students.
Purposes of level 2 analysis	Thus the purposes of a deeper, level 2 analysis are to have a closer look at the tasks/topics deemed to be worth teaching at level 1, in order to: ☐ Examine their structure and content ☐ Identify what is involved in their mastery ☐ Identify which parts give the learners most problems ☐ Generate ways of helping them to overcome these problems.
Products of level 2 analysis	The chief products of level 2 analysis are: ☐ The final test instruments and exercises ☐ The entry or prerequisite tests and standards ☐ The learning/teaching sequence (or alternatives) ☐ Lesson plans (with some idea of the methods/media) ☐ Lesson tests (for on-line evaluation during the course).
The limitations	Some insights are inevitably gained into the way that the course should be taught, and it may well be that no further analysis would be necessary before 'launching into the battle' of either teaching a class or preparing some specific instructional materials. However, the techniques of level 2 are not designed to help the designer to synthesize course materials or exercises in a systematic way. In the case of exercise or materials design it may be necessary to descend to further depths of analysis. We shall study these in later chapters.

Map 7.22 *Task analysis by the listing of elements*

Introduction	In this approach, the analyst observes the task (or uses some other technique to collect his data) and enters his findings directly on to a pre-prepared analysis form. He lists the elements or steps of the task and makes appropriate comments alongside. These comments vary depending on the type and the complexity of the task. A number of different forms exist.
The TWI method	The TWI (Training within industry) method of task analysis is one of the earliest and simplest to be used. The analyst lists the steps in one column and the key points to pay attention to in a column alongside. The method is adequate for relatively simple tasks.
Example	The example shown here has been adapted from an analysis of the task of using a duplicating machine (Boydell 1973). Note the change in the name of the key points column. Otherwise this is a classic TWI task analysis.

Steps	Safety and other factors
1. Depress feedboard drop lever, dropping feedboard to lowest position.	
2. Position feedboard centrally, using the side margin adjuster.	
3. Pull back fence fully to rear of feedboard and lay horizontal.	
4. Slacken off side fence knobs and move side fence sideways across feedboard.	
5. Separate paper stack and knock-up on a solid surface.	'Knocking-up' ensures that each sheet is separate from its neighbour. For accurate positioning of paper use scales on feedboard and cylinder guard. For sideways movement use side margin adjuster.
6. Stack paper on feedboard between side fences, fully forward towards machine.	

| A more detailed method | The example below is one way of expanding the TWI approach to attempt to capture more detail about the task elements, in a more organized manner. It was developed by the Hotel and Catering Industry Training Board (UK), but similar approaches abound. In completing this form, the analyst attempts to note down:

What is done: he lists the steps, introducing each one with a verb (eg lift, hold, open)
How it is done: (eg with left hand, by turning)
Points to ensure: factors which will affect performance and feedback that shows the trainee that he is performing correctly
Extra information needed: any special knowledge required in order to perform correctly. |
|---|---|
| Example | The form below uses this approach to analyse the same task as shown in the example above. Note the greater detail recorded. This is useful for more complex tasks. |

What is done	How it is done	Points to ensure	Other information required
1. Drop feedboard	By depressing feedboard drop lever with first finger of right hand	See that feedboard drops to lowest position	Parts of machine
2. Position feedboard centrally	By screwing side margin adjuster	See that slot in feedboard is in line with the two central holes	Parts of machine
3. Pull back fence	By lifting paper weight and pulling towards rear of feedboard, laying fence horizontal	See that fence is fully at rear of feedboard	Parts of machine
4. Open out side fences	By unscrewing side fence knobs and sliding side fences across feedboard	See that fences are wide enough to allow paper to be fitted freely	Parts of machine
5. Separate paper stack	By knocking long edge on hard surface and letting paper stack fall away, bending inwards (repeating three times)	See that paper is fanned out to separate each sheet from its neighbour, thus ensuring proper feeding into machine	Separation of paper stack
6. Stack paper on feedboard	By lowering between side fences and pushing forwards	See and feel that the paper is pushed up against the stop, otherwise it will not feed. See that the paper is between equal numbers on the scale	Parts of machine

Source: adapted from Boydell (1973)

Map 7.23 *Task analysis by listing the elements*
(paying attention to the trainee's needs)

Introduction	The TWI approach is very task-oriented in the sense that the analyst is not encouraged to 'put himself in the shoes of the trainee' in a systematic manner (of course, a good analyst does this instinctively). The expanded method, in listing points to ensure and other information is slightly more operator-orientated. However, as we are doing the analysis in order to later produce training, it would seem a good idea to become more trainee-orientated from the beginning.
The trainee's needs	The trainee differs from the skilled operator in his ability to: (a) notice the *cues (or stimuli)* that indicate *when to start* the task (or individual steps), (b) perform the *actions* required (due to lack of skill, stamina, knowledge, confidence), (c) notice the *feedback* that indicates satisfactory performance of the task. Discrepancies in the trainee's perception are more difficult to observe (items [a] and [b] above) so it would be useful to look for them systematically during task analysis.
Example 1.	This example, based on the task-detailing method of Mager and Beach (1967) lists the steps in performing the task and assigns to each step a performance type and a learning difficulty. The steps with high levels of learning difficulty merit further analysis. The simple taxonomy of types of performance will help later with the selection of instructional methods. Note also my addition of the trigger event and terminating event. Task: servicing spark plugs. Trigger: erratic engine or 3000 miles Feedback: engine runs smoothly with normal power

No.	Steps in performing the task	Type of performance	Learning difficulty
1.	Note the plug location relative to the cylinder	Recall	Easy
2.	Remove all spark plugs	Manipulation	Easy
3.	Identify the type of plugs	Discrimination	√
4.	Decide whether to adjust or replace plugs	Problem-solving	Moderately difficult
5.	Clean plugs, if necessary	Manipulation	√
6.	Adjust plugs, if appropriate	Manipulation	Moderately difficult
7.	Replace spark plugs in engine	Manipulation	√
8.	Connect ignition wires to appropriate plugs	Recall, manipulation	Moderately difficult
9.	Check for performance	Discrimination	Very difficult

Example 2.	This example shows a method we have used with much success to analyse tasks which turn out to be more difficult than they seem. This is usually a sign of important but hidden cues. Note that even in this trivial example the comments concerning cues and errors throw a lot of light on to what one should teach about tea-making.

Step	Stimulus (cue)	Response (action)	Feedback (cue)	Difficulties (cues)	Difficulties (action)	Possible errors	How to avoid
1.	Instruction: fill kettle	Fill kettle	Water must cover kettle ring and fill pot	—	—	Not covering ring (may burn out)	Look inside kettle whilst filling
2.	Sufficient water to fill pot	Plug in		How much water per pot of tea	—	Insufficient water (may have to go without tea)	
3.		Switch on	Kettle starts to boil			too much wastes power	
4.	Kettle boils	Switch off	Steam pressure decreases	Identifying boiling point		Boiling too long (may run dry)	Watch kettle (never boils) Buy whistling kettle
5.		Unplug				Adding water to hot empty kettle (may scald hand)	Let kettle cool off
6.	Tea in pot	Pour water into pot	To fill the pot	—	—		

Map 7.24 *Analysis of more complex tasks*
1. Flow charting techniques

Introduction	The direct listing of the steps or elements of a task becomes more difficult to do and the resulting task structure more difficult to communicate, as the complexity of the task increases. Sequential step tasks can be broken down directly into a list of the steps. Decision making tasks that have many alternative steps at certain points can best be analysed by first drawing a flow chart to show the interrelationship between the alternative courses of action.
Block diagram techniques Example	The simplest way of describing a complex task is by means of a block diagram. This is generally used when a very deep analysis is not warranted. It maps out the alternatives, but does not go too deeply into the decision making process involved in choosing among them.
Decision tree techniques	When there is a need to analyse the decision making process more thoroughly, the use of decision trees, or algorithms breaks down complex decisions into their elements. The fullest breakdown is the binary decision, or yes-no level. The example below analyses the top row of the previous example into more detail.

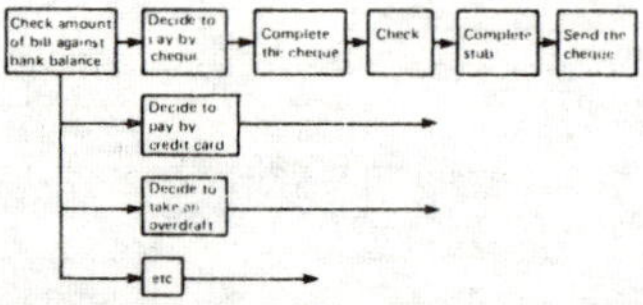

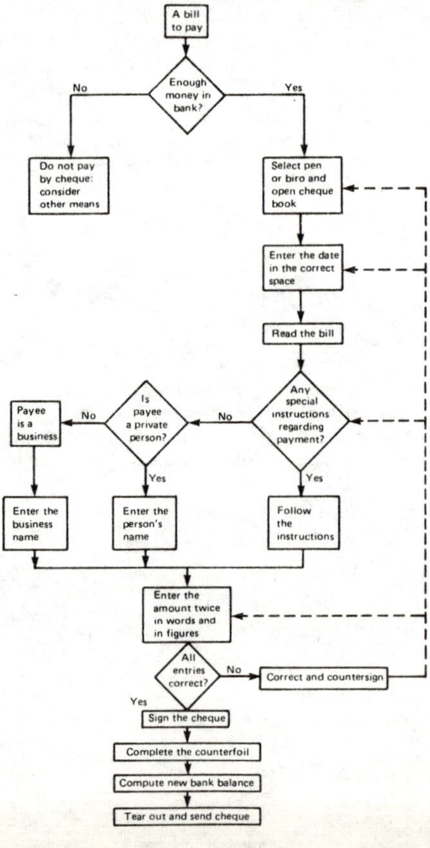

Map 7.25 *Analysis of more complex tasks*
2. The behaviour prescription

Introduction	One disadvantage of the decision tree approach is that it sometimes breaks the task down into a mechanistic form. After all, the binary decision level of analysis was developed for the programming of computers, not humans. Human beings think in larger chunks (or so it appears), so why not try to analyse human behaviour as it really is. One characteristic of human behaviour is that it generally has a reason — it is triggered off by some external event or stimulus. Thus the behavioural analyst's approach is to identify and to note down these stimuli and the resultant responses, as a behaviour prescription.
The behaviour prescription	

Notation	The basic notation for a stimulus/response analysis of a task is the operant. An operant is a unit of behaviour which identifies the stimulus and the resultant response. One can break down any behaviour to a greater or lesser degree, treating it as:

One operant

$$S \longrightarrow R$$

Telephone rings   Answer it

Many operants

S $\longrightarrow$ R	S $\longrightarrow$ R	S $\longrightarrow$ R
telephone rings	pick up handset	hand set in position	identify yourself	identified	listen to caller etc

The analyst can vary the depth and detail of the analysis to suit his problem.

Example	The example shown here is equivalent to the binary decision flow chart shown on the previous map. Compare and contrast the two techniques. We shall see in Volume II that this particular approach to analysis has many advantages. It is part of the mathetics approach to analysis and instructional design.

1

S $\longrightarrow$ R
A bill to pay / Check against bank balance (Record kept on back of counterfoil)

2

S $\longrightarrow$ R
Enough money to cover bill? / Select pen or biro and open cheque book

S $\longrightarrow$ R
Not enough money in bank? / Stop! Do not pay by cheque. (consider payment by cash or emigration or suicide another prescription may sort out these alternatives.

3

S $\longrightarrow$ R
What's today's date? / Enter date in correct space.

4

S $\longrightarrow$ R
The payee is a private person? / Enter his full name in the payee space.

S $\longrightarrow$ R
Payee is a business? / Enter the business name (use the letterhead)

S $\longrightarrow$ R
Payee is a company with special instructions for payment? (e.g. post office) / Enter payee as instructed on the bill.

5

S $\longrightarrow$ R
The amount of the bill? / Enter it twice (words and figures) leaving no gaps and starting well to the left of spaces.

6

S $\longrightarrow$ R
All data entered correctly? / Sign at bottom with standard signature.

S $\longrightarrow$ R
Data incomplete or incorrect? / Alter errors, countersign in full and sign at bottom.

7

S $\longrightarrow$ R
Cheque completed. / Transfer data to counterfoil, tear out cheque and pay.

S $\longrightarrow$ R
Cheque torn out. / Compute new bank balance on back of counterfoil.

8

Notes: (1) This is a simplified prescription. Aspects of the task such as post-dating, uncrossing, stopping a cheque have been omitted.

(2) This is one of several possible prescriptions, as banks differ in their practices.

(3) Operant numbers 2, 4, 6 are discriminations which may require appropriate practice exercises.

Map 7.26 *Identifying essential knowledge or skill*

Introduction	A list of the 'tasks worth teaching' establishes the overall objectives of the training course we are designing. A breakdown of these tasks into their elements, identifies those elements that are difficult to learn and also helps to establish an instructional sequence and the 'milestones' along that route (the intermediate objectives).
	However, there are usually some 'hidden elements' of essential knowledge or of basic skills, which are not directly observable by watching the task, but which can be inferred, by thinking about how the task is performed and by interviewing both 'master performers' and trainees. This establishes the 'enabling objectives'.
Procedure	1. Establish exactly how the task should be performed by observing and questioning master performers. This analysis can be presented as some form of flow charts. Here we have used Gilbert's prescriptions method, and algorithms. 2. Then look at each stage (or 'operant') on the chart and list all the knowledge and all the skills required to perform adequately, as shown below. 3. Check the list against what you know about the trainees (the target population). Tick those items which are already mastered. Cross those which are not. If unsure, put a question mark and then find out by testing samples of the target population.
Example	The following example continues the analysis of the task of using a cheque book correctly. (Refer to the previous maps.) The analysis below is based on the following target population: age 19—49; education generally up to 15 years of age only; average IQ; experience with a bank account not more than one week; job — operatives in light industry.

Operant No.	Knowledge	Known?	Skill	Mastered?
1.	a) Where to get original balance? Bank statements etc.	X		
	b) Why? Concept of a bank balance. Overdrawing. Debit and credit.	X		
2.	Why not use pencil? Security.	X	Discrimination between the sizes of amounts of money.	✓
3.	a) How to find today's date.	✓		
	b) Where to enter date.	?		
	c) Why must the date be entered? Validity period.	X		
4.	a) Where to enter name.	?	Discrimination between private and business names.	?
	b) Where to look on a bill for payment instructions.	X		
5.	a) Where to enter amount.	?		
	b) Why words and figures.	X		
	c) Why start well to left and fill all gaps.	X		
	d) How to fill gaps.	X		
6.	a) Where to sign	?	Identification of common errors	X
	b) How to sign. Specimen at bank. Its use.	X		
	c) How to alter errors and countersign.	X		
7.	a) Use of counterfoil as a record.	X		
	b) What data is needed for record.	X		
8.	a) Where to keep a record of balance.	X	Arithmetic skills – addition and subtraction of money.	?
	b) How to obtain a statement if needed.	X		

Comments 1.	Next stages 1. Investigate the queries above. 2. Course content is final list of Xs. 3. Select teaching method and structure a teaching sequence.
2.	When the 'hidden knowledge' elements are themselves complex, or when there are large bodies of essential knowledge, then one may need to analyse this further. The techniques of topic analysis to be described in the next two maps may then be used. When the hidden skills are very difficult to learn, a deeper skills analysis may be needed. This will be introduced later.

Map 7.27 *Level 2 analysis: topic analysis*

Topic analysis by the input/output route (the use of rule sets and Bloom's taxonomies)	
Introduction	In the educational context, we can either follow the output/input route or the input/output route. The more traditional approach is the latter, starting by the definition of topics, content and examples (information) and finishing by the definition of test instruments. Several technological tools have been developed to make this process more objective. Two of these (rulesets and Bloom's taxonomy) are combined in the methodology suggested in the example below. Both these tools are discussed in more detail in other chapters (see Chapters 3 and 12).
Procedure	1. Select a *topic worth teaching* (eg Ohm's Law). 2. Analyse it to identify the important *elements of information* (concepts, laws, procedures, etc). 3. Order the information in a *logical sequence for presentation* and expand it into a set of very short sentences which flow on (a set of *teaching points* or rules). 4. Agree on the *general aims* of teaching this topic. 5. Use the categories of Bloom's taxonomy to label each element of information with the appropriate *level of testing*. 6. Develop *appropriate test items* for each information element. 7. Build from these a *final test* of appropriate difficulty. 8. Examine the test items for necessary prerequisite skills or knowledge and prepare an *entry test* to check these. 9. Combine the logical presentation with the appropriate test items to develop an *instructional sequence*.
Example	The following diagram follows the layout style of Figure 3.5. You might refer to that to refresh your memory. The topic of Ohm's law is used to illustrate the steps. 1. Topic — Ohm's law 4. General aim — to understand and use Ohm's law 7. Final test 2. Main elements of information Charge (C) Current (I = C/t) EMF (V) Resistance (R) PD (V) Ohm's law (V = I.R) 5. Category of objective Knowledge Comprehension Comprehension Comprehension Comprehension Comprehension and application 6. Intermediate test items Define charge Is the current in a circuit equal at all points? Discriminate EMF/PD Calculate the PD; R; I in any circuit 3. A logical sequence (of presentation) *Concept of electrical charge* 1. An electric charge is produced by friction 2. The electron is the basic unit of charge 3. The electron is an impractical unit of charge 4. The coulomb is the practical unit of charge 5. Current is a flow of charge *Concept of electrical current* 5. Current is a flow of charge 6. Current is measured in coulombs per second 7. One coulomb per second is called an ampere 8. When current flows work is done 9. Energy is used when work is done 10. Energy must be supplied for current to flow *Concept of electromotive force* 10. Energy must be supplied for current to flow 11. Electromotive force is a measure of the rate at which energy is supplied 12. Energy is measured in joules 13. Electromotive force is the rate of supply of energy per unit current 14. The unit of electromotive force is the volt *Concept of resistance* (etc) 8. Entry test 9. Instructional design continues
Comment 1.	The example above of a logically sequenced set of teaching points is adapted from a complete analysis by Thomas *et al* (1963). Note the short sentences and the overlap between concepts. This method is an adaptation of the RULEG approach, which we shall examine further in later chapters.
2.	The use of Bloom's taxonomy is not always as simple as the above example would suggest. Refer to the discussion in Chapter 5 on the value of this taxonomy. Other comments regarding Bloom's taxonomies and alternative taxonomies will be encountered in Part 3.

Map 7.28 *Topic analysis by the output/input route*
(the use of a hierarchy of prerequisites)

Introduction	This approach is akin to task analysis, but uses Gagné's technique of objectives analysis. The diagram below is similar in layout to Figure 5.4.
Procedure	1. Select the *topic* (eg Ohm's law). 2. Transform it into a *task* (ie a terminal objective). 3. Produce the *final test* item to match the objective. 4. Analyse the objective into a *hierarchy* of prerequisites. 5. Produce *test items* for each *sub-objective* identified. 6. Identify entry levels and produce an *entry test*. 7. Organize the objectives into a *logical sequence for learning*. 8. Select from the topic relevant *information/examples*. 9. Continue to develop an *instructional sequence* etc.
Example	The following example may be compared with the previous map. Note the similarities and differences.

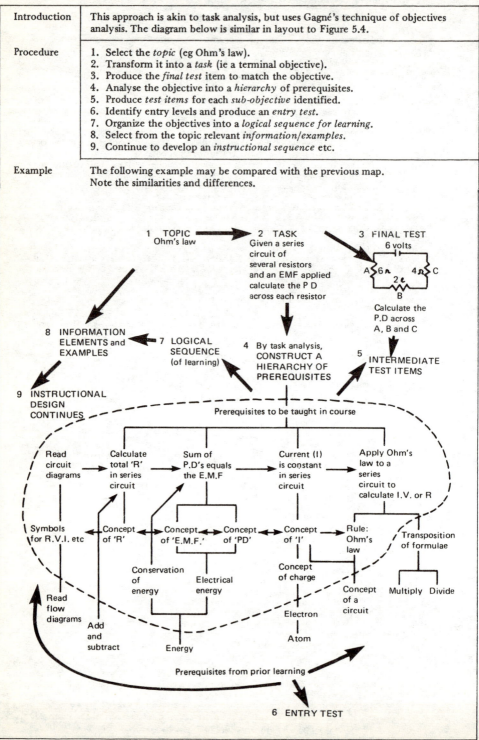

Map 7.29 *Target population analysis at level 2*

Introduction	At level 1 one sought fairly general information about the target population (see Map 7.20). At level 2 the analyst seeks more detailed data. The data required can best be organized as: job/subject-specific data and general data.
Job/subject-specific data	This is information of a more detailed nature on the existing knowledge/skills level of the probable learners. If the course design team has little or no experience of teaching the topics/tasks to the type of learners expected, there will probably be a need for the testing of a sample of the target population. This can be affected by using the final and intermediate test items already isolated as diagnostic tests.
Diagnostic tests	One argument for producing the tests early in the course design process is that they are then available for target population analysis. Usually, the tests should be followed by informal interviews with the subjects tested, in order to examine in depth any difficulties which have been noted. These tests may sometimes be actually attempting the task, but usually a more careful testing/observation procedure is required to identify the precise sources of learning difficulty (see also Map 7.25).
Entry test	One other result of this stage is the ability to specify the knowledge and skill level that will be assumed as the minimum prerequisite for entry to the course. This can be best presented straight away as a prerequisite or entry test.
General data	This is information that is not directly related to the *content* of the proposed course, but to other aspects of importance, such as course/lesson structure, sequence, methods and media.
Course structure	What amount of new information can the target population digest at one go? How many times must a new item of information be repeated in order to be learned? How much practice time/repetition is needed for a specific new skill to develop?
Sequence	Does the target population prefer a fragmented 'parts' presentation of the topic, or is an integrated 'whole' approach more acceptable? When a topic must be learned in its parts, will the learners prefer a *synthetic* (from the parts to the whole) or an *analytic* (from the whole to the parts) sequence? Would the learners prefer to master the theory fully before applying it in practice, or would they prefer to pick up the theory through practical exercises?
Methods	Do the learners prefer to study in group or individually? Do they tend to study in an active, participative manner or do they tend to be passive recipients? Do they need constant supervision and control, or do they work efficiently unsupervised?
Media	Are the target population in general 'visual' or 'aural' learners? Do they prefer to study verbal information through the spoken or the written word? Are they familiar with the various symbolic languages (eg graphs, flow charts, non verbal communication) that the study of the topic/task requires? Are they happy with inanimate media, or do they need the presence of an instructor?
The general context	Finally, one should investigate the general context in which the learning will take place and from which the learners will come. What related experience have they had which would influence the choice of meaningful examples/analogies? What are the social customs/personal habits/ working habits of the target population and how would these influence the course design?

Map 7.30 *Level 1 and 2 analysis: a summary*

Introduction	We have studied two levels of analysis in two contexts (education and training). It is time to bring together our concepts and techniques in order to show that there is a lot of common ground and that the basic 'systems approach' that we are using serves in both areas.
Compare/ contrast table	The table below has been prepared to compare and to contrast the practical procedures that we have mentioned in this chapter.
Comments 1.	Note that there are alternative procedures commonly used in education and training, but that the main stages of each procedure tally well with the general heuristics that we established in the opening chapter of this book.
2.	Note also that the distinction between education and training gradually blurs, the last stages of each procedure being more or less equivalent.

Questions in the analyst's mind (the heuristics)	Analysis techniques and procedures	
	Education context	**Training context**
AT LEVEL 1	Subject	Job
What is the system of interest? What is its boundary?	definition of the subject area/aims, definition of a notional job	definition of the job's duties and responsibilities and objectives
	Chief topics *or* Master performer	Job description
What are its components? What is its structure?	analysis of structure of subject	analysis of the job's structure
	Topic network or model *or* Topic matrix or map	Task listing or mapping
What is worth teaching/learning?	Selection of 'key' or useful topics from expert's view	Selection of key, difficult and frequently practised tasks
What needs to be taught?	Assess usefulness from learner's view. Target population analysis (existing knowledge/skill)	Specify job aids or practice as required. Target population analysis (existing related performance)
	Syllabus (course content) *or* Course objectives ⟷ Training objectives	
AT LEVEL 2		
How is each task/ topic done or structured?	Analyse topic into information elements / Analyse objectives into sub-objectives	Analyse task into steps or operations
	Teaching points *or* Objectives hierarchy *or* Task structure or list of steps	
What is involved in mastering the topic/task?	Apply a taxonomy (eg Bloom)	Look for prerequisite skills or knowledge essential for satisfactory performance
	Intermediate test items ⟷ Intermediate/enabling objectives and test items	
What will the learners bring to the learning situation?	Target population analysis of an in-depth nature, to assess suitability of sequence, pace, specific examples, methods, media, and entry levels	
What shall we do about it all?	Entry test + Learning sequence + Lesson plans + Lesson tests + Final test	

8. The Analysis of the Worth and Practicality of a Solution

8.1 Introduction

By now we have identified a problem, defined it as a discrepancy between what is and what should be, identified alternative types of actions which could contribute to a 'total' solution, identified the role that instruction would play in this solution and identified the overall instructional objectives. If we have already performed a full task or topic analysis, we may also have already specified the intermediate and enabling objectives at the lesson or exercise level of detail.

It is time to take major decisions about where (and how) we are heading before we invest any further time and effort in the project. Even before attempting a level 2 analysis, one should form some working hypotheses about how the instructional system is going to look. One never starts with a completely clean slate. There are always certain obvious restrictions on what one can do, spend, complete on time, get away with, etc. To work on, ignoring these restrictions and constraints, is sheer stupidity. There is another aspect too: we should by now also have some idea of the worth of tackling this problem at all. Is it the most pressing of our problems? Is it worth tackling? Is it perhaps possible to half-tackle it for a tenth of the cost of a full solution? Is a part-solution any use in the context of the problem under study, or do we have to go for an all-or-nothing approach? These two complex questions of worth and practicality should at this point be answered in order to decide whether to go on, and, if so, which of the available alternative approaches to adopt.

The answers to these two questions spring from several sources, the principal ones being:

- ☐ The practical constraints imposed by the context of the problem (the 'wider system')
- ☐ The practical characteristics of the problem itself, as identified in the analyses performed to date
- ☐ The theoretical standpoint that the instructional designer (or his client) has with regard to education or training (the broad aims)
- ☐ Occasional political/personal considerations which have nothing to do with solving the problem, but which must be taken into consideration.

Chapter 3 outlined various viewpoints regarding learning and instruction and laid the groundwork for Part 3. One cannot discuss instructional design in any great depth without first forming a general schema of where we are heading. Mager's comment quoted earlier ('if you don't know where you're going you may end up someplace else') is not only valid in its original context referring to the need for pre-specified objectives, but is also valid with reference to analysis and the derivation of objectives. The analyst who has only a dim idea of how (and why) the results of his analysis will be used will never be a good analyst. He will be an automaton filling in spaces on a standardized analysis sheet by asking standardized questions. If, on the other hand, he has a full understanding of where the whole project is heading, he will be alert to specific characteristics which he uncovers in his analysis that require specially careful or different treatment.

Chapter 5 dealt with level 1 and 2 analysis. The aim of both these levels of analysis is the same: to determine the objectives of instruction, or more specifically to sort out what is worth teaching from what is not. Lest this process appeared to be quite mechanical, it may be worth pointing out that it is not always easy to make the decision on what is worth teaching. Perhaps the process is more mechanical in the industrial training context as one can apparently classify the tasks as worth teaching or not by asking a few key questions such as how important is the task, how frequently is it performed, and how difficult is it?

But in the field of education, the teaching worth of a topic depends very much on the basic viewpoint or theory that one adopts regarding *why* the particular subject is being taught at all: what are the higher order aims of education which we hope to further by teaching the topic and what transfer do we hope to achieve between this topic and other objectives we hope to achieve in the future? It is quite impossible to make the necessary teaching worth discriminations except on the basis of certain theoretical positions or models that one has adopted.

The process is not all that mechanical (or at least it should not be so) even in the training field. Considerations such as personnel development for future promotions, employee interchangeability, the desirability (or not) of understanding the whole manufacturing process and not just the part of it that the trainee will execute (to say nothing of the possibility or desirability of considering the employee's own personal growth as a possible by-product of job-related training) will all exert a strong influence on what should be considered as worth teaching.

Chapter 6 served as an example of the complex analysis and decision making that should go into the definition of whether any training at all should be provided, and if so, what types of training objectives should be selected and what types of other complementary actions should be planned. The type of performance problem analysis described is based firmly on a theoretical model of the causes of job performance deficiency. The questions one asks are derived from this model. Before he starts the analyst has a clear idea of the limits which training has as a solution to job performance problems, and of the other options open to him as alternatives. We are reminded of the object of stage 2 of the systems approach: 'analyse the problem in order to identify *alternative* solutions and select the best one(s).'

Where we are going   All the groundwork for our analysis has already been laid. What we are now going to do is to bring together three bodies of knowledge that we should have:

☐ Knowledge about the problem itself (this was gained in the various analyses we have carried out).
☐ Knowledge about the wider system in which the problem is embedded. We should have this from the systems analysis we performed (see Part 1) and from the analysis of performance problems (if this was relevant to the problem).
☐ Knowledge of the instructional alternatives open to us, which are relevant to the broad characteristics of the problems (as defined by the overall instructional objectives). (In this context, the following chapter is only a brief summary of the global viewpoints commonly held, which spring from various educational philosophies and instructional theories.)

Thus we are going to make our first major planning decisions in the instructional design process. The results of these decisions will outline (tentatively — there is no reason why we cannot change our minds later when we have more information) the overall form that the proposed instructional system will have. Much of this outline will, perhaps, be in the form of estimates but we must have such estimates in order to plan where, when and for how many at a time will instruction take place: how much time will be required to develop and test the instructional system, and what resources (human, material) will be required during this time in order to complete the system on schedule?

Armed with such estimates, one can prepare a course proposal or project proposal which will probably need to be approved by someone (unless you are a 'one-man-band' — the teacher preparing the course he will teach). This 'someone', be he superior or client, will ask questions about cost. You will need to have an estimate which is as realistic as possible at this stage (particularly important to you if you are a consultant, as you will probably sign a contract based on this estimate).

Having asked the cost and been satisfied, he may or may not (but should) ask about the benefits or value which will accrue if he sanctions the cost. This question is more likely to arise spontaneously in the industrial training context than in general education. It is also easier to answer this question in that context. However, there is no reason why one should not try to answer the question (as well as is possible) even in the educational context. Indeed, it is becoming much more common to meet cost-benefit or cost-effectiveness questions being systematically raised in education, with respect to teaching methods. There is a strong movement in the USA promoting the concept of teacher accountability which would have each teacher accountable in a more or less financially quantified manner for the objectives he manages to achieve and those he fails to achieve. So, even if our 'someone' does not raise the question of value, *you* should investigate it, if only for your own good, for he is surely going to raise the question later if anything goes wrong with the project or if he is faced with a conflict of priorities. If educational and training value were quantified more carefully, perhaps we would not witness the massive educational cuts every time there is a whiff of an economic crisis (because most of the activities worth cutting would not have got started in the first place and those actually ongoing would be as valued as similar activities in other sub-systems of society or of the organization, and would, if necessary, take a proportional cut divided with those other activities). However, leaving aside this rather wishful thinking, it pays to estimate the potential value of your solution in order to:

- ☐ See if alternative solutions have different potential values
- ☐ Make sure that the value of the solution is indeed sufficiently superior to the cost in order to justify developing it
- ☐ Make sure that one should be tackling this problem, and not some other one of infinitely greater value (allocation of scarce training resources)
- ☐ Cover yourself against repercussions if anything goes wrong.

8.2 A schema of factors affecting the worth and practicality of a given solution

What could go wrong? Of course, the solution chosen could be completely inappropriate to the problem, but this is not very likely if the instructional designer is any good at all at his job. It could be poorly developed, but this again is something that should be controllable later, for we shall insist on trying out (validating) our system component by component as it is developed and feeding back information required to revise and improve the components. The more revision that is needed, the higher climbs the development cost: that is one thing that might go wrong. But even more serious a source of potential trouble is the wider system — the people and institutions who will eventually be expected to use our system, to make it work and to cooperate with it.

Thus, four main factors should be considered in analysing the worth and the practicality of a given solution:

- ☐ Its *value* (what is to be gained if the solution works?)
- ☐ Its *cost* (both development costs and running costs)

☐ Aspects of *developing the solution* which limit its practicality or its chances of success

☐ Aspects of *implementing and utilizing the solution* which limit its practicality or its chances of success.

Various subsidiary factors concerning the problem and its context combine to establish these four main 'decision factors'. The most important ones have been arranged in a schema (Figure 8.1). We shall now examine each of these subsidiary factors a little more closely, to establish its influence on the main factors.

Figure 8.1

8.3 Factors affecting the value of a solution

Size of the problem: the cost of under-performance

In the industrial training context, this is often easily estimated in terms of lost productivity, cost of errors, unnecessary scrap or wastage of raw materials, too large a workforce, etc. The further the job or occupation for which training is envisaged is separated from the production context, the harder it becomes to be accurate in our estimates of the cost of the problem we hope to eliminate. Supervisory jobs are more difficult than production line jobs; middle and top management jobs are often more difficult still. But all these are relatively easy as compared to the estimating of the cost to the community or to the individual of poor general mathematics skills or a sketchy knowledge of history.

However, if one remembers that one is looking for approximate estimates (and often only relative value between two options), our task becomes more manageable. It is useful to approach the problem by asking questions such as 'how much would one be justified in spending in order to get one person up to standard on the objectives we have identified?' or 'if you could only reach either the objectives of this project, or of another project (which is easier to quantify) which would you rate as more important/valuable/urgent?'. Such, often indirect questioning of the client at least establishes what his priorities are among the problems which face him, even if one does not always come to an agreed cash value. But it is surprising how often this line of questioning does produce a quantified value for the solution. It is a good idea to operate in terms of the value *of one person* reaching standard, as it will later be easier to compare this figure with the cost of training one person.

The intangible benefits

One should not of course ignore the intangible benefits of learning to society, to the work organization or to the learner himself. I am not including in this 'intangible' category such semi-intangibles as the image of the organization. These should be subjected to the cost of underperformance questions. For example the cost of a badly trained and rude telephone receptionist in terms of company image will vary with the company. A firm using telephone sales techniques in a highly competitive market for luxury goods (say yachts) is in a very different position from the local electricity company which has a monopoly. In balance sheet terms, telephonist performance in the first case may be as valuable as top management performance; in the second case its cash value to the sales of the electricity company may be negligible. The electricity company may nevertheless ascribe an intangible goodwill value to the performance of its telephonists, which would place this training need in its position of priority among the other (perhaps more tangible) needs. In the educational context one is often operating entirely at the level of intangibles, but this does not necessarily prevent us from ascribing relative values in order to establish priorities among curriculum alternatives.

The learner's own needs and goals

It is in the educational context particularly that the student and his own opinions regarding educational priorities come to the fore. Indeed, if general education is viewed as a service to the individual rather than a service to the establishment (a view which is now very widespread), the learner's own goals and priorities and the values that he places on alternatives come to be the most important factors to consider. This viewpoint, taken to the extreme, becomes dangerous, as we can see in certain developing countries with predominantly private educational systems. The schools offer what the client wants and the client wants a white collar profession for his children, with the resultant gross over-production of lawyers, doctors and administrators and the almost total absence of the technicians and craftsmen on which the country's rate of development will eventually depend. (Witness also the over-production of unemployable sociologists in the developed world, but at least in this case the economy can stand the luxury.)

So what we ought to be looking for here is a balanced view, taking into consideration the learners' goals together with the goals of society and, if possible, in specific cases the real costs of the problem to society or to the organization.

8.4 Factors affecting the cost of solving the problem

We are considering here specifically the costs of developing an instructional system, on the assumption that instruction has been identified as at least a part of the probable solution. The estimation of the costs of alternative solutions is outside the scope of this book. However, if there is a choice to be made between instruction as a solution and some other alternative (say selection of a higher grade person, or redesigning the job to eliminate the need for instruction) then the costs of these alternative solutions must likewise be estimated in order that the most cost-effective solution can be found.

The number of students expected

It is a good idea to operate in terms of values or costs *per student* in order to facilitate comparison. The cost of an instructional system, in common with almost any other man-made system is made up of a development cost (which may be considered more or less to be a fixed initial investment) and a running cost (which may be taken to be approximately equal for each product — student in this case — as long as the form of operation of the system does not undergo any changes). Thus the total cost per student will vary as shown in Figure 8.2, being very high for very small numbers (unless the development costs were negligible), and diminishing first rapidly and then progressively more slowly to even out at about the running cost (when the number of students who will pass through the same system are going to be very high indeed). Thus the factor of number of people who will benefit from the system is very important in comparing cost with value. This estimate should be made realistically, bearing in mind such factors as the total market for the course being planned and for the graduates of the course, the competition that exists from other institutions for the same market, the probable length of time that the course will remain up to date (before entailing further investment in its revision or replacement), etc.

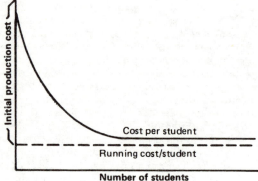

Figure 8.2 *Cost per unit diminishes with use*

The depth of analysis and design required

The 'depth of analysis and design required' factor is considered here as it is the most influential one on the cost of *development* of an instructional system. In the early days of programmed instruction, many people came out in favour of books as opposed to teaching machines on the grounds of the very high costs of teaching machines (as much as say £500 per machine) which are used by one student at one time. A classroom of teaching machines was seen as a very large, and possibly unnecessary investment. Whether it was necessary is another matter, but it soon became obvious to intensive users (as for example in the individualized remedial mathematics system devised by the author and used at the Middlesex Polytechnic since 1967 [Romiszowski 1969]) that the cost of the machines over time was not exorbitant compared to the other costs of operating the system (tutors, for example). However, once one got involved in the generating of one's own programmes (which was not the case in the above project but was the case in several industrial training projects that our centre developed), the cost of software development (for the relatively small market of one multinational company) was such as to render the cost of teaching machines an almost insignificant factor in the total investment costs.

In Chapter 7 we met two levels of analysis. The division between these two levels is an arbitrary one made to assist in this area of 'selection of the depth . . .' We shall meet deeper (level 3 and 4) analysis techniques in Chapter 10. These four levels are really only stages in a possible continuum of deeper and yet deeper detail of analysis. We shall see that there is also a similar range of depths possible in the techniques of instructional development, control and evaluation of the system.

Depth costs money here, in probably much the same way as in deep sea diving. You can go down to one level by skin-diving at relatively negligible costs of investment. You can reach another depth if you invest in an aqualung. To go any further requires the use of a full professional diver's suit.

If you need to go deeper still you need a bathyscaphe. Few people would make the economic blunder of renting a bathyscaphe to descend to lesser depths, for, coupled to the economic foolishness, the bathyscaphe is not even as useful or versatile as an aqualung at shallow depths. The worst plight of all to be in is not to have any idea of the depth you wish to go to, as you may find yourself wading waist deep wearing a full diver's suit, carrying your aqualung and towing your bathyscaphe.

So the sooner you decide on the depth of analysis that the problem merits, the less likely you are to make expensive blunders by filling up reams of analysis forms with data which will never be used. It is not easy to lay down rules for establishing the depth of analysis required. Two factors are involved. First, the ease with which the student's potential learning difficulties are likely to be isolated. This depends much on the skilled judgement of an experienced instructional designer, but also on the real difficulty that typical students have demonstrated in the past. To take an extreme (but not uncommon) example: if just about anyone normally asked to learn a topic (ie anyone who is ready to learn in terms of what he has learned before which is relevant to the desired learning) manages to learn it without the exceptional efforts of an exceptional teacher and in a reasonable time, there is probably no value to be gained from any analysis deeper than that which establishes *what* should be learned.

Thus one might stop at level 1 and certainly would stop at level 2, leaving the rest of the instructional task for an average available teacher to perform. The only exception might be if there are no available teachers or for some other reason we wish to package the instruction and eliminate the teacher's role: in such a case we may need to descend to a level 3 analysis in order to plan the details of the package.

Second, the extent to which the intended instructional system is to be *programmed* (ie to what extent are instructional planning, delivery and evaluation decisions to be left to the discretion of instructors, to occur on an 'on line' basis as the situation seems to demand, or alternatively to what extent are all the instructional events to be designed into the system. This factor is obviously linked with the previous one, as it is difficult to justify the use of an expensive highly pre-programmed approach for teaching a topic which never gave difficulty by traditional instructional methods. However there are other aspects to this factor. A highly programmed approach may not be justified on a very difficult-to-learn topic, if the market for that topic is very small or if the content of the topic is subject to frequent change. We shall come back to considering depth of design and its costs in later chapters.

Already existing, available training/ education: the make/ buy decision

Finally, as far as the cost factor is concerned, we should not forget to consider what is already available. Education and training have in the past shown a propensity to reinvent the wheel. A certain amount of variety, duplication and choice is a very healthy situation. But this is so because it enables students to choose courses more suited to their interests or needs, or may allow teachers to construct courses from available units (eg books) to meet an almost infinite variety of objectives. But when one is venturing into *instructional design*, which is quite expensive, one should justify the cost. One way is to market the instructional system in competition with already existing similar ones (the commercial justification). But if one is not a commercial publisher of instruction then the justification must spring from the lack of something suitable already on the market, or from the observation that what is available is more expensive than the home produced system would be. As a general rule, books and other media (course components) are more cheaply bought than machines (unless the number of people factor is extremely large). However, complete course packages are not necessarily bought in at a cheaper cost than making anew (management development and training is a case in point).

8.5 Factors affecting the practicality of system development

Problems in utilizing or adapting bought in solutions

The use of 'bought in' training may often be cheaper but it may bring unexpected utilization problems which reflect on the practicality of this option. The problems may include the need to modify bought in course material, or to equip with special teaching aids, or in the case of external courses to release participants at inconvenient periods, etc. Most of such problems can be designed out, but, if this proves impossible, one should seriously question the practicality of the option. Also the designing out of the problem will possibly imply an increase in cost, which should be taken into account (the factors all interact with each other).

Time available for system development

We now come to the critical questions of development resources and the most important of these resources is time. The available man hours for the instructional design project will (like no other factor) limit the depth of design that can be undertaken. We may have identified above that a level 3 or even 4 analysis would be useful for the problem on hand, but, if we have two weeks in which to prepare a two week course, we should better forget it. To perform a level 4 analysis and then use the results in the design stage and validate the component exercises typically involves in the order of 20 man hours of instructional development for each hour of instruction if *simple* media are used (eg instructor delivered lesson plans with occasional sophistications such as slides, sound presentations and simple visuals) and is known to take as much as 100 man hours if fully programmed materials are envisaged.

In the abovementioned one-to-one situation there is no way that we could do it. Even in the unlikely case of putting 20 people to work on designing the simpler course we would not be likely to succeed, as a group of that size working on one small project is totally unmanageable. How do you manage 20 people producing 80 hours of instructional materials? How do you divide the task? By the time you have solved that, you have done most of the instructional designing.

The only solution to a rush job of the type outlined is to establish objectives (at level 1) and to delegate the rest of the decisions to be taken more or less on-line by an experienced instructor. And why not? It has worked for centuries for large parts of the curriculum. Let us identify the parts where it has not worked and concentrate our deeper analysis there (but with adequate resources).

Other resources needed to develop the system

Time and human resources availability are interrelated, but not in a totally linear manner, as the example above sought to illustrate. A much more important aspect is the quality of the human resources available for instructional design. Space does not permit an analysis of the qualities required of an instructional designer, nor is this book really the place for such a discussion. Suffice it to say that the systemic thinking capability, which is stressed throughout this book is one of the most important qualities that the instructional designer should seek to develop.

Adequate financial, material and back-up resources for the design team need hardly be mentioned, if it were not for three factors which are commonly overlooked.

The first of these is more obvious: technical back-up for the subject matter expertise that may be required to approve course content as it is identified by the instructional designer. The type and nature and amount of this back-up will vary with the problem, but it is essential to define it at this stage and to check out its availability. This is another factor which must be also taken into account when assessing the total investment cost of the solution.

The second factor is the provision of adequate production back-up, for example adequate typing facilities. Many projects go way over the original time and cost estimates because inadequate or wrong provision was made for this factor. It is not adequate, for example, to rely on the typing pool of the organization to type carefully structured programmed instruction material.

The third factor is the one most often overlooked at this stage, but is probably the most dangerous one to overlook. This is the provision of adequate test facilities in the form of typical members of the target population. An instructional team that does not continually validate its production rapidly grinds to a halt. We shall return to this point later.

8.6 Factors affecting the practicality of system utilization

Adequate resources for implementation, management and evaluation

We come finally to factors which affect the practicality of utilizing the system as it was designed to be used, once it is fully developed. I am reminded of a project I was briefly connected with in a consultancy capacity a few years ago. The project objectives were to develop a correspondence course for adults (in a developing country) who had missed the normal chances of getting a secondary education. My task was to train the writers of the correspondence material (my initial advice was not to originate the material but to use existing bought in material as a basis and write only supplementary exercises, etc, but this advice was not heeded). The team set about writing the course material in five subject areas, a task that took nearly three years, though originally programmed for two. Some time in the second year, I was called on to advise on validation and implementation of the scheme. It then became apparent that whoever had concocted the project had omitted entirely to consider these aspects at an early stage, and that consequently there was no allowance in the budget to pay tutors. All that was foreseen was a letter opening and addressing service. The strongest of pleas and explanations failed to raise an extra budget. The only way to make the system work (as an interim measure till the budget question could get sorted out) was to reschedule the available resources to employ tutors. But this implied a severe restriction on the intake numbers. The course started experimentally with a maximum intake of 400 students (an average of 80 students per subject area), a ridiculously small number for a statewide correspondence course. As far as I know it is still running at this level some years later. How long will it take to recoup the three man years per subject of development time? No more needs be said as regards the consideration of the resources for system operation and control, except perhaps to remind ourselves that once again the quality of the human resources involved is at least as important as the quantity.

Existing political, ethical and philosophical climate in the wider system

Their attitude and their state of preparedness are also significant. Much can and must be done in the way of informing, orienting and training the human resources involved with our system. This will be discussed in later chapters on the implementation stage. But at this stage, when deciding among alternatives to instruction, or among alternative systems of instruction, one has the chance to possibly avoid a particularly troublesome solution. Particularly, one should look out for attitudes or positions adopted by people who can influence the viability of the system, but whom we cannot influence or control with any certainty.

Existing habits, life-styles and pre-dispositions of the intended students

Finally, many instructional systems have been rendered useless by the intended students themselves: they did not like the system; they were not accustomed to studying in the manner required by the system; their other commitments did not allow them to devote the time or to come at the appointed hour or to finish the course, etc. One cannot please everyone all the time, but equally one cannot run a successful system if it pleases no one most of the time. I am reminded of the early application of programmed learning and videotaped lessons on the Zuni Indian reservations in Arizona for the specific reason that these media were available at any time of day to any size of group. The Zuni culture does not recognize fixed start and finish times for any activity, including their religious ceremonies, and for this reason all attempts at traditional schooling had failed. This was a brave attempt to adapt the system to unusual trainee factors. Incidentally, this system did not last much longer than the research grant supporting it. The cost/value factors were all against it in the real world outside the gates of the educational research establishment.

8.7 Developing the schema

We have come to the end of our discussion of the individual factors which
influence the worth and the practicality of a given solution. We have seen that
the factors interact with each other. The reader no doubt noticed other factors
or other interactions between the factors as the discussion unfolded. If so, he
should add these observations to the conceptual schema presented to tie this
chapter's ideas together. The object is that it should become your schema, not
my schema. This, incidentally applies to all the schemata presented in the
various sections of this book: draw over them adding your own relationships
and concepts and modifying mine. If you come up with any modifications you
think I might like to know about, post them to the publisher.

8.8 Making the final decision

How do we decide, finally, between alternative solutions? Insofar as the
practicality factor is concerned, the answers we will now have for our solution
might vary from *yes* (there are no identified factors threatening practicality of
the solution) to *no* (there are insurmountable barriers to practicality) through
perhaps (practical difficulties are foreseen but there are clear and feasible
actions that can be taken to avoid or eliminate the difficulties — these actions
involve the following costs and have the following probabilities of success . . .).
A set of answers such as this can readily be ordered into priority.

The worth question is always a case of *relative worth*. This being the case,
we can use a pseudo-mathematical equation to calculate the priorities. The
equation is pseudo-mathematical as the values one calculates have no absolute
meaning. All one can do is to compare the values obtained for various solutions
against each other. The equation quoted by Gilbert (1967) is

$$P = \frac{V N}{C}$$

where P = Priority
V = Value of solution
N = Number of people
C = Cost of solution

A slight problem arises when you cannot predict the number of people with
any degree of accuracy. This is quite common in education, as it is often not
known how popular a given course will be and thus how often it will be
repeated. An approach to use in this case is to use a break-even chart.
Figure 8.3 compares two courses, one with a high development (fixed) cost
and a moderate running cost (variable in proportion to the number of students

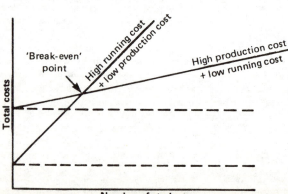

Figure 8.3 *The break-even point between two alternative courses*

using the course) and the other course with a low development cost but with high running costs. Assuming that the two courses have the same objectives and therefore the same value (this is important as it cancels the value out of the equation), the graph can be used to establish worth over time. The two alternatives might for example be a traditionally planned, teacher delivered version and a packaged version of the same course. We see that initially, with small usage, the teacher delivered version (low production cost/high running cost) works out cheaper, but with greater student numbers, the break-even point is passed and the packaged version (high production cost/low running cost) becomes the more economical alternative. Our problem of estimating student numbers is thus reduced to estimating if it is more likely that total student numbers will remain below the break-even point value, or are we fairly certain that this value will be exceeded.

Thus, we have our solutions rated in order of priority in terms of *practicality* (and some possibly already eliminated as impractical) and in terms of *worth*. You may have a solution which is rated near the top on both scales. If you get the inverse, with every solution rated highly on one scale coming at the bottom of the other, that is what the manager in your project is paid for: to make impossible decisions on flimsy evidence. At least it is good to know you tried. Which way you flip the coin might depend on such considerations as whether you are working in England or in Saudi Arabia. And there is nothing to stop you from looking for yet other possible solutions to solve the problem.

8.9 Going ahead

While making the worth and practicality decisions, you will be assembling the information necessary for three working documents which should then be prepared in full for the solution that is finally selected. These working documents are:

To obtain approval, and management support

1. *The broad proposal.* This is necessary to present the chosen solution to all concerned. It summarizes the decisions that can be taken at this point and the estimates that can be made. Typically it would include:

   ☐ The broad instructional objectives
   ☐ The probable duration, locale, methods, media, instructors, etc
   ☐ The way in which the achievement of the objectives will be evaluated
   ☐ The expected value and benefits that should accrue
   ☐ The estimated cost of development and running
   ☐ Any steps which must be taken to complement the solution
   ☐ Any steps which must be taken to ensure utilization
   ☐ Any special steps which must be taken to enable the smooth development of the solution to take place.

To assemble the necessary resources

2. *The statement of necessary resources.* This document will quantify your estimates of the resources necessary for instructional development. Typically it would include:

   ☐ The estimate of man months of each type of human resource
   ☐ The specification of the technical expertise requirements
   ☐ The specification of the back-up services required
   ☐ The specification of the validation facilities needed.

To plan the resources in time and to control progress

3. *The project management plan.* This is essentially the time chart to be used for project control, using the outsiders (experts and sample students) as management control points to check on adherence to the planned schedule.

PART 3
Macro-design

Overview

This section deals with the design of instructional systems at the *macro* level: the design of the overall plan, including the sequence and structure of the units, the principal methods to be used for each lesson, the group structure and the control and evaluation systems to be employed.

The detailed *micro* level of designing individual lessons and exercises and producing the materials will be introduced here and considered fully in Volume II.

Chapter 9. Examines the principal theoretical viewpoints on learning and instruction. In particular, the views of Skinner, Gilbert, Gagné, Piaget, Bruner, Ausubel and Landa on the objectives of instruction, the methods to be used and the individualization of the process. Finally, *mastery*, *cyclic* and *cybernetic* learning models are compared.

Chapter 10. Examines some of the more detailed models for instructional analysis and design, classifying them at two levels of detail. Level 3 approaches include the models of Gagné (categories of learning), of Mager and Beach (performance categories) and the semi-algorithmic CRAMP model developed at Cambridge (UK). Level 4 approaches include Seymour's method of skills analysis, Gilbert's mathetics and Landa's mental operations approach.

Chapter 11. Identifies some neglected areas of learning, not adequately covered by the models discussed in Chapter 10. These include interactive skills, self-control and self-actualization skills, psychomotor skills (especially those that involve planning strategies) and problem-solving skills. The need for a four-domain classification of skills is suggested, as is the need to distinguish more carefully between the acquiring of *knowledge* (information problems) and the acquiring of *skill* (performance problems).

Chapter 12. Develops a comprehensive classification of knowledge and skill categories, presenting them in the form of visual schemata. These schemata are used as the basis for the approach to instructional design developed later. The classifications presented here are alternatives to other approaches such as the Bloom taxonomies or the Gagné hierarchy.

Chapter 13. Summarizes the argument so far and indicates where we are heading. Four levels of instructional design are defined, each based on data gleaned from the four levels of analysis defined previously. These four levels approximate to designing the structure of the instructional system as a whole (the curriculum), a specific unit of the system (a module), individual lessons and the detailed steps of the activities or exercises that compose the lesson. The remainder of Part 3 deals with the first two levels.

Chapter 14. Discusses some alternatives for the overall structure and sequence within a course curriculum. Some techniques for the systematic planning of curricula are presented and illustrated.

Chapter 15. Discusses the selection of the overall strategies for a course and later of the specific methods to be used in specific modules or lessons. The selection process is linked to the use of the knowledge and skill schemata developed in Chapter 12. A directory of commonly used methods of instruction is appended, in the form of a set of information maps.

Chapter 16. Considers the choice of group size and structure, again relating the selection process to the knowledge and skills schemata developed earlier. Some aspects of group dynamics are also considered. A directory of commonly used group structures for various sizes of group is appended.

Chapter 17. Examines the question of media selection from the economic/ practical point of view and also from the viewpoint of effective communication and learning. Charts and checklists are presented as aids to media selection.

Chapter 18. Examines the control strategies that may be adopted when designing an instructional system. Norm-referenced and criterion-referenced measures are contrasted, as are also the factors that can be used to govern the time that the instructional process continues. Prescriptive, democratic and cybernetic styles of control are contrasted and some of the resultant control strategies are compared.

Chapter 19. Discusses the purposes and methods of evaluation, and the levels at which it can be performed. The use of formative and summative evaluation is examined. The problems of long-term evaluation of education are emphasized. A directory of specific evaluation techniques, to be used at various levels in the system, is appended in the form of information maps.

Chapter 20. Summarizes and concludes the analysis in this book, and introduces the themes to be discussed in Volume II.

9. Theories of Learning and Instruction

9.1 The educational psychology battleground

Teaching, or instruction (this term is preferred in the present context), has as its purpose the promotion of learning in individuals. Therefore theories of instruction are necessarily based on theories of learning. The history of learning theory has been eventful and colourful, marked by a series of feuds between partisan groups fighting under different names in different epochs.

Old battles

We have had associationists fighting the humanists, the connectionists against the *gestalt* school, and the behaviourists at loggerheads with the cognitive psychologists. Despite these changes in name, however, the battles fought in each epoch have been remarkedly similar. Each generation of psychologists has fought skirmishes on, for example, the nature/nurture controversy, the rote learning/meaningful learning question, and the aims/means argument.

Today there is a growing realization that such questions are not resolvable one way or the other, but that there is an element of validity in all the positions: that both nature (heredity) and nurture (experience) play important parts in the learning process; that some things (eg bare facts) are best learned by rote while other things (eg concepts) are better learned in some meaningful context; that one may have a variety of different aims (objectives) for teaching a topic and that these may require a variety of different instructional methods.

However, the old battle cries are still with us, often in modern updated jargon. Currently fashionable controversies include discovery *versus* exposition in teaching; products *versus* processes of learning, and learning environments *versus* knowledge structures as the keys to the control of instruction.

Some emerging controversies include algorithmic/heuristic problem-solving strategies, and deductive/conversational programming of instruction.

Is there anything new under the sun?

On analysis, however, many of these 'new' controversies are found to bear remarkable resemblances to the older ones. Indeed it is interesting to note that most of the current catch-phrases in mathematical education have been around for a long time. Young (1906) when writing on the teaching of mathematics, makes a very useful distinction between methods and modes of instruction (current equivalent terminology might be strategies and tactics). Under the methods title he lists, among others, the discovery or heuristic method, the laboratory method, and the expository method. Among his modes one finds the lecture, the Socratic dialogue, inductive and deductive presentations, and so on. It is true that Young's usage of these terms sometimes differs slightly from current usage, but one is left wondering just how many new ideas really are all that new.

Indeed one should add that current usage of many such terms is so unstandardized that it is not easy to see whether any really important changes in the basic premises underlying learning and instructional theories have taken place since the turn of the century.

An analysis of some major current theoretical viewpoints on learning and instruction, considering both their characteristics and their origins, will help to clarify the position.

9.2 The behaviourist position as exemplified by Skinner

This viewpoint, exemplified by the position of Skinner (1961b) is based on a definition of learning as an observable change in behaviour (not caused by physical maturation or growth). The structure of internal thinking and learning processes is considered irrelevant to the process of instruction, which is seen as the structuring of the environment in such a way as to maximize the probability of the desired new behaviour being learned. Desired behaviours are taught by a series of successive approximations, beginning from an already established behaviour and working towards the desired behaviour. The process is based on the principle of reinforcement expounded by Skinner, a somewhat more precise restatement of Thorndike's law of effect (1927).

Thorndike's law of effect   The law of effect states the observed phenomenon that behaviour which produces desirable or pleasant effects tends to be repeated (the corollary being that behaviour resulting in unpleasant effects tends not to be repeated).

Reinforcement theory   Skinner defined reinforcement of behaviour as the supplying of a reinforcer in order to increase the probability of given behaviour being exhibited (eg food for a hungry dog as a reward for 'begging'). A reinforcer is defined as 'any object or event which is found to reinforce', a delightfully circular definition. Instruction is equated to the conditioning of desired behaviour — termed operant conditioning. An operant is a unit of behaviour (a response), together with the environmental condition which triggers it off (the stimulus).

The instructor or trainer:

1. Arranges the stimulus.
2. Observes the learner's response.
3. Reinforces desired responses and withholds reinforcement if responses are not desired. (Sometimes punishment of undesired responses is employed, but it is not favoured.)

Shaping of behaviour   Complex behaviours are shaped by first reinforcing any already learned behaviour which approximates to the desired, and then in gradual stages only reinforcing successively closer approximation. Using the dog example, the stages might be: sitting when food is shown, sitting on haunches, but raising a paw, sitting but raising both front paws off the ground momentarily, progressively longer periods of balancing on haunches. In this example, the food is the reinforcer (the trainer arranges that this is so by not feeding the dog some time before training) and also the stimulus for the 'begging' response, but generally stimulus and reinforcer may be quite separate objects or events. They always have one characteristic in common however — they are external to the learner. The trainer manipulates and controls the learner's environment, in order to control and shape the learner's behaviour.

A black box theory   Thus Skinner's theory of instruction requires no theory of learning concerning the internal learning processes. Using systems terminology, it is an input/output learning theory, treating the learner as a 'black box'.

Two forms of conditioning   One should distinguish Skinner's operant conditioning from the 'classical' conditioning described by Pavlov. Pavlov's dogs learned to exhibit a well established and *natural behaviour* (salivating) in a *new stimulus situation* (ringing bell) by the expedient of fusing the new stimulus of the bell with the 'natural' stimulus of the sight of food. Skinner's dog, in the example above, is learning an entirely *new behaviour* to a *familiar stimulus*.

Classical conditioning serves as a paradigm for relatively little human learning, mainly very early infant learning of reflex responses and in later life the inadvertent learning of fears, attitudes and habits. It is consequently of limited relevance to the teaching of mathematics or any academic discipline. Operant conditioning, on the other hand, has been applied to the learning of subject matters, through the techniques of programmed instruction. This involved a certain amount of intellectual gymnastics (in order to equate the learning of verbal information in small units to the successive approximations to desired behaviour used as steps in the animal training laboratory) and sweeping generalizations (eg that success in intellectual tasks is reinforcing for all human learners).

The rise and fall of programmed instruction

Early developments in programmed instruction showed great promise, as De Vault and Kriewall (1969) put it:

> After a brief flurry, stirred up by the belief that a solution had been found, hopes waned considerably while criticism of the process grew. Not only was it hard to find convincing evidence that the quality of the learning experience had been enhanced by the use of these materials, but also there was a growing conviction that indeed the experience provided by such materials was the very opposite of individualization, at least insofar as the purpose was concerned. Every learner travelled the same path to the same end, varying only in the time at which he arrived at the prescribed objective.

Growth of the programming process

Although school use of programmed instruction failed to grow, indeed declined, development of the technique continued. Alternatives to the linear format included the 'branching' programmes pioneered by Crowder (1963) and the 'adjunct' programmes (based on self-marked multiple-choice testing) which actually predated Skinner's work (Pressey, 1926) was briefly in vogue. The more important long-term developments occurred in the field of programme planning techniques. Mager (1962) refined a methodology for stating objectives in behavioural terms which has had impact well outside the strict confines of programmed instruction. Gilbert (1962) developed a methodology for the

Gilbert's mathetics

analysis of behaviour and design of training which, although not generally accepted, still forms the basis of a highly successful approach to instructional problems, particularly in the industrial training field. His methodology, which he termed mathetics* classified behaviour as composed of combinations of three basic structures: chains, multiple discriminations and generalizations. He developed a basic instructional model, involving three stages to any exercise (he termed these demonstrate, prompt and release), subsidiary tactics for each of the three basic behavioural structures, and powerful rules for deciding what theoretical content to include, how to select examples, how to sequence instruction, etc.

The mathetics methodology in its original form did not live up to Gilbert's claims of being *the* technology of education. It proved well adapted to training situations where the final outcomes of instruction are observable behaviours, but somewhat difficult to use in academic disciplines, where subject matter rather than job performance was the starting point for instructional design. In this domain the rule and example (RULEG) programming technique developed by Evans *et al* (1962) was more popular. Gilbert has more recently attempted to extend the power of mathetics to the academic disciplines, with some success (Gilbert 1967 and 1969).

However, the long-term importance of mathetics, and of the other techniques associated with the beginnings of programmed instruction lies not so much in their elegance (or lack of it) as in the catalytic effect they have had on the development of theories of instruction which are capable of being tested out and verified. The programmed instruction movement was the first instructional methodology to lay itself open to experimental verification at every stage. Empirical testing and revision were key points in the process of programme development and have since become generally accepted.as key elements in any process of instructional design. In particular, the stating of instructional outcomes as specific observable behaviours has become a common practice even among instructors who would reject all other aspects of the behaviourist model of learning.

Finally, many of the behaviourist concepts have become fused into more complex, more complete theories of instruction. A good example of such an

---

*Greek: mathesis: the process of learning; mathetic: pertaining to learning; mathematic: something learned, a science. 1816 usage: mathetic exercises: exercises by which progress is made and proficiency obtained (*Source:* Oxford English Dictionary)

eclectic theory is that of Robert Gagné.

9.3 The neo-behaviourist viewpoint exemplified by R Gagné

Gagné has produced a series of books and dissertations over the last decade, expounding his views on learning and instruction (Gagné, 1965, 1970, 1974). A study of these reveals a gradual, but constant, change and evolution in his viewpoint. Certain characteristics have remained throughout and these distinguish him from the strict behaviourists on two points:

1. He admits a large variety of different types of learning (called variously, learning categories, learning outcomes, or, recently, intellectual skills). Each type of learning is associated with characteristic strategies of instruction.
2. He admits to some interest in the functioning of the internal mental processes which govern learning.

Eight categories of learning (Gagné 1965)

In his early work, Robert Gagné (1965) suggests a hierarchical list of eight categories of learning. The list is hierarchical in the sense that it proceeds from very simple conditioning-type learning, up to complex learning such as that involved in problem-solving. The list is also hierarchical in the sense that lower levels of learning are prerequisite to higher levels. Figure 9.1 presents the eight categories and illustrates their hierarchical structure. A few words about these categories may help to relate Gagné's work to our earlier discussion.

Gagné distinguished between eight different types of learning, as follows:

Signals

1. Signal learning. This may be equated with the Pavlovian conditioned response. The subject learns that a given event is the signal for another event, as the dinner bell was the signal for Pavlov's dogs. So he responds to the signal as he would to the event, ie instead of salivating when dinner arrived the dogs did so at the signal. Similarly, a child may learn that its mother's frown is the signal of pain to come, so it responds to the frown as it would to the pain itself.

It is characteristic of this type of learning that the stimulus and the response must be closely associated in time: the stimulus of course precedes the response, and it will not produce the desired learning if it takes place too many seconds before the response.

2. Stimulus/response learning. This is differentiated from signal learning in that the response is not a generalized emotional one, but a very precise act. Gagné gives the following characteristics of this type of learning:

(a) The learning is typically gradual: some repetition of the association between the stimulus and the response is usually necessary.
(b) The response becomes more precise as the repetitions take place (this is what Skinner calls 'shaping').
(c) The controlling stimulus becomes more precise.
(d) There is reward, or reinforcement, for exhibiting the required response and there is no reward when the behaviour is incorrect.

Chains

3. Chaining. Chaining is the type of learning we have already described when discussing Gilbert's work. Characteristics of this type of learning are:

(a) The individual links in the chain must be established first.
(b) Again time is a factor: the events in the chain must occur close together in time.
(c) If both the other two conditions are satisfied, learning a chain is not a gradual process, but occurs on a single occasion. In practice the occasion may have to be repeated, because the individual links may not be well enough established.

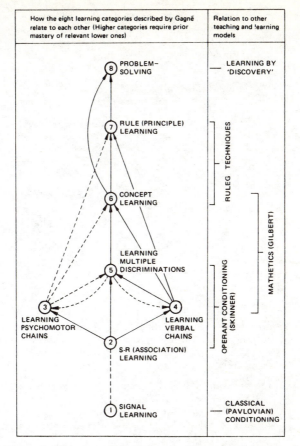

| How the eight learning categories described by Gagné relate to each other (Higher categories require prior mastery of relevant lower ones) | Relation to other teaching and learning models |

Figure 9.1 *Diagram illustrating the hierarchical nature of Gagné's categories of learning**

* The arrows indicate that certain learning categories are always (solid arrow) or occasionally (dotted arrow) prerequisite to the learning of other categories. The diagram also shows (on the right) the eclectic nature of Gagné's hierarchy, by indicating how it overlaps with the areas of work of other authors discussed.

Source: Romiszowski (1974)

Verbal association

4. Verbal chaining. Gagné says 'verbal association might well be classified as only a sub-variety of chaining . . . But because these chains are verbal and because they explain the remarkable versatility of human processes, verbal association has some unique characteristics.' He gives the example of a man learning the French for 'match' (alumette) in the following way: the word 'match' acts as a stimulus for the mental picture of a match. A match 'illuminates'. The syllable 'lum' occurs in illuminate as it does in alumette, so a chain is established.

The conditions for effective learning of verbal chains, according to Gagné, are:

(a) Each link must be established previously: the link in the individual's mind between the word match and the object match must be clear.
(b) 'Response differentiation' must have taken place; ie the individual must know how to say 'alumette' well enough so that the key syllable 'lum' means something to him and can be used as a link with the word 'illuminate'.

(c) A 'coding connection' (Gilbert uses the term mediator) must be established. The mental picture of a flaming match and the word illuminate must be associated. Clearly, people will tend to use different coding connections, depending on their previous history; highly verbal people will have more codes available than less verbal people.

Discrimi-
nations

5. Discrimination learning. This is the same category as Gilbert's multiple discriminations. The conditions of this type of learning are as follows:

(a) Necessary stimuli/responses must already be established.
(b) Interference from conflicting stimuli must be reduced to a minimum. That is to say, distinctions must be emphasized; interference is anything which might add to confusion of the stimuli and uncertainty about which of several responses is required.

Concepts

6. Concept learning. This may be compared to the 'generalization' of mathetics. In this form of learning a stimulus is classified in terms of its abstract properties, as shape, position, number etc. A child learns that a green block A is called a cube. It is then told that block B, which is twice the size of A and red in colour, is also a cube. Concept learning is the type of learning which enables him to identify a cube on the basis of an internalized representation (an idea) which is independent of the dissimilarities of the two objects — in the Platonic sense, an 'idea of cubeness'. Gagné draws a distinction between a 'concrete concept', which depends on the observable properties of objects, and a 'defined concept', which identifies a class of objects whose common properties are not determinable by observation, but are a matter of verbal definition. (For example, a broom and a screwdriver are both 'tools', but cannot be observed to have much else in common.) Conditions for this type of learning are:

(a) Necessary stimuli/responses must be established.
(b) A variety of stimuli must be presented, so that the conceptual property common to all of them can be discriminated.
(c) The learning of a new concept may be gradual, because of the need for a variety of stimuli.

Rules or
principles

7. Rule learning. In a formal sense, a rule is a chain of two or more concepts. The simplest type of rule may be 'if A, then B', eg 'if two angles in a triangle are equal, then the sides opposite the angles are equal'. This may be distinguished from a simple verbal fact to be memorized in that if the rule is correctly learned, then the learner will be able to apply it in all relevant situations, and he may not necessarily be able to state the rule in words. The conditions for this type of learning are as follows:

(a) The concepts to be linked must be clearly established: the learner must know what a 'feminine noun' is and what the 'feminine article' is.
(b) A simple process of chaining can then take place.
(c) The learning of a rule can take place on a single occasion.

Problem-
solving skills

8. Problem-solving. Once a human being has acquired some rules he can combine these rules into a great variety of higher order rules. In doing this he can use what he already knows to solve problems which are new to him, (though they may or may not be so to other people). This problem-solving takes place at all levels, from Joe Bloggs working out how to change a tyre without getting his clothes dirty, to Einstein producing the theory of relativity. The conditions of this type of learning are as follows:

(a) The learner must be able to identify the essential features of the response that will be the solution before he arrives at the solution.
(b) Relevant rules are used and recalled.
(c) The recalled rules are combined so that a new rule emerges. (Gagné admits little is known about the nature of this combining event.)

(d) Though the overall process of solving a problem may take a very long time, Gagné thinks that the solution is actually arrived at in a flash of insight.

The eclectic nature of Gagné's model

Thus we see that Gagné's model embraces the models of Skinner and of Gilbert, which we presented earlier. It also includes the very primitive type of Pavlovian conditioning which is only of marginal concern to teachers above the kindergarten level. Where it differs is that it extends these models to define categories of higher order learning. One point it makes is to stress just how much success at higher orders depends on adequate mastery of lower order learning. Another important point that Gagné (1970) makes concerning rule learning and problem-solving is that the outcomes of these two types of learning are essentially the same: the difference lies in the processes by which the learning took place. A higher order rule, formed from two or more subsidiary rules may be learned as a 'type seven' task, if the teacher recalls the relevant rules and demonstrates how they combine to give a more powerful rule. This he would do by definition and example — the expository approach.

Alternatively, the teacher might begin by presenting an example as a new problem to be solved. The learner must recall the relevant simpler rules and discover the higher order rule necessary to solve the problem, although the teacher would normally prompt or guide this process along by his use of hints and leading questions — the guided discovery approach.

Thus, for higher order intellectual learning, Gagné presents two alternative strategies — the expository (from rule to examples) strategy, which he favours on the grounds of consuming less learning time in general, and the guided discovery (from examples to rule) strategy, which he favours when long-term recall and/or transfer to other similar learning tasks is required.

In a recent book (Gagné 1974) he has further extended his model to include yet more types of learning and approach yet closer to the cognitive school, which we now turn to discuss.

9.4 The cognitive/developmental viewpoint as exemplified by Piaget and Bruner

The influence of Jerome Bruner on teaching (particularly elementary school mathematics in the USA) has been immense. He is probably the foremost living proponent of the discovery approach in mathematical education. However, he is not be any means the inventor of the discovery approach. As already noted, this concept was well known in mathematics education at the beginning of the century (Young 1906). Bruner's approach (1966) to discovery learning is characterized by three stages, which he calls enactive, iconic and symbolic. These stages are firmly based on the developmental psychology of Jean Piaget. Piaget was perhaps the most prolific researcher in developmental psychology. His interests have centred on the study and definition of the stages of cognitive development of the child. We shall not reiterate here the Piagetian stages of cognitive development. This is available in many other works (Piaget 1957, 1965). We shall concentrate on the characteristics of Piaget's view of the growth of intelligence as they may relate to the process of instruction.

Piaget's view of learning and development

Piaget views the development of intelligence as part of the more general process of biological development. Gallagher (1964) has suggested five major themes running through Piaget's work.

1. Continuous and progressive changes take place in the structures of behaviour and thought in the developing child.
2. Successive structures make their appearance in a fixed order.
3. The nature of accommodation (adaptive change to outer circumstances) suggests that the rate of development is, to a considerable degree, a function of the child's encounters with his environment.

4. Thought processes are conceived to originate through a process of internalizing actions. Intelligence increases as thought processes are loosened from their basis in perception and action and thereby become reversible, transitive, associative, and so on.

5. A close relationship exists between thought processes and properties of formal logic.

Stages of a child's development

For Piaget the child is a developing organism passing through biologically determined cognitive stages. These stages are more or less age-related, although wide variations in cultures or environments will yield differences in individual rates of development. One might view the process of cognitive growth as a drama. The script or scenario describing the drama's plot and characters is given by the biological component. The role of the director, that of determining the onset and pace of the episodes, is a function of the environment.

Although development is a continuous process of structural change, it is still possible to characterize certain growth periods by the formal logical structures most useful for describing the child's cognitive functioning during that time span. These growth periods, when a temporary stability of cognitive functioning is achieved, define for Piaget the major stages of intellectual growth.

The principle of auto-regulation

There is one other principle which is extremely important for an understanding of Piaget's system and its impact on education. This is the principle of autoregulation or equilibration. Piaget sees the development of intelligence as a sequence of successive disequilibria followed by adaptations leading to new states of equilibrium. The imbalance can occur because of a change occurring naturally as the organism matures. It can also occur in reaction to an input from the environment. Since disequilibrium is uncomfortable, the child must accommodate to new situations through active modification of his present cognitive structure.

Piaget observes that only in man can intelligence develop to the point where the domain of ideas and symbols can serve as the environmental source of disequilibrium. That is, we can construct intellectual universes, for example, 'transintuitive spaces, which can stimulate our own cognitive growth as surely as the confrontation by a baby with the problem of reaching his pacifier can lead to new insights of equilibria on his part' (Shulman 1966).

Piaget has written little specifically directed at problems of education. He has repeatedly disavowed any expertise in the pedagogical domain. Yet, either directly or through such interpreters as Bruner, his influence has been strongly felt.

Piaget's emphasis upon action as a prerequisite of the internalization of cognitive operations has stimulated the focus upon direct manipulation of concrete materials in the early grades. His description of cognitive development occurring through autoregulation has reinforced tendencies to emphasize pupil-initiated, problem-solving activities. Much of the work of such practical innovators as Z P Dienes (1960, 1964) and such theoreticians as Bruner is directly based on Piaget.

Bruner's theory of instruction

The general learning process described by Bruner (1966) occurs in the following manner. First, the child finds in his manipulation of the materials regularities that correspond with intuitive regularities he has already come to understand. Notice that what the child does, according to Bruner, is to find some sort of match between what he is doing in the outside world and some models or templates that he has already grasped intellectually. For Bruner, it is rarely something outside the learner that is discovered. Instead, the discovery involves an internal reorganization of previously known ideas in order to establish a better fit between those ideas and the regularities of an encounter to which the learner has had to accommodate.

Bruner almost always begins with a focus on the production and manipulation of materials. He describes the child as moving through three levels of representation as he learns. The first level is the enactive level, where the child manipulates materials directly. He then progresses to the iconic level, where he deals with mental images of objects but does not manipulate them directly. Finally he moves to the symbolic level, where he is strictly manipulating symbols and no longer mental images of objects. This sequence is based on Bruner's interpretation of Piaget's developmental theory. The combination of these concepts of manipulation of actual materials as part of a developmental model and the Socratic notion of learning as internal reorganization into a learning by discovery approach is the unique contribution of Bruner.

Bruner's position is in strong opposition to both Skinner's and Gagné's (1970) in that he rates the internal thought processes as of paramount importance, and the final outputs, or products, of secondary and much lower importance. The behaviourist viewpoint disregards internal processes altogether, using observable behaviours as the only measure by which to assess instruction. Gagné would allow both, though rating specific skills higher than generalized mental capabilities. However, in his recent writings (1974, 1975) Gagné has moved much closer to the cognitive position adopted by Bruner.

9.5 The subject matter viewpoint as exemplified by Ausubel

David Ausubel (1968) has been a powerful (though perhaps now a waning) influence on instructional thinking. He stands in opposition to the discovery movement, claiming that much of the apparent superiority of discovery over exposition is due to research generally comparing discovery techniques with rote learning approaches. Ausubel argues that much instruction, particularly at higher levels of education, is (and has always been) successfully performed by the process of exposition leading to *meaningful reception learning*.

He states (1968):

In reception learning (rote *or* meaningful) the entire content of what is to be learned is presented to the learner in final form. The learning task does not involve any independent discovery on his part. He is required only to internalize or incorporate the material . . . that is presented to him so that it is available or reproducible at some future date. In the case of meaningful reception learning, the potentially meaningful task or material is comprehended or made meaningful in the process of internalization. In the case of rote reception learning, the learning task either is not potentially meaningful or is not made meaningful in the process of internalization.

The essential feature of discovery learning . . . is that the principal content of what is to be learned is not given but must be discovered by the learner before he can incorporate it meaningfully into his cognitive structure. The distinctive and prior learning task, in other words, is to discover something . . . The first phase of discovery learning involves a process quite different from that of reception learning. The learner must reorganize or transform the integrated combination in such a way as to generate a desired end-product or discover a missing means/end relationship. After discovery learning itself is completed, the discovered content is made meaningful in much the same way that presented content is made meaningful in reception learning.

It is evident, therefore, that reception and discovery learning are two quite different kinds of processes, and . . . that most classroom instruction is organized along the lines of reception learning. Verbal reception learning is not necessarily rote in character. Much ideational material (concepts, generalizations) can be internalized and retained meaningfully without prior problem-solving experience, and at no stage of development does the learner have to discover principles independently in order to be able to understand and use them meaningfully.

9.6 The cybernetic viewpoint as exemplified by Landa

Leo Nakhmanovich Landa's work has been based much more on the European psychological tradition, oriented (as in the *gestalt* school) much more towards the study of internal thought processes than has been the case in the USA. It extends over a considerable period of years, parallel to the years during which most of the previously mentioned American work was published. Already in 1955 his thesis on the *Formation in Students of General Methods of Reasoning* was exploring algorithmic and heuristic methods of instruction, the construction of mathematical models of the learning and teaching process and the automatization and programming of instruction in problem-solving, all of which became important areas of research in the USA only a decade or so later. His works have only recently become available in English, with the publication in 1974 in the United States of *Algorithmization in Learning and Instruction*, first published in Russian in 1966. Much of his more recent work, published in the Soviet Union as separate papers, has appeared in the USA in 1976 as a second book *Instructional Regulation and Control – Cybernetics, Algorithmization, and Heuristics in Education.*

These works show that although working in parallel with, and geographically isolated from, North American thinkers, he was not uninformed of developments in the West. However, his different psychological background and his training in mathematics and cybernetics have combined to form a view of learning and instruction which often resolves apparent differences between opposing psychological camps.

His first book (Landa 1974) summarizes two decades of research on the learning teaching processes. Most of this work was concerned with the intellectual processes involved in the learning of mathematics and Russian grammar.

Subsequent work was concerned with investigations on how to establish problem-solving algorithms, how to identify intellectual operations which are not capable of algorithmicization, how to teach by the use of algorithms and how to teach students to develop their own algorithms for the solution of new problems.

Landa has therefore been little concerned with the lower-level type of learning, such as stimulus/response or chaining. He has been primarily interested in problem-solving activity (as in the case of geometrical proofs) and rule-following activity (as in the rules of grammar).

Mental operations used in applying rules

These two types of learning seem to correspond to Gagné's higher order categories. However, Gagné discusses these somewhat superficially and with examples drawn almost exclusively from the early elementary grades. It will therefore be interesting for our purposes to study Landa's position, based on more extensive research with older students.

In connection with rules and rule-learning Landa states:

> The application of rules, particularly the recognition of situations where the rule is applicable, is achieved by means of special operations. Just as it is impossible to solve a manufacturing problem (for example, to make something) without carrying out specific component manipulations (operations), it is also impossible to solve an intellectual problem (a grammatical, mathematical problem or one pertaining to physics, etc) without carrying out specific intellectual operations. The execution of a specific aggregate of intellectual operations to solve a problem is an objective necessity. But if this is so, then it is incorrect to think that some problems may be solved without executing the operations.
>
> The opinions that something is 'obvious at once', that something 'is immediately grasped' without any operations, 'comes to mind of itself', etc are illusions engendered by the fact that there is no awareness of many operations because of their automatization.

Landa draws our attention to the recognition of situations when and where the rule is applicable. Rule learning is incomplete until the learner can apply the rule correctly and on *appropriate occasions*. This latter aspect is not stressed by Gagné. For Gagné, the student has learned the rules for simplifying fractions when he can respond correctly to the request 'simplify this fraction in order to . . . .' For Landa a rule has been learned only once the student can respond to the request 'show me what you should do to this fraction in order to . . . .' To use Gagné-type terminology, Landa considers that rule mastery is made up of two elements: discrimination of appropriate and inappropriate occasions for application of the rule, and correct application of the rule. Landa refers to the first of these as the logical thinking component. He has the following to say concerning logical thinking:

The logical thinking component in applying a rule, and how to teach it

In pedagogy, there exist two ways to form habits of logical thinking. The first way is the unconscious mastery of logical methods by the students. This takes place during the process in which specific material from the textbooks is learned and during the solution of problems by practice. The second way is that of conscious mastery of those methods when the teacher specially draws the students' attention to those logical means with whose help the solutions of problems are achieved.

Progressive-minded pedagogues of the past always attributed great importance to the special instruction of students in methods of logical thinking. The majority of contemporary pedagogues also admit the necessity of such instruction. Then why is the first way still the most prevalent one in practice up to the present day?

The level of development in psychology and logic, even several decades ago, was such that the creation of a scientifically based general theory for the instruction in systems of intellectual operations, in particular, algorithms of intellectual activity, was hardly possible. At the present time, thanks to new ideas which have appeared in psychology, logic and cybernetics, not only is it possible to raise the question about the creation of such a theory, but it is indispensable.

Landa's theory of instruction

Landa's theory of instruction is based on two processes. First, analysis of the topic to identify the thought processes (operations) necessary to master it. This is the stage of attempting to define the algorithms that should be used for problem-solving. Second, analysis of the learners, their existing thought processes (the algorithms they have already mastered) and their psychological characteristics (individual differences, etc) in order to devise a teaching algorithm (a set of operations that should be carried out during instruction in order to ensure efficient learning.

He admits that it is not always possible to algorithmicize a process. Where such an analysis is achieved Landa is quite clear about the general, overall strategies that one should follow in teaching problem-solving:

The instruction in algorithms, like the instruction in methods of non-algorithmic character, may be achieved in different ways. One way is to present the algorithms in a ready made form so that the students have only to learn them, and then to reinforce these algorithms during exercises. With another method, algorithms are not handed to the students in prepared form, but the students discover them themselves. The instruction is arranged in such a way that the students independently find the necessary and, at the same time, efficient systems of operations. It is important, when this is done, that the assimilation of these systems of operations is achieved not by rote learning, but as a result of properly designed exercises. It is clear that, in specific cases, the first form of instruction may turn out to be expedient. But, in our opinion, the second method should be the important, basic, and leading one in instruction. It is this method which we used in experimental instruction. We did not impose algorithms on the students. We did not provide them in advance or present them in ready made form. The students did not have to specially learn them. The systems of operations forming the basis of the algorithms were gradually assembled by the students in the process of independent, active, practical, linguistic actions. The verbal formulation of the algorithms or of their separate elements and the representation of their diagrams was only the result, the sum of the formation of separate operations.

A comparison of Landa's and other writers' views on the discovery method

We note here a marked similarity of viewpoint between Landa and Gagné. Gagné's rule learning appears equivalent to Landa's learning of ready made algorithms. Gagné's problem-solving is equivalent to the discovery of the algorithm in Landa's system. The one point of difference between the two theoreticians appears to be the relative importance of these two types of learning. Gagné favours rule learning as being faster, the problem-solving approach paying off only when longer-term retention or transfer of skill are important factors. Landa seems to favour the discovery approach, perhaps because as a cybernetician his preoccupation would naturally be focused on generalization and transfer of skills between disciplines. It is doubtful if Landa would consider any skill of no transfer value as worth learning.

In this last point, Landa's viewpoint is very close to Bruner's. However, one should stress that the discovery approach suggested by Landa is far removed from the free discovery advocated by Bruner. Gagné's guided discovery approach is already much more rigorous than Bruner's. For Gagné any discovery exercise has specific pre-set objectives and the teacher has only been successful if he has guided the learner to achieve them. But he only gives general guidelines on how a teacher may attempt to do this. Landa would go much further. We can read a criticism of the position of Gagné and also of Bloom's taxonomy of objectives (Bloom *et al*, 1958) into the following paragraph (Landa, 1976).

> We note that different types of problems require the ability to perform different cognitive operations. This situation is analogous to what takes place with physical operations during various forms of physical activity: driving a car requires knowledge of one kind of operation, working a lathe requires knowledge of others. Very often in psychology and logic the characterization of cognitive activity is limited to indications of operations such as analysis, synthesis, generalization, discrimination, and a few others. This characterisation is correct, but not sufficient. The specific operations in which analysis and synthesis appear are extremely diverse (there are hundreds, if not thousands, of them), and it is possible to know some analytical operations and not to know others. The task facing psychology, especially educational psychology, requires it not to be limited by simple characterizations of cognitive activity such as that involving analysis and synthesis, but rather to discover the specific cognitive actions (operations) in which analysis and synthesis manifest themselves and which are required for the solution of a given class of problems.

9.7 Comparisons between the theories

Objectives

Skinner

The viewpoints discussed above stand in sharp contrast as regards the general objectives of instruction. Skinner, in his work on the programming of arithmetic and mathematics, considered only discrete, observable and definable behaviours. In other words, early programmes taught a specific solution algorithm for a specific type of familiar problem.

There were exceptions, notably the 'productive thinking' programmes developed at Berkeley by Covington and Crutchfield (1965) which successfully taught certain strategies of creative thinking, and several attempts to write 'conversational' problem-solving programmed courses, adopting one of the many varieties of 'branching' programmed instruction, or specially developed programming techniques (eg structural communication). Indeed, there is no reason why programmed materials cannot be used to teach certain types of problem-solving, but they must generally, in so doing, depart from the rigid Skinnerian model of programme writing.

Bruner

In direct contrast, for Bruner the emphasis is upon the kinds of processes learned by the student (rather than the specific subject matter products he may acquire). One paragraph from *Toward a Theory of Instruction* (Bruner, 1966) communicates the essence of educational objectives for Bruner.

Finally a theory of instruction seeks to take account of the fact that a curriculum reflects not only the nature of knowledge itself (the specific capabilities) but also the nature of the knower and of the knowledge-getting process. It is the enterprise *par excellence* where the line between the subject matter and the method grows necessarily indistinct. A body of knowledge, enshrined in a university faculty and embodied in a series of authoritative volumes, is the result of much prior intellectual activity. To instruct someone in these disciplines is not a matter of getting him to commit results to mind. Rather, it is to teach him to participate in the process that makes possible the establishment of knowledge. We teach a subject not to produce little living libraries on that subject, but rather to get a student to think mathematically for himself, to consider matters as a historian does, to take part in the process of knowledge-getting. Knowing is a process, not a product.

Gagné

Gagné has come out in substantial agreement with Bruner on the priority of processes over products as the objectives of instruction. His emphasis, however, is not on teaching general strategies or heuristics of discovery; he is much more concerned with the teaching of the rules or intellectual skills that are relevant to particular instructional domains. It is argued (Gagné and Briggs, 1974):

Obviously, strategies are important for problem-solving, regardless of the content of the problem. The suggestion from some writings is that they are of overriding importance as a goal of education. After all, should not formal instruction in the school have the aim of teaching the student 'how to think'? If strategies were deliberately taught, would not this produce prople who could then bring to bear superior problem-solving capabilities to any new situation? Although no one would disagree with the aims expressed, it is exceedingly doubtful that they can be brought about solely by teaching students 'strategies' or 'styles' of thinking. Even if these can be taught (and it is likely that they can), they do not provide the individual with the basic firmament of thought, which is a set of externally orientated intellectual skills.

For Gagné, the objectives of instruction are intellectual skills or capabilities that can be specified in operational terms, can be task analysed, and then can be taught. Gagné would subscribe to the position that psychology has been successful in suggesting ways of teaching only when objectives have been made operationally clear. When objectives are not clearly stated, the psychologist can be of little assistance. Objectives clearly stated in behavioural terms are the cornerstone of Gagné's position.

Ausubel

Ausubel strongly rejects the notion that any kind of process, be it strategy or skill, should hold priority among the objectives of education. He remains a militant advocate of the importance of mastering well-organized bodies of subject matter knowledge as the most important goal of education. He argues (1968):

... As far as the formal education of the individual is concerned, the educational agency largely transmits ready made concepts, classifications, and propositions. In any case, discovery methods of teaching hardly constitute an efficient primary means of transmitting the content of an academic discipline.

We may thus observe that, while Gagné and Ausubel tend to agree that exposition is a more generally useful form of instruction than discovery, they disagree regarding the appropriate objectives of instruction. Ausubel is indeed closer to Skinner in putting the *products* of learning mathematics before the *processes* involved, although he defines them in terms of subject content (inputs), whilst Skinner would refer to specific responses (outputs). Gagné and Bruner agree that processes are more important than products, but differ again in the way they define and measure the processes.

Landa

The position of Landa with respect to the objectives of instruction is stated in characteristically cybernetic terminology, but embraces all the viewpoints discussed so far, managing to mould them into a coherent whole. Concerning objectives, Landa (1976) states:

How are we to specify the structure of the processes which are to be given to the teacher as instructional objectives? How can we establish the components which constitute the process which is to be taught to the student, and the interrelationships between these components? It can be done by the same method used in other sciences, and especially cybernetics: the construction of models.

Let us assume that a particular skill, for example, the ability to prove that a given object is a member of a given class of objects is to be taught.

In order to properly map out a programme of instruction, it is first necessary to determine the components of this skill; and to do this, it is necessary to analyse the 'proving process' into elementary operations and to determine their structure. On the basis of formal considerations, observations, and, when necessary, experiments, an hypothesis is formed as to what proving membership of an object in a particular class means ie the sequence of operations which must be followed in order to carry out the proof is determined. The discovery of these operations and their structure constitutes the construction of a model of the process in question.

A correct model of a thought process should appear precisely as that programme of thinking activity which the learner should assimilate, which must be made the basis of the instructional programme and which is to be furnished to the teacher as a precisely defined objective.

Methods of instruction

In the discussion so far, we have already touched several times on the general instructional strategies favoured by the various psychologists. We have noticed a polarization between the discovery learning camp and the supporters of reception learning. The extreme supporter of the reception learning mode is Ausubel, but he is not on his own. Hess (1968) considered that not all students benefited from discovery methods and that not all teachers were skilled at employing them.

Reception or discovery

One problem, pointed out by all, is that teaching through discovery is more time-consuming than teaching through exposition. Thus the discovery approach can best be defended when some benefits will accrue from the extra time spent. These benefits, according to Gagné, are better long-term recall (in the absence of practice) and better transfer of skill to other similar problem types. This would seem to restrict discovery learning to the higher order types of learning activity, learning principles or rules and learning how to solve problems.

We have noted that whereas Bruner and Ausubel represent extreme viewpoints for or against discovery methods, most other writers adopt intermediate positions, accepting that both strategies may be used to good advantage and suggesting criteria for selection between them. We have also noted that discovery learning as defined by Bruner is quite different from the guided discovery approach of Gagné and that Landa's approach is different again.

Biggs' classification of discovery methods

A useful classification of discovery methods was suggested by Biggs (1972):

☐ Impromptu discovery
☐ Free exploratory discovery
☐ Guided discovery
☐ Directed discovery
☐ Programmed learning.

It is interesting that she should include programmed learning in a list of discovery methods. Many writers would classify programmed learning as the opposite extreme, the fully expositive technique for reception learning. Belbin *et al* 1957, for example, have even performed research comparing programmed learning and discovery learning for various tasks.

As we shall shortly be considering techniques for the individualization of instruction and as programmed learning shall be one of these, it will be useful to consider briefly this apparent confusion of terms. It is true that most linear programmed learning materials have been based on the RULEG (rule/example) model for programme writing (Evans, Homme and Glaser, 1962). This model is a classically expository approach to instruction. However, discovery type programmes have been produced, generally employing some style of branching. Even linear programmes can follow a rather restricted form of discovery model — the EG-RUL model, in which the learner has to induce the rule from given examples.

Landa (1976) speaks of:

☐ Linear programmes: both RUL-EG and EG-RUL.
☐ Intrinsic programmes: such as Crowder's (1960) branching text.
☐ Extrinsic programmes: which react not to one response of the learner but to his response pattern over a period of time. (Project PLAN is an example which is discussed later.)
☐ Adaptive programmes: which learn from the student's response pattern and adapt the programme of instruction 'on line'. (An example was the SAKI keyboard instructor of the 1960s.)
☐ Structure-diagnostic programmes: which react not only to the responses the student makes (whether they are right or wrong and why) but also diagnose the underlying psychological reasons for each mistake.

Landa describes a course in Russian grammar which has the above structure-diagnostic capabilities. Whenever a student makes a mistake, the programme enters into a diagnostic procedure to 'discover the psychological reasons for the mistake' and may therefore offer different remedial actions to different students making the same mistake.

This programme can be presented as a text, but is somewhat unwieldy and is better presented by computers. If we take programmed instruction in this very general sense to include all such variations, then indeed it is obvious that we may have programmed discovery learning. Landa's position, as outlined earlier, is that for successful instruction, even in mathematical problem-solving, the instructional process must be programmed.

Modifying Biggs' and Landa's classification somewhat we might equate the viewpoints of our theoreticians as shown in Figure 9.2.

Impromptu discovery	Unplanned learning. Occurs in every instructional situation. Sometimes useful sometimes not.
Free exploratory discovery	Bruner's position. Broad learning objectives are fixed; otherwise the learner is free to choose sub-goals, methods, etc.
Guided discovery	Gagné's model. Objectives for each learning step are fixed. The learner is free to explore methods, but with guidance and help at every stage.
Adaptive/diagnostic programmed discovery	Cybernetic approaches such as 'Dialogue CAI', Pasks's conversational programming, and Landa's structure-diagnostic programmes.
Linear/intrinsic programmed discovery	Rigidly directed. (EG-RUL, INTRINSIC PROGRAMMES).
Meaningful reception learning (a) Inductive reasoning (from particular to general)	This is really EG-RUL, but the learner receives the argument; he does not have to discover the rule. This is the way that most mathematical discovery and problem-solving takes place. It would seem to the author reasonable to use this approach, even when 'talking through' a problem solution in an expository manner. Can be programmed.
Meaningful reception learning (b) Deductive reasoning (as favoured by Ausubel)	As understanding of concepts is shown by the ability to apply them to examples. The RUL-EG model (student receives rule and demonstrates understanding by application to suitable range of examples) is an appropriate model here. Can be programmed.
Rote reception learning (drill and practice)	Learning of facts, statements and operations without understanding the concepts involved. Memorization.
Impromptu reception learning	Facts and observations, originally unplanned, supplied by the teacher, other resources, other students.

Figure 9.2 *A continuum of reception and discovery methods of instruction*

Figure 9.2 may be considered as a sort of continuum. The division between programmed discovery and inductive reception learning is very blurred. A teacher, talking through a piece of inductive reasoning is posing and answering questions, groping for rules or theorems which may help in the solution. As soon as he commences to throw those questions open to the students, he is in the rigidly directed discovery mode. Indeed a very common, if not particularly good, classroom tactic is to pose a question; if no answer is forthcoming to rephrase or prompt the question; and if still no response from the class, to answer it oneself, explain *why* that is the answer and finally get the class to recite it in chorus. Here we have descended in our hierarchy of modes, from directed discovery, through inductive reception learning to rote drills (a measure of the teacher's failure, perhaps).

To use programmed learning as an example: a sequence asking the student to induce a rule from a series of examples is discovery unless the frames are so prompted that it is obvious what the required answer shall be, or the students is given a set of multiple-choice answers where the incorrect alternatives are so *obviously* incorrect that he cannot help but choose the right one, whether he fully understands the reasons for his choice or not. This is a very common occurrence in programmed texts which use a lot of prompted frames. In effect the student's activity is little different from reading an expository text, written in an inductive style. An example is given in Figure 9.3(a).

Look at the table of coefficients of expansion of some metals on page 6.
Notice that the coefficient of expansion is positive in *all* cases.

We may say therefore that in general metals .... (expand/contract) when heated.

Figure 9.3 *Sample frame (a)*

The sequence goes from example to rule. It is inductive. The student selects the answer 'expand'. Can we really say he has 'discovered' the rule? Contrast this with (b) which illustrates strongly directed discovery.

Look at the table on page 6.
See if you can state a general rule about what happens to metals when they are heated.

Figure 9.3 *Sample frame (b)*

**The individu-
alization of
instruction**

The various theoretical viewpoints vary also in their positions regarding the individualization of the instructional process.

**The reception/
learning
viewpoint**

David Ausubel, in agreement on this point with Robert Gagné, sees the key to efficient instruction in careful sequencing and in ensuring that all necessary prerequisite learning has been satisfactorily completed. 'The most important single factor influencing learning is what the learner already knows. Ascertain this and teach him accordingly' (Ausubel 1968). The difference between Ausubel and Gagné on this point is restricted to how 'what the learner already knows' is defined. Gagné would construct a learning hierarchy in terms of his categories of learning. Ausubel would define the content, the knowledge structure that is to be or has been learned. This makes little difference from the point of view of individualization. As it is to be expected that different students will have different levels of mastery of the prerequisites, one should plan differentiated starting points and individualized remedial sequences.

How to achieve this differentiation is another matter. In a large class, the expedient of breaking the large group into small groups still leaves a problem for the proponent of the expository approach. One teacher may only give one exposition at one time. This is not a problem to the proponent of discovery learning, as he can set a common project and then monitor and guide individual progress. But for the expository approach, individualization necessarily implies the 'packaging' of the expository presentation in some reproducible medium suitable for individual or small-group use. The factors which may be individualized are:

1. Learning pace.
2. Individual or small-group learning material.
3. Alternative sets of materials employing different media, different methods or different levels of difficulty in order to achieve the same objectives. (This is limited more by economic and practical constraints than by theoretical viewpoint.)
4. Alternative sequences for the study of the lessons or units. (Only when the structure of the course allows this logically.)
5. Varied objectives or standards of assessment, adjusted to the individual needs of the learner. (Rare and only at the discretion of the teacher, not the student.)

The above statements are of course generalizations. They describe adequately the typical expository, reception learning viewpoint on individualization. Most published programmed instruction, most multi-media systems of instruction, the Keller Plan, IPI, and many other well known systems of individualized instruction falls more or less into this category.

The discovery learning viewpoint

In contrast the cognitive position can be summarized as:

1. Learning pace: may be individualized.
2. Individual or small group learning materials usually individualized (with more accent on group project work than in the reception learning camp).
3. Alternative sets of materials for the same objective: usually individualized. (The learner may exert his preferences here much more than in the expository approach, where the alternatives are generally prescribed as a result of a diagnostic process.)
4. Alternative sequences for the study of the lessons or the units: usually (whenever it is not completely ruled out by the logic of the topic).
5. Varied objectives or standards of assessment, usually adjusted to the individual needs of the learner: the aim is individual development, not mastery of specific content.

9.8 The mastery learning model

This model has been suggested and developed principally by Bloom (1968) and Carroll (1963). Its major point of difference from traditional learning models is that it does not accept differentiated achievement among students as a necessary consequence of different aptitudes.

Aptitude and achievement related to time

Carroll defined aptitudes as measuring the amount of time required to learn a task to a given level under ideal instructional conditions. In its simplest form, his model proposed that if each student was allowed the time he needed to learn to some level and he spent the required learning time, then he could be expected to attain the level. However, if the student was not allowed enough time, then the degree to which he could be expected to learn was a function of the ratio of the time actually spent in learning to the time needed:

$$\text{degree of learning} = f\left[\frac{\text{time actually spent}}{\text{time needed}}\right]$$

Bloom transformed this idea into a practical set of procedures for mastery learning. He argued that if students were normally distributed with respect to aptitude for a subject and if they were provided uniform instruction in terms of quality and learning time, achievement at the subject's completion would be normally distributed. Further the relationship between aptitude and achievement would be high. This situation is shown in Figure 9.4.

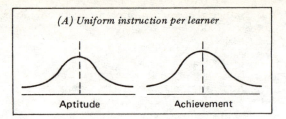

Figure 9.4 *Uniform instruction per learner*

However, if students were normally distributed on aptitude but each learner received optimal quality of instruction and the learning time he required, then a majority of students could be expected to attain mastery. There would be little or no relationship between aptitude and achievement. This situation is shown in Figure 9.5.

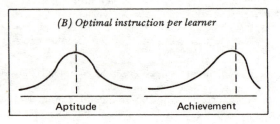

Figure 9.5 *Individualization of the rate of learning*

Individual-ization of the rate of learning   The mastery learning strategy Bloom proposed to implement these ideas was designed for use in the classroom where the time allowed for learning is relatively fixed. Mastery was defined in terms of a specific set of major objectives (content and cognitive behaviours) the student was expected to exhibit by a subject's completion. The subject was then broken into a number of smaller learning units (eg two weeks' instruction) and the unit objectives were defined whose mastery was essential for mastery of the major objectives. The instructor taught each unit using typical group-based methods, but supplemented this instruction with simple feedback correction procedures to ensure that each student's unit instruction was of optimal quality. The feedback devices were brief, diagnostic (formative) tests administered at the units' completion. Each test covered all of a particular unit's objectives and thus indicated what each student had or had not learned from the unit's group-based instruction. Supplementary instructional correctives were then applied to help the student overcome his unit learning problems before the group instruction continued (Block 1971).

Competency-based education   Thus, as originally propounded by Bloom and applied by various researchers, the mastery model was a method of implementing individualization within a large group in the school or college classroom. Since then, however, the basic concept has been adopted by various others to fully individualized learning schemes. A system of instructional design termed competency-based education has become popular in the USA. It is defined as:

Competency based education = mastery learning + modular individualized instruction

The Keller Plan (or personalized system of instruction) (Keller 1968) embraces the principle of mastery learning. Some of these plans and systems are discussed in later chapters.

The research so far on the application of the mastery learning model has been very encouraging. *Mastery Learning* (Block 1971) lists much of the research.

9.9 Cyclic learning models

The mastery learning model insists that all students should follow much the same course and towards the same objectives, receiving remedial instruction on each module or unit, until they can demonstrate total mastery, and only then being allowed to move on to study the next unit. Much of this is opposed by the developmental school of thought.

We earlier asked how to ensure the formation of a coherent schema without this sort of pre-planned sequence and tests of mastery. The answer to this is partly the personal influence of the teacher (we shall return to this point) and partly the cyclic learning process which is commonly adopted in the free exploratory discovery model of learning.

Three stages in learning
Bruner, in describing the process of mathematics learning, identified three stages in the learning of a new mathematical concept: enactive, iconic and symbolic. Optimum learning should pass through these three stages. These stages are identifiable in most of the practical procedures for working in the mathematics laboratory mode, notably in the work of Dienes (1960) although he later subdivided the three stages to give six in all (Dienes 1970). They are also discernible in the theoretical work (and in the structure of his practical textbooks) of Richard Skemp (1971) both at the level of simple concept formation with young children and at the more advanced levels in secondary school when the enactive stage may take the form of 'playing' with previously learned concepts and rules. Skemp's very useful construct of 'intuitive' and 'reflective' intelligence enables one to visualize the playing with previously learnt abstract ideas in the same terms as the play of the young child learning to discriminate shapes. Another proponent of the cyclic process at the reflective, abstract level is Polya (1963) who describes an exploratory phase, followed by a formalizing phase and leading finally to the assimilation of new ideas.

Servais and Varga (1971) paraphrase the description of Dienes (1960) and Polya (1963) to emphasize the similarities (Figure 9.6).

Dienes	Polya
The preliminary or play stage corresponds to rather undirected, seemingly purposeless activity usually described as play. In order to make play possible, freedom to experiment is necessary.	A first, exploratory phase which is close to action and perception and moves on an intuitive, heuristic level.
The second stage is more directed and purposeful. At this stage a certain degree of structured activity is desirable.	A second, formalizing phase ascends to a more conceptual level, introducing terminology, definitions and proofs.
The next stage really has two aspects: one is having a look at what has been done and seeing how it is really put together (logical analysis); the other is making use of what we have done (practice). In either case this stage completes the cycle, the concept is now safely anchored with the rest of experience and can be used as a new toy with which to play new games.	The phase of assimilation comes last: there should be an attempt to perceive the 'inner grounds' of things; the material learned should be mentally digested, absorbed into the system of knowledge, into the whole mental outlook of the learner. This phase paves the way to applications on one hand, to higher generalizations on the other.

Source: Servais and Varga (1971)

Figure 9.6 *Comparing the views of Dienes and Polya*

That Polya and Dienes should be in such close agreement is interesting, as both have extensive experience of mathematics teaching, but of different kinds.

Dienes has worked mainly with young children on concept formation; Polya has worked mainly at secondary school and university levels on problem-solving. The background of Dienes is strongly influenced by Piagetian psychology. Polya based his original studies of problem-solving on mathematical premises, particularly work of Descartes and the studies of heuristic method in the nineteenth century.

Individual-ization of the objectives and methods of learning

The value of the cyclic nature of the process of conceptual learning suggested by such different authors lies in the fact that a given student will return to previously learned concepts with regularity and each time he returns he will have the opportunity to extend his knowledge. Thus, it can be argued, there is no need to have a rigid system of predetermined modules of study, each with its own behaviourally stated objectives which all learners must master in order to gain the right to proceed. We have instead the concept of a cyclic process, passing through the enactive or 'play' stage (when certain regularities and rules are discovered) to the iconic or representational stage (when the rules and relationships are represented in some, perhaps graphical or diagrammatical form) and finally to the symbolic stage at which a language is used (perhaps even invented) by the learners to describe the relationships which have been discovered. It is natural that at this stage the learner would wish to play (in a physical or reflective sense) with something where his new knowledge can be practised, so he will naturally tend to select new activities related with the previous ones. If, from the point of view of his general education in mathematics, he has not gone as deeply as he should into a particular concept area, this will not matter in the long run, as further activities and further learning cycles will eventually throw up the need for further study in depth. The learner will return to further study of previously learned topics as he needs to in order to progress along his chosen path.

These two models for the individualization of instruction spring from two opposed viewpoints concerning the goals and methods of the instructional process. Both are applied in practice. Both work better for some than for others. Both have their critics. We shall examine several practical models for the individualization of instruction and observe that in practice not all models are totally mastery or totally free discovery cyclic. There are many hybrid models and some of these are among the most successful.

9.10 The cybernetics viewpoint — adaptive learning models

Cybernetics, the 'study of regulation and control in complex systems both living and man-made' is concerned with the discovery of general rules which govern the functioning of any system. In the field of learning, for example, one area of interest is to simulate the human learning and thinking process by machines. In educational cybernetics in particular, the concentration of the research is to discover relationships between instructional processes and learning effects which may be expressed mathematically.

Use of the computer

Not surprisingly, therefore, the concentration of effort by cybernetically oriented researchers has been in automated instructional systems, teaching machines and in particular computer assisted instruction. The attraction of computers is threefold. First, one can programme a computer to execute a particular instructional strategy faithfully. One can simulate (more or less perfectly) certain learner/tutor interactions and study them in much greater detail than is possible in a real-life situation. Second, the data collection, storage and analysis capabilities of the computer make it an ideal base for research. Third, many cyberneticians would assert that the complexity of the teaching/learning process is such that only with the help of the data processing capabilities of a computer can we hope to improve the teaching/learning process from its present primitive state of development. Only by matching the variety of response of the tutor to the variety of response possible from the learners and all other influencing factors can one ensure effective control (in the cybernetic sense) of the educational process.

Progress   Is the cybernetic approach a reality? To what extent can one analyse and simulate the student/tutor interaction? There is no room to go into great detail on this point, but it will suffice to quote the work of Gordon Pask, a British cybernetician working in the educational field.

In the late 1950s Pask developed the highly successful SAKI adaptive teaching machine for keyboard skills. The original SAKI machines were used for training punch-card operators. Typist training machines were later developed on the same basic principles. The machine presented data to be typed. The trainee would type a particular character (which was not marked on the keys so that he had to use a touch typing skill). His error pattern was used to control the programme (Lewis and Pask 1965).

The results with this machine were most impressive, learning taking place in a fraction of the normally expected time. Similar machines were built for perceptual coding skills, maintenance skills of electronic equipment, and some simple concept formation skills. These all seem rather low level learning tasks. Can the same techniques be applied to, say, mathematics? The answer is that

Drill and of course they can. For example, the drill and practice computer-based
practice   programmes at Stanford University (Suppes 1968) have certain similarities to the SAKI machine in the logic that is used to differentially branch the learners to material at an appropriate level of difficulty, though the logic of the SAKI machine is rather more complex than at Stanford.

Drill and practice is still a fairly low level learning activity as compared to say the formation of mathematical concepts or problem-solving, but by the

Serialists and 1970s Pask was working on concept formation. His well-known 'serialist/holist'
holists   experiments investigated learning styles and strategies in concept formation. Observation of subjects when they were given freedom to choose their modes of study identified two distinct groups: the serialists, who followed the linear progression of the logic of the topic under study, as it was given to them in a 'course map', and the holists, who did not follow a step by step sequence but tended to form global hypotheses concerning the problem under study, and then test it out by selecting information out of order (Pask and Scott 1972).

Armed with information from a series of such experiments, Pask and his collaborators have now constructed systems, both mechanical and manual which simulate the tutorial function, learn about the individual student's learning style, and strategies, use what they learn to adapt the instructional process to the learning style of the individual and allow the student to take over a greater proportion of the decisions concerning the content and structure of his course (Daniel 1966). In short, these experiments and others like them are beginning to achieve what the cognitive/humanist camps have been preaching as the aim of education for longer than we recall, but have never managed to implement because of the lack of effective control.

9.11 Summary and synthesis

It may be helpful to summarize, in diagrammatic form, the main similarities and differences between the various psychological viewpoints discussed in this chapter. Figure 9.7 emphasizes how some earlier viewpoints are concerned more with one aspect (eg inputs) of education and how the total systems viewpoint is beginning to act as a unifying influence. At the end of the chart are placed some existing individualized systems of instruction. Most of these are discussed at length in later chapters.

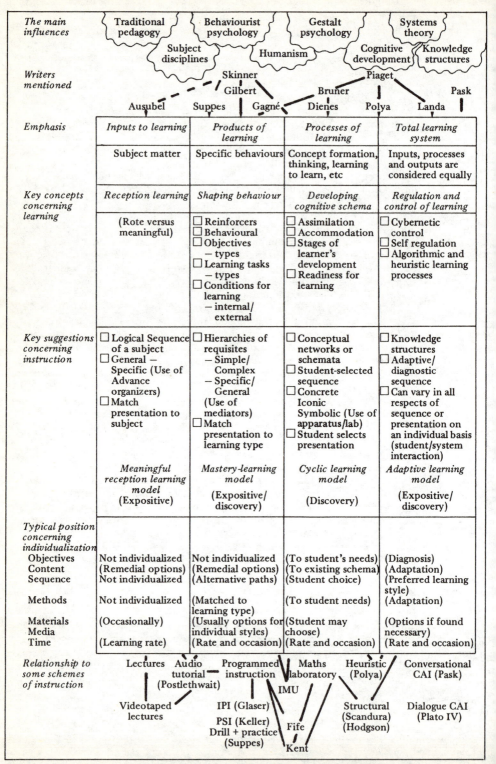

Figure 9.7 *A summary of learning theories*

10. From Instructional Objectives to Instructional Decisions: Analysis Levels 3 and 4

10.1 Where are we going?

The outcomes of analyses such as those described in chapters 6 and 7 are objectives of proposed instruction. We have considered alternatives to instruction and alternative sets of objectives for instruction at two different levels of detail. At either of these levels, we could already have taken certain instructional decisions. We may, right at the beginning during level 1 analysis,

Outcomes of level 1 analysis

have identified that the course objectives are predominantly of a 'knowledge' type that require rote memorization, that the potential students are adults who are unable to leave job or family to attend a full time course in an institution and are scattered all over the country, and that different groups of these students have substantially different needs. These observations may lead us to make such decisions as:

☐ Instructional strategy: expositive, rather than discovery
☐ Instructional media: distance education media (TV, radio, texts)
☐ Instructional grouping: therefore necessarily individual
☐ Instructional sequence: there should be several specific options to attend to the diverse needs.

Without considering for the time being whether these are very good decisions (in the light of the observations made) we note that the decisions are of a global nature and affect the course as a whole. Such decisions are and must be taken at such an early stage. However, it is obvious that all subsequent decisions will be affected. Certain types of learning/teaching experiences are possible in an individual, distance study situation and others are not. We note also that the analysis carried out at stage 1 does not enable one to make any more detailed decisions. We have only defined objectives at the level of the overall course or course unit. This only helps us to develop course and course unit final tests, to establish the sequence and interrelationship of the course units and to make some assessment of the overall course methods which are likely to be successful. Any more detailed decisions taken at this stage are taken on the basis of hunch or intuition rather than on data culled from the analysis so far undertaken. Such intuitive instructional design is in fact very common, and not always to be frowned upon, but generally more reliable instructional results are achieved if more detailed and systematic analysis is carried out.

Outcomes of level 2 analysis

Thus level 2 analysis enables more detailed instructional decisions to be taken on a systematic basis. The specification of all the intermediate and enabling objectives allows one to be more discerning as regards the appropriate instructional strategies (some groups of objectives would benefit from the discovery approach whilst other groups are better taught by expositive methods); instructional media (which parts of the distance learning course should be disseminated by radio, which by print, etc); instructional grouping (some intermediate objectives involve interaction between people and so we must arrange occasional group meetings); and instructional sequence (we can now design the sequence of lessons in the unit and even the sequence within the lessons themselves).

However, there are still many questions which our analysis has not answered.

For example, although we have a good idea of the sequence in which a certain group of objectives should be taught, our analysis has so far told us very little as regards how each of these objectives should be taught. We can, and often do, make intuitive judgements and decisions at this stage (with a level of success dependent very much on our skills as teachers). However, one aim of educational technology is to remove some of this mystique of the gifted teacher by laying bare the decision processes that he uses. For this we need to descend to a deeper level of analysis.

Aims of deeper analysis

Levels 3 and 4 of analysis have the following aims:

1. To analyse the detailed instructional objectives (which were identified at level 2) in order to identify the learning activities that the learner should engage in, in order to master the objectives.
2. To identify suitable instructional strategies and tactics to promote the learning activities identified.
3. To select the 'optimal' strategies and tactics from among the suitable ones, on the basis of cost-effectiveness and other practical considerations.

This somewhat technical sounding definition of 'where we are going' in this chapter has been put in this language to emphasize that we are still acting systemically. Indeed, the reader may notice that at each stage of analysis described so far the process of identifying alternatives and selecting from among them occurred.

In more practical terms, what we shall do is to examine several models for instructional design which attempt systematically to develop the instructional tactics for given objectives. We shall find that in general these models can be classified roughly into two degrees of detail, or as we have chosen to call it, into two levels of analysis:

Levels 3 and 4

Level 3 analysis which takes a detailed objective at the 'lesson' or 'task' level (as identified at level 2) and matches it to a specific set of instructional tactics by means of some classification or taxonomy of types of learning.
Level 4 analysis which does not take the detailed objective from level 2 as a unit, but further analyses this objective into its component behaviours (operants, skill elements, mental operations are names used by various authors). The resultant behaviour map (called a prescription by Gilbert) or mental operations map (called a problem-solving algorithm by Landa) is used as the basis for instructional decisions of a much more detailed nature than would normally be taken as a result of a level 3 analysis.

Examples of models which we classify as level 3 are:

1. Models based on the categories of learning and conditions for learning as outlined by Gagné (1965) and later modified and expanded by Gagné and Briggs (1974). The original theoretical model was developed into a very detailed set of practical procedures by Briggs (1970) in his *Handbook of Procedures for the Design of Instruction*, but there have been many other more or less complicated procedures based on the same theoretical model.
2. Models based on a simpler classification of types of learning couched in more everyday language. An example is the model for the development of vocational instruction suggested by Mager and Beach (1967), which uses the five categories of *discrimination, problem-solving, recall, manipulation* and *speech* to classify objectives and to match them to instructional tactics. Another example is the CRAMP model developed by the Industrial Training Research Unit at the University of London (ITRU 1975) in which five learning categories are identified: *comprehension, reflex skills, attitude development, memorization* and *procedural learning*.

Examples of models which are used at level 4 are:

1. The analysis of each objective into the behavioural units or operants which compose it, which was the basis of early behavioural analysis work by Skinner and was refined into the mathetics model of instructional design by Gilbert.
2. The analysis of industrial skills into the separate limb or finger movements of each operation, as developed in time and motion study and then adapted to the design of training by the Seymour brothers in England during the 1940s and 1950s (Seymour 1954, 1966) and now widely practised under the name of skills analysis training.
3. The analysis of intellectual problem-solving processes into the detailed mental operations that must take place in order for a solution to be found, as suggested by Landa (1974, 1976).

It is particularly important to note that all the techniques mentioned above are based on a theoretical model of one type or another. At level 3, the models are based on a classification of detailed and fairly complex behaviour into some system of categories, and matching instructional tactics to behaviour category. At level 4 the models are ones for further analysis of this behaviour into the minutest elements of behaviour (or internal mental activity), and then selecting the detailed instructional tactics by reference to a fairly simple general model. We shall see some of these models in action in the examples which follow in this chapter, and they are further developed in later chapters.

The theoretical background to these various models was discussed in Chapter 9. We will make frequent reference to this chapter in order to avoid repetition.

10.2 Level 3 analysis

The 'learning categories' approach of Gagné

We have already considered the eight categories of learning defined by Gagné in 1965 (in Chapters 5 and 9). In Chapter 5 we used the categories as a hierarchy to establish sequence and identify 'missing' enabling objectives which must be included to complete the sequence of instruction. In Chapter 9 a brief summary was given of the conditions for effective learning of each of the categories. By the 1970s, however, Gagné's thinking had undergone quite a significant change, resulting in a new, expanded and reorganized set of learning categories and a presentation of the conditions for learning in a more systematic manner, following a classification of 'learning phases'. These learning phases are:

☐ *Motivation*: creates expectancy in the learner
☐ *Apprehending*: creates attention and perception
☐ *Acquisition*: involves the coding and storage of information
☐ *Retention*: involves the long-term storage of information
☐ *Recall*: involves the retrieval of information
☐ *Generalization*: involves the transfer of what has been learned to new situations
☐ *Performance*: involves the using of learnt information in order to respond to specific situations
☐ *Feedback*: involves the confirmation or satisfaction of the expectancy created in the first phase.

Thus the external learning conditions (the conditions that the instructional designer seeks to create) should facilitate each of these learning phases in turn. However, things are not that simple, for the way that these phases are encouraged and developed will vary with the type of human capability which is being learned (Gagné now seems to prefer the term 'human capability' to 'learning category' which he used previously).

Gagné's reorganized model of learning

The earlier list of eight learning categories has been much reorganized. The lower level categories (signal learning, stimulus/response learning) seem to have vanished from his scheme. The 'motor chain' category has been replaced by 'motor skill' although it is by no means clear whether this is a mere change of name or whether the new names imply a redefinition of what Gagné means by them. Certainly his more recent pronouncements (Gagné and Briggs 1974; Gagné 1975) seem to suggest a much broader and more loosely defined connotation to the new terms than the rather strictly defined stimulus/ response chains of the previous terminology. The other four original categories (discriminations, concepts, rules and higher order rules, which he previously called problem-solving) are contained under the title of 'intellectual skills' (with a distinction made between concrete and defined concepts). In addition, two new categories enter the list: 'attitudes' and 'cognitive strategies'. The first of these is no newcomer and probably needs no more definition than the one that Gagné gives it: an acquired internal state that influences the choice of personal action. Gagné is also critical of the use of the term 'affective domain' (as used by Bloom and Krathwohl in their taxonomies) in that it emphasizes the emotional component of attitudes at the expense of their cognitive or behavioural aspects.

The 'cognitive strategies' capability needs a little more attention however. Gagné defines these as 'internally organized control processes' and cites a variety of examples which do not always seem to belong together. At one point he refers to the work of Bruner (1971), quoting such chestnuts as 'learning to learn' and 'learning to think'. At another point (Gagné 1975) he refers to the eight phases of learning quoted above as examples of cognitive strategies. He argues that the learner uses cognitive strategies in thinking about what he has learned and in solving problems (what Skemp refers to as 'reflective intelligence'; see Chapter 9). Whereas one can grasp a vague idea of Gagné's concept of 'cognitive strategies' from these pronouncements, there is much room for discussion yet as to what he means exactly (see later chapters for more detailed discussion of the concept).

The basic approach to analysis of objectives has not changed. All that has changed is the classification scheme for the different types of learning. As before, however, each type of learning is matched to a set of learning conditions which should be provided by the instructional strategies and tactics adopted.

These learning conditions are of two types — internal and external. The internal conditions are the prerequisite objectives which must be learned in order to enable the learning of the objective in question. These are identified by the process of constructing a learning hierarchy (as described in Chapter 5 as part of level 2 analysis). The external conditions are those which the strategies/tactics selected for the teaching of the objective in question are supposed to furnish.

Some of the external learning conditions suggested by Gagné for his original set of eight learning categories were summarized in Chapter 9. Some of those which he suggests for his revised classification are summarized below.

Present verbal information in a meaningful context

Verbal information. To assist the apprehension phase, one should present verbal information in a varied manner, using changes in tone or voice (in the case of spoken communication), or changes in type or colour or layout to emphasize important content (in the case of written communication). To assist the acquisition phase, one should present the information in a meaningful context. He suggests such techniques as the wider context advance organizer approach developed by Ausubel as part of his meaningful reception learning model, the use of mnemonics, interesting layouts or pictorial presentations, etc.

Intellectual skills. These are the bulk of Gagné's original categories, so we find the same conditions for learning specified. In general, Gagné sees the acquisition of intellectual skills as the 'snapping into place' of a combination of simpler skills that have previously been learned. The hierarchical nature of

Intellectual skills are hierarchically organized

these skills is emphasized. Thus two main stages of external learning conditions are seen to be necessary. First, the relevant lower level skills must be retrieved from memory (they must already be in memory for the internal learning conditions to be fulfilled). One therefore needs to use a tactic which will help the learner to retrieve the relevant skill. One way is to ask him to perform the skill, but there are other subtler tactics. Second, one must help the learner to put together the simpler skills into the more complex one which he is supposed to be learning. However, we should not do the putting together for him, but should guide him to do it himself. And we do this by the use of appropriate hints or cues. Third, one should take care that the intellectual skill being taught is learned as a generalizable skill and not as a memorized item of information. To ensure that this occurs one must carefully plan a variety of situations for the learner to practise the use of the skill. See Chapter 9 for further detail on the conditions for learning of intellectual skills.

Cognitive strategies are poorly defined

Cognitive strategies. Gagné is less precise concerning the external learning conditions for this newly added category. He uses this lack of precision thus: 'since cognitive strategies are internally organized control processes, the effects of external conditions on their learning is found to be less direct than is the case with verbal information and intellectual skills'. He does make the point, however, that these strategies are developed over time rather than learned 'all at once'. Thus a suggested instructional tactic is to explain the strategy verbally to the learner and then to give him the 'opportunity to practice' in a variety of situations.

This does not get us very much past the structure of traditional, unimaginative textbooks and the lessons that went with them: 'here's a new type of problem — I'll work through the first two on the blackboard now, explaining my method as I go along, then you do the rest of the set for homework'. However, the difference is that Gagné is referring to general 'thinking' strategies rather than to specific problem-solving skills. Perhaps he is referring to the general heuristics of problem-solving as suggested by Polya (see Chapter 1).

Attitudes are to do with choice

Attitudes. Gagné suggests that attitudes are either learned directly (by experiencing pleasure or success in an activity) or indirectly (by copying a human model which the learner respects or with which he identifies). Thus the main types of tactics for the development of attitudes are (a) reinforcement of participation in desirable activities or of desirable reactions to given situations, and (b) the setting of an example or the creation of a human model of the desirable attitude. Another important tactic to employ is to provide ample opportunity for the attitude to be exhibited. It is no use expecting a positive attitude to classical music to develop if the opportunities to hear classical music, to go to concerts, and to participate in discussions about classical music are very limited.

Motor skills are glossed over

Motor skills. Gagné has little to say in detail concerning motor skills. This is no doubt a reflection of his greater interest in the intellectual aspects of education. He emphasizes simply that first the sequence of activities to be carried out must be learned (learning the rule or procedure) and that then this must be followed by practice and feedback of results. We shall go into much greater detail regarding the learning and teaching of motor skills later in this chapter and in Chapter 11.

In conclusion, the Gagné model for instructional tactic selection is based on the classification of the detailed learning objectives according to a set of defined learning types (or human capabilities), and the selection of tactics that fulfil the learning conditions for the identified capability.

10.3 The 'performance-type' approach of Mager and Beach

A very similar though somewhat simpler approach was suggested by Mager and Beach (1967) in their booklet *Developing Vocational Instruction*. They suggest a classification of five types of performance:

Five types of performance

☐ Discrimination (knowing when to do it)
☐ Problem-solving (how to decide what to do)
☐ Recall (knowing what to do; knowing why to do it)
☐ Manipulation (how to do it)
☐ Speech (how to say it).

This classification, obviously designed with vocational training in mind, does not get itself involved in the intricacies of cognitive strategies or in the classifying of sub-types of intellectual skills, but comes straight to the point, which is typical of Mager. As these are categories of performance observed in real jobs it is possible to identify them even before objectives have been written, from an examination of the tasks or of the steps that make up the tasks, as Figure 10.1 illustrates.

TASK DETAILING SHEET

Vocation: X-ray Technician	Task: Take an X-ray of the chest		
No.	Steps in Performing the Task	Type of Performance	Learning Difficulty
1	Patient is asked to prepare for the X-ray by removing excess clothing	Speech	Easy
2	Correctly position the patient giving special instruction	Manipulation, speech	Moderately difficult
3	Position and check the proper distance of the tube with respect to the patient	Discrimination	Moderately difficult
4	Turn on the X-ray equipment and adjust machine	Recall	Easy
5	Insert the X-ray film and identification marker into the proper holder	Manipulation	Easy
6	Expose film and release patient from examining room	Manipulation	Moderately difficult
7	Process film	Manipulation	Difficult
8	Check film for specified positioning or developing errors	Discrimination	Very difficult
9	Release patient if film is acceptable to the radiologist	Recall	√
10	Clean examining table and film areas	Manipulation	√

Source: Mager and Beach (1967)

Figure 10.1 *Task detailing sheet*

Mager and Beach describe the main instructional tactics for each of their performance types as follows:

Discrimination is 'shaped'

Discrimination. Being able to tell whether two objects are alike or different is one form of discrimination. Another form is being able to tell whether one thing is the same or different from a mental image of what it ought to be. Discrimination between two objects is taught by showing the student pairs of the things you want him to see the difference between. The difference is gradually reduced until the student is able to make discriminations fine enough to be satisfactory. The second kind of discrimination is taught by giving the student practice in comparing single items or situations with his knowledge of what they should be like. He is given practice in saying whether a thing is or is not consistent with his picture of it.

Only one type of problem-solving is discussed

Problem-solving. Problem-solving is taught by showing the student those cues and symptoms that should lead him to conclude that problem-solving is called for, by showing him relationships between these symptoms and possible causes, and by giving him practice of the actual thing or situation needing remedial action. It is done by showing him symptoms and letting him find his way to the problem, and *not* by showing him a problem and asking him to guess what symptoms would appear.

Distinction between knowing what to do and knowing how to do it

Recall. The techniques used to teach recall depend on the nature of the performance desired. If a student is to make a certain response whenever he sees or hears something, a technique that presents the object or the sound and allows him to practice the appropriate response should be used. If the recall is related to knowing how something works, then a demonstration lecture is appropriate, followed by practice in which the student is asked to describe the relationships that go to make up the substance of how the thing works.

Manipulation. Knowing what to do is not always the same as knowing how to do it. Through recall, the student will, for example, know what to do when using certain tools, but actual practice with the tools is the best way to teach him how to use them.

Speech. For many jobs speech is merely a form of communicating knowledge. Some tasks however require that speech is used in a particular way. The principal technique for teaching speech characteristics is one involving imitation, practice and immediate knowledge of results. The tape recorder is an indispensable tool.

There have been many variations or expansions of the approach suggested by Mager and Beach, as there have of Gagné's approach. The approach is the basis of a system of training course development used in various UN projects. This system is based on the concept of 'modules of employable skill' developed by staff of the International Labour Office's vocational training branch. The typical planning sheets (see Figures 10.2 and 10.3) used in this system show the unmistakable influence of the Mager and Beach model (International Labour Office 1973).

10.4 The 'CRAMP' model

The Industrial Training Research Unit of University College London, under its director Dr Eunice Belbin, has been responsible for much useful research into various aspects of training, including a considerable amount of work on instructional methods. Work in the 1960s concentrated on the problems of training the older worker (Belbin and Belbin 1972) and on the comparison of various instructional methods, such as programmed learning texts versus the discovery approach, discrimination methods, magnification methods, deductive methods, etc (Belbin *et al* 1957; Belbin and Shimmin 1964; Belbin 1968, 1969; Belbin and Belbin 1972). The culmination of much of this work was the development of the CRAMP model for matching objectives to instructional methods. This model differs sharply from the two described already, principally in its use of an algorithmic approach to methods selection.

Five categories of learning

The initials CRAMP stand for the five categories of learning that this model identifies: Comprehension, Reflex skills, Attitude, Memorization and

Job: (01) service station mechanic   *Function:* (06) servicing tyres

ITEM	DESCRIPTION	FREQUENCY	CRITICALITY	DIFFICULTY
01.06.01	Lifting a motor vehicle	Few times daily	Medium	Some difficulty
01.06.02	Removing car wheels	Few times daily	Low	Comparatively easy
01.06.03	Dismantling tyres	Occasionally	Medium	Some difficulty
01.06.04	Inspecting tyres	Many times daily	High	Some difficulty
01.06.05	Inspecting tubes	Occasionally	High	Comparatively easy
01.06.06	Repairing tubes by simple patching	Occasionally	High	Some difficulty
01.06.07	Repairing tubeless tyres by simple patching	Occasionally	High	Considerable difficulty
01.06.08	Replacing valve cores	Occasionally	Medium	Comparatively easy
01.06.09	Mounting of tyres	Occasionally	High	Some difficulty
01.06.10	Inflating of tyres	Frequently	High	Comparatively easy
01.06.11	Mounting of wheels	Few times daily	High	Comparatively easy

Figure 10.2 *A job analysis of servicing tyres (ILO 1973)*

Function: (06) servicing tyres

TASK REFERENCE: 01.06.01 – lifting a motor vehicle

ITEM	DESCRIPTION	TYPE OF SKILL	TEACHING METHOD	EQUIPMENT
01.06.01.01	Identifying lifting points on the vehicle chassis (body)	Recall/discrimination	Demonstrations involving comparisons; exercises involving memory work	Charts and models
01.06.01.02	Selecting suitable lifting device	Discrimination/ problem-solving	Demonstrations involving comparisons; exercises involving memory work	Various lifting devices
01.06.01.03	Placing lifting device or stand under a vehicle	Manipulation	Practical assignments	Various vehicles and lifting devices
01.06.01.04	Operating hand-operated lifting device	Manipulation/recall	Practical assignments	Various vehicles and hand-operated lifting devices
01.06.01.05	Operating power-operated lifting devices	Manipulation/recall	Classroom exercises involving memory work; practical assignments	Various vehicles and power-operated lifting devices and charts
01.06.01.06	Securing vehicle and lifting device	Manipulation/recall	Demonstration involving memory; practical assignments	Various vehicles and lifting devices
01.06.01.07	Removing lifting device from the vehicle	Manipulation	Practical assignments	Various vehicles and lifting devices
01.06.01.08	Replacement of tools and equipment	Manipulation/recall	Demonstrations involving memory; practical assignments	Various tools and lifting equipment

Figure 10.3 *A task analysis and instructional design sheet for lifting a motor vehicle (ILO 1973)*

Procedural learning. These categories are defined as follows:

1. *Comprehension or C-type learning.* This involves understanding the subject matter. In general, C-type learning takes place when training involves theoretical subject matter (eg electric circuit theory, the principles of hydraulics, how a car works, etc). Comprehension embraces knowing why, how and when certain things happen or do not happen. It does not necessarily involve being able to *do* something (which is Procedural [P-type] or Reflex [R-type] learning).

2. *Reflex skills or R-type learning.* In the CRAMP system, R-type learning refers to the acquisition of skilled movements (eg operating a sewing machine) as well as skilled perceptual capacities (eg inspecting bottles on a production line for faults or defects). Typically, R-type learning is involved if the new skills can only be achieved through practice as well as instruction. This is in contrast to Procedural (P-type) learning which mainly involves simply being told what to do in order for the task to be performed successfully.

3. *Attitude development or A-type learning.* Training under this category involves an attempt to change the attitudes of the trainees. This can be broadly categorized into:

   (a) change or improvement of attitudes towards other people (eg workmates, junior staff, the public etc)
   (b) special training for adjustment to and acceptance of organizational changes (eg introduction of new techniques, new company policy, etc).

4. *Memorization or M-type learning.* This type of learning involves 'knowing what to do in a given situation'. Memorization hardly needs defining. It essentially involves committing to memory information necessary to carry out a particular job efficiently.

5. *Procedural or P-type learning.* This is another case of 'knowing what to do in a given situation'. It differs from M-type learning in that training for memorization is not required in order to perform the task correctly. This is usually because the instructions are very simple and brief, or if more complicated, they can be referred to while the task is being performed.

The matching of learning category, once identified, to instructional method is performed by the use of an algorithm (see Figure 10.4). Note that the outcomes possible in this algorithm (18 in all) are specific instructional techniques (or groups of techniques), and not general conditions for learning or tactics that the selected instructional technique should adhere to. Thus, the CRAMP approach seems to be much more prescriptive than the other two approaches previously described. However, this is not so in practice, as the following chapters will illustrate.

10.5 The three models compared

The three level 3 models discussed differ in their scope of application. Whilst the Mager and Beach approach and the CRAMP model are aimed specifically at vocational training problems, the model proposed by Gagné attempts to describe and classify all types of learning, or at any rate the major types (he refers to his new classification as the 'five major categories of human capabilities'). However, from the examples that he tends to use, it is obvious that Gagné is interested primarily in the types of learning that take place during the early years of a general education.

Perhaps due to the difference in scope between the models there exists also a marked difference in specificity: in the closeness of the match that is made between learning type and instructional tactic. The Gagné model is the least specific in its specification of tactics. It describes what the instruction should do in certain types of learning situation, but in very general terms. Gagné is operating in terms of general concepts and rules (we might call them heuristics). These should enable a teacher to make reasonable instructional decisions in specific practical situations, but would not necessarily guarantee the best, or even an adequate solution in all cases.

(2) Mager and Beach

The Mager and Beach model appears in general to be more specific and categorical in its pronouncements. As they are dealing with more specific types of learning situations, they can be more specific in their prescriptions. For example, what they say regarding problem-solving ('. . . by showing him symptoms and letting him find his way to the trouble, and *not* by showing him a trouble and asking him what symptoms would appear . . .') obviously refers to a specific, restricted category of problems. If you define the learning type more precisely, you should be able to be more specific about the instructional tactics to adopt. This has been one argument put forward for a yet more detailed level of analysis of the learning task (a level 4 analysis).

(3) CRAMP

The CRAMP model, based as it is on an algorithm, appears on first sight to be more specific still. Once the learning type has been identified, the algorithm leads the reader through further specific decisions to the selection of a specific instructional plan (a group of interrelated tactics), such as, for example, an adaptive programme, the progressive parts method, the T-group or the Skinner programme. It seems to remain only to look up the identified plan or technique in the manual that accompanies the algorithm and apply it to the instruction being designed. However, this is not so, as the descriptions of the techniques that one encounters there are very general and leave much to the imagination and experience of the reader. Thus the CRAMP model is no more specific than, for example, the Gagné model, perhaps even less so. Furthermore, the appearance of specificity given to the model by the semi-algorithmic presentation can be misleading in the same way as the performance analysis algorithm of Mager and Pipe (discussed in Chapter 6) can be misleading. The user is lulled into the feeling of being led by the hand through the decision making process. When he reaches an outcome, he will tend to accept this as the only and total solution (which is the theoretical idea behind true algorithms), whereas in fact it may only be a part of the solution as the problem under analysis is a multi-faceted one. He should go back and follow other paths as well, but the information layout hinders rather than assists him in doing so. This brings us to a third factor for consideration: the accuracy of the diagnosis of learning type that the three models enable one to perform.

Accuracy of the diagnosis

The multi-faceted nature of many training objectives is not a factor unknown to the originators of the CRAMP model. They say:

> It must again be emphasized that it is very rare for a training task to involve only one type of learning. For instance, although fairly simple tasks that don't require practice for successful performance may involve only Procedural (P-type) learning, eg operating a petrol pump, most tasks are more complicated and involve perhaps Memorization (M-type) learning as well, eg invoicing or filing (M + P). A yet more complicated task might involve comprehension, as well as memorization and procedural learning (C + M + P) eg electrical fault-finding. A complicated skill, say driving a bus in traffic, can involve all five types of learning (C + R + A + M + P).
>
> The algorithm looks complicated enough but there is little doubt that as a general guide it represents a simplified picture of the true complexity of training decisions. The absence of lines in the algorithm running between types of learning (eg linking branches C and M) does not mean that in the CRAMP system these interconnections do not exist. For the purposes of clarity and utility they have been excluded, for an over complex algorithm has little value if the user cannot follow it.

However, one could add that a semi-algorithm which presents an artificially simplified picture of the decision making process may also be of little value as a job aid if the user follows it slavishly and uncritically, to generate part-solutions made up of a limited number of instructional stereotypes. Once again, this point is recognized by the originators of the model:

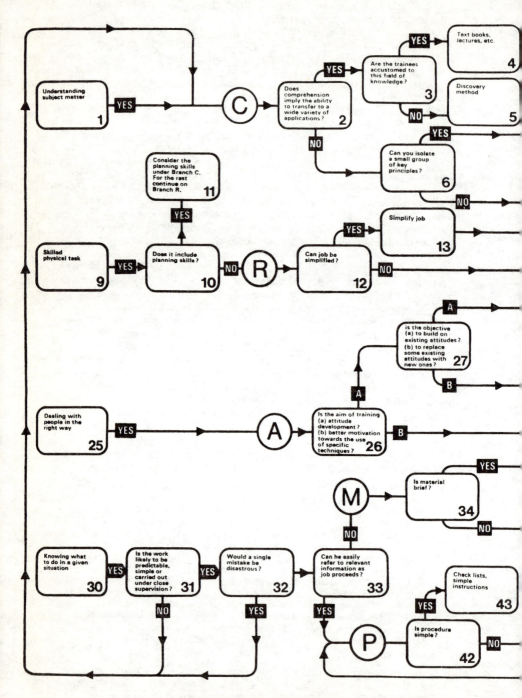

Figure 10.4 *The 'CRAMP' algorithm*
Source: CRAMP — A Guide to Training Decisions Industrial Training
Research Unit, 32 Trumpington Street, Cambridge

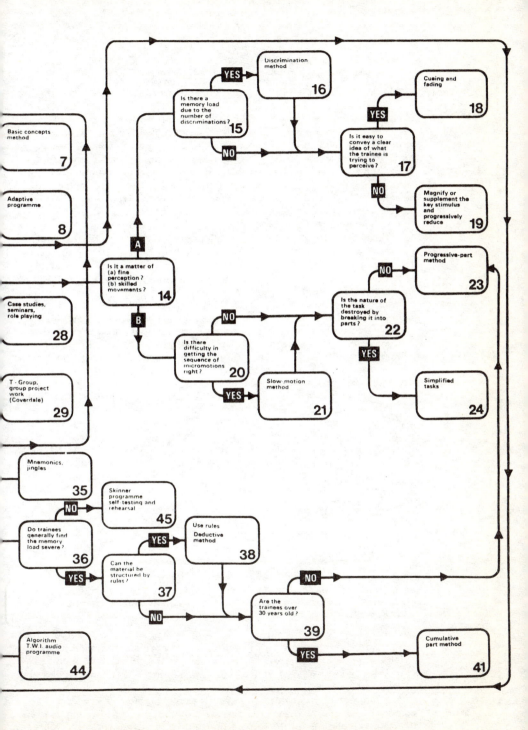

Finally it should be stressed that the PDA (algorithm) is not to be regarded as a finished product. It is hoped that the algorithm will grow not only by prescribing new training methods but also by incorporating more factors which influence the choice of training methods. This can only be achieved by putting the PDA in the hands of training officers who can test it in a variety of situations. Very positively we should welcome the opportunity of discussing the experiences of those who use CRAMP on a trial basis, since it is in this way that we can deepen understanding of how the system can be most effectively employed or refined.

Limitations of the algorithmic approach

However, there is a limit to which such an algorithmic approach can grow and still remain manageable. The author is reminded of his own attempts at algorithmicizing the process of media selection for instruction in 1967. A set of algorithms was prepared for a limited set of industrial skill training situations and was tried out in several instructor training courses, with a considerable level of success. The algorithms were published in book form (Romiszowski 1968) and were subjected to comparative studies with a basic principles approach to teaching instructional design and in particular media selection. When instructors were taught and tested on problems which were of the categories that had been used in the development of the algorithm, groups that had learned to use the algorithm were much superior to groups which had learned by studying some basic principles only, even when the basic principles group were much more experienced as instructors than the algorithms group (Romiszowski 1970). However, later attempts to extend the technique to a wider range of instructional situations proved quite difficult. One was forced to use a semi-algorithmic approach to the mapping of decisions which seemed too complex to analyse down into categorical 'yes/no' steps. These algorithms (see Romiszowski 1974) proved to be interesting ways of presenting visually a complex cluster of interrelated decisions, but in practice they proved to be of limited value as job aids and sometimes misleading in the way suggested above. Therefore, an alternative presentation technique was sought that would better present the complexity and variety of choices open to the instructional designer. The idea of structured schemata of related concepts and ideas seemed promising and is developed in this book (for performance problems in Chapter 6, for knowledge and skills analysis in Chapter 11 and for method and media selection in Chapter 17 and elsewhere).

A serious research attempt has been made to algorithmicize the whole of the instructional design process in a research project undertaken by the Admiralty Research Laboratory Applied Psychology Unit in the UK, in conjunction with Inbucon Learning Systems, Limited (see Dodd, LeHunte and Sheppard 1974). They state:

> In order to define a decision making structure we have adopted the following approach:
>
> 1. Define decisions made in instructional design.
> 2. Establish those criteria which influence decisions, including task features, learner characteristics and practical constraints.
> 3. Develop rules to link output criteria with recommendations.
>
> A system has been established providing recommendations for some 50 instructional design decisions. The scale and complexity of the decision making structure has necessitated the use of a computer to process data.

Any complete algorithm for instructional design would be so complex as to require the aid of a computer in its use. The CRAMP algorithm is thus far from being complete. Indeed, the system described in the above mentioned Admiralty article was already in its sixth version in 1974 (translator 6) and ran to a rule set of several hundreds of separate rules, yet could only '. . . accommodate motor perceptual activities and relatively low level cognitive activities. It requires further development to provide complete sets of recommendations for the broadest possible range of tasks (and possibly for "subject matter" as well).'

This considerable but necessary further development does not seem to have taken place to date. The question could be posed whether such a task will ever be completed, at any rate at the present state of development of the science of learning? And is the investment in the analysis likely to be justified by the improvements that will result in instructional design? The first question reminds me of the work of Landa on the analysis of geometry problem-solving and the use of Russian grammar rules (Landa 1976, 1977) which represents more than a decade of work to completely define the mental operations in just these two problem-solving areas. Furthermore, in such well-defined areas, Landa discovered that whereas it is possible to fully algorithmicize the processes involved in the correct use of Russian grammar, it is not possible fully to algorithmicize the processes involved in solving geometry problems. These processes are by nature heuristic and no procedure can be laid down which will guarantee that anyone following the procedure will solve correctly any possible problem of the class (see the discussion of Landa's work in Chapter 9).

Arguments for the heuristic approach

However, what is possible is to teach some general-purpose rules or heuristics, which, with guided practice in their use, will increase the probability of a correct solution. Surely this heuristics-based approach is the one to adopt to instructional design. Surely the design of instruction is at least as complex and probabilistic as the solution of certain groups of geometry problems. This does not mean that a systematic analysis should not be attempted, nor that computer assistance in the design of instruction is ruled out as a possibility. After all, chess-playing computers are programmed on a heuristic basis to apply a few basic rules of good play to the real situation that is presented to them, constructing their play as the game proceeds and learning to adapt their play to the strategy of the opponent. However, chess is played within some very fixed parameters, such as the shape and size of the board. If we suddenly invent a new game by varying the number of squares on the chess board (to 10 by 10, say, instead of 8 by 8) or changing the form of the moves possible by certain of the pieces or going to three dimensions, the skilled 'traditional' chess player can rapidly adapt to the new parameters, but the computer will need extensive pre-programming, preceded by extensive analysis of the play strategies of the new game. This 'creative adaptiveness' as opposed to 'programmed adaptiveness' seems to be a quality desirable in the instructional designer, for the variety of situations which we call education and training are not necessarily limited by strict parameters. There will always be room for the creative invention of new instructional techniques to meet new educational goals, or to meet old ones in a better (or simply different) way.

How 'water-tight' are the categories?

Thus, the heuristic approach is probably the one to adopt, and in the absence of a computer programme, one must identify the heuristic rules and then teach them, or make them available for reference, to the instructional designer. This appears to be the approach adopted by the other two models discussed above. Both the Gagné model and the Mager and Beach model specify general-purpose rules to be applied to specific categories of performance- or learning-type. However, the rules are somewhat less precise in the Gagné model, perhaps because the latter purports to be applicable to all types of human learning. There is also a difference in the accuracy of diagnosis of the two models. Mager and Beach say the following in respect of their five performance types:

> Dr Robert Gagné has presented an excellent and scholarly description of eight different kinds of performance, and has attempted to show which conditions are most appropriate for facilitating the learning of each of these performance types. In an attempt to simplify the job of course preparation, we have modified Gagné's eight categories into only five: discrimination, problem-solving, recall, manipulation and speech.
>
> If you determine which of these five types of performance is the one *primarily associated with* each of your task steps, you will be in a good position to select

course content, procedures and materials. The expression 'primarily associated with' is an important one to notice, because each task consists of several types of performance, and because each task step may involve two or more types. Performance types are interrelated. For example, although the process of mixing cake batter involves manipulation, it also involves knowing what to do and knowing how to recognize when it has been done properly.

Gagné, however, implies that all human capabilities are precisely classifiable and that required learning can be accurately diagnosed, even if we cannot then always come up with very concrete rules for the instructional prescription (Gagné 1975).

There are five major categories of learning outcome or 'learned human capabilities' (Gagné 1972). In the order in which we shall consider them here (which implies no particular order of complexity or importance), they are (1) verbal information, (2) intellectual skills, (3) cognitive strategies, (4) attitudes and (5) motor skills. It will be apparent that a greater amount of systematic knowledge is available about some of these categories than about others. However, the distinctions among them are quite adequate to make their differential properties dependably clear.

So, Mager and Beach say that objectives (at any rate at the task level) are very complex, involving a combination of several categories of learning (and even at the step level may involve two or more types), whereas Gagné claims that all human learning can be accurately classified. The one way of resolving this would be to state that *at some level of detail of analysis* one should be able to reach a point where all the elements of learning have been sufficiently subdivided so that each is identifiable as a unique category of learning. This level of detail (depth of analysis) is, however, likely to vary, being deeper for more complex skills than for simple ones.

This is yet another argument for occasionally needing to perform a more detailed level of analysis (level 4).

Completeness of the models
Finally, let us consider whether any of the three models are indeed complete. An attempt at mapping the categories on each other rapidly shows that they do not cover the same ground exactly (see Figure 10.5). Mager and Beach do not consider attitudes, whereas the other two do. However, they include 'speech' as a separate category, and it is not very clear where one should classify 'knowing *how* to say it' in the other schemes. It is a sort of reflex skill, but not really a motor skill in the full sense, and it also has connotations of 'interpersonal skill', as the task of speaking usually implies that a conversation is going on, together with all the stresses and emotional overtones that that brings.

Different types of problem-solving
Problem-solving is another problem. The definition given of the problem-solving category by Mager and Beach seems akin to Gagné's mark 1 use of the term, meaning the combination of simpler rules into a higher order rule by the process of discovery. However, Gagné now readily admits that there are different types of problem-solving, some depending more than others on the presence of well-developed 'problem-solving strategies' (Gagné would call these cognitive strategies, but we refer to them as heuristics). However, only Gagné emphasizes the existence of internal thinking processes which the learner brings to bear on the problem in a reflective manner.

What about interactive or social skills?
Thus, it appears that the Gagné model is the most complete of the three discussed, but is it in fact complete? Can any type of human capability (learning outcome) really be classified by this model? The few comments made above concerning interactive skills should serve to cast doubt on its completeness. Where would one classify the sort of interactive skills that much supervisory and management training seeks to develop? Where would one classify the human capability of 'self-actualization' (Carl Rogers claims that it is something which is learned, so it would qualify to be a 'human capability' in Gagné's usage of the term)? Where would one classify 'empathy' which presumably can also be learned? Are all these things combined under

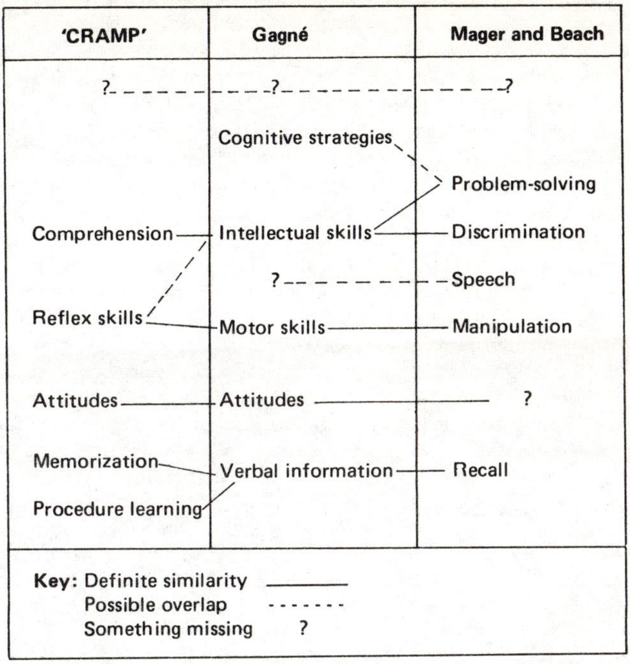

'CRAMP'	Gagné	Mager and Beach

Cognitive strategies

Problem-solving

Comprehension — Intellectual skills — Discrimination

? — — — — — — — Speech

Reflex skills — Motor skills — Manipulation

Attitudes — Attitudes — ?

Memorization — Verbal information — Recall
Procedure learning

Key: Definite similarity ————
      Possible overlap - - - - - -
      Something missing   ?

Figure 10.5 *A comparison of the three schemes for classifying learning*

'attitudes' without any subdivisions?

In Chapter 11 we shall consider in detail the nature of these missing links and shall try to construct a more complete schema of types of learning.

First, however, we shall analyse three other models, which attempt to carry the process of task or topic analysis to even greater depths. We have called this group of techniques examples of level 4 analysis.

10.6 Level 4 analysis

Skills analysis Unlike level 3 analysis, which is characterized by a more or less direct matching of objectives at the lesson level to instructional tactics, level 4 analysis analyses the objective yet further, breaking it down into component behaviours or skill elements. It is broken down in this way to identify learning difficulties with greater precision and so to specify the instructional tactics, or rather to design the detailed steps of instruction more precisely.

The descent to such a detail of analysis must be justified, and the justification is that learning difficulties (which cannot be identified at a shallower level of analysis) really do exist. The overcoming of these learning difficulties must further be judged in the economic light of whether the cost, in time and effort, of the more detailed approach is justified by the importance of the objective.

We now consider three approaches, which we may classify as examples of level 4 analysis. We shall describe two briefly and illustrate the third more fully by means of an example. It is worth mentioning all three because they related to quite different types of learning.

Seymour's approach to skills analysis Skills analysis is probably the oldest 'deep analysis' technique of a systematic nature to be widely used. It was developed out of time and motion study techniques and adapted to the design of training for complex operator skills as early as the 1940s by the Seymour brothers (Seymour 1954, 1966). We describe in some more detail the history and the underlying theoretical background to this approach later. Here we describe the method of analysis itself.

Skills analysis takes over where the level 2 type of analysis (eg listing the task steps and their level of difficulty) ends. It is particularly suited to complex semi-skilled operations in industry, particularly if they are of a repetitive nature, involve high-speed operation or a high level of manual dexterity. In such tasks it is often very difficult to identify why the novice performs so much worse than the experienced man. There is little knowledge content to learn and the novice soon masters that. However, he continues to perform way below the experienced worker's standard for weeks, months and, in some instances, years. Is it an inborn knack that is involved? It used to be thought so in some circles, but the skills analysis approach has done much to dispel this view, having been responsible for the creation of training schemes that have in days or weeks imparted the skill level that was previously considered to require months or years of on-the-job experience.

Separate the sensory and motor aspects of the task
The analysis procedure developed by Seymour is based on separating out carefully the sensory information and the motor actions for each minute step of the task. This was done by use of a multi-column form, as shown in Figure 10.6. In the first column on the left, the analyst notes down the steps involved in the task. Often, the size of step listed in a typical level 2 analysis is still too large for this purpose, as the ideal size of step for this style of analysis involves only one discrete (but coordinated) movement. Thus, for example, the task step of opening a can of beer would be split down further into the individual actions:

☐ grasp the beer can
☐ rotate the ring into correct position
☐ lift the ring
☐ pull the ring.

This is a slightly expanded version of what it says on the lid: 'lift and pull'. The complexity of this skill would not be sufficient to call for the use of a skills analysis form of the kind shown here, but if the action of opening the can was part of a more complex task of several other similar stages, some form of keeping note of one's observations is required. Thus, alongside the list of 'skill elements', as Seymour calls the individual actions, there is provision for describing what each of the limbs and the senses involved actually performs.

Identify the differences between expert and novice
This separation is important as it assists the analyst to pinpoint the exact differences between the method of working of the expert being analysed and of the novice. These differences may be in the sequence of actions performed, or in the way that certain actions are performed, or in the sensory information that is used to control the actions. This latter source of difference is most commonly the root of the different rates of performance of master and novice. The novice carries out each movement watching carefully what he is doing, whilst the expert has passed control of certain movements to other senses, particularly to touch or to the kinaesthetic sense of what it 'feels like' to be doing the job correctly. Thus, in many assembly operations that involve, for example, putting a screw into a hole, the novice flounders around trying to get it in by looking carefully at where he is putting the screw. The expert slides the screw from the side, preceded by the pad of his thumb. The touch senses in his thumb locate the hole and then his other fingers guide the screw into position, without any use at all of the sense of vision. The eyes may already be involved in planning the next stage of the operation or in controlling another action, happening in parallel, being executed by the other hand. It is this sort of level of detail that the analyst is looking for.

Once the analyst has identified the chief sources of the difference between master and novice (identified the knacks, if you like), the suggested procedures for instructional design are simple. As usually there are only a few knacks identified, even in the most complex operator task, Seymour suggests that one

ITEM	LEFT HAND	RIGHT HAND	VISION	OTHER SENSES	COMMENTS
1. Select leaf			Eyes to pile of leaves, determine leaf for selection and point of grasp.		
		Grasp leaf with T, 1 and 2 move with leaf until nose is visible.			
			Determine position on nose approximately 1" from top of leaf.		
	Grasp selected point with T and 1 on either outer sides of leaf touching stem with tips of both T and 1.				
2. Remove stem		Release hold on leaf and regrasp stem immediately below lefthand T and 1, with fingernails of T and 1 RH. Break stem and commence to draw stem out from leaf, to about 6". Pass hand holding stem behind LH and continue to draw stem leaving the leaf lightly resting against the back of the LH.			During removal of stem hold leaf in LH at right-angles to body; draw stem with RH towards body until about 6" of stem has been parted from the leaf.
	Hold leaf stationary while stem is being drawn out to 6", rotate hand once in clockwise direction while RH is wrapping leaf around back of hand during the continued drawing out of the stem process. When leaf has passed around heel of hand, and RH starts to draw leaf up back of hand, release hold of nose with T and 1 and lightly hold leaf in hand with 3 and 4 by holding leaf against palm.				
	Grasp leaf lightly as close to stem as possible with T and 1st and 2nd T. Controlling hold by applying sufficient pressure on stem against 1st knuckles of 1 and 2 to enable end of stem to be removed cleanly.	Bring stem between T and 1 LH to cross over 1 and 2 at 1st knuckle joint of LH.	Control passage of stem between fingers of LH.	Kinaesthetic (LH). Sufficient control to hold leaf while end of stem is being removed without holding up normal movement or allowing 'flags' to remain on removed stem.	
3. Place leaf on hand	Rotate hand once in anti-clockwise direction to unwrap leaf from hand. Reposition T, 1 and 2 on nose of leaf holding leaf on left hand side at nose T on front face of leaf, 1 and 2 on back.	Put aside clean stem in stem bag to RH side.			
		Grasp nose with T on front and 1st and 2nd at back on RH side of leaf at nose. Tear along stem by moving RH across in front of stationary LH quickly, holding nose of leaf firmly during tearing. Hold RH side of leaf lightly between 3 and 4 and palm and grasp nose of LH side of leaf with T on top and 1 and 2 on underside of leaf.	Control RH grasp.	Kinaesthetic (LH). Tension critical to spread leaf fully without tearing.	

Figure 10.6 *The form of skills analysis used by W D Seymour*

should teach these first. Often, this will require the preparation of special training exercises to remove these skill elements from the context of the job and to give concentrated practice in the knack. Sometimes this is possible in the context of the real job situation, but more commonly it requires the design of special training 'rigs' or 'simulators'. We shall examine some examples of such skill simulators in later chapters.

Once the skill elements of special difficulty have been learned up to a reasonable standard of performance, these elements are incorporated into the practice of the whole task. For sequential tasks, made up of a series of definite steps, the preferred tactic is the 'progressive parts' sequencing of practice. The trainee practices the first step A, the next B, then A + B, then C, then B + C, then A + B + C, and so on. If the task is an integrated one, with no fixed sequence of steps, it is practised as a whole.

The mathetics system of Gilbert

The mathetics system of task analysis and instructional design was developed by Tom Gilbert from the behavioural analysis techniques already used by psychologists in the 1950s. He published his system in a two-volume treatise called *Mathetics: The Technology of Education* (Gilbert 1962).

In Chapter 9, we made certain observations concerning Gilbert's methodology, in particular that the original claim made by Gilbert that mathetics is a complete technology of education was later retracted by him. But, despite its limitation to certain types of learning, the methodology has stood the test of time and in expanded or modified forms is still used as the basic approach of many instructional designers and training consultancy organizations.

The reason for the difficulty of the original papers on mathetics was the complex terminology that Gilbert developed for all aspects of the methodology. Much of this terminology is not perhaps all that essential and we will try to strip away the jargon in this discussion, to reveal mathetics as a very logical and thorough approach to instructional design, which is not really all that difficult to use.

Stimulus/ response notation

Mathetics is a complete system of analysis and design, replacing level 1 and 2 analysis of the more usually practised type, but capable of descending to a deeper level of analysis as and when required. The main difference between the mathetics approach to analysis and most other approaches is that it pays equal attention to the input, or *stimulus*, aspect of behaviour as it does to the output, or *response* aspect. Most other systems of analysis tend to concentrate only on the responses — on what is done — and do not give equal attention to the stimuli that control these responses: the 'when to do' and 'when not to do' aspects of the task. This is not quite true as it is always possible in any system of analysis to make a note of the when to do aspects. Indeed the formal definition of a task, quoted in Chapter 7, referred to a 'triggering event' that indicates when to perform the task. This triggering event is, of course, the stimulus in the jargon of the psychologist. However, the mathetics system is unique in insisting, through its notation used for analysis, that the triggering stimuli are always identified and specified for every task, task step, or smaller subdivision of behaviour.

The basic unit of analysis is the *operant*, which is one stimulus/response connection. An operant can be large, for example:

Stimulus: Response:
Incoming telephone call ——————▶ Connect it to the right extension

. . . or it can be small:

Stimulus: Response:
Telephone rings ——————————▶ pick it up and hold to ear

The same notation of analysis can therefore be used at various depths of detail. Rather than using a standardized form, the analyst simply uses a large sheet of paper and constructs a behaviour map or, as Gilbert calls it, a prescription. The analyst prescribes, diagrammatically, how the trainee should be able to perform after training. He does this by observing a 'master performer' and noting down his behaviour. This in principle is what any system of task analysis tries to do. However, the mathetics system does it in a particularly thorough way, passing through a series of deeper and deeper analyses (if the problem requires them) until the analyst has a clear idea of how to proceed in designing the instruction. Coupled to the range of special analyses, there are a series of rules or tactics which are brought into play depending on the *patterns of behaviour* which the analyst discovers during his analysis.

Although this approach is elaborate (therefore not always justifiable in its full form on economic grounds) and very behaviour-centred (therefore inappropriate for the initial stages of analysing subject matter or information), the more detailed stages of the method (the deeper analyses) can always be used when the detailed planning of the steps of instruction is envisaged. At this level, the analysis techniques are supplemented by detailed instructional tactics or rules.

The 'mental operations' approach of Landa

We have already discussed Landa's work in some detail in Chapter 9. His work is concerned with the analysis of the instructional needs for such subjects as Russian grammar and problem-solving in geometry. It is interesting, therefore, to examine his approach to the analysis of such 'school' subjects and compare it with the other two approaches we have discussed (which appear to be more concerned with the analysis of practical tasks).

Algorithmic and heuristic procedures

You must remember that Landa refers to the 'mental operations' that must be performed in order to solve a problem, be it a standard rule-following (algorithmic) type of procedure, as is the case of applying the rules of grammar to sentence construction, or a more open-ended (heuristic) procedure such as the solution of problems in geometry. These mental operations are what the behavioural psychologists have tended to ignore preferring to concentrate on the observable behaviour only.

Gagné's more recent position, however, has come round to acknowledging the presence of internal mental operations and the importance of knowing what they are. However, his approach to analysis leaves the impression that there are a set (how many we do not yet know) of general-purpose internal capabilities which can be developed (rather than taught) in one learning task and then transferred to many others. Such general cognitive skills or strategies possibly do exist, but Gagné's tactic of dropping the learner in at the deep end leaves a lot to be desired in the way of precision. Polya (see Chapters 1 and 9) goes further, by specifying a list of more or less general-purpose search heuristics for solving problems in mathematics.

We saw the similarity between the steps in this approach and the ones we have adopted as the problem-solving (or systems) approach to learning problems. So it would seem that there is some common structure in the approach one should adopt to problem-solving in general. However, can one make a judgement of how much the heuristics and their application to instructional design, which are presented in this book, will transfer as real skills to, say, the solution of geometry problems? To what extent will the student of this book who studies it thoroughly, applies its ideas to the design of instruction and thereby develops some reasonable level of skill in instructional design improve his performance in some other type of problem-solving activity (geometry or sentence construction). Very little probably. He may have more luck with, say, psychiatry, which also deals in the analysis of behaviour, albeit for different reasons.

Specific mental operations for specific types of problem-solving

Landa's approach differs from others, such as Gagné's, Bruner's and Polya's, in emphasizing the need to know the specific operations that are required to solve a specific type of problem. He makes a point of stressing that competence in a given type of problem-solving involves 'knowing the mental operations involved'. This 'knowing' is made up of *knowing how* to carry them out and *knowing when* to use them. (There appears to be a marked resemblance here to 'chains' and 'discriminations' but I do not know if Landa would agree.) He also emphasizes that 'one can know some of the operations involved and not know others', and that this can have a profound influence on performance in actually solving problems. (This reminds one of Gilbert's distinction between 'accomplishment' and 'acquirement', mentioned in Chapter 6, and the profound effect that a quite small deficiency in acquirement can have on accomplishment.)

The need for a deep analysis

Landa argues (as does Gilbert) that effective instruction must be based on a previous identification of *all* the mental operations (Gilbert says 'operants') that are involved and their interrelation. The teacher who is serious about wishing to instruct his students in the solution of a particular category of problem must first know the detailed mental operations that the solution of such specific problems entails, and must then plan his instruction in such a way that he can 'see' whether the learner is performing the operations correctly. A deep level of analysis is required of any category of problem-solving activity that in reality offers learning difficulties to students. The analysis performed for one type of problem-solving may not necessarily help the teacher to teach another type, unless there are marked similarities in the mental operations involved.

The methods of analysis

The publications of Landa's which have been translated into English are not very explicit on how to perform this detailed analysis of mental operations, as they do not include any complete examples of his analyses of geometry and grammar problem-solving, only isolated part-examples to illustrate certain points he is making. However, these are sufficient to illustrate the level of detail to which the analysis is taken. This is not that much unlike the depth of analysis used in the mathetics approach. However, the method of analysis and presentation is somewhat different. After all, one is attempting to analyse mental operations which are not directly observable. Therefore, the analysis must be a reflective self-examining process carried out by a master performer. The master performer is the analyst and must be included in the analysis team. There may be someone else included as well who is not skilled in the problem-solving task under analysis but who is more skilled in the analytical process being attempted. He is there to stimulate and control the master performer, but he cannot alone do the analysis. Perhaps one could visualize this process as the master performer trying to use the instructional designer as a typical student, trying to teach him the problem-solving process and both of them engaging in critical reflection of the thought processes and decisions that they have to take.

Use and misuse of the term 'algorithm'

The final object is to map out or list all the mental operations and decisions that have to be made by the competent problem-solver. These may turn out to be interrelated sequentially in a fixed manner and be of the type that can be transformed into specific instructions that, if followed correctly, guarantee the solution (ie an algorithm), or they may turn out not to be related in a specific sequence, nor to guarantee a solution, even if followed correctly but which nevertheless are the most effective way known to increase the probability of a solution being found (ie a set of heuristics).

Landa found that using Russian grammar correctly was a set of algorithmic procedures, whereas proving geometry theorems was a set of heuristic procedures. The heuristics, however, were much more specific to the type of problem than the general-purpose heuristics suggested by Polya (see Chapter 1). Concerning Landa's use of the word 'algorithm', we should note that he uses it in its mathematical sense of 'any set of instructions that, if followed correctly, will lead *anyone* to solve a relevant problem *correctly* and in the same *way*'. (The stressed words will recur later.)

It has become common practice in educational technology to use the term 'algorithm' for the flow-chart representation of an algorithm, usually in 'binary decision' (or yes/no) notation. This form of charting was developed by computer programmers to analyse decision processes into their specific operations in order to write computer programmes. It was later popularized by Cambridge Consultants (Gane, Horabin and Lewis 1966; Lewis and Wolfenden 1969) for the communication of complex procedures to people, thus often eliminating the need for much teaching. They have also been used as the basis of structuring and sequencing instructional programmes and have grown in popularity to the level of occasional overuse or misuse. As Landa points out, these charts are the graphical representation of algorithms, not the algorithms themselves. There are other, sometimes more appropriate, means of presenting the algorithm. Also the binary, yes/no, level of breakdown, so essential for computer purposes (as computers 'think' in binary notation) is not always the most appropriate for the human being. What appears in binary notation as a whole series of decisions, often appears to be handled by the human brain all at once and can therefore be treated as one decision in our algorithm. We are reminded here once more of Gilbert's basic behaviour patterns, such as discriminations — the searching for the telephone extension of a given department would require a multi-step binary decision programme for a computer (was the request for department P? — no — department Q? — no — department R? — etc). The human performer, on the other hand, seems to fetch the appropriate number out of memory in one attempt. Therefore, Gilbert treats such a discrimination as one behaviour unit. Similarly, Landa would agree that this is one mental operation, albeit a very simple one of pure recall, and would not in his algorithm break it down into binary decisions.

We have presented here an algorithm of some Latin grammar (see Figure 10.7), which was adapted (Romiszowski 1974) from an idea suggested by Evans (1964) in order to compare the instructional effectiveness of flow-chart presentations and other visual formats. The tabular form (Figure 10.8) was found to be much the easier to use, both as a job aid and as a learning aid. These findings would seem to support Landa's views concerning the degree of breakdown of the mental operations. Operations at the level of 'identify the tense required', 'identify whether the first noun in the sentence will be singular or plural', 'identify the stem ending of the verb', 'add appropriate verb endings to the verb stem', etc seem to be more in line with Landa's suggested level of breakdown of mental operations. The matching of the correct verb endings involves their memorization, a set of multiple discriminations. How the storage and recall actually occurs, in physiological terms, in the brain, is of no consequence. Perhaps the mechanism of the brain works on a binary system (which is unlikely), but it does not seem to be so to the reflective analyst of the problem-solving process. Therefore, the analyst should note the operations as they seem to occur in the human being and not be bound by a system of representation such as the binary flow-chart.

'Quasi-algorithms'   It is, moreover, quite possible to represent a decision making process as if it were an algorithmic process when in fact it is nothing of the sort. In Figure 10.9, for example, the question 'does the topic require a three dimensional presentation' is a case in point. The question can, apparently, only be answered with a 'yes' or a 'no'. But life is not really that simple. There are many factors (such as the learners' sophistication in reading two-dimensional representations of three-dimensional objects) which perhaps we do not have much data about. So our answer, be it 'yes' or 'no', has been arrived at by balancing our experience against the sketchy data we have, and going beyond the data to make a judgement in which we will not be wholly confident. We are operating in a heuristic manner in the middle of this 'algorithm'. The flow-chart is not an algorithm in the mathematical sense because it does *not* guarantee that *all* users will solve *all problems correctly* and in the *same way*. This does not, however, render this flow-chart useless. It has proved its worth as an aid to organizing one's thoughts about media selection. But perhaps it should not be called an algorithm.

The heuristic nature of responding to an algorithmic flow-chart, are equally

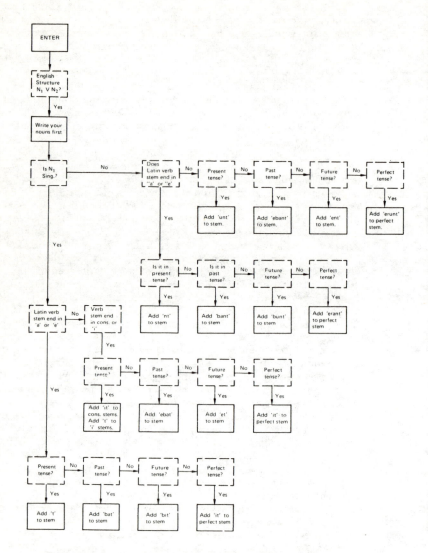

Figure 10.7 *An algorithm for obtaining Latin regular verb endings*

consider:

1 is first noun singular/plural
2 verb stem ending
3 required tense

Read off:
required verb ending
add it to the verb stem

		Present	Past	Future	Perfect
First noun is Singular	Verb stem ends in A or E	'nt'	'bant'	'bunt'	'erant'
	Other verb stem endings	'unt'	'ebant'	'ent'	'erunt'
First noun is Plural	Verb stem ends in A or E	't'	'bat'	'bit'	'it'
	Other verb stem endings ie consonant or 'i'	Stem ends with consonant: Add 'it' Stem ends with 'i': Add 't'	'ebat'	'et'	'it'

Figure 10.8 *Latin regular verb endings: an alternative chart to the algorithm*

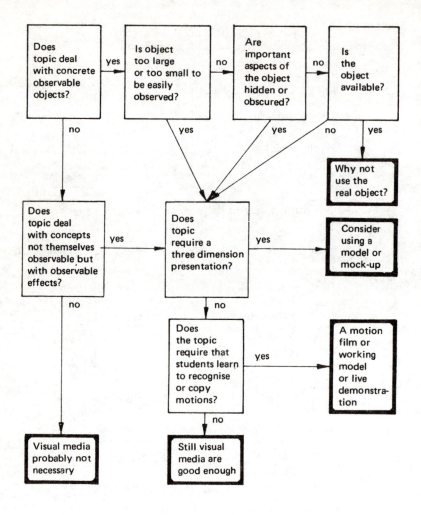

Figure 10.9 *Example of a 'quasi-algorithm':*
decisions for selecting visual media (Romiszowski 1974)

relevant to our earlier discussion in this chapter of the CRAMP system.

Incomplete
algorithms

Another possible criticism of many so-called algorithmic flow charts is that they are incomplete. Both the abovementioned examples can be considered incomplete from certain viewpoints. In the case of the media selection chart, this is because it was devised in the context of instructor training for the engineering industry and considered only the types of instructional content that such instructors would normally teach. So from a wider viewpoint the chart is quite incomplete as a general aid to selecting visual media. But for the limited category of problems for which it was designed, it has proved itself fairly complete. This illustrates the point that Landa makes concerning the need to analyse each type or category of problem-solving activity that is to be taught, and not to seek the general-purpose, all-embracing algorithm. This is where Landa's approach obviously qualifies to be classified as a level 4 type of analysis, as opposed to Gagné's level 3 approach which stops short at identifying that some sort of problem-solving activity is called for at a particular point.

10.7 Similarities and differences between the models

The
differences

The major difference between the three models for level 4 analysis that we have so far discussed is in their intended areas of application. Seymour's model was developed specifically for the analysis of industrial skills. It is easiest to apply this model to repetitive, high-speed, physical operations. It needs to be modified to be used for the analysis of tasks in which there is not a fixed sequence of operations, such as the tasks of supervising process equipment. In such tasks the difficulty rarely lies in the physical motions that are demanded by the operations, but rather in the decisions that the operator must make in order to choose between alternative operations. In a plastics production plant, for example, the operator does little actual physical work, other than the operation of some valves and switches. The difficulty lies in deciding when or whether to operate certain controls and by how much, in order to maintain the quality of the plastic being produced. He has no trouble in learning to operate the controls. His difficulty lies in interpreting the signals (or stimuli) which the various dials, meters or analysis sheets present to him.

Seymour's
skills analysis

Gilbert's
mathetics

In such tasks, Gilbert's approach pays off, as it forces the analyst to consciously look for all the stimuli that may occur and to analyse the desired responses for each one. All the alternative courses of action are explored and are mapped out (using stimulus/response notation). Important discriminations are identified, as are the generalizations (or classifications of situations that require the same response). This enables the analyst to specify the concepts that the operator should master. We are now in the cognitive domain, analysing what the learner should 'know' in order that he should be able to 'perform'. Seymour's methodology does not really get involved with the knowledge content of the task in a systematic manner. At most, some observations are made in the 'comments' column to indicate that the analyst has noticed the need for some specific knowledge. The analysis of this knowledge to ascertain whether it might not be the root of the learner's difficulties is better done by Gilbert's methodology.

However, despite Gilbert's original claims for mathetics, it becomes rather difficult for an analyst to map out a behaviour pattern when the intermediate steps of the behaviour are triggered off by internally generated stimuli, that is when the master performer is thinking rather than doing. The analyst may observe the initial stimulus (say a problem of mathematics) presented to the master performer. He may also observe the final response (the solution), but he must use indirect means (questioning or introspection) to identify the complex pattern of intermediate decisions that the master performer made to arrive at his solution. Experienced analysts will testify to the difficulty often encountered in extracting from a skilled performer the exact reasons for his actions, or the exact steps he takes in planning his designs. There is no way around this difficulty. The skilled performer must become the analyst, must become introspective, must try to identify how he makes his decisions, what internally stored knowledge he uses and what are the thinking processes that go on in his head.

Landa's analysis of mental operations

It is this type of introspective analysis by the expert that is the basis of Landa's approach. He attempts to identify all the specific mental operations that need to be performed to solve a particular category of problem, together with all the alternatives and the decisions which must be taken to choose between the alternatives. Thus Landa is mapping out the internal perceptions of an intellectual nature that are stimulated by certain aspects of the problem and the resultant intellectual decisions (or responses) that the expert makes. This perception-decision-operation sequence is akin to the stimulus-decision-response sequence used as the unit of analysis (the operant) in mathetics. The difference is that the latter is an externally observable event (at least the stimulus and the response), whereas the former may be a completely internal, not directly observable, unit of behaviour.

The similarities

Overlap

Despite the differences in the three approaches, one can observe an overlap in the areas of application for which they are best suited and a basic similarity which links them and differentiates them from the less thorough, level 3 models discussed earlier. The overlap in their levels of application can be visualized by drawing a graph (see Figure 10.10). Skills analysis is at its best when the task is composed of operations of high physical complexity (because of high-speed performance or to the need for special perceptual acuity or manual dexterity) and low intellectual complexity.

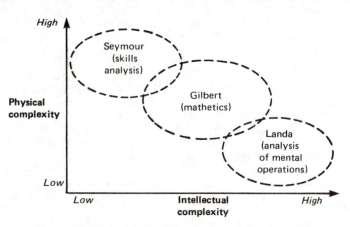

Figure 10.10 *Areas of overlap in the application of the level 4 models analysed*

Landa's approach is needed for tasks composed of intellectual operations of high complexity (intellectual problem-solving). Mathetics bridges the gap, being excellent for the analysis of tasks that have both physical and intellectual components of reasonable complexity, but the physical component does not involve high-speed repetitive operations and the intellectual component is not entirely made up of internalized reflective thinking, but is linked to external events (stimuli).

To complete the picture, one might consider the bottom-left and top-right areas of our graph (Figure 10.10). At the bottom-left, no level 4 analysis should be required, as tasks of low complexity should be effectively taught on the basis of a level 3 or even shallower analysis. The expense of a more detailed analysis is not justified. (Industry in Britain in the 1960s used a large amount of skills analysis, and there was as a result a considerable waste of time and other resources devoted to performing Seymour-type analyses of all the operations of all tasks, irrespective of their level of difficulty for the trainee.)

Combination At the top-right of the graph, there are probably few tasks that are highly complex both in their physical and intellectual aspects. Perhaps the creative arts qualify in some respects. The painter composing and painting an original picture and the jazz musician improvising freely on a basic melody use a high level of both physical and intellectual skill when performing. However, it is possible to separate out these two components, analyse and teach them separately (it is possible to appreciate a work of art and to criticize it without having the skills necessary to produce it — a conductor can 'manage' all the instruments of an orchestra without necessarily being able to play them). Thus such complex multi-faceted tasks can be analysed by a combination of techniques suited to physical operations and techniques suited to mental operations. This may be the best approach to adopt when faced with the type of task that contains 'planning skills'.

Similar approach The basic similarity in the three approaches discussed (which incidentally differentiates them from most other methods of analysis) is that all three pay attention not only to what is done (motions, responses, mental operations), but also to what triggers off action (perception of relevant signals or stimuli or characteristics of the problem). This focus on the role of perception (both in the physical and intellectual sense) in any skilled activity assists the analyst in identifying the precise roots of learning difficulties that are typically experienced by novices. More often than not, the learning difficulty does not lie in the performance of the operation (mental or physical) but in the perception and interpretation of information in order to decide what operation to perform and when. The emphasis on both perception and resultant action, together with the minute level of detail at which the observations are often made, are the chief characteristics of level 4 analysis.

10.8 When to perform a deep analysis

Such a detailed and painstaking approach costs a great deal of time. Let us close this chapter by considering briefly when one is justified in embarking on a thorough level 4 analysis. We have already mentioned the case of skills analysis and British industry. Three lessons can be drawn:

1. Do not embark on an analysis that is deeper than the complexity of the problem. Analysis is a tool to be used to understand the problems that the learner will face. As soon as we feel confident that we understand the problems sufficiently to propose solutions, we should propose solutions.

2. Do not perform analyses that no one will use. A complex and thorough analysis will result in data sufficient to develop all the instructional events required. If the overall intention is to leave the teaching to the teachers then it is probable that a centrally produced deep analysis will be a waste of effort. The teachers will probably not use it, unless they are systematically trained to use it. Thus, a deep analysis implies either that you plan to programme the instruction (by the development of highly structured instructional materials that the teachers will be expected to use), or that you plan to programme the teachers, (as is done on highly specialist teacher training courses, such as those for teaching literacy, teaching English as a foreign language, etc).

3. Do not perform analyses that you cannot afford. Many projects have come to grief by spending so much of their resources in analysis that they were never finished.

11. Plugging the Gaps in Present Approaches to Instructional Design

11.1 Where we are going in this chapter

Previous sections

We have in previous sections considered the identification and definition of a problem (performance or informational) which might require instruction. We then proceeded to the analysis of the problem in order to determine whether instruction really was the solution, whether other actions should be taken in conjunction with instruction as a 'complete' solution and what would be the expected outcomes (objectives) of instruction.

This section

In this section we have proceeded to the design of the solution. We have noticed in the last chapter that the design of instruction may often (but not always) need to be preceded by further analysis of the objectives and the content in order to obtain the sort of 'fine grained' data necessary to identify probable learning problems and design appropriate instructional solutions. We have examined several existing models for this deeper analysis and have classified them as 'level 3' and 'level 4' analysis. We have seen one common aspect in all these models — they are associated with some theory of how to go about the process of instruction. In all cases one is analysing the objectives, the content (and the target population) in order to make instructional decisions. In order to help with this decision making process, the models make use of some conceptual schema, classification or 'taxonomy' of different types of learning, types of objectives (and as we shall soon see, different types of content).

This chapter

We noticed, when analysing three examples of 'level 3' models, that the conceptual schemata were not equivalent and indeed none of them seemed to be complete. We noticed at 'level 4' a greater degree of coherence and similarity of approach and we even hinted that there may be a common way to approach the deep analysis of skills, whether physical or intellectual. In this chapter we shall examine more closely the apparent gaps in the most commonly used taxonomies and shall attempt to fill them. We shall indeed question the basic structure of some of these taxonomies. We shall also attempt to identify the common aspects of skills, whether physical, intellectual, social, interpersonal etc.

11.2 The missing domain — social, interpersonal, interactive

11.2.1 What are interactive skills?

The tripartite division

It is probably fair to blame Bloom and his associates for 'sanctifying' the division of learning into three domains, even if they were not to blame for their invention. The great impact of the work of Bloom *et al* in producing recipes for the classification of educational objectives has rendered it difficult for successive generations of educational thinkers to break away from the tripartite division of education (and often training) into:

1. The *cognitive* domain — intellectual *knowledge* and *skills*
2. The *affective* domain — feelings, attitudes and values
3. The *psychomotor* domain — physical skills.

Furthermore, general neglect of the psychomotor domain until recently has tended to delineate the area of interest of education as lying in the cognitive and affective domains — imparting knowledge, developing skills in its use and developing the 'right' attitudes to learning and to the phenomena of our society. The psychomotor domain was left to the 'training' sector.

Alternative approaches

However, the training sector has not always agreed to be bound by the 'education' view. In the first place, many trainers have traditionally preferred (and still do) to use a basic division between *knowledge* and *skills* as a basis for classification. In the second place, training has for some time distinguished a variety of different types of skill, including physical skills, intellectual skills (with various sub-divisions such as perceptual skills, sensori-motor skills, planning skills, procedural skills, problem-solving or troubleshooting skills, etc) and a further very important category of *interpersonal* or *interactive skills*.

Interactive skills

This does not imply that the education sector has habitually ignored these types of skills. On the contrary, many reports and curricula stress the social aspects of education as perhaps the most important elements in a general education. It is all the more surprising therefore that the most widely known classification of educational objectives should omit this category of skills altogether. The amount of research and development that has gone into management development in the interpersonal skill domain, into group dynamics techniques for developing interactive skills such as salesmanship, leadership, empathy, customer relations and so on, has demonstrated that this is indeed a domain of learning with its own characteristic problems and its own types of solutions.

Interactive skills as a separate class

Certainly, it is not easy to classify any of these types of skilled activity into the tripartite classification. Most interactive skills would seem to have some elements of attitude (affective domain) and would require some basic knowledge to be applied (cognitive domain). They may even call for some physical action at times, as in the case of opening doors or giving up seats to ladies in public conveyances (psychomotor domain perhaps?). Thus at some very detailed level of breakdown one could perhaps classify the elements (individual operants of behaviour) of an interactive skill into Bloom's three categories. However, an interactive skill is to do *basically* with *interaction* (between people), just as a psychomotor skill is to do *basically* with *physical action* (of people), a cognitive skill with *intellectual activity* (thinking out relationships between objects, people, phenomena etc) and (we shall argue shortly) an 'affective skill' is to do *basically* with *reacting* appropriately (to objects, events, phenomena, people etc). The work done, mainly in the 'training' context, on interactive skills suggests that it is useful to classify them in a category of their own. This we shall do in the rest of this book.

11.2.2 Interactive skills in education

The general importance of interpersonal skills has not of course been ignored by educational theorists. Education acts are full of references to 'growth to maturity as a fully participating member of society' and such-like pious intentions, often specified in more detail as 'the ability to communicate, cooperate and interact with his fellows' etc.

The 'deep end' approach

However, such phrases are still a long way from being clear and measurable instructional objectives. Indeed, the difficulties of transforming such personal skills into sets of identifiable behaviours have proved immense, as we noted in Chapter 6, on objectives. The normal reaction in education to a skill which defies analysis into its components is to use the 'throwing in at the deep end' approach. Essentially this implies putting the learner into the final 'real life' situation (or a close simulation of it) and letting him perform. We can usually supply some feedback to the learner at the end of the exercise (because we know how to identify the presence or absence of the skill to be developed) but we cannot help him much during the actual exercise (because we do not know how to identify the component sub-skills of the total skill). We can therefore tell the learner at the end of the learning session whether he has got to where we hoped he would, but cannot tell him during the session whether he is heading in the right direction or how he should change his route. It reminds one of the story of the fakir's apprentice who goes through years of aping every aspect of the life-style of his master, eventually developing the master's fire-eating and lying-on-beds-of-nails capabilities, but neither master nor apprentice being quite sure which of the characteristics of the master's life-style had contributed what to the development of these capabilities. We only got away from this sort of 'deep end' approach in the industrial apprenticeship in the last 10 years or so. We have yet to get away from it in moral and emotional education.

Given an undefined and unanalysed area, full of mystique, two tendencies appear. Entrepreneurs step in with 'instant solutions', safe in the knowledge that it will be very difficult either to prove or disprove the effectiveness of their techniques (the same type of situation is encountered in psychiatry). Inevitably, like the religious cults of California, each new technique gathers a small group of fervent supporters who, by their excessive zeal, often discredit the technique even more than it deserves. This helps to develop the other tendency — a rejection of the technique and of all connected with it by the 'scientific community', meaning those who like to see all things measured and reject anything that cannot for the moment be measured.

Interactive skills and the educational technologist   Perhaps these two tendencies explain the position of personal and interpersonal (interactive) skills with respect to developments in educational technology. One trend has been the development of simulations and games (especially in management or supervisory development and in social education in schools) which are often examples of the 'deep end' approach: 'we don't quite know what's safe to leave out, so let's make the simulation as realistic as possible.' Another trend has been the development of a variety of group-dynamic techniques for encouraging freedom of interaction, variety of interaction and depth of interaction. These techniques are not simulations in a direct sense as they usually bear no resemblance to the real-life situation which they purport to promote. Have you ever wondered exactly which job skills were being developed in a group of managers deep in transcendental meditation, or blindfolded and engaged in 'touching' exercise? Of course not all the techniques promoted are so far removed from the realities of life, but it only needs a few rum ones in the bunch for the whole group dynamics movement to be rejected by some educators.

Thus there has been a tendency for educational technology to ignore the group dynamics movement and this has no doubt been helped by a philosophical polarization between the 'social education' supporters who are staunch believers in the process-oriented approach to education (and all that implies in the way of discovery approach for all learning), and the more dyed-in-the-wool educational technologists who want to have measurable products (objectives) defined for all learning and often find it hard to justify discovery methods on a cost-effectiveness basis.

11.2.3 Interactive skills in industrial training

Turning now to the area of interactive skills in industry, as an example, one notices that several well-intentioned attempts to develop techniques of training in interpersonal skills have suffered the 'bandwagon' malady of growing rapidly in application up to a point, among a restricted group of faithful followers, then stagnating and slowly disappearing from the scene.

T-groups and other approaches   Perhaps the earliest and still the best known (but that does not imply much practised) technique, is the T-group method, developed by Lewin at the Centre for Group Dynamics in the 1940s. This is a sort of role-playing, not directed at specific job-related roles, but focusing the participants' attention on the interpersonal events which are occurring and aiming to heighten their sensitivity to these events. Participants learn by extending their awareness of their actual and possible behaviours. What a participant gets out of a session is very much what he *feels* he got out of it, as the only methods of evaluation are the participant's observations of his own behaviour and the observations of other participants on his behaviour. Thus, almost by definition, the T-group method is incapable of being evaluated objectively.

Other approaches have followed which have attempted to make interpersonal skills training more objective. This has been done in two ways: by the use of a systematic set of evaluation instruments in an attempt to avoid the subjectivity of evaluation (as in the technique of instrumented laboratory training, in which the participants complete complex evaluation instruments after every training session and maintain wall charts of their individual and group performance); or alternatively by the use of a more realistic, job-related context for the interaction exercises (as in the 'managment grid' approach in which managers classify each other on a 'grid' of management styles). However, none of these approaches manages to escape completely from the 'subjective evaluation' criticism, nor have they managed to prove conclusively their value to the participants by on-the-job results, after training.

The behaviour analysis approach

A recently developed approach seems to be overcoming these difficulties and merits especial mention here as it seems to be an excellent example of a 'level 3' analysis. This is the method based on 'behaviour analysis' which was first developed by Neil Rackham and Terry Morgan at BOAC* in the UK.

It is interesting to review rapidly how Rackham and Morgan became involved with the analysis and classifying of interactive behaviour. Their interest started from some weaknesses identified in an 'administrative skills' course that they attempted to revise in 1968. Since that date research and development has continued into ways of identifying and classifying interactive behaviours and techniques for developing the desired ones. Rackham and Morgan describe the beginnings of their interest as follows (Rackham and Morgan 1977):

> The course was traditional in its design. That is, it contained a lot of information giving of the 'how to do it' or 'traps to avoid' kind, interspersed with case studies, and a little bit of role-playing. By the standards of many other companies, it would have been rated a good course of its kind. So why were the training staff dissatisfied with it? There were two main reasons.
>
> First, although participants generally rated the course as enjoyable and useful, there was little evidence that it actually made them more skilful in the areas covered by the course. The problem with the course, as trainers saw it, was that while it gave supervisors knowledge *about* various supervisory skills, it lacked two features crucial for skill improvement — namely, opportunities for practice of the skills, and information (feedback) on how well, or badly, the skills were being performed. No trainer worth his salt would attempt to train someone in a psycho-motor skill without allowing him to practice, and giving him feedback on his performance. Yet the BOAC Administrative Skills course (in common, let it be said, with much supervisory training conducted elsewhere) did not take account of these 'home truths' of skill learning.
>
> Second, the balance of the course was not in keeping with the reality of the supervisor's job as it was coming to be understood. That is, the emphasis in the course on *people* skills (or *interactive* skills as we will call them in this book) was less than their importance in the job situation seemed to warrant. The conclusion did not stem from analyses of training needs based on the conventional job description approach: indeed such analyses tended to support an emphasis on the procedural skills of supervision. Thus, among a group of supervisors, when procedural and interactive skill needs were compared, the relative proportion of training needs arising from the job description approach was 80 per cent procedural and 20 per cent interactive. From which it would seem fair to conclude that a supervisory training course should give priority to procedural skills over interactive skills — as the Administrative Skills course did. However, when the training needs of the same group of supervisors were investigated using another approach, the critical incident technique, which asked them to describe those incidents in any time period which gave them difficulty, the results were quite different. The training needs identified were 30 per cent procedural and 70 per cent interactive — an

* BOAC now forms part of British Airways.

almost complete reversal of the results from the job description approach.

The comments regarding job analysis by task-based methods and 'critical incident' methods, and the different pattern of needs that was thrown up, are particularly interesting. We see that the way in which the 'level 1 and 2' analysis is carried out can strongly influence what comes to the top as being 'worth teaching'.

Having identified that the existing training was not what was wanted, they looked at other techniques, including those mentioned above, and rejected all of them on the grounds of insufficient evidence of contributing to job-performance improvement. They therefore set out to create a more objective technique, as follows:

The first and most basic assumption was that interactive competence — the facility to work effectively with others — is primarily a skill, rather than a matter of attitudes or knowledge. From this assumption followed conclusions about the nature of the training required to develop competence: that it should provide opportunities for trainees to interact, and that feedback on their performance should be available to trainees. Had we adopted an assumption that interactive competence is primarily dependent on attitudes, or on knowledge, it hardly needs to be said that the course design requirements would have been very different.

The second assumption, almost as basic as the first in terms of its influence on the development, was that a key component of interactive skill is verbal behaviour. From the viewpoint of training people to improve their skill, it is the most profitable component on which to concentrate because it is readily observable and measurable. This assumption led directly to the development of behaviour analysis as a tool for monitoring performance and providing feedback.

The global theory
Next we took what might be called a *global* view of interactive skill. We assumed that the skill of dealing with people is a general one, relatively independent of the specific situation in which it is practised. The corollaries of this assumption are that a person who is good at dealing with one kind of situation will be equally competent in other situations, and that one interactive task is as good as another for giving practice in the skill of dealing with people.

> There is a generalized skill of interacting which is largely independent of specific situations
>
> THEREFORE
> there must be particular behaviours which will be helpful to an individual across the majority of situations
>
> THEREFORE
> individuals from different jobs have very similar training needs and objectives
>
> THEREFORE
> there are likely to be 'right' and 'wrong' behaviours in a general sense
>
> THEREFORE
> because these behaviours are useful in almost all situations then they can be developed by almost any interactive training task (eg Lego bricks).

Figure 11.1 *The 'global' theory of interactive skills development (from Rackham, N and Morgan, T [1977])*

The behaviour analysis instrument referred to above was developed as a set of verbal behaviour categories which went through several versions and modifications (the final version presented in their 1977 book being the fifth main version developed). Each version of the classification was extensively field-tested and a considerable amount of data was amassed on whether the classifications were usable and useful as means of supplying feedback to course participants.

Proposing Behaviour which puts forward a new concept suggestion or course of action (and is actionable).

Building Behaviour which extends or develops a proposal which has been made by another person (and is actionable).

Supporting Behaviour which involves a conscious and direct declaration of support or agreement with another person or his concepts.

Disagreeing Behaviour which involves a conscious, direct and reasoned declaration of difference of opinion, or criticism of another person's concepts.

Defending/attacking Behaviour which attacks another person or defensively strengthens an individual's own position. Defending/attacking behaviours usually involve overt value judgements and often contain emotional overtones.

Blocking/difficulty stating Behaviour which places a difficulty or block in the path of a proposal or concept without offering any alternative proposal and without offering a reasoned statement of disagreement. Blocking/difficulty stating behaviour therefore tends to be rather bald: eg, 'It won't work,' or 'We couldn't possibly accept that.'

Open Behaviour which exposes the individual who makes it to risk of ridicule or loss of status. This behaviour may be considered as the opposite of defending/ attacking, including within this category admissions of mistakes or inadequacies provided that these are made in a non-defensive manner.

Testing understanding Behaviour which seeks to establish whether or not an earlier contribution has been understood.

Summarizing Behaviour which summarizes, or otherwise restates in a compact form, the content of previous discussions or considerations.

Seeking information Behaviour which seeks facts, opinions or clarification from another individual or individuals.

Giving information Behaviour which offers facts, opinions or clarification to other individuals.

Shutting out Behaviour which excludes, or attempts to exclude, another group member (eg, interrupting, talking over).

Bringing in Behaviour which is a direct and positive attempt to involve another group member.

Figure 11.2 *A classification of interactive behaviours (from Rackham, N and Morgan, T [1977])*

A level 3 analysis

Note that the approach so far has many of the characteristics of a 'level 2' analysis. The interactive behaviour of the supervisors has been analysed and certain generalized categories of interactive behaviour have been established.

One can now set about the development of a course by deciding which of the behaviour categories to include and then selecting or developing appropriate exercises (a process analogous to the use of Bloom's taxonomy in the cognitive domain, or to the use of Gagné's categories of learning). The course would have general applicability for any group of supervisors — *if* the 'global theory' of interactive skills holds water.

The 'specific' theory

However, another development took place over the years. The early 'global theory' of interactive skills, which suggests that almost any interactive exercise can develop almost any of the types of interactive behaviour, was gradually abandoned. In its place there grew up a 'specific' theory, which in outline is as shown in Figure 11.3.

Level 3 analysis

This change in outlook of course implied the need to match *behaviour type* to *specific exercise*. Note that now we have the characteristics of a 'level 3' analysis. All we need is a 'model for instructional design' to complete an approach almost as rigorous as mathetics, but in a rather specialized area of learning. This model is identified by Rackham and Morgan as follows:

> Effective interaction depends almost entirely on the
> specific situation in which the interaction takes place
>
> THEREFORE
>
> the usefulness of particular behaviours to an individual
> will depend on the context or situation in which they
> are used
>
> THEREFORE
>
> individuals from different jobs have very different
> training needs and objectives
>
> THEREFORE
>
> there are unlikely to be 'right' and 'wrong' behaviours in
> a general sense
>
> THEREFORE
>
> because the appropriateness of a behaviour is dependent
> on the situation such behaviours can only be developed
> by specific tasks geared to the situation and the
> individual's need.

Figure 11.3 *The 'specific' theory of interactive skills development
(from Rackham, N and Morgan, T [1977])*

We hypothesized a number of conditions necessary for skilled interaction:

A person must be able to perceive accurately the behaviours he is using, and the behaviours those with whom he is interacting are using. To do this he must have a language for recognizing and describing behaviour — a workable categorization system.

A person must know which behaviours are likely to be appropriate in different situations — or be capable of finding out by experimenting with his behaviours and observing the results.

A person must be able to 'produce' the appropriate behaviours at will. To do this, he must have a wide repertoire of 'available' behaviours, and be flexible in his use of behaviours.

The reader will note that the three conditions for skilled interaction are, in general terms, a *perception* condition, a *knowledge* condition and an *ability to act* condition. We shall meet these same three types of conditions in other types of skill. Indeed it may be possible to generalize that all skills require these three types of conditions for performance, which in turn require three different types of conditions for learning (more about this in the next chapter).

To conclude, the work of Rackham and Morgan summarized here is interesting on various counts. First, it shows that an area of learning for long considered un-measurable and un-programmable was capable of being measured and programmed to a high degree by the concentration of research and development effort on the problem in a systematic manner. Second, it shows the amount of time and effort that is required to bring order and measurability into quite a small and well-defined area of interactive skills (supervisory skills). Much more research and development would have to be expended in order to treat other areas of interpersonal and social skills in the same manner. Third, whereas the resources to perform such research and development may be forthcoming in areas linked to productive job performance, it is unlikely at the moment that similar resources could be found to develop similar rigorous analyses of the sort of social skills that the general school curriculum is supposed to promote.

11.2.4 Use of simulation for interactive skills training

A simpler
approach

However, there is another approach — the 'deep end' approach we mentioned earlier. It takes the form of simulations and games. The learner is asked to participate in activities which are a close simulation of the real-life situation for which we are preparing him (in the case of simulations) or (in the case of games) he participates in exercises that may perhaps simulate only one aspect (one skill) of reality. The instructional designer, being unable or unwilling to analyse in great depth the behaviours that he wishes to teach, simply constructs a set of simulation exercises or a full-blown 'replica' of the situation for which he wishes to prepare the learner. The learner, by participating, practises the behaviours he will be called upon to exhibit in reality.

Simulation in the training context
Well known examples of the use of such techniques for the development of interactive skills in industry include:

- management games, involving role-playing and dealing with various aspects of employer-employee relations;
- role-playing for the development of interviewing skills;
- 'microteaching' exercises for the development of the classroom — teaching skills of the teacher;
- simulations of customer/salesman interactions in courses on salesmanship;
- simulated telephone calls used in the training of telephonists.

Simulation in the education context
In education, the use of simulation games for 'social education' has been a growing trend for some years. By 'social education' one should understand more than merely 'social interactions'. One would include a lot of conceptual learning about the structure of society and how it operates, but certainly the development of interactive skills would form a part of social education. The skills that would be included in a general school course would necessarily be less specific on the whole. Rather than 'correct customer handling' one would expect to see 'discussing without arguing', or 'controlling one's temper'.

The techniques used in schools are similar to those in training — role-playing, dramatization — but often the behaviours expected of the participants are less fully defined. The main aim is to participate usually in a competitive, 'game' situation. As Coleman (1974) put it:

Simulation games for social skills
A game is a way of partitioning off a portion of action from the complex stream-of-life activities. It partitions off a set of players, a set of allowable actions, a segment of time, and establishes a framework within which the action takes place. It establishes what one might describe as a minute system of activities, and if the game contains more than a single player (as most games do), the game can even be described as a minute social system.

It is undoubtedly for this reason that games are such an important part of the socialization of young children. For the playing of a game allows a child to practise, in this limited framework, action that is interdependent with the actions of others, carried out within a set of rules, and in pursuit of a goal. As Piaget's observations of children playing the game of marbles show, children do not immediately learn the idea of playing a game, and only slowly gain a sense of the nature of its rules. Piaget suggests that the learning of the nature of rules in a game is, in fact, the learning of the nature of a moral order.

Thus, games may be regarded as a special invention in which children or adults practise with the components of life itself, a kind of play within the larger play of life. Because they are constructed of these components of life, games as means by which children learn deserve more serious attention than they have received.

Such combined simulations of life, with a gaming element, are called 'simulation games'. We will define them further in Chapter 15.

Experiential learning
Simulation games are techniques which promote what has come to be called 'experiential learning', ie learning through direct experience or involvement with the problems or issues of real life. Of course there are other techniques which do this, project work for example. However, in our present context simulations and games are of special interest in that they are more highly structured and pre-prepared than the average project, yet not as highly structured as, say, an audiovisual package or a programmed text. Also, the instructional strategy used by most simulation games is quite different from that typically employed in instructional materials developed from a deep analysis of the objectives.

A good simulation game should have objectives, but these would be derived from a 'level 1' or 'level 2' analysis. Once we have identified the critical tasks in a job, we can begin to devise exercises that will simulate those tasks (and those only), thus giving the learner a 'simplified model of reality' to play with Alternatively we can descend to 'level 2' and identify the critical operations in a given task. Then we can proceed directly to devising exercises that will give practise in those operations, and those only.

We shall leave the details of how to design simulations and games, and further considerations of when it is desirable to use such techniques, for later chapters. Here, our concern has been to identify 'interactive skills' as worthy of consideration as a separate category of skilled human behaviour, capable of being analysed to greater or lesser depth of detail and therefore capable of being developed by 'instruction'. To what extent simulations and games should be considered as 'instructional techniques' is a question on which people differ. However, in the light of the definition of 'instruction' that has been adopted in this book (has precise objectives and has precise methods pre-prepared to achieve them) at least some types of simulation games would qualify.

Furthermore, simulations and games have particular applicability to the development of interactive skills.

11.3 The affective domain — feelings or skills?

We commenced the previous discussion of interactive skills by observing that it was not easy to classify many of these into the three domains identified by Bloom. However, we saw a certain affinity between these skills and the affective domain, in particular. After all it is difficult to separate how we react (to people or events) from how we feel about them. The difficulty for the salesgirl learning that 'the customer is always right' is exactly this — she must behave overtly *as if* the customer was right, pleasant, intelligent etc, when in reality she may be feeling scorn for his lack of intelligence, anger for the unpleasant way he treated her and exasperation because she knows that really the customer is quite wrong.

It is a moot point to what extent we could teach the salesgirl *not to feel* scorn, anger or exasperation in situations which would quite naturally raise these feelings in any normal person. Rather, we are concerned with teaching her to control her emotions — *not to show* her feelings. In doing this, we are attempting to develop certain *skills* of self-control.

As Ebel (1974) points out, it is indeed a moot point whether we should talk of the 'teaching of feelings'. He says:

Feelings are essentially unteachable. They cannot be passed along from teacher to learner in the way that information is transmitted. Nor can the learner acquire them by pursuing them directly as he might acquire understanding by study. Feelings are almost always the consequence of something — of success or failure, of duty done or duty ignored, of danger encountered or danger escaped. Further, good feelings (and bad feelings also, fortunately) are seldom if ever permanent possessions. They tend to be highly ephemeral. The surest prediction that one can make when he feels particularly good, strong, wise, or happy is that sooner or later he is going to feel bad, weak, foolish, or sad. In these circumstances it is hardly surprising that feelings are difficult to teach.

Nor do they need to be taught. A new-born infant has, or quickly develops, a full complement of them — pain, rage, satiety, drowsiness, vitality, joy, love, and all the rest. Experience may attach these feelings to new objects. It may teach the wisdom of curbing the expression of certain feelings at inappropriate times or in inappropriate ways. And while such attachments and curbings may be desirable, and may be seen as part of the task of the school, they hardly qualify as one of its major missions.

The conditioning of attitudes

However, it is possible to transfer, or attach, certain specific feelings or emotions to certain specific objects, events or people. This can be done, for instance, by the classic Pavlovian conditioning method of pairing a new 'neutral' stimulus with one that already evokes the desired reaction, as a response. Watson (1920) demonstrated the power of this technique by 'teaching' a small boy (little Albert) to fear a white rabbit. The procedure was simple. Albert disliked and feared loud noises. Every time there was a loud, unexpected noise, Albert demonstrated the symptoms of fear. Watson presented the rabbit to Albert and at the same moment caused a loud noise to occur. After a few repetitions, Albert showed fear at the sight of the rabbit, even when there was no loud noise.

By similar pairing of stimuli, one can elicit feelings of pleasure to new stimuli. Roden and Hapkiewicz (1974) argue that much of what happens in typical classrooms produces undesirable feelings towards learning, as the subject in question is paired with 'failure', 'ridicule' or some other feared or hated situation. They argue that skilful use of Pavlov's principle could reverse this. Learning can be paired with pleasant stimuli that naturally produce feelings of pleasure, interest and curiosity. In his booklet *Developing Attitude Toward Learning*, Mager (1968) suggests various practical ways in which the teacher may plan to develop positive attitudes to his teaching. He refers to the identification of 'approach behaviours' and 'avoidance behaviours' as indicators of the attitude of the learner. He tends, however, to favour the 'operant conditioning' principles developed by Skinner as a technique of developing positive attitudes. By reinforcing the approach behaviours, by means of suitable 'pleasant' consequences, one seeks to increase the frequency of their occurrence.

An example from the education context

Thus, whichever method one adopts, one is manipulating the environment in order to condition the learner to exhibit positive attitudes (approach behaviours) when faced with specific circumstances. This implies that our sphere of activity, in school or training centre, in so far as 'teaching' feelings is concerned, is severely limited by the types of circumstances that we can arrange.

To take social science as an example, it is quite feasible to attempt to form the learner's attitudes towards the study of social science, because the activities and events involved in this study occur in the school and are under our control. It is quite another matter to try to form the students' attitudes towards a specific social problem, say racial strife. This does not (generally) happen in the classroom and is certainly not under our control. How do we arrange to pair stimuli that give the learner a pleasant feeling with the appearance of a face of a different colour? Or how do we arrange to reinforce approach behaviours and extinguish avoidance behaviours that our students might exhibit on meeting strange foreigners? The best we can do is to talk about the problem (which is not at all effective) or to try to simulate the problem situation in school (which can be effective, provided that the environment outside of school is not more efficient at pairing unpleasant stimuli or reinforcing avoidance behaviours). Often, the limitations of the school environment, however well planned, are dooming it to failure in its competition with the living environment of our students.

Finally, it follows from the preceding discussion that it is absolute nonsense to talk of 'teaching positive attitudes or feelings' in the general sense. As Ebel said, we do not teach feelings; we can at best attach certain feelings to certain situations. We can form a specific attitude towards a specific class of objects or events or people.

An example from the training context

Let us now return to consider our salesgirl. The type of experiences that she has undergone, either in training or in real life, may have formed a specific attitude towards customers (or different attitudes towards different types of customers). This will have occurred through some form of conditioning process, either planned or accidental. The attitude of our salesgirl will certainly influence how easily we can train her to treat all customers with civility, but whatever her attitude, however negative, it is still possible (at least theoretically) to train her to behave *as if* she had a positive attitude to all customers. This would imply that she had mastered a type of interactive skill. In practising this skill, she controls her feelings in order to achieve certain objectives she has set herself — in this case the achievement of sales figures, company image, and so on (her objective may even simply be to hold on to her job).

The forming of values   Now let us consider a writer who hates the process of writing books, but slogs through his third attempt. What keeps him going? Or the diplomat who hates cocktail parties, but attends an average of three a week and is always the model of politeness. Or the child who likes reading comics, but has foregone them in order to spend his pocket money on a classic. They have all taken personal decisions, made value judgements and followed them through, often at some personal short-term sacrifice. Rather like the salesgirl, they are controlling their immediate desires, feelings, emotions, in order to achieve some long-term goal that they have set themselves. This long-term goal may be a practical, external event such as promotion or passing an exam. But it may also be a moral, internal goal, such as a particular lifestyle that the person has chosen to lead, a particular set of religious principles he wishes to adopt, or some set of cultural or aesthetic values that he espouses.

The skill of self-control   Whatever the nature of the goal, the problem for the person is the same, namely to control his own behaviour so that it leads to the long-term goal, despite the fact that in the short term this may not be the easiest or the most pleasant path to follow. Those who do this well may quite justifiably be said to have developed a skill — a skill of self-control, or of 'self-actualization' (to use Carl Roger's terminology), or of living according to their value system (to use a term from Krathwohl's and Bloom's taxonomy of the affective domain).

Does this sort of behaviour exhibit the characteristics of a skill? It certainly requires practise and repetition to acquire, as do skills in general. It certainly may be acquired to varying degrees of perfection, as can skills in general (in opposition to knowledge, which one either has or has not — imperfect knowledge of a subject means that one knows some parts and not others; imperfect mastery of a skill *may* mean that one can perform *all* parts but at diminished rates of precision or productivity). Finally, the type of behaviour we have described exhibits the typical stages of a skilled activity:

— *perception* (of one's own options)
— *decision* (involving the planning and selection of actions)
— *action* (directed towards a clear purpose)
— *evaluation* (involving perception of results, further decisions, actions, etc).

We saw a similar set of stages in the case of interactive skills (perception of the other persons' behaviour, decision on how to react and the actual reaction etc) and we shall meet similar stages in the physical and intellectual skills areas.

Attitudes and values   Thus the affective domain seems to be composed of two different types of behaviour:

— reflexive, conditioned reactions to certain specific stimuli (situations); we can call these *attitudes*;
— voluntary reactions and actions, planned to lead to certain goals and involving the exercise of skills of self-control; we can call these *value-systems*.

These two distinct types do not shine out too clearly in the list of major classifications used in the Krathwohl/Bloom taxonomy.

Attending to specific phenomena may be considered a conditioned approach behaviour, but it may also conceivably be voluntary effort to attend to something uninteresting, but potentially useful (which requires a certain amount of self-control).

Responding could similarly be reflexive or planned.

Valuing the phenomenon appears more to be a voluntarily planned behaviour (but the man with a drinking habit obviously 'values' his whisky to the extent of the best part of his salary, yet may not consciously include drink in his value system — what he *lacks* are the self-control skills).

Organizing one's values and establishing a personal *value system* are quite clearly planned voluntary activities; however it is one thing to do the organizing (an intellectual activity) and quite another to live by one's values (a skill).

The categories of the affective domain's taxonomy are not different *types* of attitude, but different stages of development of an attitude. As such they may be useful for evaluating progress, but not for the prescription of instructional methods. The division into reflexive reactions and planned life-style may be more useful, as this division suggests specific instructional techniques.

We shall attempt to develop this theme further in the next part of this chapter.

11.4 The neglected domain — physical skills

The analysis and training of physical skills (or psychomotor skills) seems to have had a history quite divorced from the mainstream of educational research and development. This is probably because for a long time educators tended to look down on the physical skills domain as unworthy of their attention. After all, practical skills seem to be learned by simply 'watching and doing'. Anything that can be learned without the aid of the skilled human teacher must surely be so easy to learn as not to warrant close analysis. In any case, training in most skills (apart from sports and some 'recreative' manual skills such as home carpentry) were traditionally the domain of industrial schools, technical and trade colleges, outside the mainstream of the formal educational system.

Thus, in 1956, when Bloom's taxonomy was published, it dealt with the cognitive domain. It was not until 1964 that the second handbook, dealing with the affective domain was published. As its preface says:

> The success of *Taxonomy of Educational Objectives, Handbook 1 Cognitive Domain*, has spurred our work on the affective domain . . . we found the affective domain much more difficult to structure . . . our hope is, however, that it will represent enough of an advance in the field to call attention to the problem of affective domain terminology . . . (Krathwohl *et al* 1964).

And not a word concerning the psychomotor domain!

Bloom's taxonomies describe levels of competence

However, the taxonomies of Bloom and Krathwohl are essentially hierarchical descriptions of 'levels of competence' or 'level of mastery'. *Handbook 1* suggests that cognitive development follows a sequence, from *knowledge* (of specific facts or procedures of classifications etc), through *comprehension* of the knowledge, its *application* in particular situations, to the higher order mental skills of *analysis*, *synthesis* and *evaluation* — all involved in the problem-solving process.

In the affective domain, the categories of *attending* to specific phenomena, then *responding* to them, then learning to *value* them, then *organizing* one's values in relation to each other, finally creating a *generalized* 'set' or personal *value system* to guide one's life, have a definite sequential 'developmental' flavour about them. One can see them applied to the practical skill of salesmanship, in the 'AIDA' model for salesman training. In this model, the salesman follows a four-step sequence in closing a sale. He is expected to:

A — Gain the potential client's *attention*

I — Arouse their *interest* (responding ?)

D — Kindle their *desire* (valuing ?)

A — Gain their *acceptance* of the product (decision to live according to the value?)

The salesman in a sense 'trains' the customer, developing his attitudes to the product and building it into his system of values.

In this example, the affective behaviour of the clients in relation to the salesman's product develops through all the stages outlined in the taxonomy during a brief period, maybe as short as a few minutes, maybe spread over a period of weeks. Of course, the taxonomy is concerned more with the stages of development of moral, ethical or aesthetic values than the desire for particular products, but the analogy is obvious, and is a useful starting-point for our examination of the *psychometer* domain.

Early work on the development of physical skills

Taking this view of the taxonomies as 'stages of development' or 'milestones on the road to mastery', then a taxonomy of the psychomotor domain existed even before Bloom's and Krathwohl's work was published. However, this was overlooked as the work behind this taxonomy (which was never called by such a name) was performed in a different area (work study) in a different country (UK).

The TWI approach

The myth of the relative unimportance and simplicity of training in physical skills was finally shattered by World War II. The sudden need for large numbers of workers in highly mechanized industries focused the attention of all the countries involved in the problem of more effective and more rapid training. In the USA this led to the formation of the 'training within industry' (TWI) service.

In England no similar formal organization was set up, but private enterprise efforts were made to improve training methods, notably the work of the Seymour brothers. Both TWI and the Seymour brothers based their initial approach on the existing techniques of work study. However, in the USA the TWI service concentrated on job breakdown into parts and on a method of instruction which we might call the 'parts' method. A simple, low-depth analysis of the job into parts and their 'key-points' served as a guide to the instructor who then followed a seven-step method of instruction (McCord 1976):

1. Show workers how to do it.
2. Explain key points.
3. Let them watch you do it again.
4. Let them do the simple parts of the job.
5. Help them do the whole job.
6. Let them do the whole job but watch them.
7. Put them on their own.

Skills analysis training

In the UK, on the other hand, the Seymour brothers, whilst following much the same lines of development (including investigations of alternative instructional tactics — 'parts to whole', 'whole to parts', 'progressive parts') went further into the study of the nature of physical skill, developing a much deeper approach to analysis, originally christened 'process analysis' but now known almost universally as 'skills analysis'. This was described in some detail in the previous chapter.

This work continued after the end of World War II, in various private and public companies. Thus in the UK by the end of the 1950s there was a strong movement towards training of operator skills based on a detailed skills analysis. The original work study basis of practical observation, documentation and breakdown of jobs and tasks was supplemented by a theory base drawn from psychology and physiology. The original practical decision to observe and analyse not only the detailed steps of each operation but also the perceptual cues which control these steps, was a direct parallel to the stimulus-response analysis of behaviour advocated by the behavioural psychologists. However, the characteristics of skilled behaviour — its apparent automatization, the number of different functions that seem to be performed in parallel (planning, initiating actions, controlling actions, evaluating results of actions, etc) — led

Seymour to consider also the special psychological aspects of skilled physical behaviour.

Stages in mastery of a physical skill

The observed stages in the development of a physical skill can be summarized as follows:

1. *Acquiring knowledge* of what should be done, to what purpose, in what sequence and how.

2. *Executing the responses in a step-by-step manner*, for each of the steps of the skilled operation. The characteristics of this stage are:
   (a) that there is a conscious application of the knowledge. The 'what and how to do' aspects of the operation are controlled by the conscious thinking out of each step; and
   (b) the perceptual information necessary to initiate and control action — the 'when to do and how well done' aspects of the operation — is supplied almost entirely by the eyes. Exceptions to this are where vision is replaced or supplemented by specific signals perceived by the other senses. (For example the noise of an alarm buzzer is the natural and only signal available to an operator to signal that he should perform an emergency shut-down operation of a given machine.)

The observable result of these two characteristics is that the execution of the action is erratic and jumpy. Each step is performed as a separate unit before the next is attempted. The time taken to perform a given step may vary considerably between attempts.

3. *Transfer of control* from the eyes to other senses. For example, in car-driving the signal that triggers off the decision to change up a gear becomes the sound of the engine turning at the requisite rpm (perceived through the ears) whereas originally it tended to be the reading on the revolution-counter, or the speed registered on the speedometer (perceived through the eyes). The reaching down to grasp the gear lever in order to change gear, which initially is a movement controlled by the eyes (the driver glances down in order to locate the position of the gear lever) becomes increasingly controlled by the kinaesthetic sense (the hand automatically finds the gear lever, being guided by the 'feel' in the arm muscles of the correct position). This transfer of control releases the eyes to attend to other aspects of the skilled task, in particular to the planning of subsequent actions. The observable change in this stage is a marked increase in the fluidity and regularity of action. Practice has made the timing and precision of individual movements more regular and predictable. The release of the sense of vision from the direct control of each movement allows for more efficient 'advanced planning' of subsequent movements in the sequence. Whilst changing gear, the driver is already planning to turn right, give a signal, etc. Whilst trapping and controlling the football, the player is already planning whether to pass it, to whom and how. The subsequent actions therefore flow on directly without any apparent break between one movement and the next.

4. *Automatization* of the skill. This stage is characterized by a reduction of the need for conscious attention and 'thinking through' of the actions. The skill becomes almost a set of reflex actions, one triggering off the next, without direct conscious effort being called for from the operator. Of course he must continue to pay attention, to perceive the information necessary to plan, control and evaluate the activities, but the planning, control and evaluation occur 'unconciously'. The observable result of this stage is that the operator may perform skilled activity and at the same time be thinking or talking about other matters, and to some extent may even attend to or perform other things not related to the skill, without this having any appreciable effect on the quality of execution of the skill. Thus a skilled motorist may discuss other matters, or may, to some

extent, appreciate the passing scenery without detrimental effect on his driving. The skilled copy typist may answer a boss's question concerning an earlier phone call, without stopping or reducing the speed of her typing, the skilled sewing machinist in the clothing industry may be relating to other workmates all the details of last night's date, interspersed with giggles and sighs, whilst carrying out all the complex activities and making all the decisions necessary to turn out a high-quality garment in minimum time.

5. *Generalization* of the skill to a continually greater range of application situations. This last stage only really applies to non-repetitive skilled activities, such as most sports, most 'crafts' and most 'design' skills. Car driving is a good example. No matter how well one has learned the basic rules and procedures of driving, no matter how well one has learned to apply this knowledge to the execution of specific components of the skill (eg to gear changing), no matter how efficiently these components flow together to form a continuous and fluid driving activity and no matter to what extent the whole activity has been automatized and subjected to unconscious control, the driver continues to learn and to improve his skill in dealing with unusual and unexpected road situations. It is still possible to discriminate more and less skilled drivers, although they are both equally proficient in the basic manipulative skills of driving a car, by the 'road sense' which they exhibit in dealing with a variety of situations. Another good example is football where again, two players equal in competence 'off the field' as far as ball control is concerned, may be strikingly different in their level of skill 'on the field' during a match, when rapid interpretation and reaction to unique occurrences call for the instant planning and execution of original play strategies.

This last stage is what has been in recent years called the development of 'planning skills' or 'strategy skills'.

The wording of the five stages in the development of physical skills, outlined above, is my own. However, the stages themselves are based on well documented work. The first four are based on the observations of Douglas Seymour from the 1940s onwards, and published at about the same time as the Bloom taxonomies (Seymour 1957, 1966). The fifth, although only hinted at in Seymour's work (which was concerned primarily with repetitive industrial 'operative' skills, generally requiring only a low level of planning skill) is primarily based on observations made by the research team at Perkins Engineering Limited of Peterborough, England, during the late 1960s, sponsored by the Engineering Industry Training Board. In his book on training in physical skills, John Wellens (1974) emphasizes the importance of this research in formally identifying the 'planning' or 'strategy' skill element in complex skilled activities (an element that was always acknowledged as present on a commonsense basis — the 'experience ' element, if you like). The importance of formally identifying and measuring this element is that it leads to considerations of how to teach the planning skills. Can one in fact formally 'teach' experience? More of this in later sections of the book.

A taxonomy of the psychomotor domain

For the time being let us review the 'taxonomy' (if it merits the name) presented above and note why I said earlier that in reality a taxonomy of the psychomotor domain has existed as long as the other two taxonomies.

First, note that the information supplied by the five-stage taxonomy is of much the same type as the information supplied by the major categories of the Bloom/Krathwohl taxonomies. It could serve as efficiently as they do to develop appropriate types of test items for evaluating the stage of development of a given physical skill. True, there are no sub-divisions in the taxonomy as presented, as there are in the Bloom/Krathwohl taxonomies. But there could be.

One could, for example, classify different types of basic physical activities in category 2 (learning to execute the responses) or different types of transfer of control (eg vision to hearing, vision to kinaesthetics etc) and so on. How useful such sub-divisions would be, we are not quite sure, just as we are not quite convinced of the usefulness of some of the sub-divisions in the Bloom/ Krathwohl taxonomies.

Second, note that the stages had been identified and were already being used to guide trainers in decision making in the 1960s, the period when the Bloom/Krathwohl taxonomies came into vogue with educators.

Do we need a taxonomy? One might conjecture why the ideas and observations concerning physical skills, outlined above, never became integrated with the ideas and observations concerning the cognitive and affective domains into one coherent methodology for developing objectives. Was it that the cognitive/affective domains are of principal interest to educators and lead to 'educational' objectives (as the titles of the taxonomies, handbooks 1 and 2, suggest) whereas the psychomotor domain is of principal interest to 'trainers' (industrial or sports) and lead to 'training' objectives (a sort of 'lower-class' area of interest?) or was it simply that the work described above on physical skills was performed on one side of the Atlantic (UK) whilst the work in the cognitive and affective domains was performed on the other side (USA), so that perhaps there never was a 'confrontation' of the two trends? Or was it that there is no real practical need for such a taxonomy of psychomotor skills? This last question is worth investigating seriously. In my opinion, a hierarchical list of the main stages in the development of a skill, as outlined above, has some value in orienting trainers to 'what to look for' as signs of a developing skill. It does not help at all, however, in deciding what to do in order to develop the skill. Does the skill in question have a large or small element of planning skills? And what do we do about it anyway? How would we teach a 'planning-intensive' skill, as opposed to a 'non-planning-intensive' skill? Thus a taxonomy of hierarchical stages of psychomotor skill development suffers from a limitation (which is also a limitation of the Bloom/Krathwohl taxonomies) that it does not tell us much about how to instruct. It might help a bit with deciding the sequence of instruction, but not at all with the methods to be employed.

The use of Bloom's taxonomy for selecting content However, there is one use that the Bloom taxonomy, for example, has, which is not so apparent in the case of a psychomotor skills taxonomy. One can use Bloom's taxonomy of the cognitive domain as an aid in the *selection of content* for a course. When following the 'input-output' route of course design (as we christened it earlier), the course designer starts with a subject and some overall aims. These overall aims may be translated into more objective terms by matching them to a specific category in the taxonomy. Then, still aided by the examples of relevant test items given in the *Handbook*, our course designer performs a 'search operation' of the subject in order to identify examples of content in *this* subject which could be used to teach and test *that* category of objective. This search operation in effect identifies the 'topics worth teaching' in a subject (level 1 analysis) or at a more detailed level (level 2 analysis) the 'information elements worth teaching' in a topic.

Its limitations Now, this use of the taxonomy vanishes if one adopts the 'outputs-inputs' route of course design. In this case the course designer starts by defining terminal tasks, analyses these into task elements and derives directly from the enabling cognitive objectives. It is quite easy to derive a coherent set of well sequenced objectives when following the 'output-input' route, without the use of any taxonomy.

Seymour's 'taxonomy' in the education context By analogy, in the psychomotor domain, we could apply an 'input-output' approach in the case of, say, designing a physical education curriculum. The curriculum designer might find a taxonomy useful to decide in general terms what the proposed programme should achieve. For example, should it attempt to develop planning skills and what type of planning skills? Then he might look at the 'subject' of physical education to select sports or activities which may be used to promote the defined skills. For example, long-distance running involves a considerable amount of planning skill, as compared to short sprints. However, this is a special case, taken from the educational context.

The industrial training context

Most instruction for psychomotor skills takes place in the industrial training context. In this context, training is job-related. The development of instructional objectives necessarily follows the output-input route, starting from the analysis of the job or occupation into the tasks and operations to be performed. This in turn helps to define the essential physical skills, essential knowledge, etc. No taxonomy is required to classify the types of skill or knowledge to be taught. The exact skills and the exact knowledge required to perform on the job are identified directly from the job and task analyses.

Limitations of the use of a 'taxonomy' of psycho-motor skill development

Thus there is limited need for the use of a taxonomy of psychomotor skill development as a tool for the selection of course content. However, it is a useful conceptual framework for the evaluation of a learner's progress in the development of a skill — one can check the learner's observed progress against the list of stages in skill development.

1. Has he got the necessary prerequisites — the knowledge of what should be done, why and how; any essential basic skills; requisite perceptual acuity etc?
2. Is he applying what he knows correctly — is he performing all the necessary steps and in the correct sequence?
3. Is his performance still jumpy and very step-by-step, or has he commenced to transfer control to other senses than the eyes and achieve a smoother, more integrated pattern of work?
4. Does he still require to concentrate on the execution of the skilled work to the exclusion of all else, or has he commenced to 'automatize' the skill?
5. To what extent is he already capable of handling variety? Can he generalize the newly learnt skills to other similar situations? To what extent is he being creative in his execution of the skilled activity? How well is he planning the execution of the skilled activity?

Another approach: the skill cycle

Let us investigate a little more closely the nature of physical skills. Many writers refer to a 'skill cycle', that is a cycle of events which occur during the performance of skilled activity. Wheatcroft (1973) outlines the cycle of skilled performance as composed of:

1. *Purpose:* what you wish to achieve (eg to apply the brakes of a car in order to achieve the correct speed for turning a corner).
2. *Information reception:* making the sensory checks that are necessary (eg estimation of braking distance, condition of road in front, traffic conditions front and rear).
3. *Perception:* selecting that sensory information which is relevant to the purpose and ignoring the rest.
4. *Decision:* deciding what (and how) to do in the light of the relevant sensory information (eg how hard to brake).
5. *Action:* carrying out the action (eg braking).
6. *Then check:* Information reception, perception (of results of action), decision, remedial action (or none).

We have used a somewhat simplified version of such a skill cycle (although we did not call it by that name) when discussing interactive skills and self-control skills in previous sections of this chapter. We referred simply to perception (of others or of self), decision (how to react), action (reaction, interaction) and finally, evaluation (involving modification). However, these categories of skill also must have a purpose, albeit sometimes a little more difficult to define (self-improvement may take many forms), and there is just as much need for the selective processing of sensory information when observing oneself or other people as when observing a road and its traffic conditions. Thus, one might surmise (and we will argue) that all skilled activity follows much the same sort of cycle. For the time being, however, let us visualize and perhaps rephrase the cycle of physical skill performance. The diagram which follows is an attempt to represent schematically the process of skilled activity.

Key events in the skill performance cycle The top circle represents the 'doer' — the person who is performing the skilled activity. The bottom circle is the 'situation being affected' — the object, machine, or system that is being operated, *together with its immediate environment*. The two sausage-like links are the 'extensions of man'; on the left, his senses (and any technological aids to his senses such as instruments, meters), and on the right, his limbs (and any tools he may use).

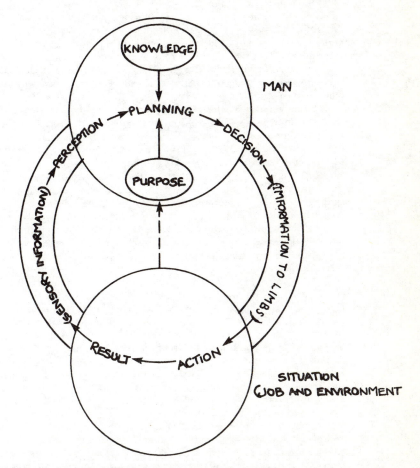

Figure 11.4 *The cycle of physical skill performance*

The skill cycle is quite clear:

information is collected by the senses about the situation;

perception selects the information relevant to the immediate purpose (this purpose may also be perceived from information received about the situation, or it may be generated quite separately);

planning, in which the information perceived and the purpose are compared with other information previously stored (knowledge), in order to generate and evaluate (internally) alternatives for action;

decisions as to the chosen action are fed to the limbs;

actions are executed and these produce —
results, which act as new information to be *collected, perceived, evaluated,*
new *plans* and decisions, etc.

The planning
element

We have now included one extra element in the skill cycle — the *planning*
element. This is an internal process which we may hypothesize as taking place
and giving rise to the decisions on what action to take. This planning may be
complex and to some extent executed at the conscious level (as in the case of
an artist or craftsman deciding on the composition of his work, how best to use
his raw materials, what sequence of operations to adopt etc) or it may be
unconscious and almost non-existent (as in the case of repetitive high-speed
tasks on a mass-production line — the skill in such tasks lies principally in the
levels of perceptive acuity, manual dexterity and speed of reaction and stamina
developed by the operator). The planning element may also be quite complex
and yet executed at the subconscious level (as in the case of a skilled footballer
trapping a ball, or placing himself correctly on the field, a skilled driver coping
with heavy and fast traffic etc). It is, incidentally, this complex-yet-
subconscious planning element which is the most difficult to pin-point and
analyse in practice.

We have referred to this planning element already, earlier on. It is something
that Seymour, in his work devoted mainly to repetitive industrial skills, did not
identify as of great importance. However, work on the analysis of craft skills,
pioneered in the 1960s at Perkins Engines Ltd in Britain, identified the concept
of 'planning skills' or 'strategy skills' as perhaps the most important category of
sub-skills that the craftsman or artisan (or indeed artist) possesses. These are
the skills of decision making which complement any manual or perceptual
skills that the man must have and render him versatile, perhaps even creative.
Another way of looking at these skills is to refer to them as the 'experience'
element in the job. But the point brought out by the Perkins Engines research
was that often these planning skills may be identified and analysed and
appropriate instruction developed. In other words, experience can be taught, if
you can analyse it.

The analysis
of planning
skills

Wellens (1974) gives several examples of simple skills such as bricklaying,
crazy paving laying, wallpapering, which nevertheless have quite considerable
elements of planning skill. The aesthetic/artistic/economic-use-of-materials/etc
results distinguish those craftsmen who have well developed planning skills
from those who have not. The isolation and analysis of these skills is another
matter. When the planning is carried out at a conscious level, as in the case of
planning a sequence of operations to economize time or materials, then the
analysis is relatively simple. It is more difficult, however, to analyse the
subconscious planning that goes into positioning oneself to catch a ball, driving
a car, or playing a pin-ball machine. In these cases, the skill has generally been
gained through experience and practice — the master performer is not even
aware that he is planning his actions, let alone exactly *how* he makes his
complex decisions. Other examples may be found in the arts — the intuitive
composition of a picture by a 'naive' painter, the unrehearsed variations on
a melody by a jazz musician, or indeed the free flow of powerful prose from
the pen of a writer (not this one).

We shall come back to the consideration of how to teach the planning skills
in a task, later on. Once again, as in the case of interactive skills and the skills
of self-control, we shall find that simulation techniques can be most useful.

For the time being, however, let us observe that as in the case of the
affective domain, the psychomotor domain may be divided into the *reflexive*
skills (simple repetitive stimulus-response types of activity involving little or no
planning, often referred to as sensori-motor skills), and the *planning-intensive*
skills (involving complex decision making at the conscious or subconscious
level — we might call them craft skills or even creative skills). It is obvious that
the instructional methods best suited to these two distinct categories of skill

will be different. For this reason alone it may be useful to make the distinction as part of one's methodology of instructional design.

It is also quite gratifying to see some 'symmetry' in the subject, that is to find similarities between such different domains as the interactive, affective and physical. We shall attempt to capitalize on these similarities in the next chapter, in drawing up a fairly comprehensive model for the design of instruction. First, however, let us investigate the cognitive domain, to see whether we can identify any similarities or differences — can we find the same symmetry, or is the cognitive domain a law unto itself?

11.5 The cognitive domain: knowledge or skill?

We have already indicated in earlier chapters the limitations of the Bloom taxonomy (and similar taxonomies) as aids to the *design* of instruction, however useful they may be as aids to the evaluation of learning (ie to test construction). We have seen attempts to develop categories of learning or of objectives which are more directly linked to specific instructional tactics, so that the identification of the category of a given objective leads more or less automatically to a specification of the way that the instruction ought to be organized. The best known of these systems for instructional design is the one devised by Robert Gagné and his collaborators. We have seen that this system is based on an 'outputs-inputs' approach, in that it first identifies the required objectives and their sequence, deriving the exact content later on in the process. We have also seen that it is possible to adopt an alternative 'inputs-outputs' approach, starting by a subject/topic analysis, selecting the topics that seem 'worth teaching' and only then proceeding to the definition of objectives (perhaps with the aid of Bloom's taxonomy). These approaches have been with us for well over a decade now, have been very widely publicized, but have not resulted in sweeping revolutions in any national educational system, to my knowledge. They have indeed caused as much opposition and confusion as they have created converts.

Before we go on therefore, let us consider why, in 1977, Williams felt forced to suggest a new approach to topic analysis and the stating of cognitive objectives. He sees it necessary to get away from the 'intellectual capability' statements of Bloom's taxonomy, but does not see the categories of learning defined by Gagné as sufficiently clear in behavioural terms. He sees them more as categories of *information*, on which certain *operations* have to be performed. Williams describes his 'typology' as follows:

> The categories of the typology are based on the assumption that most tasks required of learners have two components: *learning task content* and applying generic intellectual *operations* to that content. To perform the task stated in an objective or required by a test question, the learner must first learn (or have previously learned) certain *information* basic to and determined by the task. For convenience these basics will be referred to as the content of the task. Task *content* is subdivided into the following types: facts, concepts (classes of objects or events), principles (statements of relationships among objects or events) and procedures (tasks with psychomotor aspects).
>
> *Operation* refers to the way in which the content is used. 'A stitch in time saves nine' is an often quoted principle or rule. As such, it is content which is often learned. Once learned, this content may be used in various ways. It may be recited verbatim (Memorization). It may be restated in different words (Summarization). Cases where the rule has been applied may be identified (Instantiation). The rule may be used to anticipate the consequences of certain acts eg sewing or failing to sew up small rips in clothing (Prediction). The rule or principle may also be used to arrange conditions so that a desired outcome results (Application). Finally, knowledge of the rule may be used in conjunction with values to select the most desirable action in a given situation (Evaluation). These same intellectual operations may be applied to almost all types of content.
>
> A third dimension, *test mode*, influences placement of objectives in the

typology. Test mode is divided into two classifications using a common distinction in the field of educational measurement. The *recognition* mode refers to selection from alternative choices as in multiple-choice or true-false test items. The *production* mode refers to any task requiring the learner to determine available choices as part of the selection process. All open-ended evaluation procedures, including performance tests which use naturalistic observation as the measurement too, are included in this mode.

The trend back to information content analysis

William's approach illustrates an interesting, current 'back to information' trend in considering the types and patterns of information *input* that should be supplied for effective learning. The four types of information *content* listed by Williams,

FACTS	PROCEDURES
CONCEPTS	PRINCIPLES

could act as a basis for the classifying of information (though the author would argue with Williams whether procedures need *necessarily* have psychomotor aspects).

It is important to keep the information (the inputs) in mind. Consider the case of a book such as this. The author may not really have any clear idea of his audience. What are the entry-level skills and knowledge? What are the objectives that *they* have? This book is not an instructional system, but an information system. It may perhaps be used by someone as a component of an instructional system. In that case, that someone will need to specify precise objectives — the author does not need to!

But what he does need to do is to ensure that the information he is trying to communicate 'hangs together'. To do this he needs some rules for the *classifying of information types* and the *organizing* of each type for *effective communication*. In so doing he is trying to facilitate the *inputting* of the information into the reader's mind. What the reader does with the information is only of secondary concern to him. However, once this book has been incorporated into an instructional system, he is (by definition of the term instruction) establishing certain objectives. They are needed to define the *outputs* of learning in performance terms (to use William's terminology, he needs to specify the operations to be performed on the content).

We therefore need three types of activity:

1. Analysis of outputs (or performance or operations)
2. Analysis of inputs (or information or content)   } both leading to
3. Design of instructional processes (or methods).

Gagné's methodology has much to say about methods of instruction (the process), but little about the content. *Information analysis* (or the analysis of knowledge structures) has much to say about content, but has been largely ignored of late (due, no doubt, to the 'swing of the pendulum' away from content-oriented course planning towards the objectives-oriented approach).

But there are signs that the pendulum is swinging back.

The design cycle

At the end of Chapter 2 (on approaches to problem-solving in education) we mentioned that the pendulum has been swinging about quite erratically over the years, tending at one time to favour the inputs-oriented approach (content) at others the outputs-oriented approach (objectives) and at yet others the instructional process-oriented approach. We expressed the view that in fact all three are important, and that one can imagine a 'design cycle' giving due weight to all three. We can now see that the analysis levels are tending to flow round this cycle. By the end of 'level 1' analysis, whether we started from 'subject' or 'job', we have reached the same point; some very complete and precise output-statements in the form of objectives and tests.

Whichever route we followed, we also have some (but not as precise) idea of the content which we should include in the course.

In level 3 analysis, we are trying to define or select systematically:

(a) the instructional methods;
(b) the information content and its detailed structure.

Gagné's
approach to
the design of
instruction

We have already seen that the Bloom model has nothing to say about instructional methods, but Gilbert's model and Gagné's model had much to contribute. The best part of Gagné's books was devoted to the 'conditions for learning' each of his learning categories. These conditions were:

(a) The internal conditions — readiness to learn. What has to be learned prior to the new learning taking place.
(b) The external conditions — the particular instructional tactics to be employed.

Limitations
of Gagné's
early model

What we notice about Gagné's model is:

(a) It is rather woolly about the conditions (particularly the external conditions) for learning problem-solving. One thing Gagné does say is that whereas at the lower levels (including concept learning) the 'discovery approach' does not pay off particularly (except perhaps in terms of motivation) at the higher levels there are benefits in terms of long-term retention and the ability to transfer the skill to a greater variety of problems.
(b) Many writers have commented that problem-solving is a learning category (perhaps several categories) worthy of more attention. Even Bloom's model identifies three types of mental processes involved just in problem-solving: analysis, synthesis and evaluation (we have been using these constantly in this book, as the basis for the systems approach — a problem-solving approach). Polya (1945), Landa (1976) and many other writers draw a distinction between algorithmic and heuristic problem-solving (Landa even subdivides these). It is not all that clear to which type of problem-solving Gagné is referring and which are missing from his scheme.
(c) Other writers (Bruner 1966) commented that creativity and such capabilities as 'learning to learn' are overlooked. Others (Merril 1974) suggest essentially very similar categories but with some differences in definitions and nomenclature.

Gagné's
revised
model

Thus in the 1970s Gagné drastically modified his thinking of the 1960s, or rather, he attempted to modify and enlarge his model to take into consideration the indicated shortcomings, to placate the humanists, the 'mental process' fans, the 'information processing theory' fans and cyberneticians. At the same time, he played down the behaviourist roots of many of his earlier concepts, whilst attempting to keep most of them in his model.

After all, they had given good service. Several practical systems of instructional design have been developed, based on the model. As examples one might quote the *Handbook of Procedures for the Design of Instruction*, (Briggs 1970) and the earlier *Instructional Media* (Briggs, Campeau, Gagné and May, 1967) aimed at the general education field, and *Instructional Systems Development for Vocational and Technical Training* (Butler 1972) in the field of training. The present author had also both taught and used the earlier model with success (within its limitations) for some years.

Limitations
of the new
model

However, in trying to please everybody, the new model is in danger of pleasing no one. Launched in 1974 (Gagné and Briggs 1974) as the *Principles of Instructional Design* the model focuses first on the *processes of learning* and the external events (in general terms) that influence these processes.

This is a mixed bag of internal processes (storage, retrieval) and outputs (responding). It then presents a new set of learning outcomes. This seems to imply *outputs*, but it actually means types of learned capabilities — the results of learning. This list includes five of the previous eight learning categories (lumped together under the generic title of 'intellectual skills'). In addition there are: verbal information (which would seem to include the earlier categories of stimulus-response learning, and verbal chaining), attitude (which n doubt has swallowed up Pavlovian conditioning, though Gagné does not make this clear) and which is treated in a way very different from the Krathwohl and Bloom taxonomy; motor skill (which must have swallowed up motor chains) and the one completely new category of 'cognitive strategies'. Judging by the examples Gagné gives and the description of the process, he seems to be referring here to what we have called heuristic problem-solving (though he does not use this name). He also implies that there is a great variety of these strategies, but does not identify many of them. He also goes to great pains to define them in a general sense by contrasting them to intellectual skills:

> Intellectual skills are oriented towards aspects of the learner's environment; they enable him to deal with numbers, words and symbols which are 'out there'. In contrast, cognitive strategies govern the learner's own behaviour in dealing with his environment; they are in a sense 'in here'. Cognitive strategies are ways the learner has of managing the process of learning (as well as retention and thinking).

But when one looks at the examples given of human performance (see Figure 10.1) the distinction between 'cognitive strategy' and 'higher order rule' (previously 'problem-solving) is not all that strong. And if one studies the critical learning conditions for these two capabilities (see Figure 10.2) one also observes little difference.

Confusion among the categories

So Gagné's new expanded model does not take him much further than the previous one, and the new terminology adds confusion rather than clarity. As further examples, why are 'higher order rules' (problem-solving) and 'discrimination' and 'concept' all lumped together as 'intellectual skills'? One aspect that differentiates knowledge and skill is that you either have knowledge or you do not, whereas a skill may be mastered to various levels of proficiency. Problem-solving is a skill — including the heuristic type that Gagné classifies as a cognitive strategy — whereas a simple discrimination between printed 'b' and 'd' is patently knowledge — either you can discriminate them or you cannot. There is no half-way point. Concepts are a moot point, as one can classify examples into a given category with different degrees of success — the child learning the concept of 'red' classifies some borderline shades which are really orange or pink, as red. With time he learns to identify the colour 'red' with greater precision. Is he developing a higher level of skill in the use of the concept of 'red', or is he learning 'knowledge'? However, the defined concept examples quoted by Gagné (Figure 10.1) and also the example of 'rules' are patently examples of 'knowledge' (or information).

The need to analyse 'knowledge'

One source of weakness, which was pointed out by Williams (1977), in the Gagné model, is the playing down of knowledge, or 'information' as a characteristic to be analysed.

Williams identified four basic categories of information; facts, procedures, concepts and principles (unlike Gagné's new terminology which labels most of them as skills). In his short article, however, Williams does not elaborate on the procedures for communicating these categories of information.

However, Robert Horn and his associates in their work over the last decade, on the technique of information mapping, have developed an excellent working system for the analysis of information and the matching of information to appropriate communication tactics (Horn *et al* 1969, Horn 1973, 1974).

Horn's classification of types of information

Horn's classification of information includes the following categories:

Facts stand on their own, do not need examples (names of objects, etc; statements of fact; answer questions such as what is this called?)

Concepts properties or ideas which require examples and non-examples in order to define their limit; (agrees with Gagné's definition, including concrete and defined concepts); answer questions such as what is this an example of?

Structures interrelated groups of objects or concepts (theories, organizations, etc); answer questions such as how is it organized?

Processes structures which change with time (administrative, mechanical etc); answer questions such as how does it work?

Procedures actions to be performed by the reader (processes in which he is involved); answer questions such as what do I do?

The categories seem to be in rough agreement with Williams, except for the subdivision of 'principles' into 'structures' and 'processes'. Williams does not define his terms, so it is difficult to analyse this difference. However, as his model is based on Gagné's work, among others, we might assume the same meaning as Gagné ascribes to them.

The need for further clarification

Gagné's original use of 'principle' (which he later equated to 'rule') implies a *chain of concepts* (eg an if/then relationship: if it stands still, paint it white; if it moves, shoot it). Higher order principles, on the other hand, are combinations of such simple ones (into, for example, a 'model of military mentality' which Horn would classify no doubt as 'structure'). I see some value in not labelling simple if/then rules as structures, but rather keeping a separate category. There are other expansions to this classification which I would also like to make.

A basic division into skills and knowledge

However, before going on to suggest a revised classification (which we attempt to do in Chapter 12), let us identify the chief revision which should be made. We should encourage a return to the use of a basic division between skills and knowledge. This is commonly made but does not feature as a basic conceptual discriminator in any of the well-publicized *education-based* models for instructional design. It does feature in models for the analysis of industrial tasks and the design of job-related training (see Chapter 5). However, the use of the terms knowledge and skill is often rather unspecific in these models. They tend to be used as synonyms for theory and practice.

Knowledge is stored as usable information

We prefer to use the term knowledge for information stored in the mind and would sub-classify this into the four categories suggested by Williams: facts, concepts, principles and procedures. Being able to recall any of these constitutes proof of the presence of that information in the mind, that is of the presence of knowledge. Furthermore, being able to restate the knowledge in other words, being able to explain it, or to state its usefulness, signifies that the knowledge is usable (ie signifies understanding).

However, the actual use of that knowledge in a given (practical or theoretical) situation, constitutes an activity which can be performed to a greater or lesser degree of proficiency. This is the chief characteristic of a skilled activity, as defined earlier.

This application of knowledge can be in two forms: (a) the rigorous following of a known procedure, step by step, (applying an *algorithm*), and (b) the use of known concepts and principles in order to deal with a situation for which we do not know a standard procedure (*heuristic* problem-solving).

Algorithmic problem-solving skills

In the first instance, little real thinking or planning is involved. It is sufficient to recognize which of the various known procedures is applicable to the problem (should we really grace such simple activity with the name 'problem'?). Once identified, the known procedure is 'retrieved from store' and applied. Differences in proficiency may arise in terms of speed and accuracy, as they do in other simple procedural skills (eg sensori-motor skills).

Heuristic problem-solving skills

In the second instance, a great deal of thinking and planning may be involved. There is no guarantee that the concepts and principles needed to solve the problem will be recognized as such immediately. Attempts may be made to solve the problem in different ways. Some general principles of how to approach problem-solving may be applied, as well as the more specific principles linked to the subject matter of the problem. There is no guarantee that a solution will be found, nor that all solvers of the problem will use the same procedures. In the process of searching for and finding the solution, new higher order principles may be developed which will be stored for eventual future use, or new procedures will be learned and stored, which will enable that type of problem to be tackled by a 'standard known procedure' next time.

We shall go into more detail on these two types of cognitive skill in Chapter 12. But we should note that, by hiving off the 'knowledge' categories as a separate domain, we are left with a cognitive or intellectual skill domain which subdivides into two main types of skill analogous to the two main types identified in the other skill domains. These are: *algorithm following* (analogous to reflexive skills or reactions), and *heuristic problem-solving* (analogous to the planning-intensive psychomotor skills, interactive skills and self-control skills).

12. Analysis of Knowledge and Skills: A Modified Approach

The learner as a system

The following approach to knowledge and skills analysis is based firmly on systems thinking as practised throughout this book so far. Therefore we start with our learner represented as a 'black box' receiving *information* as input and outputting certain performances which are indicators that learning has taken place.

The two tangible things that we can analyse are:
— the information we feed the learner
— the performance he achieves (the results).

Definitions of knowledge and skill

Now let us define 'knowledge' and 'skill':

Knowledge shall be used to refer to information stored in the learner's mind. This is akin to the normal use of the word when we say that we 'know' something.

Skill shall be used to refer to actions (intellectual or physical) and indeed 'reactions' (to ideas, things or people) which a person performs in a competent way in order to achieve a goal. In practising a skill, one uses certain items of knowledge that are stored in the mind. One uses perception (of the situation/ problem/object) to gain new information which is combined with the knowledge and one acts on the basis of planning decisions. Any skilled action may have four component activities — perception, planning, recall of prerequisite knowledge, and finally the execution, or performance, of the action.

An important discrimination: knowledge is a 'go-no go' quantity. Either you have it or you do not. Either it is stored or it is not. If you 'know' part of a subject it means that you know certain elements of information and you do not know others.

Skill, on the other hand, is something which develops with experience and practice. You can be highly skilled, or not so highly skilled, in *using* information to achieve a certain purpose.

Facts and concepts

Turning now to the 'performance' side of our black box, what are the performances normally accepted as proof of the possession of knowledge or skill?

'Knowledge' generally implies two categories of capability:

(a) remembering
(b) understanding

The two related categories of skilled behaviour are:

(a) recalling/repeating etc
(b) explaining/recognizing instances etc.

These two categories of knowledge are technically referred to as factual and conceptual.

Factual knowledge can take various forms, the most common being:

(a) knowing objects, events or people (either directly as concrete experiences, or as verbal information);
(b) knowing what to do in given situations (knowing the procedure).

Conceptual knowledge can also take two common forms:

(a) specific concepts or groups of concepts (being able to give or recognize instances of a given phenomenon, being able to define it, etc);
(b) rules or principles which link certain concepts or facts in specific ways (enabling one to explain or predict phenomena).

The four categories of knowledge

Thus we have four categories into which we can classify knowledge:

1. Facts.
2. Procedures.
3. Concepts.
4. Principles.

These are the four categories of information used by Williams (1977) in his suggested improvements to the taxonomies of Bloom and Gagné. They are also not so different from the categories of information used by Horn (1969) as the basis of information mapping.

The four categories of skills

Skills are divided into a wide variety of categories by various writers and are given various names. We shall adopt a basic division into four categories:

1. Thinking, or cognitive skills (I will avoid using 'intellectual skills' so as not to create confusion with Gagné's terminology).
2. Acting — physical or motor skill (psychomotor to be exact).
3. Reacting — to things, situations or people, in terms of values, emotions, feelings (this is largely synonymous with attitudes).
4. Interacting — with people in order to achieve some goal, such as communication, education, acceptance, persuasion, etc.

Note the main difference between reactive skills and interactive skills is that the former are concerned only with the behaviour (overt or covert) of the learner when confronted with particular situations, whereas the latter are concerned with the behaviours the learner adopts in order to influence or modify the situation. Note that we plan to treat attitudes (the affective domain of Bloom's taxonomy) as skills. Insofar as attitudes can be learned and are exhibited by the learner's behaviour, it is quite useful to treat them as acquired skills. They have the characteristics of skills, in that one may hold a particular attitude in varying degrees or strengths. They do not have the characteristics of knowledge, as defined above.

The first three of my categories equate approximately with the cognitive, psychomotor and affective domains as defined by Bloom, except that Bloom's cognitive domain combines 'knowledge' and 'cognitive skills' in its subdivisions. I see a lot of value in separating out knowledge and skill in two quite distinct classifications. The need for the fourth category, of interactive skills, was clearly demonstrated in our earlier discussions of the gaps which exist in the classifications of Bloom and Gagné.

12.1 The 'knowledge schema'

Let us now expand the basic concepts presented above into a more comprehensive schema which can act as the basis for our system of classifying types of learning. Firstly let us consider the 'knowledge' domain.

Purpose of the schema

The schema presented here subdivides our four main basic types of knowledge (facts, procedures, concepts and principles) in order to illustrate several aspects of knowledge:

☐ That the information stored (the knowledge) may have been gained directly through concrete experience ('observation' of the outside world by any one of our senses) or it may have been gained through 'vicarious' experience, usually by means of the spoken or written word but also through the use of other symbolic languages (this implies the previous mastery of the language in question).

☐ That the information may be stored as discrete items (individual facts, concepts, rules, etc) or it may be combined into information systems (or schemata) which relate the discrete items to each other in particular ways (note that the form of these systems or schemata may have been received 'from outside' as part of the way in which the information was communicated in the first instance, or else they may have been constructed 'internally' by the student himself when he tries to relate new information received to information previously stored — the processes of assimilation and adaptation described by Piaget).

☐ That knowledge of a particular topic is seldom of one type, but is usually a combination of several types of factual and conceptual knowledge, both concrete and verbal, some stored as coherent schemata and some as discrete unrelated items. Hence the circular nature of our diagram (Figure 12.1) is once again intended to emphasize the non-exclusive, non-hierarchical nature of the categories.

We shall now pass to an analysis of each of the sub-divisions.

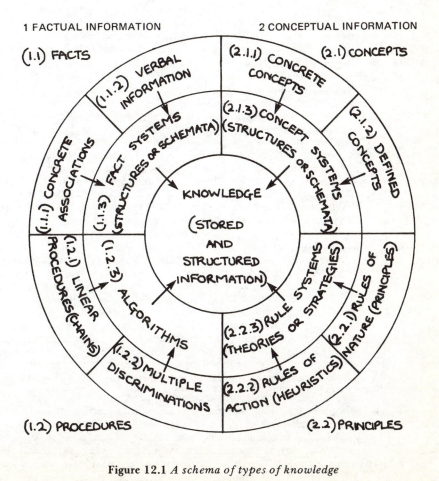

Figure 12.1 *A schema of types of knowledge*

1. Factual information (specific information which exists — no examples exist)

1.1 Facts (knowing objects, events, names, etc)

1.1.1 Concrete facts

(Concrete associations; things observed and remembered.) This category includes all knowledge that has been gained by direct experience, exemplified by the ability to recognize objects or people or places. Usually the name of the object etc, is associated with it and is used as a means of verifying that recognition has taken place, but the verbal element is not an essential part of the learning process. For example, one finds one's way home by recalling and recognizing certain landmarks and one does not need language to either learn or to demonstrate knowledge of these landmarks — getting home is proof enough of one's state of knowledge.

1.1.2 Verbal (symbolic) information

(Including languages such as logic, maths.) This category includes all knowledge of a factual nature that has been gained by means of a symbolic language; statements of fact, descriptions of events, specifications of a motor car part by means of a code number, etc. Note that usually the verbal or symbolic message refers to concrete facts. Rain on your face is a fact that you recognize in a most direct and concrete way. Associating the name 'rain' with this fact is the most simple of verbal associations. The fact that the lump of land hanging off the south-western corner of Europe is called Spain is a somewhat more complex bit of verbal information, probably learned through a combination of two languages — verbal communication and the symbolic language of maps. 'The rain in Spain stays mainly in the plain' is a yet more complex statement of fact (of doubtful truth perhaps).

1.1.3 Fact systems

(Or schemata.) This category includes the more complex interrelated factual knowledge that one acquires. Perhaps not the one sentence quoted above, but certainly the words of the song from *My Fair Lady* in their entirety would be classified as a fact system, as would any long and complex bit of prose (I am referring here to the memorization and recall of the information contained and not to its understanding, which may well classify as conceptual knowledge). Similarly, other complex factual information, such as the symbols of Morse code, the conventions of geography maps, the international road signs, and so on, are examples of fact systems. Note that fact systems are composed of a set of facts (concrete and/or symbolic) which are interrelated in a specific way. These interrelations will influence both the learning and the recall of the facts.

Learning and teaching factual information

The learning of facts requires certain conditions. At a relatively shallow (level 3) level of analysis, the conditions for learning factual information (whether concrete or verbal) are as suggested by Gagné for his equivalent categories (S-R learning in 1968, verbal information in 1972). Although such information may sometimes be learnt 'at one go', usually there is a need for planned repetition and review, this need being greater when the information to be learned is more complex (when the fact system is large). At deeper levels of analysis, however, there is much already known about the learning of facts. The immense literature in psychology on paired-associate learning, learning of multiple discriminations, learning of rote text, learning through mnemonics, and so on, is of relevance here. The 'level 4' technique of mathetical analysis, which looks for sources of competition and facilitation is a powerful tool for the organizing of the instruction of factual information. The literature and research on fantastic 'memory men' and the techniques used in 'memory development' courses are also of interest in the teaching of factual information.

1.2 Procedures (knowing how to proceed in specific situations)

1.2.1 Chains

(Simple step-by-step procedures.) This category includes the type of learning described exhaustively by Skinner in his work on the training of rats and pigeons. The training procedures of 'shaping of behaviour' which he describes are of particular relevance to this category. Note that Skinner was concerned with the study of behaviour (ie performance) rather than of knowledge (ie of information stored). Our contention here is that an organism, be it a rat or a human being, that exhibits the ability to perform a procedure, carrying out all the steps in the correct sequence, whenever he is called upon to do so, has stored within him certain information regarding the steps and their sequence, etc. Thus we are quite justified in talking of the 'knowledge' of a procedure. The performance of this procedure in practice may involve more than the knowledge of the steps — it may also involve specific skills necessary for its performance. The separation of these two aspects is considered a valuable aspect of the model we are presenting in this chapter. We can see the difference between the person who 'knows' the procedure and the one who 'can perform' the procedure in such cases as that of a supervisor and his subordinates. The supervisor knows exactly what each subordinate should be doing, can observe and identify good and bad performance and will notice if any steps are omitted. But the supervisor may not be as capable at executing the procedures as are his subordinates, because he has not had as much practice (lack of opportunity to develop skill) or because he has ceased to practice for some time (neglected skill).

Many athletics events (running, high jumping, etc) are examples of chains that some people develop to a high level of proficiency. However, if the abovementioned distinction between 'knowing' a procedure and 'performing' it were not valid, then the concept of an athletics coach training an Olympics team (when he himself does not perform to Olympic standard) would also be invalid.

1.2.2 Dis-
criminations
(Distinguishing similar information.) This category equates to the 'multiple discrimination' type of learning referred to by Skinner, Gilbert, Gagné and many other writers. Whereas a chain is built up of a series of 'stimulus-response' associations joined 'end-on' as it were, a multiple discrimination is built up of a set of associations 'in parallel'. We have already seen examples of both chains and discriminations in the discussion of the 'mathetics' approach to analysis of behaviour, in Chapter 10. Whereas picking up and speaking into a telephone is a simple chain, the decisions on how to connect the phone call to the correct extension depend on the presence of a stored multiple discrimination (a set of associations linking the correct extension number to the correct person/department). The above example illustrates why we are justified in labelling such discriminations as 'knowledge'. The name-number associations are pure factual information, which may just as well be stored in written form in a telephone number directory. Nobody would disagree that such a directory is an information store. If by chance someone memorizes the directory, he then simply retrieves the information from a different source when it is required (from his memory as opposed to the directory). This does not alter the nature of what is retrieved — it is information. By our definition, information stored in the mind is called 'knowledge'. The performance characteristics of a person recalling such information also exhibit the characteristics we identified for 'knowledge'. Either he remembers a specific number or he does not. If he can remember, say, half the extension numbers in his organization, this is not a measure of his skill, but rather of the completeness of his schema (the information stored in a useable manner represents only half the information that exists). But each individual number is either recalled or not — the 'go-no go' characteristic of knowledge.

1.2.3
Algorithms
(Procedures which may be complex but which guarantee correct performance if followed correctly.) This category includes the more complex procedures that involve decision making between alternative courses of action. However, all the alternatives are clearly defined and all the courses of action are clearly specified. Remembering Landa's definition of an algorithm (when correctly used, *all people solve* the problem, *correctly* and *in the same way*), we can see that such complex procedures exhibit the characteristics of an algorithm. Each decision point is a discrimination between alternatives (a simple binary discrimination or a more complex multiple discrimination). Each alternative is a procedural chain, fully specified in advance. Note that

(as Landa pointed out) it is not always necessary to break down such procedures into binary yes/no decisions. This is necessary when we wish to programme computers, because computers operate on a binary system of logic. However, human beings appear, from all external indications, to be able to handle more complex decisions 'in one go' as it were. Thus the approach to the analysis of procedures that is embodied in Gilbert's mathetics seems more apt than the computer programmer's flowcharting approach. This latter would tend to break down the decision making processes involved in the procedure to too fine a level of detail, and may lead the instructional designer to teach the procedure in an over-mechanistic, artificial way, devaluing the higher level decision making capabilities (the ability to store very complex multiple discriminations) of the human brain.

Procedures are factual knowledge

It should be obvious from the above discussion that the knowledge of procedures (chains, discriminations or more complex procedural algorithms) is still very much in the domain of *factual* knowledge. Procedures are a form of fact systems. It is useful to distinguish the more structurally oriented fact systems (which answer questions such as, how is it constructed? where is it located? etc) from the more procedurally oriented fact systems (which tend to answer questions such as, what should I do?). However, the distinction is not always clear-cut. Each road sign is a unit of information for the motorist. Knowing the meaning of a road sign is a unit of factual knowledge — an association of symbol with hazard, for example. This knowledge may have been gained by verbal learning or through concrete experience. All the road signs listed in the *Highway Code* form a fact system. Being able to distinguish the different signs and state the meaning of each demonstrates the presence of this information as knowledge in the mind. However, doing this is an example of discrimination and may well form part of a more complex procedure that has been learned (for example the procedure to decide whether one can legally park in a given place).

Learning and teaching 'procedures'

The teaching of procedures may be accomplished by two main strategies. One is the inductive strategy, which involves the 'programming' of the learner to master the procedure. Skinner's methods of operant conditioning are one set of tactics that may be used. Gilbert's 'Demonstration-Prompt-Release' model is a tactic better suited to the training of human beings. The alternative strategy is the deductive approach, favoured by Landa. He argues that although it is without doubt very efficient to teach a procedure by (1) presenting the algorithm, and (2) giving practice in its use (an inductive strategy), it is more beneficial to the learner (for reasons of long-term recall, possible transfer to other learning and basic self-satisfaction) if the learner is led to develop his own algorithm, through the controlled exposure to selected problem-solving situations (obviously a deductive strategy). One is reminded of Gagné's views on the teaching of 'rules', which he says can be taught either by expositive teaching methods (faster in general) or by guided discovery means (generally better for long-term recall and for transfer).

The choice of strategy may therefore be principally determined by the context of the learning and the broader objectives. Procedures which are taught in order to be practised on a regular basis as part of a job, do not raise problems of long-term recall (they are used regularly and so not forgotten). Also they do not require (in general) to be used in a variety of situations which differ widely (so the need for ability to transfer to other similar but slightly different situations does not arise). Thus the inductive strategy would be the more cost-effective one to adopt, without the penalty of limiting the ability of the learner to adapt to the variety existing in his place of work. On the other hand, procedures that are being taught as part of a wider, educational course may not be practised with great regularity. Similarly some job performance procedures are practised only at intervals, as for instance the procedures on reporting industrial accidents, the performance of first-aid, dealing with exceptional conditions on the job, etc. In these cases, an inductive strategy may carry the penalty of poor long-term recall. It may well be more effective, and economically justifiable, to adopt a deductive strategy. The use of games and simulations as instructional tactics is one way of teaching procedures deductively.

If the procedures form part of a course of instruction that has mainly conceptual learning as its objectives (most general education) then there may be even more reason for promoting transfer, by adopting a deductive instructional strategy.

2. Conceptual information (requires understanding, to be used in many ways)

2.1 Concepts (names of classes of items or ideas that can be exemplified)

2.1.1 Concrete concepts

(Primary concepts.) This category includes concepts which are classes of real objects or situations, etc. Thus 'red' is a concrete, or primary, concept as it is a word which defines a particular class of real objects (objects which are red in colour). A child can learn this concept by direct experience of a variety of red objects and other objects which are not red. The word 'red' is a useful learning aid (in order to check that the concept is being learned) but it is not essential to the learning process. Professor Skinner's pigeons, for example, learned to respond (by pecking a key) to a red light but not to lights of other colours. The precision with which the pigeon pecks at red lights but does not peck at 'nearly red' lights (say pink or orange) is a measure of the precision of the concept it has formed, just as the child, in naming objects by colour demonstrates the precision of the concepts 'red', 'blue' etc that he has formed. Such ideas as 'higher', 'bigger', 'same', 'different', 'first', 'last' are also primary concepts, because they too can be developed entirely through direct experience, without the essential need of a language.

2.1.2 Defined concepts

(Secondary concepts.) This category includes concepts which are classes of other concepts. These cannot be learned without the use of a suitable language. Whereas one can demonstrate one's possession of the concept 'red' or 'bigger' by pointing at appropriate real objects, one cannot do this to demonstrate one's understanding of 'colour' or 'size'. The examples that make up the class described by these words are themselves concepts. Every real object has a colour and a size. One needs language, and the previous mastery of simpler concepts, in order to communicate to the learner the meaning of 'colour'. 'Red' is a colour, and so is 'blue' and 'green' and so on. By quoting such examples of colours, one can communicate the concept of 'colour'. But if the learner does not yet have the concepts of 'red', 'blue' etc, then the sentences we use to communicate the concept 'colour' will be meaningless to him.

Similarly, the concept of the 'size' of an object can only be communicated by the use of language and by reference to previously learned simpler concepts, such as 'big', 'bigger' etc.

At a further level of complexity, the concept of 'physical properties' requires to be communicated by a yet more complex verbal definition (say 'any characteristic of an object which can be observed or measured . . .') supported by suitable examples which are themselves secondary concepts (eg 'size and colour are examples of the physical properties of an object').

2.1.3 Concept-systems

(Schemata.) This category includes sets of related concepts which (it is hypothesized) the learner stores in memory in such a way that the relations between the concepts as well as the concepts themselves are remembered and can be recalled. The concept 'physical properties' together with the properties themselves may be thought of as a system of interrelated concepts. Thus such physical properties as mass, weight, density, size (or rather volume), may be stored in such a way that the interrelationships between them are also remembered, or alternatively they may be stored as relatively separate concepts. In the former case, the observation that one object floats whilst another sinks would lead, apart from the direct conclusion that one is more dense than water and the other is less dense, to other correct conclusions about the relative masses of the objects in relation to their apparent volume. In the latter case, it is less likely that such secondary conclusions would be made correctly. Many psychologists consider that all new concepts are in some way grafted onto the previously stored concepts (ie that all conceptual information is stored as schemata). Piaget's thinking is that the learner 'assimilates' any new concept into his existing schema of knowledge, in order to make sense of it. If the learner fails to assimilate the new concept into his schema, he needs to reorganize, or 'adapt' his schema to fit the new concept. Thus 'whale' might seem to fit the learner's 'fish' schema better than it fits his 'mammals' schema. To make sense of this apparent 'misfit', the learner needs to adapt his concepts of 'fish' and 'mammal'. Most of Piaget's experiments on the early learning of concepts such as 'size' and 'volume' (the famous 'conservation of volume' experiments, for example) illustrate these processes of assimilation and adaptation in action.

Learning and teaching conceptual information

Once again, the literature on concept learning is very large. At a relatively shallow level of analysis, the rules for teaching concepts suggested by Gagné are useful general tactics. The main rule is to teach through examples and non-examples and to arrange practice and tests involving different examples and non-examples. At a deeper level of analysis, however, there is much more known concerning the learning of particular types of conceptual information. Much yet remains unknown however. For example little is known about the process of formation of conceptual schemata. Many writers consider that the learner should form his own schemata and that each learner's schemata may well be different. Others consider that the structure of the information itself suggests useful ways of presenting it and storing it and that such insights should be communicated to the learner — he should whenever possible be aided and guided in the formation of appropriate schemata, by the presentation of complex information already pre-structured in easy-to-remember patterns. Examples of attempts to do this are mnemonics, analogies, summary diagrams and charts (such as the schemata used in this book). Only by deep (level 4) analysis and subsequent evaluation of the resultant instructional systems, will one be able to resolve such differences of opinion. The truth may not be all that straightforward either. It may be that some learners learn better when left to structure their own schemata whereas others benefit from programmed help in structuring their knowledge. It may be that certain types of information benefit more from one approach than do other types.

2.2 Principles (or rules that guide action or explain change)

2.2.1 Principles of nature

(Rules that govern the behaviour of our environment.) This category includes all principles or rules that we can observe to be in operation in the world around us, either by direct observation or by inference from their effects. A rule is a statement of a relationship that exists between two or more concepts or phenomena. For example, the statement 'metals expand when heated' is a rule or principle of nature. It is an explicit statement of an interrelationship which exists between the concepts 'metals', 'heat' and 'expansion' — *if* metal *and if* heated *then* expands. The *if-then* type of rule is the most common form. Not all rules are as clear-cut as this example. The statement, 'red sky at night, shepherd's delight' is a figurative way of expressing a rule of probability — *if* red sky at night, *then* increased probability of good weather tomorrow (*therefore* shepherd's delight).

2.2.2 Principles of action

(Rules that govern the principle-holder's behaviour.) This somewhat clumsy expression is intended to include the knowledge that one acquires regarding the appropriate actions or reactions to specific situations, whether they be real-life or purely reflective (conceptual) situations. Thus such rules as 'if I identify a problem situation, I should also examine the wider system to establish whether the problem is "real" or whether it is a symptom of a more general problem' is a rule that one may use to guide one's actions in a problem-solving situation — both a real situation (solving the problems of one's factory) or a purely imaginary situation (solving problems presented by the teacher). These are the sort of principles that Polya (1945) refers to as 'heuristics' for problem-solving. We have also used this term throughout this book in the same sense, except that we have differentiated between general heuristics (applicable to a wide variety of situations) and highly specific heuristic strategies (applicable to a certain defined category of problem). The heuristics suggested by Polya are generally applicable to any type of mathematics problem (and even other non-mathematical problems — remember that at the beginning of this book we used Polya's heuristics as a guide to construct our own for instructional design). The heuristic strategies described by Landa (1976) for the solution of problems in geometry are highly specific. They relate to only this category of problem and they specify as precisely as is possible the most efficient strategies for solution.

This category of knowledge — the general principles of action — contains the Polya-type general heuristics. The specific strategies belong in the category to be described below.

2.2.3 Rule systems

(Theories and strategies.) Just as discrete facts combine to form fact systems, or as discrete but related concepts combine to form concept systems (or schemata), so discrete but related rules combine to form rule-systems. As an example, the Landa-type heuristic strategies for problem-solving, mentioned above, are a combination of specific knowledge of geometry (the individual geometry theorems are rules or principles of nature, in my classification) with knowledge of how to search for solutions to maths problems (general heuristics, or principles of action, in my classification). The result is a set of highly specific problem-solving strategies, suitable for a given class of problems. Similarly, the combination of certain observed principles of physics, together with the application of certain general principles of thought (scientific inference etc) might lead to the formulation of a new, highly specific theory or hypothesis (a higher order rule or principle, to use Gagné's terminology).

The learning and teaching of principles

Two approaches compete in popularity in this area — the direct expositive approach (as favoured by Ausubel — see Chapter 9) and the discovery approach (as favoured by Bruner, Piaget and the developmental psychologists — see Chapter 9). The two opposing viewpoints have often clashed in the literature of education and teachers have tended to 'take sides' espousing one or other of the approaches as a universal strategy of instruction. A somewhat more balanced view has been argued by Gagné, who admits that both methods can be effective in the teaching of principles, but the discovery approach (or rather 'guided discovery'), in which the learner is led to form the principle for himself, tends to lead to better long-term recall. On the other hand, there is a time penalty — it usually takes longer to lead the learner to the discovery of a principle than to expound and explain it to him. A further advantage that may spring from the discovering of principles is the increased chance of successful transfer of learning to other similar situations.

Practising cognitive skills whilst learning knowledge

After all, much of education is concerned with the development of capabilities of logical thinking, of problem-solving, etc. The discovery approach requires the learner to practise these skills as part of the learning process of a new principle. Thus the learner is working towards two types of objectives at one and the same time — he is learning an item of knowledge (a principle that is new to him) and he is learning to analyse what he already knows, restructure it in more complex ways (synthesize new relationships), put these new ideas to the test, either in reality or by internalized reflection (evaluation) eventually arriving at the formulation of the new principle. This latter process is the use of problem-solving skills.

It is probable that the expositive strategy is less successful in terms of transfer in that it does not directly make the learner practise his problem-solving skills. It concentrates on the one objective — the acquisition of knowledge of the new principle. Some authors argue that the 'reflective lecturing' technique (in which the lecturer goes through a simulated process of discovery, explaining his problem-solving strategy as he goes) can combine the benefits of short learning times with the promotion of problem-solving skills and consequent transfer to other learning tasks. The learners, as a group, participate as observers of the problem-solving strategy in action. Whether this is, in fact, as effective as having to go through the process of problem-solving oneself, is doubtful, but on the other hand there is not sufficient time available to allow learners to discover everything that they are to learn. Thus, for practical reasons, one has to adopt a judicious mix of expositive and discovery methods in teaching.

The importance of examples

As concerns the detailed steps of teaching principles, it is important to provide sufficient variety of example situations. As in the case of the teaching of concepts it is necessary to discriminate problems to which the new principle applies from other similar problems to which it does not apply. Sometimes the mere statement of the principle is sufficient. A principle is in a sense a 'chain of concepts' linked by the grammar of the language in which it is expressed. For example, the principle of nature 'metals expand when heated' is expressed here in English and establishes a relationship between the concepts 'metals', 'heat' and 'expansion'; the principle of algebra, $(a + b)^2 = a^2 + 2ab + b^2$, is expressed here in the language of mathematical notation and establishes a relationship between the concepts 'square', 'sum of two quantities', 'square of the sum', etc. In these examples, anyone who has already stored in memory the component concepts and who has learned the language used (factual information) should understand the principle merely from its statement. Learning the principle requires no more than the restructuring of already stored information. Few examples are required to establish the area of applicability of these principles.

On the other hand, the principle of action (taught to salesgirls) that 'the customer is always right' requires further explanation or illustration of the context. Obviously the customer is not right, if, for example, he mis-reads a price or mis-calculates the change he should get. What is the range of situations to which the principle *does* apply? Examples are needed to define this. Similarly the principle of geometry (Pythagoras' Theorem) when stated as $c^2 = a^2 + b^2$ still requires the definition of the context — the rule only applies in right-angled triangles in which the hypotenuse has been named 'c'. A full definition of the context is needed as part of the statement of the principle.

12.2 The skills schema

The four skill categories

I have already suggested the division of skills into four main categories — cognitive, psychomotor, reactive and interactive. In the last chapter we discussed the reasons for the subdivision of the 'affective' domain into two. One might refer to these two areas as 'managing oneself' and 'managing others'. They are obviously interlinked, but also there are quite clear differences. We can all think of people we know who lead exemplary personal lives but who do not shine at the skills of getting on with, or of influencing, others. Similarly, many 'born leaders' who excel at the skills of influencing or controlling others, do not stand out as examples of self-control. There seem to be, therefore, strong practical reasons for discriminating between these two 'affective' areas of skilled behaviour.

Reflexive skills and strategy skills

We also noticed in the last chapter that in each of the four categories, one could identify examples of skills that were more or less 'reflexive' in nature, that were repetitive and that showed little variation in execution from one instance to another. Examples include the execution of routines (say the division of two numbers), the execution of repetitive tasks (say typewriting), the exhibition of 'approach behaviours' towards a certain type of situation (eg welcoming and seeking opportunities to dance), and the execution of routine social habits (eg saying 'thank you', giving precedence to ladies or older colleagues, etc). But we noted that each category also contained examples of skilled behaviour that required a certain amount of planning, that involved the use of some strategy for decision making, that showed substantial variations in execution from one instance to another. Examples include the solving of mathematical problems, the artistic or aesthetic layout of a page of typescript, the planning of one's life around a set of values or principles (religious, aesthetic, political, etc) and the persuasion of a group of people to accept a certain set of values or principles.

Productive and reproductive skills

We shall call the first type 'reproductive' skills and the second type 'productive' skills. I use these terms in the sense in which several educational psychologists have applied them when discussing learning and instruction. Briggs (1970), used the terms 'reproductive learning' and 'productive learning' as the two grand categories of educational objectives. Bloom's main categories of cognitive objectives can be classified into these two groups with a high degree of accuracy (knowledge, comprehension and application — reproductive: analysis, synthesis and evaluation — productive). A little reflection on the types of test items that one would use to test for these categories of objectives should illustrate the difference. In the first case, one tests whether the student can *reproduce* what he has learned, either exactly as learned or put into his own words or applied to standard types of tasks. In the second case, the tests should seek to establish whether the student can apply what he has learned to novel situations and tasks — whether he can *produce* a novel solution to a novel problem. Covington and Crutchfield (1965) have used the term 'productive thinking' in exactly this sense. Their productive thinking programmes of instruction sought to teach the student to apply some general problem-solving strategies to a variety of situations of a 'detective story' nature. Others have used the term as a near-synonym for creative thinking. My use of the term in relation to skills certainly includes the creative element in skilled performance. As Wellens (1974) points out, even basically simple psychomotor tasks such as laying crazy paving or wallpapering a room have an element of creative planning in deciding how to get a more pleasing visual effect. Analysis of the performance of the craftsman who achieves the more pleasing effect can give us insights concerning the 'problem-solving strategies' this craftsman uses and the general principles upon which these strategies are based.

The analysis of 'creative design' and 'creative management' has also revealed the existence of specific strategies which apply certain general principles. Thus, productive skills depend on the presence of a body of knowledge, built up through experience or through instruction, composed of relevant general principles and structured into specific strategies of thought or action.

The 'productive-reproductive continuum'

Different tasks require different strategies for their 'productive' execution and the complexity of the necessary strategies also varies. For example, the painter and decorator requires very little knowledge in order to apply paint to a wall uniformly. He needs to know the recommended *procedures* for mixing paints, for laying on the paint and for spreading it out without leaving brushmarks. He does not need to know any general principles or problem-solving strategies. When wallpapering, however, the decorator needs to know not only the *procedures* for measuring up the room, cutting the wallpaper, mixing and applying paste, etc, but also certain aesthetic *principles* concerning the positioning of patterns and joins in the wallpaper so as to obtain an acceptably pleasing effect. These principles combine into a decision-making *strategy* that enable him to decide, for a room of any shape or size, which parts of which walls to paper first, which corners to use as reference points, how to 'balance' the pattern around features such as doors and windows, how to accentuate or 'hide' such features as excessive height, asymmetry, irregularity, etc. The interior decorator/consultant, who is contracted to design the decorative scheme of a house, may not require the reproductive skills of the painter/decorator, (unless he will also execute the work), but he will need to know the procedures that the craftsman employs (in order not to demand the impossible), the principles of obtaining a high quality of finish (in order to visualize the finished product) and in addition he will need many more general principles (eg of colour combinations). This much larger knowledge-base is structured into a much more complex set of decision-making strategies. The painter of works of art will require an even larger knowledge base — both *procedures* (eg how to build up thickness and leave brushmarks when required) and *principles* (eg of the use of texture and relief to achieve desired visual effects).

Thus the terms 'reproductive' and 'productive', when applied to the classification of skills, should not be taken as two 'watertight compartments'. Most skilled activities are partly reproductive and partly productive. One could place a given activity at some point on a 'mainly reproductive — mainly productive' scale.

A more detailed analysis of the skilled activity will however identify the sub-skills, or component-skills, involved. At this more detailed level of analysis, some of the sub-skills may appear to be purely 'reproductive' whilst others will appear as very much 'productive'. Such a level of analysis is useful, as the techniques of instruction for the development of these two categories of sub-skills are quite different.

How to read the skills schema
Thus the schema of skill categories (Figure 12.2) can be read in two ways, depending on the depth of analysis. At 'level 2' (when analysis has provided us with a list of the operations for each task or with a list of detailed instructional objectives) we can look at each operation or objective in turn, identify the skills involved in performance (cognitive, psychomotor, reactive and interactive) and place each skill identified on a 'reproductive — productive' scale. At 'level 3' however, we would analyse the skills into their respective (reproductive and productive) component sub-skills, and would be able to classify these sub-skills more accurately into the cells of our schema. At this stage we will have identified those sub-skills that are the most difficult to learn and to perform to required standard. Some of these may require to be analysed even further (level 4) in order that we may discover the precise sources of difficulty. At this depth of analysis special techniques may be needed, depending on the skill category. We met some of these techniques in Chapter 10. For psychomotor skills the in-depth analysis methods developed by Douglas Seymour are useful. For cognitive skills we can perform a mathetical analysis (more useful for reproductive skills) or an analysis of mental operations as suggested by Landa (more useful for productive skills). For interactive skills, techniques such as those developed at the British Overseas Airways Corporation (now British Airways), for supervisory skills, may be developed. These techniques were developed by Rackham and Morgan and were described at length in Chapter 11.

12.3 The skill cycle

12.3.1 The four components necessary for skilled performance

The stimulus response model of skill
In the last chapter, when discussing the psychomotor skill domain, we introduced the idea of a cycle of stages in the performance of a skilled activity. We also saw that the other categories of skill showed a marked similarity, in that all of them involve the perception of external signals or 'stimuli' (emanating from objects or people in the environment) and the execution of appropriate 'responses' to these stimuli. Also, there is always a 'self-checking' or 'feedback' stage when the performer observes the effect that his responses have had and, if necessary, executes further responses. The universality of this model of performance is seen in the widespread acceptance of behaviourism as an explanation of all manner of learning. However, the strongest criticisms made of the behaviourist position centre on the tendency to ignore the *processes* that go on inside the performer. The *stimulus-response-feedback*

	TYPE OF 'KNOWLEDGE CONTENT'	
MAIN SKILL CATEGORY	**REPRODUCTIVE SKILLS** Applying procedures (algorithms).	**PRODUCTIVE SKILLS** Applying principles and strategies.
COGNITIVE SKILLS Decision-making, problem-solving, logical thinking, etc.	Applying a known procedure to a known category of 'problem', eg dividing numbers, writing a grammatically correct sentence.	Solving 'new' problems; 'inventing' a new procedure, eg proving a theorem, writing creatively.
PSYCHOMOTOR SKILLS Physical action, perceptual acuity, etc	Sensori-motor skills; repetitive or automated action, eg typewriting, changing gear, running fast.	'Strategy' skills or 'planning' skills; arts and crafts, eg page layout design, 'road sense', playing football.
REACTIVE SKILLS Dealing with oneself; attitudes, feelings, habits, self-control.	Conditioned habits and attitudes, eg 'attending, responding and valuing' (Bloom taxonomy), 'approach/ avoid behaviours' (Mager).	'Personal control' skills, developing a 'mental set' or a value system (Bloom) 'self-actualization' (Rogers).
INTERACTIVE SKILLS Dealing with others.	Social habits; conditioned responses, eg good manners, pleasant tone, verbal habits.	'Interpersonal control' skills, eg leadership, supervision, persuasion, discussion, salesmanship.

Figure 12.2 *The skills schema*

model treats the skilled performer as a 'black box'. It does not offer any hypotheses concerning how the performer *decides* to execute a particular response (or series of responses) to a particular stimulus (or series of stimuli). In terms of evaluating the skilled performance, the 'black box' model is quite adequate. One may observe a skilled performer, observe the input information that he received (the stimuli) and the output performance that he exhibits (the responses). Comparing this observed situation against some criteria one can form an opinion concerning the quality of the performance (is it up to standard or is it deficient) and one can also evaluate whether the input information was in any way deficient. One can thus come to a conclusion whether the source of any performance discrepancy lies in the performer or in his environment. We have done exactly this in earlier chapters, under the name of 'front end' or performance deficiency analysis.

Opening the 'black box'   However, if there is a serious performance deficiency that appears to have causes that lie within the performer, we may need to 'open up' the black box in order to discover just exactly what is causing the problem. To do this, we need a model of what should be going on 'inside' during the performance of a skill. We shall now attempt to build up such a model, which is sufficiently general to serve for any skill category.

The skilled performer does two things that are quite obvious to any observer: he *perceives* the stimuli that trigger specific actions and he then *performs* those actions.

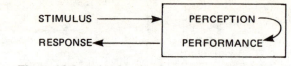

Figure 12.3 *A simple stimulus-response process*

The non-observable aspects of the skilled performance are the internal processes that link the perception stage to the performance stage. Our previous discussion of skilled performance and of category of skills has suggested two types of process that must be involved in making this link. First, in all cases the performer must recognize the stimulus as being of a type that requires a characteristic response. He must *know* the significance of the stimulus and he must have gained this knowledge through previous learning. In other words, there are certain learning *prerequisites* that must be 'in store' as it were, and that are available to the performer. Secondly, in most cases the performer must process the new information (the stimulus) in the light of the stored information (the knowledge prerequisites) in order to decide what response is required. In other words, he must *plan* his response. We noted that certain ('reproductive') skills are low on the need for planning. They require only the recall of the appropriate response or series of responses (procedure). However other ('productive') skills are high on the need for planning. No standard response is required, but rather a specific response or procedure needs to be designed for the specific stimulus situation encountered, through the application, in a heuristic manner, of relevant general principles.

The four-stage cycle   Thus, our model now has the form of a four-stage cycle of *perception* of the stimulus situation, recall of the relevant *prerequisites* (procedures or principles), *planning* of the response and *performance* of the response (finally closing the cycle by once again perceiving the results of his actions). Note that the planning stage does not occur in all skills, giving us, sometimes, a 'short cut' round the cycle.

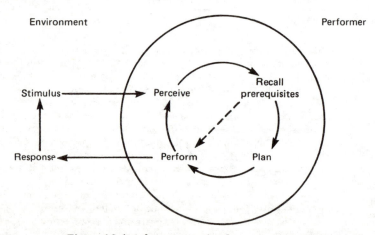

Figure 12.4 *A four-stage stimulus-response cycle*

Causes of poor performance   This simple model enables us to postulate four possible causes of poor performance: the performer cannot

— perceive the stimulus situation,
— recall the necessary prerequisites,
— plan his response effectively, or
— actually perform the required response.

**(1)
Perception**

Inability to perceive the stimulus may be caused by a low level of 'perceptual acuity', as for example:

- ☐ (cognitive skill) — inability to 'see' a problem;
- ☐ (psychomotor skill) — inability to discriminate colour, tone, size, shape, etc to the degree necessary;
- ☐ (reactive skill) — inability to notice the signs and events occurring around one (a lack of attention);
- ☐ (interactive skills) — inability to notice the responses (including non-verbal responses) of other people.

In all these cases the performer shows a low level of acuity in perceiving the necessary stimulus information even when that information is quite clearly presented. However, sometimes the information is not clearly presented. There are distractions. All manner of other irrelevant information is being picked up as well (engineers call this 'noise'). Our performer may be adept at perceiving the stimulus when it is presented 'on its own' but may have trouble in picking it out in a 'noisy environment'. For example:

- ☐ (cognitive) — ability to notice punctuation error in a given single sentence, but inability to notice them when the sentence is part of a larger paragraph;
- ☐ (psychomotor) — the car driver who can identify danger signals in light traffic conditions but fails to identify them in heavy traffic conditions;
- ☐ (reactive) — the music lover who perceives opportunities to listen to good music when directly invited, but fails to notice them in the general life of his community;
- ☐ (interactive) — the manager who can identify signs of employee insecurity in a specific interview situation, but fails to identify the same signs in a more general casual conversation.

**(2)
Prerequisites**

Inability to recall prerequisites may be caused by a lack of these prerequisites. The performer simply *does not know what to do* in a particular situation. The relevant procedure has not been learned (or has been forgotten). The relevant principles that would enable him to invent or develop an appropriate procedure are not available from his memory store.

Alternatively, the performer may fail to recall the relevant knowledge, although it is in store, due to a failure on his part to interpret the perceived stimulus information in the correct way. The new information is compared with the stored experience (knowledge structures or schemata) and is mis-classified. Thus the wrong procedure is recalled and applied:

- ☐ (cognitive skill) — a given Portuguese noun (the stimulus information) is mis-classified as to gender; this leads to the recall of the wrong form of the adjective to be coupled to it;
- ☐ (psychomotor skill) — a given road sign is mis-interpreted by the motorist, leading to the recall of an incorrect strategy — the motorist accelerates instead of braking;
- ☐ (reactive skill) — a student's examination errors are mis-interpreted by the teacher as due to laziness, leading to the development of an unduly negative attitude towards the student in question. This negative *feeling* (reaction) may *later* influence actions (interactions);
- ☐ (interactive skill) — the salesman who mis-interprets a potential customer's reactions and as a result applies an inappropriate selling strategy.

Thus we have two aspects involved in recalling prerequisite knowledge schemata, procedures or principles:

1. Ability to interpret the stimulus information in order to identify what

knowledge is required.
2. Having that knowledge in memory store in a useable form.

(3) Planning

Inability to plan may also have two main causes. One is planning one's immediate actions. This involves considering the alternatives open to us and deciding among these. The causes of failure in the planning of an action may be due to inability to generate the list of possible alternative courses of action, or to inability to make the best choice. The first implies inability to use the relevant principles in order to 'invent' alternative procedures (assuming of course that the relevant principles are 'in store'). The second implies inability to evaluate the alternatives by 'thinking through' the implications of each one. For example, the structural engineer may (or may not) come up with, say, four alternative solutions for the construction of a given bridge and he then may (or may not) select the most cost-effective solution. The manager faced with an industrial relations problem may (or may not) consider all the alternative courses of action open to him (eg sackings, warnings, suspensions, ignoring the problem, etc) and he may (or may not) evaluate correctly the hazards of each one (strikes, loss of productivity, etc).

(4) Performance

Inability to perform can also spring from two types of deficiencies — inability to initiate the necessary action or inability to 'see it through'. Assuming once again that the performer has perceived the stimuli, interpreted them correctly, recalled relevant knowledge, considered all the alternatives and decided which is the 'best' one, he may yet fail to perform. Examples:

☐ (cognitive) — having 'seen' the problem (in, say, maths) the student works out the stages of the 'best' solution, but he does not actually work out the solution (due to lack of motivation, time, relevance, etc); alternatively, he commences to work it out but gets 'bogged down' in the detail of calculation and gives up (due to lack of persistence or 'mental stamina', etc);

☐ (psychomotor) — the industrial operative responds as is expected, but his productivity/quality of work is below standard (due to deficiencies in strength, stamina, dexterity);

☐ (reactive) — practical difficulties are encountered in attempting to 'live by one's values', leading to compromises;

☐ (interactive) — a supervisor fails to initiate necessary disciplinary action (due to lack of moral courage) or fails to 'see it through' correctly (due to lack of tact).

12.3.2 The 'expanded' skill cycle

The 12 factors in skilled performance

Combining the factors we have just discussed, it is possible to conceptualize an 'expanded' version of our skill cycle, as shown in the diagram (Figure 12.5) below. This shows the 12 types of abilities which *may* have to be present for the efficient performance of a skilled activity. I stress the word 'may', as I am not implying that all skills depend in equal measure on all 12 of these factors. We have already seen, for example, that the reproductive skills require very little planning and thus rely little on the presence of analytical, synthetical or evaluative abilities. Indeed, some completely automated, reflexive skills, such as typing, may require none of these abilities at all. Typing does require, however, a high degree of attention to the stimulus material (the manuscript). If this is already typed, or very clearly written, there may be no great need for a high level of perceptual discrimination. In the case of a typist in a typing pool, however, having to deal with the poor handwriting of all manner of people, the perceptual discrimination element takes on greater importance.

An example of skills analysis (psycho-motor skill)

At the other end of the cycle, poor typing performance could result from difficulties in actually initiating and performing the necessary responses. Acute arthritis, for example, may make it impossible to build up any reasonable speed. Or insufficient dexterity and muscular control may make certain errors

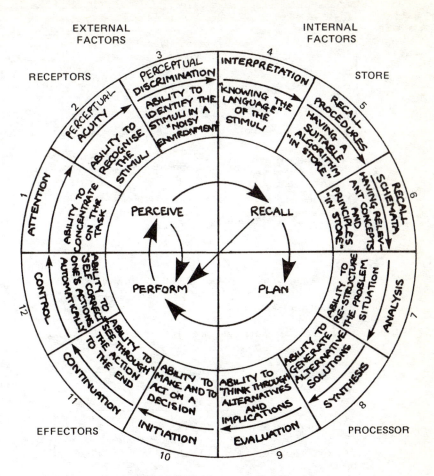

Figure 12.5 *The 'expanded' skill-cycle*

occur with high frequency. It is common for typists to have more trouble initially in controlling the movements and pressure exerted by the little fingers, thus making errors likely in the typing of letters such as 'a', 'q' and 'z'. Another factor — fatigue — creeps in to cause higher error rates as the day progresses. Thus continuation of the task is jeopardized by lack of sufficient stamina.

This typing example should suffice to illustrate the basic idea behind the expanded skill cycle. It is merely a conceptual tool to aid the analysis of any given activity in order to identify the causes of poor performance. It is a language for analysing skills — a taxonomy if you like. But no hierarchical dependencies are implied. Any given skilled activity may require any combination of the 12 factors in varying degrees. Any trainee may come to the learning situation with any combination of any of them, in different degrees. The function of skills analysis is to identify the 'gap' between performance requirements (the 'what should be') and existing trainee abilities (the 'what is'). The analyst must identify, for the particular case in hand, the exact combination of factors that make up the 'what should be' and through target population analysis, compare this with 'what is'.

A practical example may illustrate the depth of analysis implied. This time let us choose a cognitive skill — that of performing long division.

1. **Attention**	Ability to concentrate on arithmetic tasks.
2. **Perceptual acuity**	Ability to recognize numbers and division signs, whether presented symbolically or verbally.
3. **'Noisy environment'** *(discrimination)*	Ability to recognize the need for division when this is implied indirectly (eg 'Joe gets a third of the money').
4. **Ability to interpret**	Ability to analyse the problem to identify what is divided by what (eg $3 \div 9$ or $9 \div 3$).
5. **Relevant knowledge**	Ability to recall the procedure (the algorithm) for long division, in all its steps. Also one's 'tables' (facts).
Further	
6. — schemata, or	Not involved, as long division is a reproductive skill.
7. — analysis, or	One simply recalls the algorithm and applies it step by
8. — synthesis, or	step to the data.
9. — evaluation	
10. **Initiation**	Merely requires the physical abilities of writing figures.
11. **Continuation**	May require some degree of perseverance in the case of large numbers.
12. **Control**	Ability to automatically check the 'scale' of the answer.

The above analysis is not necessarily complete, but is sufficient to illustrate that the approach can be applied to the cognitive area. An interesting aspect is observed when one passes to the analysis of the present level of performance of our trainees. Why does a given student make errors in long division? In what combination of factors is he deficient, and to what degree. I am reminded in this context of an example once given by Tom Gilbert (1967), of three students who had taken a test on long division.

Tom, Dick and Harry

> Tom scored 100% correct answers.
> Dick scored 50% correct answers.
> Harry scored 0. Every answer was incorrect.

The question posed was: 'who knows most and who knows least about long division?' Gilbert argued that the answer is not at all that clear. It may be the case for example that Harry knows just about all there is to know, *except* the meaning of the division sign. He thus reads $[90 \div 3]$ as $[3 \div 90]$, for example. He then proceeds to solve these (inverted) problems correctly, problems which are generally harder to solve than those originally set $[90 \div 3 = 30$ but $3 \div 90 = 0.033333$ recurring]. Dick, on the other hand, is making a variety of mistakes associated with the use of the long division procedure (eg he forgets to bring down a zero, or he writes his figures in the wrong columns), which result in occasional mistakes in the final answer. Thus, once we know all this we might say that Harry actually knows considerably more about long division than Dick and at least as much as (possibly even more than) Tom. The difference that Gilbert is emphasizing is that between 'accomplishment' and 'acquirement', or in other words, between 'execution' and 'knowledge'.

My expanded skill cycle illustrates that there are many possible causes of a failure to execute. The example above is one of an inability to interpret the stimulus in the intended manner. Harry has all the necessary knowledge, but for some reason he insists on mis-interpreting the division sign. This may be a knowledge deficiency in itself — he has learned the wrong meaning somehow. But it may also be some strange aberration that occurred on the day of the test, due to the stress of the situation — inability to perform under stress, or inability to discriminate in a 'noisy environment'.

The four critical sub-systems of the learner

Thus we see that the analysis of deficiencies in skilled activities can be quite a complex process. In effect, four elements of the learner may need to be developed:

— his abilities to perceive the relevant events, situations, moods, or problems that should instigate his actions — we can refer to this as the development of his *receptor* mechanisms;

— his abilities to recall relevant facts, concepts, procedures or principles — we can refer to this as the development of his *store of knowledge*;

— his abilities to analyse, synthesize and evaluate alternative courses of action, in the process recalling relevant conceptual schemata and if necessary restructuring them — we can refer to this as the development of his *processing* mechanisms;

— his abilities to actually perform the responses which the situation calls for — we can refer to this as the development of his *effector* mechanisms.

A simple 'model' of the learner

These four terms have occasionally been used in the building up of cybernetic models of the human learner. It is not my intention to be over-mechanistic in my approach, but in order to explain the way in which the skills schemata (and the knowledge schemata) presented here are used in practice, it is convenient to construct a simple model of the learning process.

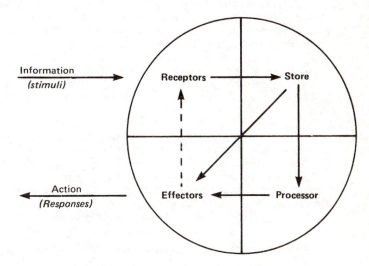

Figure 12.6 *A simple model of the learner*

We could conceptualize our learner as composed of the four types of components — *receptors*, *effectors*, (which interact with the 'outside world') and *store* and *processor* (which form the 'inside world' or brain). The arrows in the diagram summarize the interactions between these components, which have already been discussed fully above, in our analysis of the skills cycle.

The 'imbalance' of most approaches to skills development

The planning of a course aiming to develop a skilled capability (and that includes just about any course worth giving) should give due consideration to the development of each of the four components.

— psycho-motor domain

In the case of psychomotor skills, emphasis has in the past been placed on perceptual development (the receptors) and performance development (the effectors). Only in recent years have we become interested in systematically analysing the knowledge content in skilled performance (even now the tendency is to simply list the necessary knowledge without much consideration of just exactly how that knowledge should be stored in the brain). We have only started to scratch the surface of the planning elements in skills of a higher order, such as the arts and crafts.

— reactive domain

In the affective domain (reactive skills) we have concentrated on imparting knowledge. We have traditionally gone no further than to *tell* people that

'Beethoven is good', or that 'race discrimination is bad'. The next step was often to get involved with the processors, by discussing *why* Beethoven is good. It is more seldom that we meet systematically developed programmes that aim to sharpen our students' perceptions of 'good' and 'bad' in reality and still less often do we meet systematic programmes to get our students to respond. Mager's booklet on developing attitudes towards learning offers a model of how, through the rewarding of 'approach behaviours' one can develop specific reactive skills. But how often is this done in practice?

— interactive domain

In the domain of interactive skills, a similar situation of imbalance was the rule. One exhorts people to behave towards others in particular ways. One demonstrates the desired behaviour by 'setting an example'. But how often does one stop to consider whether the learner must *know* anything in order to help him to react appropriately? Rackham and Morgan's work on supervisor training indicated that effective verbal interaction required a conceptual structure (schema) for classifying the statements of others as an aid to deciding on one's response (and it took some years of research to develop an effective schema).

— cognitive domain

Finally, in the cognitive domain, how often do we really understand the structure of the knowledge that we expect our students to acquire? Some work has been done on this in recent years, but there is still much to do. Likewise, the difficulties that students have in 'seeing' the essential information in a problem (say in mathematics) are not fully understood. Nor are the processes by which students search their knowledge stores in order to try to identify relevant schemata for problem solution. Here again, Landa spent some years working on the processes for solving problems in geometry —but that is only one class of problems.

The problem of 'problem-solving'

Indeed, the whole question of problem-solving is at the core of understanding many of the difficulties that learners experience. This is true in all four domains. It will be of interest to close this chapter by considering a few learning situations, particularly ones involving problem-solving, to see how the concepts we have used in building up our knowledge and skills schemata behave in practice. Do they help us to think clearly about the learning process? Do they help us to make decisions concerning the instructional process? Let us concentrate on the cognitive aspects of learning in the examples that follow.

12.4 Analysis of some learning situations

Let us conceptualize (or rather idealize) the learning process in systems terms. Imagine the simplest possible model of the learner, with two basic functions in his brain:

— store (or memory) and
— processor (or thinking box).

We are ignoring such sophistications to the model as long and short-term memory. Le us get right to the root of the matter.

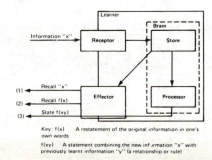

Figure 12.7 *An idealized model of the learning process*

The recall of stored knowledge

Information 'X' is received in the store, or so we hope, because that was the objective of instruction. In order to test whether it is still in store, we need to 'call it up' rather like the memory button on a pocket calculator. If the information is factual, and we ask the learner to repeat it, then we have an 'X-in': 'X-out' situation (case 1 above). On other occasions, when the information was not verbal (and we ask the student to verbalize it) or if it was verbal and we ask him to use it, then the performance elicited is some 'function of X' (a verbal description of X, for example). This is case 2 above. Note that the higher mental processes (the processor) are not involved. Thus, assuming that we are dealing with learners who can speak and/or write (not with very young children or exceptional cases) the most direct operation for simple factual information (to prove that it is known) is to ask the learner to *state* it. An alternative is to reverse the process. For example, given an object → state its name or given the name → point to the object.

When the information is complex — a system of facts, the same applies in principle, but for reasons of motivation and interest one may use a less direct operation which nevertheless, *proves* recall of the facts and how they are related.

Morse code is an example of a system of facts. It is a bit boring to simply recite it as a test, so using it to send or receive messages is commonly used. This involves other activities (writing, banging a key) but it nevertheless proves unequivocally whether the 'facts' of Morse code are known or unknown. One word of caution: is not the use of Morse code a skill? Yes, it is. So let us analyse what we mean.

Separating knowledge and skill

Using Morse code is perhaps an example of the simplest type of skilled activity. The letter 'A' appears as a 'stimulus', generating immediately the reaction (dot-dash) from the key operator. In so doing, the key operator proves that

(a) he *knows* the Morse code symbol for 'A'
(b) he *can operate* the transmission key.

Now imagine a rapid stream of letters flashing onto a screen. At some given rate of presentation, the operator's performance will break down. He cannot keep up. He has reached the 'limit of his skill'. He makes errors in transcribing letters, including the letter 'A'. Yet, *we know* that *he knows* the symbol. (He was keying it correctly at lower speeds.)

Therefore, if we wish to test his *knowledge* level, as opposed to his skill in using the knowledge, we must choose an operation which we are sure is well within his present level of skill. Another example would be asking a child to write an essay about Roman Britain, in order to assess his factual knowledge of the topic, and then 'marking him down' for poor expression — the problem is not in his factual knowledge but in his creative writing skills.

I referred to 'using Morse code' as a simple type of skill, because the operation involves only the information being perceived at the moment. It is a simple transformation: $X \to f(X)$.

A more complex skill involves the combination of perceived information and previously stored information or symbolically: $X \to f(XY)$ where X is perceived and Y is stored information. A typical case here is algorithmic problem solving, (or in Gagné's terms rule-following). The stored information Y is the algorithm or set of rules on how to, for example, solve simultaneous equations. In order to test for factual knowledge of these rules, it is sufficient to ask the student to state them; for conceptual knowledge, to recognize instances in which they were used, or to explain how and why the rules work. But for skill in application, we must look for an operation which combines the knowledge (stored information) with actual examples of simultaneous equations (input information). Certain other important points arise. For example, if the information Y was originally inputted into store by means of a particular example of simultaneous equations, then it is possible (although not certain) that the particular example is also stored. If so, then effectively we have f (XY) in store already. The part-information X is sufficient to cause retrieval of the ready-made combination f (XY). No new processing (in thinking) has occurred. In order to be *certain* that information processing of the type desired is occurring (that the operation f (XY) is being performed) we must be sure that the results of this operation are not already available in store, that is, we must use examples unfamiliar to the student.

Analysing poor performance   Another point: success in performing the desired operation proves at least that the information Y was in store. There is no need to test separately for knowledge. But failure to operate correctly entails checking for both the knowledge and the skill component of the task separately, ie

— was the necessary information in store?
— did the processor work properly?
— was the new input information perceived correctly?
— was the correct stored information called up?
— was the operation f (XY) executed correctly? etc

To analyse a problem-solving task, one can follow a procedure of 'elimination of causes of failure'. Starting with the simplest types of knowledge (facts) one tests out by suitable questions the presence of relevant knowledge 'in store'. One then passes to part-test the execution of the skill, looking separately at perception, planning and performance factors. The flow chart below (Figure 12.8) illustrates the procedure and some typical test modes that would be used to diagnose the causes of failure.

Example 1 — a simple skilled task   In the case of the Morse code:

— there is factual knowledge — recognizing and producing the symbols correctly;
— there is no conceptual element directly involved;
— the operator must demonstrate that he can hear/see the symbols correctly in the practical situation;
— there is no real conscious planning involved (no deep analysis or synthesis is required) ie decision-making. Thus, very quickly, the skill becomes automated. The operator does not need to think;
— performance skills are composed of the accuracy and speed of reaction of the fingers of the operator. Control skills are involved in checking performance and correcting errors immediately. (Sensori-motor skills are involved but they are not new to the trainee — anyone knows how to press a button.)

Thus, the training plan would:

1. Ensure that the necessary knowledge is stored.
2. Arrange an appropriate distraction-free environment.
3. Arrange for practice of the sensori-motor skill, as a whole.

Thus the Morse code task is essentially a combination of a fact system and a physical skill.

Example 2 — a complex skilled task   Let us now consider a somewhat more complex skill — that of solving simultaneous equations. There are several 'standard' procedures for solving simultaneous equations. These can be applied quite mechanically if 'known' (ie if stored and recalled correctly). Furthermore, several types of simultaneous equations exist, some soluble best by one method, some by another. There exists a classification schema (a concept system) relating 'types of equations' to 'best procedures for solution'. This schema may, or may not, be 'known' in the case of a given student. Finally, there are different ways of posing the problem. Let us consider two ways: (1) *solve example 'A' by procedure 'B'* and (2) *solve example 'A' by the 'best' method.*

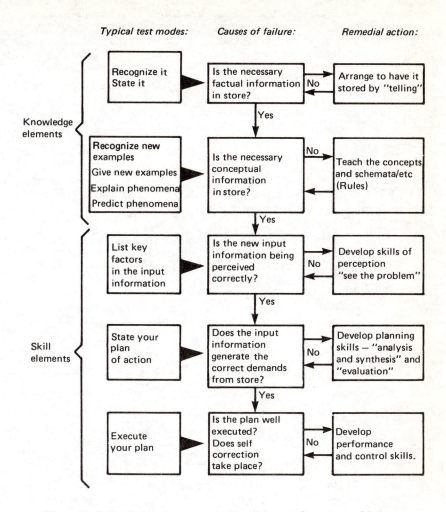

Figure 12.8 *Typical test modes used to diagnose the causes of failure*

In Figure 12.9 there is an analysis of the first problem statement. Note that the probability of a correct solution depends very much on what is already 'in store'.

In Figure 12.10 there is a suggestion of what happens in the case of problem statements of the second type. Note that a correct solution can never be guaranteed.

The difficulty of the problem depends on the 'state of the learner'

These two analyses are of course simplified, but they serve to illustrate the point that the same problem may take on quite different characteristics for the learner, depending on his current 'state of knowledge'.

In example (1) (a) If the necessary factual procedure is in store, there is no reason (apart from carelessness) why the student should not give the solution required. Furthermore the student does not need to 'understand' conceptually the steps of the procedure (this is an algorithmic procedure).

(b) If the procedure (in all its minute steps) is not stored (has been forgotten perhaps) but a conceptual understanding of the procedure exists (he would recognize the procedure if he saw it/he can explain the purpose of the main steps) then there is nothing to stop the student from deriving it. This is the 'prove from first principles' type of problem. The student solves it if he

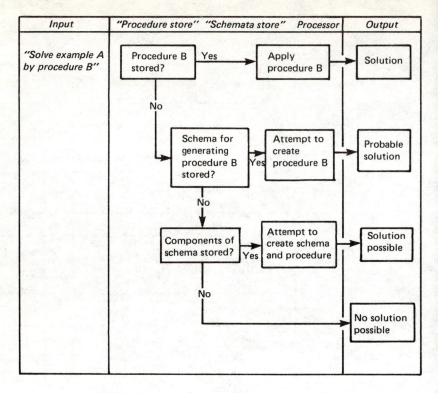

Figure 12.9 *Solution of problem statement (1)*

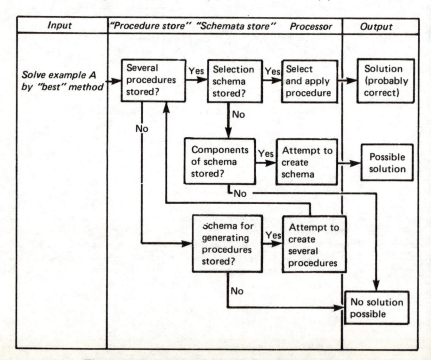

Figure 12.10 *Solution of problem statement (2)*

has all the *conceptual* elements required to recreate the forgotten *procedural* (factual) elements.

(c) However, if there is no ready-made schema for recreating the forgotten procedure, the problem takes on even greater proportions. If the student has the component concepts necessary to construct the appropriate procedure (but they have not in the past been related to each other with the specific purpose of creating methods of solving simultaneous equations) he may *possibly* nevertheless 'hit on the procedure' by playing around in his head with the relevant conceptual ideas. He may 'discover' the conceptual relationship which in turn will enable him to recreate the procedure. (The mental activity of the student in this case is on a higher plane than in case (b).)

We may continue the analysis to even more complex levels. Consider the case when the student has to 'solve by the best method' and he has neither methods nor a classification schema in store.

He may succeed in — generating several methods, including the best one (by chance);
— generating a classification schema;
— applying the best method.

Solution would be a chance process, but it is theoretically possible, so long as all the conceptual information necessary to construct the methods and the schema are in store (albeit not yet related to each other in appropriate ways).

12.5 Conclusion

The 'knowledge' schema

This chapter has outlined an approach to the analysis of learning difficulties and learning needs based on the age-old distinction between 'knowledge' and 'skill'. A schema of categories of knowledge was developed, to assist in the analysis of 'what is in store', (or what should be 'in store') in the learner's mind. The emphasis here was on the *structure of the knowledge*, that is, on the way in which discrete items of factual information, or discrete concepts, are interrelated to each other, forming systems, or schemata. The structure of these schemata is dictated largely by the structure of the information content itself. We do not want our students to form incorrect interrelationships. Many writers (eg Bruner) argue that students should be left alone to form their own conceptual schemata and that the schemata of one student are quite different from those of another. Whereas the latter point is no doubt true in the overall sense (each human being has undergone a unique set of experiences which have left their unique marks in his 'store'), we disagree that one can accept significant differences in specific schemata which relate to specific bodies of information.

The word 'significant' is used here in the sense that the difference impairs the individual's ability to use that specific knowledge in practical situations. Whereas there may be several acceptable ways of 'filing' and 'cross-indexing' a body of information, there are also many inefficient, and therefore unacceptable ways.

The formation of conceptual schemata

We therefore disagree with the first point, that all learners should be left to form their own conceptual schemata. Whereas *some* learners, in *some* situations, develop acceptable 'filing systems', it is common observation that this does not always happen. We rather agree with the position (argued by Landa) that it is good (given the time) to allow learners to form their own schemata, through a process of guided discovery but it remains the teacher's responsibility to:

(a) know what the acceptable schema (or alternative schemata) should be like; and
(b) check the schemata being formed by the learners, for acceptability; and
(c) assist the learners to form acceptable schemata.

One also has to admit that, in reality, there is seldom enough time to develop all one's teaching by discovery learning techniques. Therefore these techniques are best reserved for areas where they really seem to pay off. These areas are conceptual information in general and principles and heuristic problem-solving strategies in particular.

The 'skills' schema   A second schema was developed for the skills area. This postulates four domains of skilled activity, rather than the commonly accepted three domains (of Bloom *et al*). The reasons for subdividing the 'affective' domain into reactive and interactive skills domains were outlined in this and the previous chapter. Within each of the four domains, one sees a continuum of skills, from the fully automated 'reflexive' actions that make up sensori-motor skills, attitudes, habits and the following of algorithms, to the more complex types of skilled activity based on a high level of planning and decision making. These two dimensions of a skill were termed the reproductive and productive elements, suggesting that at a given, sufficiently deep level of analysis, one can separate out the productive and reproductive sub-skills composing the complex skilled activity.

The 'skills' cycle   A further schema was developed for the skills area, identifying the factors which influence the successful execution of skilled activity. This schema was based on the idea of a 'skill-cycle' involving *perception* of the relevant stimuli, recall of necessary *prerequisite* knowledge, *planning* what to do, and actually doing it (*performing*). Four types of 'essential' sub-systems are therefore involved – the 'receptors', the memory 'store', the 'processor' of higher mental activity and the 'effectors'. The development of a skilled capability may involve different degrees of attention to each of these four sub-systems. Analysis of these led to the identification of 12 factors to consider when analysing a skilled activity.

The 'interface' between knowledge and skill   This 'extended skills cycle' illustrated clearly the 'interface' between knowledge and skill. Any activity can be considered (as a whole) a skilled activity, in that inevitably some people 'learn to do it better than others', due to differences in the development of some of the 12 factors. However, three of these factors (interpretation, procedures and schemata) are in fact the relevant knowledge. Thus, the knowledge schema and the skills schema interlink.

If one is in the business of transmitting *information*, then one would use the knowledge schema by itself, as a tool to assist in the analysis of the information to be transmitted, the selection of suitable transmission methods and the design of the message itself.

If, on the other hand, one is in the business of developing *performance*, then one would commence by using the general skills schema to identify the type (or combination of types) of skilled activity to be developed, together with an idea of how far along the 'productive-reproductive' continuum they lie. The more 'productive' the skill, the more will knowledge play a part in its efficient execution. Passing to a more detailed level of analysis of each skill involved, one would use the 'extended skills cycle' as a conceptual tool to search for the sources of difficulty in execution. One now considers the perceptual factors involved and the psychological/physiological factors governing performance. But also (and especially in the productive skills area), one considers the exact knowledge requirements.

The 'skills' of analysis, synthesis and evaluation   Finally, one should say a few words regarding the 'planning' segment of the skills cycle. The three factors identified here were labelled 'analysis', 'synthesis' and 'evaluation'. The suggestion is that these are the three principal activities performed by the 'processor' sub-system. The examples of the solution of simultaneous equations, shown above, give some (but only some) insight into how these activities take place. Bloom, in his taxonomy, used these three terms as the three highest categories of cognitive objectives. We have used the terms throughout this book, referring to the principal types of activity involved in the application of the systems approach. We also saw, in Chapters 10 and 11, that the activity that Gagné refers to as 'problem-solving' involves these three component activities. We also saw, right back in Chapter 1, that approaches to the teaching of mathematical problem-solving transform these three activities into heuristics for action (Polya, 1945). We drew up some heuristics for instructional design at the end of Chapter 1, and in this chapter we have included a special category in our 'knowledge' schema for such heuristics (we called it 'heuristics' or 'rules of action').

General heuristics, or specific strategies?

The question remains — to what extent are such heuristics of general applicability and to what extent are they different for different categories of problem? We have seen, in previous chapters, that the approaches to a variety of problems bear quite marked similarities (for example, in mathematics, interior decorating, engineering design, instruction design and organizational development). However, the skilled mathematician is not necessarily an excellent instructional designer or craftsman or manager. Thus the application of general heuristics to specific categories of problems requires something more. This 'something' is (in part) experience of the 'context', or in other words, past practice at the solution of similar problems. Through this practice, the general heuristics, or 'rules of action', are combined with knowledge of the type of problem and its context (we called this 'rules of nature') to form highly specific and powerful problem-solving strategies.

Innate individual differences

Yet there is another part to that 'something more'. Given the same instruction and the same amount of planned experience, people differ in their mastery of a skilled task. In the reproductive or reflexive skills this is often explicable through the presence of individual differences in the receptor or effector sub-systems. Poor eyesight, slow reflexes, lack of strength or stamina may limit the level of an individual's performance in a sport, no matter how hard he trains. Surely, for the planning of productive skills, a similar restriction can be expected, imposed by the individual differences in the 'processor' sub-system. Poor analytical ability, lack of creativity in synthesizing, or inability to reflect intuitively and evaluate the possible consequences of a given course of action, may limit the individual's performance in an intellectual task, no matter how hard he practises.

However, there are exercises that can develop the general efficiency of the effectors and the receptors. Kim's game has been used for generations to develop attention and observation of detail. Perceptual acuity exercises are often used in industrial training, in the training of quality control inspectors, of fault-finding and such tasks. Perceptual discrimination in a 'noisy environment' was the object of much military training aimed at the recognition of the noises of enemy ships or planes when mixed in with other sounds. Strength, stamina, perseverance, self-assurance can all be developed by appropriate exercises. In all these areas, exercises exist which 'work', in that they develop the individual's capability. But they do not develop each individual's capabilities to the same extent. Individual differences are not eliminated.

One can expect a similar situation in the 'processor' sub-system. Exercises can be devised to develop, up to a point, the analytical, synthetical and evaluative capabilities of an individual. However, individual differences will persist and will result in different levels of skilled intellectual activity.

Summary

We have thus come full circle in this chapter, back to our definitions of knowledge and skill. Knowledge is 'information stored' — it is something an individual possesses. He either has it, or he has not — a go/no-go quality. Individuals differ in the quantity of knowledge that they possess. Skill is the ability to perform. It usually depends on the possession of specific knowledge, but it depends on much more. It depends on the efficiency of functioning of the four essential sub-systems (receptors, effectors, store and processor) and this efficiency depends in part on the practice that these sub-systems receive (the 'exercise' one gives them) and in part on innate individual differences between people. Individuals will always differ in the quality of the results they achieve when they apply knowledge to practical tasks.

Preview   In the chapters that follow, we shall examine the details of instructional design. We shall see that the instructional design process can be developed at several levels of detail, analogous to the levels of analysis we have already encountered. We shall see that at each level of detail, the instructional design decisions become more specific and more based on a full understanding of the difficulties that the learning task presents to the learner. As we proceed, therefore, to greater detail of design, we will require greater precision in our analysis. The ideas presented in this chapter, together with the 'language' of classification used in the schemata of 'knowledge' and 'skill' should act as a system of analysis both more precise and more complete than the majority to be encountered in the existing literature on learning and instruction.

13. The Four Levels of Instructional Design

13.1 The four levels of analysis reviewed

We have now examined four levels of analysis which can be described in summary as follows:

Level 1: Defines the overall instructional objectives for our system, as well as certain other non-instructional actions that should be taken to ensure success in overcoming the initially defined problems.

Level 2: Defines (a) the detailed objectives that have to be achieved in order to enable us to achieve the overall objectives (hence the term 'enabling objectives'), (b) the sequence of interrelationship between these objectives (in terms of prerequisites) and (c) the level of entry (defined by those objectives which will not be taught but which the learner must have mastered before entering the instructional system).

Level 3: Classifies the detailed objectives according to some system or taxonomy of types of learning and assigns specific instructional tactics to each objective or group of similar objectives. Thus typically one might find that the objectives of one lesson were all of the same category or type (say 'verbal information') so one would 'dip into' one's bag of tactics and pull out a bunch labelled 'for teaching verbal information' and use it.

Level 4: Does not take the objective 'as found' from level 2, but (a) analyses it further in order to discover exactly what is entailed in achieving this objective (in terms of basic motions, for physical skills, in terms of basic behaviour patterns or in terms of basic mental operations for other skills and for knowledge) and then (b) matches instructional tactics at this micro level.

We have also seen that it is possible to take certain instructional design decisions at each of these levels, indeed certain global decisions may have to be taken in order to decide whether to proceed with the project at all, and, if so, whether to continue to a more detailed level of analysis by formal means, whether to delegate the further stages to others whom we trust (eg the skilled instructor) or whether to avoid further design entirely by buying in existing instructional systems.

So far, we have only mentioned these various possible outcomes in passing, leaving the details of what instructional design decisions are possible at each level to be treated all together. We shall examine the 'synthesis' aspects of instructional design, therefore, in much the same way as we treated the 'analysis' aspects, by identifying four broad levels of decision making. These four levels are in a sense arbitrary, having been chosen as a convenient way of organizing the content of this book, but they do have some usefulness in guiding the instructional designer, as they correspond more or less to four levels of system with which the instructional designer has to deal.

13.2 The four design levels

These four system levels are as follows (note the similarity to one of the schemes for classifying objectives mentioned in Part 2).

Level 1: The course system (or, in a large course with many main objectives and possible options, the 'course unit or module level' — the term 'unit' is preferred because the term 'module' has many connotations).

Level 2: The 'lesson' level, a lesson being taken more in the sense of the instruction necessary to achieve one objective (or a small number of closely related objectives), rather than its other meaning of a fixed period of time in the timetable.

Level 3: The 'instructional event' level, this term being used in the sense given to it by Gagné of one specific act (among others) that should be made in order to achieve effective learning of a specific objective (a fuller definition is given below).

Level 4: The 'learning step' level, this implying that each 'instructional event' is planned in all its detail.

Thus, at level 1 we will treat the course more or less as a black box, concentrating on the specification of the outputs, inputs and control mechanisms for the course as a whole. At level 2, the course structure will become apparent in terms of the sequence and interrelationship of the lessons that will make up the course and each lesson will be specified in terms of its outputs, inputs and control mechanisms. However the lessons themselves (their internal structure and sequence and the detailed events which will take place during each lesson) will remain to a large extent 'black boxes'. At level 3, the structure of each lesson becomes apparent in its overall detail. We will have a specification of the sequence of instructional events which should take place. But we will not necessarily know exactly *how* each instructional event will take place. For example, the planned event may be 'recall previously learned relevant concepts'; it will be clear to any instructor what these concepts are from the sequence of the objectives in the course (level 2 analysis). However, it is not specified exactly *how* the instructor should get the learners to recall these prerequisite concepts: what questions to use and in what order, whether to do it in group activity or by an individual test, etc. Thus the instructional events are specified in terms of their intended outcome, but the internal structure of each remains in general terms a black box.

Finally, at level 4, the instructional events themselves become 'transparent', allowing us to see exactly how they will take place.

It should be obvious, therefore, that all four levels of design *always take place* whenever any course is given, because the giving of the course implies the executiion or arrangement of certain instructional events in particular ways, and these instructional events were chosen in preference to others by some process of examination of the course-giver's intentions. I specifically avoided the term 'objective' here to avoid the implication that the four levels of design necessarily occur in an objectives-based systematic manner (less still in a systemic manner). All we imply is that a course will not take place unless *somebody* makes certain overall decisions at the *course* level (be they objectives- or content-based), that then *somebody* makes some further decisions at the course-structure, or lessons level (in order to assign teachers and timetable hours if for no other reason), that then *somebody* makes further decisions at the instructional event level (plans a lesson) and that finally somebody actually gives the lesson, carrying out the lesson plan.

The aim of this book is to promote the 'systemic' execution of these four levels of design. This means somewhat more than being merely 'systematic'. By 'systemic' we mean 'applying the systems approach in all its aspects and in particular those aspects to do with creative problem solving'. One can be

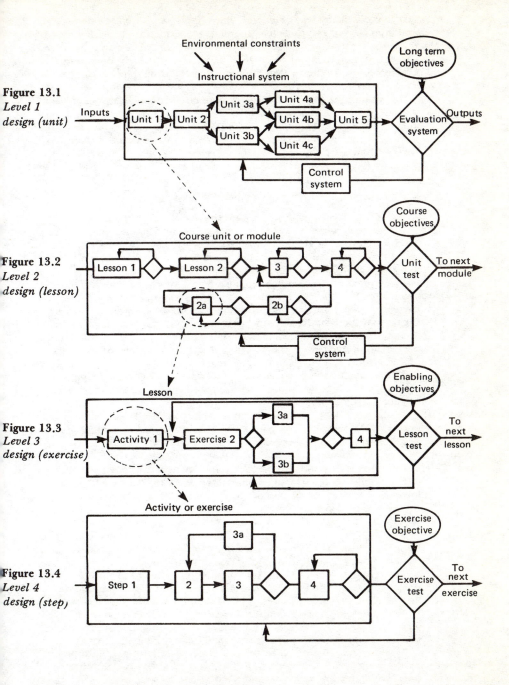

Figure 13.1
Level 1 design (unit)

Figure 13.2
Level 2 design (lesson)

Figure 13.3
Level 3 design (exercise)

Figure 13.4
Level 4 design (step)

Figures 13.1 to 13.4 illustrate the increasingly detailed design decisions that are made as instructional design progresses systematic in many ways, some of which imply the systematic use of a preferred class of solutions (eg programmed instruction, television, etc) with very little regard for the suitability of the solution as compared to other alternatives and with not a vestige of creativity. This raises the question of who the 'somebody' mentioned in the last paragraph should be for each of the four levels of design.

Let us imagine that we form part of an instructional design team trained in the systems approach and that we are following the stages of analysis outlined in earlier chapters. At any one of the four stages we may choose to continue to the next stage ourselves, or to *delegate* the rest of the design process to others. We have four alternatives (four alternative 'exit points' from the design process). Let us examine the implications of each of these four alternatives.

13.3 Alternative 1: exit after level 1 analysis

At the end of level 1 analysis we have the overall course objectives specified. This gives us all we need in order to design the terminal test instruments that will be used to evaluate the course. We may also have an overall idea of the sequence of instruction that should be adopted, if these objectives are related in a close sequential fashion. (Often they are not, as they deal with unrelated tasks that make up a complex job, or discrete topics that only come together much later, if at all.) We also have a pretty good idea of the need for the particular course, in terms of the number of students per annum to cater for, the flow of these students (a constant dribble/one annual intake/several intakes?) and the overall, general level of student that we will receive. Also, we are performing our front-end analyses of alternative causes of the original problem and alternative solutions, in parallel with our job/subject analyses and our target population analyses, so we have by now a good idea to what extent an instructional solution *by itself* is likely to resolve the problem originally diagnosed.

Management information   We have most of the information necessary to specify the outputs and inputs to our course (although the inputs information concerning costs and necessary resources will be tentative, and based more on our previous experience with similar instructional design projects than on a detailed costing of this one). We should also be able to specify how the course will be managed and controlled at the overall administrative level. In short, we have most of the information that the manager of an educational or training institution may need in order to give the 'go ahead' to the project and to assign the necessary resources — human, material and time resources.

Trade-off   This is the first point at which one may be forced to compromise to seek trade-offs between what one would like to do (or feels one ought to do) and what one can in reality do with the resources available.

One may be forced into making some overall strategic decisions, such as deciding that despite the philosophical inclination to 'individualize' the instruction to as great a degree as possible, the available resources will only suffice to develop a very traditional large group instruction system (we often have the painful choice of deciding between our principles as educational technologists and the hard facts of educational/training life).

Delegating the project   One may even be forced to delegate the project at this stage to others. For example, our institution's management sees that as this project does not warrant the detailed systemic treatment necessary for individualization (but there are other projects which do), our time would be spent more usefully working on some other project. But the original project goes on. What can we hand over?

It is obvious that we can hand over a fairly detailed brief of the projected course's outputs, inputs and control mechanisms, but very little detail concerning the internal design of the course. Thus, how well the detailed course design is executed will depend very much on the skills of those who take over. If they are as skilled as ourselves, (trained perhaps in the same systemic approach) then very little has changed apart from the names of the members of the course design team. If, however, they are less skilled, or have a totally different approach, we effectively do not know how well the course will turn out until it is implemented and we have a chance to evaluate the results. However, this does not necessarily mean that the course is going to turn out to be a terrible failure. In any case, the evaluation results can be used, resources permitting, to improve the course by identifying weaknesses and improving those parts of the course that are causing the weaknesses.

Similarity to educational traditions
Notice the similarity here to what has been for centuries the most common approach to course design. Some team of 'experts' by some means (presumably based on an analysis of the needs as they saw them) drew up a course syllabus of topics to be taught and set up an examining system that drew up examinations of this syllabus (in an indirect way transforming the topics into objectives that will be tested). From then on, it was up to the schools. The schools would then either set up a course design team to plan the curriculum or pass the whole problem straight on to the teachers, defining only the hours to be spent on the course, in the form of the school's timetable.

Buying in an existing system
There is one further option at this stage. This is to buy in an existing instructional system that meets the requirements, as defined by the objectives we have already derived. This is not an option to be overlooked, as it is often the most economical solution. One should however be careful to ensure that the system is likely to meet requirements *in practice*, as well as in theory. It is not sufficient to examine the system's objectives and compare them with our own. We must also seek data to show that the objectives are being achieved. Some systems may have evaluation data available, but more often it will be necessary to arrange a trial validation of the system in our own typical 'field conditions' before making a final decision.

13.4 Alternative 2: exit after level 2 analysis

Now let us imagine that we continue on with the project, to complete a level 2 analysis of our problem. We now have all the detailed intermediate objectives specified and sequenced in order of prerequisites. We can divide the objectives into convenient teaching units or lessons. We can devise appropriate exit tests for each of the lessons. We can estimate the time and teaching resources necessary for each group of related lessons and thus 'work back' to obtain a much more realistic estimate of the resources needed for designing and implementing the course. Also we can be much more precise about entry requirements than we could be at level 1, presenting them in the form of an entry test of prerequisite objectives.

Better costing information
As far as the detailed instructional procedures that should be followed, our information is as yet incomplete. However, we have more information than at level 1 to temper our philosophical and theoretical inclinations. We will already be forming some idea of how the course will turn out from the beginning of the design/analysis process, but, whereas at level 1 we had little to go on apart from our global feelings concerning the strategies to adopt, we can now attempt to match these strategies a little more closely to the types of objectives

Differentiated strategy decisions
that we are encountering in different parts of the course. For example, we may, right from the outset, have been inclined to make the course individualized (to continue with the earlier example) but have seen that our resources were not up to this task. Now, by examining the objectives a little more closely at the lesson level, we might see that individualization of certain sections of the course is particularly desirable. This may lead us to what we shall call 'differentiated strategy decisions' in that one is still operating at the level of specifying an overall strategy, but for a certain section of the course. Thus we might decide that certain sections will be taught by teacher-led group instruction activities, others by project work in the workshop or laboratory,

Trade-off

others by self-instructional texts to be studied in the student's spare time, etc.

Once again, we will be forced to compromise and to seek the optimal trade-off between what seems desirable and what is practically feasible in the light of available resources and prevailing constraints. This will lead us to look, even more closely than at level 1, at what is available already on the market, in order to incorporate existing materials whenever they are appropriate and avoid elevating our costs by reinventing the wheel.

Delegating the project

Once again we may have to delegate the project at this stage to others. In this case we will be able to pass on a detailed course plan, in terms of the outputs expected from each group of lessons, the sequence and structure of the course, the control mechanisms that should operate during the course (eg should a mastery learning plan be followed, assuring that each learner achieves each group of objectives before being allowed to proceed, or should a less rigorous developmental or growth plan be followed, allowing learners to achieve according to their abilities and then to recycle to that group of objectives later on if needs be, etc) and some suggestions on the general instructional strategies to be adopted in each lesson or group of lessons. We may also have selected some existing materials that meet the objectives of some of the lessons.

Whoever inherits the project at this stage will need to knit these suggestions and the selected ready made materials into an effective course of lessons.

Similarity to modern curriculum planning

Notice the similarity between this model and the currently popular curriculum planning approach, wherein a special team (that might be composed of the eventual teachers of the course, or else might be a team of experts, eg the Nuffield projects) plan the structure of a proposed course to the level of detailed lesson objectives and suggestions as to how these lessons could be carried out, together with a certain amount of ready made ideas and materials that the teacher may incorporate into his lesson plans, but it still rests with the teacher to prepare his own detailed lesson plans. Note also the disclaimer in most such curriculum projects that what the teacher's guides contain are 'suggestions for the teacher to incorporate into his teaching together with his own ideas', no doubt an attempt to pander to the concept of academic freedom in the classroom so dearly cherished by the teaching profession. Such academic freedom is much less encountered in the industrial training context, where instructors are often expected to follow the manuals prepared for them.

This is not the place to enter a philosophical discussion on the pros and cons of academic freedom in the choice of instructional methods. Suffice it to say that the more progress is made in developing a technology which matches means to ends (and much progress has been made even if there is still far to go), the more suspect becomes the concept of total freedom in selection of means. As an example, if one can show conclusively that a discovery approach is superior for certain types of objectives, whereas an expositive approach is superior for other types, it becomes unrealistic to continue to believe in the overall preference of one or other of these strategies.

It is the appearance of developments of this type which makes a level 3 analysis possible in a systematic way, and thus open the door to a methodology for level 3 instructional design.

13.5 Alternative 3: exit after level 3 analysis

Level 3 analysis attempts to classify the objectives identified at level 2, by use of a taxonomy of types or categories of learning. Each category has associated with it a series of specific tactics which are recommended for effective instruction. Thus the mere act of classifying the objectives and identifying the desirable instructional tactics should enable the instructional designer to plan the detailed steps of each lesson, or the producer of a media presentation to plan the sequence and structure of the intended final product. However, it does not produce the details of the final product. A tactic such as the one suggested for teaching concepts ('define and illustrate by a variety of examples chosen to clearly delineate the boundaries of the concept, then test comprehension with other examples, not used in the presentation') is fairly definite and precise, but it does not actually select the examples for the teacher.

Lesson plans The main products, therefore, at level 3 are detailed lesson plans which specify the instructional events which should take place during the intended lesson, but not necessarily much detail on how the events are to be realized in practice. A teacher would, in practice, wish to enter the classroom with a somewhat clearer idea of what he will do. He will have chosen his examples to illustrate his concept as best he can, in the light of what he knows about the topic and the students he is teaching. He may perform this choosing of examples in a more or less intuitive manner, based on his experience as a teacher, or he may use some more systematic approach — a level 4 analysis.

Who should produce the lesson plans? Opinions differ widely as to who should make the level 3 and 4 decisions. Perhaps the majority opinion in the education sector considers that each individual teacher should be responsible for the planning of his own lessons. If he does not have freedom to choose the course objectives, nor the intermediate objectives, nor the basic structure and media for the course, he should at least be responsible for the detailed planning of the events that he will be called upon to execute. Thus the tendency in education is to teach every teacher the skills of lesson planning and then leave him to apply these skills to the courses he will teach. In the training sector this approach is also very common, but one does also meet the alternative approach in which all training is prepared to the level of detailed lesson plans, which remain only to be executed 'according to plan' by the instructor. This approach is defended sometimes by arguing that instructors in industry are not full-time instructors, nor should they be (as they tend to stagnate and fail to keep up with developments if they stay away from their specialism too long). Thus a course design based on detailed lesson plans will enable such a master performer to communicate his knowledge and skills to others effectively, without his necessarily having to undergo extensive training in the skills of instruction. There are some excellent examples in industrial training of this approach having been successful, but there are also failures. Even in the industrial training context, there have been cases in which the instructors were just not prepared to execute the limited role expected of them in such a system, insisting on greater control over the course design.

The course team approach Thus, on entry into level 3 one should consider carefully the question of who should do the designing. The professional instructional designer is loth to delegate it, as he feels that the majority of teachers and instructors have not been adequately trained to perform the design with the rigour that it requires. The teachers and instructors are loth to simply execute a set of lesson plans prepared by someone else, especially when that someone is not a specialist in their subject or job. One possible compromise is to involve both groups in a course team approach. This has worked well at the school level in various team teaching projects, which have successfully divided the tasks of course design among the team of teachers involved, based on a communally developed plan. At the higher education level the supreme example is the Open University in the UK, which uses the course team approach for virtually all its course design effort.

13.6 Alternative 4: continue through to level 4 analysis

As level 4 analysis goes to a very detailed level, examining all the individual behaviours or mental operations that make up each objective, it is very time-consuming and is normally justified on a formal basis only when the objectives under analysis have proved to be generally difficult to achieve and when there is a reasonably large market for the achievement of the objectives.

Thus, the idea discussed above in reference to level 3 design (that each teacher should do his own) is impossible. Every teacher who is giving a course has to make some form of decision concerning the details of each step in the instructional process. But to make these decisions formally, on the basis of a full behavioural analysis, would take so much time, in relation to the time of instruction involved, as to be totally uneconomical. In reality most teachers make many of these minute decisions on line as the lesson unfolds, in a semi-unconscious manner, somewhat akin to the unconscious decision making that goes on constantly while one is driving a car. One reacts instinctively to situations, steering to left or right, accelerating, slowing down, changing gear and stopping when required. So the skilled teacher reacts to the situations occurring during a lesson with a type of teacher's 'road sense' gained through experience. That human beings can rapidly acquire this type of 'road sense', or 'planning skills' as we shall call them, is very fortunate, or the educational system (as well as the traffic system) would be a much less predictable, and more dangerous, experience for the learner.

Thus, level 4 analysis is reserved for the preparation of materials that many teachers will use to teach many students, or alternatively for the preparation of teacher-less instructional systems such as programmed instruction.

13.7 Defining the terminology

We have already, in various parts of this book, used the terms instructional *method*, *strategy* and *tactic* to describe various aspects of 'what the instructor will do during instruction'. It has not been necessary to discriminate the meanings ascribed to these terms until now, but in the discussion which follows, these terms will be used in definite ways which we define as follows:

Methods   *Instructional methods:* a generic term used to mean 'ways of doing something'. There are some commonly recognized 'methods' of instruction, such as the lecture method, the discussion method, the tutorial method, or the practical demonstration method. However there is no end to the different methods that one might 'invent' given sufficient time and creativity. In designing or selecting a method one makes decisions.

These decisions may be made at various levels of generality. For example, the discovery method is used by some to describe their overall approach to teaching, ie the overall strategy that they apply whenever possible. For others, the same term (eg 'guided discovery' as used by Gagné) has a less global, more specific significance — a method to be applied to teaching certain types of objectives only (more a 'tactic' than a 'strategy').

For this reason it may be a good idea to avoid the use of the term 'method', or rather to supplement it by other more precise terms that indicate the level of generality that is implied. Let us define four levels of method.

1. Strategies   *Instructional strategies* are the general viewpoints and line of action that one adopts in order to choose the instructional methods. Thus a strategy which advocates 'active learner participation in the lesson' will tend to minimize the use of the lecture method, in which the student is relatively passive, and promote the choice of more 'learner active' methods such as group seminars, group project work, individual tutorials or self-instructional packages. A further strategy advocating the preference of individualized instruction to group instruction would tend to support a choice from among the latter two of this set of four methods, as opposed to the first two 'group' methods. Yet another strategy which supports teacher-intensive methods as opposed to methods with little or no teacher contact would tend to favour seminars and tutorials as opposed to projects and packages.

Decisions as to strategies are generally taken quite early on in the instructional design process, typically at level 1, as soon as a decision has been made that there is a need for instruction. It is often possible, however, to delay such decisions until a deeper level of analysis has been completed. The strategy then develops from the more detailed decisions taken at the level of lesson design, rather than being imposed from the start and thus constraining the options at later stages.

In this case, one is more likely to end up with a differentiated, rather than a global, strategy. One will probably have more variety in the methods selected and a better match between methods and objectives. It is exactly this mix of methods, resulting from a differentiated strategy, that is the sign of a good instructional plan.

2. Plans   *Instructional plans* are the specific combinations of methods that one decides to adopt in a given course of instruction. As suggested above, the plan may be simple, involving the use of only one or two methods throughout, or it may be complex, using a great variety of methods and media.

Usually, the plan of the course develops at level 2, once we have a complete definition of the intermediate objectives and the necessary content. Often it is imposed by a global decision, or by practical constraints. For example the Keller Plan has been adopted by some institutions in South America and the USA as the standard plan for all courses (in such a case, the plan is elevated almost to the status of a strategy). The plans of courses given by the Open University, on the other hand, whilst constrained in their variety by restrictions imposed by the overall strategy of 'distance education for adults who work', do nevertheless exhibit some adaptation to the particular content and objectives of the course. Not all courses use TV or radio and not in the same proportions or for the same purposes.

3. Tactics   *Instructional tactics* are the specific ways that one chooses to implement a particular method in a particular case. There is some possible confusion here, if one starts to talk in terms of the 'methods of getting students interested in the topic' without specifying whether one is referring to methods which are particularly good at doing this (eg the project method) or to tactics, which can be used as a part of various methods (eg 'create an impact' with an unusual and perhaps spectacular or amusing demonstration or anecdote). We shall try to be careful not to confuse the issue, by using systematically the term 'method' for a recognized way of going about giving a lesson, and reserve the term 'tactic' for the detailed steps of instruction.

Tactics are decided by means of a level 3 analysis, which matches the detailed objectives to appropriate tactics by means of some type of classification or taxonomy. This matching takes place at a fairly fine level of detail, the resultant prescription, or lesson plan specifying in depth what will occur (or should occur) at each step of the lesson.

In practice, the instructional designer sometimes delegates the specification of tactics to the classroom instructor. Indeed, instructor training tends to concentrate on this tactical level. However, practical experience shows that not all instructors plan their lessons effectively, either because they have not learned to match tactics to objectives, or because they prefer to do this on line, as the lesson goes on. It is true that the good teacher should be prepared to change his tactics if necessary, during a lesson, but it is dangerous practice to have no original lesson plan at all.

4. Exercises   *Instructional exercises* are the actual activities and events that occur when a particular tactic, or a set of tactics that make up a lesson, are put into practice. Thus the tactic suggested for the teaching of concrete concepts (present a sufficient variety of examples and non-examples, then test with different examples and non-examples) will give rise to quite a different exercise for every different concept to be taught. The choice of the examples, their sequencing, how many and so on, are all decisions that are made at the exercise design level. This is level 4 in our system.

Exercises are what the learner gets involved with. He may never be conscious of the strategic, planning and tactical *decisions* that lie behind the actual exercises. But all those prior decisions are made in order to ensure that the learner does actually learn from the exercises. Therefore, the evaluation of the decision making process and its improvement for future applications depends on the measure of success that the learner has with the exercises finally developed. In the end the student is the judge.

It is even more common, in traditional education, for the exercise design level of decision making to be left to the classroom teacher. He most often develops the details of the exercises on line as the lesson progresses. If he is a good teacher and has a clear lesson plan to work from, this method is quite successful. The lesson plan states 'teach the concept of "triangle" by presenting a sufficient number of examples and non-examples, as well as a formal definition, then test with other examples'. The teacher decides on line, by the feedback that he gets from the learners, how many examples are required. He involves all of them in responding. He varies the shape and the size of the triangles. He includes a variety of other shapes that 'almost look like triangles' until he observes that all the learners are classifying the shapes correctly.

However, the efforts of this good teacher, whilst successful, are lost to posterity. There is no record of just how many and which particular examples led to successful learning. There is no way of deciding whether the exercise used was the most efficient: whether for example the choice of other examples might have reduced the quantity of examples needed and, therefore, the learning time.

Systematic exercise design, on the other hand, leaves behind a lot of data, which can be used for improving performance of future teachers of the same material. Obviously, in cases where, generally, the on line approach gives good results, there is no economic justification for a full level 4 analysis and exercise design. There are many cases in general education where this is so. But there are also instances of subjects or of specific topics in subjects that invariably give problems to successive generations of students. Mathematics is an example of a problematical subject area. The concept of 'entropy' is an example of a particularly problematical topic for most science students. In such cases, detailed exercise designs, to be used by all teachers, are a viable and economically justifiable approach.

The other reason for getting involved with exercise design is when the on line approach is impossible, because of, for example, a shortage of teachers or a desire to use them in a different role. Then programmed exercises act as a substitute for the teacher. This is the case in all 'mediated' instruction. But if the medium is to substitute the teacher, it had better substitute the *good* teacher. Thus it is important that the quality of our exercise design is good. Hence the need for a deep and thorough (ie level 4) analysis, followed by the application of appropriate instructional tactics in efficient practical ways.

13.8 Designing the instructional process

At the beginning of this chapter we used the black box concept to visualize the instructional design process at four levels of increasing detail. Let us return to this basic systems diagram (see Figure 13.5) in order to consider the questions that face the instructional designer.

The key questions

At any of the four levels of design, the prior steps of *analysis* have defined:

What should be achieved (the desired outputs, or *objectives*).
With what (the principal inputs — *content, learners, resources*).
In what context (the environmental *climate* and *constraints*).

The main questions the designer must answer are:

When (the *sequence* of events that should occur).
How (the *strategies, methods* and *tactics* that should be used).
Who (the *structure* and *grouping* to be used).
With what (the instruments, or *media* to be used).
How well (the *tests* and *control mechanisms* needed).

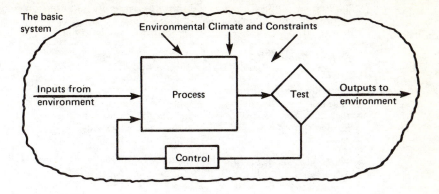

Figure 13.5 *The basic system*

The first four of these questions refer to the 'process' box in the diagram. the last refers to the 'test' and 'control' boxes.

In Chapters 14 to 17 we shall examine the four questions referring to the instructional process — the questions of *sequence, methods, structure and grouping*, and *media*. We shall discuss the 'how well' question in Chapters 18 and 19, although, in practice, it is often a good idea to design the tests and control systems before geting involved in the details of the process.

Interaction between the questions
We shall also see, as we reach a deeper and more detailed level of design, that the more difficult it is to treat these questions separately. Even at level 1 or 2 there are obvious interactions between the choice of methods, groupings and media. Certain overall decisions on structure (say the adoption of a distance education model like the Open University) immediately impose severe restrictions on our choice of instructional methods and limit us to perhaps only three or four possible media. However, it is possible to perform analyses of, say, the costs of alternative media, or their viability in practice, without too much regard to the content they will transmit and the precise instructional methods to be adopted.

When we reach the level of designing individual lessons or exercises, however, the various questions become so interdependent that it is impossible to treat them in isolation.

13.9 Overview of the design process

As an introduction to the chapters which follow, let us summarize, in two diagrams, some of the chief aspects of the instructional design process. Figure 13.6 shows some of the considerations that will be dealt with in depth, relating them to the 'key questions of instructional design' that we have just outlined and to the chief types of information that the instructional designer has already collected, through general study and experience or through specific study and analysis of the problem.

The chart only gives a sample of the chief considerations that will be examined in the coming chapters. We shall examine each of the four key questions in turn, considering first the decisions that can be taken at level 1 concerning the course as a whole, the decisions at level 2 concerning the principal course units and the lessons they will contain. We shall only briefly refer to level 3 and 4 decisions in the next four chapters. These are discussed fully in Volume II, which presents some examples of instructional materials developed through the application of level 4 analysis and design techniques. The chief topics dealt with in the next four chapters are as shown in Figure 13.7.

Information already available	Questions to answer in the design process			
	When (sequence)	How (methods)	Whom (grouping)	With what (media)
Desired outputs (objectives)	Objectives hierarchy	Matching means to ends	Group or individual behaviours	Matching media to objectives
Probable inputs (content and learners and resources)	Flexibility, choice by learners	Matching methods to learners content	Practical limits on group size/ structure	Selecting the channels of communication
Preferred processes (theories and philosophies)	Backward chaining/ forward chaining	Discovery/ exposition	Cooperation/ competition/ individualization	Theories of media selection
Constraints (practical, social or economic	Practical opportunities for practice of skills	Ethical and cultural traditions	Geographical distribution of students	What is economically available

Figure 13.6 *The complexity of the design process*

	Chapter 14	Chapter 15	Chapter 16	Chapter 17
	The question of sequence	The question of methods	The question of grouping	The question of media
Level 1 (the course)	Overall curriculum structure	Overall instructional stratgies	Overall grouping decisions	Overall media options
Level 2 (the unit)	Sequence of units and lessons	Specific plans and methods to be used	Grouping for each lesson	Matching to essential media characteristics

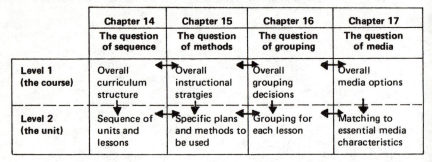

Figure 13.7 *Overview of the design process at the macro level*

14. The Question of Sequence

14.1 Decisions at level 1

We shall first consider the question of sequence as it is one of the first aspects of the instructional design to become defined as the process of analysis progresses.

Overall curriculum structure Already at the stage of level 1 analysis, the main instructional objectives can be seen to have a certain interrelationship to each other. This relationship may be a strict sequential dependence, one objective being impossible to achieve until another has been learned, or it may be a thematic relationship of a looser character (for example, some objectives cohere because they deal with the same general topic).

Thus already at this stage the instructional designer will be able to make certain decisions concerning the overall sequence and structure of the course. His decisions will be influenced by the type of instructional course he is planning (eg is it part of a programme of general education destined to develop certain skills or habits in the students, up to the limit of each student's ability, or is it part of a programme of job-related or professional training, in which each student should achieve mastery of all the key objectives). A further influencing factor will be the general philosophical or theoretical viewpoint held by the instructional designer respecting the nature of the learning and instructional processes (as discussed in Chapter 9).

The linear curriculum An overall curriculum structure may commence to emerge at this stage. Most commonly, a linear curriculum structure is adopted, but we shall see that there are several alternatives. A linear structure is most justified in the case of objectives which are closely related to each other sequentially and which are 'obligatory learning' (as in the case of job-related training). In such a case the final job, or task to be performed after training, is made up of separate sections, each one producing an input to the next. Thus, for example, learning to mark out a workpiece involves various measuring and planning skills, learning to machine the workpiece roughly to size on a lathe involves the mastery of another set of skills, learning to finish the workpiece to a high level of dimensional accuracy and surface finish involves yet other knowledge and skills. Each of these three stages of training of an engineering craftsman may involve several weeks of training.

Yet each may well appear as one overall objective at the stage of level 1 analysis. Nevertheless, because of the difficulties of starting stage 2 without a workpiece already marked out, or of stage 3 without the rough machining having been completed, we are more or less forced to adopt a linear 1-2-3 curriculum sequence for this training. Otherwise we would need instructors or instructor's aides to use their valuable time in manufacturing part-prepared workpieces for the trainees.

However, the linear 'A to Z' approach to curriculum structuring is used more often than is necessary. The type of difficulty just described is not often encountered. In conceptual learning, where the exercises the student performs are more often than not of a 'paper and pencil' variety, it is quite feasible to part-prepare exercises. For example, one may present a written passage to the student in order that he may practice the correct punctuation. It is not necessary that the student himself practises the writing of passages beforehand. This opens the choice of whether one would teach punctuation before or after the rudiments of composition, the rules of sentence construction and so forth. As we shall see later, the answer to such questions is not always a simple one, although there are some rules that one may apply (but these are at the detailed objectives level, requiring therefore a deeper level of initial analysis).

The spiral curriculum   In such a case, the overall structure of the main objectives may already suggest that there is no one answer — that some rules of sentence construction must be taught early while others can wait, and indeed depend on prior teaching of some rules of punctuation. Thus one wishes to treat a topic at a relatively shallow depth, then study another topic and later come back to the original topic. This gives rise to the concept of the *spiral curriculum*.

It is useful, early in the design process, to identify the overall structure that the course will probably take on, as this will influence later analysis and design decisions. In the case of adopting a spiral curriculum model, for example, one will need, at the level 2 of analysis, to examine very closely the interrelationships between the objectives in different topics, in order to ensure that all the detailed objectives of topic A which are prerequisite of the learning of topic B are so sequenced and divided that they are both an acceptable sequence of teaching topic A and at the same time are always being achieved ahead of the related objectives of topic B.

Thus on the first time round the spiral, one learns all of the first topic that will be required as prerequisites of the content planned for the 'first time round' for all the other topics. Similarly the 'first time round' for these other topics must include all the prerequisites for the 'second time round' of the earlier topics in the sequence (see Figure 14.1). This gives an added dimension of difficulty which does not exist in the planning of the sequence of a linear curriculum, as in that case one treats the internal sequences of each topic as more or less independent of other topics once the topics themselves have been sequenced.

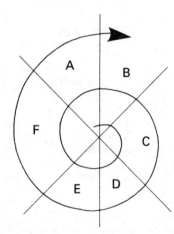

Figure 14.1 *The spiral curriculum: schematic representation of the concept of the spiral curriculum with 6 topics — A to F*

Thus the adoption of a spiral curriculum structure in a course of any size, involving several instructional designers or teachers, requires a higher level of coordination and teamwork in the early stages of design, than in the case of a course made up of separate, unrelated units, or of a sequence of units, each one taught completely before proceeding to the next. Note the similarity here between the spiral curriculum concept and the situation in most schools, where several closely related subjects (say, mathematics, physics, chemistry and statistics) are taught in parallel, by different teachers, over a period which often extends to years. We might conceptualize this as a 'tight spiral' as each subject is taught every week and they are very closely interrelated. We all know the problems of keeping the separate subjects in step. One approach to this problem has been to scrap the divisions, at least as far as the sciences are concerned, and to make one teacher responsible for the teaching of an 'integrated science curriculum' to one particular group of students. This cuts out the need for close cooperation between different teachers, but throws the burden of teaching a wider area of curriculum and of integrating it into a coherent, well-sequenced course on to the teacher involved. The other approach which has been tried is the 'team teaching' method of course planning and execution, in which the teachers of the related subjects work as a team on course design, on the division of teaching tasks and on course evaluation (this provides the framework for the necessary cooperation but often at a cost of much extra teacher time). Yet another approach has been the centralized development of integrated curricula (eg the Nuffield Science Project) in the hope that groups of teachers in a school will adopt it (or adapt it), thus cutting down on the amount of planning time the individual school needs to invest.

Thus we see that decisions regarding the overall curriculum shape taken at level 1 carry with them quite sweeping implications concerning how the rest of the instructional design project will be performed and managed (see Figure 14.2).

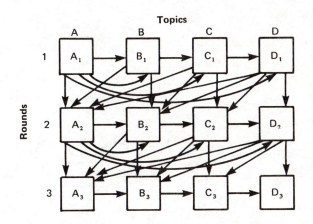

Figure 14.2 *The network of possible prerequisites in a four-topic spiral curriculum during three rounds*

The 'pyramidal' curriculum and the 'core' curriculum

Other curricular 'shapes' one may opt for include the 'pyramidal' structure (Figure 14.3) described in some detail in Chapter 4. This shape intends to communicate that a course has a common base that all students will study and that later they will tend to specialize in one or more specific areas. This shape is not perhaps as useful in conceptualizing a whole curriculum. It communicates rather the type of path that one particular student might follow. When used to conceptualize the various options, one may be led to start talking in terms of 'multi-peaked pyramids', as was the case in the experience quoted in Chapter 4.

Perhaps a more useful way to visualize such a curriculum structure is to use the 'core curriculum' concept — the idea of a curriculum being something like an apple which you can bite at here or there, not necessarily eating all of it, but with a core that must be swallowed whole by everyone (see Figure 14.4).

Figure 14.3 *The pyramidal curriculum*

The design problem raised by the adoption of a pyramidal or common core plus options model for the course is to ensure that the common part of the course is *necessary and sufficient* as a background to the specialist options that will follow.

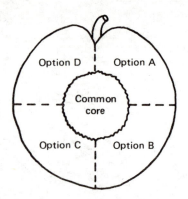

Figure 14.4 *The common core curriculum*

There is a danger of putting in too much common core ('just in case it proves necessary') or too little (because of an insufficiently thorough analysis of the prerequisites). I am reminded of an analysis some years ago of a common core mathematics and statistics course for university graduates who would later specialize in one or other of the social sciences. The course was not fulfilling the need for which it had been designed. Analysis of the content of this course *in the context of the specialisms that were to follow later* showed that the course was extremely strong on techniques but rather weak on concepts. What I mean by this is that the student learned to perform various statistical calculations by a variety of methods and to a high degree of competence (which later he did not do as the college had a sophisticated set of computer programmes to do it for him and he was encouraged in later courses to use the computer as much as possible). However, he did *not* learn to identify the techniques which he *should be applying* to specific types of social science problems. Thus his problem-solving skill in social science was low because although he knew *how* to perform he was not able to perceive *when* the performance was called for.

Thus once again we see that the adoption of a particular overall course structure implies the need for further specific analysis and design actions. In this case the specification of the core should be preceded by a deep (perhaps level 3 or 4) analysis of the specialisms. This is often not the case in practice. As the common core is the simplest (most basic) part of the course and as it is taught first (usually in the 'base' year of the pyramid) it is designed first, more on the basis of intuition concerning the specialisms that are to follow, than on a full specification of the objectives of the specialism (and therefore their prerequisites).

Topic networks and project-centred curricula
One can plump for yet other overall shapes for the course curriculum. Particularly if the level 1 analysis has been performed in the 'inputs to outputs' manner, starting by an analysis of the subject matter into its principle 'teachable topics', there is a tendency at this stage to see shape in the subject itself. This may be linear (as is often the case with strictly sequenced subjects such as mathematics) or spiral (geography is sometimes taught in this way, as each new country or region is introduced one goes once round the spiral of main topics such as climate, products, way of life, geological formations, etc). However an alternative structure is the network of topics (see Figure 14.5).

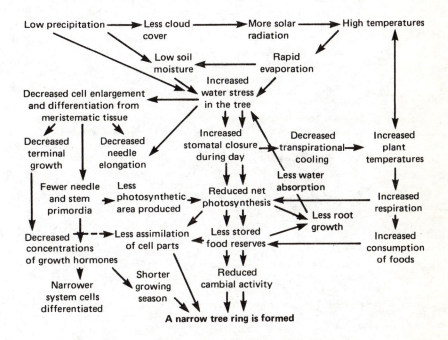

Figure 14.5 *A topic network (from Rowntree 1974)*

This approach is often the basis for a 'project-centred curriculum' approach, in which the students are given the network of topics as an overall map of where they are supposed to get to in a given period of time, but the sequence in which they cover the topics is left to be decided by the students themselves on an individual or small group basis (with help from the teacher). The topics are followed up by mini-research projects, sometimes involving field work in the community, practical experiments, individual study, etc. Such an approach is used, for example, in the Nuffield curriculum for teaching Environmental Studies in the primary school, developed by Colin Kefford and his collaborators (1970). This approach to the shape of the curriculum is based on the identification of a few main themes, such as 'transport', 'food', etc and the development of a network of interrelated topics around each theme. Once the network has been developed, at least provisionally, the instructional designer turns his attention to defining the specific objectives of teaching each of the topics and then to the selection or development of 'resource materials' that will act as the basic information for the research and study projects of which the final course is to be composed.

Inquiry-centred curricula

Another type of curriculum design is often referred to as the 'inquiry-centred curriculum'. The basic idea is that the curriculum should be structured around questions which the student has in his mind. This approach is supported strongly by the philosophical viewpoint which argues that education should answer first and foremost to the needs of the student as he sees them. Without necessarily disagreeing with this viewpoint (expressed, for example, by Postman and Weingarter in *Teaching As A Subversive Activity* 1969) one notes that in practice some students seem to have surprisingly few questions in their mind until their interest and attention are stimulated by some external phenomenon. Thus the teacher planning an inquiry based curriculum cannot simply sit back and hope that inquiries worth following up will necessarily occur. He will need to plan a strategy to promote inquiries of the type that he is competent to answer (and charged with answering by the overall aims of the course he is planning).

Whereas at the early schooling level, almost any inquiry could conceivably be used to lead into a worthwhile learning experience, this is not so as we progress up the educational ladder and enter into more specialist fields. The inquiries have to be channelled in some way.

This does not mean however that the structure and sequence needs to be entirely pre-planned by the teacher. As Mager and McCann (1961) showed, even in quite complex subject areas, such as electronics, it is quite possible, and in many cases even more efficient, to let the student choose the order of learning a subject. Their students tended to choose to start learning from the 'complex' rather than the 'simple' by immediately asking questions about actual pieces of home equipment with which they were familiar (radios and television) and the answers to these questions immediately led to discussion of the main components (valves, amplifiers, transformers, etc). Questions raised about these led in turn to more detailed questions and thus eventually the students were led to ask questions at the 'basic principles' level of electricity flow, electric current, potential difference, electron theory and so forth (usually the starting point of most courses on this subject).

But it is important to note that the students were *led* to ask the more detailed questions by the presentation of earlier situations that would naturally lead to these questions. This implies the careful planning of the instructional sequence (keeping in mind not only the interrelation of the topics and the objectives of the proposed course, but also the ways in which the proposed target population is likely to be interested and stimulated to inquire) the types of inquiries that are likely to occur, and the way in which these can be used by the teacher to lead eventually to the overall mastery of the course objectives. A somewhat special approach to the deeper stages of analysis will be required, paying more than usual attention to the learners, their characteristics and the environment to which they are accustomed.

One can also adopt the inquiry-centred approach without necessarily adopting the totally learner-centred philosophy advocated by the 'progressive movement'.

Deriving a questions-based curriculum systematically

Tom Gilbert, in an article extending his mathetics approach to the information-based part of education (we saw earlier that mathetics *seems* to be best suited to problems stated in performance terms) shows how an inquiry based, integrated, social science curriculum could be systematically derived from the separate subjects that compose the social sciences at school level (Gilbert 1969). As usual, Gilbert starts with his concept of the master performer — what is our model of the type of performance (the imaginary or notional job) that the graduates of our course should be prepared for? We discussed this concept in relation to the teaching of history in Chapter 6 quoting four possible models: 'archivist', 'storyteller', 'maker of history' and 'real-life problem solver'. Gilbert's choice among these four options is for the 'problem solver' model. He then asks what this would involve: what questions should such a problem solver be capable of answering? By listing such questions one can arrive at the final *intellectual behaviour* that the course should promote, or at any rate an operationalized selection from this behaviour. So we use these questions both in the teaching and the subsequent testing of our course (not the same questions on both occasions, of course, but questions of a similar type).

Example 1: A social sciences curriculum (multi-disciplinary) In the case of wishing to design a more complex course, such as an integrated social science course, Gilbert advocates a similar approach. In this case, however, the question answering behaviour is not restricted to explaining how some current event is related to, or could be compared to, some previous event of history, but is extended to answering questions of an inter-disciplinary nature such as 'how could a group of idealistic and religious people, especially opposed to infringements of human rights and liberties, be induced to forsake their own rights and liberties to the extent of subjugating their destiny totally to the whims of a fanatical leader (for example, the mass suicide of the 'disciples' of Jim Jones in Guyana in 1978)? This example is mine. Gilbert quotes the well known 'cargo cult' phenomenon that was observed during the second world war (parachute drops of provisions went astray and were received by groups of natives in the jungle, with the result that the natives stopped hunting, buried their weapons and developed a ritual of praying for the cargo drops). Gilbert's master performer (a hypothetical student of his hypothetical course) should be able to explain such phenomena, or, better still, to predict that they will occur, by the process of identification of certain basic characteristics of the phenomenon (in this case a sociological one), and seeing some types of similarity or analogy with problems he has already met in some other area. In the case of the cargo cult, for example, Gilbert suggests that the student might well draw an analogy from psychology — the random and intermittent reinforcement of no particular behaviour which leads to what Skinner refers to as 'superstitious' behaviour in the learner, be he rat, pigeon or human. So here we have a group of people receiving random reinforcement; the result one can predict is group based superstitious behaviour, which becomes ritual or cult.

It is not much help to the instructional designer to hit upon such a cross-disciplinary question by chance, nor to simply tell him that he should look for similar types of questions. What he needs is a system for generating such questions. For the integrated social sciences curriculum Gilbert suggests that one draws up a matrix of the subjects involved, as shown in Figure 14.6. Using one axis of this matrix as the cause and the other as the effect one first identifies the cells of the matrix that seem likely to include useful questions. For example, taking the subjects geography and sociology one might decide that there are useful questions to ask regarding the way that the geography of a region affects the way that the inhabitants live, and also there are useful questions worth asking regarding the effects of the way people live on the geography of the region. What are these questions? To look for them systematically one subdivides the cells of the matrix into topic headings (say, geological structure, weather, flora and fauna, etc, for the geography cell and life- and work-style, group organization, family structure and customs, etc for the sociology cell).

Thus our large cells now are subdivided into a large number of small cells in which we can register whether the interrelation of various topics is likely to be a source of useful questions. For example the effect of weather on the life-style of the inhabitants is likely to be of major interest, whereas the effect of the

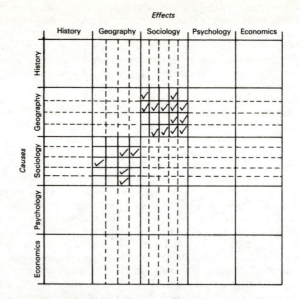

Figure 14.6 *A matrix for the planning of a questions-centred and inter-disciplinary curriculum, based on Gilbert 1969*

In the example only the relationships between geography and sociology are being investigated. Sociology has been subdivided into five topics and geography into four. The names of the topics have been omitted for clarity. Thus in theory there are 20 sub-cells describing the effects of geography on sociology and similarly 20 sub-cells for the effects of sociology on geography. The analyst has identified 12 worthwhile cells in the 'effects of geography on sociology' domain and only five in the 'effects of sociology on geography' domain. He has thus identified 17 types of 'worthwhile questions' to ask. This technique is quite subjective. The matrix merely organizes one's thoughts.

weather on family structure is probably a less fertile cell to explore, and the effect of family structure on the weather is of no interest at all (at any rate not at our present state of scientific knowledge). Thus we cross off the cells of no interest and establish a priority among the others. As often the time available for a course of this nature is defined in advance by certain immutable constraints, the task of the instructional designer (or rather at this stage the curriculum designer) is reduced to identifying the cells of greatest priority that can be investigated in a course of the length proposed. One then starts on the top priority cells and analyses them further, into sub-topics if necessary, or, alternatively, proceeds straight to the generation of questions that exemplify the relationships mapped out on the matrix. As the number of questions grows, one can go back and revise one's judgement on the question of which cells are of top priority. One can also estimate the number of questions that can reasonably be dealt with in one area of the course, without encroaching on the time requirements of other areas.

Finally, as similar types of questions (though different in substance) would be used to test achievement and transfer of the problem-solving skills being taught, one can estimate and generate the total number of questions required as building bricks to construct the course. As this goes on, one is also making notes on the generally applicable principles that one is trying to teach, practice and test by the questions. Thus at the end of the exercise one has generated all the data one needs to structure and sequence a questions-based curriculum which will, throughout the course, be transferring principles first encountered in one area of social studies to other relevant areas.

Example 2: An educational technology introductory course

The author has tested out the transferability of this idea with some success in a project to develop an academic course on educational technology. If the objectives of the course were in real-job terms (ie if the master performer was, for example, an instructional designer) I would have set about the course design in a task-oriented approach, as the main theme of this book indicates. I would have encouraged the learners to apply a systems approach, in all its stages, to a series of problems, using prepared exercises and simulations. However, the master performers were more in the line of 'storytellers' and 'customers', in the sense that they either had later to write essays describing the work of the educational technologist, or they were expected to be more favourably inclined to the use of educational technology (in all its guises) in their educational institutions. Thus a curriculum based on *one key question* (incidentally the title of the course) was envisaged. This question was 'what is educational technology?' The short answer to this is the definition used in Chapter 2: 'the creative application of science to the solution of practical problems in education'. Modifying Gilbert's idea, I drew up the matrix shown overleaf. The cells indicate the relevance of one particular area of science to one particular type of educational problem area. There was already some choice made at this stage (although the matrix shown is only an extract from the original). The stars indicate the cells that were chosen as high-priority ones to investigate, bearing in mind what I had to say and with what the target audience was most likely to be concerned. The next stage of course development followed Gilbert's ideas — dividing the sciences and problem areas more finely and identifying the sub-cells that really mattered. Then some questions (and case studies in my case) for each cell were selected. Finally a reasonable sequence of presentation was established. This sequence could quite easily be amended to act as the basis for a lecture course, or it could be flexible, by presenting the main questions in matrix form to the group and letting them choose the ones that interested them most. Given the preparation that had taken place, I found myself quite equipped to take the questions in any order or combination that the particular group on the particular occasion desired. Figure 14.7 illustrates this process.

Knowledge structures and learning styles

There are many other possible approaches to establishing a flexible sequence. Gordon Pask and his collaborators (Pask and Scott 1972) have been working on the mapping of subject matter in ways similar to those described above, which they term 'knowledge structures', and have discovered that learners can use these structures in order to follow their own most effective learning style, as far as sequence is concerned. Pask has identified two characteristic types of learner that he has named 'holists' and 'serialists' who differ in their approach to study by, in the former case, 'aiming high' and attempting material for which they have not really completed the prerequisite learning steps (only returning to these steps if they fail to grasp the difficult material unaided) and in the latter case following the most logical step-by-step learning path in the indicated sequence (hence serialists).

Curriculum structures based on PERT networks

Others, among them Wyant (1971, 1973) and Vaughan (1972) have developed the use of network diagrams drawn from the Network Analysis or PERT technique of project planning and control, for the mapping of course curricula. The application of this technique to curriculum plans is not a full use of the power of network analysis, which has its uses in the overall planning and implementation of instructional systems. However the use of a network diagram of this type to map a curriculum is an excellent visual guide to the course structure, as it clearly shows all the interrelationships between the topics, both sequential and parallel. Thus the learner may choose to start his study along any one of the several parallel streams (starting incidentally at his present level of competence in that stream). As he comes to a confluence of two streams, he should check back along the other stream (by trying

Applied science/ know-how of	A Content and objectives	B Organization and control	C Teaching methods and media	D Motivation and interest	E Assessment and evaluation
1 Individuals (Psychology) Learning	*	*	*	*	*
2 Groups Learning (Sociology and Psychology)	*	*	*	*	
3 Management Sciences (including Cybernetics)		*			*
4 Mathematics and Computer Science		*	*		*
5 Physical Sciences (including Engineering and Architecture)		*	*		
6 Communication Sciences and Arts			*	*	

Figure 14.7 *A matrix for generating a questions-based curriculum on educational technology (first step)*

appropriate topic tests) to see what he needs to study in that stream before progressing further along the stream of his choice.

14.2 Decisions at level 2

Much of what has been said above concerning techniques of sequencing of course curricula is equally applicable at levels 1 and 2. The grain of detail at which the techniques are applied, will, however, be much finer as we are now working with all the detailed objectives of the course rather than only the key terminal objectives. One is at the level of dividing the objectives into convenient groups to be taught in one lesson and in the sequencing of the lessons. It is much more likely at this level of detail that one will encounter whole groups of objectives and therefore lessons that are very closely linked in a sequential manner. For example, in mathematics, at the topic level of say algebra, geometry, statistics, etc, there is much choice of possible sequences, but within, say, algebra the choice is much more limited, as all the concepts and methods are closely dependent on previous learning. Within a particular technique, such as say 'solving quadratic equations', the interdependence of the learning steps is greater still.

Prerequisite sequence established by the objectives hierarchy

Thus, techniques which help to examine the sequence and dependence of the individual objectives are of particular use now. It is at this level of detail that one might use the hierarchical approach to analysing the main objectives and identifying the intermediate and enabling objectives, as already described in Chapter 10. Once the hierarchy has been constructed, it is an immensely useful tool for deciding sequence, dividing topics into lessons and identifying the prerequisite entry behaviour.

Alternative sequences are still encountered in most analyses. At the level 2 stage of analysis we have little concrete evidence on the best way to organize the instruction of a sequence or group of related objectives. There are however a number of rules of thumb or general-purpose tactics, which are often brought into play.

Examples of such general-purpose tactics are:

1. *From simple to complex*, implying that the simpler to learn subject matter should be taught first, or that new ideas should be introduced by simple examples and applications first.
2. *From known to unknown*, implying that learning should be so planned as always to commence from a concept or procedure that the learner has already mastered and expanding his abilities by carefully building on this base.
3. *From particular to general*, implying that general principles should be introduced by means of examples first.
4. *From concrete to abstract*, overlapping in one sense with the previous rule but also being taken in the sense implied by the viewpoints of Piaget, Bruner and their followers (see Chapter 9), concerning the 'learning cycle' of concrete experiences followed by analysis followed by generalization in abstract terms and then back to more concrete experiences.

In addition there are some general purpose tactics for instruction in practical tasks (the above refer more to intellectual learning). These include:

1. *The progressive parts method* of sequencing the practical exercises for a task made up of a series of sequentially linked stages.
2. *The cumulative parts method* which organizes the sequence and structure of the exercises somewhat differently.
3. *The backward chaining* method, which is the inverse of the cumulative parts method.

Considering a three-stage task, involving steps A, B and C, normally executed in that order, the instructional sequences would be more or less as follows.

Progressive parts: practise A; then B; then A and B; then C; then A, B and C.
Cumulative parts: practise A; then A and B; then A and B and C.
Backward chaining: practise C; then B and C; then A and B and C.

We shall study these sequences in more detail later.

Summary

Major sequence decisions are decided (both at level 1 and at level 2) by the pattern of interrelationships which is discovered between the objectives (or between the topics, if you are still working in terms of subject matter). This pattern usually leaves many options yet open to the instructional designer. To decide between the options the instructional designer uses his judgement and certain pre-formed dispositions to structure the course in a certain way. The differences between the approaches at levels 1 and 2 (apart from the obvious difference in the level of detail at which the decisions are being taken) are that at level 1 the designer is establishing the overall structure and philosophy of the course, and will therefore be strongly influenced by the particular theories of instruction that he happens to agree with, whereas at the more detailed, level 2 of design, he will be bound more by the interrelationship of the detailed objectives, in terms of learning prerequisites, relative difficulty, relative familiarity to the learner, relative ease of explanation and similar factors which affect learning in a general way.

At level 1, decisions on sequence are thus taken in terms largely of *overall strategies*, whereas at level 2 they are taken largely on the basis of *general-purpose methods*.

15. Strategies, Plans and Methods

In Chapter 13, when introducing the four-level model of instructional design, we defined the sense in which we use the terms 'strategies', 'plans', 'tactics' and 'exercises'. This is summarized in Figure 15.1.

	Applying our:	In the light of:	Determines our:
1.	Philosophies and theories of instruction	☐ Final objectives ☐ Target population ☐ Wider system	Instructional *strategies*
2.	Instructional strategies	☐ Detailed objectives ☐ Entry skills ☐ Actual resources and constraints	Instructional *plans* (sets of *methods*, in sequence)
3.	Instructional plans	☐ Content ☐ Enabling objectives ☐ Knowledge and skill taxonomies	Instructional *tactics* (for each step of each lesson)
4.	Instructional tactics	Actual practical experience in applying them to specific learning/teaching problems	Specific instructional *exercises* (in any medium)

Figure 15.1 *Summary of the four-level model of instructional design*

In this chapter we examine some typical strategies, plans and methods, and consider the procedures for deciding which to apply in specific situations. We shall begin at level 1, considering the overall instructional strategies.

15.1 Level 1: overall instructional strategies

Overall instructional strategies are the translation of a philosophical or theoretical position regarding instruction into a statement of the way in which instruction should be carried out in specific types of circumstances. In Chapter 9, we examined current theoretical viewpoints and found that we could identify two more or less opposed positions (concerning the process of learning and instruction).

Reception-learning and discovery learning

Reception learning: the strongest open supporter of this position is Ausubel, but the behaviourist camp also largely favours this position.
Discovery learning: the strongest supporters of this approach are Piaget and Bruner, most of the cognitive school of psychology and the humanists.

Both groups have tended to support their position in preference to the alternative for all, or most, of learning. Hence, they would tend to translate their view into a global strategy of instruction, to be applied whenever possible.
An intermediate position has been adopted by Gagné and writers such as Landa, who argue that for some types of learning situations the reception

learning position (leading to expositive strategies) is more effective and efficient, whilst for other types the discovery learning position (leading to experiential strategies) is better. Such intermediate positions tend to lead to the adoption of differentiated strategies, which often require the need for more information than is available at level 1 before a choice of strategy is made.

The two contrasting strategies are well summarized in a report of the Centre for Social Organization of Schools of John Hopkins University (Stadsklev 1974). This report refers to two processes of learning, which it calls 'information processing' and 'experience processing'; they might also be called, respectively, reception learning and experiential learning.

Reception learning as 'information processing'

Information processing (or reception learning) is the process by which much of school learning takes place. Its main steps are:

1. *Reception* of information, concerning a general principle or rule and using specific examples as illustrations.
2. *Understanding* of the general principle takes place. This can be tested by tests requiring restatement of the principle or giving examples.
3. *Particularizing*, ie being able to infer a particular application from the general principle, tested by explaining how a general principle applies in a particular instance, or what general principle applies to the particular instance.
4. *Acting*, ie moving from the cognitive and symbol processing sphere to the sphere of action. It involves the use of the information received in step 1, applying it to real problems.

Discovery learning as 'experience processing'

Experience processing (or experiential learning) follows almost a reverse sequence:

1. *Acting* in a particular instance. One carries out the action and sees the effects. The effects may act as rewards or punishments (as in operant conditioning) or may simply supply information about a cause-effect relationship that exists.
2. *Understanding* the particular case, so that if the same set of circumstances reappeared, one could anticipate the effects. The person has learned the consequences of the action and thus has learned how to act in order to obtain his goals in this particular case.
3. *Generalizing* from the particular instance to the understanding of the general principle under which the particular instance falls. This may require action over a range of instances before the general principle becomes apparent. Understanding of the general principle does not necessarily imply an ability to express it in a symbolic medium such as writing.
4. *Acting* in a new circumstance, to which the principle applies and anticipating the effects of the action.

The two strategies that spring from these processes of learning would have the following main steps.

A basic expositive strategy

Expositive strategy:
1. Present information. This may be symbolic through explanation, or practical through demonstration.
2. Test for reception, recall and understanding. Repeat or rephrase the message if it proves to be necessary.
3. Present practice opportunities for applying the general principle to a range of examples. Test for correct application. Modify the quantity and difficulty of the examples as necessary, to ensure correct performance.
4. Present opportunities for the application of the newly learned information to real situations and problems.

A basic discovery strategy

Discovery strategy:

1. Present opportunities to act and observe the consequences of one's actions.
2. Test for understanding of the cause-effect relationship. This may be done by questioning or simply by observation of the reactions of the learner. Present further opportunities to act, if this proves necessary.
3. Either by questioning, or by observing further activity, test for the formation of the general principle underlying the cases presented. Present further cases as required until the general principle has been learned.
4. Present opportunities for the application of the newly learned information to real situations and problems.

Variations on the theme

There are, of course, many variations on these two basic strategies. In Chapter 9 we constructed a continuum of discovery/expositive strategies, ranging from totally free discovery to totally controlled expositive rote learning (see Figure 15.2).

Impromptu discovery	Unplanned learning: no instruction was involved directly (eg free use of a library/resource centre)
Free exploratory discovery	Bruner's approach: broad learning goals are fixed; otherwise the learner is free to choose (eg resource-based learning systems)
Guided discovery	Gagné's approach: objectives are fixed; learner is guided as to appropriate methods, conclusion, etc (eg typical Polya methods for problems)
Adaptively programmed discovery	Guidance and feedback correction is given on an individual basis, (eg computer-based learning systems)
Intrinsically programmed discovery	Guidance and feedback according to a pre-planned programme, based on the typical student (eg some programmed instruction materials)
Inductive exposition	Also called 'reflective lecturing': the teacher 'talks through' the discovery process
Deductive exposition	The 'meaningful reception learning' process favoured by Ausubel (mainly lectures)
Drill and practice	Rote reception learning: instruction demonstrates what to do and provides practice. No conceptual understanding is necessarily involved (memorization)

Figure 15.2 *The range of learning strategies*

The discovery-expositive continuum

Related to curriculum structure

The discovery-expositive continuum is perhaps the most important group of strategies as regards the actual process of instruction. Other important strategy decisions concern the overall sequence and structure of the course. We discussed in the last chapter the rationale behind the linear, spiral, pyramidal and inquiry-based curricula. Choosing a particular overall curriculum structure is a strategic decision. Sometimes this decision is influenced by one's knowledge of the subject. For example, the pyramidal and common core curriculum structures are dictated by the structure of the content we wish to teach and the use that the learners will make of it. At other times, however, the sequence strategy is related to one's choice of instructional strategy. For example, the spiral curriculum is particularly well suited to the application of a free exploratory discovery strategy. The matricial inquiry-based curriculum is ideally suited to adaptively programmed discovery. Linear curricula are not so well adapted to discovery strategies, but are ideally suited to expositive strategies.

Other important strategic decisions

We shall meet in the next chapters the decision areas of individual/small group/large group organization of the instructional process and teacher-led/mediated systems of delivery. Once again we shall see that there are interactions between these various decisions on strategy.

Output measures

Other very important strategy decisions refer to the 'test' and 'control' sub-systems. These also interact with the instructional process. As far as output is concerned, the important strategic decision is between norm-referenced and criterion-referenced measures of evaluation. Do we compare students to each other, or to a quantified standard or criterion of terminal performance? Another important strategy decision concerns what we should do if students fail to perform to standard. Do we adopt the mastery

Output control

learning strategy or the individual development strategy of output control? This latter decision is closely bound to one's choice of instructional strategy. For example, the mastery learning strategy is quite incompatible with the principles of Bruner's free exploratory discovery but quite compatible with Gagné's guided discovery strategy. Finally, concerning control of the process,

Input control

an important decision concerns who exerts the control over inputs — teacher, learner, the mediated system or some combination of the three. This decision interacts with media decisions and instructional method decisions.

The undesirability of a global strategy

It is the presence of such interactions between strategy decisions that makes it difficult, indeed undesirable, to adopt one overall strategy from the beginning of the instructional design process. Yet this is often done in practice. Teachers, and indeed writers on instruction, adopt a discovery or an expositive approach to all instructional problems. As we have seen, authors such as Skinner and Ausubel have at least been interpreted as arguing for an expositive, guided approach in all instruction, whereas Piaget and Bruner advocate a free discovery approach across the board.

These interpretations are, however, somewhat erroneous. For example, the operant conditioning procedures of the animal laboratory, developed by Skinner are closer to the discovery than the expositive camp. The animal acts, observes cause-effect relationships, learns to anticipate the consequences of action in specific cases and in some instances (such as learning to find food always under the 'different' container of a set of three or under the 'biggest' of a given set) the animal learns to generalize, forming general concepts or principles of action that it then applies correctly to novel problems of the same type.

The misunderstanding of Skinner

Thus, the expositive strategy used by Skinner in early examples of linear programmed instruction is substantially different from the discovery strategy used in the conditioning laboratory. Early examples of linear programmes created the impression that programmed instruction necessarily applies an expositive strategy. But the above observations should indicate that this is not necessarily so, and, indeed, there are many examples of programmed instruction materials that do follow an experiential learning approach (for example, programmed laboratory exercises or the 'productive thinking programmes' developed by Covington and Crutchfield to teach creative problem-solving).

— of Ausubel

Similarly, Ausubel has been misinterpreted as arguing for reception learning exclusively. In fact, he argues that reception learning works well enough in most cases, but that there is simply not sufficient time for everyone to discover everything he needs to know. Thus reception learning, which is faster, must continue to form the bulk (but not necessarily the whole) of the strategies adopted in practice.

— and of Bruner

One might also interpret Bruner's argument from the standpoint of the 'knowledge explosion'. As there is so much to learn, much learning must occur out of the formal school situation and must indeed go on throughout life (the concept of permanent education popularized by Edgar Faure, 1972). Therefore an important (if not the principal) function of formal education should be to teach people how to learn independently. As we have mentioned earlier, the discovery approach has an advantage in this respect. It engages the learner in exercising his problem-solving and solution-seeking skills, as a by-product of his learning of the actual content presented.

The content as a vehicle for the process

Many proponents of discovery strategies argue that the content of instruction is merely the vehicle for the exercise of cognitive skills. As a *general* rule, this is an overstatement of the case; often the content of instruction is of critical importance, either for immediate vocational reasons, or for long-term reasons of development of specific conceptual schemata which will need to be present for successful future learning. As a *partial* rule, however, the argument is quite correct. Education must develop the learning skills of the learner, and should make specific planned efforts to do so. In developing an instructional system aimed specifically at the development of cognitive skills, one may select content which is particularly suitable as a vehicle for the development of these skills, but which has no special value to the learner as 'knowledge'. We see the need to define our aims clearly.

How to select the best strategy

A course of instruction usually has a variety of aims and objectives. We would, therefore, expect to see both discovery and expositive strategies used. The question is: when is each strategy used?

There are no hard and fast rules but, on the basis of existing research and our conceptual schemata of knowledge and skills, it is possible to establish some guidelines. We shall use the classification schemata developed in Chapter 12, but only to the more general, first level of resolution. Let us first consider the learning of knowledge. This is essentially an information storage task.

15.2 Strategies for the teaching of knowledge

The information to be stored falls into four basic categories: facts, concepts, procedures and principles. Remembering the definitions of these four categories given in Chapter 12, and the use that is made of these types of information in subsequent skilled activity, we can delineate the areas of application for discovery and expositive strategies (see Figure 15.3).

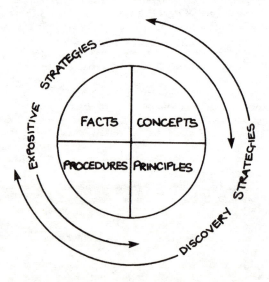

Figure 15.3 *Strategies for teaching knowledge*

The rationale for this division is as follows:

Facts

1. *Facts.* It is possible to discover facts. We discover facts of all sorts every day and this constitutes a large part of the unplanned, incidental learning that goes on throughout life. We need to know a great number of facts in order to survive in life. Others we do not need to know but simply need to know where to look up when required (contrast the need to know the meaning of road signs and the need to look up telephone numbers in a diary).

By definition, facts do not have examples — they exist on their own. Thus the learning of one set of facts does not greatly help the learning of some other set. There is little transfer value, and what there is relates to the development of memorization and recall skills. These are not as highly valued in education today, as they used to be and still are in, for example, the Arab world, where it is still common practice in education to memorize large tracts of the Koran. Much time is spent in such memorization activities, which invariably employ expository strategies. It is difficult to imagine a group of children being asked to 'discover' what the Koran says in its tenth chapter. Would they watch the teachers act out a charade which aims to depict the content of Chapter 10?

An example: language learning

The cultural tradition of memorization prevalent in the Arab world and in other regions, where the word of mouth (rather than the presence of abundant reference books) is the normal way of transmitting information, accounts for the superior capabilities of these nations to master foreign languages, even when the learner is at quite an advanced age. The learning of a new language is principally factual learning, once the learner has previously mastered his own language. Few new concepts are learned, but simply new labels for previously formed concepts (this may not be completely true for very widely different cultures based on quite different concepts, but the exceptions are few). Similarly, the grammar structure is at least in part algorithmic (as Landa showed in the case of a grammar as complex as Russian) and thus also largely factual.

The 'direct' method

One of the most popular methods of language teaching is the 'direct' method, based on the principle of not using the native tongue. Rather, the new vocabulary (factual information) has to be acquired by a process of discovery of the meanings of words, from their context in previously learned word structures or by observing the teacher (or some other visual aid) 'act out' or 'demonstrate' the meaning. There is no doubt that the direct method works and is enjoyable, but it is slow. How far do schoolchildren get in four or five years of studying French at school, compared to the businessman on a short 'crash' language laboratory course. The latter employs the direct method, in conversation practice, for *some* of the time, but it also uses expositive drill-and-practice methods.

There is nothing wrong with the direct method, in moderation. It is indeed a good *simulation* of the process of using the new language (including even the stress situations which occur when one cannot get oneself understood). But it is not the most efficient way of learning the language's factual content. A mixture of methods, both discovery-based and exposition-based should be employed. The use of a dictionary as a regular tool should feature more prominently in language teaching in schools. It is probably the most efficient text book yet invented for the instruction of the *facts* of a language.

Principles

2. *Principles.* Just as facts can be learned through discovery methods, principles can be learned through expositive methods. However, the evidence is overwhelming that principles learned through discovery are remembered more efficiently and applied in transfer of learning situations with more success than when they are learned through reception learning. The price one has to pay for this is an increase in the initial learning time.

Furthermore, the principle learned through a process of discovery is more easily rediscovered if, by chance, it is forgotten through lack of use. Finally, the learning of principles by discovery (which employs the solution of problems as an instructional method) exercises the learner's problem-solving

298   *Macro-design*

skills. In addition to mastering a new 'principle of nature' he is using and developing his 'principles of action' or heuristics. Thus he is likely to become better at the solving of other types of problems related to other sets (schemata) of concepts and principles. For all these reasons it would seem reasonable to use discovery strategies for the teaching of principles whenever this is practically possible and economically justifiable.

The context of job-specific training

In an industrial training context, where speed of learning and instant employability on a defined task are the valued criteria, it is more difficult to justify the extra time involved in discovery learning. The trainee will use what he is learning on a daily, continual basis and so will not have the opportunity to forget. The employer does not wish to encourage transfer capabilities that the specific job does not require, or he runs the risk of losing the employee soon after training. He is not directly concerned with the employee's general education but with his firm's profitability, so is unlikely to be interested in developing the employee's learning skills in a general way.

The context of general education

However, in the general educational context, the vocational training context (for an occupational group or an industry in general) and also where the job is ill-defined and often changing (eg management), the opposite is true. Forgetting is a serious problem, and transfer of learning is an important factor to encourage and the learner's general learning and problem-solving skills should be developed as much as possible.

Procedures

3. *Procedures.* By our definition procedures are algorithmic, composed of associations and discriminations of discrete stimulus situations. As such they are a category of fact systems that answer the question 'how do I do it' in a unique and unambiguous way. It would seem, therefore, that, like facts, procedures should be taught by expositive strategies. This is, in fact, commonly the case. Most industrial procedures are taught through the method of demonstration, followed by imitative practice (unstructured, as in 'sitting next to Nellie', or structured, as in the TWI method). So are most procedures in school subjects (eg long division, or the rules of grammar). One often hears the complaint, however, that children can carry out a long division sum correctly, but they do not 'understand the concept of division'. This is important, as they need to have a working concept of the operation in order to decide, in 'open' problem situations, whether they need to divide or not and what two numbers they need to divide. They also need a working concept in order to visualize the result of a division and thus be able to assess their computed answer as 'reasonable and probably correct', or as 'obviously incorrect'.

Guided discovery

It is possible to teach long division, by a guided discovery approach, in which the teacher asks the learner to deduce the next step, by applying the concepts and principles of number and of the basic operations. Thus, the learner constructs the algorithm for himself, during the learning process. Subsequently, he simply recalls the algorithm 'from store' when required and applies it mechanically. There is no long-term advantage, as far as performance of long division is concerned, so long as the algorithm remains completely remembered. However, if it is seldom used, it may be partly, or completely forgotten with time. As in the case of principles, this is less likely to occur if a process of reflection and construction took place during the initial learning. Also, if forgotten, the conceptual schema used in the original construction may still be 'in store', allowing the learner to reconstruct the forgotten steps. The process of construction during learning strengthens the conceptual schemata and the problem-solving schemata (heuristics) used in the proof of the algorithm. This not only aids in the reconstruction of that particular algorithm, if forgotten, but also in the solution of other future problems (say the construction of the algorithm for calculating the square root of a number).

Exposition

However, not all procedures are based on concepts or principles that are worth building into one's schemata and strengthening. This is the case of many administrative and bureaucratic procedures. It is best not to waste time considering why a given form must be completed in four copies when three of them end up in the same filing cabinet (unless one is studying organization and methods). It is also the case with, for example, the procedures of using tables of logarithms as an aid to calculations. Learning the concept of a logarithm and the principles behind the development and use of a table of logarithms does not greatly assist learning the procedures of use (although an understanding of exponents and powers may help one remember that one adds logarithms in order to multiply numbers).

Furthermore, the time-span between the learner's readiness to learn how to use tables of logarithms as a job aid, and his readiness to understand 'why they work' is a matter of years. Should he be deprived of the use of this job aid until he reaches a level of conceptual development at which he could be expected to learn by discovery? Certainly not!

Thus we see that the decision between the two strategies, in the case of procedures, requires a somewhat deeper analysis of the particular case. If forgetting is likely, if the concepts and principles needed to discover the procedure in a meaningful way are already in store (or there are good reasons for wishing to put them into store), there is a strong case for the use of a discovery strategy. If the likelihood of forgetting is low, or if the concepts etc are not in store (and it is unnecessary or premature to put them there), the case is stronger for an expositive strategy. All this is tempered by the consideration that, in most cases, the expositive strategy will be more economical on time.

Beware of 'pseudo-discovery' methods. I have seen a teacher distribute tables of logarithms to a class and say: 'I'm not going to explain these to you; go away and find out how they are used.' Those who succeed, have usually asked their brother or father to show them. The research project approach adopted by the teacher is really a delegation of the task of exposition.

Few students would discover as complex a procedure as the use of logarithms without the aid of a considerable amount of guidance, even if they are equipped with the requisite conceptual schema. As in the case above, the students had not yet studied logarithms, success by trial and error methods is a very remote possibility. Furthermore, the student who does succeed in 'breaking the code' has done just that: he has broken a code, useful for one purpose only, namely the use of the table. He has invested a lot of time, time which could have been better invested, to make little progress.

4. *Concepts.* These come in two forms: primary, or concrete, concepts, and secondary, or defined, concepts. The situation is slightly different for each type. Concrete concepts can, up to a point, be learned without verbal communication. We saw above that Skinner's animals in the laboratory can learn simple concrete concepts, such as 'red', 'circle', 'biggest', 'different from' and so on. They do not, of course, learn these verbal labels, but they demonstrate that they 'have' the concept by exhibiting correct 'classifying behaviour'. For example the pigeon pecks at a red object but not at other colours (including near-reds such as pink or orange), or it pecks at circular objects, but not at oval objects. The monkey learns to expect food under the biggest container presented, whatever its shape or colour or absolute size, or alternatively, under the container which is a different shape from the rest, irrespective of other properties such as colour or size. The operant conditioning method used in such animal training, whilst based on the principles of reinforcement by food, is nevertheless an example of a discovery learning strategy. Mastery of the concept depends on experiencing sufficient numbers of instances of the concept to enable the learning organism to generalize the classifying principles involved.

Human beings learn primary (concrete) concepts in exactly the same way. We also learn verbal labels as we go along. This helps to define what we are about. When a child is presented with a coloured disc, it helps greatly to establish the context of the exercise by verbal questions such as 'what's the

---

Marginal notes:

Need for deeper analysis

Pseudo-discovery methods

Concepts

Concrete concepts

colour?' or 'what's the shape?' (at an earlier stage of learning when the secondary, defined, concepts of colour and shape have not yet been learned, we would say 'is it red?' or 'is it round?'). However, language only establishes the context. The child needs a range of examples similar to those presented to the pigeon in order to classify red objects with precision and not include the borderline non-examples.

In the case of concrete concepts, therefore, we have no option but to apply discovery learning strategies.

Defined concepts

In the case of defined concepts, however, the case is somewhat different. A defined concept is, in a sense, a rule for the classification of simpler concepts. Let us examine some examples.

Example 1

'Red', 'blue', 'green', 'pink' and 'yellow' are examples of the concept 'colour'. It is impossible to learn this concept without first learning at least some colours and their respective verbal labels. Given that prior learning, it is possible to learn the concept of colour either by expositive means (eg by the presentation of the definition in the first sentence of this paragraph) or by discovery strategies (eg by presenting a large set of concrete examples of objects of a variety of known colours and, instead of associating the specific labels of the colours, associate the generalized label colour every time). The latter procedure will be more time-consuming and more likely to confuse the student. The former is, however, rather abstract, being entirely in the form of language. A compromise is to exhibit examples and say 'this is red —red is a colour', 'this is blue — blue is also a colour' and so on. This approach is expositive.

Example 2

'Colour', 'shape', 'size', 'weight' are examples of the 'properties' of an object. We have now gone one step further up the ladder of abstraction. We now have the problem that almost everything we can describe about an object can be called its property. Where are the non-examples? In the case of 'red' it was easy to locate any number of non-red objects, some of them being near-red. In the case of 'colour' we can point to other properties of the object as non-examples of colour ('round' is not an example of 'colour'). In the case of 'property' we are more hard pressed. 'Nearby' or 'far away' are its position and not its property.

It would seem to me to be the duty of the teacher to identify and present sufficient non-examples to make the concept usable in further work. Can we afford to let the critical non-examples appear with time? Can we afford the time needed for the development of the concept through discovery? Can we justify ignoring the power of language, which, through definitions, is the tool that distinguishes men from animals (at least in the sense of being able to master secondary, abstract concepts)? I think not.

In the case of defined concepts, therefore, the use of clearly worded definitions, and thus of expositive strategies, is indicated.

15.3 Matching instructional strategy to skill category

In separating carefully the two main classes of learning (knowledge and skill), I have separated the two main types of problems which face the instructional designer. These were referred to in Chapter 2 as problems of information deficiency and problems of performance deficiency. In Chapter 6 we considered some cases where a performance deficiency (especially in an organizational context) may be the result of factors other than a lack of knowledge or skill. The organizational structure may make it difficult to perform correctly. The reward or 'consequence' structure may militate against correct performance. We also noted that the performer may be performing unsatisfactorily because he has never learned what is necessary, or because he no longer remembers (because of lack of practice opportunities) or because he has 'drifted' from the correct procedures (through lack of feedback), or for a number of other reasons.

The causes
of learning
difficulties
in skills

We shall now consider a little more closely the causes of poor performance in the case of the *new learner*. His performance deficiency may be the result of a 'knowledge deficiency', a 'skill deficiency' or to a combination of both. All skilled performance involves the execution of a *cycle* of activities which can be summarized as:

1. *Perception* of the relevant stimuli.
2. *Recall* of the relevant *prerequisite* knowledge.
3. *Planning* of the appropriate responses.
4. *Performance* of these responses (followed by *perception* of the results, etc).

Some skills are highly dependent on the *planning* element (strategy skills, planning skills, or preferably *productive* skills), while other similar skills involve very little original planning, requiring simply the recall of a standard procedure (reflexive skills, or *reproductive* skills). Reproductive skills are thus always much the same in their execution. There is little need for further learning of *knowledge* once the basic procedure involved has been learned. These skills improve in time because of improvements in the performer's skills of perception, and of performance (dexterity, speed, precision, etc). Productive skills, on the other hand, involve an element of novel problem-solving in the planning of a response. There is a great deal of variety in the stimuli that present themselves to the performer. Although the basic principles of planning may always be the same, the examples which present themselves are always different. Thus the performer's experience grows with practice, both in terms of *knowledge* (the variety of different problems that can present themselves) and *skill* (in perceiving and interpreting the problem, deciding a course of action and executing it).

The threshold
of mastery for
reproductive
skills

One could argue that there is a 'threshold' for mastery of a reproductive skill, which may be reached by a certain finite amount of practice. This threshold is different for each performer and is determined by characteristics other than the knowledge that he possesses. We may observe this in such skills as typing. A given typist reaches a level of performance after some months of training and on-the-job experience, which he or she never exceeds, even after years of further experience. There have been experiments in 'forcing' the pace of typing skills by the paced presentation of the stimulus material (letters and other symbols), which have demonstrated the existence of such personal thresholds. Forcing the pace above a certain limit leads to an increase in the error rate and eventually to a total breakdown of skilled performance. No amount of practice raises the performance level above this threshold.

The planning
aspect of
productive
skills

For a productive skill, it is doubtful whether such a definite threshold exists. Further practice, provided that it continues to present further variety and does not just repeat previously solved problems, continues to add to the richness of the conceptual schemata associated with the activity. Thus the planning aspect of the skill could continue to improve indefinitely, even when the physiological aspects (perception, dexterity, coordination, etc) have reached their respective thresholds of development.

Given a well-planned training schedule and a good trainer, a sprinter may reach the threshold of his performance in one or two seasons. He may then maintain this level of performance for a few years without much improvement. A long-distance runner, on the other hand, may also reach the peak of physical fitness in one or two seasons of training, but his skill at winning races will continue to improve as long as he continues to study his opponents and their strategies and adapts his own strategies to the new problems that each race poses. His is a planning skill to a much greater degree than the sprinter's.

The productive-reproductive measure is a continuum. Most skills (even the sprinter's) involve a certain amount of planning. The typist may have little need of planning when performing copy typing and the only criteria applied to the finished product are speed and accuracy. The requirement to justify the right-hand margin of the text immediately introduces a certain element of planning into the task. This is fairly easily mastered and may become nearly as automated as plain copy typing. The requirements for aesthetic layout of letters, for symmetrical layout of lists and tables, for the correct usage of conventions in business letters, and so on, all increase the planning elements in the job of the skilled typist. Some of her tasks are routine, reproductive skills. Others are well towards the problem-solving or productive side of the continuum. The composition of a letter from a short note or comment made by the boss, is indeed, quite a creative activity, (usually the domain of a personal secretary rather than a typist and remunerated accordingly).

An approach to the teaching of skills

The approach suggested for matching instructional strategies to skills is based on the aforementioned considerations, and two others:

☐ Skilled activity is useful
☐ Skilled activity is enjoyable once a reasonable standard of performance has been reached.

One should, therefore, attempt to make the learner perform at a reasonable (not necessarily exceptionally high) standard of performance as quickly as possible. In order to achieve this, the procedure outlined below (see Figure 15.4 for a summary) is suggested.

	Reproductive skills	Productive skills
Imparting the knowledge content	Expositive or discovery methods (dependent on the type of knowledge)	Discovery methods (principle learning is always involved)
Imparting the practical application	Expositive methods (demonstration and prompted practice) *Note:* Imparting the knowledge and skills content may be combined	Expositive methods (demonstration and prompted practice)
Developing proficiency	Supervised practice of whole task and/or special exercises Continuing feedback of results	Discovery methods (guided problem-solving) Continuing feedback of results

Figure 15.4 *Instructional strategies for the development of skills*

1. Teach the basic knowledge

1. Teach the knowledge necessary for reasonable performance. In the case of reproductive skills this may well be all the knowledge necessary. In the case of productive skills it will be basic knowledge required to start at a reasonable level of proficiency. The choice of strategy at this stage should be governed by the considerations presented in the previous section on the matching of instructional strategies to knowledge categories.

2. Use an expositive strategy to make initial progress

2. Apply an *expositive* strategy to aid the learner's initial performance of the skill (mainly because it achieves results faster. This strategy would follow a three-stage procedure:

(a) *Demonstrate* the skill that is required, both in its entirety and in its main parts, or key points. (This may on occasions be done concomitantly with the teaching of the essential knowledge — demonstration plus explanation.)

(b) Arrange *simplified or prompted practice* of the skill by the learner. The prompting may be achieved by guidance, by simplifying the task artificially, by dividing the task into stages or parts to be practised one at a time, or by other tactics.

(c) Arrange *supervised free practice* of the complete skilled activity by the learner, supplying *feedback* in the form of knowledge of results, appropriate praise or other reinforcers. The feedback should be in a form capable of interpretation by the learner so that he may correct any errors. It should also demonstrate clearly to the learner both the usefulness and the enjoyment of the skill.

3. Once the learner is performing at a reasonable standard, the strategy will depend on whether the skill is basically reproductive or productive.

3a For reproductive skills: arrange practice exercises

(a) In the case of reproductive skill, no third stage of planned instruction is called for, as far as the knowledge content is concerned. Often, the continuation of step 2c is all that is required for the skill to develop to the required standard. In some cases, when performance depends on exceptional levels of perceptual acuity, dexterity, strength, stamina, patience or persistence, etc, special training exercises, quite apart from the practice of the actual skilled task, may accelerate the process of skill development. We shall examine some such exercises later on.

3b For productive skills: continue by use of a discovery learning strategy

(b) In the case of a productive skill, a *discovery* strategy should be adopted in further instruction. Rather than leave the learner to develop his skill as best he can, the instructional system should:

(i) Arrange as wide a variety of problems as are likely to be encountered in real life, in the shortest possible time, thus concentrating the variety that may, in reality, be met over years into a period of weeks or months. This can be achieved by various techniques of *simulation*. (It may not be necessary to simulate reality, if the requisite variety of real-life experiences can be arranged in a reasonable period.)

(ii) Arrange for the analysis of these situations by the learner, in such a way that he demonstrates the growth of his conceptual schemata to encompass the ever greater variety of problems that he has encountered. He should demonstrate that he is applying the principles that he has learned and, in the light of new experiences, is modifying, complementing, or reorganizing these principles. As we are dealing here with conceptual learning, an element of verbal interaction between teacher and learner is almost inevitable at this stage, even if the skilled task itself does not call for verbal responses. The verbal communication is necessary for the learner to demonstrate to the instructor the processes of analysis (of new situations), of synthesis (of new principles or schemata) and of evaluation (of the new principles in yet further situations). The instructor, by observing the learner's performance on new and ever more difficult problems can assess whether the learner is, or is not, developing his skills satisfactorily. But only through verbal interchange can he hope to get 'inside the mind' of the learner in order to assess why a skill is not developing and what should be done in order to help it to develop.

The importance of verbal analysis and reflection in learning productive skills

Thus, in simulation exercises (when used to develop productive skills), the debriefing or analysis session is of paramount importance. For example, a supervisor knows that he handled a simulated disciplinary problem rather badly. It is important that he analyses why, suggests improvements and tries them out later on, repeating the whole analysis, synthesis and evaluation cycle. Similarly, a young child knows he reacted inappropriately to a simulated race relations problem. Again it is important he should analyse *why*, suggest *how* he should have reacted and *generalize* this new reaction, applying it as a *heuristic* in the future.

Example 1: Car driving skills

The car driver learns initially by basically reception learning methods. The instructor explains the theory and demonstrates the application, simplifying the task by division into sub-tasks such as changing gear, reversing, etc. He guides the learner and supplies constant feedback through comments. Little, if anything, is left to discovery in the early stages. Once a certain level of performance is reached, progress continues by supervised but 'free' practice, with all manner of feedback, until the driving test is taken.

This is usually the end of formal instruction for most drivers, but not so for racing drivers or rally drivers or police drivers. In these cases, the drivers themselves, or their instructors, seek out opportunities to simulate the requisite variety of experience (simulators are used occasionally but skid pans and special test tracks are more common) and arrange thorough briefing and debriefing sessions. In the police driver training at Hendon, the trainee, who is already a competent driver by normal standards, is obliged to drive for many hours in a variety of traffic conditions, talking constantly to his trainer in the passenger seat. He describes the traffic conditions ahead, states his decisions in advance of executing them, justifies them, argues with the trainer over debatable decisions, and so on.

Example 2: Professional football

Footballers use a combination of reproductive (reflexive) skills and productive (strategy) skills. Their regular training is composed of playing the game as a whole, of special perception and dexterity exercises (eg heading and dribbling), of stamina building exercises, and of elaborate verbal simulations of strategies and later detailed debriefing and analysis.

Example 3: Mathematical problem-solving skills

The mathematics teacher, in teaching an algorithmic task, such as long division, may either present the algorithm 'ready made' to the learners (an expositive strategy), or he may get the learners to construct the algorithm from first principles (by a guided discovery strategy). He will then give prompted practice in the use of the procedure until he is satisfied that the learners can tackle long division of the requisite level of difficulty. He then arranges some supervised practice, perhaps in the form of homework which he marks and returns with comments.

In teaching a mathematical problem-solving skill, such as the proof of geometrical theorems, he will explain some basic methods of approach (or heuristics). He will then demonstrate these in action on a few problems. He will arrange prompted practice on similar problems to allow the learners to reach a minimum level of performance. He will then 'open up' the variety of problems presented to the learners and switch to a discovery strategy, asking the learners to tackle the problems (in small groups or individually in front of the whole class). He will require the problem-solvers to explain their approach, justify it, test it out, evaluate its success, rethink their approach and try again if necessary, draw general conclusions applicable to other problems of the class, and revise or augment their schema of problem-solving heuristics.

Example 4: Reactive skills

The principle also applies to attitudes. Reflexive reactions and habits are learned by a process of conditioning or by the imitation of a respected model of the required behaviour. Value systems and life-styles are developed by self-discovery, effected through a process of the analysis of one's reactions, followed by the synthesis and evaluation of new general 'rules of reaction'.

15.4 Level 2: developing a plan

Analysis of the task or topic leads to the development of a hierarchy of intermediate objectives, or a network of sub-topics, which allow quite detailed decisions to be made with respect to the sequence of units and individual lessons in the proposed training system. This sequence may be now

The plan

transformed into a *plan* of the overall structure of the instructional system. This may be a linear, pre-ordained plan which defines the exact sequence of lessons that will be given, or it may be a flexible plan allowing for alternative routes, for student choice of certain objectives, for elective topics complementing a common core, or many other variations. A further aspect of the system that this plan would specify is the method, or combination of methods that will be used to achieve each of the intermediate objectives.

Recording the plan

One will be building up some record of the decisions being made, which may take the form of a list of the objectives, in sequence, and other aspects of the design in columns alongside (see Figure 15.5).

Objective	Test items	Methods	Grouping	Media	Materials and equipment

Figure 15.5 *Suggested notation form for level 2 instructional design*

The exact layout of the list is of no special significance. The column headings may vary (combining, for example, the decisions about instructional methods and about group organization in one heading). These headings correspond to the chapter divisions of this part of the book, and the general sequence of decision making which we recommend.

Note that one can complete a column of test items as soon as one has the objectives defined. This is a good practice to follow, as the development of viable and valid test items, which are really capable of being used during instruction to evaluate whether it is effective, is an excellent test of the validity and clarity of the objectives themselves.

Deciding on the methods   The third column refers to instructional methods, the particular topic of this chapter. Let us consider to what extent we are ready to complete this column. It is probable that even before the analysis of the problem commences in earnest, some views already exist as to the most desirable instructional methods to adopt. These views have to a large extent been formed by tradition, by the educational theories and philosophies espoused and by previous experience of similar problems. At many points in this book, we have already seen the danger of following these preconceived viewpoints too slavishly. We have seen the need for a more detailed analysis of the problem and of the context (the wider system) in which it is embedded. We have seen how front-end analysis may reveal that instruction (or instruction by itself) may not be an effective solution to the problem.

The levels of analysis and design   In Chapters 5 and 10 we saw that progressively deeper analyses may be carried out in order to decide exactly what should be taught and what are the learning difficulties that students encounter. We saw also, however, that the deeper we go in our analysis, the longer, and therefore the more costly, is the instructional design process. We concluded that not all learning problems are of sufficient worth to justify the full treatment and that often we have quite effective means at our disposal to deal with the problem, without the need to descend to level 3 or level 4 analysis. In Chapter 13, therefore, we postulated four levels of instructional design, with the possibility of exiting from the formal design process at any one of these levels.

Level 1 design   Exiting at level 1 in effect leaves almost all the instructional planning (of a detailed nature) to the individual teacher to perform. This is the traditional situation that existed (and still largely exists) when teachers received a syllabus defining the course content in broad terms and some past copies of the final examination which indirectly defined the terminal objectives, the standard expected and the criteria which would be used for final assessment. The rest was left to the individual teacher. Whereas this approach is often defensible on various grounds (eg it utilizes the skills of an existing well-trained body of teachers), it is not usually a satisfactory approach to the type of problem that the professional instructional designer is called in to tackle. The need for more careful, more professional instructional design is recognized exactly because the gross level 1 syllabus design, followed by delegation to the teachers has not worked or is not viable (eg there are no trained teachers).

Level 2 design

Exiting at 'level 2' is the next possibility to consider. This takes the design process one stage further, based on the data collected in a somewhat deeper analysis of the objectives and content of the proposed course of instruction. The result is a curriculum or course plan which may be quite rigid (ie in specifying the sequence and objectives of each lesson and the methods to be used) or quite flexible (ie simply making suggestions to the teacher as to how he could set about teaching in order to achieve the course objectives). Examples of the rigid approach include many of the currently popular modular training systems used in vocational and industrial training. Examples of the more flexible approach include various recent curricular schemes, such as the Nuffield projects.

However, whether they are presented as rigid instructions or as flexible suggestions, the content of the plans refer to the same basic parameters: objectives, content, sequence, methods and activities, media and materials, systems of control and evaluation and (occasionally) lists of recommended existing materials, books, exercises, references, etc.

The column headings in Figure 15.5 are useful as a guide to level 2 design whether one is working in the training or the educational context, with the intention of preparing a rigid, more or less 'autocratic' instructional system, or a flexible, 'democratic' system. We shall assume that the first two columns have been more or less completed and shall consider the third column — instructional methods. We have already considered in some depth the basic instructional strategies that we may be led to consider, partly through our philosophical predispositions, but mainly (we hope) through an objective consideration of the overall objectives and content of the course, the general characteristics of the target population and other important factors that we have identified in our analysis of the wider system.

A procedure for method selection

Armed with the more detailed breakdown of the instructional objectives, a more precise idea of the necessary content and a more thorough analysis of the existing levels of knowledge and skill in the target population, we are in a position to turn our views regarding appropriate strategies, into more detailed suggestions of the methods that should be adopted in order to put these strategies into operation.

Knowledge and/or skill?

The procedure we shall follow is:

1. Determine, from the *objectives*, whether we are dealing with:
   (a) An *information* problem (the need to instil knowledge)
   (b) A *performance* problem (the need to develop skills)
   (c) A combination of information and performance problem.

What basic knowledge or skill categories?

Each objective should be considered in turn.

2. Consider, for each objective the basic category of knowledge or skill that we intend to teach:
   (a) If knowledge, is it factual information, concepts, procedures or principles (or what combination)?
   (b) If skill, is it basically a simple reproductive skill or a more complex productive skill (or a combination of both reproductive and productive skills)?

Exposition or discovery

3. In the light of considerations 1 and 2, decide whether *expositive* or *discovery* methods are more indicated for the objective.

Practical constraints

4. Consider now the practical constraints that have already been identified at level 1 as 'immutable'. These might include such factors as:
   (a) *Resources:* what quality and quantity of teachers, books, audiovisual equipment, etc can we expect?
   (b) *Target population:* what is the geographical distribution of our student population, its level of study skills, social habits, etc?
   (c) *Wider system:* what are the political decisions or social pressures that affect our system's design, etc?

Final selection

Consider what restrictions these constraints impose on your selection of specific instructional methods.

5. Select a method (or several alternative methods) that is (are) both appropriate and viable, in the light of the considerations outlined above. As one is working at the level of overall recommendations, there is no need to describe exactly *how* the method will be put into practice. This is a later stage, that may be delegated to the individual teacher. If it is not to be delegated, it should be done on the basis of a more detailed level 3 analysis of the knowledge and skills content of each objective. We shall come back to this in Volume II.

At level 2 we are simply suggesting the *basic type* of instructional method that should be used for a given objective. What are these basic types? The remainder of this chapter presents, in information maps, a short directory to some basic types of instructional methods.

15.5 A directory of commonly used instructional methods

The pages that follow review, in information mapping format, some of the basic methods that might be indicated at the end of a level 2 analysis. Figure 15.6 presents the methods subdivided into those that are principally expositive and those that are principally discovery. The figure also relates these groups of methods to the basic categories of our knowledge and skills schemata, thus summarizing the recommendations made in this chapter. The maps which follow describe most of these methods and indicate their areas of application.

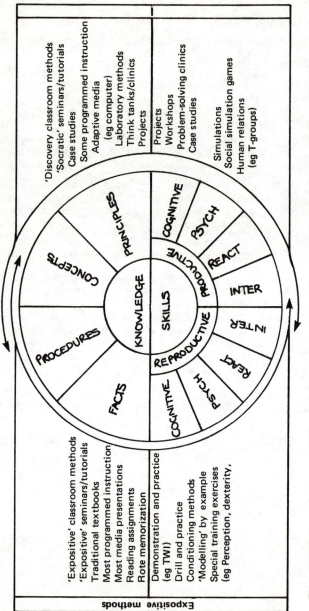

Figure 15.6 *Some basic expositive and discovery methods and their relation to the knowledge/skills schemata*

Map 15.1 *Expositive classroom instruction*

Introduction	Classroom instruction can encompass a great variety of strategies and tactics. The procedures depend very much on the particular instructor involved, on the objectives, on group size and many other factors. We shall review here only two basic methods, which may be considered as two extremes of a continuum.
One-way system (teacher input system) Example: lecturing	The one-way communication characteristic of the typical lecture situation has been termed 'direct teacher input system' by M M Broadwell (1976). As this name implies, all the responsibility for the transfer of information rests with the teacher. The learners have no say in what is communicated, in how it is communicated and in whether it needs to be recommunicated. There is no effective feedback from the learners to the teacher, except perhaps through groans or non-verbal signals of pleasure or displeasure. The presentation is pre-planned, expositive, usually content-oriented rather than objectives-oriented and controlled by a predetermined time limit. Lecturing is the most common, but not the only way of applying this system; it is in operation whenever the teacher uses a pre-recorded TV or radio programme, for example. It is not a bad system in its right place, being effective for most factual information and simple conceptual learning.
Two-way system (teacher modification system)	Broadwell (1976) used the term 'teacher modification' to stress that the above one-way system immediately turns into a two-way system when the teacher asks for feedback that proves correct reception of the message. This feedback modifies the teacher's presentation to ensure that the learners have understood. Also, the learner's responses are modified by the teacher, if they were incorrect. The method is still wholly expositive. Only the teacher inputs information which is new. The learner contributions serve to check reception and interpretation but do not add new content to the lesson. This is more of an 'instructional' technique than a lecture or similar one-way teaching method (which is 'informational').

Map 15.2 *Discovery classroom instruction*

Introduction	The discovery learning strategy is best applied in small group learning (as we shall see in Chapter 16). Nevertheless, it can be applied in the larger group, though generally this does not involve all the learners equally in the process of discovery. However, as a basic presentation technique the discovery approach has much to commend it. Once again, it may be applied in a one-way or two-way communication mode (dependent usually on the group size).
One-way system (reflective lecturing)	This approach is really a hybrid, as it is based on a one-way presentation (exposition) made by the teacher. However, the structure of the teacher's presentation is an attempt to *simulate* the discovery process in front of the class. A problem is posed by the teacher and *he* then proceeds to solve it, but in doing so he acts out the steps of discovering the solution. He does not expound the rules and theories which apply to the solution of the problem, but rather he questions the audience as to what he should do in order to search for the rules. Leaving suitable pauses for reflection, he then answers his own questions. Thus the problem's solution appears, step by step, in the sequence in which it might have been discovered by any one of the learners, if he had worked alone on it. The teacher hopes that the learners, as a whole, succeed in accompanying him through the problem-solving process, answering at a reflective level the questions that he poses. There is no guarantee that all, or indeed any, of the learners will actually experience the discovery process ahead of the teacher's exposition. However that is the idea, and when well done, it does seem to give very good results. In the hands of some skilful university lecturers, it has given results (in large groups) equivalent to those achieved by 'true' discovery learning in much smaller groups. It requires excellent presentation and timing on the part of the teacher, as well as the ability to anticipate the difficulties that individuals in the audience are experiencing.
Two-way system (guided discovery)	Once the audience is involved in responding to the questions posed by the teacher, we have a two-way system of communication, in which the learners make the discoveries and the teacher guides them in the right direction. This is essentially the style of instruction that Gagné called 'guided discovery', though in the classroom-sized group of say 20 to 30 learners, only some of them actually make the discoveries. The others participate vicariously in the discovery process, just as under the reflective lecturing system described above. In smaller groups, the teacher may involve most of the learners in the process. Once again, skill is needed on the part of the teacher to provide the correct amount and type of guidance. He needs to diagnose the learner's difficulties with the problem and supply appropriate hints, but not so strongly as to answer the question for the learner, thus once again turning the method into reflective lecturing.

Map 15.3 *Small group instruction techniques*

Introduction	When group size is reduced to 10 or less participants, it is much easier to maintain effective two-way communication. Many special techniques may be developed for small group learning activities. Here we shall only mention the more common general-purpose techniques for instruction in the medium or small group situation.
Individual tutorial·	The tutorial is often held up as the ideal method of learning: one tutor to one learner. this is an overgeneralization, as many types of objectives require the presence of other learners and of interactions between them. It is in the development of skills and conceptual knowledge that the tutorial method ranks above others. The one-to-one relationship ensures that the tutor can diagnose precisely the difficulties and misconceptions of the learner.

Many tutorials are, in reality, no more than individually adapted expositions. The tutor presents and the learner absorbs. It is no more than the 'teacher modification system' under ideal conditions. It is possible however to adopt a discovery strategy in a tutorial. The 'socratic dialogue' technique is an example. |
Group tutorial	Although traditionally a tutorial was on the basis of a one-to-one relationship, it is now common to refer to 'group tutorials' for five, eight or more students at a time. Somewhere along this line, the tutorial technique becomes indistinguishable from classroom instruction.
Seminar	Seminars are characterized by the previous preparation of a topic by the learners. One (or several) of the group members carry out a study/project/research on a topic given by the teacher and present their findings/viewpoint to the rest of the group. There follows a discussion of the findings, organized by the teacher in order to reach general conclusions. Thus much of the learning and instruction responsibility is delegated to the learners themselves.
Workshop	Workshops generally have a practical applications aspect. The teacher may present information, procedures and principles by any one of many instructional methods. The participants apply this new information to a real task, often of their own choosing, under the teacher's supervision.
Clinic	This is a diagnostic, problem-solving session. It may deal with the problems of individual group members (eg difficulties with other parts of the course), or with problems in the organization or society at large. The clinic method usually deals with real life, ongoing problems. Occasionally, however, simplifed or simulated situations are used (see simulations, case study, role-play).
Open group discussion	Group discussion forms part of all the abovementioned methods, and of many others. In the sense used here, the leader only defines the topic and acts as chairman. Learning occurs only through interchange among members.

Map 15.4 *Student-directed learning systems*
(learner-controlled instruction)

Definition	Student-directed, or learner controlled, instructional systems place the responsibility for the learning with the learner himself. The teacher does not take a directive role in the system, but rather becomes one of the learning resources available to the learner when he so wishes. The teacher would normally offer advice to the learner regarding what and how to study, but the final decision is the learner's. In practice, systems vary in the extent of total student freedom. At one extreme, all decisions are open. At the other, the objectives and the evaluation procedures are fixed, but the student may choose the methods he uses to reach the objectives. In the middle are the 'learning contract' systems, in which student and instructor negotiate and agree on the objectives and time-scale for each course unit on an individual basis. Once agreed, the contract is considered binding, to be renegotiated only in extenuating circumstances.
Justification	Different justifications are given for this approach at different levels in the educational/training system. At the primary levels, this method is justified on the philosophy of individual development (as opposed to mastery of pre-ordained objectives), propounded by the humanists and supported also by Bruner, Piaget and most of the *gestalt* psychologists. The 'open classroom' system makes extensive use of learner-controlled instruction. In adult education, studies of the special needs of the adult learner (andragogy) suggest that adults learn more effectively if they see the practical relevance of what they are learning, have the opportunity to apply what they learn in their particular job/life context and are in control of the learning process (Knowles 1969). The two most widespread areas of current application of learner-controlled instructional systems are in primary education and in management education and development.
Resource-based learning systems	These are generally highly structured systems, with a variety of tested, effective learning materials for each of the objectives that the learner is expected (or may choose) to attain. The resources are indexed in some form of learning map to help the learner to choose among them. Usually the materials will vary in the instructional strategies they adopt and in the media they use for instruction. The learner is expected to work principally within the confines of the pre-planned system of resources.
Project-based learning systems	Project-based systems are more loosely structured. Usually only the objectives are defined and agreed. The means for reaching them may be suggested by the teacher, through advice or by means of reading lists, but it is up to the students to locate and organize the learning resources they will require to use. Project-based systems are a close simulation of the research/development process in real-life industrial or academic institutions. As such they have a dual function — the immediate one concerned with the content of the project and a long-term 'learning to learn' function.

Map 15.5 *Programmed self-instructional methods*

Introduction	Programmed instruction can be taken in either the 'process' sense, as a general process for the design of instructional materials, or in its 'product' sense as a type of instructional system in which the learner studies, usually on his own and at his own pace, in order to achieve precise behavioural objectives, using pre-prepared instructional materials which require no (or very little) support from a live teacher. This latter restricted sense is the one used here.
Programmed texts — linear	Programmed self-instructional systems are most commonly based on the use of programmed texts. The structure of the text may be basically linear. In this case the instructional exercises of which the text is composed follow on in a linear, sequential pattern. All learners follow the same path through the material, though occasionally there may be built-in diagnostic tests that may allow the occasional learner to skip ahead if he can show prior mastery of a topic. Linear texts are generally composed of a series of exercises written in an expositive style. Each exercise presents information and opportunities to practice its use. Each exercise has its built in test item. Mastery is expected of each exercise before proceeding to further exercises.
— branching	It is possible to write linear programmes in a discovery learning style, but this is achieved more easily if 'branches' are used. A branching programme has alternative tracks for the rapid and slow learner, follows up certain errors in detail, can pose a question without effectively demanding one unique correct answer. Whereas the style of the linear programme is closer to expositive classroom instruction, the style of the branching programme is closer to the tutorial.
— mixed styles	The branching and linear techniques may be mixed at will, giving a hybrid style of programme, that uses the most appropriate technique for each exercise. It is possible to mix programmed and unprogrammed sections as well, resulting in part-programmed instruction.
— semi-programmed styles	There are also many styles of text writing that espouse some of the principles of programmed instruction, but do not follow all the rules. Among these there are various forms of active and interactive text, the best known possibly being the information mapping format and the 'structural communication' style of open ended programming.
Programmed media	It is possible to apply the principles of programming to other instructional media. Audiotape has been used widely as a carrier for programmed self-instruction, notably in the Postlethwaite Audio Tutorial System. Videotape is now coming into use supplementing the slide cassette programmes that have been produced over the years.

Map 15.6 *The TWI method (description)*

Origin	TWI (Training Within Industry) was established in the USA during the second World War to promote and develop training for the war effort. It developed a standard approach to job instruction training (JIT) for industry, which has remained a popular basis for the training of not too complex industrial procedures ever since. It is probably the most commonly used approach in both the USA and the UK. The approach was based on the pioneering work of Frederick Taylor in the early 1900s, on 'work measurement' and on later work by Charles Allen, during World War I. Allen's method was based on four stages: show, tell, do, check.
Application	There were several TWI methods, developed for leadership training, safety, methods improvement, etc. The method described here was developed specifically for *job instruction*.
Basis: the job breakdown	The basis of the TWI method is the job breakdown. This is effectively a level 2 job/task analysis, using a two-column form for recording the steps in the task and the key points concerning performance.
Example	

Job breakdown sheet

Job: *Writing a cheque*

Important steps (what to do)	Key points (how to do it)
1. Verify that your balance is OK	It must be greater than the amount you wish to pay
2. Write in the date	This is the date on which the cheque becomes valid
3. Write in the name of the payee	Check if it is a private or a company name
4. Write in the amount in words and figures	Leave no spaces and start well to the left
5. Sign the cheque	The signature must agree with the one at your bank
6. Cross, if necessary	If being sent by post
7. Compute your new balance	
8. Send the cheque	

Map 15.7 *The TWI method (procedure)*

Basis of the procedure	The TWI procedure sets out to orient the instructor: ☐ To prepare himself to instruct ☐ To follow an expanded version of Allen's four steps. These two 'before' and 'during' procedures are summarized on a card, which the instructor carries on his person, as a job aid. The gist of this card is reproduced below.
Procedure	*(a) Before* *(b) During*

<table>
<tr><th>How to prepare instruction</th><th>How to instruct</th></tr>
<tr>
<td>

Have a timetable:
how much skill you expect him to have and how soon

Break down the job:
list the principal steps and pick out the key points

Have everything ready:
the right equipment, materials and supplies

Have the work place
properly arranged:
just as the worker will be expected to keep it

Job training
War Manpower Commission
TWI

KEEP THIS CARD HANDY

</td>
<td>

Step 1: *Prepare the worker*
☐ Put him at ease
☐ Find out what he already knows about the job
☐ Stimulate his interest in learning the job
☐ Place him in the correct position

Step 2: *Present operation*
☐ Tell, show, illustrate, question (carefully)
☐ Stress key points
☐ Instruct clearly and completely, one point at a time

Step 3: *Try out performance*
☐ Test him by having him perform the job
☐ Have him *tell* and *show* you
☐ Have him *explain* key points
☐ Ask questions and correct
☐ Continue until you know that *he* knows

Step 4: *Follow up*
☐ Put him on his own
☐ Designate to whom he goes for help
☐ Check frequently
☐ Encourage questions
☐ Taper off and close the follow up

</td>
</tr>
<tr>
<td></td>
<td>If worker has not learned the instructor has not taught</td>
</tr>
</table>

Comment	As shown by the 'cheque' example the TWI procedure can be adapted to office procedures, simple cognitive skills and so on.

Map 15.8 *Instruction by example: demonstration, illustration and modelling*

Introduction	The power of example is often underrated in education and training. Teachers spend too much time 'telling' and not enough time 'showing'. This is true, in different ways for all the four skills domains.
Cognitive domain	The presentation of examples for analysis is a basic technique useful both for the acquisition of knowledge (especially conceptual knowledge) and for the development of cognitive skills. The discovery technique of teaching concepts is an example. A series of instances of the concept are presented illustrating the concept and all its ramifications. No definition and no explanations are given. The learner has to formulate the definition through analysis of the examples and identification of the common properties. This technique has been called EG-RUL (examples leading to rules), and has been contrasted to the expositive RUL-EG approach (the rule stated and then illustrated by examples).

The discovery technique based on examples provides practice for the analytical, synthetical and evaluative cognitive skills. This is one of the justifications for the case study method, which is, after all, the open ended analysis of examples. |
| Psychomotor domain | Many simple psychomotor skills can be effectively learned simply by observation of a demonstration by a master performer, with little or no need for explanations. The success of the silent single concept loop film in scientific and nursing training illustrates the power of the visual demonstration, which does not always need to be supported by verbal commentaries. Some interesting work using videotape in the training of illiterates to perform industrial and agricultural tasks showed that the soundtrack was seldom necessary and sometimes caused more distraction than instruction. |
| Reactive and interactive domains | These are the domains where example is one of the most powerful and important techniques available. Most attitudes and social habits (and even quite complex interactive skills) are learned through the imitation of one's peers or superiors. The systematic provision of a behavioural model to copy has been termed 'modelling'. It is important to be systematic about modelling and to ensure that the learners accept, respect and therefore choose to identify with the model. Much research has been done on the effects of modelling and on how to set up the right models. The controversy over the effects of television on children revolves around this issue. |

Map 15.9 *Conditioning techniques: classical and operant conditioning*

Classical (or Pavlovian) conditioning — the process	Classical conditioning is the technique described by the Russian psychologist Pavlov (with referencc to his famous dog conditioning experiment). Pavlov's dog learned to salivate (a natural, previously learned, response) when a bell was rung, by the simple juxtaposition in time of the ringing of the bell and the presentation of food. After a few such contiguous presentations of the two stimuli (the dogs salivating at the sight of the food), the dogs would salivate when the bell was rung without the presence of food. The response of salivation was transferred to the new stimulus (bell).
— its applications	Human beings also learn many of their basic attitudes through the classical conditioning process. They already have basic natural responses (reactions) such as pleasure, hate, love, fear, etc. There are also natural stimuli that elicit these reactions — pain, abnormality, etc. With time, other, non-natural stimuli become associated with certain natural ones and thus a new stimulus-response bond is formed. A time of economic difficulty is associated in time with a period of growth in immigration. The association immigrants-economic hardship-hate may become established even through there are no facts to support such a relationship. Equally, the juxtaposition of two stimuli may be used as a technique systematically to form desirable attitudes. The use of popular music as a medium of religious communication has succeeded in changing many peoples' reactions towards religious services and eventually to the religion itself.
Operant (or Skinnerian) conditioning? — the process	The operant conditioning technique, developed in the animal laboratory by Skinner, is based on the principle of reward or reinforcement of a desired response. This technique has already been described elsewhere in this book. The important difference is that (unlike classical conditioning) a specific new response is taught by rewarding the odd occasions when it occurs, almost by accident. By shaping (successively rewarding more complex or precise responses) one can condition quite complicated behaviour patterns (for example, Skinner taught pigeons to play table tennis).
— its applications	This is not exactly the technique used in programmed instruction. However, it is a very powerful technique for the development of habits: hygiene, social manners, habits of speech, habits of dress, etc. As such, it is a technique of great importance in the reactive and interactive domains.

Map 15.10 *Simulation techniques*

Introduction	Simulation techniques are used, in the general sense of the word, in almost any course of instruction. Applying the general principle of instructional design that whatever behaviours are required by the final objectives should be practised during the learning process, then any skills training must be carried out either in the *real life situation* for which the person is being trained (eg on the job) or, failing this, in situations that *simulate the essential characteristics* of the real life situation. In this sense, your early morning physical exercises could be considered a simulation of the real-life exertions you will perform during the day. We shall, however, limit our use of the term to cases in which an attempt has been made closely to simulate, in training, some *specific* situation or task that the learner will later encounter. Simulation techniques are used in all four categories of skill: cognitive, psychomotor, reactive and interactive. They are particularly useful for developing the more complex, productive skills.
Simulation in the cognitive domain	Specific problem-solving, planning and decision making tasks may be simulated, by the presentation of real or invented situations and data to the learners, who adopt the roles of the decision makers or planners. The benefit of simulation is the 'safety' factor in that the learners may make errors of judgement without the dire consequences that these may bring in reality. Many business and management training applications are to be found. A further advantage of a simulation is to 'compress time' so that the results of decisions which normally appear after weeks or months may be examined in the space of a few hours. The presentation of such business simulations may be as simple as a printed case study or as complex as a computer-based data bank.
Simulation in the psychomotor domain	Off-the-job training on simulators is used in all branches of psychomotor skills training. The advantages include compression of experience, elimination of on-job dangers, release of expensive production equipment, and increased training effectiveness. Very complex total system simulators (eg space flight trainers) are well known, though not very common. Simple simulators of hand or machine tools are less spectacular but much more widely used in training.
Simulation in the reactive domain	Simulations of social and other phenomena are used to develop appropriate attitudes and values. Race relations, poor housing or other problems can be enacted, either through case studies, or more commonly through dramatized 'socio-dramas'. The learner has the opportunity to identify with other social classes and to see and feel problems from the viewpoints of other social groups.
Simulation in the interactive domain	Similarly, dramatizations in which the learners take part, or role-play may be used to develop interactive skills for both social and business situations.

Map 15.11 *Case study methods*

Introduction	Case study methods may be considered a form of simulation, aiming to give experience in the sort of decision making that the learner will have to do later. Used principally in business applications, it is possible also to prepare social case studies for the training of social workers or for the affective training members of society in general.
Real cases	Case studies may be written based on real events that have occurred in business or in society. The writing of such cases is relatively easy as one is using existing sources of information. The problem is to decide what to leave out in order to simplify the case study for the learners.
Abbreviated or invented case studies	It is often useful to abbreviate a real case, in order to present the aspect of interest uncluttered by other irrelevant information. If this is not possible, one may invent a simple case in order to illustrate one's point. There are dangers, however, in the oversimplification of a case, which may lead to a loss of realism and through this, to a loss of instructional effectiveness.
Using case study methods 1. Practice the real life behaviours under life-like conditions	As the case study is intended to give simulated practice in the sort of decision making that occurs in real life, it is important to maintain the real-life aspects of the case. For this reason it is dangerous to oversimplify. A simplified case will appear to have a unique 'best' solution when in reality the other related factors complicate the issue, so that there is no 'best' solution but merely positive and negative aspects to any one of several reasonable solutions. If real-life demands the taking of decisions on the basis of incomplete data and in the face of uncertainties, the case study should simulate this incompleteness and uncertainty.
2. Analyse the results and the process used to obtain them	Hence the importance (sometimes overlooked) of the debriefing session which should always close the use of simulation techniques of this nature. This session engages the participants in self-analysis: 'We have considered the case presented to us and come to certain conclusions; now let us consider the case of ourselves. How did we attack the problem? How could we have attacked it? What can we learn of general application concerning our approach to case studies?'
Role of the leader	The instructor, or leader as he is commonly called, has the role of presenting the basic case description and some of the data. He may withhold other data, in certain cases, until the learners discover the need and ask for it. He may prompt or question the approach adopted by the learners, but he should not suggest it nor should he assist in actually solving the case. He is more data bank, referee and critic than instructor. The case study method is 'true' discovery.

Map 15.12 *Role-playing*

Introduction	Role-playing, or socio-drama technique, is a type of simulation technique, most commonly used for social and human relations education. It is related to the case study, but the case involves individual human beings and their behaviour or interaction is dramatized. The learners may participate as role-players or as observers, depending on the objectives of the particular application.
Objectives of role-playing	According to Shaw (1967), role-playing may be employed to promote four types of learning: 1. Learning by doing: the learners act out roles that they will have to take in reality later on. This may be aimed at the development of interactive skills (eg supervision or interviewing), or reactive skills (learning what it 'feels' like to wield power or responsibility or to be snubbed or slighted). 2. Learning through imitation: the observers of the drama identify with the actors and their behaviours. 3. Learning through feedback: the observers comment on the performance of the role-players, during the debriefing session. This may promote the learning of the cognitive procedures and principles which underlie the performance of the skill. 4. Learning through analysis, evaluation and repetition. The participants may perfect their skills by repeating the role-play and debriefing cycle.
Organization of role-playing	In order to get the best out of the role-play exercise, it is necessary to adapt the organization pattern to the objectives, in particular to whether the objectives require participation as players, or just observation and analysis of the play. Three common patterns are used: 1. Single role-play. The majority of the learners observe whilst the play is enacted. This is characteristic of socio-drama, aimed at forming attitudes and values. 2. Multiple role-play. The learners are divided into groups of a number equal to the number of roles. Each group enacts the play so that all learners are participants in one role or another. Also used for attitudes. 3. Role repetition. The key role (say of the interviewer in an interviewing skill exercise) is taken by all the learners in turn. The interviewee may even by a professional actor. Learning occurs through performing, observing and comparing performances. This approach is good for interactive skills.
Role of the leader	The instructor, or leader, has an important function to play at the beginning of the exercise, explaining the roles and the precise objectives of the exercise. He should also attempt to dispel nervousness and create the right climate for playing without embarrassment. At the end, the leader may supply feedback of a constructive nature and lead the debriefing towards useful generalized conclusions. He also acts as referee, attempting to avoid the destructive criticism that participants sometimes level at each other.

Map 15.13 *Instructional games and simulation games*

Introduction	Games have been used for educational purposes since time immemorial. Recently there has been an unprecedented growth in the design of games specifically for instructional purposes. An essential element in games is the competition factor. This may be competition between participants, against a standard, or simply against the forces of chance.
Educational game	Any game from which the participants can learn something of more general value. 'Snakes and ladders' is hardly educational, but one could argue that 'Monopoly' is educational as it is based on the application of certain general business principles and optimization strategies that the players may find useful in other ways.
Instructional game	A game which sets out specifically to teach something of general use. Usually there is an element of repetition (drill) involved, aimed at developing certain skills. The game of 'snap' is hardly instructional, but the substitution of the normal pack by a pack marked with English and French verbs transforms the game into an instructional exercise in learning a new vocabulary.
Simulation game	A simulation exercise that is also a game. The competition factor is present and so is the representation in simplified form of a real-life situation of importance to the learners. 'Monopoly' could be considered a form of simulation game, in that it represents the wheeling and dealing of the property business. However, it has no very precise instructional objectives, and is not therefore the kind of simulation game that interests us here — an *instructional* simulation game. Applications include *business games* that simulate accurately the real life factors that influence the course of business decision making and *social simulations* which use the competitive element of the game to stimulate interest and motivation of the learners.
Diagram of the simulation and gaming spectrum	The following diagram illustrates the relationships between the various types of games and simulations used in education (for the development of reactive and interactive skills). 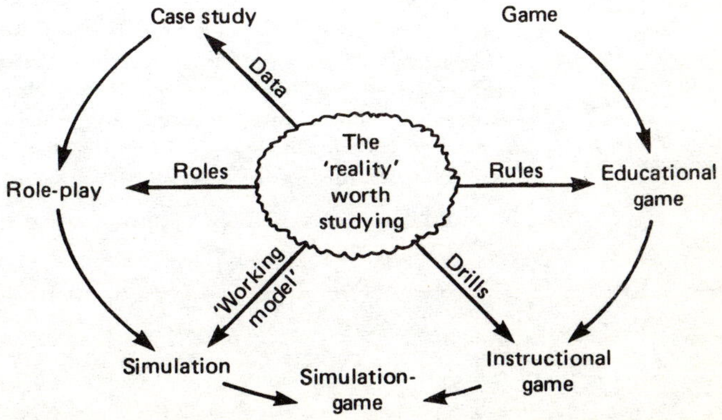

Map 15.14 *Group dynamics methods for creativity*
(brainstorming and DACUM, instructional think tanks)

Brainstorming and think tanks — purpose	The brainstorming technique was developed specifically to promote creative problem-solving in groups. The advantage of working in groups is that the thoughts of one individual may stimulate new directions of thought in another. Thus the communal effort is likely to be more productive than the efforts of the individual members separately. Various ways have been evolved for the running of brainstorming sessions, or think tanks as they are sometimes called (the term sometimes reserved for a group who meet regularly for creative problem-solving sessions).
— procedure	In order to get the best out of a session, it is necessary to have certain rules designed to focus effort on creation of new ideas rather than on the analysis or criticism of the ideas of others. A typical routine is as follows: 1. Define the problem or objective of the session. 2. Set a time-limit (say half an hour) during which members may contribute ideas for the solution of the problem/attainment of the objective. All manner of contributions are welcome and all are noted down. Criticism or objection to contributions is forbidden during this period. 3. Once the time is up (or if ideas dry up earlier) the second stage, which involves analysis, criticism, evaluation and organization of the contributions begins. 4. Depending on the success of this round, the group may decide to repeat the cycle.
DACUM process	Originally, the DACUM technique was developed as a tool for curriculum design (hence the name: *Design A CUrriculuM*). It is a form of brainstorming, with the added refinement that all the contributions are written on separate cards and are organized as a wall display. This helps to illustrate the *structure* of any complex problem. Thus, the DACUM idea is now used widely for the conduct of any problem-solving or system design group session. The cards can be moved about to experiment with different structures, to reveal missing items of information, etc. One important rule is to keep the items on the cards in any one structure of the 'same order of magnitude' (for example, in analysing a job, not to mix cards describing tasks with cards describing sub-tasks or operations). However, it is possible to build up structures at different levels of detail, alongside each other, giving further opportunities for insights and creative solutions. The card displays may later be photographed or otherwise copied to maintain records.

Map 15.15 *Group dynamics methods (laboratory training)*

Introduction	There are several varieties of 'human relations laboratory training' techniques in use today. They include various self-analysis techniques, inhibition reducing techniques (eg touching), transactional analysis techniques, 'instrumented laboratory training' and so on. However, the oldest and best known technique is the T-group (ie training group). It is not clear whether these techniques should be listed as 'instructional' methods because, although there are clearly laid out procedures for conducting the training, there are no precisely stated objectives. Rather the purposes are to develop a broad band of self-awareness. However, we include the following description for the sake of completeness.
Purposes of laboratory training	The chief purposes of laboratory training are to learn: ☐ How individuals behave, in particular to learn about one's own behaviour. The aims are to develop self-analysis, openness, awareness of feelings, flexibility, etc ☐ How groups behave ☐ How organizations behave.
Methods of laboratory training	Most laboratory training methods take the form of a one or more week, residential course, away from the person's normal working or social environment. In this new context, various tasks are set and various ways of organizing the learners to perform the tasks are experimented. The tasks are not necessarily in any way directly related to the types of job performed by the participants, but they do demand that they work together in groups and organize the work of the groups effectively and efficiently. In so doing they experience the sorts of organizational and personal problems that occur in any working group. The approach used in the T-group, developed by Lewin (1951) is termed the 'unfreezing-changing-refreezing' cycle. Initially the participants are presented with a novel, poorly defined and ambiguous problem to solve. No rules are given as to method, roles, leadership, etc. The group members have to 'unfreeze' from their habitual roles and adapt to the novel situation. As work progresses on the problem, they develop new and often unexpected roles. These behaviour changes are then subjected to study by the group members. Further tasks are set and further changes in group and individual behaviour induced, followed by further analysis.
Role of the leader	The skill and experience of the leader, or trainer, is critical, especially in the early stages of the process, when he has to strive to 'unfreeze' the participants for the first time. Later, the participants often take over much of the trainer's role. He is thus principally a catalyst or animator who starts the participants on the task.

16. Grouping

16.1 Decisions at level 1: the data we have so far

The data that we have available after a level 1 analysis may help us to make some overall strategic decisions regarding the group structure of the instructional system that we plan to design. It may even force us to adopt certain overall grouping decisions, because of the existence of immutable constraints imposed by the wider system in which our problem is embedded. Some of the information we now have would concern the following.

Relation of objectives and learning group structure

1. *The tasks or topics to be learned.* Job analysis (or subject analysis) together with a gross analysis of the target population, its needs and present level of preparation, lead us to defining the tasks (or topics) that are 'worth teaching'. The nature of these tasks and topics may suggest that certain methods of instruction and certain forms of *learning group structure* should predominate in the final instructional system. One may see the need for individual self-instruction, or for 'group dynamics' learning methods, or for a mixture of approaches to cater for different types of learning. Much basic learning of facts and concepts can be achieved in the individual self-instructional situation (indeed, in part at least, *must* be achieved by the individual on his own). However, the application of that knowledge to the development of skilled activity often benefits from the group learning situation (indeed some skills can only be learned under group learning conditions). Thus, the nature of the *final objectives may indicate the types of learning structures* that should, in general, be employed.

Relation of the target population to the choice of learning group

2. *The analysis of needs* (that is the quantitative aspect of the gross target population analysis) also provides much information regarding the geographical location of the target population (concentrated or scattered), distribution according to needs (large groups at a given time of year or a constant dribble of trainees) and the life-style and preferred (customary) study styles of the potential students.

This information will possibly impose some constraints on the type of grouping that is economically or practically feasible. The seasonal output of the traditional school system forces the designer of an industrial training system (for craft apprentices) to think in terms of groups, whereas the content of training (learning to operate a series of specialist machines of which the company has one of each type for training purposes) would rather suggest an individualized approach, with intake spread out during the year. The constant turnover at unpredictable moments of the sales staff of a chain of department stores suggests the adoption of an individualized self-instructional system, which is in opposition to an extent to the needs for group learning activities in order to master the interpersonal skills of salesmanship. Groups of learners brought up in verbally delivered group learning may not be well-suited to a print based self-instructional system.

Practical and economic constraints

3. *The analysis of the wider system* should have given a clear picture of the scale of resources that are available for the design and implementation of the system with which we are concerned. This may impose obvious constraints on the approaches that we may economically adopt. Large scale use of

pre-prepared materials may be out of the question, because of cost limitations or insufficient time for development. There may be limits imposed on the minimum staff/student ratio to be employed in our system, imposed either by economic or by legal factors. A combination of such factors may limit severely the use that our system can make of individualized or of small group working methods, despite the possible desirability of the use of such techniques being suggested by the objectives and content of the proposed instruction.

Traditions and philosophy of the wider system

4. *The philosophical viewpoints* (and traditions) of the wider system may create obstacles to the adoption of certain course structures. For example, the limits of the staff/student ratio could be ameliorated by the use of other, non-traditional human resources in our system (eg the parents, teacher's aids, the students themselves through a monitorial system, etc), but cultural, legal or trade union objections render these options difficult or impossible to implement.

We should consider here the influence of the philosophical viewpoints of the instructional designers themselves, who may (perhaps subconsciously) refuse to consider certain possible alternative solutions. The disciple of group dynamics may force the use of small group techniques for objectives that do not need them, or the supporter of individualization may confuse this concept with 'individual study' and may neglect to use group methods when the nature of the objectives demands them. We shall see, in later chapters, that individualization as a philosophy of instructional design does not necessarily imply self-instruction nor a one-to-one teacher/learner relationship.

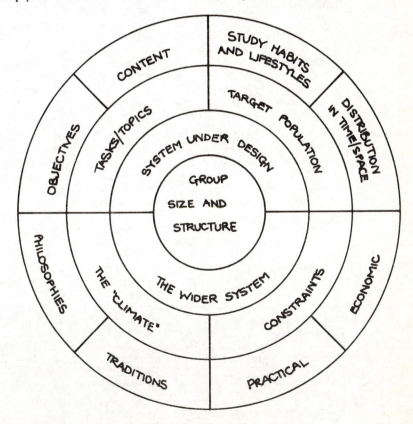

Figure 16.1 *Factors influencing decisions concerning group size and structure*

Individualization may be achieved equally in certain groups and, indeed, group dynamics techniques are one way of ensuring some individually adapted learning in the group situation.

Let us now consider how the four factors mentioned above influence decisions concerning group structure.

16.2 Group or individual learning?

Reasons for the debate

There has been a tendency in recent years for instructors to favour either group or individual learning methods as an overall instructional philosophy. There are several reasons for this trend:

1. Philosophically opposed positions

1. A basic philosophic position concerning the nature of learning. 'The learner alone must do the learning – nobody can do it for him' is an often quoted phrase. This is then extrapolated to imply (which it does not) that the learner should *be* alone when he is learning. 'Man is a social animal, who lives, works and learns in groups' is another shibboleth, extrapolated to imply that *all* organized learning should therefore be in groups. 'There is no substitute for the human teacher' is a position which, apart from being dubious (if it is taken to mean that no part of the teacher's functions can be substituted) is often extrapolated to imply that large group instruction must be used in the absence of economic conditions which would enable small group or individual tutorial methods to be adopted.

2. A tendency to over-generalize

2. A tendency to apply in the wider context the practical experience gained in a specific area of instruction. The experience with self-instruction, first applied to the teaching of basic reading, writing and arithmetical skills, was extrapolated to the development of self-instructional programmes for all categories of skills and knowledge. The emphasis on social education in the lower school has led to the development of simulation and game techniques involving group participation. The gaming 'fever' then leads to the development of group participative learning for the whole curriculum, including basic skills such as arithmetic.

A mix of group and individual learning is best

There are appropriate learning applications for both group and individual study techniques. Indeed, any instructional system will almost invariably use both strategies, though in varying proportions. There are extreme cases, such as certain distance education systems, in which all learning (planned learning that is) takes place through individual study. However, research has shown that even a small amount of group learning activities greatly enhances the effectiveness of such a system.

There are systems in which all the planned instruction takes place in groups and yet most of the actual learning takes place through direct teacher/learner contact, as if the other learners were not there at all. This is the case in most lectures, for example. What is the difference between an Open University student watching a televised lesson in the privacy of his home and (as is now quite common) a student in any other (closed?) university watching a videotape of the same lesson together with a group of his colleagues? During the actual television presentation, there is no difference. What learning takes place is an individual, unique experience for each viewer. However, in the latter case, there are opportunities for further learning activities, which may be initiated by the teacher or by the learners themselves as a group. A number of other learning resources come into play: the teacher and his experience, relevant experiences of the learners, the difficulties expressed by individual learners that make the others recall, restate and reorganize what they learned during the programme.

When to use which?

The question, therefore, is not whether to use group or individual study methods, but *when* to use *which*. We are, as instructional designers, concerned with the specification of an effective mix of group structures, taking into account both educational and practical considerations. Let us first consider the educational considerations.

In Chapter 12, we developed classification schemata for the categories of knowledge and skill with which we are normally concerned in instructional design. We shall now consider the grouping question in relation to these categories, but for the time being only to the first level of resolution. At level 1 of analysis we as yet have only a very general idea of the principal categories of knowledge and skill that will need to be taught. In reality, only the terminal objectives have been defined. However, this is generally sufficient to see whether the instructional content is primarily knowledge or skill and to identify the main knowledge and skill categories.

16.3 Grouping decisions for knowledge content

There are four main categories of knowledge in our classification schema — facts, concepts, procedures and principles. The areas for which individual and group learning are favoured can be indicated on our schema as shown in the diagram below.

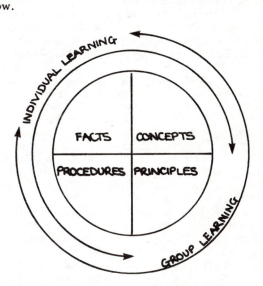

Figure 16.2 *Suggested areas for the use of group and individual learning methods*

The arrows in this diagram should be read as suggestions, not as immutable rules. After all, any item of knowledge may be learned either by individual or group learning methods. The critical factor is not so much the group structure as the form in which the information reaches the learner. Is it clear? Can he perceive it? Can he interpret it sufficiently to store it in a sensible way, related meaningfully to other information already in store?

In some situations, however, the presence of a group of learners may help the individual to perceive what is important, to interpret and store it and to reorganize the schemata already in store in order to accommodate the new information more comfortably (the processes of assimilation and of accommodation, described by Piaget, Bruner, Skemp and others).

Facts In the learning of discrete *facts*, or of simple factual information, there is comparatively little to be gained from group learning, as opposed to self-instruction. The learning of facts is very much drill and practice. Different learners require different amounts of practice. The more concentrated and personal this practice, the quicker will be the learning. Contrast the learning of a list of 10 new French words (a) on your own, and (b) through discussion methods in class. What do the discussions contribute? One is not challenging the meanings of the words. One, presumably, already knows the equivalent English words and the concepts associated with them, so one is not trying to clarify the meaning of the words. Organized drill and practice in the classroom (for example, reciting the meanings of the words spoken by the teacher) is no more than a group form of *individual learning*. The only exchanges are between teacher and learner. The presence of the other learners does not contribute any extra factor to the learning situation. So you might as well do the learning on your own, in your own time, at your own pace.

Principles

The learning of *principles*, on the other hand, has much to gain from well-organized *group learning*. In order to learn a principle and be able to apply it effectively in the future, in a variety of situations, the learner must experience as wide a variety of situations as is possible during the actual learning. He must also reflect on the relations that exist between the new principle and previously learned principles and concepts, in order to forge meaningful links and store the newly learned principle as part of a wider schema of conceptual knowledge.

In order to encourage this process of reflection, recall and restructuring the instructional system should provide the maximum opportunity for analytical conversations. The lone student must have these conversations with himself, reflecting internally on the relationships between what he has learned before and what he is learning now. He is stimulated to do this only by his own curiosity as a learner and by the structure of the learning materials which he is using. Some learning materials can indeed be quite effective in stimulating the appropriate form of reflective activity (eg the 'structural communication' technique that we shall discuss later). However, the mutual sharing of insights between a group of learners and the mutual overcoming of misconceptions can enhance the richness of the reflective processes and hence improve the quality of the conceptual learning taking place. A learning group, through discussion, ensures that the individual learners *cooperate*, helping each other to form and reform their conceptual schemata in order better to accommodate the new principles being learned.

Concepts

Much of what has been said concerning the learning of principles also applies to the learning of *concepts*. However, a fair proportion of concept learning is at a lower level of difficulty than the learning of principles. In the case of primary (concrete) concepts, learning depends on the exposure to a sufficient quantity and range of concrete examples of the concept. There is little to discuss in this case. Each learner has to observe and classify the examples. It matters little if he does this on his own or in a group. Group methods may be more fun, but there is no reason for them to be more efficient than individual methods. There is not that much difficulty with simple defined concepts either. A defined concept that is only one step removed from the concrete (eg the concept of colour which is a classification of concrete concepts — red, blue, green, etc), is easy to define clearly and leaves little room for fruitful discussion of its meaning. As we climb up the ladder of abstraction however (eg from 'red' to 'colour' to 'property' to 'physical property' and 'chemical property', etc), the room for misunderstanding increases, as does the web of interrelationships between the concept being learned and other previously learned concepts. The need for analytic reflection grows and so, therefore, does the need for learning that stimulates and encourages such reflection. Hence, as the degree of abstraction of conceptual learning increases, so does the need for group learning techniques that capitalize on the communal store of insights and experiences, and share them in cooperative group discussions and activities.

Procedures

The case of *procedures* is governed by a somewhat different consideration. The knowledge of a procedure, as discussed in Chapter 12, simply implies that the steps of the procedure (the algorithm) have been learned and stored in a

usable manner (ie they can be recalled correctly and in the right sequence).
In Chapter 15 we saw that the algorithm may have been acquired through
reception learning (eg by observing the procedure being performed) or through
discovery learning (eg by attempting a problem-solving approach). We also saw
that the discovery approach was favoured when the steps of the algorithm
were deducible by the application of previously learned concepts and
principles. We may argue, therefore, that when a procedure is learned through
reception learning techniques, without investigation into the reasons (the 'why
to do') behind actions ('what to do'), individual learning is quite adequate.
When, however, the procedure is to be learned through a discovery approach,
deducing the steps of the procedure from the reasons for the procedure,
group-based problem-solving strategies may be superior, as, once again, they
provide greater opportunities for reflective discussion and the sharing of
difficulties and insights.

There is one other factor that influences the learning group structure in the
case of procedures. Some procedures are performed individually and some in
groups. For example, operating a lathe in a factory is a one-man job, but
operating a hydraulic press that punches out car body panels is a highly
coordinated team job. It is probable that, in practice, most of the procedures in
both of these jobs would be learned on the job, combining the theory and the
practice elements. In such a case, the lathe operator would inevitably learn in
an individual mode whilst the press operator would learn in a group. Indeed,
in the latter case, most of the instruction could probably be done by the other
group members.

16.4 Grouping decisions for the skills content

The form of the learning task

The most influential factors on the grouping of learners for the teaching of
skills are probably the *task/topic* factors. Tasks that are performed in groups
are usually taught much more easily in groups, because the post-training
situation can be simulated. Some categories of skill, in particular the interactive
skills, rely on the presence of other persons as sources of the stimuli that
control the skilled activity. Such skills can only be learned and practised
effectively in a certain kind of group. In the training of salesmanship skills, for
example, it is necessary to provide experience of interaction with customers
(the source of the controlling stimuli). This experience may be difficult to
provide in practice, in a controlled manner. Hence the importance of various
simulation and gaming techniques in the development of interactive skills.

Similarly, it is often only possible to teach tasks that are practised on one's
own in an individual learning situation. A lathe operator could receive a part of
his training in a group — the basic theory (knowledge) content of his job and
perhaps a demonstration of the basic operations to be carried out. But, since
the practice of these operations is since the task will eventually be the
responsibility of one man, even the instructor takes a background role,
restricted to providing guidance and feedback. The main learning occurs
through the interactions of man and machine. The learning pace is controlled
in part by the man's responses and in part by the machine itself. The task is
a one-man task and so is learning.

The choice of instructional strategy

When the characteristics of the task do not dictate the type of learning
group, one can follow the decisions made with respect to instructional strategy.
When an expositive instructional strategy is used, there is less value in group
learning activity. The interchanges on the whole occur between the teacher (or
some substitute medium) and the learner (either as an individual or as one of
the mass in the lecture hall). No significant learner/learner interchanges occur.
Indeed, it is sobering to consider that in a large group 'lecture' or 'formal
classroom' situation, each learner is learning largely as if he were in an
individual learning situation. He receives little from the other learners and
contributes little to their learning. Only as a group size becomes such as to

allow questions and interchanges do the participants begin to learn through the experiences, viewpoints or difficulties of their colleagues.

We may thus conclude that when expositive strategies are employed, there is little to choose between the individual learning situation and the large group learning situation.

When discovery learning strategies are employed, however, then there is always something to be gained through exploratory and analytical discussion and reflection. This can best be promoted in the small- or medium-sized group. Furthermore, as much of the work of such a group is made up of learner/ learner interchanges, it is usually possible to reorganize a large group into several smaller groups for discovery learning.

16.5 Decisions at level 2: the group structure

The general strategies established as a result of a level 1 analysis define the overall structure and approach to be adopted. After the completion of a more detailed level 2 analysis, we are in a position to design the structure and approach to be used in individual lessons. We can now develop a course plan, which would normally specify, for each lesson or group of lessons, the following information: objectives, test items, methods, grouping, media, and materials and equipment to be used.

Be more specific
The least information that could be given on grouping at this stage is to define for each objective whether it is to be achieved by individual or by group methods. However, it is better to try to specify not only the size band of the learning group but also the *type* of group structure or the type of group activity that is to be adopted. To specify 'large-group lecture plus debate' is more informative than simply 'large group'. 'Small groups cooperating to solve the problem' tells us more than simply 'small group methods'. 'Individuals compete to solve most problems in half an hour' is much more specific than just 'individual practice'. The course plan will be more useful if it is more specific.

Cooperative, and competitive groups
A few basic concepts may help us to be more specific in defining the sort of group or individual activity that we wish to employ in our instructional design. In addition to the *group/individual* dimension of learning it is useful to consider the *cooperation/competition* dimension. The latter refers to the type of group interactions that take place between students when they are learning There may be a *cooperative* atmosphere, in which students help each other to achieve the objectives of the lesson. There may be a *competitive* atmosphere, one student attempting to do better than another. Finally, there may be an

Independent study
independent atmosphere, in which one student is not particularly concerned with any other student. Note that it is not necessary to be on your own in order to be learning independently. In a large lecture, for example, the students are, in effect, learning independently. There is neither cooperation nor overt competition between students.

'Goal structures'
Johnson and Johnson (1975) referred to these three modes of learning in groups as three basic 'goal structures' (they used the terms *cooperative*, *competitive* and *individualistic*). The term is quite descriptive: 'structure' emphasizes that it is necessary to consider and plan the interdependencies that exist between the learners. One should plan a group structure for each objective; 'goal' emphasizes that the structure we plan should take into account the long-term objectives of the system we are designing. A certain type of learning can be better achieved by a certain goal structure.

Which goal structure to use
Johnson and Johnson come out strongly in favour of the cooperative structure for most types of learning, although they allow the superiority of the other two in certain cases. Their suggestions are summarized in the tables below (Figures 16.3 and 16.4). The reader may find it interesting to compare Johnson and Johnson's list of cognitive and affective outcomes with our own knowledge and skills schemata.

Cognitive outcome	Cooperative	Competitive	Individualistic
Mastery of factual information			x
Retention, application and transfer of factual information, concepts, principles	x		
Mastery of concepts and principles	x		
Verbal abilities	x		
Problem-solving ability and success	x		
Cooperative skills	x		
Creative ability: divergent and risk-taking thinking, productive controversy	x		
Awareness and utilization of one's capabilities	x		
Perspective- (role-) taking abilities	x		
Speed and quantity of work on simple drill activities		x	
Competitive skills		x	
Individualistic skills			x
Simple mechanical skills			x

Figure 16.3 *Suggested group structures for various cognitive outcomes (from Johnson and Johnson 1975)*

Affective outcomes	Cooperative	Competitive	Individualistic
Interpersonal skills for humanness	x		
Group skills for humanness	x		
Pluralistic, democratic values	x		
Acceptance and appreciation of cultural, ethnic, and individual differences	x		
Reduction of prejudice and bias	x		
Valuing education	x		
Positive attitudes toward school, subject area, instructional activities, school personnel, and other students	x		
Enjoyment and satisfaction from learning	x		
Moderate levels of anxiety to promote learning	x		
Positive self attitudes	x		
Emotional capacity	x		

Figure 16.4 *Suggested group structures for various affective outcomes (from Johnson and Johnson 1975)*

How to implement a given goal structure

It is obvious that the adoption of a particular goal structure brings with it various implications concerning the way in which the lessons will be given. Students will communicate with each other in different ways when they are requested to work as a team and when they are asked to compete. The nature of the student/teacher interactions will also be different. There are also practical organizational considerations. Johnson and Johnson's analysis of three goal structures is shown in Figure 16.5.

Relation between group structure and group size

Structure is not independent of 'size'. Whereas it is quite easy to apply any of the three goal structures in a small group, this is not so in the larger group or in the individualized instruction mode. A comparison of the two dimensions is shown in Figure 16.6.

Figure 16.6 illustrates one probable reason for the preponderance of competitive and individualistic structures in traditional education, when research such as that listed by Johnson and Johnson (1975) suggests the superiority of cooperative structures for most learning. In the typical large group situation, it is far easier to adopt competitive or independent structures.

Self-instruction is also not very suitable for the use of cooperative structures.

	Cooperation	Individualistic	Competition
Student access to each other	Use each other as major resource. Free movement and talking between students. Students grouped in variety of ways, heterogeneous groups are best.	Minimal use of each other as resource. Students working on their own with very little movement or talking between students. Students not grouped.	Observing or other means of keeping track of each other. Students working in clusters with some movement and talking between students. Students grouped in clusters emphasizing equal chance at winning.
Student access to the teacher	Less use of the teacher for ideas and solutions as they use each other more.	High use of teacher for ideas and feedback.	Less use of teacher for ideas, feedback or solutions as criteria of winning are set by each other's performance.
Teacher statements	'Check with your group.' 'Does anyone round you know?' 'Add your idea to the others on the board.'	'Don't bother David while he's working.' 'Raise your hand if you need help.' 'Let me know when you're finished.'	'Who has the most so far?' 'What do you need to do to win next time?'
Student access to materials	Centrally located, shared set of materials. Large variety with minimal duplication. Need knowledge of what is available and of ways to share.	Complete set of materials for each student. Need complete instructions on use of materials initially.	Set of materials for each cluster of students, or individual sets for each student. Need rules on how to take turns with common materials.
Room arrangement	Clusters of chairs or use of tables (probably without ownership feelings toward any particular chair).	Separate desks or carrels with as much space between students as can be provided.	Clusters of desks or tables with separation possibilities (moving desks away from each other).

Figure 16.5 *A comparison of three goal structures (from Johnson and Johnson 1975)*

And, though the small group approach has gained much ground in recent years, particularly in non-formal education (eg management training and all sorts of interpersonal skills training), and in lower primary education, as a whole, however, small group work is as often competitive as it is cooperative. This is an instructional design factor worthy of more careful attention.

Mixed group structures

One may well develop group structures that are hybrids of these three basic types.

One may have, in the same instructional exercise, small groups cooperating to achieve a goal, in competition with the other groups. This is a very common strategy in many business games and in management training in general. This approach combines the positive training aspects of cooperation (eg the future job demands cooperation) with the positive motivational aspects of competition.

	Large group	Small group	Individual
Competitive	Very easy to arrange.	Quite easy to arrange (although the small group tends toward cooperation).	Indirect competition can be induced by setting a standard or by supplying data on other students' performance.
Cooperative	Not feasible unless one divides the large group into task groups.	Very easy to arrange.	Not possible because of lack of contact with other students.
Independent (individualistic)	Quite easy to arrange (often difficult to avoid).	Quite easy to arrange.	Very easy to arrange.

Figure 16.6 *Comparisons of group size and structure*

One may combine cooperative and independent structures most effectively in types of learning that demand a group effort but allow for delegation of specific tasks to specific people. A group of children preparing a class newsletter as a part of communication studies must work as a coordinated team with common objectives, but the individual students in the group might each be responsible for specific articles or features.

Some of the most carefully designed group structures are found in educational simulations and grames. In these types of instruction it is usually desirable to reproduce in the simulation or game the same type of interpersonal and group interactions that exist in the aspect of real life that is being studied. In the case of games and simulation games the element of competition is also built in. The instructional designer must be careful to ensure that these two requirements — the life-like simulation of group interactions and the artificial game element of competition — do not enter into conflict.

16.6 Commonly used group structures

The group structures presented in the information maps that follow are not meant to form a comprehensive directory, but represent the variety of possible structures, classified according to certain important parameters.

First, the structures are classified according to group size. Thus, apart from Map 16.1, which presents the main theoretical and practical considerations that should be taken into account, the maps deal with specific group size bands.

In Map 16.2, large groups are sub-classified into very large groups (mass instruction) and medium to large groups (class instruction). The other parameter used in the classification is whether communication channels are one-way, two-way or multi-way.

In Maps 16.3, 16.4 and 16.5 the structures for small group instruction are sub-classified into three size bands. All the small group methods listed involve two-way or multi-way communication.

In all cases, the prevalent interaction pattern (or goal structure) is identified as being individualistic, competitive or cooperative. We also show how the basic structures — lecture, class, group discussion and tutorial — may be varied to serve various purposes.

Map 16.1 *Selecting an appropriate group structure*

Introduction	Two sets of considerations have to be considered when selecting a group structure. These are: — group size (how many learners work together) — group interactions (how the learners work together). The group size is dictated both by the interactions desired and by a host of practical and economic factors, many of which are beyond the control of the instructional designer. As usual, the group structure decision is a trade-off between the theoretically desirable and the practically feasible.		
Theoretical considerations: factors favouring certain group structures	**Individualistic**	**Competitive**	**Cooperative**
	Learning of basic information. Practice of one-man skills (especially the initial learning and practice stages). Development of perseverance and personal skills.	Recall and reinforcement of knowledge. Development of proficiency in skilled tasks. Motivation to work on dull learning tasks.	Learning and practice of group skills. Development of cognitive skills, problem-solving and conceptual schemata. Development of social skills.
Practical and economic considerations	1. *Staff/student ratio:* This may be fixed by tradition, by politics or by financial constraints. Sometimes an unfavourable staff/student ratio may be ameliorated by the use of other resources and structures, such as self-instruction, resource-based learning, monitors and peer teaching systems, team teaching, etc. This will release teachers of certain functions, enabling them to operate with smaller groups for at least part of the time. 2. *Available learning space:* This may be unsuitable for small group work. Usually such restrictions are at least partly capable of being overcome by inventive planning and lobbying. 3. *Available time:* As small group learning methods are generally discovery-based, they usually require extra time. This is not always available. A mixture of group structures must take this into consideration and use the small group methods where they will give the best pay-off. 4. *Existing theories, traditions and teaching skills:* These must be taken into account in the introduction of any innovative methods. Do not expect success if the teachers are against you or lack the skills.		
Preview	The following four maps present some typical group structures to be used with various sizes of group.		

Map 16.2 *Some structures for large groups*

Introduction	Large groups may be divided into two size bands: — very large (mass instruction); groups of over 50 members — medium-large (class instruction); groups of 20 to 50 members. The larger the group, the more difficult it is to generate effective two-way communication and the more difficult it becomes to avoid independent learning structures. However, some group structures may provide opportunities for cooperation or competition for at least part of the session's time.
Structures for mass instruction	**One-way communication** / **Two-way communication**
	Lecture. One speaker addressing a large audience. No feedback. No group interaction. Independent learning. / *Forum.* Lecture followed by open discussion. A limited amount of group interaction, but mainly speaker-listener exchanges. Independent learning.
	Panel. Three to six speakers discuss a topic in front of an audience. No feedback. Independent learning. / *Panel forum.* A panel followed by audience participation. This may be by 'live' comments or by written questions.
	Symposium. A modified lecture. Three to six speakers each address a large audience on the same topic. No feedback. Independent learning. / *Symposium forum.* Several formal addresses followed by open discussion. When the speakers are either 'for' or 'against' a motion, this becomes a *debate*.
	Colloquy. A modified panel. Six to eight people, some 'experts' and some 'audience', discuss a topic in front of the rest of the audience. Independent learning. / *Colloquy forum.* A colloquy followed by audience participation. In this case, the forum allows the audience to join in the argument developed in the colloquy.
Structures for class instruction	**Two-way communication** / **Multi-way communication**
	Active class. The teacher expounds, demanding little or no response from the learners. Mini versions of all the above structures may be employed in a class. Tasks may be set during the class, but they demand individual effort, with perhaps a competitive comparison of results. Teacher controls what is learned (and how). / *Interactive class.* The teacher makes every effort to involve all the learners. He may use expositive or discovery strategies, may set tasks that demand cooperative, competitive or independent learning. Students learn from each other and from the teacher.

Map 16.3 *The medium/small group*

Introduction	Small groups may also be conveniently divided into two size bands: — medium/small (group instruction); groups of five to 20 members — very small (individual instruction); groups of one to five members. Below about 20 members there is really no excuse for using exclusively one-way or even two-way communication patterns. Whenever feasible, one should attempt to promote interactions between the group members, so that learners learn from each other and stimulate each other to reflect and reorganize their conceptual structures.
Structures for medium/small group instruction	*Group discussion.* This is the basic ingredient of most group instruction methods, because of the richness of possible interactions that may take place (see the diagram opposite). To control these interactions, it is important to have a well-defined topic, an agenda and a skilful, well-trained group leader, who encourages cooperative rather than competitive interactions.
	Seminar. Although often used loosely, the term 'seminar' implies a three-stage process of instruction: 1. Prior research and preparation of a topic by one or more of the group members (this is individual or cooperative project work). 2. Presentation of the findings or viewpoints by the researcher(s) (ie a mini-lecture). 3. Group discussion of the findings and conclusions reached by the whole group (guided by the leader).
	Workshop. This is used for the development of skills, of any type. It usually follows the stages of: 1. Demonstration of the skill and explanation of the theoretical background and essential knowledge (this may follow a 'class instruction' model). 2. Practice of the skill, usually on problems or tasks of special interest to each individual member or sub-group (members choose the tasks and work individually or in cooperation. 3. Interchange of results, self evaluation and group discussion to reinforce or restructure the basic concepts and principles involved.
	Clinic. This is a type of workshop devoted to the solution of problems, usually real-life problems affecting the group members. Techniques such as brainstorming, games and role-play may be used.

Map 16.4 *The individual tutorial*

Introduction	Instruction in very small groups takes on many of the characteristics of individual instruction, but retains much of the benefit of group interactions. In many ways the small group of three or four learners and a teacher offers better learning conditions than the one-to-one tutorial. We can see these advantages if we analyse the one-to-one situation.
The one-to-one tutorial — reinforcing or restructuring of prior learning	Even in the one-to-one situation, it is still the learner who does the learning. The teacher can only guide, inform, evaluate, provide feedback, etc. The benefits of the tutorial situation do *not* rest on the use of the teacher as a medium of primary communication. This is extremely wasteful. Effective tutorials are based on *prior learning* that the student is expected to have achieved, on his own or in a group. New learning may take place during the tutorial by reinforcement or by restructuring of previous learning.
The reinforcing tutorial	Tutorials for *reinforcement* of learning are those that diagnose the student's mastery of a certain body of knowledge, or of a skill, correct wrong interpretations, provide extra practice where this is required, complete the knowledge where this is incomplete and continue the process until the individual student has reached the *specified standard of performance on specified objectives*. As such, it tends to apply the *mastery* model of control of a student's progress. In practice, there are often time limits which prevent all students achieving equal levels of mastery, even under the tutorial regime. It is difficult to imagine a more effective (and more expensive) system for achieving pre-set cognitive objectives. However, much of the opportunity for incidental learning through group interactions is lost.
The restructuring tutorial	Tutorials for restructuring of learning are more concerned with the formation of useful conceptual schemata and with individual development rather than with predetermined objectives. In this form of tutorial the tutor does not follow a pre-set path but rather follows the path that develops from the conversation as it unwinds. The tutor does not show and tell, but seeks and asks for demonstrations and explanations from the learner. He is the sounding board against which the learner tries out his ideas. Often, the presence of one or two other learners enhances the value of the learning sessions.
Comment	The reinforcing tutorial is often referred to as 'cramming' by the teachers who do not agree that examinations are there to be passed. The restructuring tutorial is sometimes described as 'Socratic'.

Map 16.5 *The very small group*

Introduction	As suggested in the previous discussion of the individual tutorial, tutorials for reinforcement of prescribed learning are most efficient when a one-to-one tutor/learner relationship is maintained. However, this is usually ruled out by economic considerations.
	Tutorials for restructuring of previous learning and for individual development of conceptual and problem-solving schemata may however benefit from the added richness and variety of small group learning. Hence the importance of the very small learning group of two to five individuals.
Structures for very small group instruction — group tutorials	*The group tutorial.* This has all the characteristics of an individual tutorial, but takes place in groups of two to five students with one tutor. It is always based on a prior learning assignment, which may have been individual, small group or large group based. It may take the form of a *reinforcing tutorial*, as when time is devoted to problems encountered by the students in previously set learning tasks. In this case the tutorial may almost take the form of a mini-seminar. On the other hand, a *restructuring tutorial* in a small group becomes effectively a group discussion, though much more controlled by the tutor than by the group members. Cooperative problem-solving is promoted.
— special group discussion structures	*The 'Phillips 66' technique and derivatives.* Originally this technique involved groups of six learners who each had to address the group on a given topic for six minutes (hence '66'). Various modifications of this structure are possible, bringing elements of the *seminar*, the *symposium* and the *colloquy* into the small group learning. It is an excellent way to start a restructuring tutorial. It may promote competition.
— small group projects and assignments	*Small group projects and assignments.* This is a very important way of using the group as a self-instructional device. Highly specific learning assignments may be set, or very open ended problem situations posed. The emphasis is on the small group organizing itself in an efficient and cooperative manner to carry out the task. The common structure is 'cooperation within groups and competition between groups'.
— compensatory grouping	*Compensatory grouping.* This technique may be used with any of the above. It aims to balance the skills or other factors in a group by the careful selection of the members. Learning 'diads' (two members) or 'triads' (three members) are formed of members who complement each other and can therefore do much to teach each other. This is essentially cooperative.

17. Media Selection

17.1 Introduction

What are
media?
To some people instructional media refer only to complex items of equipment such as television or film. An alternative point of view, expressed by Marshall McLuhan in *Understanding Media*, is that media are any extensions of man which allow him to affect other people who are not in face-to-face contact with him. Thus to McLuhan, communication media include letters, television, film and telephone, and even roads and railways as these are extensions by which one man can communicate with another.

However, we shall take a middle course between these two extremes, defining 'media' narrowly to include only those media which can effectively be used for the process of planned instruction, but sufficiently broadly to include not only complex electronic communication media but also simpler devices such as slides, photographs, teacher-made diagrams and charts, real objects and visits to places outside the school. We would even include the teacher as one of the presentation media, because after all teachers, like radio and television, spend much of their time transmitting information to learners. Teachers have other functions to perform too, for example the planning and evaluation of lessons.

Defining
'media'
We define 'media' as *the carriers of messages, from some transmitting source* (which may be a human being or an inanimate object), *to the receiver of the message* (which in our case is the learner). These carriers of information interact with the learner through his senses. The learner may be called upon to use any of his senses to receive information, including the often overlooked kinaesthetic sense, which is the sense of muscular coordination (of 'feeling' that one is doing a job correctly). Quite often messages are received by a combination of senses in order to render the desired communication complete.

The selection
of media for
instruction
The traditional approach to selecting media for instruction has often been based on a search for applications for a new item of equipment which has come on the market. Somebody invented videotape and the education industry set about finding educational applications. Looking back over the last 10 years or so, we can now see that some of these applications were valid and useful, whereas others were a waste of time and money. Whereas it is quite legitimate as a research activity to look for applications for a new invention, this is usually an early stage (the pure research stage). A later stage (the development stage) usually starts the other way round, that is, the designer has a problem already in front of him and he sets about looking for a solution to this problem among what is already known to him. The approach to instructional planning based on first specifying objectives and then designing lessons, is obviously this second 'development' type of activity, rather than the 'pure research' activity. In other words, the practising teacher is more concerned with finding solutions to a given problem than in looking for problems which a given solution might solve.

Although both approaches outlined above have their value, for the practising teacher the developmental approach is more appropriate and is indeed the one that we are adopting.

The basis for
selection

The basis of each selection procedure is in the analysis stages when we identify the content of the lesson and the appropriate information which the learner should receive in order to learn. We can refer to this as the appropriate stimuli that the learner must receive. But, of course, the learner must react to this information; he must do something with it; he must respond. Our analysis also identifies the appropriate learning activities, whether practical, overt activities or internalized, covert activities.

It is this analysis which is used as a starting point for our media selection process. The media that we use for instruction must be capable of transmitting all the information, supplying all the instructional stimuli which the lesson content requires, and, second, the media should also help the learner to engage in the appropriate learning activities (at any rate the media selected should not hinder the learner in actively participating as required).

Many approaches to the selection of media have been outlined, some very complicated, others extremely simple, even simplistic. At the simplistic level we have the point of view that any media of communication can teach any lesson content within broad limits and the only important factors in media selection are the economic and practical constraints that exist in any given situation. Thus we use television in the Open University because it is available and can be economically justified in some way or other.

However, others notice that not all media seem to be as well adapted to a given lesson content and suggest that one should match media choice to the particular lesson content or the objectives of the lesson. The problem is how to do this. This has led to complex systematic schemes for the analysis of individual learner differences, in how they react to different media and schemes for the analysis of lesson content so that it can be matched to appropriate media and so on. Some of these schemes have proved to be rather difficult to use in practice and certainly difficult to teach to all teachers, so we are going to steer a middle course and try to suggest some basic rules which might be applied in order to:

1. Eliminate any media which would be quite inappropriate for a given lesson or part of a lesson. We use here the principle that an appropriate medium should be capable of supplying all the stimuli essential for learning. So this first stage might be referred to as 'Selection by Rejection'.
2. Select from the short list of media left, on the basis of the economic and practical constraints and teacher and learner preferences and skills.

Factors
affecting the
choice of
media

The factors which we ought to consider during this process are summarized in Figure 17.1. During the first stage (of selection by rejection) we consider only the factors which influence effective communication. These include learner factors, content factors and the objectives of the lesson. Then, in the second stage we consider those factors which influence cost, practical factors and finally human factors which might influence the acceptability of the solution which we are designing.

The four
levels of
decision
making

However, the decisions concerning effective communication may be taken early or late in the instructional design process, and may be made in greater or lesser depths of detail.

It is useful, once again, to conceptualize the instructional design process as occurring at four levels of detail, which we have called levels 1, 2, 3 and 4. In Figure 17.2 we summarize these four levels of instructional design (which have been fully described in earlier chapters), the chief types of analysis, their chief outcomes and the types of instructional decisions commonly made.

One notes that this four-level model of the instructional design process suggests that certain decisions concerning the selection of media may be taken at any of the four levels. The decisions need not always be taken at each level of detail. For example, one may not make any final decisions concerning the principal media to be used until one has completed a much more detailed

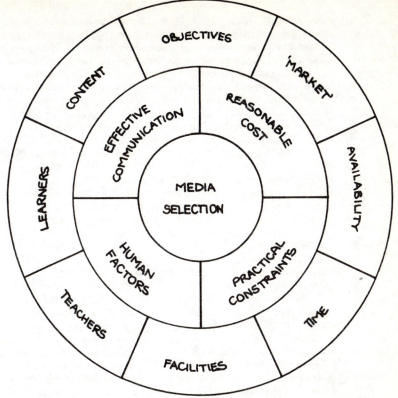

Figure 17.1 *Factors affecting the selection of media for instruction*

Level of analysis	Chief outcomes at this level of design	Instructional decisions commonly made at this level of design
1. Job analysis. Subject analysis.	Final objectives. Tasks to teach. Topics to teach.	Final evaluation. Syllabus/curriculum. Overall sequence (of units in the course). Overall choice of principal methods/media.
2. Task analysis. Topic analysis.	Intermediate objectives. Prerequisites. Task/topic structure.	Formative evaluation. Diagnostic tests. Lesson structure. Sequence of lessons. Selection of methods/media for each lesson.
3. Knowledge and skills analysis.	Enabling objectives. Type of learning for each objective.	Detailed lesson plans. Instructional events for each objective. Methods/media matched to each objective type.
4. Detailed analysis of the learning behaviour/problems.	Exercise design for each learning step.	Programmed learning exercises — in any *suitable* media (text, practical, audiovisual, human presenter, computer).

Figure 17.2 *The four-level design process*

(level 2 or 3) analysis. Then, by summing the detailed media choices for
individual lessons, or even individual objectives, one establishes the overall
'media mix' in the course as a whole. However, very often, one is forced to
make early decisions concerning the principal media to be used. Almost before
any analysis is started, certain overriding practical, economic, social or political
factors will dictate the principal media available and may even prescribe the
proportional 'mix' of these media in the final course. In the case of the Open
University, for example, only certain media are available and there are various
pressures to use these in fairly well-defined proportions. The 'principal
medium' in this case is print, because of its availability, flexibility in terms of
the variety of instructional methods possible, low cost and individualized
nature, and because of the economic limits of the availability of the other
available media (radio, television, tutors, summer schools). On the other hand,
there are pressures to use these other media to the limits of their availability.
Consequently a course may be allotted so much television time, to be filled in
the best way possible (this will appear in subsequent deeper analysis).

**Reality
forces early
decisions**

Such 'early' decisions naturally limit the variety of choice open to the
instructional designer in the later stages. It is, therefore, probably a good idea
to delay decisions on media selection until a sufficiently deep level of analysis
has been performed to supply all the data needed for achieving the best match
between the media to be used and the objectives, learner characteristics and
content characteristics of the instructional system under design.

**Early
decisions
limit later
choice**

However, in practice, one can seldom go very deep into the detail of
instructional design without coming across economic, practical or human
(including social and political) constraints that are 'outside our sphere of
influence'. As one cannot eliminate or neutralize these constraints, one had
better work within their confines. In such cases it is a waste of time to
continue the instructional design process as if the constraints did not exist. It is
more logical (and more efficient) to make the necessary overall media decisions
and then to continue the deeper design process taking into account the
limitations that these decisions impose on later decisions.

Fortunately, these limitations are not usually too severe. There are usually
many media that can be used to satisfy the essential characteristics of the
message being transmitted. The first stage of selection by rejection reduces the
list of all available media to a short list of available *suitable* media. We are
unlucky indeed if none of the suitable media are practically available.

**Take only
unavoidable
decisions
early on . . .**

Thus, in practice, one may find it necessary to make global
cost-effectiveness decisions, decisions regarding practicability or political
decisions in advance of the (logically more important) effective communication
decisions. We represent the key factors involved in all these decisions in the
form of a conceptual schema (see Figure 17.1). This diagram, unlike a flow
chart, does not try to impose a sequence on the decisions to be made, but
rather suggests that the decisions are interrelated — that effectiveness factors
and cost factors are connected, that practical and human constraints may
influence choice between viable cost-effective alternatives or may, from the
start, render some theoretically effective solutions non-viable.

**. . . and take
them with
care**

However, such early decisions should be taken intelligently so as not to limit
later stages of instructional design unduly or unnecessarily. They should only
be made if they are unavoidable. Otherwise the instructional designer's options
should be left open. Often they may be presented as recommendations rather
than as hard decisions: for example, 'avoid the use of projected visuals if at all
possible as we cannot guarantee the supply of the necessary projectors'.
Sometimes, however, the constraints are such that a clear early decision is
called for, eg 'do not use projected media or recorded sound as 90 per cent of
schools have no electricity'.

In particular, one should avoid early decisions relating the exact form that
the solution should take (the 'solutions seeking problems' syndrome). There
are certain global decisions concerning effective communication that can

legitimately be taken at level 1. But as our analysis at this stage is fairly shallow, these decisions are restricted. A greater range of decisions can be taken once we have completed a level 2 analysis and have identified the intermediate objectives, the sequence and structure of the tasks and/or topics to be taught, etc. An even greater precision is possible at level 3, and so on.

17.2 Media selection decisions at level 1

Effectiveness   Analysis at level 1 involves, in the training context, the identification of the tasks that make up the job of the people to be trained, or, in the educational context, the identification of the topics that compose the subject matter to be taught and their interrelation with each other and with what the intended learners already know. Further analysis of the intended learners (the target population) and the job/subject in the wider context helps to identify the tasks or the topics that *need* to be taught (instruction required), those that are too easy to need teaching (information required), those that are too rarely practised or used to justify teaching (reference materials required) and those that are already well known by the target population (prerequisites).

Instruction or   Analysis at this depth gives little insight as yet into *how* to teach. We are
information?   primarily concerned with *what* to 'teach' and what to package as 'information'. Thus one valid decision which can be made is whether we require *instructional* media or *informational* media. The difference is important and is quite simple. Information may be disseminated by unidirectional (one-way) media. Instruction requires two-way communication between the transmitter and the receiver.

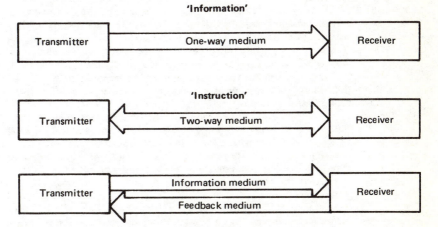

Figure 17.3 *'Instructing' and 'informing' contrasted*

This entails the use of two-way communication media, or a combination of one-way media that effectively provides the necessary two-way communication. Note that the feedback channel may not be in use all the time, but only at key stages in the process. Hence one-way media, such as television, may be used for instruction, if supported by the necessary feedback media (eg letters in distance education systems, or discussions in normal schools or practical applications exercises in vocational training).

Quantitative   The gross analysis of 'level 1' also tells us quite a lot about the *quantitative*
aspects   aspects of the target population (eg how many people are to be taught, with what frequency, in what size of groups, how dispersed geographically, etc). This leads to the identification of many constraints and also of certain factors related to effective communication. Our choice of media must be able to reach the learners (and at reasonable cost). We are naturally led to consider the gross

alternatives of distance education (mass media are the principal media) and face-to-face education (teachers are the principal media, supported by teaching aids). This distinction was nicely put by Wilbur Schramm when he referred to 'big media' and 'little media'.

Types of objectives

Finally, at level 1, we form an overall view of the final (terminal) objectives of the course we are about to design. These objectives may be 'obligatory', in the sense that all learners should achieve mastery of all objectives (this is the case in most vocational training and also in educational courses that apply the mastery learning model), or they may be optional, in the sense that there is room for individual students to choose which objectives they wish to master and to what level of proficiency they wish to master them. This is the case with many non-vocational educational courses, necessary in courses based on the 'cyclic learning' model of the curriculum favoured by Bruner, and is used by proponents of 'open classroom' and resource-based discovery learning fans, etc). Thus, we may at this level be led to decide (for practical or philosophical reasons) between media that are capable of presenting a fixed message (thus controlling the uniformity of the message) and media that are capable of presenting information in such a way that it is easy for teachers or learners to modify the content or the sequence of the message (thus allowing freedom of choice and a measure of 'individualization').

Thus to summarize, effective communication, at the overall level, would lead us to consider:

Learner factors: big or little media?
Content factors: one-way or two-way media?
Objectives: fixed or flexible?

A schema for initial media decisions

The way in which these interact is shown in Figure 17.4. The upper half of the wheel lists, in the outer ring, some 'big' or mass media' together with necessary additions to render the system instructional (which requires feedback), or flexible in use (which requires alternatives and a guide). The lower half of the wheel lists, in the outer rim, some 'little media' combinations.

The outer rim has intentionally been left open at the edge, to indicate that the examples given are not a complete and exhaustive listing, but only examples of a category.

The choices within a category would be influenced very much by the economic, practical and other constraints that exist in the organization or society that is sponsoring the design of the course. Such constraints would render some choices more attractive, and others simply impossible. Thus one may be forced to make definite choices from the examples in these categories, or one may be able to leave the options open a little longer, while indicating preferences.

Cost-effectiveness

Costs enter as an important consideration at the very beginning of any project. It is, therefore, quite legitimate, and even necessary, to eliminate from the media shortlist any that are quite impossible for reasons of cost. The important concepts to apply at this stage are presented in Figure 17.5.

Initial cost estimates are approximate

Applying the concepts of cost-effectiveness, of cost over time and of break-even points enables a more balanced judgement to be made of the economic factors at play in media selection. One may only, at this early stage, have a 'hunch' regarding the relative effectiveness of alternative media choices. One has not gone deeply enough into the analysis of the problem to formulate clear hypotheses, nor to be certain how to form hypotheses concerning effectiveness. There may not be sufficient experience nor sufficient reliable empirical data to be able to predict with any certainty the probable effectiveness of a proposed course structure. In this respect, the accumulated research on media comparisons for total courses is singularly unhelpful (Briggs, Campeau and Gagné, 1966).

In such cases it is advisable to postpone final decisions to a later stage of the instructional design process, either until later stages of deeper analysis have

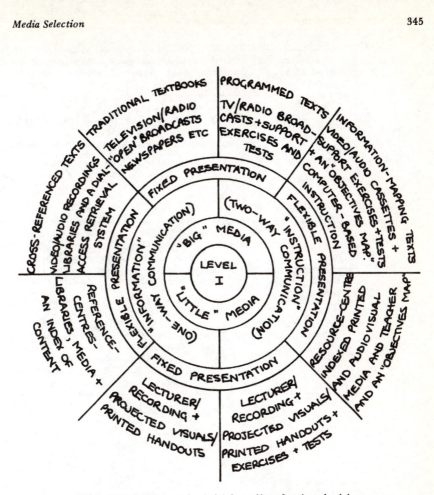

Figure 17.4 *Schema for initial media selection decisions*

given reliable indicators as to probable effectiveness or, if this fails, until one can collect one's own empirical data during the pilot project stages of course validation (this would imply the testing out of alternatives on a small scale before making final decisions).

Using
existing
materials
cuts costs

At this stage, an overall analysis of what is already available in the way of media and instructional materials should also be made, to avoid 'reinventing the wheel', which often occurs in educational and training innovations. A great deal of time and money is spent in the design of courses that already exist and are readily available for adaptation. We stress 'adaptation' as almost invariably the commercially available product will not be exactly suitable. It may need some extensive modification, or it may only need some notes to integrate it into the overall course structure. In either case, the costs of adaptation of existing high-quality materials are much lower than the costs of originating high-quality materials.

The one problem is to recognize whether the available materials are suitable and are of a high quality. To do this we need to compare the materials' objectives and evaluation results against our own objectives and criteria. If no reliable published data exists for the commercial materials, we once again need to find out for ourselves, by mounting some pilot projects. This implies, once again, that final decisions are left to a later stage of the instructional design process.

Effectiveness of a presentation	Are the objectives achieved? Is the message communicated and understood? Either the presentation achieves its objectives or it does not.
Efficiency of a presentation	How well are the objectives achieved? This is a relative measure. Two presentations may both be effective, but one may be more efficient, in that it used less resources to achieve the objectives. These resources may be: ☐ Time required to achieve the objectives ☐ Quantity of human resources (teachers, etc) needed ☐ Quantity of other resources (materials, support services, etc).
Cost-effectiveness	As most resources can be expressed in terms of their cost, a useful overall concept for media comparison is cost-effectiveness, which may be defined as: 'The relative costs of achieving objectives by alternative media'.
Capital and running costs (definitions)	All costs can be classified as: Capital: development costs, overheads. Running: costs incurred during use.
(Implications)	1. Therefore, the cost per student of a presentation diminishes as the number of students using it increases (see Figure 17.6). 2. And sometimes, media with high development costs, but lower running costs may in the long time be more cost-effective (see Figure 17.7).

Figure 17.5 *Important concepts to apply at level 1*

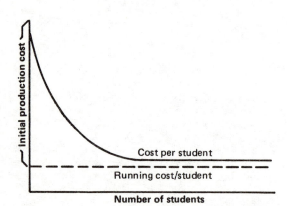

Figure 17.6 *The cost/usage relationship:*
cost per student diminishes with use

Practicality   At level 1, certain overall considerations of practicality influence initial preferences for media. Perhaps the most important of these is the time available for course preparation, as, if this is limited, some options may become impossible to implement. Other important factors are the existing availability of the necessary resources, both human and material.

Time   Up to a point it is possible to control the time necessary for the production of instructional media by the allocation of more or less resources, by, for example, doubling the number of programme writers. However, in general, doubling human resources (even when this is possible whilst maintaining their

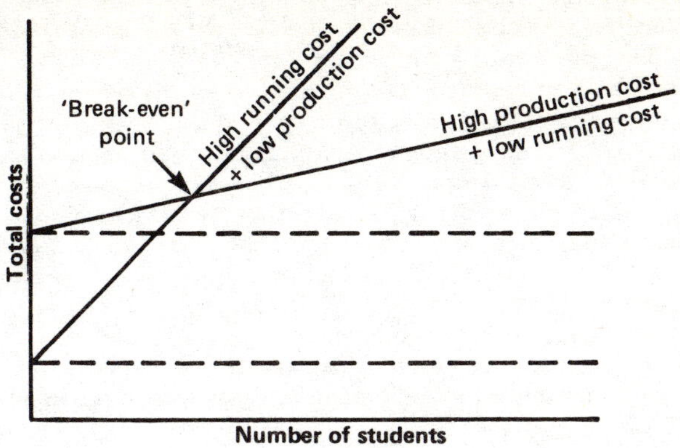

Figure 17.7 *The 'break-even' point between two alternative courses*

quality) will not generally result in a doubling of productivity. There are always certain uncontrollable factors which set certain time-limits on certain production activities. For example, expert technical assistance is not always available in unlimited quantities, the opportunities for the experimental validation of the materials cannot always be arranged when required, certain sub-contracted production processes, such as film development, take their time irrespective of the pressures existing in our project, and so on. Many of these are capable of being solved, at a price, but the price may be too high. It is important at this early stage to make reliable time estimates for the production of different media alternatives.

Material resources

The availability of the necessary production services, such as television or recording studios, film development laboratories, photographic equipment, printing equipment, etc should be verified. One should examine not only the existence of these services but also their reliability and quality. One may be forced to consider the installation of one's own 'in-house' specialist facilities and this adds another factor to the cost-effectiveness equation. It is important to make some accurate estimates of what services can be relied on and at what cost.

Human resources

The specialist human resources necessary for the preparation of media must likewise be estimated. Do they exist in sufficient quantity? Can they be trained? How much do they cost?

Overall human considerations

At this level, it is premature to make many detailed decisions regarding the learners, as the level of target population analysis carried out is a gross, quantitative, assessment of who will study the course and what are their needs, in terms of objectives to be reached or topics to be covered. We know little, at this stage, of how the potential students will react to specific instructional methods or media. All we might know is the 'traditions' – the way the students have been accustomed to learn on other courses in the past. We know this not so much from a target population analysis, as from our knowledge of the typical form that educational and training systems take in our society or our organization. This small amount of information may lead us to make certain conclusions concerning the types of media that are already familiar to our students. But this should not be taken as a constraint. On the contrary, a novel instructional method or medium often produces superior results (at least in the short run), not so much because it is intrinsically superior, but simply because it is new (the famous 'Hawthorne effect').

Preferred learning styles

Preferred teaching styles

A more serious consideration is whether the medium is new and strange to the people involved in delivering and administering the course. Are the teachers familiar with the medium? Are they afraid of getting involved with gadgetry, or with novel course administration systems? Are they resistant to delegating some of their teaching tasks to media? Are they worried about their status or about being put out of a job?

Taking human factors in the broad sense, is the system into which we are to implant our new course ready to accept and use it? Are the administrators of education or training willing to make the necessary reorganization to accommodate, for example, a resource-based, individualized instructional system? Do they have the skills and resources to manage such a course effectively? Will they oppose the use of specific media either from a practical or theoretical standpoint? Does the prevailing educational philosophy clash with the use of certain methods or media?

In many cases no strong answers will appear to such questions, indicating that no insuperable constraints exist. In other cases, however, one may identify real constraints that should be taken into account in media selection at level 1.

17.3 Media selection decisions at level 2

General considerations   Unless, at level 1, the constraints were such as to completely define the medium (or media) of presentation, we now have the opportunity to select our media with more precision (or to allocate different learning objectives among the media selected according to their suitability).

The products of level 2 analysis   Analysis at level 2 involves, in the training context, the analysis of the tasks to be taught into the operations or steps that must be executed, or, in the educational context, the analysis of the topics to be taught into the sub-topics or elements of information that must be learned. In each case, the sequence and structure of the tasks/topics is identified, which gives insights into the way they should be taught, the prerequisite knowledge or skills that the learner should possess and the intermediate objectives that must be attained during the course as stepping stones to the final objectives.

We now also get some insights into *how* to teach, at least to the extent of establishing the content of individual course units and lessons and determining the possible sequence (or alternative sequences) in which the lessons should be learned.

Often, formal analysis goes no further. At this stage, the rest of the task of course design is left to individual teachers, to plan their lessons as they see fit, in the light of the overall course structure (curriculum) that they have been given. Sometimes, however, the planning of the curriculum goes further, suggesting to the teacher the instructional methods, media and content that he should use. The Nuffield projects (Nuffield maths, science, environmental studies, etc) are examples of well-known curriculum projects that have made such a thorough analysis. In these cases, the teacher receives complete, or virtually complete, lesson plans to apply in his teaching.

'Little media' decisions   Note that we are now concerned principally with the 'little media'. If mass media have been chosen, this is usually a level 1 decision and our task now would be to develop instruction that made good use of these media. However, there is no reason why we may not at this stage decide to use some of the 'big media' such as television, in the classroom setting.

Let us now look at the factors indicated in Figure 17.1 at this more detailed level of analysis.

Communication effectiveness   Level 2 analysis establishes the objectives for each lesson at a level of specificity that enables one to match appropriate media with a high degree of confidence. The approach is based on only two general rules, which are given below.

Rule 1   *If you expect a certain behaviour from the learner after instruction, you should give him opportunities to practice that behaviour during instruction.* Thus if the learner is expected to be able to give examples of a certain concept, he should be presented with examples during instruction, if he is expected to *perform* a procedure after training he should *practice performing* the procedure and not observing it or hearing it described (although these may both be steps to getting him to perform correctly).

Rule 2   *Use the most appropriate sensory channels for communicating the information to be learned.* Thus, one should attempt to match the sensory channels to the message. Often this is not a significant factor, as the information to be communicated is verbal, and the only choice open to us is between the spoken and the written word. But in other cases, as the figure below shows, a wider variety of sensory channels may be involved.

Sensory channels	Sensory channels are the senses through which the learner receives the information. Media use the following channels of communication:	
Types	Vision –	most commonly used, often in combination (audiovisual) for all
	Sound –	types of learning tasks.
	Touch –	less commonly used but important in learning perceptual and
	Kinaesthesis –	psychomotor skills.
	Smell –	rarely used in school learning (only in very specialized skill learning –
	Taste –	eg cookery)
Examples of sensory channels used by certain media	Media	Sensory channels used
	Television	Sound and vision
	Book	Vision
	Wine-tasting session	Taste, smell and vision or sound for the verbal label description
	Samples of textiles	Vision and touch (again perhaps sound for the name)
	Pilot trainer (simulator)	Vision, sound, touch, kinaesthesis

Figure 17.8 *Sensory channels used by certain media*

The teacher is himself a medium   The teacher has many functions. One of these is to communicate information (messages) to the learners. When performing this function the teacher is himself a medium of communication. He employs the following sensory channels:

Sound   when he speaks.
Vision   in non-verbal communication (eg smiling, scowling).
Touch/kinaesthesis   in physically guiding the motions of the learner (eg in sports training).

Note that when, for example, he writes something on the blackboard, the medium of communication is the blackboard and not (directly) the teacher. The teacher has in a sense programmed the blackboard to communicate a given message.

The teacher controls other media   The teacher's other functions include the observation and evaluation of what happens during the learning process, modifying the sequence or the actual presentation, and, most importantly, providing feedback on the learner's progress. There is often a case, therefore, for the instructional media to be under the teacher's control. The extent of his control may vary from almost absolute, as in the case of teacher-prepared visuals on the blackboard, to nearly non-existent, as in the case of educational broadcasts.

The use of media taxonomies   One approach to the selection of media, which can be applied at level 2 is the use of some media classification, or taxonomy. A rather complex taxonomy has been suggested by Bretz (1971). A somewhat similar approach has been used by Anderson (1976). Both of these classify existing media into groups according to the types of stimuli or information that they can present. A somewhat different approach, using the two factors of 'sensory channel' and 'extent of teacher-control' has been used by the author to draw up, rather than fixed categories, a sort of media map that places commonly used media in relation to each other and to the two factors used as the basis for classification (Romiszowski 1974). The use of the chart (see Figure 7.9) involves the selection of any combination of the media listed to form the right mix for a given task or topic, at the desired level of teacher control. For individualized, student-directed or resource-based systems, one should restructure the chart considering learner control as the vertical scale.

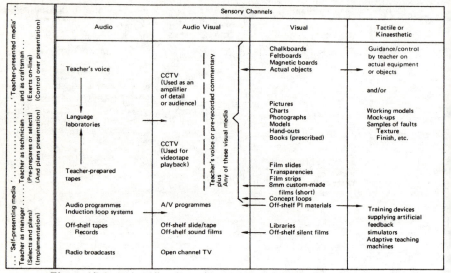

Figure 17.9 *A classification of instructional media (Romiszowski 1974)*

Flowcharts as aids to media selection

As a further aid to selection from this chart, a set of flowcharts were drawn up. The first flowchart (see Figure 7.10) is for the analysis of tasks that have a visual stimulus content.

The second flowchart (see Figure 7.11) is of more application to the analysis of topics, in order to decide whether the verbal information to be communicated should be presented live or packaged, and, in the latter case, whether written or recorded audio media should be preferred. Note that this chart also considers when audio is an essential part of the information to be communicated.

The third flowchart (see Figure 7.12) assists the instructional designer to apply the other golden rule, of providing appropriate practice of the behaviours required by the objectives. This chart concentrates on the responses that the learner should make during learning. This leads to certain choices of instructional exercise, which in turn indicate certain essential characteristics that the media should have, in order to provide optimal learning conditions. The identification of these characteristics helps one to select appropriate media from the chart.

Thus, so far, we have considered, in some detail:

Stimulus and response factors

Content factors — by identifying the types of *stimuli* that the content should present to the learner, and hence the sensory channels that are essential characteristics of appropriate media. We also considered the content's structure, learning difficulty, etc, in order to form an opinion regarding what extent of teacher control we should plan for our presentation. Highly structured, difficult to learn, often variable or debatable content requires greater teacher control over the presentation than does descriptive and factual, easy to learn, unchanging and unchallengeable content.

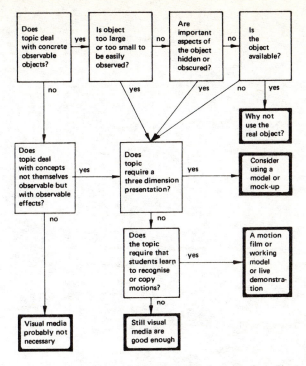

Figure 17.10 *Decisions for selecting visual media*

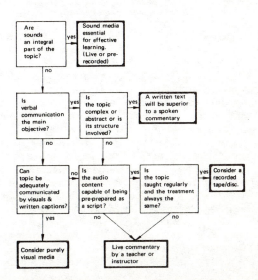

Figure 17.11 *Decisions for selecting verbal and sound media*

Objectives — by ensuring that the media chosen will assist (and certainly will not hinder) the learner in practising during the lesson the *same behaviours* that are demanded by the objectives (as identified in the task or topic analysis).

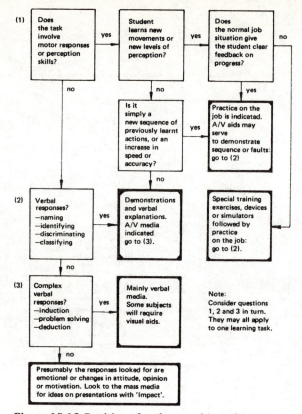

Figure 17.12 *Decisions for the matching of learning task*
to media characteristics

Learner factors to consider

There is one further group of factors to consider from the viewpoint of effective communication — *learner factors*. Much lip service is paid to the importance of individual differences in the planning of instruction, but less is actually done about them. This is partly because we do not really know all that much about how to allow for learner differences. Certainly, a deeper level of analysis is required to identify the learner differences that matter in a specific instructional exercise. At level 2 we can only, from our target population analysis, identify a few general types of learner differences which may influence our choice of media at this stage. The chief types of general learner differences (not specific to a particular learning task) are listed in Figure 17.13, which also presents three other types of learner factors which may be identified at this stage.

Possible decisions resulting from the identification of the presence of some of these learner factors are suggested in Figure 17.14.

Deciding among viable alternatives

We have now considered the influence of the three main groups of factors (objectives, content and learners) on the identification of the characteristics that our presentation media should have. Each instructional design project poses particular problems. Different specific factors are of prime importance and lead to the identification of unique sets of essential characteristics. Fortunately, the variety of media capable of satisfying quite complex demands is very large, so we are rarely unable to find a suitable medium. Rather more often we are yet faced with a shortlist of suitable media.

We are then able to make a final choice by considering any non-essential, but desirable, characteristics of our planned presentation. These may include

Individual differences	Research suggests that learners differ in: ☐ Their preference for learning by observing/by listening (visual learners/aural learners) ☐ Their perceptions of a given message; this is mainly a factor of past experience, and often a cultural difference exists (eg perception of perspective) ☐ Their understanding of the conventions used by various media (eg the grammar of language, the 'grammar' of technical drawing, etc).
Attention span	How long a learner can attend to one type of task. Factors affecting this are: ☐ Age: young children seldom attend to one style of presentation for more than a few minutes, whilst adults may attend for hours ☐ Interest, generated either by the content itself or by the style of its presentation ☐ Motivation on the part of the learner to achieve the objectives of the learning task presented.
Number of learners	The group size to be taught renders certain media difficult or impossible to use; others become uneconomical.
Physical disablities of learners	Poor vision, hearing, dyslexia, colour blindness, etc.

Figure 17.13 *Some learner factors*

For differences in preference for specific media.	Use a multi-media approach, offering both audio and visual options for the same objectives or content.
For differences in perception.	Either avoid the types of presentation that give difficulty, or arrange extra perception training.
For differences in the understanding of symbolic language or conventions.	Either avoid the types of symbolic language that gives problems, or teach it first, to all students.
For groups with a short attention span.	Use a variety of media, in order to change the style of presentation at intervals shorter than the span.
For dealing with groups of different sizes.	Select media that are well suited to the group size you have, or, if this is difficult, modify the group size or structure to suit the media you have.

Figure 17.14 *Selecting media in the light of learner factors at level 2 analysis*

the use of colour (when colour is not essential to the message), use of illustrations (when the text is basically sufficient for effective communication), using film (when a still slide presentation is adequate), etc.

Example 1: Deciding between alternatives
To illustrate the variety of interrelated factors which might influence our decisions, let us consider one decision which might be called for in a hypothetical course. Suppose we wished to teach the working of a mechanism (perhaps the internal combustion engine). Suppose we have identified that

visual stimuli are essential. Suppose furthermore that we may practicably make available a set of still diagrams (overhead projector transparencies) or a film, or a working (but simplified) model. As the cost increases considerably for each of these options, we wish to assess whether we will get away with the still pictures, or whether the more expensive options are worth considering. Figure 17.15 presents a set of considerations which should be weighed up in making our decision.

Try for yourself the internal combustion engine example. See how closely you agree with our rating (there is no reason why you should agree exactly, as some of the questions call for value judgements).

Our rating on the first ten are: A − 6; B − 4; C − 3. In other words the task factors favour a working model over a still or moving visual.

Let us consider the learner factors for two distinct target groups: (1) undergraduate engineering students (highly selected, above average IQ, proven learning skills, probably well-motivated as they selected this course of study); and (2) people preparing for car mechanics questions to be set as part of a car driving test (a common practice in some European countries). They probably have a wide range of IQs, little previous mechanical experience, low motivation in most cases.

Keep a score of the letters A, B, and C for those questions where you answer *yes*. Select the high scoring medium.

A − model; B − still visual; C − film.

Note Questions 1—7 relate to real objects only. They may be ignored if you are attempting to visually explain an abstract concept, etc.

Task content	1. Complex shape or inside details which should be studied?	A: C.
	2. Many interrelated parts, the relative position being of importance to the learner?	A: B.
	3. Are the functions of the parts to be studied?	A: C.
	4. Are the relative sizes important to learner?	A: B.
	5. Is it so complex that detailed breakdown and analysis is required to fully understand it?	A: B.
	6. Is the motion of the object or its parts to be studied?	A: C.
	7. Is the sequence of operation to be studied?	A: B.
Objectives	8. Is the purpose to demonstrate the performance of a manipulative or motor skill?	C.
	9. Will student apply what he learns in an identical situation?	A: C.
	10. Will student apply what he learns as general principles in a number of similar situations?	B.
Learner factors	11. Are students of above average IQ?	B.
	12. Average or below average IQ?	A: C.
	13. Do students need motivation?	C.
	14. Are they already well-motivated?	B.
	15. Do they already have experience of the topic?	B.
	16. Do they lack relevant experience?	C.
	17. Do your students learn well from verbal or from visual material?	B: C.
	18. Do they need to handle or operate equipment to ensure efficient learning?	A.
	19. Do they have good mechanical ability?	B: C.
	20. Do they have poor mechanical ability?	A.
	Your score	A .... B .... C ....

Figure 17.15 *Media characteristics: model, still visual or film — checklist*

Our ratings on the questions are:

Group 1: A — 6; B — 8; C — 5
Group 2: A — 8; B — 5; C — 5

It seems the more expensive media choices may be a waste of money for Group 1, but certainly the expense of a model may pay off for Group 2.

This example is presented here purely to illustrate that weighing up the final choice of media is complex and is in part subjective.

Example 2: Selecting available media (film)

In many ways, the problems of selecting an appropriate training film off-the-shelf are similar to those of evaluation. One selects a film with certain objectives, aimed at a certain type of student, and tests its effectiveness. However, off-the-shelf films are rarely explicit about their target population, and still more rarely have any statement of objectives, let alone one phrased in terms of student behaviour. There is no alternative but to sit down and preview it. Teachers have always done this, but all too often with a view solely to checking the factual accuracy of the material presented. While this is of vital importance, the factors of film structure are equally important in deciding whether a film is worth screening to your students. For example, if the objectives differ widely from your own, or if the commentary assumes vast amounts of pre-knowledge which your students do not have, then it is a waste of time to even attempt to use the film. Greenhill (1956) produced, as part of an extensive study into instructional films, a set of questions the potential film user should attempt to answer when deciding the merits of a film.

The final version of his 'film analysis form' contains 17 questions on the structure of the film, and 10 on the subject matter content. Each question can be answered as a matter of degree, and is rated on a six-point scale. High scores indicate a strong yes, low scores indicate a strong no. The questions dealing with structure are:

*1. Are the objectives clear?
*2. Will the *target audience* find the film interesting?
 3. Does the film build on previous knowledge, skills or experience of the target audience?
*4. Is the subject matter appropriate for the course of training?
 5. Does the content relate directly to the main objectives?
 6. Is the content presented in a well-organized, systematic pattern?
 7. Are the important ideas or procedures clearly emphasized?
 8. Does the film attempt to present too much material for the audience?
 9. Are new facts, ideas, terminology or procedures introduced at a rate which will permit efficient learning (not too fast or too slow)?
 10. Does the film provide for adequate repetition of the important content (eg revision, summaries, outlines)?
 11. Is the method of presentation suitable to the subject matter?
 12. Is the difficulty of the *pictorial presentation* appropriate for the target audience?
 13. Are the details of the information or demonstration clearly presented pictorially (camera angle, lighting, close-up etc)?
 14. Is the verbal difficulty of the commentary appropriate?
 15. Does the commentator contribute to the effectiveness of the film (appearance, tone, manner, speed)?
*16. Is the sound track clearly audible?
 17. Is the information presented in the commentary well integrated with that presented in the pictures?

Another set of questions should be asked regarding the film's content:

*1. Is the information *technically* accurate?
 2. What is the relative importance of any inaccuracies?
 3. Is the content up-to-date?

*4. Is the content specific (precise factual material rather than broad abstract generalizatons)?

*5. Is it highly probable that the information or procedures presented will be confirmed by subsequent experience?

*6. Is it highly probable that the target population will be able to *use* or *apply* the information or procedures presented?

*7. Is the subject treated more effectively than it would be through some other medium? (Lecture, demonstration slide show, textbook.)

8. Is it the most feasible or economic way of teaching the subject?

9. Does the kind of film used (colour or black and white) effectively show the essential details of the subject matter?

10. Does the film show common errors (in the performance of a skill), or common misconceptions (in understanding of theory), and how to correct them?

The answers to most of these questions are of course subjective. Individuals will differ in the exact rating given to a specific question. However, Greenhill found that if training was given in the use of the film analysis form, by practising on standard films, a surprisingly consistent and reliable level of rating was achieved. It is suggested that when rating a film, a low score (1 or 2) on any of the questions marked with an asterisk is sufficient to disqualify the film. Those without an asterisk are deemed less important and one or two low scores can be tolerated. The analysis form was originally developed for pinpointing weaknesses in film during production. It has, however, been extensively used for the systematic selection of off-the-shelf films. Finally, we should not ignore the possibility of using only part of a commercially available film. More and more film users are employing the technique of analysing a range of available films, and using only those parts which pass the test.

Cost-effectiveness The cost questions to ask at level 2 are essentially those discussed at level 1. But now we are likely to have more precise data to make our cost estimates. We have specified our media, lesson by lesson, objective by objective, so we can now get quite accurate estimates of the proportion of our course that any given medium will present. We could derive a fair estimate of the study hours through television, the study hours in direct contact with the teacher, the study hours on self-instructional materials and so on. Given the 'standard' costs for the preparation of each of the types of media to be used, one can estimate the costs of media production with a fair degree of accuracy.

One should not forget also to question from the cost-effectiveness viewpoint whether a particular presentation should indeed be developed.

Availability Are there suitable materials already available on the market, which can be bought in at a fraction of the production cost and can be incorporated into the course (with or without some adaptation)? This consideration can now be treated at a micro level (eg are there any suitable slides or photos or verbal descriptions in existing materials) whereas at level 1 it is treated at the macro level (eg are there any complete courses, textbooks, sets of TV programmes that we can adopt/adapt).

Market How much will the individual media be used? At level 1 this was a consideration of how many students will take the whole course. Now we should consider whether a particular presentation will perhaps be used many times by each student (as is the case with single concept 8mm films) or whether perhaps it is optional and will be chosen and used by only a small proportion of all students.

Objectives Can the presentation be obtained or made at an economical price, in relation to the importance of the objectives. One is attempting here to make a worth/cost analysis for each individual media presentation, before deciding finally whether to select that option or to go for a more economical solution.

Once again we note that these three types of cost factors interrelate with each other and also with the effectiveness factors to render media choice a complex task.

Practicality
Once again the procedure at level 2 is similar to level 1 in terms of the chief categories of factors to consider, but the decisions can now be taken on better data and at a micro level of detail.

Time
One can now estimate production times for each group of lessons, or for each specific presentation. Thus, in the case of time constraints, one might assign priorities, so that the media most important to the effectiveness of the course are produced early and without delay.

Resources
These can now be allocated on an item-by-item basis, giving a method for the control of media production. Once again, if resources are scarce, it should be possible to establish priorities (from consideration of effective communication), and prune down our ambitions to the size of our pockets, by opting for less problematic and more easily produced media for the less essential objectives. (This may perhaps only marginally reduce course effectiveness and thus, by definition, increases cost-effectiveness — equal results for less resources.)

We should also ask some *practical usage* questions, such as:

☐ Will the medium operate in the conditions of the training area (temperature, humidity, power sources, transportation)?
☐ Is the environment well-adapted to its use (space, layout, black-out facilities, acoustics, annoyance to/from others)?
☐ Is the medium 'student-proof' (robust, withstands careless handling, not prone to disintegrate, etc)?
☐ Is it capable of being easily maintained at low cost?
☐ Will it have a reasonable working life (bearing in mind its development costs) before it is rendered obsolete by changes in the subject or in teaching methods?

To assist in formulating and answering questions at this level, it is useful to consider the practical advantages and limitations of individual media or groups of related media. Figure 17.16 lists some characteristics of commonly used types of little media.

Human factors
We have already considered human factors under other headings: *learner factors* affecting the effectiveness of a message, and *human resources* for the production of media. Under the present heading we are considering constraints that may make a potentially effective media choice ineffective. Among the human factors to consider now are *teacher factors*.

Teacher factors
At level 1, we looked at some of the overall constraints that may be encountered in the system as a whole, in relation to certain types of media used on a large scale. These constraints arise from the educational philosophies, prejudices, habits and fears of the people involved in the system. Naturally these constraints, if they are found to exist, should be taken into account in the selection of media, or should be overcome. To a certain extent, they may be overcome or even eliminated by effective promotion of the proposed system, and if necessary by training the people who will be involved in running it in the new skills that are required to operate it efficiently.

Consideration of a detailed nature should therefore be given at level 2 to ways of preparing teachers to accept and to use any novel instructional medium that we plan to adopt.

Any media presentations that are not absolutely essential and that demand significant changes in practice, or substantial learning to use, on the part of teachers, might perhaps be avoided.

Particular care should be taken to allay any fears or negative attitudes that specific complex gadgetry sometimes produces, as these attitudes may easily be transferred from the specific case in point to whole classes of methods and media, thus increasing future difficulties for innovation.

Learner factors
One should consider in a similar way any learner factors which might produce fears or negative attitudes. This would be particularly important to

Material	Advantages	Limitations
Photographic print series	1. Permit close-up detailed study at individual's own pacing. 2. Are useful as simple self-study materials and for display. 3. Require no equipment for use.	1. Not adaptable for large groups. 2. Require photographic skills, equipment, and darkroom for preparation.
Slide series	1. Require only filming, with processing and mounting by film laboratory. 2. Result in colourful, realistic reproductions of original subjects. 3. Prepared with any 35mm camera for most uses. 4. Easily revised and updated. 5. Easily handled, stored, and rearranged for various uses. 6. Increased usefulness with tray storage and automatic projection. 7. Can be combined with taped narration for greater effectiveness. 8. May be adapted to group or to individual use.	1. Require some skill in photography 2. Require special equipment for close-up photography and copying. 3. Can get out of sequence and be projected incorrectly if slides are handled individually.
Filmstrips	1. Are compact, easily handled, and always in proper sequence. 2. Can be supplemented with captions or recordings. 3. Are inexpensive when quantity reproduction is required. 4. Are useful for group or individual study at projection rate controlled by instructor or user. 5. Are projected with simple lightweight equipment.	1. Are relatively difficult to prepare locally. 2. Require film laboratory service to convert slides to filmstrip form. 3. Are in permanent sequence and cannot be rearranged or revised.
Recordings	1. Easy to prepare with regular tape recorders. 2. Can provide applications in most subject areas. 3. Equipment for use, compact, portable, easy to operate. 4. Flexible and adaptable as either individual elements of instruction or in correlation with programmed materials. 5. Duplication easy and economical.	1. Have a tendency for over-use, as lecture or oral textbook reading. 2. Fixed rate of information flow.
Overhead transparencies	1. Can present information in systematic, developmental sequences. 2. Use simple-to-operate projector with presentation rate controlled by instructor. 3. Require only limited planning. 4. Can be prepared by variety of simple, inexpensive methods. 5. Particularly useful with large groups.	1. Require special equipment, facilities and skills for preparation. 2. Are large and present storage problem.
Videotape/ videocassette	1. Permit selecting the best audiovisual media to serve program needs. 2. Permit normally unavailable resources to be presented. 3. Playback capability of video recording permits analysis of on-the-spot action.	1. Do not exist alone, but are part of total television production. 2. Must fit technical requirements of television.
Multi-media presentations (eg slide/tape)	1. Combine presentation of slides with other media forms for presentations. 2. Use photographs, slides, filmstrips and recordings in combination for independent study. 3. Provide for more effective communications in certain situations than when only a single medium is used.	1. Require additional equipment and careful coordination during planning, preparation, and use.

Figure 17.16 *Practicality factors for little media*

consider in the planning of individualized or resource-based courses, in which the learners come into direct contact with the hardware, having to load their own projectors, recorders, or videocassettes. If the learners are not prepared adequately, then, apart from possible operational difficulties and consequent rejection, one will have a high and costly breakdown rate, which may totally disrupt course efficiency.

18. Control

18.1 Control strategies

Before we leave the discussion of general strategies and decisions at levels 1 and 2, it is necessary to give some consideration to the 'control strategies' that we plan to adopt.

In this context control strategies refer to the following questions:

1. How are we going to assess the results of our instructional efforts (*output measures*)?
2. What factors control when instruction should stop (*output controls*)?
3. Who decides how instruction should begin, proceed or stop (*the control system*) and on what basis is the decision made?

18.2 The output measures

There are two more or less opposed philosophies concerning what we have called the output measures. They refer to the way in which one should view the learning results obtained by the learners in one's system. One approach is to view the results in relation to what is *normally expected*. This is the *norm-referenced* approach. It has been the traditional approach in the assessment and grading of students, basing itself on the assumption that the curve of normal distribution (the Gaussian curve, see Figure 18.1) which applies to the distribution of so many human characteristics (eg height, weight, intelligence) should also apply to the distribution of the learning which occurs in any instructional course.

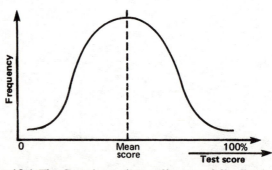

Figure 18.1 *The Gaussian or 'normal' curve of distribution*

The norm-referenced approach has its attractions, particularly for administrators, as it gives a mathematical technique for deciding who should pass and fail in a given examination. It can be used to compensate for 'easy' or 'difficult' examinations (by scaling the passing mark to the norm), for 'hard' and 'soft' examiners (by scaling the assessments of each examiner to a 'norm'), and for changes in the 'demand' for qualified people higher up the educational/social ladder (by ensuring that a predetermined proportion of the learners pass the examination). In all, the norm-referenced approach to assessing the learning output is well suited to an educational system which is (from the viewpoint of its administrators) principally a *selection* system and a *certification* system.

It is not such a well-suited approach for a system that sees itself as principally an *instructional* system. In particular, it ensures mediocrity in the instructional process, for it does not reward exceptional instructional efficiency. Any significant improvement in instruction, resulting in significantly improved learning, is seen as more a problem than a benefit. Something must be done, by scaling the exceptional results, to balance the normal distribution curve. One reaches the ludicrous sort of situation of a university that adopted a more efficient system of individualized instruction, in one discipline, and then adopted an especially 'hard' examination policy in this discipline, in order to normalize the exceptional results.

The alternative approach, which has gained much ground in recent years, principally through the efforts of educational technologists, is the *criterion-referenced* approach. This simply implies that a precise standard (or criterion) of the learning that is desired should be established, even before the learning process begins. The success of the learner should be measured only against this criterion. In such a case, any improved efficiency in the instructional process should be reflected in an increased number of students 'making the grade'. The student is compared against a performance standard which can be made available to him as a guide, *not* against the performance of his colleagues, which has nothing to do with his own learning efforts and cannot be predicted in advance. It seems fairer to both the learner and the teacher.

However, there are difficulties in implementing a criterion-referenced approach, which have delayed its widespread adoption. Apart from considerations of the wider system (such as the one mentioned above concerning the instruction/selection conflict in the aims of educational systems) there are practical problems. One of these is that you have to define the criteria with some precision and in good time. This is a time-consuming task and not always easy. In the training context it is much easier to define precise objectives both for job performance and for the prior learning that must occur. Hence the criterion-referenced approach is widely adopted. In the educational context, however, the specification of objectives is much more difficult and open to more debate, as there is no precise 'job' to use as the final arbitrator.

Another practical difficulty is that the application of the criterion-referenced approach in a long course of study generally requires a change in the evaluation procedures. A long course has many objectives and, hence, many criteria. Therefore, many test items are required to measure success in achieving the criteria. It no longer becomes feasible to sample the course content in a final examination, as has been the tradition. All the criteria must be evaluated. If left to the end of the course, this leads to excessively long testing procedures. The alternative is to adopt some form of continuous assessment procedure.

18.3 Output controls

Output controls are the factors that control when and how the student can 'get out' of the system. There are three principal factors:

☐ Time in the system
☐ The individual student's needs
☐ Mastery of the content/objectives.

Time in the system is the traditional approach. The curriculum defines the number of hours to be devoted to a given subject, topic or task. The learners learn as well as they are able in the given time. It is no wonder that their performance is often below expectations (because of poor prediction by the system of the time needed for a topic) and always distributed (because of individual differences in learning rates), though not necessarily in a neat Gaussian fashion. Usually the distribution is 'skewed' either to the left or the right (see Figure 18.2). If the allowed time is very short, few students will do at all well. If there was plenty of learning time, a larger number of students will do well.

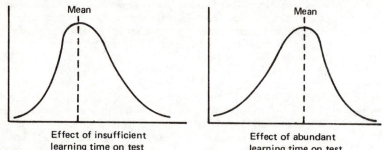

Effect of insufficient learning time on test score distribution

Effect of abundant learning time on test score distribution

Figure 18.2 *Skewed distributions*

It is clear that when learning time is fixed, there is a reasonable case for using the norm-referenced approach. There is no hope that all will learn equally. What we are testing is who can learn more in the time. We are really testing the student's ability to learn the given subject rather than what has been learned about the subject. Sometimes this is what we really wish to evaluate. So sometimes a norm-referenced approach is justifiable.

2. Individual needs

The individual student's needs are more seldom used as a 'get out' criterion, though it is an approach that has been growing in the last few decades, particularly in the tertiary and adult education fields. The credit system of degrees, which offers many options open to the student, is an example of a plan which allows a given student to do as much of a given topic as he wishes or needs. At a more detailed level of design, the use of differentiated objectives, as in some resource-based instructional plans, allow a student to follow up his interests to the level that he desires, needs or can cope with at that moment. Cyclic instructional processes, favoured by the cognitive school, are an attempt to allow the learner to 'get out' of a particular topic when he has had enough and later to return to the same topic, strengthened by other related learning that has occurred in the meantime. Instructional plans which attempt to embody this principle have sometimes been called 'student-centred'. The 'cyclic' learning model was discussed fully in Chapter 9. Such student-centred plans may use either norm-referenced or criterion-referenced systems of assessment.

3. Mastery

Mastery of the objectives seems a logical factor to select as an output control. However it has not been all that common outside of the job-related training context until recently when the mastery learning concept was popularized in the United States by Bloom and others. This model was also discussed fully in Chapter 9. The essential aspect of the mastery model is that performance on each course unit is the output control, defined at a predetermined level (often 100 per cent) of mastery of the unit's objectives. The learner only proceeds to the next unit when he has achieved this defined criterion on the previous unit. Thus mastery learning implies criterion-referenced measures and implies that 'time in the system' is *not* used as an output control.

18.4 The control system

The controllers are those who decide:

- ☐ When a learner should 'get out'
- ☐ When he should 'recycle'
- ☐ What options (in terms of objectives, methods, learning materials, etc) he should take.

Typically the controllers might be the teacher, the learner himself, or the system (in this case neither teacher or learner have many options open to them). Most commonly, control of learning is exercised by a combination of two, or even all three, of these types of controllers. What is important is not so much the exact components in this combination, but rather the resultant *style* of control. Three principal styles may be identified.

Prescriptive control

Prescriptive control. This is the style which predetermines all, or most, of the options in the original instructional plan. Very little is left to be decided on line as the instruction proceeds. There is, as it were, an algorithm of the steps of instruction and the allowable alternatives laid out in advance for the whole course.

Such prescriptive control is usually exercised by the instructional system itself, which dictates, either to the teacher or directly to the learner, what steps to take in specific circumstances.

Democratic control

Democratic control. This is the style in which the participants decide. The principal participants in learning are the learners. Their decisions are usually influenced by the advice of the teachers or sometimes of some special guidance components built into the system (eg an objectives map). However, the main decision makers (as opposed to advisers) are the students themselves.

Instructional plans that incorporate the principle of democratic control are often called student-directed or learner-controlled.

Adaptive control

Adaptive control. This is the style in which not everything is pre-planned and not everything is left to the discretion of the learner. Rather, the decisions of when to get out, and when and how to recycle are taken on line on the basis of data generated by the instructional system as it operates. Decisions are made in a systematic manner on an individual student basis in the light of that student's performance. The decision making process is quite carefully planned, but it does not take the form of an algorithm. Rather, there are some precise heuristics built into the system to assist the teacher and learner in planning the detailed steps of the instructional process as it is proceeding. Systems using adaptive control are termed cybernetic systems.

Combining the factors into a control strategy

The combination of the choice of output measures, output control and control style leads to a variety of different possible control strategies for a course of instruction. Almost any combination of these factors can be encountered in actual projects. However, there are a few combinations which do not (or should not) occur as the factors are mutually exclusive. For example, the mastery learning philosophy is based on a total adoption of a criterion-referenced approach to the measurement of results. Furthermore, it is

Mastery implies criterion-referenced measures

highly unlikely that a given group of learners could all reach mastery performance in a given fixed learning time. Therefore, at least in theory, the mastery model does not consider time to be in any way a limiting control factor. In reality, one never has an unlimited amount of time, so there is always a cut-off point after which it is no longer possible or economical to continue to instruct a particularly slow learner. Each learner does as much as he can in the available time. One crucial difference between the mastery learning model and the traditional model, and an important argument in favour of the former, is that, whereas in traditional learning all learners cover the same ground but do not necessarily learn much of the content, under mastery learning each learner does what he can in the time but learns all the content that he covers up to a high level of performance.

Time constraints lead to norm-referenced measures

Similarly, the various types of traditional learning, such as normal classroom instruction, are usually severely bound by timetables and are usually evaluated in the end by the use of norm-referenced measures. However, this does not prevent some teachers in some situations from applying a criterion-referenced approach and from extending time on a topic, or organizing extra small group tuition, in an attempt to get all the learners in the group up to a satisfactory level of mastery of the topic. This is the case in early education, with the basic skills of reading, writing and counting. A teacher might insist on mastery of these to a minimum predetermined standard by all his pupils, while allowing them to follow a much more democratic, learner-controlled, norm-referenced strategy for other topics.

The need for differentiated control strategies

Once again, we observe that it may be unwise to adopt an overall strategy at the beginning. The content, objectives and the relative importance of different objectives may suggest a mastery learning strategy for some and a norm-referenced, learner-controlled strategy for others. Consider, for example, the training of a doctor. He may progress to further study and research in medicine later, but he may leave the university and commence practising his profession. Some of what he learns in his first years is directly related to practising as a doctor. Some is related to preparing him for further research.

Only some doctors stay on to do research, and it is proper that these should be chosen from among their colleagues, on a norm-referenced basis, as the ones who show the most promise as researchers. But all of them will complete their studies with a certificate to practice. This certification should surely be on the basis of proven competence in the skills of medicine, that is, it should be a criterion-referenced procedure. The implications of this view for the curriculum are that some of the doctor's training should be organized on the mastery learning model and its contents should be prescribed by the system, whilst other parts may better be organized on a learner-controlled, democratic model, more closely simulating the atmosphere of scientific research. Exactly which parts of the curriculum should be treated in which way may not become fully clear until a level 2 analysis has been performed.

The tendency to select an overall control strategy

However, it is quite common to prescribe a general control strategy for a course from the beginning. Sometimes this happens because of the strongly held theoretical position of the course designer, who might insist that, for example, all learning activities should be chosen exclusively by the individual learners themselves (the 'free school' philosophy). At other times this happens because of the adoption of a practical plan for the course, without due thought given to the implications this has for possible control strategies. For example, the widespread adoption of the Keller Plan as the standard way of running courses, by institutions of higher education in both North and South America, suggests that little consideration has been given to the control strategies inherent in this plan. The typical Keller course follows the mastery learning model and has all its content and objectives prescribed in advance, through the use of pre-prepared study assignments and learning materials. Most specialists in higher education would agree that a criterion-referenced, mastery learning, prescriptive control strategy is not suitable for *all* the objectives of higher education. It is excellent for the training of specific job skills or the learning of specific information, but less good for the development of general learning and research skills, creative problem-solving, attitudes and values.

The structure of typical control strategies

It would seem to be a good idea, therefore, to analyse the control strategies inherent in commonly used instructional methods. Figure 18.3 attempts to relate the three aspects: output measures, output control factor, and control style. In combination, these lead to a number of typical control strategies. The names we have used for these strategies are not standardized in any way. We have chosen them to attempt to illustrate the types of control procedures that the particular strategy implies, and have illustrated the strategies by reference to well-known systems or 'plans' for instruction. This diagram is only meant as a conceptual guide to the types of control strategies that might be employed,

Output measure	Control factor for output	Style of control	Typical control ∴ strategy	Examples of typical plans
Norm-referenced	Time	Prescriptive	Traditional classroom	Lecture course
		Democratic	Open classroom	Primary school integrated day
		Cybernetic	Traditional tutorial	Oxbridge
Norm- or criterion-referenced	Learner's needs	Prescriptive	Individually prescribed	Manager's individual development plan
		Democratic	Student-controlled	Resource-based learning
		Cybernetic	Adaptive tutorial	Project PLAN/CMI
Criterion-referenced	Mastery	Prescriptive	Pre-programmed	Keller Plan
		Democratic	Learning contract	Individually pro-grammed instruction
		Cybernetic	Adaptive programme	Computer-based learning

Figure 18.3 *Some typical control strategies and examples of their application*

or that are commonly employed. It is often necessary to use more than one control strategy in a given course, in order to deal adequately with different types of objectives. Nevertheless, there will usually be a principal control strategy, applied for the majority of the course units. This often reflects more the theoretical inclinations of the course designers (or of the examiners) than the particular characteristics of the course's content or objectives.

However, the instructional plans that one adopts should temper one's theoretical position with due regard to the nature of the particular learning problem being solved.

19. Evaluation

19.1 The evaluation process

Evaluation implies that one is seeking to assess the *value* of a certain activity or product of our system. As an instructional system is generally concerned with preparing people for the future, one should assess the value *in the future* of what the student has gained as a result of passing through our instructional system. In practice, evaluation often stops short and only assesses whether the immediate instructional objectives have been met. This is also important. If the learner has learned nothing on our course we cannot expect any effects in the future. But it is not the whole story.

Evaluation starts with the wider system

Thus our decisions concerning what to evaluate should take into consideration the wider system or client system in which our trainees will find themselves in the future. In the case of a vocational training course, this would be the organization (or the sector of industry) for which the trainee is being prepared. In the case of general education, the wider system is society itself.

The problem of evaluating educational systems

We have already noticed how much harder it is to assess the needs of 'society' (and of the learner as a part of this system), compared to the needs of a given organization. Thus, the evaluation of long-term effects of education is a difficult, and therefore often ignored, task.

We shall, however, attempt to map out a path which might be followed, however difficult and uncertain the results. First, let us select the basic route. As evaluation requires that measures should be taken, the sooner we are dealing with measurable goals, the easier will be our task. Let us therefore select the outputs/inputs route, treating education in a manner analogous to training. While realizing that many educators will disagree that education, in all its aspects, should be treated in this way, we can justify this approach by arguing that it may be better to start somewhere, and develop an approach which works for at least some parts of education. Then it may be easier to tackle the other parts by observing what it is about our model that does not work and modifying it accordingly. This would appear to be a better strategy than to continue discussing the evaluation of education in an abstract way without any model to guide us.

Applying the training model

Level 1 analysis looks at the job that the trainee will perform. In the case of education, one may postulate a notional job by describing the kinds of capabilities that the educated person should be able to demonstrate. However, the performance requirements of the job were looked at in the context of the wider system, where the job is performed and who uses the outputs of the job. Analysis of the wider system considered whether learning was necessary, or whether there were other causes of poor job performance that would require other types of solutions. This was done by the process of front-end analysis. One can imagine a similar form of analysis being applied to specific situations in society, in order to determine to what extent a person's schooling, however effective, could in fact equip him to cope with life. The 'deschooling' movement is attempting to perform just this sort of analysis (Illich 1971; Postman and Weingartner 1969).

There is no reason why one could not, in education as in training, seek to draw up an explicit contract which specifies to what extent the educational system can contribute to the solution of a given problem in society and on what other actions a total solution depends. An attempt to do this might lead to the specification of some measurable and realistic criteria for the long-term evaluation of the effects of education.

The limits of one's sphere of influence

One should acknowledge that, apart from the practical difficulties of defining and measuring the desired long-term changes, it is usually outside the terms of reference of the instructional designer to go so far into the design of the wider system. Even in the training context, the evaluation of long-term effects involves the production departments, finance and accounts, after sales service records and so on, all of which are normally outside the sphere of influence of the training manager, let alone the instructional designer.

The overall evaluation model

The model that we shall draw up here is, therefore, not always applicable in practice in all its stages or levels. However, it is important to have a complete model, even if in a particular project one applies only a part of it. One should, at least, consider in the analysis stages implications at least one step beyond the synthesis stages that one is briefed to carry out. Thus, if one is preparing course materials for a given lesson, one must study at least how this lesson fits into the overall course structure and objectives. If one is charged with designing the whole course, one should at least consider the post-instructional situations in which the participants might make use of the course content. If the educational or training system as a whole is being redesigned, the role of this system in the overall organizational or society system must be considered. (By 'consider', we mean apply the steps of problem definition and analysis as outlined in Parts 1 and 2.)

In Figure 19.1 we map out the overall model of the evaluation process, in the context of the overall instructional design process. This diagram illustrates very clearly the concept of various 'depths' of instructional design.

The depth at which one is working

One may, in given circumstances, be concerned only with level 1 analysis, design and evaluation. This may be the position of the administrator, whether training manager or headmaster. Instructional designers are more likely to be involved at least to level 2. This is the case of curriculum planners, training officers responsible for a given course or heads of department in a school. Teachers are involved in levels 2 and 3 in a formal way. They may take level 1 as given and apply existing materials without concerning themselves systematically with their evaluation. Finally, the instructional designer who develops course materials may receive most of the previous decisions already made. This would be the case of staff working in an audiovisual service unit of an institution, who are consulted by teachers on the preparation of specific transparencies or slide/sound presentations.

The purpose of this chapter

Here, we shall be concerned with the first and second levels of detail, levels 3 and 4 are considered in Volume 2 which deals with detailed instructional design. Before we consider specific methods for evaluation at levels 1 and 2, let us consider, in general, some of the philosophical positions and resultant strategies that may be applied to the evaluation of instructional systems.

We started this section by noting that evaluation was to do with assessing value. But why should we wish to do that? In the next section, two possible reasons are examined: to *prove* or to *improve*.

19.2 Evaluation strategies

The question of evaluation is closely interlinked with the question of control. Whereas our control strategy defines *how* we shall measure the results of our instructional system, our evaluation strategies define *what* we shall measure and *why*. These are decisions which must be taken early on in the instructional design process, as they influence the way that we should set about later stages. We have already seen how defining job performance standards and the ways in

The training context

which they are to be assessed helps us to define the instructional objectives (what is 'worth teaching') and separate these from performance aspects that can

Analysis process   The design process   The evaluation process

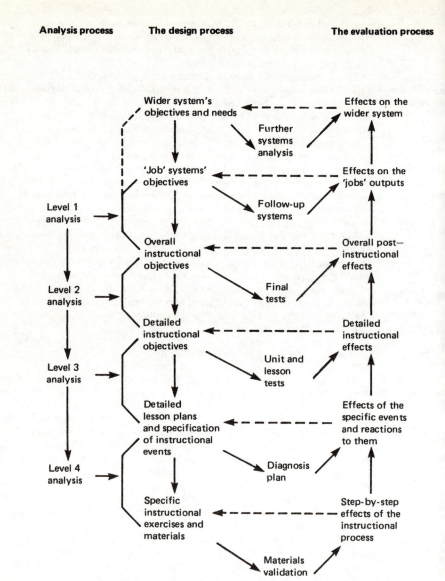

Figure 19.1 *The overall process of evaluation*

be developed through on-the-job supervision, through the provision of job aids, or through other non-training means. Thus job analysis, together with front-end analysis help us define with some precision both what we shall measure (by defining the final objectives in performance terms) and why (by relating these objectives directly to jobs after training).

The education context   Unfortunately, in the educational context, things are not nearly as clear-cut. There is no specific job that we can analyse to derive in an impersonal and unambiguous way the exact standards of performance on precisely defined tasks that should be applied as our evaluation criteria. Hence, as we have seen, controversy rages on all questions related to the specification of course objectives and the ways one should adopt to evaluate course outcomes. The approach adopted is always based on a blend of instructional theory, actual or supposed learner needs and practical expediency.

In Chapter 9 we summarized theoretical viewpoints concerning learning and the instructional process. We have attempted, in subsequent chapters, to combine some of these viewpoints to form a more comprehensive picture of the types of learning involved in most education and training systems. We have shown that most of the theoretical viewpoints have some part to play in the design of appropriate instruction but that none of them is the complete answer.

The need to define an evaluation strategy

The same applies to theoretical positions regarding evaluation. Often the rationale behind a course's evaluation scheme has not been made explicit. It has simply developed from tradition, and often an analysis of the evaluation scheme shows it to be quite inappropriate to the overall aims of the course. Thus, when designing or redesigning any instructional system, it is a good idea to consider the evaluation strategies to be adopted and to do so quite early on in the instructional design process.

Defining the outcomes of learning

The drive towards greater efficiency, relevance and accountability in traditional educational systems, produced by the rapid expansion of demand in the last few generations, has led many people to seek ways of defining more precisely the objectives of education. As we saw in Chapter 3, two routes have been followed:

1. The output/input route, which seeks to treat education systems as if they were training systems, by defining a master performer and an imaginary notional job, thus adapting the techniques of task analysis and job analysis to the educational context.
2. The input/output route, which seeks to be more precise and scientific in following the traditional paths of curriculum design, which start with a body of information (a subject) and through analysis of this information define the topics 'worth teaching' and define the activities in which the learner should engage in order to learn and to show that he has learned.

Indicators of learning are only a part of the evaluation strategy

Both routes eventually reach the same point, but in a different sequence. This point is the definition of precise and measurable performances which can be used as *indicators* that the desired learning has taken place. But this is not the whole story. We must now consider whether there are other aspects of the course design that need to be measured and evaluated. Let us begin by summarizing some basic ideas concerning evaluation.

19.3 Basic concepts in evaluation

Evaluating the outcomes of a course of instruction has three functions:

Why evaluate course outputs?

1. To quantify them, for the purposes of student certification or grading.
2. To measure and improve the effectiveness of the course (this is equivalent to quality control and product development in industry).
3. To test out some hypothesis about the course structure and processes which may give us some insights into the general problems of course design (the research function).

It has become fashionable to speak of:

Summative and formative evaluation

1. *Summative evaluation*, which *sums up* the results or outputs of a course. This normally takes place after the course is over and has no effect on the structure or processes of the course.
2. *Formative evaluation*, which measures the outputs specifically in order to change the *form* of the course to modify either its structure or the processes which go on. Formative evaluation takes place during the course as well as at the end of the course.

Feedback

In systems jargon the, formative evaluation is designed to produce feedback which modifies the course or the inputs to the course. Summative evaluation

What outputs can we evaluate, and how?

has no intention of producing such feedback.

Figure 19.2 lists, in very condensed form, some of the outputs which can be measured, together with suggestions of appropriate indicators and some reasonably valid instruments of measurement.

When studying this chart, the reader may well observe how often, in practice, totally inappropriate instruments of measurement are applied.

Effects of instruction	Indicators (outputs)	Instruments of measurement
Do teachers like course?	Teacher attitudes	Teacher questionnaires/report cards. Audience ratings (if use is governed by teacher's decision)
Do students like course?	Student attitudes (to course)	Student report cards/questionnaires, audience ratings/course drop-out (if use is governed by students' decision)
Are students influenced by course?	Changes in student attitudes (to subject or content)	Teachers' observations. Surveys of student attitudes
Are students motivated by course?	Voluntary student activity (reading, discussion, etc)	Teacher observations. 'Sales' (eg usage of certain library books)
Do students learn the course content?	Changes in student performance/capability	Performance tests

Figure 19.2 *Possible methods of evaluation*

Measuring the affective outcomes (reactions)

Although all the outcomes listed above are of importance, the one to which most attention is given is the last one — do students learn from the course? This is not because the other outcomes are undervalued. Indeed, great lip service is payed to motivating, interesting and developing attitudes. Less is done about formally evaluating these outcomes simply because it is more difficult.

1. It is more difficult to define precisely the indicators and measure which would be appropriate.
2. Only very little can be done during or immediately after a course to evaluate attitude changes. These generally require long-term follow-up which may be difficult or impossible to arrange.

Measuring the learning outcomes

The knowledge or the skills that students gain from a course are more capable of immediate assessment. Hence the emphasis in evaluation of courses has followed the easy route and has concentrated (perhaps too much) on testing the mastery of course content.

Moreover, it is easier to define the aims and objectives of a course in terms of what a student should know or should be able to perform after successful learning than in terms of what he should feel about it or how he should apply his new knowledge and skills in the outside world.

Tradition

Thus, formal education has not traditionally been based on a detailed analysis of the long-term objectives, leading to specification of short-term objectives and finally course content (as is the case with systematic vocational/industrial training) but rather has started from the selection of content, or disciplines, and the grafting on of short-term objectives (desired course outcomes) later. This process of selection of objectives was clearly influenced by the 'outside world' as the general aims of education are to prepare us for life. As the outside world is competitive and imperfect, it is hardly surprising that the educational system also grew to be competitive and necessarily imperfect and that the processes of evaluation were based on the premise that 'if you can survive and win at school, you'll probably survive and win in life'. This is an almost classical application of the simulation or role-playing technique of teaching, a technique in which the detailed content or events are of secondary importance as compared to the reproduction of the patterns and stresses of 'reality'.

Present change

However, the simulation of reality only remains the most efficient way of education as long as we do not come to terms with the reality. Once we analyse the real situation and identify key points we can improve the efficiency of the educational process by concentrating on these. We can insist that certain defined standards are reached in certain skills, as we now know that these are prerequisites for success in the real world. We are led to prescribe specific criteria for specific educational activities.

Criterion-referenced and norm-referenced testing

The traditional approach to evaluating courses has therefore been based on norm-referenced testing, the process of comparing the test scores of individual students. No effort to develop tests which cover *all* the course content is made, for a sample is sufficient to sort out the 'better' and 'poorer' students. Students are graded on the curve of normal distribution. Provided the tests are well-designed (appropriate, valid and statistically reliable), which is seldom, students who have learned more will score higher, but their score bears no relation to the total content of the course. The test may be referenced (a) to the immediate peer group (as is the case in most classroom tests) or (b) to a distant peer group (as is the case in the UK with GCE examinations where all scores are adjusted to the national norm).

The current trend is towards criterion-referenced testing, whereby the individual student's performance is compared with a predetermined standard. Students are not compared with each other but receive usually only a pass/fail grade depending in whether their performance is up to a standard or, where their progress towards the criterion can be *reliably* measured, a percentage score.

Two main arguments are advanced for criterion-referencing:

1. It is fairer to the students who should know the criterion they are aiming to achieve and need not compete in stressful and poorly defined situations against each other.
2. It is fairer to the 'course', in that the criteria define the aims and objectives of the course. The course design may be more easily analysed and revised when criteria are typically not being achieved, but on the other hand no one can blame the course for not achieving objectives that were not planned for in the first place.

Implications of the criterion-referenced approach

The criterion-referenced approach is more difficult to implement and certain considerations must be borne in mind:

1. In order to avoid bias creeping in later and standards being adjusted, it is necessary to establish the criteria before running the course, indeed before getting too far involved in course development. You design the tests *before* the lessons. The evaluation scheme is an early stage in course development.
2. This implies that teaching for an examination becomes the normal and desired procedure rather than the frowned on but generally unavoidable pressure in the current educational system.
3. But there is nothing wrong with this examination oriented approach provided that the criteria in the examination are relevant to the needs of the student/his employers/society at large.
4. The criteria must, therefore, be developed from a much closer and deeper analysis of the course's aims and objectives than is usually the case.
5. As the criteria are measures of some observable student activity, it is

necessary to specify the detailed objectives of the course in terms of performance or behaviour. If this proves impossible or undesirable, criterion-referenced testing is by definition, impossible.

6. There is, therefore, the need to change the whole process of course development, away from a discipline-based or content-based process to one which is based on first defining the course outputs in measurable terms.

7. A change in the way that courses are run is necessary. As there is usually a hierarchical structure between the various elements of a course, one criterion being a prerequisite for study towards another, students should master the first criterion completely before passing to further study. This would imply modular courses, individually independent study rates, and a near total mastery of all course objectives, stage by stage.

This is the mastery learning model currently very popular among US educators at all levels, including higher education where it is the philosophical basis of the Keller Plan, the Postlethwaite Audio Tutorial System and various other innovatory schemes.

Summary: Combining the two approaches

As is usually the case, the truth lies somewhere in the middle. We need to *select* outstanding individuals for some purposes (norm-referenced) whilst teaching *most* individuals to an acceptable basic standard. The two needs exist together. Who would wish to undergo an operation under the knife of the year's top PhD in surgical research if he had failed to reach complete mastery in any one basic surgery skill — it may be the one he needs today.

Figure 19.3 may help to integrate the concepts discussed and to stimulate thought over the mix of evaluation strategies appropriate for a given course.

	Formative evaluation	Summative evaluation
Criterion-referenced procedures	Course improvement. Diagnostic testing for student's learning problems	Testing mastery of the objectives. Certification
Norm-referenced procedures	Possibly for streaming (doubtful)	Grading against the national average Selection (possibly)

Figure 19.3 *Combining criterion- and norm-referenced methods*

19.4 Decisions at level 1

At level 1 we are treating the course as a 'black box' which is expected to produce specified outputs when functioning correctly. These outputs are the instructional objectives defined through our level 1 analysis.

Evaluation instruments prepared at level 1

The information we have so far is sufficient to enable us to prepare the final test. We may also go one step further up the design and evaluation process and consider how we will be able to evaluate the long-term changes in post-instructional performance.

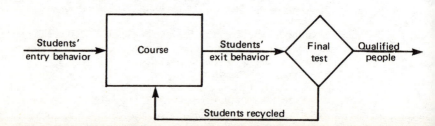

Figure 19.4 *Evaluating course objectives at level 1*

These measures are sufficient to enable us to make a judgement regarding the overall effectiveness of the course, but are not detailed enough to enable us to make judgements concerning exactly what parts of the course are as efficient as they might be and what parts should yet be improved. Thus, the results of these measures are more likely to be used for *summative* purposes than for formative purposes.

Used for summative evaluation

One may use the results to prepare a summative report to our client or our administrative bosses, in order to prove that the course is fulfilling its objectives, or to prove that further development (requiring more time and greater resources) is needed.

Used for control purposes

The results may also be used to certify the students as qualified, or not qualified, to perform a certain task or job. One may also identify which students are ready to pass out of the system, and which should be recycled through certain parts of the system. The results may, therefore, be used as part of the overall control strategy.

All the above uses require the test results to be treated in a criterion-referenced manner, comparing the individual's performance to a predetermined standard, or establishing the proportion of the group who have reached this standard.

Used for grading and selection

The results may, however, also be used to grade the students on a scale of attainment. Their position on this scale might then be used for the purposes of selecting a smaller group for further training or for a specific job. In this case, the results would have to be treated in a norm-referenced manner, by mapping out the frequency distribution of all the students' scores and then possibly applying correction factors to the scores in order to make the distribution approximate to a Gaussian curve.

The only *formative* value of the final tests, by themselves, is to indicate (from an analysis of the error patterns) that the instructional system needs to be improved, and, if the error patterns indicate particular peaks on specific questions, roughly which parts of the system should be looked at more closely.

Test only the overall objectives

As the functions of final evaluation are principally summative it is quite in order to test only a representative sample of the objectives that are taught during the whole course. Normally, these would be the overall, or job, objectives, as these generally require the application of many of the intermediate objectives in combination. One should attempt to look for test items which integrate the maximum number of lower level objectives. As an example, the division of 87 by 7 is a better test of long division than the division of 77 by 7. The second example does not test many of the intermediate steps of the procedure.

Also, one seldom needs to test for knowledge separately, if the final objective requires the performance of a task in which the knowledge is used in order to perform. The act of performing the task correctly proves that the necessary prerequisite knowledge is indeed known. However, a failure to perform the task correctly does not indicate whether the failure was due to lack of knowledge, or lack of other skill elements necessary to apply the knowledge effectively in practice.

We could extend the testing procedure by asking subsidiary questions designed to diagnose the cause of failure to perform. However, this will probably need a somewhat more detailed analysis of the objectives to decide exactly what subsidiary questions should be asked. Moreover, if all objectives are treated in this detailed manner in the final test instrument, the testing procedure will become too long and bulky.

19.5 Decisions at level 2

Test the detailed objectives

It is best to leave the more detailed testing of all the intermediate objectives to the individual unit and lesson tests. This spreads out the load on the student and also supplies evaluation data at a time when something can be done about any observed weaknesses in the instructional process. As the course of instruction progresses, lesson by lesson and course unit by unit, the individual lesson tests supply detailed information on the effectiveness of the process. The teacher can, if he has the time and resources, repeat any lessons that did not achieve reasonable standards of efficiency, modifying and improving them in the light of the evaluation data collected.

In some control systems, this is an obligatory aspect (as in the mastery model which attempts to ensure that every learner achieves complete mastery of one unit before proceeding to the next). In other control systems, where time is a controlling factor, the teacher cannot spend an unlimited amount of time in ensuring that all students reach mastery. However, he can aim at a reasonable standard of performance from most students and certainly not proceed to new material if essential prerequisite learning has not been achieved by the majority of the students.

Used for formative evaluation
The actions described above are all *formative*. The teacher compares performance against a standard, objective by objective, step by step. Any weaknesses in the instructional process are corrected on line so that the students actually studying the course at the moment benefit from improvements made as a result of their own performance on detailed objective tests.

On line improvements
This on line formative action, taken by the teacher, instils a certain element of *adaptiveness* in the system. The system does not, however, become fully adaptive (cybernetic) unless it manages to adapt to each individual student's learning needs and problems. This is not very easy to achieve in the classroom, where the teacher tends to adapt the instructional process to suit the average student in the group.

Long-term improvements
There is a further set of formative decisions that the teacher, or the instructional designer in this case, can take on the basis of level 2 evaluation data. He can modify the design of certain parts of the system for the future. He can revise lesson plans, select different or more examples, rewrite materials, redraw visuals, etc.

This formative activity may be carried out later, after the present students have passed through the system. The benefits of this revision will be felt by future groups of students.

General improvements in the design process
Finally, the experience of evaluation and revision of one system may give the designer insights into the general principles of instructional system design. He may develop better personal procedures or even better general principles that can be applied by other designers in other courses.

Thus the results of evaluation may have both a development and a research application. In both these applications the results must be treated in a criterion-referenced manner.

19.6 Specific evaluation techniques

At the beginning of this chapter, we developed an overall model of the evaluation process as part of the general instructional design process. At the highest level in this model, we have the wider system. In the training context, this is the organization in which the job (for which training is being designed) is performed. In the education context, the wider system is society itself.

The evaluation of wider system effects is difficult
The highest level of evaluation involves examining the effects of our training or educational system on this wider system, in the light of the objectives and needs of this system as they are understood. Even in the training context, this is not an easy thing to do, although progressive companies do attempt to perform cost-effectiveness evaluations of their overall training effort. In the educational context, where not all benefits are measurable in terms of cost and where current techniques of control do not allow many things to be measured in any way at all, the difficulties are much greater.

When considering not a total educational or training system, but only the contribution of one particular instructional course, it becomes meaningless to attempt to evaluate the overall wider system effects in a systematic manner. Only occasionally are some effects so marked as to stand out.

The other levels are much easier

We shall therefore concentrate on listing some of the techniques most useful at the level of designing:

☐ Follow-up systems to evaluate long-term effects on the job, or in the notional job in society (Map 19.1)

☐ Post-instructional systems to evaluate the overall learning from the course, in a summative manner (Map 19.2)

☐ Detailed formative evaluation systems (Maps 19.3 and 19.4).

Map 19.1 *Long-term follow-up techniques*

Introduction	In follow-up, it is never possible to say for sure whether the measured improvements are due entirely (or even in part) to the learning that has occurred. There are usually other factors at play that must, if possible, be controlled or allowed for in the assessment of effects. The evaluation of follow-up data must therefore be done carefully. Usually there is need for 'before' and 'after' data in situations where all other factors that may influence job performance have been kept from changing. This is easier said than done. However, many viable techniques do exist.	
Techniques for measuring long-term performance changes	One may obtain information about past and present performance levels by three main routes: ☐ Direct observation (of the performers) ☐ Indirect measures (of the effects of the performance) ☐ Secondary measures (by asking someone else). Some practical techniques that may be used, both in the educational and training contexts, are given below.	
	Training context	Educational context
Direct measurement techniques	Job performance evaluation system, by regular formal reports from supervisor. Observer diary, kept by an expert, over a given period, recording changes in post-training performance. Critical incident methods: an analysis of how the trainee deals with exceptional job situations.	As there is no formal job, no formal system of reporting is possible. A sample of past students may be observed and a diary kept. A sophisticated example is Project 'TALENT'. Very effective in the educational context. Does schooling contribute to success/happiness?
Indirect measures of effects	Changes in productivity, error rates, speed or quality of work, rates of wasteage/scrap, human relations, turnover.	Changes in standard of living, quality of life, social awareness, participation in government.
Secondary information	Interviews of performers. Questionnaires. Diaries kept by the performers. Interviews of superiors.	All the sociological techniques of interviews and questionnaires used to investigate people's life-styles.
Techniques for measuring long-term reactions	Direct observations of attitude to the job. Indirect measures of job changes, drop-out rates, etc. Secondary information through attitude questionnaires or interviews, on reasons for job change.	Direct observations of voluntary continuing education efforts. Indirect measures of demand for education. Secondary information through questionnaires and interviews.

Map 19.2 *Post-instruction techniques*

Techniques for the evaluation of skilled performance	We may use our schema of skill categories to list some of the more useful techniques.	
	Reproductive skills	Productive skills
— cognitive skills	Problems of a *familiar* type to be solved to predetermined standards of accuracy, speed, etc (eg long division drills) (closed, objective methods)	Problems of *unfamiliar* type to be solved, often with no unique solution. Evaluation of the process as well as the solution (open ended methods)
— psychomotor skills	Performance tests on real or simulated task. Criteria of speed, accuracy, quality applied objectively (eg typing drills, machine operation skills)	Productive tasks which require planning of a strategy. Evaluation of result and of planning process by observation and discussion
— reactive skills	Directly, by objective counts of 'approach' or 'avoidance' behaviours. Indirectly by attitude questionnaires, etc (see Mager 1968 for approach/avoidance)	Directly through observing people's value systems in action, outside school. Indirectly through analysis of positions taken during debates on key issues and the arguments used
— interactive skills	Directly, by counts of frequency of 'good' habits, manners, etc, being displayed under voluntary conditions	Observation of complex interactive skills under real or simulated social conditions, followed by evaluation debriefings to examine the planning element
Techniques for the evaluation of knowledge	At the post-instructional stage, the separate evaluation of knowledge is only necessary if the objectives are purely to acquire knowledge (ie we are dealing with an information problem). In the case of performance problems, the necessary knowledge is indirectly tested by the skills testing, as above. If necessary, knowledge may be tested as follows:	
— recognition	Multiple-choice questions demanding identification of the correct fact, definition, example, etc	
— recall	Direct open-ended questions, phrased so as to elicit one unique answer	
— comprehension	Multiple-choice questions demanding the identification of errors, correct/incorrect statements, conclusions or classifications. Matching lists of concepts and examples, rules and applications, steps and sequence, etc Open ended essay questions requesting explanations, restatement in own words, examples, etc	

Map 19.3 *Detailed evaluation of skilled performance*

Introduction	Remembering that the principal function of evaluation *during* the instructional process is to *improve* the instruction. The evaluation techniques and instruments must be sufficiently sensitive to indicate exactly what parts of the instructional plan are working and what parts need to be improved. We may no longer test for prerequisite knowledge indirectly by testing its application in skilled performance. We need to have instruments which will identify what aspect of the skilled performance is poorly mastered.
Use of the skill cycle	We may employ our basic skills cycle to identify the questions we should be asking in the detailed evaluation of a skill.
Perception tests — cognitive skills	Does the learner understand the problem? Can he restate it/put it into symbolic form/identify the unknown quantity that he should seek/recognize when it has been solved/recognize degrees of difficulty in the problem?
— psychomotor skills	Can the learner perceive the external signals that guide the skilled activity? Can he discriminate between relevant and irrelevant information? Does he have the requisite level of perceptual acuity?
— reactive skills	Does the learner attend to external events and show an interest in them? Is he sensitive to events?
— interactive skills	Does the learner attend to the reactions of others and is he sensitive to their feelings?
Prerequisite tests — all skill categories	Tests of the requisite knowledge: the procedures and the principles that must be stored (see Map 19.4 for more detail).
Strategy tests — productive skills	Tests of the requisite ability to analyse relevant problems, generate alternative solution strategies and pre-evaluate them by thinking through at a reflective level (open ended verbal tests).
Performance tests — cognitive skills	Can the learner put it all together in order to perform the cognitive task to required standards of accuracy, speed, long-term productivity, etc.
— psychomotor skills	Can the learner perform and continue performing at required productivity, accuracy and quality standards?
— reactive skills	Does the learner actively respond in appropriate manner at all opportunities? Does he seek opportunities, practise his values and life skills?
— interactive skills	Does the learner actually respond to others in the expected manner? Does he seek to interact effectively and frequently? Does he seek to improve his skills?
Observation	Naturally, the above suggestions are very general. Every skill requires its own set of specifications.

Map 19.4 *Detailed evaluation of the knowledge content*

Introduction	The comments made on Map 19.2 regarding the evaluation of knowledge referred only to the type of testing instruments that may be used for the testing of knowledge. After level 2 analysis, we have a more detailed picture of the knowledge to be taught. We can classify the items of knowledge into the four basic categories of *facts, concepts, procedures* and *principles.* Furthermore, we can build up a sequence, or hierarchy, for the learning of this knowledge. Certain facts must first be learned in order to be linked together into procedures. Certain concepts must first be learned in order to enable the learning of further more complex concepts and to later be linked with other concepts in order to form rules, rule sets and finally complex problem-solving strategies. The *knowledge structure* that we uncover helps us to determine the sequence of lessons in our course and the content of each lesson.
	Thus, for each lesson, we are in a position to develop appropriate tests.
Questions for various types of knowledge	The table below suggests typical questions that should be asked at the lesson level, for each of the four main categories of knowledge.

	For *recall*, ask student to:	For *comprehension*, ask student to:
Facts — verbal — concrete	State the facts Recognize the fact	Restate in own words Explain its significance
Concepts — concrete — defined	Recognize examples State definition	Classify examples and non-examples Classify examples and non-examples
Procedures	State the steps in correct sequence	Explain the key points which govern effective performance
Principles	State the rule or set of rules	Give an example of their application. State if they apply to a given example

Observations (1)	Only recall and comprehension are included as the aspects of knowledge that are worth testing by direct questioning. Recognition is a somewhat simpler behaviour than recall. It may be tested as a step towards the testing of unaided recall, but, at the end of a lesson, or unit of instruction essential knowledge at least should be recallable. Testing for comprehension is an attempt to ensure that the knowledge is stored in an efficient way, related to other knowledge as a meaningful schema.
(2)	The other categories of Bloom's taxonomy are not used, as *application* of knowledge is tested via the performance of *all skills* and the *creation* of new knowledge (through analysis, synthesis and evaluation) is tested through evaluation of *productive skills.*

20. Why Projects Fail

20.1 Stages in implementing the plan

The design
stages lead
to a plan

We have now reached the stage of having taken strategic decisions on most of the aspects of our proposed course of instruction. We have defined our overall objectives and policy (level 1 decisions), and have outlined course sequence, structure of the curriculum, principal methods to be employed, group size and structure for various sections of the course, media to be employed in each section, and control and evaluation strategies. All these are level 2 decisions, which combine to form our *instructional plan*.

Key points
for
approval by
management

This plan would now need to be approved by our client or employer, before we proceed to its realization. This is the second point at which approval should be sought from the client. The first was at the end of the problem analysis stage, when a first proposal was drawn up, stating that some instruction appears necessary, and detailing the overall objectives of this instruction, the value of achieving these objectives, and the estimated cost of developing and implementing the instructional system. Now the instructional system is planned in much greater detail and we have much more information to report. We have much closer cost and time estimates, much clearer ideas of the human and material resources required for development and implementation, an idea of the methods that will be employed and whether they are novel or well-known to existing staff, an idea of the disruption that will be caused to existing systems by the new system that we are about to develop, and so on. All these aspects of the new system may be unexpected by the management, and so they should be justified, explained and approved, or later, if problems occur, they may be used as reasons for criticism or excuse.

The
development
stages lead
to a pilot
project

Once the plan is approved, we pass to the development or production stages, which will eventually lead to a prototype instruction system, ready to be implemented in a *pilot project*. These stages would normally include further design at level 3 (lesson plans and exercises) and/or level 4 (specially prepared instructional materials), followed by the production and testing of individual materials, before assembly of a prototype of the full instructional system.

The pilot project would normally take the form of one or more carefully controlled test runs of the course, with close attention being paid to all effects that appear during the implementation and use of the system.

These effects would normally include the intended and expected learning effects, for which special measuring instruments will no doubt have been prepared, and also unexpected, unplanned effects, both in terms of student reaction and operational problems. These unplanned effects must also be monitored and taken account of in the subsequent evaluation of the pilot project and revision of the prototype system.

System is
approved for
dissemination

The revised system may need to be further tested under pilot conditions, or, if few serious revisions were required, may be deemed to be ready for large-scale dissemination and use. Once again, the formal approval of management should be sought at this stage.

Dissemination
stages lead to
a full-scale
project

Once the system is approved for dissemination, we pass to what may be termed the *full-scale project* stage. This is the stage in which the instructional system is used in the way in which we originally envisaged, under the normal field conditions and with no more supervisory or management attention than was planned in the first place. Some measure of special evaluation activity goes on for some time, in order to make certain that no problems arise under the full-scale field conditions that were not encountered in the pilot project stage. Almost inevitably some unexpected problems do occur at this stage, often a result of the 'scale effect'.

20.2 Scale effect

Concept of scale effect

Many large-scale applications of educational technology seem to run into problems, either when (a) an originally successful small-scale (micro) project grows in size or is 'multiplied' (applied in many institutions), or (b) a project is planned as a large-scale (macro) project from the start, but the techniques that it uses have been developed and tried out mainly at the micro level. Problems may occur at three stages:

1. Training system and materials development (the 'manufacturing' stage).
2. Implementation and dissemination of the system (the 'distribution' stage).
3. Long-term operation of the system (the 'utilization' stage).

Very few guidelines exist on how to predict and avoid problems in macro projects, although many retrospective analyses of such problems exist.

John Cowan (1975) described the concept of scale effect in relation to the problems appearing during the growth of a resources centre. Elsewhere (Romiszowski 1978) Cowan's findings have been summarized as a matrix relating specific growth factors to the problems that they created (see Figure 20.1).

Key problems when the factor was:	Factors which created problems			
	1. Number of students	2. Frequency of use of centre	3. Quantity and variety of materials	4. Number of staff in centre
Small	Justify existence and costs of centre	Part-time staffing. Limited budget	Integrating self-instruction with traditional courses	Need for jacks of all trades
Medium	Loss of personal contact	Organizing; utilization. Queuing problems	Storage and retrieval	Need for specialist and teamwork 'team-building'
Large	Predicting demand. Losses and damage	Loss of flexible study hours	Need to decentralize. 'Satellite departments'	Personnel: — training — motivation — control

Figure 20.1 *Matrix of problems encountered in a resource centre, owing to the scale effect (adapted from Cowan 1975)*

Scale effect in instructional systems

During a recent conference, the author had the opportunity to investigate, together with 30 other instructional designers and educational technologists, how the scale effect seems to show itself when instructional systems grow in size (Romiszowski 1979a).

Three groups were formed, to consider separately the problems of:

1. Instructional system design and development.
2. Implementation of instructional systems.
3. Long-term management of instructional systems.

Size bands were defined for each group as shown in Figure 20.2.

	Group (1) criterion	**Group (2) criterion**	**Group (3) criterion**
	Number of instructional designers on the project	Number of 'client' institutions in the project	Number of students ('consumers') per year using the instructional system
Small project	1 to 5	1 to 5	about 100
Medium project	10 to 20	10 to 20	about 1000
Large project	about 50	about 50	about 5000

Figure 20.2 *Definition of size bands*

Through the use of brainstorming techniques each group attempted to list the key problems for the project manager in each of the size bands. The ideas were then brought together and complimented or criticized in large group discussion.

Each group also suggested some types of problems that exist in projects of any scale but tend to grow as the size of project. The main types of problems mentioned are summarized in Figure 20.3.

Key problems when the project is:	**Stages in which problems are encountered**		
	(1) Instructional design/ production stages	**(2) Implementation/ dissemination stages**	**(3) Long-term management and control**
Small	Promoting a creative approach Adapting project to existing skills	Availability of resources Personnel changes and personalities	Integration within the institution Performing long-term evaluation
Medium	Standardizing the language and documents Scheduling time and budgeting	Creating 'receptive' environment Controlling 'drift' in the system	Maintaining individualization Staff development, control, delegation
Large	Coordination of several teams Task scheduling and teamwork Planning regular validation/learning opportunities (for the designers)	Support of the 'supra-system' Ensuring long-term resources Controlling waste of resources/time Ensuring the system is 'self-correcting'	Management information systems that work Support-staff requirements Student opinions, objectives, welfare Systematic procedures of project management
Factors which create problems in projects of any size but which increase as the project grows	Changes in the team or in the team management Duration of the design stages and continuity in time Sheer quantity of materials to be produced	Training of the teachers/monitors Extent of centralized control Maintenance of interest/ momentum Ensuring adequate installation budget	Overcoming tendencies towards inertia Establishing effective command-chains Predicting and defining future changes in system Ensuring adequate running resources

Figure 20.3 *Matrix of problems encountered in instructional system development/use (drawn up by the participants in the workshop)*

The following information maps offer a refinement of the model developed by the author earlier (Romiszowski 1979b).

Map 20.1 *The principal stages of an instructional design and development project*

Introduction	Any project that is worth carrying through should produce results, that is, it should solve a problem, to convert 'what is' into 'what should be'.

The three main stages of a project	To achieve this the project passes through three principal stages:
	
	1. *Design stage:* proposals, objectives, methods, content, etc leading to a *plan*.
	2. *Development stage:* detailed design, production and validation of materials, development of implementation and management systems, etc leading to a *pilot project*.
	3. *Dissemination stage:* application of the tested system on a large scale in many institutions, building up to the *full-scale project*. 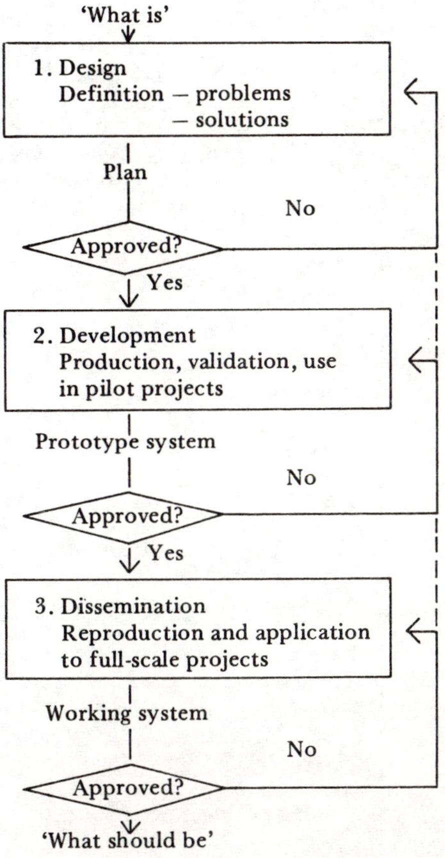
	
	'What is'
	
	1. Design
	   Definition — problems
	   — solutions
	
	Plan
	
	Approved? No
	  ↓ Yes
	
	2. Development
	   Production, validation, use in pilot projects
	
	Prototype system
	
	Approved? No
	  ↓ Yes
	
	3. Dissemination
	   Reproduction and application to full-scale projects
	
	Working system
	
	Approved? No
	  ↓
	'What should be'

Comment	Each stage should have its own evaluation, approval and feedback provision, as shown above.

Map 20.2 *The main sub-systems of the development stage*

Introduction	Each of the principal stages may be regarded as a system made up of a series of *essential* sub-systems. If any one of these essential sub-systems functions badly, the system as a whole is likely to fail.
The instructional development stage	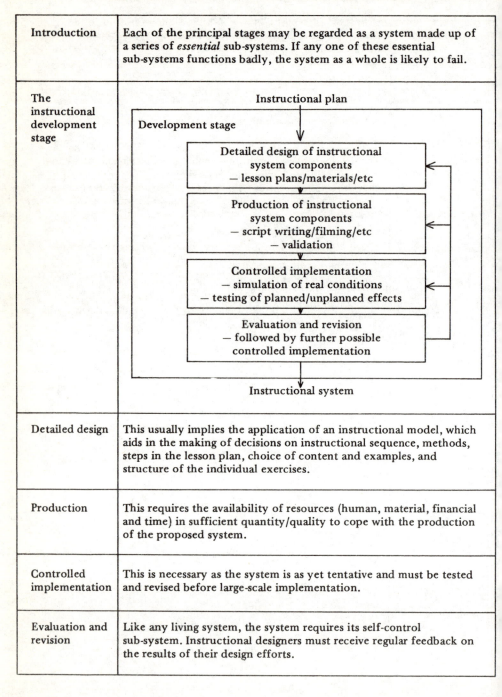
Detailed design	This usually implies the application of an instructional model, which aids in the making of decisions on instructional sequence, methods, steps in the lesson plan, choice of content and examples, and structure of the individual exercises.
Production	This requires the availability of resources (human, material, financial and time) in sufficient quantity/quality to cope with the production of the proposed system.
Controlled implementation	This is necessary as the system is as yet tentative and must be tested and revised before large-scale implementation.
Evaluation and revision	Like any living system, the system requires its self-control sub-system. Instructional designers must receive regular feedback on the results of their design efforts.

Map 20.3 *Sources of failure in the 'detailed design' sub-system*

The need for an instructional design model	The detailed design sub-system develops, and indeed often originates, the lesson plans, reading assignments, tests, media, materials and exercises, etc that do much of the instructing. If the design of these system components is not based on a clear instructional design model, it is difficult for instructional designers to check their work, learn from their successes and failures, communicate to other designers and learn from others.
Sources of failure 1. Lack of a defined model	The designers follow traditions, including objectives, content and methods, which are commonly applied in similar courses, without checking the real needs of the specific problem they are trying to solve. If they do not succeed, they just prescribe more of the same instructional medicine applying the same techniques for any situation.
— examples (a) (b) (c)	The traditional belief that any performance problem can be solved through training, or any behavioural deficiency needs a course. The traditional belief that there is no substitute for the 'personal contact' between teacher and pupil. The vogue for programmed instruction, ETV, Keller Plan, etc.
2. Use of the wrong model	Not all learning problems can be solved by applying the same instructional model. Some models apply to only certain categories of learning problems, or to only certain steps in the total instructional process.
— examples (a) (b) (c)	The behaviourist model of Skinner is excellent for teaching some reflexive or reproductive skills, but is inadequate for higher level productive skills and for knowledge. Bloom's taxonomy was developed solely to assist in the preparation of tests for subject-based curricula, but has been applied as an instructional model, even in the (inappropriate) training context. The use of a model imported without adaptation to allow for cultural differences, different levels of sophistication, or different data.
3. Lack of experience in using the model	The model may be adequate, but the designers lack skill and experience in its application. They go through the motions, but without understanding or creativity.
— examples (a) (b)	Task analysis forms, duly filled in with useless information. Long lists of objectives that bear no relation to subsequent lesson exercises.

Map 20.4 *Sources of failure in the 'production' sub-system*

Production requires adequate inputs	As any other production system, the production of instructional system components requires specific quantities and qualities of inputs: resources (human, material and financial) and of time. Failure to provide and maintain these inputs will lead to failure of the sub-system.
Sources of failure 1. Human resources	Both the quality and the quantity of production staff is critical. *Quantity* is related inversely to the time at our disposal. One should budget in terms of 'man-months' for most production tasks. *Quality* depends in part on the previous detailed design phase. The specification of sophisticated media, such as television, raises the need for quality in the production staff and calls for specialist staff. More ambitious objectives may call for more creative producers.
— examples	(a) Many instructional design projects have failed principally for lack of adequate simple support staff (eg typists who can lay out a page, artists who can think in terms of learning rather than decoration, etc). (b) A resource frequently overlooked, is the very necessary sample of the target population, for validation purposes.
2. Material resources	Lack of material resources, equipment, physical space, may also upset the progress of an instructional design project.
— examples	(a) Small, or badly organized/ventilated/lighted working space. (b) Working conditions that impede creative activity (eg that are noisy, distracting, have too rigid an organization, etc). (c) Lack of access to trainees and their working environment for the purposes of task analysis, testing, evaluation, etc. (d) Lack of basic equipment, or poor maintenance, materials, etc. (e) Lack of adequate control over externally bought in support services (eg printing, photography, recording, etc).
3. Time	Although one can usually compensate insufficient human resources by extending the project time, one can not always reduce time by increasing resources. Many other factors combine to set a minimum project time.
— examples	(a) Time required for outside support services that are not under the control of the project management. (b) Available times for subject specialists or target population samples. (c) Waiting time for postal or other delays.
4. Money	Clearly the provision of all other necessary resources, even if correctly predicted and theoretically available, ultimately depends on adequate financial resources.

Map 20.5 *Sources of failure in the 'controlled implementation' sub-system*

Experimental try-out: the most important of the developmental phases	Probably the most common fault in this sub-system is the absence of control. Many projects that are launched under the educational technology banner, do not deserve to be so-called, as they break the cardinal rule of validating and developmentally testing the system *before* large-scale implementation. Any technological project needs to be systematically evaluated throughout the developmental stages for three reasons: 1. To improve the results of the project Development 2. To improve the performance of the design team functions 3. To improve and contribute to the growth Research of the technology. function But even when a controlled experimental try-out is organized, other sources of failure may appear.
Sources of failure 1. The sample of the target population — examples (a) (b)	It is not always easy to obtain an appropriate sample of the target population at the time when validation and developmental testing must be carried out. Sometimes one is led to simulate the target population by using other available persons whose characteristics (relevant to the learning task) approximate to those of the real target population. Sometimes however this produces distorted results. The use of a group of schoolchildren to stand in for adult learners has often produced most misleading, non-transferrable results. The use of the faster students in an individualized course to spearhead the validation of further modules as they are produced, gives a non-representative sample and can demotivate and even alienate the 'high flyers'.
2. The measuring instruments — examples (a) (b)	It is not always easy to match the test instruments to the instructional objectives. This may be due to a design error or to real practical difficulties. A common type of error is inversion, for example, asking the learner to list the symptoms of given failure, instead of identifying the type of failure, from a given set of symptoms. Mass media such as television are often evaluated by mis-matched instruments, (eg teachers' reactions rather than students' learning, written verbal tests of visual and aural learning, etc).
3. Artificial conditions	It is not always easy to evaluate in the real-life situation. The task may seem lacking in reality. Also the students know that they are participating in an experiment and this affects their performance.

Map 20.6 *Sources of failure in the 'evaluation and revision' sub-system*

Formative evaluation	The main function of any evaluation performed in the development stage is *formative*: that is to *improve* the system or its components, rather than to *prove* anything.
Sources of failure 1. Little/no validity in the results — examples	If controlled implementation is poorly planned, or poorly controlled, there is a possibility that the wrong data will be collected, or that the data will be affected by spurious, uncontrolled and unknown effects, diminishing the reliability of any subsequent decisions. (a) Testing out a programmed text in conditions that do not control whether learners respond before or after verifying the correct response. (b) Testing a given sequence in a manner that does not distinguish whether a given difficulty exhibited by a learner is due to the actual material being presented, or to deficiencies in prior learning.
2. Poor interpretation of the results — example	Results of doubtful validity make the process of interpretation and diagnosis of weaknesses in the system, very difficult. A poor or non-existent instructional model makes matters worse, particularly in terms of deciding on remedial actions. It is necessary to be able to discriminate difficulties caused by inability to attend, or generalize, a lack of prerequisite learning, inability to solve problems, etc.
3. Lack of resources to make necessary revisions — example	Many projects suffer the problem of an insufficiency of budgeted resources for the implementation of necessary revisions, indicated by the developmental evaluation phase. Revisions are left to some future date, but, unfortunately, the people most closely concerned with the planning and design stages have often left the project by then. This renders revisions more difficult and throws away the self-instructional effect of feedback of results to the original designer. It is well to remember that professional producers of self-instructional (programmed) materials used to quote between 50 and 100 design/development hours for each student hour of material and about half of that time was budgeted for the phases of controlled implementation, evaluation and revision.
4. 'Selling the system'	Sometimes, political or commercial pressures lead designers to feel the need to justify their work, at any cost. This may lead to distortion in the validation procedures, in an attempt to hide any weaknesses. The aim changes from 'improve the system' to 'sell the system'.

Map 20.7 *The main sub-systems of the dissemination stage*

Introduction	Many instructional design projects that pass successfully through a stage of small-scale implementation (the pilot project) then fail at the stage of large-scale implementation (the full-scale project). New and often unexpected problems appear. Many of these could however be predicted. On the following maps we shall examine some of the sources of failure.
The main sub-systems of the dissemination stage	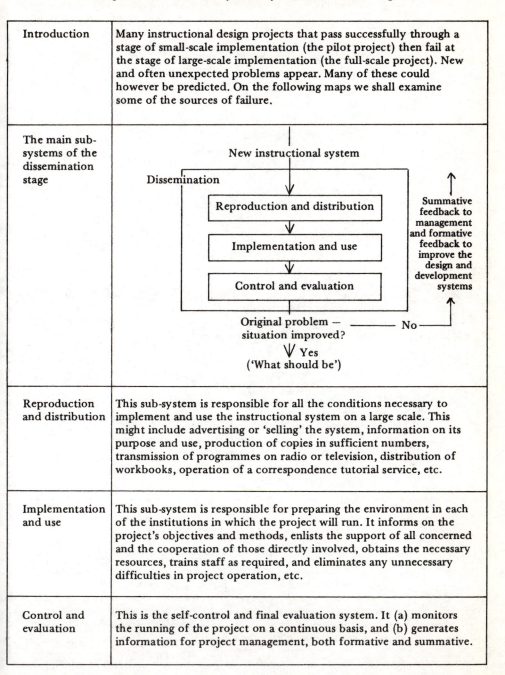
Reproduction and distribution	This sub-system is responsible for all the conditions necessary to implement and use the instructional system on a large scale. This might include advertising or 'selling' the system, information on its purpose and use, production of copies in sufficient numbers, transmission of programmes on radio or television, distribution of workbooks, operation of a correspondence tutorial service, etc.
Implementation and use	This sub-system is responsible for preparing the environment in each of the institutions in which the project will run. It informs on the project's objectives and methods, enlists the support of all concerned and the cooperation of those directly involved, obtains the necessary resources, trains staff as required, and eliminates any unnecessary difficulties in project operation, etc.
Control and evaluation	This is the self-control and final evaluation system. It (a) monitors the running of the project on a continuous basis, and (b) generates information for project management, both formative and summative.

Map 20.8 *Sources of failure in the 'reproduction/distribution' sub-system*

1. The lines of communication	Dissemination requires efficient lines of communication, both for the spreading of information to popularize the project and for the maintenance of contact during the life of the project (particularly in distance education projects). Often, projects fail due to weakness in their lines of communication.
— examples	(a) Radio or television projects with a weak signal distribution, giving poor reception, noise, or frequent breakdowns. (b) Correspondence courses with an excessive turnround time for letters, due either to postal delays or to bad organization at the headquarters of the school. (c) Lack of a planned communication system in the project. Institutions do not communicate, literature is circulated irregularly, nobody is responsible for public relations on behalf of the project. (d) Lack of an effective information feedback system to designers, developers and implementers, designed to ensure the maintenance and improvement of personal performance.
2. Scale effect	The scale effect was mentioned at length earlier. It often appears when a project passes from a micro scale of implementation to a macro scale. New and often quite unexpected problems appear as the project grows (see also Figure 20.1).
— examples	(a) Difficulties with material storage and handling, rewriting, etc. (b) Problems of predicting the necessary print runs, etc to keep ahead of demand. (c) Preventive maintenance of equipment, distribution/transmission systems, etc. (d) Planning of convenient transmission times, etc. (e) Planning for the variability of demand for services. (f) Need for more staff, more specialist staff, more professionalism. (g) Loss of personalization in the communication system. (h) Growth of bureaucracy.
3. The necessary resources	It is very common for projects that were adequately financed in the pilot and initial stages to run out of money (and therefore out of steam) as they grow. Projects are allowed to grow faster than their resources will allow and this leads to a dilution of services, a drop in results, disenchantment and sometimes total failure. Sometimes the project never makes the step from pilot to full scale, because someone forgot to calculate the true costs of full implementaton. The project dies as a promising experiment.

Map 20.9 *Sources of failure in the 'implementation/use' sub-system*

Introduction	In the dissemination stage, when a project goes to large-scale implementation and use, things are very different from the well-controlled pilot stage. The people involved are generally less interested, less enthusiastic, less well prepared, less committed to the project's success. We are now in the real world rather than the laboratory.
Sources of failure **1. A poorly prepared environment** — examples	The people whom we shall involve in our project already have their own attitudes and feelings, philosophies, traditions, etc. If the project requires any serious changes in these entrenched positions, a great deal of preparatory work must be done. Sources of failure include: (a) Projects that attempt to force a change in theoretical viewpoint (eg over the use or not of objectives). (b) Projects that appear to create more work without offering any obvious reward to the personnel involved. (c) Projects that require a change in the life-style or organizational pattern of the persons and institutions involved, that may cause some practical hardships, etc.
2. Conflict among objectives or methods — examples	The project will be implanted in an organization that already has its own objectives, methods of operation, etc. Sometimes our project may enter in conflict with the super-system that it is supposed to serve. (a) Individualized instruction projects that proceed at the pace of the learner are difficult to implant in institutions where all other courses follow a traditional lock-step pattern. (b) Projects using criterion-referenced measures almost always enter in conflict with systems that apply norm-referenced measures.
3. Preparation of the human resources — examples	It is necessary to orient, inform and train the people involved with the project to a much greater extent than is often realized. Sometimes this is not done and leads to problems. (a) Immediate distortions in the project's methodology. Each institution or teacher makes what he can of the system. (b) Distortions which only appear after some time, when the original project personnel begin to be replaced or supplemented.
4. Scale effect — examples	Scale effect also can play its part in this phase, principally in the project management area. (a) Organization of time, avoidance of queuing, overbooking, etc. (b) An insufficient level of decentralization of resources and decisions. (c) Financial hold-ups, because of the growth in bureaucracy, etc.

Map 20.10 *Sources of failure in the 'control/evaluation' sub-system*

Introduction	Educational technology projects are generally based on the philosophy of 'management by instructional objectives' (ie competency-based learning or mastery learning). This may follow approximately the following stages: ☐ Statement of the objectives to be accomplished ☐ Agreement with the learner to pursue specific objectives ☐ Revision of individual programmes, in the light of results achieved. This is a clear application (to education) of the general management by objectives model. To avoid conflict, the administrative aspects of the course should also be managed by objectives. However, many projects are implanted in systems that do not follow anything like this philosophy of management. Conflicts then occur.
Sources of failure 1. The administrative philosophy of the institution — example	The execution of an individualized instruction project, for example, requires quite a different set of activities in the classroom than more traditional group methods. If the top management of the institution does not understand and accept these differences, and the underlying rationale, conflict and potential failure of the project may occur. There is a traditional tendency to evaluate the efficiency of instruction by observing the *behaviour* of teachers and learners in the class (teacher standing/talking, learners sitting/quiet, etc), rather than in terms of their *performance* (objectives achieved).
2. Organizational structure of the project	To manage by objectives effectively, it is generally necessary to adopt a project management organizational structure. The traditional line management organizational model, with overcentralized authority, tends to fragment the project, which inevitably cuts across several line responsibilities. In large organizations a matrix structure is desirable, with line management possibly responsible for strategic decisions or approvals, but each project manager, responsible for all tactical decisions.
3. Human relations in the project	Finally, to manage by objectives, it is necessary to involve all project personnel in the setting and evaluation of their immediate objectives, by means of individual contracts between manager and subordinates. Lack of maturity, self-confidence or mutual respect among project personnel can seriously affect the smooth running of a management by objectives project.

Map 20.11 *The main sub-systems of the initial design stage*

Introduction	We have left this, the first stage of the project, to be discussed last for two reasons: 1. It should now be obvious that there are many factors that can affect the smooth running of the development and dissemination stages that can be foreseen and planned for in the initial design stage. 2. It is this stage that this book has mainly considered. It may now also be obvious to the reader why we have laid so much emphasis throughout on considering alternatives, thinking them through and always taking the wider system viewpoint to look for possible snags in later stages.
	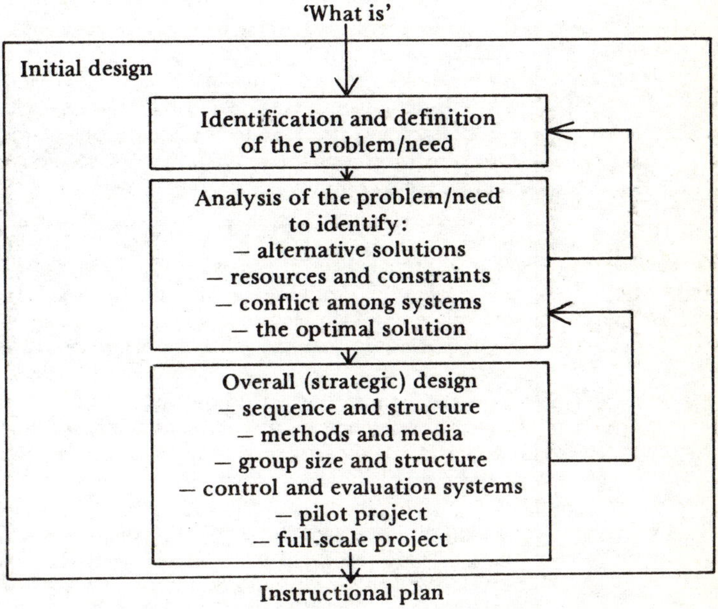
Definition of the problem	This is not always 'as the problem is first presented'. See Part 1 for a treatment of problem definition.
Analysis of the problem	This is the most critical phase, as it describes whether an instructional solution or some other will be adopted. See Part 2 for various approaches to analysis.
Overall design	There are many decisions that may be taken here, some critical, some not. Part 3 gives a full treatment of this design stage.

Map 20.12 *A guide to this book's structure in relation to the 'initial design' stage*

Introduction	The initial design stage should follow the steps of the systems approach, as outlined in Chapter 1. At each of the five steps, one should apply appropriate heuristics for decision making.
1. The problem definition phase	This phase serves to clarify the overall objectives of the project (if there is indeed to be a project), and to evaluate the value and the chances of achieving the project objectives. The heuristics listed in Map 1.1 should help to avoid failure at this phase (eg by attempting impossible objectives). Part 1 gives further background.
2. The problem analysis phase	This phase serves to analyse the project objectives further to establish whether the project is to be an instructional design project (or some other type of solution) and if so, to establish the precise instructional objectives. The heuristics listed in Map 1.2 help to avoid failure at this phase (eg by attempting to teach what is already known or what is not required). Part 2 gives further background, examples and techniques.
3. The overall (strategic) design phase	What is important in this phase is that design and planning are both 'global' and forward-looking. One should think through the consequences of all decisions right to the full-scale dissemination stage, passing through the pilot project stage. Many potential snags may be identified and attempts should be made to avoid or to minimize them by the selection of alternative strategies. Those that cannot be avoided can at least be documented, so that ample preparation of the project and its environment to accommodate to these snags may be undertaken in good time. To help do this, one should apply during this stage the heuristics in Maps 1.3; 1.4 and 1.5. Part 3 details the types of decisions that can be made and the techniques that may help in making them. This present chapter summarizes the looking forward that should be done in order to pre-evaluate one's decisions in the light of predicted future problems.

Map 20.13 *How to avoid failure in the 'initial design' stage*

Introduction	Naturally, however carefully we plan ahead, we are never likely to predict all difficulties and problems that will arise. Therefore a two-pronged attack is suggested: 1. Adopt a planning approach that will facilitate the identification of future problems and difficulties. 2. Be flexible and adaptive.
Maximum administrative flexibility	Right from the start of a project, plan and insist on the maximum possible levels of administrative and decision-making flexibility, in order to adapt the project to unexpected developments as they occur. Such developments are most likely to develop for reasons of resources shortages, scheduling errors, human relations and personality problems and the scale effect. The greatest number of such unpredicted problems are likely to occur when the project passes from the pilot stage to the full-scale dissemination and implementation stage.
Retrogressive planning	Normally, one tends to plan from the beginning to the end of a project (eg first objectives, analysis, etc, then a pilot project). However, a much more effective way of predicting probable future problem areas is to plan retrogressively. First draw up a blueprint of the full-scale project. Estimate its effects, costs, manpower needs, its effect on related systems, its political, ethical, social or philosophical implications. Get the blueprint agreed in principle, if only informally, by your client. Modify it if it is not realistic in any way. From this you can develop a blueprint of the pilot project, which should simulate all important characteristics of the full-scale situation, except the size and cost. If any potential problem in the full-scale model was identified, plan to experiment with alternative solutions to it in the pilot project. Thus the pilot project can be used to evaluate much more than the instructional materials to be disseminated. Finally, get down to the initial design of the instructional system, keeping your two forward-looking blueprints in mind.
Maintain an overall 'systems' view of the design process	Whilst working backwards, do not forget that instructional design is a complex systemic process. One decision often involves or influences others. This book should have helped you build up a systems view of the instructional design process. To summarize, the Maps 20.14 and 20.15 present a sort of 'world map' of the major activities and decisions and their interrelationships.
Visual aids to the systems view	Map 20.14 details the *design* stage of the project. This is a very condensed summary of the contents of this book. It is laid out on a grid which shows the stages of the systems approach involved and the level of instructional design adopted. Map 20.15 details the *development* stage of the project. This is the subject of Volume 2, *Producing Instructional Systems*, a companion volume to this book, that will shortly be in print.
Comment	No map is presented for the *dissemination* stage. This would be very different depending on the type of project (eg face-to-face courses or distance education) and on its size (eg institutional or national). You should start any project by drawing up for yourself a similar world map of what needs to be done to get your particular project operational at the full-scale.

Map 20.14 *World map of the 'initial design' stage of an instructional design project*

		Stages in the systems approach			
		Define problem	Analyse problem	Design/develop solution	Implement	Control/evaluate
Level 1 design	Analysis	Identify problem — what should be done/known? — what is done/known?	Front-end analysis — is instruction part of the required solution	Consider other types of solution		Has the problem really been solved?
	Synthesis	Transform discrepancy into measurable project objectives	Perform a full job/ subject analysis to derive the post-instruction objectives	Design evaluation instruments	Administrative steps to make use of existing system	Perform a long-term evaluation of the effects on society or organization
	Evaluation	Are the project objectives viable? Stop or revise	Do appropriate instructional systems exist already? (No)	(Yes) Evaluate and select existing systems		Produce and validate the long-term evaluation instruments
Level 2 design	Analysis		Perform target pop/task/ topic analysis of what seems 'worth teaching'	What are the characteristics of the knowledge and skills content	Identify probable difficulties of implementation	Analyse the effects of instruction
	Synthesis		Derive detailed instructional objectives and content	Develop the instructional plan — structure/sequence — strategies/methods — media — control/evaluation	Dissemination of plan to teachers. Orientation and preparation	Control and evaluate the full-scale project
	Evaluation	What is the 'climate' and philosophy of the wider system?	What is the worth and practicality of the proposed system?	What level of design is required?		Produce and validate the final tests

'Initial' design is principally concerned with the first three stages: define problem, analyse problem and design/develop the solution.
We include the implementation, control and evaluation stages in this matrix only to demonstrate the feedback loops for project revision
which exist at each level.

Map 20.15 *World map of the 'development' stage of an instructional design project*

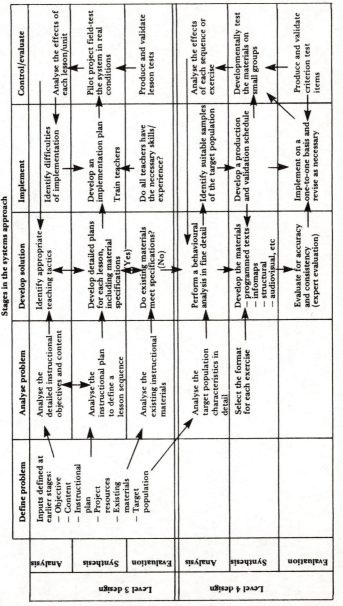

Stages in the systems approach

	Define problem	Analyse problem	Develop solution	Implement	Control/evaluate
Level 3 design — Analysis	Inputs defined at earlier stages: — Objective — Content — Instructional plan — Project resources — Existing materials — Target population	Analyse the detailed instructional objectives and content	Identify appropriate teaching tactics	Identify difficulties of implementation	Analyse the effects of each lesson/unit
Level 3 design — Synthesis		Analyse the instructional plan to define a lesson sequence	Develop detailed plans for each lesson, including material specifications	Develop an implementation plan Train teachers	Pilot project field-test the system in real conditions
Level 3 design — Evaluation		Analyse the existing instructional materials	Do existing materials meet specifications? (Yes) / (No)	Do all teachers have the necessary skills/experience?	Produce and validate lesson tests
Level 4 design — Analysis		Analyse the target population characteristics in detail	Perform a behavioural analysis in fine detail	Identify suitable samples of the target population	Analyse the effects of each sequence or exercise
Level 4 design — Synthesis		Select the format for each exercise	Develop the materials — programmed texts — infomaps — structural — audiovisual, etc	Develop a production and validation schedule	Developmentally test the materials on small groups
Level 4 design — Evaluation			Evaluate for accuracy and consistency (expert evaluation)	Implement on a one-to-one basis and revise as necessary	Produce and validate criterion test items

The 'problem' has been fully defined at levels 1 and 2, as has the overall form of the solution. Level 3 is concerned with the detailed tactics of each lesson — what learners and teachers should do at each stage of the instructional process. Level 4 is concerned with the development of special instructional materials.

References

Anderson, R H (1976) *Selecting and Developing Media for Instruction* Van Nostrand Reinhold: New York

Armstrong, R J *et al* (1970) *The Development and Evaluation of Behavioral Objectives* Charles A Jones: Ohio

Armstrong, R J *et al* (1971) A scheme for evaluation. *Educational Accountability* Educational Technology Publications: Englewood Cliffs, New Jersey

Ashby, W R (1956) *An Introduction to Cybernetics* Chapman and Hall: London

Austwick, K (1972) The message, the medium and post-literate man. In eds: Austwick, K and Harris, N D C *Aspects of Educational Technology VI* Pitman: London

Ausubel, D P (1968) *Educational Psychology: A Cognitive View* Holt, Rinehart and Winston: New York

Banathy, B H (1973) *Developing a Systems View of Education: The Systems-Model Approach* Fearon: California

Belbin, E, Belbin, R M and Hill, F (1957) A comparison of different methods of operator training. *Ergonomics* Vol 1, No 1

Belbin, E and Belbin, R M (1972) *Problems of Adult Retraining* Heinemann: London

Belbin, E and Shimmin, S (1964) Training the middle aged for inspection work. *Occupational Psychology,* Vol 38, No 1

Belbin, R M (1969) CRAMP. *Industrial Training International* No 4

Biggs, E E (1972) Investigational methods. In ed: Chapman, L R *The Process of Learning Mathematics* Pergamon Press: Oxford

Block, J H (1971) *Mastery Learning: Theory and Practice* Holt, Rinehart and Winston, New York

Bloom, B S *et al* (1956) *Taxonomy of Educational Objectives, Handbook 1: Cognitive Domain* David McKay Inc, New York. Reprinted in paperback in 1972 by Longman: New York and London

Bloom, B S (1968) Learning for mastery. *Evaluation Comment,* Vol 1, No 2, UCLA: California, USA

Bloom, B S, Hastings, J T and Madeus, G F (1971) *Handbook of Formative and Summative Evaluation of Student Learning* McGraw-Hill: New York

Boydell, T H (1973) *A Guide to Job Analysis* British Association for Commercial and Industrial Education (BACIE): London

Bretz, R (1971) *A Taxonomy of Communication Media* Educational Technology Publications: Englewood Cliffs, New Jersey, USA

Briggs, L J (1970) *Handbook of Procedures for the Design of Instruction* American Institutes for Research: Pittsburgh, Pennsylvania, USA

Briggs, L J, Campeau, P L, Gagné, R M and May, M A (1966) *Instructional Media* American Institutes for Research: Pittsburgh, Pennsylvania, USA

Broadwell, M M (1976) Classroom instruction. In ed: Craig, R L *Training and Development Handbook* McGraw-Hill: New York

Bruner, J S (1966) *Towards a Theory of Instruction* Norton: New York

Butler, F C (1972) *Instructional Systems Development for Vocational and Technical Training* Educational Technology Publications: Englewood Cliffs, New Jersey, USA

Carroll, J B (1963) A model of school learning. *Teachers College Record* No 64

Clarke, J (1970) The learning of mathematics in the primary school through the use of concrete materials. In eds: Bajpai, A J and Leedham, J F *Aspects of Educational Technology IV* Pitman: London

Coleman, J S (1974) Academic games and learning: a rationale. In ed: Stadsklev, R *Handbook of Simulation Gaming in Social Education* Institute of Higher Education Research and Services, University of Alabama: USA

Coombes, P and Tiffin, J (1978) *Television Production for Education* Focal Press: London

Covington, M V and Crutchfield, R S (1965) Facilitation of creative problem-solving *Programmed Instruction* Vol 4, No 4 NSPI: Washington, USA

Cowan, J (1975) Scale effect and its relevance to resource-based learning. In eds: Clarke, J and Leedham, J *Aspects of Educational Technology X* Kogan Page: London

Craig, R L (ed) (1976) *Training and Development Handbook: A Guide to Human Resource Development* McGraw-Hill: New York

Crowder, N A (1963) Intrinsic programming: facts, fallacies and future. In ed: Filep, R T *Prospectives in Programming* Macmillan: USA

Croxton, P C L and Martin, L M (1970) The application of programmed learning in higher education. In eds: Bajpai, A J and Leedham, J *Aspects of Educational Technology IV* Pitman: London

Daniel, J S (1976) Learning styles and strategies: the work of Gordon Pask. In *How Students Learn* Quebec University: Canada

Davies, I K (1971) *The Management of Learning* McGraw-Hill: London

Davies, I K and Hartley, J (1972) *Contributions to an Educational Technology* Butterworths: London

De Bono, E (1967) *The Use of Lateral Thinking* Penguin: Harmondsworth, UK

DeVault, M V and Kierwall, T E (1969) *Perspectives in Elementary School Mathematics* Charles E Merril Publishing Co: New York

Diamond, R M *et al* (1975) *Instructional Development for Individualized Learning in Higher Education* Educational Technology Publications: Englewood Cliffs, New Jersey, USA

Dienes, Z P (1960) *Building Up Mathematics* Hutchinson: London

Dienes, Z P (1964) *The Power of Mathematics* Hutchinson: London

Dienes, Z P (1973) *The Six Stages in the Process of Learning Mathematics* OCDL, Paris. Translated by Seaborne, P L (1973) NFER: London

Dodd, B T, LeHunte, R J G and Shephard, C (1974) Decision making in instructional design. In eds: Baggaley, J *et al Aspects of Educational Technology VIII* Kogan Page: London

Drumheller, S J (1971) *Handbook of Curriculum Design for Individualized Instruction: A Systems Approach* Educational Technology Publications: Englewood Cliffs, New Jersey

Ebel, R L (1974) What are schools for? In eds: Charizio, H F *et al Contemporary Issues in Educational Psychology* Allyn and Bacon: Boston, USA

Emery, F E (ed) (1969) *Systems Thinking* Penguin Books, Harmondsworth, UK

Evans, J L (1964) A pot pourri of programming technology. In *Trends in Programmed Instruction* DAVI, National Educational Association: USA

Evans, J L, Homme, L E and Glazer, R (1962) The RulEg system for the construction of programmed verbal learning sequences. In *Programmed Instruction: Data and Direction* DAVI, National Educational Association: USA

Food, Drink and Tobacco Industry Training Board *Creating a Training Programme for Technicians* Training Recommendations, No 2. *Assessing your Company's Training Needs* Systematic Training Guide No 1. *How to Use Job Analysis for Profitable Training* Systematic Training Guide No 2. FDTITB: Croydon, UK

Faure, E (1972) *Learning to Be* UNESCO: Paris

French, W L and Bell, C H (1973) *Organization Development: Behavioral Science Interventions for Organization Improvement* Prentice-Hall: Englewood Cliffs, New Jersey, USA

Gagné, R M (1965) *The Conditions for Learning* Holt, Rinehart and Winston: New York. Second edition 1970

Gagné, R M (1975) *Essentials of Learning for Instruction* Dryden Press: Illinois, USA

Gagné, R M and Briggs, L J (1974) *Principles of Instructional Design* Holt, Rinehart and Winston: New York

Gallaher, J J (1964) Productive thinking. In eds: Hoffman, M L and Hoffman, L W *Review of Child Development Research* Russell Sage Foundation: USA

Gane, G P, Horabin, I S and Lewis, B N (1966) The simplification and avoidance of instruction. *Industrial Training International* Vol 1, No 4, pp 160-6. Reprinted (1972) in Davies, I K and Hartley, J (eds) *Contributions to an Educational Technology* Butterworth: London

Gibbons, M (1971) *Individualized Instruction: A Descriptive Analysis* Teachers College Press, Columbia University: USA

Gilbert, T F (1961) Mathetics: the technology of education. *Journal of Mathetics*, Vols 1 and 2. Reprinted (1969) as supplement No 1 of the *Reivew of Educational Cybernetics and Applied Linguistics* Longman: London

Gilbert, T F (1967) Praxeonomy: a systematic approach to identifying training needs. *Management of Personnel Quarterly* 6 No 3. University of Ann Arbor: Michigan.

Reprinted (1972) in eds: Davies, I K and Hartley, J *Contributions to an Educational Technology* Butterworth: London

Gilbert, T F (1969a) The sensible teaching of social science, or mathetics revisited. *NSPI Journal* Vol **8** No 1 National Society for Performance and Instruction: USA

Gilbert, T F (1969b) Some issues in mathetics: saying what a subject matter is *NSPI Journal* Vol **8** No 2 National Society for Performance and Instruction: USA

Godycki, R (1968) Strukturalny zapis swiazkow matematycznych w nauczaniu przedmiotow elektrycznych. (The structural notation of mathetmatical relationships in the teaching of electrical subject matter). In *Szkola Zawodowa* Nasza Ksiegarnia: Warsaw, Poland

Godycki, R and Romiszowski, A J (1970) A structural approach to the teaching of formulae in physics and technical subjects. *Visual Education* February 1970 NCAVAE: London

Greenhill, L P (1956) The evaluation of instructional films by a travel panel, using a film analysis form. Instructional Film Research Reports Vol 2, Instructional Device Centre, USA

Hamblin, A C (1974) *Evaluation and Control of Training* McGraw-Hill: London

Harless, J (1968) (1971) *An Ounce of Analysis (is Worth a Pound of Programming)* Harless Performance Guild Inc: Washington

Harrow, A J (1972) *A Taxonomy of the Psychomotor Domain: A Guide for Developing Behavioral Objectives* David McKay: New York

Harrow, A J (1977) The behavioral objectives movement: its impact on physical education. *Educational Technology* Vol 17, No 6

Hartley, J (1978) *Designing Instructional Text* Kogan Page: London

Hartley, J and Davies, I K (1979) *Contributions to an Educational Technology*, Vol 2 Kogan Page: London

HMSO (1975) *Making Work More Satisfying* Tripartite Steering Group on Job Satisfaction HMSO: London

Holmberg, B (1977) *Distance Education* Kogan Page: London

Horabin, I S (1971) *Toward Greater Employee Productivity* Ivan Horabin: Summit Point, West Virginia, USA

Horn, R E *et al* (1969) *Information Mapping for Learning and Reference* Information Resources Inc, Lexington, Mass, USA

Horn, R E (1973) *Introduction to Information Mapping* Information Resources Inc, Lexington, Mass, USA

Horn, R E (1974) *Course Notes for Information Mapping Workshop* Information Resources Inc: Lexington, Mass, USA

Illich, I D (1971) *Deschooling Society* Harper and Row: New York

Industrial Training Research Unit (1975) *CRAMP: A Guide to Training Decisions — Users' Manual* ITRU Research Paper TR1. Industrial Training Research Unit, University College: London

International Labour Office (1973) *Introduction of a Vocational Training System Using Modules of Employable Skill* ILO: Geneva

International Labour Office (1977) *Modules of Employable Skill: Principles and Practices* ILO: Geneva

International Labour Office (1979a) *Report on the Development Phase (1974-78) of the ILO/SIDA Research and Development Project in Vocational Training Methods and Techniques* ILO: Geneva

International Labour Office (1979b) *Modules of Employable Skill: Handbook on Practices* ILO: Geneva

Johnson, D W and Johnson, R T (1975) *Learning Together and Alone: Cooperation, Competition and Individualization* Prentice-Hall: Englewood Cliffs, New Jersey, USA

Johnson, R B and Johnson, S R (1973) *Assuring Learning with Self-Instructional Packages* Addison-Wesley: USA

Kefford, C (1970) *A Programmed Approach to Environmental Studies* Blandford Press, London

Keller, F S (1968) Goodbye teacher. *Journal of Applied Behavioral Analysis* No 1

Keller, F S and Sherman, J G (1974) *The Keller Plan Handbook* W A Benjamin: USA

Kaufman, R (1976) *Identifying and Solving Problems: A Systems Approach* University Associates: California

King Taylor, L (1973) *Not for Bread Alone: An Appreciation of Job Enrichment* Business Books: London

Knowles, M S (1969) *The Modern Practice of Adult Education* Association Press: New York

Krathwohl, D R, Bloom, B S and Masia, B B (1964) *Taxonomy of Educational Objectives, Handbook II: Affective Domain* David McKay: New York. Reprinted in paperback (1972) by Longman: London

Landa, L N (1974) *Algorithmization in Learning and Instruction* Educational Technology Publications: Englewood Cliffs, New Jersey, USA

Landa, L N (1976) *Instructional Regulation and Control: Cybernetics, Algorithmization and Heuristics in Education* Educational Technology Publications: Englewood Cliffs, New Jersey, USA

Langdon, D G (1973) *Interactive Instructional Designs for Individualized Learning* Educational Technology Publications: Englewood Cliffs, New Jersey, USA

Lenn, P D (1974) *Five Ways to Help Your Students: A Workshop on Instructional Techniques* American Analysis Corporation: San Francisco

Levins, R (1968) *Evolution in a Changing Environment* Princeton University Press: Princeton, USA

Lewin, K (1951) *Field Theory in Social Science* Harper and Brothers: New York

Lewis, B N and Woolfenden, P J (1969) *Algorithms and Logical Trees: A Self-Instructional Course* Algorithms Press: Cambridge, UK

Lumsdaine, A A (1964) Educational technology: issues and problems. In ed: Lange, P C *Programmed Instruction: The Sixty Sixth Yearbook of the National Society for the Study of Education* NSSE: Chicago, USA

Macdonald-Ross, M (1972) Behavioural objectives and the structure of knowledge. In eds: Austwick, K and Harris, NDC *Aspects of Educational Technology VI* Pitman: London

Mager, R F (1962) *Preparing Objectives for Programmed Instruction* Reprinted (1975) as *Preparing Instructional Objectives* Fearon Publishers: Belmont, California, USA

Mager, R F (1968a) *Goal Analysis* Fearon Publishers: Belmont, California, USA

Mager, R F (1968b) *Developing Attitude Toward Learning* Fearon Publishers: Belmont, California, USA

Mager, R F (1973) *Measuring Instructional Intent* Fearon Publishers: Belmont, California, USA

Mager, R F and Beach, K H (1967) *Developing Vocational Instruction* Fearon Publishers: Belmont, California, USA

Mager, R F and McCann, J (1961) *Learner Controlled Instruction* Varian Associates: Palo Alto, California, USA

Mager, R F and Pipe, P (1970) *Analysing Performance Problems* Fearon Publishers: Belmont, California, USA

Markle, S (1969) *Good Frames and Bad: A Grammar of Frame Writing* John Wiley & Sons: New York

McAleese, R (ed) (1978) *Perspectives on Academic Gaming & Simulation 3* Kogan Page: London

McCord, B (1976) Job instruction. In ed: Craig, R L *Training and Development Handbook* McGraw-Hill: New York

McLuhan, M (1964) *Understanding Media: The Extensions of Man* McGraw-Hill: New York

Mechner, F (1965) Science education and behavioral technology. In ed: Glaser, R *Teaching Machines and Programmed Learning II: Data and Directions* Department of Audiovisual Instruction, National Education Association of the United States, Washington: USA

Megarry, J (1978) *Perspectives on Academic Gaming & Simulation 1 & 2* Kogan Page: London

Megarry, J (1979) *Perspectives on Academic Gaming & Simulation 4* Kogan Page: London

Merrill, M D and Wood, N D (1974) *Instructional Strategies: A Preliminary Taxonomy* ERIC Information Analysis Center for Science Mathematics and Environmental Education: Columbus, Ohio, USA

Milholland, J E (1966) *An Empirical Examination of the Categories of the Taxonomy of Educational Objectives: Cognitive Domain* American Educational Research Association, 1966 Conference Proceedings, Chicago, Illinois, USA

Miller, R B (1962) Task description and analysis. In ed: Gagné, R M *Psychological Principles in System Development* Holt, Rinehart and Winston: New York

Mitchell, P D (1977) Educational technology. In *Encyclopaedia of Educational Media, Communications and Technology* Macmillan: London

Neill, M W (1970) A systems approach to course planning in the Open University. In ed: Romiszowski, A J *A Systems Approach to Education and Training* APLET Occasional Publication No 1. Kogan Page: London

Newsom Report (1963) *Half Our Future* HMSO: London
Norwood Report (1943) *Curriculum Examinations in Secondary Schools* HMSO: London
Page, G T and Thomas, J B (1977) *International Dictionary of Education* Kogan Page: London
Pask, G (1960) *The Teaching Machine as a Control Mechanism* Transactions of the Society of Instrument Technology: UK
Pask, G (1976) Conversational techniques in the study and practice of education. *British Journal of Educational Psychology* Vol 46. Reprinted in eds: Hartley, J and Davies, I K (1978) *Contributions to an Educational Technology 2* Kogan Page: London
Pask, G and Scott, B C E (1972) Learning strategies and individual competence. *International Journal of Man-Machine Studies* Vol 4, No 3
Paul, W J and Robertson, K B (1970) *Job Enrichment and Employee Motivation* Gower Press: Epping, UK
Peters, R S (1969) Session two introduction. In *Conference on Objectives in Higher Education* University of London Institute of Education: London
Piaget, J (1957) *Logic and Psychology* Basic Books: USA
Piaget, J (1965) *The Child's Conception of Number* W W Norton and Co Inc: New York
Polya, G (1945) *How to Solve It: A New Aspect of Mathematical Method* Princeton University Press: Princeton, New Jersey, USA. Second edition 1957. First paperback printing 1971
Polya, G (1963) On learning, teaching and learning teaching *American Mathematical Monthly*, Vol 70
Popham, W J (1968) *Objectives and Instruction* Rand McNally: Chicago, USA
Postman, N and Weingartner, C (1969) *Teaching as a Subversive Activity* Penguin: Harmondsworth, UK
Powell, L S (1969) *Communication and Learning* Pitman: London
Pressey, S L (1926) A simple device for teaching, testing and research. *School and Society*, No 23
Rackham, N and Morgan, T (1977) *Behaviour Analysis in Training* McGraw-Hill: London
Roden, A H and Hapkiewicz, W G (1974) Respondent learning and classroom practice. In ed: Charizio, H F *et al Contemporary Issues in Educational Psychology* Allyn and Bacon: Boston, USA
Rogers, C R (1969) *Freedom to Learn* Merril: Ohio, USA
Romiszowski, A J (1969) *Report on the Use of a Computer-Managed Remedial Mathematics Course at Undergraduate Level* PIC Occasional Publication, Enfield College of Technology (Middlesex Polytechnic): Enfield, UK
Romiszowski, A J (ed) (1970a) *The Systems Approach to Education and Training* Kogan Page: London
Romiszowski, A J (1970b) Classifications, algorithms and checklists as aids to the selection of instructional methods and media. In eds: Bajpai, A C and Leedham, J *Aspects of Educational Technology IV* Pitman: London
Romiszowski, A J (1972) The systems approach to instruction with particular reference to the evaluation of course materials. *Educational Broadcasting International*, special issue on evaluation of instruction, Centre for Educational Development Overseas: London
Romiszowski, A J (1974) *Selection and Use of Instructional Media: A Systems Approach* Kogan Page: London
Romiszowski, A J (1976) Individualisation in higher education. *Programmed Learning and Educational Technology* Vol 13, No 1
Romiszowski, A J (1977) A study of individualised systems of mathematics instruction at the post-secondary levels. Doctoral thesis presented to the University of Technology, Loughborough, UK
Romiszowski, A J (1978) Alguns cuidados na apliçãcao de tecnologia educacional em grandes projetos de treinamento (Dangers in the application of educational technology in large scale training projects). Paper delivered at the Congress of the Brazilian Association for Training and Development, São Paulo
Romiszowski, A J (1979a) The management of large scale instructional technology projects. In eds: Page, G T and Whitlock, Q *Aspects of Educational Technology XIII* Kogan Page: London
Romiszowski, A J (1979b) Porque os projetos fracassam? (Why do projects fail?). Paper presented at the 1979 Conference of the Brazilian Association for Educational Technology, Salvador, Brazil.
Romiszowski, A J (1980a) Problem solving in instructional design: an heuristic approach. In ed: Howe, A *International Yearbook of Educational and Instructional Technology 1980/81* Kogan Page: London

Romiszowski, A J (1980b) A new approach to the analysis of knowledge and skills. In eds: Winterburn, R and Evans, L *Aspects of Educational Technology XIV* Kogan Page: London

Romiszowski, A J and Atherton, B (1979) Creativity and control: neglected factors within self-instructional programme design. In eds: Page, G T and Whitlock, Q *Aspects of Educational Technology XIII* Kogan Page: London

Rowntree, D (1974) *Educational Technology in Curriculum Development* Harper and Row: London

Schramm, W (1967) *Big Media — Little Media* Sage Publications: Beverly Hills, USA

Servais, W and Varga, T (1971) *Teaching School Mathematics: A UNESCO Source Book* Penguin: Harmondsworth, UK

Seymour, W D (1954) *Industrial Training for Manual Operations* Pitman: London

Seymour, W D (1966) *Industrial Skills* Pitman: London

Seymour, W D (1968) *Skills Analysis Training* Pitman: London

Shaw, M E (1967) Role playing. In eds: Craig, R L and Bittel, L R *Training and Development Handbook* McGraw-Hill: New York

Shulman, L S and Keislar, E R (eds) (1966) *Learning by Discovery: A Critical Appraisal* Rand McNally: Chicago, USA

Silber, K H (1970) What field are we in, anyhow? *Audiovisual Instruction*, AECT, Washington, USA

Simpson, E J (1967) Educational objectives in the psychomotor domain. In eds: Kapfer, M B *Behavioral Objectives in Curriculum Development* Educational Technology Publications: Englewood Cliffs, New Jersey, USA

Simpson, E J (1969) *Psychomotor Domain: A Tentative Classification* University of Illinois: Urbana, USA

Singleton, W T (1974) *Man-Machine Systems* Penguin: Harmondsworth, UK

Skemp, R (1971) *The Psychology of Learning Mathematics* Penguin: Harmondsworth, UK

Skinner, B F (1961a) Why we need teaching machines. *Harvard Educational Review*, No 31

Skinner, B F (1961b) Teaching machines. *Scientific American*, No 205

Skinner, B F (1968) *The Technology of Teaching* Appleton-Century-Crofts: New York

Stadsklev, R (1974) *Handbook of Simulation Gaming in Social Education* Institute of Higher Education Research and Services: University of Alabama, USA

Stoker, H W and Kropp, R P (1964) Measurement of cognitive processes. *Journal of Educational Measurement* Vol 1, No 1

Suppes, P et al (1968) *Computer-Assisted Instruction: Stanford's 1956-66 Arithmetic Program* Stanford University Institute for Mathematical Studies in Social Science: California, USA

Tansey, P J (1971) *Educational Aspects of Simulation* McGraw-Hill: London

Taylor, L C (1971) *Resources for Learning* Penguin: Harmondsworth, UK

Thomas, C A, Davies, I K, Openshaw, D and Bird, J (1963) *Programmed Learning in Perspective: A Guide to Program Writing* Educational Methods: Chicago, Illinois, USA

Thornley, D H and Valentine, G A (1968) Job enlargement: some implications of longer cycle jobs on fan heater production *Philips Personnel Management Review*

Tyler, L L (1966) The taxonomy of educational objectives: cognitive domain — its use in evaluating programmed instruction. *California Journal of Educational Research* Vol 17, No 1

UNESCO (1975) *A Systems Approach to Teaching and Learning Procedures: A Guide for Educators in Developing Countries* UNESCO: Paris

Vargas, J S (1972) *Writing Worthwhile Behavioral Objectives* Harper and Row: New York

Vaughan, B W (1972) The application of the operational research technique of network analysis to primary mathematics. In *Aspects of Educational Technology VI* Pitman: London

Wadsworth, B J (1971) *Piaget's Theory of Cognitive Development* David McKay: New York

Warren, M W (1978) Performance technologies for human resources management. In eds: Howe, A and Romiszowski, A J *International Yearbook of Educational and Instructional Technology 1978/79* Kogan Page: London

Watson, J B and Rayner, R (1920) Conditioned emotional reactions. *Journal of Experimental Psychology* Vol 20, No 3

Wellens, J (1974) *Training in Physical Skills* Business Books: London

Wheatcroft, E (1973) *Simulation for Skill* McGraw-Hill: London

Wheatley, D M and Unwin, A W (1972) *The Algorithm Writer's Guide* Longman: London

Williams, R G (1977) A behavioral typology of educational objectives for the cognitive domain. *Educational Technology* Vol 17, No 6

Winfield, I S (1979) *Learning to Teach Practical Skills* Kogan Page: London

Woodcock, J A D (1972) *Cost Reduction Through Operator Training and Retraining* Kogan Page: London

Woodward, J (1965) *Industrial Organization: Theory and Practice* Oxford University Press: London

Woodward, J (1970) *Industrial Organization: Behaviour and Control* Oxford University Press: London

Wyant, T G (1972) Learner controlled self-instruction. In eds: Austwick, K and Harris, N D L *Aspects of Educational Technology VI* Pitman: London

Wyant, T G (1973) Syllabus analysis. In eds: Budgett, R and Leedham, J *Aspects of Educational Technology VI* Pitman: London

Wyant, T G (1974) Network analysis. In eds: Howe, A and Romiszowski, A J *APLET Yearbook of Educational and Instructional Technology 1974/75* Kogan Page: London

Young, H W A (1906) *The Teaching of Mathematics in the Elementary and Secondary School* Longmans Green: London

Subject Index

verbal information, 244

wider system, 6, 65, 66
workshop (method of group instruction), 311

Author Index